International Child Law

D0082337

International Child Law examines and discusses the international legal framework and issues relating to children. Analysing both public and private international legal aspects, this cross-disciplinary text promotes an understanding of the ongoing development of child law, children's rights and the protection of the child.

Examining the theoretical background to the law, and providing a concise and clear overview of the instruments and institutions that protect children internationally, this text then focuses on key themes and issues in child law and children's rights. This new edition has been updated and revised throughout, including expanded material on the UN Convention on the Rights of the Child, as well as discussion of recent landmark developments on the law relating to recruiting child soldiers as a result of *Lubanga* (2012). The third edition also includes a new case study feature that critically considers key themes and issues in international child law in a real world context.

Drawing on a range of legal and other disciplines, *International Child Law* is a valuable resource for those in the course of study and research in this area.

International Public Law

International Child Law

Third Edition

Trevor Buck

Routledge
Taylor & Francis Group

LONDON AND NEW YORK

First published 2014
by Routledge
2 Park Square, Milton Park, Abingdon, Oxon, OX14 4RN

and by Routledge
711 Third Avenue, New York, NY 10017

Routledge is an imprint of the Taylor & Francis Group, an informa business

© 2014 Trevor Buck

British Library Cataloguing in Publication Data
A catalogue record for this book is available from the British Library

Library of Congress Cataloging-in-Publication Data
Buck, Trevor, 1951- author.
International child law / Trevor Buck. -- Third edition.
pages cm
ISBN 978-0-415-82591-7 (hardback) -- ISBN 978-0-415-82592-4 (pbk) --
ISBN 978-0-203-53813-5 (ebk) 1. Children (International law) 2. Children--
Legal status, laws, etc. I. Title.
K639.B83 2014
346.01'35--dc23
2013048580

ISBN: 978-0-415-82591-7 (hbk)
ISBN: 978-0-415-82592-4 (pbk)
ISBN: 978-0-203-53813-5 (ebk)

Typeset in Baskerville by
Servis Filmsetting Ltd, Stockport, Cheshire

Printed and bound by CPI Group (UK) Ltd, Croydon, CR0 4YY

*This edition of International Child Law
is dedicated to
Trevor Buck's four granddaughters
Sara, Ella, Sofia and Alba*

Contents

Acknowledgements   xii
Preface   xiii
List of Contributors   xv
Table of Cases   xvi
Table of International Legal Instruments   xx
List of Abbreviations   xxv
List of Tables and Figures   xxviii
Case Studies   xxix

1   Childhood and children's rights   **1**

1.1   Childhood   1
      1.1.1   Historical perspective   2
      1.1.2   Psychological perspectives   6
      1.1.3   Sociological perspective   9
      1.1.4   Social policy perspectives   14
1.2   Human rights   18
      1.2.1   Children's rights   21
      1.2.2   International children's rights   35
1.3   Childhood, children's rights and cultural relativism   37

2   International law sources and institutions   **40**

2.1   Introduction   40
2.2   Sources of international law   41
      2.2.1   International treaties and conventions   41
      2.2.2   International customary law   46
      2.2.3   General principles of law recognised by civilised nations 49
      2.2.4   Judicial decisions and publicists' writings   50
      2.2.5   Hierarchy of sources and *jus cogens*   51
      2.2.6   'Soft law'   52
2.3   The relationship between domestic and international law   53
2.4   International organisations and institutions   55

	2.4.1	The United Nations (UN)	55
	2.4.2	The Hague Conference on Private International Law	70
	2.4.3	The International Criminal Court	72
2.5	Human rights protection		74
	2.5.1	Global protection: UN machinery	75

3   The UN Convention on the Rights of the Child   **87**

3.1	Introduction	87
3.2	Background and history	89
3.3	Failure to ratify the Convention on the Rights of the Child	91
3.4	The Committee on the Rights of the Child	95
3.5	The reporting process under the Convention	98
3.6	The optional protocols	107

3.6.1   Optional Protocol to the Convention on the Rights of the Child on the Sale of Children, Child Prostitution and Child Pornography (OPSC)   108

3.6.2   Optional Protocol to the Convention on the Rights of the Child on the Involvement of Children in Armed Conflict (OPAC)   110

3.6.3   Optional Protocol to the Convention on the Rights of the Child on a Communications Procedure (OPIC)   112

3.7   The implementation of the Convention on the Rights of the Child   117

3.7.1   General measures of implementation: Articles 4, 42 and 44(6)   118

3.7.2   Definition of the child: Article 1   126

3.7.3   General principles: Articles 2, 3, 6 and 12   131

3.7.4   Civil rights and freedoms: Articles 7, 8, 13–17, 28(2) and 37(a)   150

3.7.5   Family environment and alternative care: Articles 5, 18(1), (2), 9–11, 19–21, 25, 27(4) and 39   165

3.7.6   Violence against children: Articles 19, 37(a), 34 and 39   175

3.7.7   Disability, basic health and welfare: Articles 6, 18(3), 23, 24, 26, 27(1), (2) and (3), and 33   184

3.7.8   Education, leisure and cultural activities: Articles 28, 29 and 31   199

3.7.9   Special protection measures: Articles 22, 30, 32–36, 37(b)–(d), 38–40   205

4   Child labour   **227**

4.1	The phenomenon of child labour	227
	4.1.1	Difficulties of definition and types of child labour	227
	4.1.2	Identifying the causes of child labour	231

	4.1.3	The extent and location of exploitative child labour	234
	4.1.4	Cultural relativism and child labour	237
	4.1.5	Covert nature of child labour	238
	4.1.6	Measuring the extent of child labour	238
4.2	International legal protection of child labour		240
	4.2.1	The Minimum Age Convention of 1973	242
	4.2.2	The UN Convention on the Rights of the Child and Child Labour	249
	4.2.3	Elimination of the Worst Forms of Child Labour Convention of 1999	250
	4.2.4	Other international instruments relating to child labour	257
	4.2.5	The wider role of the International Labour Organization (ILO)	260
	4.2.6	ILO reporting, representation and complaints procedures	263
4.3	Progressing the elimination of exploitative child labour		267
	4.3.1	Child labour in international law: assessing the role of law and the enforceability problem	268
	4.3.2	Partnership and coordination	269
	4.3.3	Linking trade and labour standards	270

5   International parental child abduction   **274**

5.1	International parental child abduction		274
5.2	Introduction to the international legal instruments		277
	5.2.1	UN Convention on the Rights of the Child	278
	5.2.2	European Convention on Recognition and Enforcement of Decisions Concerning Custody of Children and on Restoration of Custody of Children of 1980	279
	5.2.3	The Revised Brussels II Regulation of 2003	280
5.3	The Hague Convention on the civil aspects of international child abduction (1980)		283
	5.3.1	Wrongful removal or retention	286
	5.3.2	The duty to make a return order	296
	5.3.3	Exceptions from the duty to make a return order	298
	5.3.4	Exercising discretion	311
5.4	International parental abduction and non-convention countries		314
5.5	The use of mediation in international parental child abduction		318
5.6	Concluding remarks		320

6   Inter-country adoption   **321**

6.1	Introduction		321
	6.1.1	Inter-country adoption: the statistics	323
	6.1.2	The sending and receiving countries	326

6.2   The need for international legal regulation   326
   6.2.1   The Hague Convention of 1965   326
   6.2.2   Adoption and the UN Convention on the Rights of the
       Child   327
   6.2.3   The Special Commission and the Hague Convention of
       1993   328
   6.2.4   UNICEF's Position   331
6.3   The Hague Convention on Intercountry Adoption of 1993   333
   6.3.1   The best interests of the child are paramount 335
   6.3.2   Subsidiarity principle   339
   6.3.3   Safeguards to protect children from abduction, sale and
       trafficking   339
   6.3.4   Cooperation between states and within states   342
   6.3.5   Automatic recognition of adoption decisions   343
   6.3.6   Competent authorities, central authorities and accredited
       bodies   344
6.4   Hague Conference International Centre for Judicial Studies and
     Technical Assistance   346
6.5   Concluding remarks   352

7   Sexual exploitation   **353**

7.1   Introduction   353
   7.1.1   What is sexual exploitation?   353
7.2   International action   356
   7.2.1   Global bodies   356
   7.2.2   Regional bodies   359
   7.2.3   Industry   361
7.3   International instruments   364
   7.3.1   UN Convention on the Rights of the Child   364
   7.3.2   Convention on the Worst Forms of Child Labour (1999) 365
   7.3.3   Optional Protocol to the Convention on the Rights of the
       Child on the sale of children, child prostitution and child
       pornography of 2000 (OPSC)   366
7.4   States' responsibilities   368
   7.4.1   Criminalisation   368
   7.4.2   Establishing jurisdiction   373
   7.4.3   International cooperation and support   376
   7.4.4   Assisting victims   376
7.5   Reporting mechanisms   378

8   Children and armed conflict   **384**

8.1   Children and armed conflict: the international law framework 384
   8.1.1   International humanitarian law   385

		8.1.2 International human rights law	393
8.2		The United Nations and children associated with armed forces or armed groups	404
	8.2.1	Security Council resolutions	404
	8.2.2	The Paris Principles	407
	8.2.3	The Special Representative of the Secretary-General for children and armed conflict	409
8.3		International courts and tribunals	412
	8.3.1	The International Criminal Tribunal for the former Yugoslavia (ICTY)	412
	8.3.2	International Criminal Tribunal for Rwanda (ICTR)	413
	8.3.3	Special Court for Sierra Leone (SCSL)	415
	8.3.4	International Criminal Court (ICC)	416

9   Indigenous children   **425**

9.1		Indigenous children: introduction	425
	9.1.1	Overview	425
	9.1.2	Who are indigenous peoples?	425
9.2		Indigenous peoples: international law and policy	427
	9.2.1	United Nations human rights treaties	427
	9.2.2	Convention on the Rights of the Child	430
	9.2.3	ILO Indigenous and Tribal Peoples Convention	435
	9.2.4	United Nations Declaration on the Rights of Indigenous Peoples	437
9.3		Indigenous peoples and United Nations mechanisms	440
	9.3.1	United Nations Permanent Forum on Indigenous Peoples	441
	9.3.2	The Special Rapporteur on the situation of human rights and fundamental freedoms of indigenous people	442
	9.3.3	Expert Mechanism on the Rights of Indigenous Peoples	447
9.4		Concluding remarks	448

Bibliography   449
Index   467

Acknowledgements

The author and publishers would like to thank the following for providing permission to reprint material in this textbook:

A.C. v. Manitoba (Director of Child and Family Services), 2009 SCC 30 (2009), 26 June 2009 reproduced with the permission of the Supreme Court of Canada, 2013.

Hague Conference of Private International Law, Report of Mission to Kazakhstan (9–12 May 2011), Jennifer Degeling and Laura Martínez-Mora, (July 2011), Permanent Bureau: The Hague, Netherlands (copyright 2011, United Nations), reprinted with the permission of the United Nations.

International Court of Justice: Application of the Convention of 1902 Governing the Guardianship of Infants (Netherlands v Sweden) (Judgment) [1958] ICJ Re p 55, reprinting with the permission of the International Court of Justice (ICJ).

Re S (A Child) (Abduction: Rights of Custody)[2012] UKSC 10, [2012] 2 A.C. 257; Re M. (Children) (Abduction: Rights of Custody) [2007] UKHL 55, [2008] 1 AC 1288, HC/E/UKe 937; Re J. (A child) (Return to foreign jurisdiction: convention rights), [2005] UKHL 40, [2006] 1 AC 80, HC/E/UKe 801; and Gillick v. West Norfolk and Wisbech Area Health Authority [1986] AC 112, [1985] 3 All ER 402 all reprinted with the permission of The Incorporated Council of Law Reporting for England and Wales (ICLR).

'UNICEF's position on Inter-country adoption' (2010) <http://www.unicef.org/media/media_41918.html> (accessed 9 November 2013) courtesy of UNICEF.

The Prosecutor v Thomas Lubanga Dyilo (Judgement), (International Criminal Court, Trial Chamber I, Case No ICC-01/04-01/06, 14 March 2012), [1351-1363]; and The Prosecutor v Thomas Lubanga Dyilo (Decision on Sentence), (International Criminal Court, Trial Chamber I, Case No ICC-01/04-01/06, 10 July 2012) [92-110] reproduced here courtesy of the International Criminal Court, Public information and Documentation section.

Every effort has been made to trace and contact copyright holders prior to publication. If notified, the publisher will undertake to rectify any errors or omissions at the earliest opportunity.

Preface

The aim of this book has been to provide the reader with an accessible, informed, critical and scholarly account of the international law framework relating to children. The third edition of *International Child Law* has been updated and revised throughout since the appearance of the second edition in 2010. Chapter 1 (Childhood and Children's Rights) and Chapter 2 (International Law Sources and Institutions) set the scene with introductions to the key disciplinary perspectives on the nature of childhood, the international movement and theoretical debates about children's rights and a narrative account of international law sources and institutions. Chapter 3 (UN Convention on the Rights of the Child) has been expanded substantially from the last edition to include more detailed commentary on the articles of this landmark Convention which has established comprehensive normative legal standards of international child law. Chapters 4 to 9 focus on more specialist concerns: child labour, international parental child abduction, inter-country adoption, sexual exploitation, children and armed conflict, and indigenous children. These chapters examine the social phenomenon under discussion and then provide an account of the relevant matrix of international law and its institutional regimes. My hope is that the reader will be provoked to question whether the international law frameworks established have been appropriate responses to the phenomena examined. Cross-cutting themes and debates appear in most chapters: for example, issues relating to the autonomy and participation rights of children, the 'universalism v cultural relativity' debate, the gap between the aspirations of international law texts and their implementation in domestic legal systems.

Thanks are due to a number of individuals who have, in different ways, contributed to the production of this edition: in particular to my former colleague and mentor, Professor Malcolm Shaw QC (University of Leicester), who first suggested to me some years ago that I should write this book; and to Professor Alisdair Gillespie (Lancaster University) who has authored Chapter 7; and to Conrad Nyamutatu, one of my PhD students who kindly read and commented on Chapter 8. A number of staff members at Routledge have been extremely helpful in bringing this project to completion. My thanks in particular to: Emma Nugent (associate editor), Rebekah Jenkins (editorial assistant), Nicola Prior (copy editor), and Hayley Kennard (production editor). My thanks also to my under-graduate, postgraduate and doctoral research students who have all engaged with *International Child Law* since the first edition appeared in 2005 and provide continuous, constructive feedback. Finally, and most importantly, my thanks go to my wife, Barbara, who has given me with excellent support during the writing process.

Trevor Buck
Professor of Socio-Legal Studies
De Montfort University
United Kingdom
March 2014

List of Contributors

Trevor Buck is Professor of Socio-Legal Studies in the School of Law at De Montfort University, Leicester. His main teaching and research interests include international child law, administrative justice and social security law. He has been appointed a member of the Law sub-panel for the Research Excellence Framework 2014 in the UK.

Alisdair A. Gillespie is Professor of Criminal Law and Justice at Lancaster University. His main research interests are in the fields of the sexual abuse of children, particularly where it is facilitated by Information and Communication Technologies, and cybercrime. Alisdair is responsible for writing Chapter 7 (Sexual Exploitation) of this book.

Table of Cases

Australia

Director-General, Department of Families, Youth and Community Care v Rhonda May Bennett [2000] Fam CA 253; HC/E/AU 275 309

Austria

Ob256/09t , *Oberster Gerichtshof*, HC/E/AT 1049 302

Canada

A.C. v Manitoba (Director of Child and Family Services) 2009 SCC 30 29
BJG v DLG. 2010 YKSC 44 149
Canada (Prime Minister) v Khadr 2010 SCC 3, [2010] 1 SCR 44 221
Crnkovich v Hortensius [2009] WDFL 337, 62 RFL (6th) 351, 2008; HC/E/ CA1028 308
W(V) v S(D) (1996) 2 SCR 108, (1996) 134 DLR 4th 481m, HC/E/CA 17 284

England and Wales

A v A (Children: Habitual Residence) [2013] UKSC 60; HC/E/UKe 1233 295
Cannon v. Cannon [2004] EWCA Civ 1330, [2005] 1 FLR 169, [2005] 1 W.L.R. 32 299
Derbyshire County Council v Times Newspapers Ltd [1992] QB 770 55
Garland v British Rail Engineering Ltd [1983] 2 AC 751 55
Gillick v West Norfolk and Wisbech Area Health Authority [1986] AC 112, [1985] 3 All ER 402 27
Nottinghamshire County Council v KB and KB [2011] IESC 48; HC/E/IE 1139 310
R v Barnet London Borough Council, ex p Shah [1983] 2 AC 309 296
R v Bow Street Metropolitan Stipendiary Magistrate, ex p Pinochete Ugarte (No 3) [2000] 1 AC 147 54
R v Secretary of State for the Home Department, ex p Brind [1991] 1 AC 696 55
Re B (A Minor) (Abduction) [1994] 2 FLR 249; HC/E/UKe 4 288
Re D (A Child) (Abduction: Rights of Custody) [2006] UKHL 51, [2007] 1 AC 619 281

Re D (A Child) (Abduction: Rights of Custody) [2006] UKHL 51, [2007] 1 AC 619, HC/E/UKe 880..288

Re D. (A Child) (Abduction: Rights of Custody) [2006] UKHL 51, [2007] 1 A.C. 619, HC/E/UKe 880..290

Re G (Child Abduction) (Unmarried Father: Rights of Custody) [2002] EWHC 2219 (Fam), HC/E/UKe 506 288

Re H (A Minor) (Abduction: Rights of Custody) [2002] 2 AC 291............................289

Re H (Abduction: Acquiescence) [1998] AC 72 302

Re HB (Abduction: Child's Objections) (No 2) [1998] 1 FLR 564...........................308

Re I (Abduction: Acquiescence) [1999] 1 FLR 778..303

Re J (A child) (Return to foreign jurisdiction: Convention rights) [2005] UKHL 40, [2006] 1 AC 80; HC/E/UKe 801 315

Re JS (Private International Adoption) [2000] 2 FLR 638 289

Re M (Abduction: Zimbabwe), [2007] UKHL 55; [2008] 1 FLR 251...................309

Re M. (Children) (Abduction: Rights of Custody) [2007] UKHL 55, [2008] 1 AC 1288, HC/E/UKe 937...312

Re S (A Child) (Abduction: Grave Risk of Harm) [2002] EWCA Civ 908, HC/E/ UKe 469 307

Re S (A Child) (Abduction: Rights of Custody) [2012] UKSC 10, [2012] 2 AC 257..305

Re V.-B. (Abduction: Custody Rights) [1999] 2 FLR 192, HC/E/UKe 261 289

Re W (Abduction: Procedure) [1995] 1 FLR 878; HC/E/UKe 37 301

TB v JB (formerly JH) (Abduction: Grave Risk of Harm) [2001] 2 FLR 515; W v. W [2004] 2 FLR 499 307

Trendtex Trading Corp v Central Bank of Nigeria [1977] QB 529..............................54

European Court of Human Rights

Ahmed v Turkey (1997) 24 EHRR 278..375

JPC v SLW and SMW (Abduction) [2007] EWHC 1349 (Fam) [2007] 2 FLR 900..283

Neulinger and Shuruk v Switzerland (Application No 41615/07), Grand Chamber (2012) 54 EHRR 31, HC/E/ 1323 304

Re A (Custody Decision after Maltese Non-Return Order) [2006] EWHC 3397 (Fam), [2007] 1 FLR 1923..283

Re F (Abduction: Child's Wishes) [2007] EWCA Civ 468 282

Re M (A Child) (Abduction: Child's Objections to Return) [2007] EWCA Civ 260, [2007] 2 FLR 72 282

Šneersone and Kampanella v Italy (Application No 14737/09) (12 July 2011) 279

Soering v United Kingdom (1989) 11 EHRR 439 375

European Court of Justice

McB. v L.E. Case C–400/10 PPU J, HC/E/ 1104 (5 October 2010)...............288

Inter-American Court of Human Rights

Mayagna (Sumo) Awas Tingni Community v Nicaragua (Judgment) 31 August 2001, Series C, No 79...426

International Court of Justice (and PCIJ)

Application of the Convention of 1902 Governing the Guardianship of Infants (Netherlands v Sweden) (Judgment) [1958] ICJ Rep 55 (the 'Boll case')..............................51
Corfu Channel Case (UK v Albania) (Merits) [1949] ICJ Rep 4 64
Factory at Chorzów (Germany v Poland) (Merits) [1928] PCIJ Ser A No 17 50
Nicaragua v United States (Military and Paramilitary Activities in and against Nicaragua) (Judgment) [1986] ICJ Rep 14 49
Nuclear Tests (New Zealand v France) (Judgment) [1974] ICJ Rep 457, 473 50
Legality of the Use by a State of Nuclear Weapons in Armed Conflict, Advisory Opinion of 8 July 1996 [1996] ICJ Reports 226 65
Legal Consequences of the Construction of a Wall in the Occupied Palestinian Territory, Advisory Opinion of 9 July 2004 [1994] ICJ Rep 136................................65

International Criminal Court

Prosecutor v Thomas Lubanga Dyilo (Decision on Sentence), Trial Chamber I, Case No ICC-01/04-01/06 (10 July 2012) 421
Prosecutor v Thomas Lubanga Dyilo (Judgment), International Criminal Court, Trial Chamber I, Case No ICC-01/04-01/06 (14 March 2012).............418
Prosecutor v Thomas Lubanga Dyilo (Warrant of Arrest), Pre-Trial Chamber I, Case No ICC-01/04-01/06 (10 February 2006).......................................417

International Criminal Tribunal for Rwanda

Prosecutor v Akayesu (Judgement), Trial Chamber I, Case No ICTR-96-4-T, 2 September 1998..414
Prosecutor v Bosco Ntaganda, (Decision on the Prosecutor's Application under Article 58), Pre-Trial Chamber II, Case No ICC-01/04-02/06 (13 July 2012) ... 418
Prosecutor v Kambanda (Judgement and Sentence), Trial Chamber I, Case No ICTR-97-23-S, 2 September 1998..414

Ireland

H.I. v M.G. [1999] 2 ILRM 1, [2000] 1 IR 110; HC/E/IE 284......................288
M. S. H. v L. H. [2000] 3 IR 390..302
W.P.P. v S.R.W. [2001] ILRM 371, HC/E/IE 271 289

Director-General, Department of Child Safety v Stratford [2005] Fam CA 1115; HC/E/UKe 830..302
Re W (Abduction: Procedure) [1995] 1 FLR 878; HC/E/UKe 37 302
Re K (Abduction: Consent) [1997] 2 FLR 212; HC/E/UKe 55............................302
Re H (Abduction: Acquiescence) [1998] AC 72 302

Israel

Anonymous et al v The High Rabbinical Court et al (25 June 2008) HCJ 1073/05.... 141
Anonymous et al v The Shari'a' Court of Appeals et al (5 June 2006) HCJ 1129/06 141

New Zealand
Anderson v Paterson [2002] NZFLR 641; HC/E/NZ 471 288
Fairfax v. Ireton [2009] NZFLR 433 (NZ CA), HC/E/NZ 1018 291
RCL v APBL [2012] NZHC 1292, HC/E/NZ 1231 292

Scotland
AQ v JQ Outer House of the Court of Session (12 December 2001); HC/E/
    UK 415 308
N.J.C. v N.P.C. [2008] CSIH 34, 2008 S.C. 571 310
O. v O. 2002 SC 430; HC/E/UKs 507 302
S. v S. 2003 SLT 344; HC/E/UKs 577 302

South Africa
Sonderup v Tondelli 2001 (1) SA 1171 (CC) (Constitutional Court of South Africa) .. 307

Special Court for Sierra Leone
Prosecutor v Brima, Kamara and Kanu (AFRC case) (Appeal Judgment), Trial
    Chamber II, Case No SCSL-2004-16-A (22 February 2008) 415
Prosecutor v Brima, Kamara and Kanu (AFRC case) (Sentencing Judgment), Trial
    Chamber II, Case No SCSL-04-16-T (19 July 2007) 415
Prosecutor v Charles Ghankay Taylor (Appeal Judgment), Appeals Chamber,
    Case No SCSL-03-01-A (26 September 2013) 416
Prosecutor v Charles Ghankay Taylor (Sentencing Judgment), Case No SCSL-03-
    01-T-1285 (30 May 2012) 416
Prosecutor v Charles Ghankay Taylor (Trial Judgment), Case No SCSL-03-
    01-T-1283 (18 May 2012) 416
Prosecutor v Fofana and Kondewa (CDF Case) (Appeal Judgement), Appeals
    Chamber, Case No SCSL-04-14-A, (28 May 2008) 416
Prosecutor v Fofana and Kondewa (CDF case) (Sentencing Judgment), Trial
    Chamber I, Case No SCSL-04-14-T (9 October 2007) 415
Prosecutor v Sam Hinga Norman (Moinina Fofana intervening), Decision on
    Preliminary Motion Based on Lack of Jurisdiction (Child Recruitment),
    Appeals Chamber, Case No SCSL-2004-14-AR72(E) (31 May 2004) 415
Prosecutor v Sesay, Kallon and Gbao (RUF case) (Judgment), Trial Chamber I,
    Case No SCSL-04-15-T (2 March 2009) 415

United States
Abbot v Abbott 130 S. Ct. 1983 (2010); HC/E/USf 1029 288
Chafin v Chafin, 133 S. Ct. 1017, 185 L. Ed. 2d 1 (2013); HC/E/US 1206 284
Re Gault, 387 US 1 (1967) 33
Roper v Simmons, 543 U.S. 551 (2005) 93
Walsh v Walsh No. 99–1747 (1st Cir July 25, 2000) (US Court of Appeals for
    the First Circuit) 307
Whallon v Lynn 230 F.3d 450 (1st Cir. 2000), HC/E/USf 388 288

Table of International Legal Instruments

Hague Conference on Private International Law

Guide to Good Practice: Mediation 2012.. 320

Guide to Good Practice No 1: The Implementation and Operation of the
    1993 Hague Intercountry Adoption Convention 335

Guide to Good Practice No 2: Accreditation and Adoption Accredited
    Bodies 2012.. 346

Hague Convention Concerning the Powers of Authorities and the
Law Applicable in Respect of the Protection of Infants 1961........................... 64

Hague Convention on the Settlement of Guardianship of Minors,
    Guardianship 1902 51

Hague Convention on Jurisdiction, Applicable Law and Recognition
of Decrees Relating to Adoptions 1965 326

Hague Convention on Jurisdiction, Applicable Law, Recognition,
    Enforcement and Co-operation
in respect of Parental Responsibility and Measures for the Protection of
    Children 1996 51

Hague Convention on Protection of Children and Cooperation
in respect of Intercountry Adoption 1993 333

Hague Convention on the Civil Aspects of International
Child Abduction 1980... 283

Hague Convention on the International Recovery of Child Support
and Other Forms of Family Maintenance 2007... 72

Hague Convention Protocol on the Law Applicable
to Maintenance Obligations 2007 72

Hague Convention Protocol on the Law Applicable to Maintenance
    Obligations 2007.. 72

Statute of the Hague Convention on Private International Law 1955 70

International Labour Organization

Abolition of Forced Labour Convention 1957 (No 105) 251

Constitution of the International Labour Organisation 1919.......................... 237

Decent Work for Domestic Workers 2011 (No 189) 212

Declaration of Philadelphia 1944 261
Declaration on Fundamental Principles and Rights at Work and its Follow-
    up 1998 262
Discrimination (Employment and Occupation) Convention 1958 (No. 111) ... 251
Employment Policy Convention of 1964 (No 122) 264
Equal Remuneration Convention 1951 (No. 100) 251
Forced Labour Convention 1930 (No. 29) 251
Freedom of Association and Protection of the Right to Organise Convention
    1948 (No. 87) 251
Indigenous and Tribal Peoples Convention (ILO Convention No. 169) 1989 .. 435
Indigenous and Tribal Populations Convention (ILO Convention No. 107)
    1957 435
International Labour Organization Constitution 1919 69
Labour Inspection (Agriculture) Convention of 1969 (No 129) 264
Minimum Age (Agriculture) Convention 1921 (No10) 241
Minimum Age (Fishermen) Convention 1959 (No 112) 242
Minimum Age (Industry) Convention 1919 (No 5) 241
Minimum Age (Industry) Convention (Revised) 1937 (No 59) 241
Minimum Age (Non-industrial Employment) Convention (Revised) 1937
    (No 60) 241
Minimum Age (Non-Industrial Employment) Convention 1932 (No 33) 241
Minimum Age (Sea) Convention 1920 (No 7) 241
Minimum Age (Sea) Convention (Revised) of 1936 (No 58) 241
Minimum Age (Trimmers and Stokers) Convention 1921 (No 15) 241
Minimum Age (Underground Work) Convention 1965 (No 123) 242
Minimum Age Convention (No. 138) 1973 242
Minimum Age Recommendation 1973 (R146) 242
Right to Organize and Collective Bargaining Convention 1949 (No. 98) 251
Tripartite Consultation (International Labour Standards) Convention of
    1976 (No 144) 264
Worst Forms of Child Labour 1999 (No. 182) 250
Worst Forms of Child Labour Recommendation 1999 (R190) 239

Regional International Instruments

Africa

African Charter on Human and Peoples' Rights (the 'Banjul Charter')
    1981 20
African Charter on the Rights and Welfare of the Child 1990 38

America

American Convention on Human Rights (the 'Pact of San Jose') 1969 20

Asia

Asian Human Rights Charter: A Peoples Charter 1998 20

South Asian Association for Regional Co-operation (SAARC) Convention
on Preventing and Combating Trafficking in Women and Children for
Prostitution 359

Europe
  (i) Council of Europe
Convention for the Protection of Human Rights and Fundamental
Freedoms 1950 16
Convention on Action against Trafficking in Human Beings 2005 360
Convention on Contact Concerning Children 2003 15
Convention on Cybercrime 2001 360
Convention on Recognition and Enforcement of Decisions Concerning
Custody of Children and on Restoration of Custody of Children of
1980 279
Convention on the Adoption of Children 196 14
Convention on the Adoption of Children (revised) 2007 15
Convention on the Exercise of Children's Rights 1996 15
Convention on the Legal Status of Children Born out of Wedlock 1975 14
Convention on the Protection of Children against Sexual Exploitation and
Sexual Abuse 2007 360
European Social Charter 1961 14
European Social Charter (revised) 1996 15

  (ii) European Union
Charter of Fundamental Rights of the European Union 2007 282
Council Decision 2000/375/JHA of 29 May 2000 to Combat Child
Pornography on the Internet [2000] OJ L138/1 360
Council Framework Decision 2004/68/JHA of 22 December 2003 on
Combating the Sexual Exploitation of Children and Child Pornography
[2004] OJ L13/44 360
Council Regulation (EU) 2201/2003 (the 'Revised Brussels II Regulation') 280
Directive 2011/92/ EU of 13 December 2011 on Combating the Sexual
Abuse and Sexual Exploitation of Children and Child Pornography
and replacing Council Framework Decision 2004/68/JHA [2011] OJ
L335/1 361
Treaty on European Union ('Maastricht Treaty') 1992 360

United Nations
Charter of the United Nations 1945 19
Convention against Torture and Other Cruel, Inhuman and Degrading
Treatment or Punishment 1984 84
Convention on Psychotropic Substances 1971 215
Convention on the Elimination of All Forms of Discrimination against
Women 1979 67

Convention on the Elimination of All Forms of Racial Discrimination 1965 .. 93
Convention on the High Seas 1958 68
Convention on the Law of the Sea 1982 48
Convention on the Reduction of Statelessness 1961 206
Convention on the Reduction of Statelessness 1975 206
Convention on the Rights of Persons with Disabilities 2006 196
Convention on the Rights of the Child 1989 87
Convention Relating to the Status of Refugees 1951 206
Convention Relating to the Status of Stateless Persons 1954 156
Declaration of the Rights of the Child 1924 21
Declaration of the Rights of the Child 1959 22
Declaration on Social and Legal Principles relating to the Protection and
    Welfare of Children, with special reference to Foster Placement and
    Adoption, Nationally and Internationally 1986 173
Declaration on the Protection of Women and Children in Emergency and
    Armed Conflict 1974 390
Declaration on the Rights of Indigenous People 2007 437
Durban Declaration and Programme of Action adopted at the World
    Conference against Racism, Racial Discrimination, Xenophobia and
    Related Intolerance 2001 136
Geneva Convention IV: Relative to the Protection of Civilian Persons in
    Time of War 1949 386
Guidelines for the Prevention of Juvenile Delinquency (the 'Riyadh
    Guidelines') 1990 222
Guidelines on Justice in Matters Involving Child Victims and Witnesses of
    Crime 2005 226
ILC Draft Articles on the Responsibility of States for Internationally
    Wrongful Acts 2001 68
ILC Guide to Practice on Reservations to Treaties (2011) 68
International Bill of Human Rights 75
International Code of Marketing of Breast-milk Substitutes 1981 193
International Convention for the Protection of All Persons from Enforced
    Disappearance 2006 155
International Convention on the Protection of the Rights of All Migrant
    Workers and Members of their Families 1990 84
International Convention on the Rights of Persons with Disabilities
    2006 84
International Covenant on Civil and Political Rights 1966 19
International Covenant on Economic, Social and Cultural Rights 1966 19
Millennium Declaration 2000 17
Optional Protocol of the International Covenant on Economic, Social and
    Cultural Rights 2008 19
Optional Protocol to the Convention on the Rights of the Child on a
    Communications Procedure 2012 112

Optional Protocol to the Convention on the Rights of the Child on the
    Involvement of Children in Armed Conflict 2000 110
Optional Protocol to the Convention on the Rights of the Child on the Sale
    of Children, Child Prostitution and Child Pornography 2000.................. 108
Optional Protocol of the Convention against Torture 2002 84
Optional Protocol to the Convention on the Rights of Persons with
    Disabilities 2006.. 186
Paris Commitments to Protect Children Unlawfully Recruited or Used by
    Armed Forces or Armed Groups of 2007 407
Paris Principles and Guidelines on Children associated with Armed Forces
    or Armed Groups of 2007... 407
Principles Relating to the Status of Independent National Human Rights
    Institutions (the 'Paris Principles') 1993 124
Protocol Additional to the Geneva Conventions of 12 August 1949, the
    Protection of Victims of International Armed Conflicts (Protocol I)
    1977 391
Protocol Additional to the Geneva Conventions of 12 August 1949, the
    Protection of Victims of Non-International Armed Conflicts (Protocol
    II) 1977... 392
Protocol relating to the Status of Refugees 1967 206
Rules for the Protection of Juveniles Deprived of their Liberty (the 'Havana
    Rules') 1990.. 222
Rome Statute of the International Criminal Court 1998................................. 416
Single Convention on Narcotic Drugs 1961 215
Standard Minimum Rules for the Administration of Juvenile Justice (the
    'Beijing Rules') 1985 129
Standard Rules on the Equalization of Opportunities for Persons with
    Disabilities 1993.. 188
Statute of the International Court of Justice 1945 62
Statute of the International Criminal Tribunal for the Former Yugoslavia
    2002 413
Statute of the International Law Commission 1947 67
Supplementary Convention on the Abolition of Slavery, the Slave Trade
    and Institutions and Practices Similar to Slavery of 1956........................ 258
Treaty of Versailles 1919 69
Universal Declaration of Human Rights 1948.. 19
Vienna Convention on Diplomatic Relations 1961 68
Vienna Convention on the Law of Treaties 1969 52
Vienna Declaration and Programme of Action 1993 75
Vienna Guidelines for Action on Children in the Criminal Justice System
    1997 222

List of Abbreviations

Armed Forces Revolutionary Council	AFRC
Child-rights impact assessment	CRIA
Civil Defence Forces	CDF
Committee Against Torture	CAT
Committee of Experts on the Application of Conventions and Recommendations	CEACR
Committee on Economic, Social and Cultural Rights	CESCR
Committee on Enforced Disappearances	CED
Committee on Migrant Workers	CMW
Committee on the Elimination of Discrimination Against Women	CEDAW
Committee on the Elimination of Racial Discrimination	CERD
Committee on the Rights of Persons with Disabilities	CRPD
Committee on the Rights of the Child	CRC
Democratic Republic of the Congo	DRC
Economic and Social Council	ECOSOC
Ending Child Prostitution And Trafficking	ECPAT
European Convention for the Protection of Human Rights	ECHR
European Court of Human Rights	ECtHR
European Union	EU
European Union Law Enforcement Agency	EUROPOL
Female Genital Mutilation	FGM
Food and Agriculture Organization	FAO
Gross National Income per capita	GNI
Gross per capita Domestic Product	GDP
Human Rights Committee	CCPR
International Atomic Energy Agency	IAEA
International Child Abduction and Contact Unit	ICACU
International Child Abduction Database	INCADAT
International Civil Aviation Organization	ICAO
International Committee of the Red Cross	ICRC
International Court of Justice	ICJ
International Covenant on Civil and Political Rights	ICCPR

International Covenant on Economic, Social and Cultural Rights	ICESCR
International Criminal Court	ICC
International Criminal Police Organization	INTERPOL
International Criminal Tribunal for Rwanda	ICTR
International Criminal Tribunal for the former Yugoslavia	ICTY
International Fund for Agricultural Development	IFAD
International Labour Organization	ILO
The International Law Commission	ILC
International Maritime Organization	IMO
International Monetary Fund	IMF
International Non-Governmental Organisation	INGO
International Programme on the Elimination of Child Labour	IPEC
International Telecommunication Union	ITU
Middle East and North African region	MENA
Millennium Development Goal	MDG
National human rights institution	NHRI
Non-Communicable Disease	NCD
Non-Governmental Organisation	NGO
Office of the United Nations High Commissioner for Human Rights	OHCHR
Open-Ended Working Group	OEWG
Optional Protocol of the International Covenant on Economic, Social and Cultural Rights	OP-ICESCR
Optional Protocol to the Convention on the Rights of the Child on a Communications Procedure	OPIC
Optional Protocol to the Convention on the Rights of the Child on the Involvement of Children in Armed Conflict	OPAC
Optional Protocol to the Convention on the Rights of the Child on the Sale of Children, Child Prostitution and Child Pornography	OPSC
Organization of African Unity	OAU
Permanent Court of International Justice	PCIJ
Revolutionary United Front	RUF
Sexually Transmitted Disease	STD
South Asian Association for Regional Co-operation	SAARC
Special Court for Sierra Leone	SCSL
Special Representative of the Secretary General	SRSG
Statistical Information and Monitoring Programme on Child Labour	SIMPOC
Subcommittee on Prevention of Torture and other Cruel, Inhuman or Degrading Treatment or Punishment	SPT
System of National Accounts	SNA
United Nations	UN
United Nations Children's Fund	UNICEF
United Nations Commission on Human Rights (1945–2006)	UNCHR
United Nations Convention on the Rights of the Child	CRC

United Nations Development Programme	UNDP
United Nations Educational, Scientific and Cultural Organization	UNESCO
United Nations High Commissioner for Refugees	UNHCR
United Nations Human Rights Council (2006 – to present)	UNHRC
United Nations Industrial Development Organization	UNIDO
United Nations Office on Drugs and Crime	UNODC
United Nations Population Fund	UNFPA
United Nations Programme on HIV/AIDS	UNAIDS
Universal Declaration of Human Rights	UDHR
Universal Periodic Review	UPR
Universal Postal Union	UPU
Virtual Global Taskforce	VGT
West European and Others Group	WEOG
World Bank	WB
World Food Programme	WFP
World Health Organization	WHO
World Intellectual Property Organization	WIPO
World Meteorological Organization	WMO
World Tourism Organization	UNWTO
World Trade Organization	WTO

List of Tables and Figures

Figure 1.1	The orb web model	12
Table 2.1	International Human Rights Treaty Bodies	84
Table 2.2	International Human Rights Treaty Bodies: communication/ complaints Procedures	85
Figure 3.1	United Nations Convention on the Rights of the Child: signatures (140), ratifications (193), accessions (47) and successions (8) by year	88
Table 3.1	General Comments of the Committee on the Rights of the Child	96
Table 3.2	Number of state reports considered by the Committee on the Rights of the Child in 2014 and 2015, under the Convention and the two substantive Optional Protocols	103
Table 4.1	Global child labour by level of national income, 2012	232
Table 4.2	Global estimates of number of children (age 5–17) in child labour and hazardous work, 2008 and 2012	235
Table 4.3	Regional estimates of child labour, 5–17 years old, 2012	235
Table 4.4	Regional estimates of children in hazardous work, 5–17 years old, 2012	235
Figure 4.1	Child labour by sector in 2012	236
Table 5.1	Outcomes of return applications in 2008 under the Hague Convention	277
Figure 5.1	Structure of the Hague Convention of 1980	286
Table 5.2	Reasons for judicial refusal	298
Table 6.1	Estimated numbers of children adopted via inter-country adoption 1948–2010: total 970,000 adoptions	324
Table 6.2	Inter-country adoptions to 23 receiving states 2003–2011	324
Table 6.3	15 countries sending most children for inter-country adoption to the 23 receiving states in Table 6.2 above: 2003–2011	325

Case Studies

Chapter 1

Case study 1.1   **27–8**
Gillick v West Norfolk and Wisbech Area Health Authority [1986] AC 112, [1985] 3 All
    ER 402

Case study 1.2   **29–30**
A.C. v Manitoba (Director of Child and Family Services) 2009 SCC 30 (2009), 26 June
    2009

Chapter 2

Case study 2.1   **64–5**
*Application of the Convention of 1902 Governing the Guardianship of Infants (Netherlands v
    Sweden) (Judgment)* [1958] ICJ Rep 55 (the 'Boll case')

Case study 2.2   **77–80**
United Nations: Youth Assembly on 'Malala Day' in New York on 12 July 2013

Chapter 3

(None)

Chapter 4

Case study 4.1   **273**
Concluding observations on the combined third and fourth periodic reports of
    Uzbekistan, adopted by the Committee at its 63rd session (27 May–14 June
    2013) CRC/C/UZB/CO/3-4 (14 June 2013) paras 65–66

Chapter 5

Case study 5.1   **292–95**
High Court of New Zealand: *RCL v APBL* [2012] NZHC 1292; HC/E/NZ 1231
    (J W Gendall J) Judgment, 11 June 2012.

Case study 5.2   **305–07**
In re S (A Child) (Abduction: Rights of Custody) [2012] UKSC 10, [2012] 2 AC 257

Case study 5.3   **312–14**
Re M (Children) (Abduction: Rights of Custody) [2007] UKHL 55, [2008] 1 AC 1288:
   HC/E/UKe 937

Case study 5.4   **315–17**
Re J (A child) (Return to foreign jurisdiction: Convention rights) [2005] UKHL 40, [2006]
   1 AC 80; HC/E/UKe 801

Chapter 6
Case study 6.1   **348–52**
Extract from: Hague Conference of Private International Law, *Report of Mission
   to Kazakhstan* (9–12 May 2011), Jennifer Degeling and Laura Martínez-Mora
   (July 2011) Permanent Bureau: The Hague, Netherlands.

Chapter 7
Case study 7.1   **379–83**
Child Sex Tourism

Chapter 8
Case study 8.1   **400–04**
Extract from: Concluding observations on the initial report of China submitted
   under Article 8 of the Optional Protocol to the Convention on the Rights of
   the Child on the involvement of children in armed conflict, adopted by the
   Committee at its 64th session (16 September–4 October 2013), CRC/C/
   OPAC/CHN/CO/1 (29 October 2013).

Case study 8.2   **418–24**
The Lubanga Case

Chapter 9
Case study 9.1   **443–47**
Statement upon conclusion of the visit to Canada by the United Nations Special
   Rapporteur on the rights of indigenous peoples, James Anaya

Chapter 1

Childhood and children's rights

The international law relating to children is best understood by considering at the outset what we mean when we talk about 'childhood' and 'children's rights'. At first sight, these two concepts seem straightforward, but on closer examination they turn out to be contestable notions. 'Childhood' assumes some kind of understanding of what it means to be a child and, by implication, an adult. 'Children's rights' assumes a background framework of knowledge about 'human rights' of which children's rights can be considered an integral part. To an extent, the project of international law relating to children is one which is predicated on the existence of a universally held definition of 'child',[1] and yet it is self-evident that 'childhood' is experienced very differently by groups of children even within the same nation state. Furthermore, the way in which we perceive childhood and children's rights will have a highly significant bearing on how we view international child law and the international community's approach to legal regulation and standard-setting in this area. This chapter seeks to introduce the reader to these two important concepts.

1.1   Childhood

The following sections include a brief overview of the historical, psychological, sociological and social policy perspectives on childhood. The study of childhood has become a truly multi-disciplinary activity. However, while the focus on childhood tends to be favoured within the academic community, research initiatives that are more highly linked to policy and specific projects have, since the 1990s, tended to concern themselves primarily with child protection (Ennew 2008). Indeed, there are many research centres dedicated to the study of childhood,[2] and the number of 'childhood studies' programmes in higher education has grown.

---

1 The UN Convention on the Rights of the Child (1989) art 1 defines the child thus: 'For the purposes of the present Convention, a child means every human being below the age of eighteen years unless under the law applicable to the child, majority is attained earlier'.
2 For example Norwegian Centre for Child Research, Norwegian University of Science and Technology http://www.ntnu.edu/noseb. Centre for the Study of Childhood and Youth, University of Sheffield http://cscy.group.shef.ac.uk/ (accessed 2 January 2013). Centre for Applied

1.1.1   Historical perspective

As one commentator has observed, '[f]or much of history children have not been of particular interest to academics or policy-makers' (Kelly 2005: 375). However, Ariès's (1962) work was the classic historical study of the notion of childhood and his analysis is often referred to in the literature as simply the 'Ariès thesis'. Ariès examined the iconography in art and literature over several centuries to identify an emerging 'discovery of childhood'. He suggested famously that 'in mediaeval society the idea of childhood did not exist'. He stated that there had been no distinctive vocabulary of childhood, nor any distinct dress or games. He argued that infants below seven years old were recognised as physically vulnerable, but their parents were largely indifferent to them, probably because of the high levels of infant mortality. After seven years of age, the child was simply regarded as another (smaller) adult.

By contrast, from about the 15th to the 17th centuries, Ariès suggested a transition had occurred in the prevalent notion of childhood: the child was perceived as a significant family member, to be nurtured and protected. Change started, first in wealthy households where there were increasing concerns for the moral and educational development of children. Children were becoming creatures to be nurtured and reformed by a combination of rationality and discipline. Ariès reinforced his views by pointing to the historical development of education for the young and the establishment of the 'child' as a central figure in the appearance of the 'family', itself a newly developing institution emerging over the centuries. Ariès argued that these new attitudes to children were then transmitted to the bourgeois class, where there was additionally concern for the health and hygiene of children as well as their education. The expansion of the school system brought with it a lengthening in the period of childhood.

Some later studies reinforced these views by examining the history of child-rearing practices. For example, Stone (1990) asserted that in earlier centuries high infant mortality had prompted a low level of affection for children by their parents/carers. In the 18th century a new, more affectionate style of child-rearing emerged and traditional practices such as wet-nursing, swaddling and excessive punishment declined. However, by the mid-19th century a reaction, caused by the Methodist revival, had set in whereby the child was perceived as naturally tending towards sinful behaviour and in need of correction by parents and other adults by means of stern discipline designed to break the will (and wilfulness) of a child. This reversion to a more authoritarian family type in turn gave way to a more permissive style in the later Victorian era.

> Only in the closing decades of the Victorian period was there a gradual return to child-centredness and permissiveness caused by a variety of new

Childhood Studies, University of Huddersfield http://www.hud.ac.uk/research/researchcentres/cacs/ (accessed 2 January 2012).

influences – the decline of religiosity, women's emancipation, family limitation and the new psychological theories of child development. These trends
ultimately affected all social classes in the twentieth century, resulting in the
small, modern family characterised by high concentration of affection, a
decline in paternal authority, more 'natural' child-rearing practices and more
democratic sharing of roles.

(Burnett 1983: 1)

Subsequent commentators have questioned Ariès's thesis and methodology
(Pollock 1983) and, indeed, some of his conclusions do not appear to be sufficiently supported by the evidence. In short, his work:

> ... sparked off a whole series of strictly historical debates: on whether the
> mediaeval period did in fact have an awareness of childhood, on the key peri-
> ods in 'the discovery of childhood', on the nature of parent–child relations at
> various periods, and on the role of the schools to name a few.

(Heywood 2001: 5)

Both Ariès and another historian, Lloyd De Mause, believed in essence that the
further one went back in history the worse would be the level of treatment of
children. Indeed, De Mause stated that: '[t]he history of childhood is a nightmare
from which we have only recently begun to awaken' and that '[t]he further back
in history one goes, the lower the level of child care, and the more likely children
are to be killed, abandoned, beaten, terrorised, and sexually abused' (De Mause
1976: 1–2).

Archard (1993), amongst others, has provided a carefully crafted deconstruc-
tion of Ariès's influential thesis. He points not only to the weak evidential basis but
also to Ariès's 'predisposition to interpret the past in the light of present-day attitudes, assumptions and concerns'. Furthermore, he argues that Ariès subscribes
(wrongly) to a historical understanding of 'modernity' as a linear progression to
moral enlightenment. Instead, Archard argues, one can employ a distinction
between a 'concept' and a 'conception' to better analyse Ariès's thesis. The argument, in brief, is that to have a 'concept' of childhood is to recognise that there is
a distinction between children and adults. To have a 'conception' of childhood is
a specification of what the distinguishing attributes are. Archard concludes that
all societies at all times have had a concept of childhood, but there have been a
number of different conceptions. Historically, we cannot be confident about the
reliability of our knowledge in relation to these conceptions. He therefore concludes that Ariès's thesis is flawed by what he refers to as an 'ill-judged leap' from
'concept' to 'conception'.

Archard also provides an interesting conceptual framework to accommodate
the examination of different 'conceptions' of childhood. He introduces three elements to the notion of childhood: its 'boundaries', 'dimensions' and 'divisions'.
The boundary for childhood he defines as the point at which it ends. He argues

that any particular society's conception of this boundary may differ according to its culture. Conceptions of childhood frequently locate the relevant boundary in relation to cultural 'rites of passage or initiation ceremonies which celebrate the end of childhood and beginning of adulthood'; according to Archard: '[t]hese are likely to be associated with permission to marry, departure from the parental home or assumption of the responsibility to provide for oneself ' (Archard 1993: 23).

Conceptions of childhood may also differ according to their 'dimensions'. Archard suggested that a number of perspectives would render a distinction between children and adults; for example, moral, juridical, philosophical and political. Each society will have its own particular value system which may at any one time favour one or more of these perspectives. Sometimes a society sets the legal age of majority according to a view about one or more of these dimensions.

A majority age need not necessarily be consistent with the 'boundary' implied by other dimensions. By way of illustration of this point, Archard points to the origins (in Europe) of the age of majority, which was fixed in the Middle Ages by the capacity of a young boy to bear arms, and changed as armour became increasingly heavier and thus demanded greater strength to wear it (Archard 1993: 25). If, however, rationality is the key dimension, then the acquisition of reason is a better test of majority age. Similarly, in societies that focus on the overriding importance of sustaining and reproducing life, 'the ability to work and bear offspring is a strikingly obvious mark of maturity' (Archard 1993: 26).

Archard argues that conceptions of childhood will also depend on how its 'divisions' are ordered and managed. There are in most societies a number of sub-categories between birth and adulthood. Most cultures recognise a period of very early infancy where the child is particularly vulnerable and deserving of adult care; a point that is consistent with the findings of developmental psychology outlined in the following discussion. Some cultures attach importance to weaning: the point where close maternal care finishes. Some societies put particular significance on the point at which a child acquires speech. Roman law specified three age periods of childhood: *infantia* (child incapable of speech); *tutela impuberes* (pre-pubescent child requiring a tutor); and *cura minores* (post-pubescent young person requiring the care of a guardian prior to attaining majority).

At any rate, the notion of 'adolescence' or 'youth' in the modern conception of childhood is widely recognised as a period usually involving an apprenticeship for the roles to be required of adulthood. Indeed, the inclusion of the 'middle-aged child', that is, the post-infantile seven-year-old to the pre-adolescent 12-year-old, is arguably a key element of the modern conception of childhood. Archard (1993: 27) concluded that:

> ... any conception of childhood will vary according to the ways in which its boundaries are set, its dimensions ordered and its divisions managed. This will determine how a culture thinks about the extent, nature and significance of childhood. The adoption of one conception rather than another will reflect

prevailing general beliefs, assumptions and priorities. Is what matters to a society that a human can speak, be able to distinguish good from evil, exercise reason, learn and acquire knowledge, fend for itself, procreate, participate in running the society or work alongside its other members?

In an influential and controversial work, Pollock (1983) challenged what had become the orthodoxy of Ariès, DeMause and Stone. She argued that the experience of childhood was not as unremittingly gloomy as had been portrayed. Her study was based on her doctoral work, which examined over 500 published diaries and autobiographies. She rebutted the notion that there were any fundamental changes in the way parents viewed or reared their children in the period from 1500–1900: '[t]he texts reveal no significant change in the quality of parental care given to, or the amount of affection felt for infants for the period 1500–1900' (Pollock 1983: 3).

The controversies in historical research about childhood are not made easier by the difficulties in locating reliable source materials. One commentator puts it thus:

> Ideas about childhood in the past exist in plenitude; it is not so easy to find out about the lives of children. There are sources which can tell us about their numbers in relation to adults, their life expectancy, the ages at which they were likely to start work and leave home and so on, but those seeking to recapture the emotional quality of the lives of children in the past encounter formidable hurdles. The letters and diaries of parents seem to be one way of surmounting the hurdles, but they tend to be written only by the articulate and well-to-do, and in them our view of the child is mediated through the perceptions of the adult. Children themselves have sometimes left behind written materials, but too often what they write in their diaries tells us more about the genre of diary writing and the desires and expectations of adult readers than about the experience of being a child.
>
> (Cunningham 2005: 2)

In essence, what emerges from the historical analyses is that the notion of childhood is a culturally transmitted idea that may have changed significantly over past centuries, although there is little consensus about the detail of how and why these changes in perception have occurred. At the least, this brief survey of the historical perspective of childhood ought to suggest that the aim of universal norm-creation underlying international human rights instruments, such as the United Nations Convention on the Rights of the Child,[3] may not necessarily be consistent with the core notion of childhood prevalent in any one society at any one time in history. In recent years there appears to have been some renewed academic interest in the history of childhood. Indeed, in 2003, the History Faculty at the

---

3 Convention on the Rights of the Child, opened for signature 20 November 1989, 1577 UNTS 3 (entered into force 2 September 1990). See generally ch 3.

University of Oxford established the first Centre for the History of Childhood in the United Kingdom.[4]

The definition of the 'child' contained in the Convention on the Rights of the Child[5] is, in Archard's terminology, a 'boundary' of the conception of childhood. Given the high degree of 'cultural relativity' (see section 1.3 below) inherent in the conception of childhood, it is perhaps surprising that the international community was ever able to agree on this important age limit of 18 years. Equally, the definition contained in Article 1 of the Convention on the Rights of the Child (see further section 3.7.2) does also allow for a majority age of less than 18 years, a result achieved partly by virtue of sensitivity to cultural diversity and in part by the diplomatic awareness that such flexibility would encourage a maximum number of states that could ratify the Convention. International human rights instruments, aimed at achieving a universalist code, are likely to be vulnerable to the criticism that the negotiation and implementation of such agreements will carry the cultural preferences of the most powerful actors responsible for their creation and implementation. If we view the Convention as a paradigm of international norm-creation, then equally we must address carefully the cultural relativist critique (Harris-Short 2001). The issue of cultural relativity is examined in more detail in section 1.3 below.

1.1.2 Psychological perspectives

Sigmund Freud emphasised the significance of an individual's experiences in childhood, and much of his work focused on mental disorders rather than normal functioning. He conceptualised child development as a series of 'psychosexual' stages: oral, anal, phallic, latent and genital. Libidinal desire could be satisfied at each stage, but if it was not, an individual would be at risk of developing a range of personality and behavioural disorders in later life (Freud 1920). Erik Erikson, much influenced by Freud and also by cultural anthropology, later devised a theory of eight 'psychosocial' stages of development. At each stage, Erikson thought that an individual would experience a conflict that had the potential to become a beneficial or damaging developmental turning point. In addition to Freud's reliance on universal drives within the psyche to explain development, Erikson also pointed to the way in which an individual's personality could be shaped by the wider society and the culture in which that person lived (Erikson 1995).

As we have seen in the previous section, Ariès pointed to the development of education as historical evidence of a major shift in historical attitudes towards the nature of childhood. Similarly, an understanding of the developmental psychology of children has been enhanced by the adoption of universal education, at least in some countries. It is perhaps unsurprising that such an investment of resources

---

4 Centre for the History of Childhood http://www.history.ox.ac.uk/research/centre/centre-for-the-history-of-childhood.html (accessed 4 January 2013).

5 See n 3 above.

is based upon some pre-existing theory of learning. The particular shape of an education system in any society must be based on a view about the ability of children to receive and process knowledge, in other words, cognitive development.

Piaget (1952, 1960) provided a highly influential analysis of how the processes of thought were structured through his theory of learning. He realised that a child's mind was different from merely being a small version of an adult's mind. In essence, Piagetian theory attempts to explain how humans adapt to their environment via the process of the child's 'assimilation' (taking in new encounters) and 'accommodation' (revising cognitive constructs) of experience. Piaget suggested that the developmental process involved the individual in a search to achieve a balance between assimilation and accommodation. This balance is what Piaget describes as 'equilibrium'.

On the basis of empirical studies, Piaget identified a model of the child's intellectual growth through separate chronological stages. First, the sensory-motor stage (infancy) immediately after birth. In this period, which he asserted lasted until around two years old, the infant's adaptation to his or her environment is shown by motor activity without the use of abstract reasoning. At first, infants use motor reflexes to interact with their environment. The infant relies on seeing, feeling, sucking and touching to learn about his or her environment. Infants eventually learn that their environment is not simply an extension of themselves, and they develop a sense of causation in learning to move an object by hand.

Children acquire the concept of 'object permanence' at about seven months old, that is, an understanding that an object (or person) still exists when not in view. For example, a young infant will lose interest in a toy when it is covered up, but an older infant will actively seek it out. Following an understanding of object permanence, the infant performs motor experiments ('directed groping') and learns how to manipulate objects. An increase in the child's physical mobility allows the child to develop new intellectual abilities. Some symbolic abilities, for example language, are developed at the end of this stage.

Piaget's second 'pre-operational stage' (toddler and early childhood) lasts until the child is around two to seven years old. In this period, a child will acquire language skills, and memory and imagination are developed, but thinking is done in a non-logical, non-reversible manner. This stage is characterised by what Piaget terms 'egocentric thinking'; that is, children will only view the outside world from their own perspective. For example, a three-year-old may well hide behind a chair in the belief that, as she cannot see anyone else, no-one else can see her. Pre-operational children will develop an internal representation of the outside environment that allows them to provide a description of people, events and feelings. Children can be observed using memory and imagination during this stage.

Piaget's third stage, 'concrete operations' (elementary and early adolescence), was said to last for children from around seven to twelve years old. Such children are capable of taking into account another person's point of view and can appreciate more than one perspective at the same time. The beginning of this period is marked by the acquisition of the principle of 'conservation'. This is an understanding that the number, volume, mass, liquid, weight, area and length of objects does not change when the particular configuration of the object(s) is changed. For example, a child will appreciate that two identical lengths of ribbon, one rolled up into a ball and the other laid flat, retain the same length.

Children also acquire the idea of reversibility; that is, some changes can be undone by reversing an earlier action. For example, one can regain the flat ribbon by rolling out the ball. Children become capable of mentally visualising this type of action without the need to see it actually performed. Egocentric thought decreases. A child develops the ability to coordinate two dimensions of an object simultaneously, arrange structures in sequence, and transpose differences between items in a series, and will have a better idea of time and space. During this stage, a child begins to reason logically, but can only think about actual, concrete, physical objects; the child cannot yet manage abstract reasoning.

The final stage of Piaget's theory is 'formal operations' (adolescence and adulthood), acquired by children from around 11 or 12 years old into adulthood. Children at this stage will be capable of thinking logically and in the abstract and can reason theoretically, although some people may never reach this stage. Early on at this stage there is a return to egocentric thought processes. However, thinking is not tied exclusively to events that can be observed. The stage is characterised by the ability to construct hypotheses and systematically to test these to resolve a problem. In particular, the ability to reason hypothetically or contrary to the known facts appears. For example, an argument based on the premise that the world is flat could be processed.

The impact of thinkers such as Freud, Erikson and Piaget has been profound. Piaget's theory in particular has had a significant influence in shaping education curricula. The lasting influence of Piaget can be seen in the proliferation of 'Early Childhood Studies' courses available in university education and other departments.[6] One key point to his theory should be noted. This is that a child could only pass from one stage to another when the appropriate levels of maturity and external stimuli were present. The theory thus acknowledges both the importance of the child's biological maturation and the differential influence of the external environment; in other words, 'nature and nurture'. In the absence of good conditions to sustain both, a child is unlikely to progress to his or her fullest potential.

However, subsequent researchers in developmental psychology do not accept Piaget's theory uncritically. For example, the theory does not clearly explain why development from one stage to another happens. The theory largely ignores individual differences in cognitive development and provides little explanation for why some individuals may proceed faster than others from one stage to another. Also, the actual functioning of a person at a particular time may vary considerably in relation to the understanding of spatial, mathematical and other concepts, to

6 A UCAS search in the UK produced 249 such courses available in 2013. See http://www.ucas. ac.uk/students/coursesearch/2013searcheu/ (accessed 4 January 2013).

the point where placing that individual in one of Piaget's stages becomes artificial. In order to remove some of these weaknesses scholars, known as 'neo-Piagetian' theorists – for example, Demetriou and others (2000) – have adapted Piaget's theory to develop new understanding of cognitive and developmental psychology.

Indeed, there is an increasing body of evidence in the last 30 years that young babies, for example, do far more representational 'thinking' than merely the motor reflexes that Piaget underlined at his first 'stage' (Sutherland 1992). Nevertheless, Piaget's contribution has been enduring and, indeed, the very concept of the cognitive development of the child makes much sense when applied, as in the *Gillick* case (see Case study 1.1 below) in the United Kingdom, to determine the point at which teenagers can be regarded as sufficiently mature to understand the meaning and consequences of important decision-making that may have significant effects upon their lives.

As we shall see, one of the key dilemmas in discussions of 'children's rights' (section 1.2.1) is the nature and extent of the child's autonomy across a range of decision-making areas. The insights of developmental psychology have much to contribute towards a more rounded understanding of children's ability to conduct and understand fully the consequences of their own independent action.

1.1.3 Sociological perspective

In the 1980s and 1990s, academic societies started to pay specific attention to an emerging *sociology of childhood*. For example, in 1998 a research committee of the International Sociological Association was dedicated to the study of childhood.[7]

One explanation for the sidelining of interest in children is their general marginalisation in society. Adult perspectives on children often focus on what children are to become rather than appreciate what they are. Since all children are expected to grow up, there is a tendency to focus on the end product, that is, the adult, rather than to concentrate on the child and the 'here and now' aspects of childhood. Children are often viewed as passive consumers of a culture already established by adults. Society can be seen, within traditional social theory, as maintaining its integrity through a process of 'socialisation'. Individuals are in effect guided into suitable roles via a wide range of institutional and other processes. The notion of socialisation itself involves society's values being lodged into individuals' personalities. Social theory has often recognised the child as particularly in need of such socialisation in order to provide the appropriate induction into the adult world.

However, it is the family that has the expected primary role to ensure that this process of socialising the child is carried out effectively. It is useful in this context to distinguish two different versions of the socialisation process: the deterministic and constructivist models (Corsaro 2011).

---

7 International Sociological Association: Research Committee 53 (Sociology of Children) http://www.isa-sociology.org/rc53.htm (accessed 8 January 2013).

The deterministic model is based on the idea that the child is essentially appropriated by society, that is, trained into becoming a useful member of society. On the one hand, the child's potential future contribution to society is recognised. On the other hand, the underlying assumption is that without the appropriate application of socialisation the child will remain a threat to the good order of society. The child's role in this conceptualisation is essentially a passive one. Furthermore, there are 'functionalist' and 'reproductive' models contained within this deterministic approach.

The functionalist approach in the 1950s and 1960s emphasised the need to maintain order and balance in society and therefore looked at children in terms of how they can best be prepared to take up useful places in the adult world. Theorists such as Talcott Parsons advocated such an approach and viewed the child as a threat to the intricate balance required to maintain society. Parsons saw the child as a 'pebble "thrown" by the fact of birth into the social pond' (Parsons and Bales 1956).

The child's point of origin, the family, will be the first element to feel the effects of this potential disruption, followed by schools and then other social institutions and processes. Eventually, the child internalises the values, norms and standards of the wider society. A key criticism of the functionalist approach was that the internalisation of the requirements for society's good order could simply be viewed as a sophisticated method of social control. It assumed that the status quo would be maintained. In other words, these socialisation processes were viewed as a means to reproduce social inequalities.

The reproductive model of society therefore tended to analyse the nature of such inequality in a more critical manner and not just assume that the function of society was merely to reproduce itself without improvement or any fundamental change. As regards the impact on children, such an approach takes greater note of the existence and nature of social conflict and inequality. The deterministic approach as a whole can be criticised in that it will tend to over-emphasise the outcomes of socialisation and underestimate the active roles played by the individual. Some advocates of the deterministic approach have advanced a behaviourist understanding of childhood, emphasising the value of training in skills needed for functional living and the need for a clear system of rewards and punishment which would determine appropriate socialisation.

In contrast to the notion of society appropriating the child, the 'constructivist' model focuses on how the child appropriates society. The contribution of developmental psychology, in particular Piagetian theory, is particularly important here. The child is conceptualised as extracting information from his or her environment in order to construct his or her own interpretation of society. Piaget's 'stage' analysis of intellectual development (see section 1.1.2 above) confirms children's differing qualitative understandings of their environment and their interactions with it as compared with adults. Piaget's concept of 'equilibrium' also provides a view of the child as being more active and self-determining than a picture of the child determined by irresistible societal forces. Although Piaget believed there was an inherent tendency for children to compensate for environmental intrusions (he termed this 'equilibrium'), nevertheless, 'the nature of the compensations is dependent on the activities of children in their social-ecological worlds' (Corsaro 2011: 13–14).

Lev Vygotsky is another significant constructivist theorist who underlined children's active rather than passive roles. He believed that their social development was based on *collective* rather than individual action. He argued that language and other cultural tools are developed collectively by societies over the course of history and are acquired by children in order actively to participate and contribute to that culture. Vygotsky had a notion of 'internalisation', whereby every function in the child's development appeared not only on the social level at first, that is, *between* people (interpsychological), but also on the individual level, that is, *inside* the child (intrapsychological) (Vygotsky 1962). The following commentary provides a useful illustration of how such a conception can be seen to operate:

> Consider Vygotsky's conceptions of self-directed and inner speech. With *self-directed speech*, Vygotsky is referring to the tendency of young children to speak out loud to themselves, especially in problematic situations. Piaget saw such speech as egocentric or emotional and serving no social function. Vygotsky, on the other hand, saw self-directed speech as a form of interpersonal communication, except that in this case the child is addressing himself as another. In a sense, the child is directing and advising himself on how to deal with a problem. In experimental work, Vygotsky found that such speech increased when children were given tasks such as building a car with construction toys or were told to draw a picture. Vygotsky believed that over time, self-directed speech was transformed or internalized from the interpersonal to the intrapersonal, becoming inner speech or a form of thought. We can grasp his ideas when we think about how we first learn to read. Most of our early reading as young children is done out loud as we read to ourselves and others. Over time we begin to mumble and then to mouth the words as we read, and eventually we read entirely at a mental level. In short, the intrapsychological function or skill of reading has its origins in social or collective activity–reading out loud for others and oneself. For Vygotsky internalization occurs gradually over an extended period of time.
>
> (Corsaro 2011: 16–17)

In addition, Vygotsky posed a model of development in which children were constantly in between their actual and potential developmental levels (the 'zone of proximal development'), interacting with others in order to acquire more skills and information. Children gradually appropriated the norms and values of society through this collective process of sharing and creating culture. Although constructivist models are capable of providing a picture of the child as a more active participant in society, there are two essential weaknesses with this general approach.

First, most constructivist theory focuses on *individual* child development. Even Vygotsky's notion of *collective* action at the interpersonal level becomes obscured with an over-emphasis on the intrapersonal level; the process of an individual child's internalisation of culture. Secondly, the focus is usually on the endpoint of the developmental cycle, the transition from immaturity to adult maturity. Corsaro (2011: 20–21) offers the notion of 'interpretive reproduction' as a theoretical perspective which refocuses attention on collective interactions and children's own creative generation of culture:

> The term *interpretive* captures the innovative and creative aspects of children's participation in society. In fact … children create and participate in their own unique peer cultures by creatively taking or appropriating information from the adult world to address their own peer concerns. The term *reproduction* captures the idea that children are not simply internalizing society and culture, but are actively contributing to cultural production and change. The term also implies that children are, by their very participation in society, constrained by the existing social structure and by societal reproduction. That is, children and their childhoods are affected by the societies and cultures of which they are members. These societies and cultures have, in turn, been shaped and affected by processes of historical change.

Corsaro has produced a graphic representation of his model (Figure 1.1). The spokes represent a range of fields that comprise various social institutions. Cultural information flows to all parts of the web along these spokes.

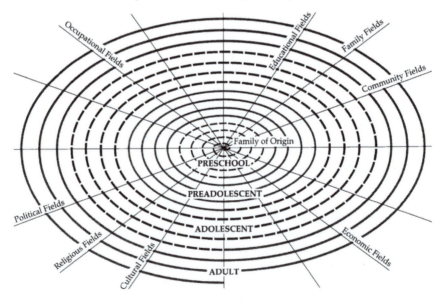

Figure 1.1 The orb web model
Source: Corsaro (2011: 27).

The child enters his or her culture at the point of origin, the family. However, children begin to participate in relations outside the family from an early age, as is represented in the figure by the spiral lines. They 'begin to produce and participate in a series of peer cultures' (Corsaro 2011: 28). Four distinct peer cultures are represented: pre-school, pre-adolescent, adolescent and adult. Corsaro argues that these peer cultures are not stages through which children progress. They are not, for the most part, pre-existing structures, but are produced and participated in by the children themselves. It can be seen that one key element of the recent sociological theorising about childhood has been the focus on the child as an active social agent:

> In sociology this has been codified ... as a call for children to be understood as social actors, shaping as well as shaped by their social circumstances. This represents a definitive move away from the more or less inescapable implication of the concept of socialization: that children are to be seen as a defective form of adult, social only in their future potential but not in their present being. And yet this rallying point of children's agency is embedded in and related to a much wider process through which the individual voices and presence of children is now being recognised and accounted for.
>
> (James and others 1998: 6)

Consequently, this approach avoids viewing children as somehow outside of the mainstream of society and also avoids any marginalisation of children by viewing them only as emerging members of the wider community.

Another key theme in the sociological perspective on childhood, sometimes referred to as 'generational order', has been the way in which children are categorised by age for different purposes, which does not necessarily reflect children's own needs but instead may be seen as structural requirements in society to maintain social order (Mayall 2003). Consequently, social inequalities are also intimately related to the sociological understanding of childhood. Some sociological work focuses on the accounts that children themselves have of their lives and relations with parents and other adults. Children themselves make important points on questions relating to autonomy and interdependence. Some commentators have called for more attention to be paid to children's own perspectives:

> Whilst Western liberal thinkers have regarded the autonomous, independent moral agent as the highest form of life, children regard relationships as the cornerstone of their lives. It is of crucial importance to them to work with and through family relationships, to care about those who live elsewhere as well as those they live with. ... Thus any account of how the social order works, in terms of values ascribed by varying social groups to dependence, independence, and inter-dependence, needs to take account of children's views.
>
> (Mayall 2000: 256)

One commentator has observed that the 'new sociology of childhood'[8] has become 'the dominant theoretical framework, for anyone seeking a sociological understanding of childhood and children' (King 2007: 194). He observes that the new sociology of childhood is distinct from the socialisation and development psychology research of previous decades. It can also be seen that this renewed sociological emphasis on the child's competence, autonomy and active agency and 'voice' fits comfortably around the legal-oriented perspective of 'children's rights', which is examined in further detail in section 1.2.1 below. Indeed, as King (2007: 194) observes:

> One of the difficulties faced by the new sociology of childhood has been that of establishing a clear demarcation line between what claims to be a new theoretical understanding of children and the discourse of children's rights.

1.1.4   Social policy perspectives

The way in which the concept of childhood has been viewed historically, the theories of child development and the constructivist account of childhood from the sociological perspective, discussed above, cannot provide a complete picture without an understanding of society's approach to formulating and developing social policy in child-related matters. To an extent, the approach to building social policy relating to children will reflect a society's distilled understanding (derived from many disciplines) of how children fit into the overall order of that society. An understanding of international child law is enhanced by an ability to locate it within the context of the wider social policy framework at the international, regional or national level.

At the international level, this can be identified in the programmes pursued by the United Nations, for example, via the United Nations Children's Fund (UNICEF) (see section 2.4.1.2). At the regional level; in Europe for example, one needs to look at the key institutions – the Council of Europe and the European Union (EU) – to determine how policy is determined and delivered. Indeed, there are indications that both these latter institutions are becoming active participants in progressing child policy. The Council of Europe has issued a number of conventions related to family and child matters.[9] The EU has in the past sidelined

---

8 For example Corsaro (2011), James and Prout (1997), James and others (1998), Jenks (1996) and Qvortrup and others (1994).

9 Convention for the Protection of Human Rights and Fundamental Freedoms, opened for signature 4 November 1950, CETS No 005 (entry into force 3 September 1953); European Social Charter, opened for signature 18 October 1961, CETS No 035 (entry into force 26 February 1965); European Convention on the Adoption of Children, opened for signature 24 April 1967, CETS No 058 (entry into force 26 April 1968); European Convention on the Legal Status of Children born out of Wedlock, opened for signature 15 October 1975, CETS No 085, (entry into force 11 August 1978); European Convention on Recognition and Enforcement of Decisions concerning Custody of Children and on Restoration of Custody of Children, opened for signature 20 May

child-related issues on the basis that they are not directly related to the overall EU project of the single market. However, this appears to be changing:

> In recent years, the pendulum has swung from a steadfast resistance on the part of the EU and nation States to EU intervention in children's rights, towards a growing eagerness to engage the institutions in a range of issues affecting children. Indeed, the broadening scope of EU activity has made it increasingly difficult to justify maintaining a hands off approach; all aspects of EU law and policy have a direct or indirect impact on children's lives such that it is no longer a question of why the EU should be enacting child-focused provision, but rather, what it should be doing to minimise the adverse effects of EU law and policy for children.
>
> (Stalford and Drywood 2009: 170–71)

Finally, at the national level, government activity in the relevant ministries, in addition to local government organs and voluntary agencies, will implement policy and feedback both strategic and operational lessons learned from such implementation.

It would appear that a key driver of social policy formulation in relation to children is a society's dominant perception of the *state–family* relationship. Fox Harding (1996) has described seven potential models describing this relationship. At one end of this typology there is an authoritarian model, where the state sets out to compel and prohibit certain family behaviour, thereby severely limiting personal freedom. At the other end there is a *laissez-faire* model where state intervention is minimal and where family life is seen as a private matter unsuitable for legal intervention. It is arguable that at present the British Government, for example, best reflects one of Fox Harding's models located between these two extremes, in which the state will substitute for and support families when they fail. In this model the state recognises that, in the normal course of affairs, the family should be left alone and is the best place for children to be raised.

However, when the family breaks down a state duty arises to mitigate the resulting damage, protect family members and support the formation of a substitute family, for example, by arranging an adoption. Indeed, this approach is probably comparable to the position in several other European Member States

1980, CETS No 105 (entry into force 1 September 1983); European Convention on the Exercise of Children's Rights, opened for signature 25 January 1996, CETS No 160 (entry into force 1 July 2000); European Social Charter (revised), opened for signature 3 May 1996, CETS No 163 (entry into force 1 July 1999); Convention on Cybercrime, opened for signature 23 November 2001, CETS No 185 (entry into force 1 July 2004); Convention on Contact concerning Children, opened for signature 15 May 2003, CETS No 192 (entry into force 1 September 2005); Convention on the Protection of Children against Sexual Exploitation and Sexual Abuse, opened for signature 25 October 2007, CETS No 201 (entry into force 1 July 2010); European Convention on the Adoption of Children (Revised), opened for signature 25 October 2007, CETS No 202 (entry into force 1 July 2010).

and elsewhere. The way in which the right to respect for private and family life, home and correspondence in the European Convention on Human Rights[10] (ECHR) is drafted, and its practical operation, are based on the assumption that the individual is in need of protection from arbitrary interference by the state and therefore any state interference must be justified on specified grounds. It can be seen that those grounds in effect may describe circumstances where private and family life have become dysfunctional and therefore justify a higher degree of state involvement, subject always to the proportionality principle that requires the particularities of state interference to be commensurate with the overall aims of that interference.

In countries where this type of state–family relationship prevails, the social policies in relation to children have tended to focus on interventions deemed necessary to address situations where families fail. The classic example is where parents, for a variety of reasons, are no longer perceived as capable or available to look after their children properly. Consequently, in many countries child policy has often tended to gravitate towards a concentration on the state's social services for children. A comparable child welfare approach is also found in the education and health sectors. In these sectors, the state only intervenes, at least with coercive techniques, when clear dysfunctions are evident.

Furthermore, social policy relating to children is often viewed as either 'welfarist' or 'rights-based', although these two approaches are not necessarily mutually exclusive. The former usually refers to an underlying policy aimed at protecting children who are seen as vulnerable members of society in need of guidance and control. The role of parents, schools, social services and the state is to protect, nurture and provide fulfilling opportunities for children's development. Rights-based policy is designed to support children's own participation in decision-making and is based on a conception of children having distinct rights that can be asserted, both morally and legally.

As we have seen, this approach also very much resonates with the dominant sociological image of the child as a competent, autonomous and active social agent. The dichotomy in current debates between welfarist and rights-based policy should not hide other complexities of child welfare policy and the subtle changes in perception of the acceptability of state intervention in the family. For example, Hendrick showed, in an examination of British child welfare, that there was a shift in around the 1870s 'from a simple concern with child reformation and rescue, usually by placing children in either philanthropic or Poor Law institutional care, to a far more complex notion and practice of welfare' (Hendrick 1997).

The precise boundaries of state intervention also depend on the way in which the major social problems involving children are perceived. If the physical, emotional or sexual abuse of children is regarded as a manifestation of the individual pathology of the abuser, then detection, treatment and/or punishment of the

10 Convention for the Protection of Human Rights and Fundamental Freedoms, opened for signature 4 November 1950, CETS No 005 (entry into force 3 September 1953) art 8.

offender are likely to be of central concern in social policy initiatives. On the other hand, if child abuse can be explained to an extent by a social structure that harbours poverty and inequality, then other initiatives are required.

Child protection policy that is based on intervention only in circumstances where the family unit has broken down obviously raises issues about the extent of family dysfunction that might justify such intervention, for example by means of family care and supervision orders.[11] In addition, our understanding of the background state–family configuration will also impact upon the decision-making involved in placing children once they are ingested into the public care system.

Consistently with the standards about the family environment set out in the Convention on the Rights of the Child (1989) (see section 3.7.5), planning the child's future will take place initially on the understanding that the ultimate aim is to rehabilitate the family unit. Where this is not possible 'permanency planning' will follow, that is, placing the child with a new adoptive family. However, such decision-making is of course fraught with difficulties; in what circumstances does the underlying aim of rehabilitation become a hopeless cause and the alternative of adoption a realistic one?

At the international level, a significant landmark in setting social policy goals was the adoption by the United Nations General Assembly of the United Nations Millennium Declaration in September 2000.[12] This Declaration committed states to a global partnership that would tackle extreme poverty and establish a series of targets to be achieved by 2015. These are known as the 'Millennium Development Goals' (MDGs). They have particular relevance in providing a broad framework for child policy formulation. For example, MDG 4 (reduce child mortality) aims to '[r]educe by two thirds, between 1990 and 2015, the under-five mortality rate'; MDG 2 (achieve university primary education) aims to '[e]nsure that, by 2015, children everywhere, boys and girls alike, will be able to complete a full course of primary education'; MDG 3 (promote gender equality and empower women) aims to '[e]liminate gender disparity in primary and secondary education, prefer-ably by 2005, and in all levels of education no later than 2015'. UNICEF under-takes important development and other work for children and reports annually on the state of the world's children (see section 2.4.1.2). A recent report, for example, focuses on the plight of children living in cities (UNICEF 2012).

It may often be difficult to identify clearly what is the social policy of a particu-lar community towards its children. Sometimes this is precisely because the policy, if it exists at all, is relatively incoherent and uncoordinated. As we shall see, the 'concluding observations' emanating from the Committee on the Rights of the Child (section 3.4) in response to states parties' reports are full of such criticisms.

---

11 In some countries the legal threshold test that will trigger state power to take a child into care is a 'significant harm' formulation: eg in the United Kingdom's Children Act 1989 s 31(2).

12 UNGA Res 55/2 (8 September 2000) UN Doc A/RES/55/2, adopted without a vote. The General Assembly (see section 2.4.1) is the chief deliberative, policy-making and representative organ of the United Nations.

States parties' reports submitted to the Committee and the latter's 'concluding observations' are a useful source of information about a state's policy on
child-related matters. Another informative source is the official documentation,
along with critical commentary from non-governmental organisations (NGOs)
and academic commentary.

1.2   Human rights

Children's rights can be properly understood only in the context of the wider
human rights framework. The devastating impact of the Second World War and
the founding of the United Nations in its aftermath have been the most recent
modern inspiration behind the human rights movement in the 20th century.
Early legal codes in mediaeval times, which appear to include 'rights', on closer
inspection turn out merely to reflect how powerful groups in that society at that
time were realigning themselves. Thus, the Magna Carta (1215)[13] in England, for
example, is concerned more with the privileges of the barons and church–state
relationships than with matters of common humanity. Similarly, the English Bill
of Rights in the 17th century[14] set out the ground rules for a new constitutional
settlement between the Crown and Parliament. Philosophers in the 18th and 19th
centuries generated thinking about 'natural rights' and 'natural law'; that is, the
rights attached to a human by virtue of nature, rather than by status or any other
classification.

The American (1776) and French (1789) Revolutions drew on such ideas for
their inspiration. The US Declaration of Independence (4 July 1776) famously
stated that: 'we hold these truths to be self-evident; … that all men are created
equal, that they are endowed by their Creator with certain unalienable Rights,
that among these are Life, Liberty and the pursuit of Happiness'. John Locke
(1632–1704), the English philosopher, believed there was a natural-law right to
life, liberty and property. The French Republic produced its Declaration of the
Rights of Man and of Citizens (26 August 1789) and the US Constitution and Bill
of Rights (15 December 1791) followed shortly after.

In the 19th century a number of recognisable human rights issues were becoming increasingly controversial; for example, slavery, serfdom, bad working conditions and child labour. Social movements sprang up in response; for example,
labour unions, racial and religious minority groups, women's rights and national
liberation movements. The idea that every human being was equally deserving
of respect and dignity and could be regarded as a right holder was emerging.
Individuals were recognised as capable of asserting rights against other individuals
and the state and governments had a duty to respect, promote and protect such
rights.

---

13   Confirmed and reissued in the reign of King Edward I, Magna Carta 1297 (c9).
14   1688 (c 2) 1 Will and Mar Sess 2.

The political consensus achieved by the allies in the immediate postwar period allowed the conditions necessary for a synthesis of these ideas to emerge. There are several references in the United Nations Charter of 1945[15] to human rights, in particular in the preamble, where it is stated that the peoples of the United Nations are determined 'to reaffirm faith in fundamental human rights, in the dignity and worth of the human person, in the equal rights of men and women and of nations large and small'.

Article 68 of the Charter required the UN's Economic and Social Council (ECOSOC) to set up a UN Commission on Human Rights (UNCHR).[16] Its first task, through the chairmanship of Eleanor Roosevelt, was to produce an International Bill of Human Rights. It was decided that this should be in the form of a Declaration (not binding in international law) rather than a binding Treaty. It was envisaged that the document should be short, inspirational and accessible, and would be followed at a later date with more detailed (and binding) treaty provisions.

The result was the Universal Declaration of Human Rights of 1948 (UDHR).[17] Article 1 stated that '[a]ll human beings are born free and equal in dignity and rights. They are endowed with reason and conscience and should act towards one another in a spirit of brotherhood'. Eighteen years later the (binding) treaty provisions appeared in the form of the International Covenant on Civil and Political Rights of 1966 (ICCPR) and the International Covenant on Economic, Social and Cultural Rights of 1966 (ICESCR).[18] The ICCPR and the ICESCR, together with the (non-binding) UDHR, are now collectively referred to as the International Bill of Human Rights. The two international covenants reflect respectively the so-called 'first generation' (civil and political) and 'second generation' (economic, social and cultural) rights. Human rights scholars have questioned the justiciability of the latter type of rights as they necessarily vary according to the resources available to state authorities.

Following the adoption of an Optional Protocol that established a communication/complaints procedure under ICESCR[19] in 2008, 'it became more difficult to sustain objections to the justiciability of economic, social and cultural rights' (Buck and Wabwile 2013: 207). This approach is consistent with

---

15 Charter of the United Nations (24 October 1945) 1 UNTS XVI.

16 The UNCHR was replaced by a United Nations Human Rights Council (UNHRC) in 2006: see section 2.5.1.1.

17 UN General Assembly, Universal Declaration of Human Rights (10 December 1948) 217 A (III). The UDHR was adopted by the then 56 members of the United Nations; the vote was unanimous, although eight nations chose to abstain.

18 International Covenant on Civil and Political Rights, opened for signature 16 December 1966, 999 UNTS 171 (entered into force 23 March 1976); International Covenant on Economic, Social and Cultural Rights, opened for signature 16 December 1966, 993 UNTS 3 (entered into force 3 January 1976).

19 Optional Protocol of the International Covenant on Economic, Social and Cultural Rights, opened for signature 10 December 2008, UN Doc A/RES/63/117 (entered into force 5 May 2013).

the general view that human rights are: 'interdependent', that is, the full range of rights constitutes a complementary framework in which the exercise of one right affects the exercise of others; and 'indivisible', that is, each individual right is equally important – there should be no 'hierarchy' of rights.

Despite its formal non-binding status, the UDHR has become the accepted universal standard of international human rights. It has almost certainly become part of what is termed 'international customary law' (see section 2.2.2). It has inspired similar human rights instruments to be produced at the regional level. For example, the European Convention on Human Rights (Rome, 1950), the American Convention on Human Rights (the 'Pact of San José', Costa Rica, 1969) and the African Charter on Human and Peoples' Rights (the 'Banjul Charter', Nairobi, 1981). The 50th anniversary of the UDHR was celebrated by the adoption of the Asian Human Rights Charter: A People's Charter (Kwangju, South Korea, 1998). Individual countries too are increasingly incorporating these now well-known human rights standards into their own domestic law.[20]

Some of the provisions of the UDHR relate to the family and children. Article 12, for example, states that: '[n]o one shall be subjected to arbitrary interference with his privacy, family, home or correspondence, nor to attacks upon his honour and reputation. Everyone has the right to the protection of the law against such interference or attacks'. Article 16(3) states that: '[t]he family is the natural and fundamental group unit of society and is entitled to protection by society and the State'. Article 25(2) interestingly provides that: '[m]otherhood and childhood are entitled to special care and assistance. All children, whether born in or out of wedlock, shall enjoy the same social protection'. Article 26 contains a right to education which should be free and compulsory at the elementary stage and 'directed to the full development of the human personality and to the strengthening of respect for human rights and fundamental freedoms'.

The historical development of human rights outlined in the preceding discussion and the emergence of the UN 'Treaty bodies' (section 2.5.1.2 and Table 2.1) that now deal with particular categories of human rights issues, including the Committee on the Rights of the Child supervision and monitoring of the Convention on the Rights of the Child (1989), have raised the issue of how far children's rights should be differentiated from the general international human rights instruments. The problem with the latter is that they have tended to focus on the rights of *parents*. There may also be obligations on parents and institutions towards children but these are likely to be unenforceable by children. Arguably, the recognition of children's rights may lead to an assumption that children have different rights from adults, with different justifications, rather than accommodating children as an integral part of the same human rights protection regime. However, it would seem preferable to regard children as part of the human family with each individual equally entitled to rights. Any special or additional

---

20 For example the UK's Human Rights Act in 1998 and the Australian Capital Territory produced Australia's first Bill of Rights in its Human Rights Act of 2004.

formulations of human rights would need to be premised on children's particular vulnerability or inexperience (Sawyer 2006: 13).

This reinforces the point that in order to be effective, any instrument that purports to provide for children must be child-centred and independent of adult bias. Hence the view that a more appropriate way forward in providing for children would be to grant them defined 'rights'; a trend that became increasingly popular following the end of the First World War and which eventually led to a fully-fledged code of children's rights in the form of the Convention on the Rights of the Child (1989).

As will be seen in Chapter 3, the Convention on the Rights of the Child contains some particular principles customised to apply to children (eg the 'best interests' and 'participation' principles) as distinct from adults and there are a number of rights that resonate with general human rights instruments but are formulated in a way that provides a child-centred focus or context to those rights. It is interesting to note that the same arguments raised in opposition to the Convention on the Rights of the Child on the basis that general international human rights law applied equally to the whole human family irrespective of their age, are being revisited in relation to the current debate in the UN about whether to adopt a UN 'Convention on the Rights of Older Persons'.[21] The delineation of a meaningful category of 'older persons' is, arguably, even more difficult than the definition of the 'child' in the Convention on the Rights of the Child. Could such a Convention 'age-proof' human rights in the way that the Convention on the Rights of the Child provides an attempt to 'child-proof' human rights?

1.2.1 Children's rights

Even before the modern development of international human rights law, as outlined in the preceding section, the League of Nations (1919–1946) had shown an interest in protecting and providing welfare services for children, in particular those orphaned and displaced following the First World War. In 1919 a Committee for the Protection of Children was set up by the League of Nations. Eglantyne Jebb (1876–1928), the founder of the British Save the Children Fund and the Save the Children International Union in Geneva, was an early campaigner for children and succeeded in getting the League of Nations to adopt a Declaration of the Rights of the Child (1924).[22]

This was in fact the first declaration of human rights adopted by any inter-governmental organisation and preceded the UDHR by 24 years. The

---

21 United Nations Department of Economic and Social Affairs, Division for Social Policy and Development. Programme on Ageing, 'Report of the Expert Group Meeting "Rights of Older Persons"', convened in preparation for the report of the Secretary-General to the 64th session of the General Assembly (5–7 May 2009) Bonn, Germany http://www.globalaging.org/aging watch/desa/aging/mipaa/egm_report.pdf (accessed 11 January 2013).

22 Geneva Declaration of the Rights of the Child, adopted 26 September 1924, League of Nations OJ Spec Supp 21 at 43 (1924).

Declaration was reaffirmed by the League of Nations in 1934. It contains five principles directed to creating the conditions necessary for children to be protected and to enable them to develop into citizens who will contribute to their communities. However, the text of this document implies that the child is a *passive* object of concern rather than as an *active* subject capable of asserting rights against others.

The intention behind the Declaration of 1924 was not to create a binding treaty but merely to create guiding principles for those working in international child welfare. The Declaration reflects a paternalistic view of child welfare where adults are clearly in total control of children's destinies. There is no suggestion here about welcoming or encouraging children's participation in decision-making or other aspects of children's self-determination.

The Declaration was revisited and revised by the United Nations in the form of the Declaration of the Rights of the Child (1959).[23] A much more robust language of rights is deployed in this Declaration. It sets out 10 principles in a more expanded form than the 1924 document. Indeed, some commentators have regarded the Declaration of 1959 as the 'conceptual parent' to the UN Convention on the Rights of the Child of 1989 (Van Bueren 1998: 14). Although the UDHR contains some material specifically addressed to children, there are more specific formulations of rights directly affecting family and child issues contained in the ICCPR and ICESCR.

The ICCPR contains a robust right of the child to be protected from discrimination, a right to a name and nationality:

> 1. Every child shall have, without any discrimination as to race, colour, sex, language, religion, national or social origin, property or birth, the right to such measures of protection as are required by his status as a minor, on the part of his family, society and the State.
>
> 2. Every child shall be registered immediately after birth and shall have a name.
>
> 3. Every child has the right to acquire a nationality.[24]

The status of the family as 'the natural and fundamental group unit of society' referred to in the UDHR is reaffirmed in Article 23, which also sets out a principle of equality of spouses during marriage and at dissolution and that '[i]n the case of dissolution, provision shall be made for the necessary protection of any children'. The ICESCR contains a strongly worded provision giving protection to children against economic and social exploitation, in particular setting out standards to regulate child labour. State parties to the Covenant recognise that, inter alia:

---

23 Declaration of the Rights of the Child, GA res 1386 (XIV) 14 UN GAOR Supp (No 16) at 19, UN Doc A/4354 (1959).

24 International Covenant on Civil and Political Rights, opened for signature 16 December 1966, 999 UNTS 171 (entered into force 23 March 1976) art 24.

Special measures of protection and assistance should be taken on behalf of all children and young persons without any discrimination for reasons of parentage or other conditions. Children and young persons should be protected from economic and social exploitation. Their employment in work harmful to their morals or health or dangerous to life or likely to hamper their normal development should be punishable by law. States should also set age limits below which the paid employment of child labour should be prohibited and punishable by law.[25]

Rights to health (Article 12) and education (Article 13) are also included in detailed formulations in the ICESCR.

In short, the modern human rights movement in the post-war era has involved an increased concern for the rights of children. This has been reflected both in the development of the more robust textual formulations found in the two international covenants of 1966 and in the further development of UNICEF and other inter-governmental organisations and NGOs working for improvements in children's lives. The account of how the UN's International Year of the Child in 1979 eventually led to the production of the Convention on the Rights of the Child in 1989, which has become, in effect, the template for the international legal rights of the child, is taken up in more detail in section 3.2. For the purposes of this chapter, however, it is useful to consider further what 'children's rights' means.

There is now a considerable body of academic literature relating to the subject of children's rights. As Fortin (2009: 3) notes, the literature gravitates around three themes: how to identify children's rights; how to balance one set of rights against another in the event of a conflict between them; and how to mediate between children's rights and those of adults.

1.2.1.1   Theories of children's rights[26]

It is useful to make a preliminary distinction between positive 'legal rights' and 'moral rights', the latter being rights that are recognised by a moral theory. Most states readily acknowledge children's legal rights, as evidenced by the near-universal ratification of the Convention on the Rights of the Child. The controversy about children's rights usually gravitates around more fundamental questions of whether there is a credible account of children's moral rights. Furthermore, '[t]hat children have "positive" rights does not then settle the question of whether they do or should have moral rights' (Archard 2010).

There are two fundamental, moral and philosophical debates that have exercised theorists who have grappled with the notion of children's rights. First, there

25 International Covenant on Economic, Social and Cultural Rights, opened for signature 16 December 1966, 993 UNTS 3 (entered into force 3 January 1976) art 10(3).
26 See generally Freeman (1983: ch 2); Fortin (2009: 3–30); Archard (2010).

is a 'choice' or 'will' theory of rights.[27] This theory assumes that the person asserting those rights will have a choice as to when and whether to exercise them. As
children at various levels of maturation will not be likely to have the capacity or
competence to exercise such choices in all circumstances, it has been questioned
whether they can properly be described as having 'rights' at all. If rights are basi-
cally premised on the notion that the right holder must be capable and competent
to make such choices, then it might follow that, at least in circumstances where
it is clear that a child would lack competence to choose, that child could not be
properly described as a right holder.

There are a number of difficulties with this approach. As Fortin (2009: 12)
remarks: '[t]he assertion that children, who are too young and incompetent to
claim rights, therefore have no rights, has an unattractive logic'. Indeed, if one
applied the same approach to, for example, the position of a severely mentally
ill or disabled adult, the 'unattractiveness' of the logic is exposed. In order to
circumnavigate such a stark conclusion, it could be conceded that there may be
correlative duties on parents and other adults or institutions to provide a remedy
for children (or severely mentally ill or disabled adults) who are not competent to
make their own choices.

Put another way, the choice theory can still be seen as delivering rights for
children if one accepts that adults act in effect as proxies for the choices a child
would make if endowed with sufficient capacity or competence. Thus, a child's
right might obtain some, albeit indirect, recognition from the existence of such
correlative duties placed on adults in respect of (incompetent) children.

However, this theory can be criticised on the basis that it over-emphasises the
existence of remedies. MacCormick (1982), for example, argues that it is only
because a child has a right to care and nurture that the legal imposition on adults
and institutions to provide such protection is justified; the existence of the right
presupposes the remedy. In addition, the will/choice theory fails to provide children with a secure standpoint in the face of parents or institutions who are failing
in their correlative duties to protect. Furthermore, how should the identification
of representatives of children's choices be tested? Parents would not necessarily
be the best option. As we know from the considerable literature on child abuse, it
is frequently the case that the greatest threat to a child's emotional, physical and
sexual integrity comes from parents and other close family members and friends.

Secondly, there is the 'interest' theory of rights[28] intended to address some of
the problems of the 'choice' theory. According to this theory, rights are based
upon whether a child has an interest that is in need of protection, rather than
merely based upon whether the right holder is actually capable of asserting or
waiving his or her claim. If society generally recognises that children have a need

---

27 Advocates of the 'choice' theory include: Feinberg (1980); Hart (1984); Sumner (1987); and Steiner
   (1994).
28 Advocates of the 'interest' theory include: MacCormick (1982); Campbell (1992); Raz (1996); and
   Kramer (1998).

for care and protection, then it ought to be possible to construct rights upon such foundations.

It is also convenient to think about the distinctions between choice and interest theories in parallel to a distinction of the content of rights into categories of 'liberty rights' and 'welfare rights'. Archard (2010) characterises liberty rights as 'rights to choose, such as to vote, to practise a religion and to associate' and welfare rights as 'rights that protect important interests such as health'. Even if children lack the capacity or competence to 'choose', they surely have fundamental interests worthy of protection and thus have 'welfare rights' (Brighouse 2002).

Once children's 'interests' have been identified it can be seen that it should not be too difficult to formulate a credible set of 'moral rights' applying to children. One formulation of a moral right is 'a good of such importance that it would be wrong to deny it or withhold it' from any member of a given class (MacCormick 1982: 160). However, this does not assist greatly in the task of identifying which interests can be transformed into moral rights and on what basis; it appears merely to beg the same question using different terminology. What constitutes a 'good' of 'such importance' that it would be 'wrong' to deny or withhold it? Even if a set of moral rights can be reliably formulated, there still remains the issue of the basis upon which moral rights ought to be transformed into concrete legal rights. Many commentators accept that such transformation occurs 'if there is some recognition of their importance by the rest of society and consequently the imposition of correlative legal duties on others regarding the fulfilment of those rights' (Fortin 2009: 15).

The core point of the interest theory is that children ought not to be denied access to concrete legal rights merely because some children will not be sufficiently mature to make informed choices in their exercise and operation. However, the proponents of the interest theory would not claim that all children's interests are suitable to be transformed into moral rights and subsequently legal rights. A weakness of the interest theory is the uncertainty involved in identifying the relevant interests and the mechanisms that might operate to transform such interests into moral and then into legal rights. Which 'interests' should be rights-protected and why? By what criteria are we to assess the various interests of children for inclusion in a list of potential moral and legal rights?

Although there is no definitive resolution to this problem, Eekelaar at least provides a practical classification of children's interests, which might be capable of transformation into moral/legal rights. In order to meet the problem that children might not be competent properly to formulate their interests, he suggested that the adult should 'make some kind of imaginative leap and guess what a child might retrospectively have wanted once it reaches a position of maturity' (Eekelaar 1986: 170). He ordered children's interests into three groups: 'basic', 'developmental' and 'autonomy' interests. Children's basic interests refer to the child's need for immediate physical, emotional and intellectual care. Children's developmental interests are concerned with children's needs to optimise their full developmental potential by having equal access to appropriate resources. A child's autonomy interests relate to the need for children to be free to make independent decisions about their lives. Eekelaar (1986: 171) argued that where autonomy interests conflicted with basic and/or developmental interests the latter interests should prevail:

> The problem is that a child's autonomy interest may conflict with the developmental interest and even the basic interest. While it is possible that some adults retrospectively approve that they were, when children, allowed the exercise of their autonomy at the price of putting them at a disadvantage as against other children in realizing their life-chances in adulthood, it seems improbable that this would be a common view. We may therefore rank the autonomy interests subordinate to the basic and the developmental interests. However, where they may be exercised without threatening these two interests, the claim for their satisfaction must be high.

So, for example, the autonomy demonstrated by a child's decision to smoke cigarettes would be overridden by the recognition of basic (and development) health interests. Using the 'imaginative leap' notion referred to earlier, Eekelaar justifies this view on the basis that adults would be unlikely retrospectively to approve behaviour that would clearly prejudice their life-chances in adulthood.

As regards the underlying debate between the application of 'choice/will' or 'interest' theory, Fortin has argued that the emerging case law under the Human Rights Act 1998 has suggested that a young person's claim to exercise autonomy based on Convention rights has been dependent on that person's ability to comprehend what is involved in the decision itself (Fortin 2006: 325). This is an approach that conforms to the 'choice/will' theory but which, in practice, is neither a logical nor a safe approach. On the other hand , an interest theory of rights 'allows conceptions of the child's welfare to be accommodated within conceptions of his interests or rights', and the interest theory does not compel any rejection of the idea of children making choices.

> Children may indeed have some rights to self-determination based on their interest in choice, without having a right to complete autonomy. An analysis based on an interest theory of rights withholds the right to complete autonomy, including the right to make all fundamental decisions regarding his future, until the teenager reaches a required level of maturity, measured not only by reference to his powers of comprehension. At this level, he is deemed to be on a par with adult rights holders, with no paternalistic interventions available to protect him from the hazards of dangerous decision-making. Before then the courts are entitled to deny him the right to reach decisions which will materially threaten his adult wellbeing. Such a stance is a morally coherent one, reflecting the view that the status of minority carries a legal significance. It is designed to protect children from the dangers of adulthood, more particularly from making life-threatening decisions.

1.2.1.2   Autonomy, paternalism and participation

The review of theories of children's rights above exposes significant issues relating to the capacity and competence of children to make choices that justify the attribution of rights. A key controversy in child law and policy is the extent to which the child can be properly regarded as having a right to autonomy or self-determination. This reflects the focus on the active *agency* of the child identified in our discussion of the sociological perspective on childhood (section 1.1.3). It also reflects the way in which childhood is a 'social construction', a point brought out by our discussion of the historical perspective on childhood (section 1.1.2). The notion of active agency has been increasingly recognised and supported by the strengthening of a global human rights culture since the UDHR in 1948.

In the United Kingdom, for example, the process of the legal recognition of children's autonomy was given a significant boost in the landmark case of *Gillick*.

Case study 1.1

Gillick v West Norfolk and Wisbech Area Health Authority [1986] AC 112, [1985] 3 All ER 402

Facts: In this case, the Department of Health and Social Security had issued guidance to area health authorities on family planning which contained a section dealing with contraceptive advice and treatment for young people. It stated that attempts would always be made to persuade children under the age of 16 who attended clinics to involve their parent or guardian at the earliest stage of consultation, and that it would be most unusual to provide contraceptive advice to such children without parental consent. However, the guidance underlined the need not to abandon the principle of confidentiality between doctor and patient, and stated that in exceptional cases it was for a doctor exercising his or her clinical judgment to decide whether to prescribe contraception. The plaintiff, who was the mother of five girls under the age of 16 years, wrote to her local area health authority seeking an assurance from them that no contraceptive advice or treatment would be given to any of her daughters without her knowledge and consent. The area health authority refused to give such an assurance and stated that in accordance with the guidance the final decision must be for the doctor's clinical judgment. The plaintiff challenged the legality of the guidance.

Held: The House of Lords held that the National Health Service legislation indicated that Parliament regarded contraceptive advice and treatment as essentially medical matters and that there was no statutory limit on the age of the persons to whom contraceptive facilities might be supplied; and that a girl under the age of 16 years had the legal capacity to consent to medical examination and treatment, including contraceptive treatment, if she had sufficient maturity and intelligence to understand the nature and implications of the proposed treatment; that the parental right to control a minor child deriving from parental duty was a dwindling right which existed only in so far as it was required for the child's benefit and protection; that the extent and duration of that right could not be ascertained by reference to a fixed age, but depended on the degree of intelligence and understanding of that particular child and a judgment of what was best for the welfare of the child; that the parents' right to determine whether a child under 16 should have medical treatment terminated when the child achieved sufficient intelligence and understanding to make that decision itself; that although in the majority of cases parents were the best judges of matters concerning the child's welfare, there might be exceptional cases in which a doctor was a better judge of the medical advice and treatment that would conduce to a girl's welfare and where it might be desirable for a doctor to give a girl, in her own best interests, contraceptive advice and treatment, if necessary without the consent or even the knowledge of the parents; and that, accordingly, the department's guidance did not contain advice that was an infringement of parents' rights.

The support which this case appeared to give to a child's autonomy of decision-making, subject to being recognised as of sufficient understanding and maturity in relation to the decision, was much heralded at the time, and the appearance of the iconic '*Gillick*-mature child' in public debate in the United Kingdom and elsewhere has persisted.[29] Shortly after the House of Lords' decision in *Gillick*, the 'mature minor' doctrine was applied in Canada.[30] More recently, the Supreme Court of Canada, in *A.C. v. Manitoba (Director of Child and Family Services)*, had to grapple with the question of a child's autonomous decision-making in the context of a life-threatening scenario.

29 *Gillick* was followed in the early 1990s by two decisions that arguably diminished the child's right to make autonomous decisions (Douglas 1992): see *Re R (A Minor) (Wardship: Consent to Treatment)* [1992] Fam 11, [1991] 4 All ER 177; and *Re W (A Minor) (Medical Treatment: Court's Jurisdiction)* [1993] Fam 64, [1992] 4 All ER 627. The Court of Appeal ruled that the court could override a young person's decision to withhold consent from life-saving treatment (anti-psychotic drug treatment and treatment for *anorexia nervosa* respectively).

30 *J.S.C. v. Wren* (1986) 76 AR 115 (CA), where a 16-year-old girl had received medical approval for a therapeutic abortion, but her parents sought an injunction to prevent it because the age of majority was 18. Based on *Gillick*, Kerans JA concluded that the girl was capable of consenting to the abortion on her own behalf.

Case study 1.2

A.C. v Manitoba (Director of Child and Family Services) 2009
SCC 30 (2009), 26 June 2009

Facts: C, a devout Jehovah's Witness, was admitted to hospital when she
was 14 years and 10 months old, suffering from lower gastrointestinal bleed-
ing caused by Crohn's disease. She refused consent to the receipt of blood.
The Director of Child and Family Services apprehended her as a child in
need of protection, and sought a treatment order from the court under
section 25(8) of the Manitoba Child and Family Services Act, by which the
court may authorise treatment that it considers to be in the child's 'best
interests'. There is a presumption in section 25(9) of the Act that the best
interests of a child 16 or over will be most effectively promoted by allowing
the child's views to be determinative, unless it can be shown that the child
does not understand the decision or appreciate its consequences. Where the
child is under 16, however, no such presumption exists. The applications
judge ordered that C receive blood transfusions, concluding that when
a child is under 16 there are no legislated restrictions of authority on the
court's ability to order medical treatment in the child's 'best interests'. C
and her parents appealed the order, arguing that the legislative scheme was
unconstitutional because it unjustifiably infringed C's rights under sections
2(a), 7 and 15 of the Canadian Charter of Rights and Freedoms. The Court
of Appeal upheld the constitutional validity of the impugned provisions and
the treatment order.

Held: The Supreme Court of Canada held (Binnie J dissenting) that the
appeal should be dismissed and that section 25(8) and 25(9) of the Child and
Family Services Act were constitutional. The majority (LeBel, Deschamps,
Charron and Abella JJ) found that when a young person's best interests are
interpreted in a way that sufficiently respects his or her capacity for mature,
independent judgment in a particular medical decision-making context,
the constitutionality of the legislation was preserved. The statutory scheme
struck a constitutional balance between what the law has consistently seen
as an individual's fundamental right to autonomous decision-making in
connection with his or her body, and the law's equally persistent attempts
to protect vulnerable children from harm. The 'best interests' standard in
section 25(8) operated as a sliding scale of scrutiny, with the child's views
becoming increasingly determinative depending on his or her maturity.
The more serious the nature of the decision and the more severe its potential impact on life or health, the greater the degree of scrutiny required.
Interpreting the 'best interests' standard in this way navigates the tension
between an adolescent's increasing entitlement to autonomy as he or she

> matures and society's interest in ensuring that young people who are vulnerable are protected from harm. The Supreme Court took the view that this approach brought the 'best interests' standard in line with the evolution of the common law (including *Gillick*) and with international principles.

The mention of 'international principles' here was a reference to the Convention on the Rights of the Child in which Article 3 describes 'the best interests of the child' as a primary consideration in all actions concerning children (see section 3.7.3.2). Articles 5 and 14 of the Convention on the Rights of the Child require state parties to respect the responsibilities, rights and duties of parents to provide direction to the child in exercising his or her rights 'in a manner consistent with the evolving capacities of the child'.

Similarly, Article 12 requires state parties to 'assure to the child who is capable of forming his or her own views the right to express those views freely in all matters affecting the child, the views of the child being given due weight in accordance with the age and maturity of the child' (section 3.7.3.4). Archard (2012: 329) pinpoints a 'central tension' between two of the foundational principles of the Convention on the Rights of the Child, the best interests principle (Article 3) and the child's right to be heard (Article 12):

> The tension between a best interest principle and a child's right to express her own views on matters affecting her interests is not simply an abstract or theoretical conflict of attitudes toward the child. It is a tension that yields conflicting practical recommendations in those situations where we must decide what to do in respect of a child, and where what the child wants is at odds with what adults who must make that decision judge is best.

In essence, this reflects the need for a balance between the elements of *protection* and *empowerment* in the Convention.

There are, of course, a number of legal duties to take into account children's views in child law in many countries.[31] Although these may fall short of full participation rights in decision-making, at least they indicate a fuller acknowledgement of children's capacities and autonomy. It may be inappropriate, even positively damaging, to give a younger child the final decision about which parent he or she wants to live with, in the context of a parental dispute; however, it may be suitable to ensure some consultation with the child to ascertain his or her wishes and feelings in order to improve the overall decision-making process. After all, the

---

31 For example under the 'welfare principle' contained in section 1 of the Children Act 1989, when a court is considering making, varying or discharging an order under Part IV of the Act, or making etc a section 8 order, where that order is opposed, it must have regard in particular to a welfare checklist which includes 'the ascertainable wishes and feelings of the child concerned (considered in the light of his age and understanding)' (s 1(3)(a)).

airing of a child's views is good practice for more central participation in decision-making to be undertaken later in adulthood.

If a child cannot be regarded as fully autonomous, then it follows that there is a need for some adult or state constraint on a child's autonomy, commensurate with the maturity and competence of the developing child and the prevalent view within that society of the respective responsibilities of parents, the wider family and the state. Most commentators now accept the justification for at least some paternalistic intervention. Raz (1996) justifies paternalistic coercion on the basis that it may be grounded on the general trust reposed by the child in the person or body exercising such coercion. Thus, a child may trust and respect his or her parents to understand at least the legitimacy of their coercive action in relation to specific behaviours. Paternalism is often identified as an agent of oppression; paternalistic structures of society are frequently used to explain sex discrimination and gender-based inequalities. In the context of the child-parent relationship, however, paternalism is arguably a key component once it has been accepted that the best interests of children lie in both welfarist protection and the encouragement of participatory decision-making.

Fortin argues that the theories of rights 'provide a substantial body of wisdom supporting the view that paternalism can be justified as a means of protecting children's long term interests' (Fortin 2006: 325). Other advocates of children's rights, while affirming that '[t]he language of rights can make visible what has for too long been suppressed' (Freeman MDA 2007: 6), have had little difficulty in retaining a suitable place for liberal paternalistic intervention, particularly in relation to life-threatening decision-making by adolescents (Freeman MDA 1983: 54–60; Freeman MDA 2007: 15).

If the principle of the need for at least some paternalistic intervention is accepted, then the argument will often turn to how the occasions on which such intervention is appropriate can be properly identified. This has remained an almost irresolvable issue in the literature. On the one hand, there is a need to respect children's interests in making choices, in deploying their autonomy. On the other hand, there is a need to override some of their decisions which would otherwise damage their lives.

The problem is particularly acute at the threshold of adult responsibility seen in older teenagers. Most parents of adolescents will have experienced the dilemma of when to exert authority over their children on the basis that this is in their best interests, or to allow a child to follow his or her own choices which, although disapproved, will provide the child with a sense of being taken seriously and an opportunity to learn better the practice of autonomous decision-making. As Fortin (2009: 29) wisely puts it:

> The ideal formula would authorise paternalistic interventions to protect adolescents from making life-threatening mistakes, but restrain autocratic and arbitrary adult restrictions on their potential for autonomy. Finding it may prove problematic.

Perhaps a more pragmatic way to examine children's rights is to focus on their 'participation rights'. This phrase refers to the way in which a child may participate in a range of decision-making. The advantage of using this type of language is that it allows a finer calibration of the extent to which a child may participate in any one particular decision according to the child's own maturity and the nature of the decision in question. Article 12 of the Convention on the Rights of the Child obliges states parties to assure to the child who is capable of forming his or her own views a right to express views about matters affecting him or her; it also confers on the child a right to be heard in any judicial or administrative proceedings affecting the child (section 3.7.3.4). As will be seen, this right is one of the foundational principles of the Convention, and its importance has been underlined by the Committee on the Rights of the Child's production of recommendations following a 'Day of General Discussion'[32] and a detailed and analytical 'General Comment' (section 3.4).[33]

A widespread practice has emerged in recent years, which has been broadly conceptualised as 'participation', although this term itself does not appear in the text of Article 12. The term has evolved and is now widely used to describe ongoing processes, which include information-sharing and dialogue between children and adults based on mutual respect, and in which children can learn how their views and those of adults are taken into account and shape the outcome of such processes.[34]

This idea of a continuum of children's participation has an immediate practical appeal and, indeed, has been taken up enthusiastically by child advocates and practitioners. Hart (1992: 8) produced a useful model of a 'ladder of participation'.[35] The first three rungs of the ladder ('manipulation', 'decoration' and 'tokenism') are not categorised as true child participation. 'Manipulation' refers to situations where children may be used as a means to an (adult) end. 'Decoration' refers, 'for example, to those occasions when children are given T-shirts related to some cause' and this rung is distinguishable from 'manipulation' in that 'adults do not pretend that the cause is inspired by children; they simply use the children to bolster their cause in a relatively indirect way' (Hart 1992: 9). 'Tokenism' refers to situations where children are apparently given a voice but have little or no choice about the subject or style of communicating it and little or no opportunity to formulate their own opinions. The remaining five rungs of the ladder are categorised as constituting differing degrees of children's participation.

---

32 Committee on the Rights of the Child, 'Day of General Discussion on the right of the child to be heard', 43rd session, CRC/C/43/3 (16 July 2007) [980–1041].

33 Committee on the Rights of the Child, 'General Comment No 12: The right of the child to be heard', 51st session, UN Doc CRC/C/GC/12 (20 July 2009).

34 ibid para 3.

35 This model was based on Arnstein's (1969) model relating to adult participation in the political process.

A useful critique of Hart's 'ladder of participation' and related theories of children's participation is provided by Thomas (2007: 215). He concludes that the components of a theory of children's participation should:

a) encompass all the sites where children's participation may or may not take place;
b) be located in a broader context of inter-generational relations;
c) understand the distinction between 'participation' meaning activity that children engage in conjointly with adults, and children and young people's autonomous activity;
d) accommodate the new kinds of participatory practice with children and young people that have been developed (particularly in countries of the majority world);
e) account for the demands for children and young people to have the same political rights as adults.

1.2.1.3   Children's rights movement

The growing international recognition of children's rights can be regarded as one element of a more general interest in human rights that followed the Second World War. In Europe this was characterised by the European Convention on Human Rights in 1950,[36] prompted by the previous experience of arbitrary state interference with individual liberties. There has been an increased awareness of sex and race discrimination issues. Indeed, the civil rights movement in the United States demonstrated a broad concern about the 'rights' of minority groups. The US Supreme Court had ruled in *Re Gault* that 'neither the Fourteenth Amendment nor the Bill of Rights is for adults alone'[37] and that children could likewise benefit from the US Constitution's procedural safeguards.

The minority legal status of children came to be regarded in some quarters as oppressive and as a means to conceal the abuse of power over children, both by parents and the state. The American so-called 'child liberationists' took this to extremes. They suggested that it was essentially a form of oppression to exclude children from the adult world and adult freedoms. Holt (1974), for example, argued that children of any age should have the vote, they should be able to work for money, direct their own education and be paid a guaranteed minimum state income. Thus, the movement for children's rights was unfortunately closely associated with simply giving adult freedoms to children. This was a gross distortion of the true position, as any cursory examination of the structure and content of the Convention on the Rights of the Child would reveal.

---

36 European Convention for the Protection of Human Rights and Fundamental Freedoms, opened for signature 4 November 1950, 213 UNTS 221 (entered into force 3 September 1953).
37 *Re Gault*, 387 US 1, 13 (Fortas J) (1967).

Some commentators now believe that the liberationists did little to serve the cause of children's rights precisely because of this lasting association (Fortin 2009: 4). However, other social movements have equally gone through stages of militant ideology in their development. Such militant interludes have arguably performed the valuable function of challenging conventional orthodoxies, but also have acted as precursors to more measured responses.

In retrospect, the liberationists' views do appear to have been formulated without due regard to the obvious facts of varying physical and mental competence found in children. Their views ignore, for example, all the carefully worked and tested body of knowledge concerning children's cognitive development. The liberationists' views can also be regarded as potentially damaging to the extent that they may encourage children to shoulder adult responsibilities before proper preparation for such roles.

Campbell (1992), for example, stressed the need for children not to have their experience of childhood stolen from them under the guise of offering them adult responsibilities. On one view, the focus on the need for children to make their own decisions and exercise autonomy, if taken too far, would inevitably lead to the boundary of adulthood and childhood being redefined. However, the radical approach of the liberationists has at least established that children are not inherently incapable of informed and rational decision-making, at even quite young ages, contrary to what many people might have otherwise thought.

Some commentators, in particular Goldstein and others (1973, 1980), have argued strongly for family autonomy from the state, that is, a model of minimum state interference in the privacy of family life.[38] There have been recent public debates influenced by this orientation. An authoritative historian of childhood (Cunningham 2006: 245) has noted the significant differences between the experience of childhood now and in past centuries:

> Children in the past have been assumed to have capabilities that we now rarely think they have. ... So fixated are we on giving our children a long and happy childhood that we downplay their abilities and their resilience.

Gill further develops this picture of children and argues that childhood is becoming undermined by 'risk aversion'. For example, a range of childhood activities previously enjoyed by children have been 'relabelled as troubling or dangerous, while the adults who still permit them are branded as irresponsible'. He detected 'a pattern of growing adult intervention to minimise risk at the expense of childhood experience' (Gill 2007: 10–11).

The assumption of those advocating a minimalist state intervention role is that parents should be entitled to raise their children as they think best. While this perspective is reflective of the general human rights drive to prevent arbitrary

38 A similar position to the *laissez-faire* model of Fox Harding (1996) outlined in section 1.1.4 above.

state interference, it also poses a threat to the integrity of children's rights. If legal systems are premised on minimum state intervention in family life, as many are, there equally may be little opportunity for supporting children's choices where these conflict with parental views.

The assumption underlying the minimalist state intervention model of the centrality of parental roles may be in danger of being translated into a parental immunity from any type of appropriate accountability. However, these positions need not be mutually exclusive. It is no doubt possible to constrain both state and parental authority within reasonable limits, thus reflecting a desired balance of authority in relation to children.

1.2.2 International children's rights

Although it is reassuring to find theoretical justifications for children's rights, the approach of legal positivism has simply been to point to the existence of such rights in contemporary legal instruments. At the international level one can identify, in addition to the references contained in the International Bill of Human Rights, 40 substantive rights as set out in the 54 articles of the Convention on the Rights of the Child. The speed at which the Convention on the Rights of the Child was ratified (see Figure 3.1), and the number of states parties involved, strengthen the argument, at least on a pragmatic basis, that this Convention has established itself as the key international instrument that sets out the fundamental principles of international children's rights.

Indeed, this argument is further advanced by the view that the Convention may constitute a special form of international law which can be regarded as having a 'fundamental' status, that is, *jus cogens* (see section 2.2.5). On the other hand, it has been said that the Convention, and indeed other international treaties, are vehicles for 'manifesto' rights, that is, rights that reflect mere aspirations. Some commentators note that the proliferation of international human rights instruments may have led to a 'devaluation' in the currency of rights talk (Wellman 1999).

Fortin identifies Article 27 of the Convention on the Rights of the Child (the child's right to an adequate standard of living – see section 3.7.7.6) as a provision that is difficult to imagine could ever be legally enforced owing to its 'extreme vagueness' (Fortin 2009: 18). However, once we move away from expectations of concrete legal enforceability, even such provisions as Article 27 may be seen as offering more than mere rhetoric. Upon closer examination, Article 27 does at least provide a useful normative legal standard, namely that parents have the 'primary responsibility' for securing favourable living conditions, and the state by implication has a secondary responsibility to assist parents and other carers in these tasks and 'in case of need provide material assistance and support programmes, particularly with regard to nutrition, clothing and housing'. It thus provides a useful structure, defining the relationship between parents and state, in which the right to an adequate standard of living can be operationalised.

It also contains a more detailed obligation on states to secure the recovery of maintenance for children.[39]

Lawyers and policy-makers are often concerned more with the way in which legal rights, that is, those contained in valid international and domestic instruments, are formulated and structured, rather than their philosophical pedigree. How do individual rights relate to other associated rights in the same or related instrument? For example, Article 27 of the Convention on the Rights of the Child is linked to Article 6(2) ('child's right to survival and development') and Article 24 ('the right to enjoyment of the highest attainable standard of health'). Inevitably most rights, especially social, economic and cultural rights, can only be successfully implemented by balancing them against other rights and interests.

One of the reasons for the wide recognition of the important status of the Convention on the Rights of the Child is precisely its form and structure and the origins of its drafting. Chapter 3 deals with this in greater detail, but suffice it to say here that the Convention combines civil and political rights ('first generation rights') – for example, Articles 13, 14 and 15 – with social, economic and cultural rights ('second generation rights') – for example, Articles 24, 26 and 27. Indeed, consistently with the structure of general human rights instruments, securing second generation rights often proved to be a necessary precondition for meeting first generation rights.

Freedom of expression, for example, can be conducted more effectively only when a society has created reasonable conditions of economic security and social order. The way in which the international community continues to perceive children's rights through its legal instruments and programmes provides a unique opportunity to examine how that community is constantly revising and setting its priorities in relation to children.

As will be seen (section 3.5), the 'Concluding Observations' of the Committee on the Rights of the Child on states parties' periodic reports give specific direction to state parties about the shortcomings that need to be addressed in order to further the cause of children's rights as formulated in the Convention on the Rights of the Child. However, one of the key weaknesses in the system is the lack of 'teeth' if the state party is somewhat dilatory in addressing these issues. It remains to be seen whether the addition of the Optional Protocol to the UN Convention on the Rights of the Child on a Communications Procedure[40] to the Committee's remit will be capable of enhancing the implementation of children's rights (Buck and Wabwile 2013).

---

39 Convention on the Rights of the Child art 27(2)–27(4).
40 Optional Protocol to the UN Convention on the Rights of the Child on a Communications Procedure (28 February 2012) UN Doc A/RES/66/138 (entered into force 14 April 2014).

1.3   Childhood, children's rights and cultural relativism

The discussion of both the concepts of childhood and children's rights in this chapter also raises the issue of 'cultural relativism'; a term first used in anthropological research, implying that human beliefs and activities can only be understood in terms of their own culture. It should be noted that this concept should not be confused with 'moral relativism'; a belief that all cultures are both separate and equal and that any value system, however different from another, is equally valid. The problem of cultural relativism in international human rights law was highlighted at the time the United Nations was in the process of preparing the UDHR in 1947–48. The Executive Board of the American Anthropological Association (1947: 539) produced a statement on human rights and put the question thus:

> The problem is thus to formulate a statement of human rights that will do more than just phrase respect for the individual as an individual. It must also take into full account the individual as a member of the social group of which he is a part, whose sanctioned modes of life shape his behavior, and with whose fate his own is thus inextricably bound.
>
> Because of the great numbers of societies that are in intimate contact in the modern world, and because of the diversity of their ways of life, the primary task confronting those who would draw up a Declaration on the Rights of Man is thus, in essence, to resolve the following problem: How can the proposed Declaration [UDHR] be applicable to all human beings, and not be a statement of rights conceived only in terms of the values prevalent in the countries of Western Europe and America?

Consequently, one can see how any international human rights instrument, such as the Convention on the Rights of the Child which seeks to achieve a universal standard, may be significantly weakened in terms of its legitimacy and ultimately its implementation if it is seen to be an exclusive product of the cultural values held principally by the powerful nations who were in a position to manage and direct its drafting. It would appear, for example, that at least in the early years of the drafting process of the Convention, '[t]he industrialised countries were significantly over-represented at all stages' and fears that the outcome would be 'a heavily Northern-oriented text were widespread and justified' and only mitigated by the participation of a few developing countries in combination with a last-minute surge of delegates from the south, many from states with Islamic law (Cantwell 1992: 23).

Equally, although cultural differences must be respected, conversely this must not become an excuse for practices that are widely perceived as unacceptable (Harris-Short 2001: 306). International human rights law has frequently been criticised on two grounds: first, that it lacks universality and in fact has been construed according to an ethnocentric view of the world usually associated with the influence of the more powerful nations of the north; and second, it is conceded that the normative standards may be culturally 'neutral', but consequently they will lack any substantial meaning in terms of their practical implementation. It is certainly true that any perusal of the Convention's preparatory works (*travaux préparatoires*) (Detrick 1992) shows the negotiated and mediated nature of some of the legal standards that eventually emerged in the final text. Some would argue that a high number of active state participants in the drafting process should ensure that there is reasonable attention to cultural diversity in framing such standards in the first place.

Cultural relativism is also a significant aspect of how international legal standards are viewed by individual nations and put into practice. For example, a state that has become politically and economically weak, which may have suffered years of warfare, civil strife, poverty and hunger, is likely to have very different priorities from some of the well established and relatively secure industrialised nations. There will not only be a difference in the resources available for deployment on appropriate programmes, but there will also be differences in how such states may construe the key underlying assumptions, relationships and concepts behind the standards. For example, it can be seen that the African nations, in their production of the African Charter on the Rights and Welfare of the Child,[41] have proceeded on the basis of a different view about the nature of the family unit and the relationship of individuals to the family and to the wider community.

The way in which the Convention on the Rights of the Child was drafted, the nature of the standards finally agreed, and the way in which the Committee on the Rights of the Child has interacted with states parties in their examination of reports, are all alive with cultural implications. As will be seen in the detailed discussion of the Convention on the Rights of the Child in Chapter 3, it contains an ideological commitment to a relatively modest extent of state interference in family affairs, shown both by the way in which certain articles of the Convention have been framed and the Committee's comments in respect of countries that appear to have a quite different view of the relationship between the state and the family (section 3.7.5). 'Traditional and customary practices' are also frequently criticised by the Committee as obstacles in achieving the standards set out in the Convention – for example, in relation to another foundational principle of the Convention, the right to life, survival and development (section 3.7.3.3). Yet anthropologists may well point out that such practices can have a positive influence, underwriting the community's social solidarity and shared belief systems.

In theory, the ability to make *declarations* and *reservations* (section 2.2.1) on ratifying the Convention[42] allows room to accommodate such differences, but within a unified international framework. It can be argued that a generous provision for reservations and declarations in international treaties should be a mandatory element of the required consensus-building in the international community.

---

41 See African Charter on the Rights and Welfare of the Child, adopted 11 July 1990, OAU Doc CAB/LEG/24.9/49 (1990) (entered into force 29 November 1999).
42 See Convention on the Rights of the Child art 51.

Equally, the way in which the Committee on the Rights of the Child probes individual states parties for their reasons and justifications for such departures from international normative standards reflects a mechanism of dialogue that is actively exploring cultural sensitivities but remains within the overall international framework. The balance to be achieved in advancing concrete international rights in this area and allowing sufficient flexibility to encompass cultural sensitivity is not an easy one to strike.

Chapter 2

International law sources and institutions

2.1 Introduction

This chapter provides an outline of some of the key sources, concepts and institutions that are necessary for an understanding of the international law relating to children. Those already familiar with international law sources and institutions might wish to omit this chapter, although it contains references to child law related examples that illustrate some of the general international law points discussed. A number of topics, discussed in some detail in general international law textbooks (eg Dixon 2013; Klabbers 2013; Crawford 2012; Aust 2010; Evans 2010; Kaczorowska 2010; Shaw 2008), are omitted here as they have little connection specifically with the realm of international child law. Thus the reader will find little about the law of the sea, territorial sovereignty, state succession and other concepts and institutions which do not relate directly to the subject of this book. However, an understanding of international child law will require some basic knowledge of the international legal system, how disputes are resolved and the nature of some of the key international institutions that have an important role to play in this field.

The study of international law is characteristically divided into private international law (more accurately described as 'conflict of laws') and public international law. 'Conflict of laws' refers to the body of laws that regulate private relationships across national borders. It deals largely with cases within legal systems where there is a foreign element to consider. It has been described as 'the body of rules of the domestic law of a State that is applicable when a legal issue contains a foreign element, and it has to be decided whether a domestic rule should apply foreign law or relinquish jurisdiction to a foreign court' (Aust 2010: 1).

Public international law, on the other hand, deals mainly with relations between states and the operation of international bodies. International child law in fact encompasses both subdivisions of international law. For example, there are a number of conventions emanating from the Hague Conference on Private International Law (section 2.4.2) that seek to enhance judicial and administrative cooperation on inter-country adoption and child abduction. There are also a number of human rights standards from the United Nations and from regional institutions that are directly relevant to children.

2.2   Sources of international law

Unlike most domestic legal orders that are based on the existence, in some form or another, of a distinct legislature, an executive and a judicial power, the international legal order is not constructed in this way. As yet there is no unified world government with law-making and executive authority to issue international laws that will be applied and interpreted by a global court system. The arrangement of international institutions does have some similar features to state governance, but there are important points of distinction. There is an authoritative statement of the sources of international law to be found in Article 38 of the Statute of the International Court of Justice (1945),[1] which most commentators would agree has been universally accepted, even though it technically applies only to the sources that the International Court of Justice (ICJ) (section 2.4.1.1) must apply:

(1) The Court, whose function is to decide in accordance with international law such disputes as are submitted to it, shall apply:

   (a) international conventions, whether general or particular, establishing rules expressly recognised by the contesting states;
   (b) international custom, as evidence of a general practice accepted as law;
   (c) the general principles of law recognised by civilized nations;
   (d) subject to the provisions of Article 59, judicial decisions and the teachings of the most highly qualified publicists of the various nations, as subsidiary means for the determination of rules of law.

(2) This provision shall not prejudice the power of the Court to decide a case *ex aequo et bono*, if the parties agree thereto.[2]

These sources of international law, that is, conventions/treaties, international customary rules, the general principles, judicial decisions and teachings, are discussed in the following sections.

2.2.1   International treaties and conventions

'Treaties' are known by a number of different names: eg Agreements, Statutes, Declarations, Pacts, Conventions, Charters, Covenants and Protocols etc. In essence, they involve the creation of a written agreement with which the states

1 Charter of the United Nations and Statute of the International Court of Justice, concluded 26 June 1945, 1 UNTS XVI (entered into force 23 October 1945).
2 Statute of the International Court of Justice art 38. Article 59 states: 'The decision of the Court has no binding force except between the parties and in respect of that particular case'. The Latin phrase in art 38(2) means 'according to what is right and good; in equity and good conscience'.

participating in them will be bound in international law. The procedural and other matters relating to the making of treaties have developed over time into rules of customary international law, which have been consolidated and extended by the Vienna Convention on the Law of Treaties[3] (1969) (Vienna Convention).

Treaties are traditionally divided into two types: there are 'law-making treaties' that are intended to have a general relevance; and 'treaty-contracts' that are intended to be binding only as between two or a few states. A good example of a law-making treaty in this context is the United Nations Convention on the Rights of the Child[4] (1989) (CRC). The CRC is, as we shall see in Chapter 3, a comprehensive statement of an agreed international vision of children's rights.

An example of a treaty-contract is any one of the many bilateral extradition treaties that regulate the surrender by one government to another of an accused or convicted person. The United Kingdom, for example, has extradition relations with more than 100 territories by way of both multilateral extradition conventions and agreements, or under bilateral extradition treaties. Extradition relations are regulated in the United Kingdom by the Extradition Act 2003.

It is in the nature of a multilateral law-making treaty that its success in establishing anything approaching a global or general effect will often depend on the political support that it receives from the nations of the world. Thus, for example, although the Hague Convention on Jurisdiction, Applicable Law and Recognition of Decrees Relating to Adoptions[5] (1965) represented an attempt to manage certain adoption issues at the international level, the lack of state ratifications deprived this instrument of ever having any significant impact. This convention has now been 'denounced' by each of the ratifying countries and has ceased to have effect in international law. A new international instrument, the Hague Convention on Protection of Children and Co-operation in respect of Intercountry Adoption[6] (1993) (see Chapter 6), has superseded it.

A treaty will normally specify two commencement dates: first, when it comes into force in international law; and, second, the date when any particular ratifying state is bound by it in international law. For example, the Hague Convention on Protection of Children and Co-operation in respect of Intercountry Adoption specifies, first, that it will enter into force in international law 'on the first day of the month following the expiration of 3 months after the deposit of the third instrument of ratification, acceptance or approval'.

---

3 Opened for signature 23 May 1969, 1155 UNTS 331 (entered into force 27 January 1980).
4 Opened for signature 20 November 1989, 1577 UNTS 3 (entered into force 2 September 1990).
5 Hague Conference on Private International Law, concluded 15 November 1965, (denounced and ceased to have effect 23 October 2008). Austria, Switzerland and the United Kingdom were the only states to have ratified this Convention; see further, section 6.2.1.
6 Hague Conference on Private International Law, concluded 29 May 1993 (entered into force 1 May 1995).

Secondly, it will 'thereafter' enter into force 'for each State ratifying, accepting or approving it subsequently, or acceding to it, on the first day of the month following the expiration of 3 months after the deposit of its instrument of ratification, acceptance, approval or accession'.[7] All other things being equal, the greater the international support for such international instruments, the more likely their underlying aims will be realised.

States that have not ratified a treaty will not be bound by its terms in international law. Thus, the United States and Somalia are not bound by the CRC. Remarkably, all the other (193) countries of the world have ratified this Convention. However, even if a state has not ratified an international treaty there are two ways in which it might nevertheless be bound by it, or at least by parts of the treaty. First, the treaty may contain some provision(s) that could be regarded as 'international customary law' (section 2.2.2), which is deemed to bind all nations. Secondly, a state may have appended its 'signature' to the treaty but then failed to follow this with the next usual step of final 'ratification'.

The act of signature is not without any legal effect. The Vienna Convention provides that once a state has signed a treaty it is 'obliged to refrain from acts which would defeat the object and purpose of a treaty', at least until it has made clear its intention not to become a party to the treaty; this is often referred to as the 'compatibility test'.[8] States will normally 'sign' treaties as a preliminary step to indicate their forthcoming agreement in the later 'ratification'. Signature in effect qualifies the state to proceed to ratification and creates an obligation of good faith not to 'defeat the object and purpose of a treaty'.[9]

The use of treaties as a primary means of international law-making has been so widespread that there was a need for an authoritative statement of the principles and formalities of treaty-making. This was achieved in the Vienna Convention, which reflected and codified pre-existing international customary law relating to the machinery of treaty-making, for example, the basic international law principle that treaties bind the parties to them and must be performed in good faith (*pacta sunt servanda*).[10] It also contains some general guidance about the approach to be taken to the interpretation of treaties.

---

7 Hague Convention on Protection of Children and Co-operation in respect of Intercountry Adoption arts 46(1), (2)(a). This Convention had been ratified by 93 states at the time of writing.

8 Article 18. A state may deposit an instrument expressly clarifying that, despite its signature, it does not intend to become a party to the treaty and that accordingly it 'has no legal obligations arising from its signature'. An example of this is the United States' signature (31 December 2000) of the Rome Statute of the International Criminal Court (1998), followed by its later statement (6 May 2002) that it did not intend to become a party to this treaty.

9 Although Somalia and the United States of America have famously not ratified the CRC, they are both signatories to it, on 9 May 2002 and 16 February 1995 respectively.

10 'Every treaty in force is binding upon the parties to it and must be performed by them in good faith': Vienna Convention art 26.

Article 31
General rule of interpretation

1. A treaty shall be interpreted in good faith in accordance with the ordinary meaning to be given to the terms of the treaty in their context and in the light of its object and purpose.
2. The context for the purpose of the interpretation of a treaty shall comprise, in addition to the text, including its preamble and annexes:

   (a) any agreement relating to the treaty which was made between all the parties in connection with the conclusion of the treaty;
   (b) any instrument which was made by one or more parties in connection with the conclusion of the treaty and accepted by the other parties as an instrument related to the treaty.

3. There shall be taken into account, together with the context:

   (a) any subsequent agreement between the parties regarding the interpretation of the treaty or the application of its provisions;
   (b) any subsequent practice in the application of the treaty which establishes the agreement of the parties regarding its interpretation;
   (c) any relevant rules of international law applicable in the relations between the parties.

4. A special meaning shall be given to a term if it is established that the parties so intended.

The Vienna Convention also permits recourse to 'supplementary means' of interpretation, including 'preparatory works' (*travaux préparatoires*), in three cases:

   i.   To confirm the meaning resulting from the application of Article 31;
   ii. To determine the meaning when the interpretation according to Article 31 leaves the meaning ambiguous or obscure; or
   iii. To determine the meaning when the interpretation according to Article 31 leads to a result which is manifestly absurd or unreasonable.

Preparatory works can provide an authoritative source of background and contextual information relating to the origins, objects and purpose and drafting history of the treaty in question. Detrick's (1992) work on the CRC is a good example. Background documentation on International Labour Organisation (ILO) Conventions is now collected on a website[11] containing texts of the preparatory reports, discussions at the International Labour Conference, committee reports, votes and texts of all up-to-date ILO Conventions. There are also 'explanatory reports' available in respect of the Hague Conventions: eg the reports by Pérez-Vera (1980) on child abduction and by Parra-Aranguren (1994) on inter-country

---

11 See http://labordoc.ilo.org/collection/ILOconventions (accessed 8 February 2013).

adoption. Regional international organisations also produce explanatory reports in relation to their legal instruments.

International law and international relations are closely entwined and the process of a state agreeing to any particular treaty is often influenced by political considerations at the domestic, regional and international levels. Multilateral treaties between a larger number of countries will often involve both compromise in the drafting process and some flexibility in the treaty text as to the extent to which states are bound with respect to some specific provisions.

Such flexibility is achieved by two methods. First, the text of the treaty may stipulate that states can opt in or opt out of a particular provision.[12] Secondly, states may make certain 'reservations', 'understandings' or 'declarations' upon signature and/or ratification of a treaty. A separate instrument containing such statements are usually lodged by states with the depositary of the treaty and then communicated to the other contracting states.[13] Such statements may affect the degree to which a state is bound by any particular provision of the treaty in question. Where such a statement is formulated expressly as a 'reservation' this indicates that the state intends that it should not be bound by a particular Article of the treaty. A state reserving its agreement to a particular Article may withdraw its reservation subsequently.[14]

Some ground rules about reservations have been formulated in the Vienna Convention.[15] Usually, the facility and procedure for making reservations in a treaty are set out expressly in the text of the individual treaty. Consequently, it is important to read any relevant provisions of the particular treaty at issue alongside the Vienna Convention to understand fully the precise scope of reservation-making that is available to contracting states. The Vienna Convention provides authority for states to formulate any reservations when signing or ratifying a treaty, subject to three exceptions:

- where the reservation is prohibited by the treaty
- where the treaty provides that only specified reservations may be made and
- where the reservation is 'incompatible with the object and purpose' of the treaty.

An example of the first exception can be found in the Hague Convention on Protection of Children and Co-operation in respect of Intercountry Adoption,

---

12 For example, there is provision to *opt in* to the interstate communications procedure and provision to *opt out* of the inquiry procedure in the Optional Protocol to the Convention on the Rights of the Child on a Communications Procedure (2012). See further ch 3 sections 3.6.3.2–3.6.3.3.

13 The depositary for the CRC is the Secretary-General of the UN; the depositary for ILO conventions is the Director-General of the ILO.

14 For example, the UK made four reservations upon its ratification; they had all been withdrawn by November 2008.

15 Articles 19–23.

which stipulates that 'no reservation to the Convention shall be permitted'.[16] An illustration of the second exception is contained in the Hague Convention on the Civil Aspects of International Child Abduction[17] (1980), which specifies that reservations are only permitted in two rather narrow areas[18] and furthermore reiterates the customary provision that a state can 'at any time withdraw a reservation it has made' (Pérez-Vera 1980: para 150). The third exception articulates the customary rule that prohibits making a reservation which is incompatible with the object and purpose of the treaty.

Some treaties expressly adopt this formula. For example, the CRC provides that a 'reservation incompatible with the object and purpose of the present Convention shall not be permitted'.[19] Of course, this begs the question as to which reservations can be regarded as striking sufficiently at the root of a treaty's 'object and purpose'. In this regard, the Committee on the Rights of the Child (Committee) has expressed concerns that some reservations are plainly incompatible with the CRC's 'object and purpose'; for example, those suggesting 'that respect for the Convention is limited by the State's existing Constitution or legislation, including in some cases religious law'.[20]

There have also been general concerns at the widespread use of reservations, declarations and understandings in relation specifically to multilateral human rights treaties, including the CRC.[21] International human rights treaties tend to provide a minimum standard of protection, and any departure from these is often criticised as contributing to a weakening of their overall legitimacy and effectiveness.

2.2.2 *International customary law*

The law on international treaties was first developed by the emergence of rules of 'international customary law' relating to a wide range of subject matter. It is tempting to think in modern times that the role of custom as a source of law is merely a residual one. This is generally the case within many municipal (that is, domestic) legal systems of developed nations. However, at the international level,

---

16 Hague Conference on Private International Law, concluded 29 May 1993 (entered into force 1 May 1995) art 40. This was required because of the 'the mandatory character of the Convention's rules' (Parra-Aranguren 1994: para 578).

17 Hague Conference on Private International Law, concluded 25 October 1980 (entered into force 1 December 1983) art 42.

18 In relation to the choice of language translation into French or English of documents sent to the Central Authority of the requested state (art 24); and in relation to the assumption of costs and expenses of proceedings (art 26).

19 CRC art 51(2).

20 Committee on the Rights of the Child, *General Comment No 5: General Measures of Implementation of the Convention on the Rights of the Child (Arts 4, 42 and 44, para 6)*, UNCRC/GC/2003/5, 34th session (27 November 2003). On reservations to the CRC see generally Schabas (1996).

21 At the time of writing there were 71 states parties to the CRC that had lodged reservations or declarations.

the role of custom as a source of law has remained creative rather than merely residual, precisely because the international legal order lacks the better defined and authoritative institutional framework generally found in domestic legal orders.

The appearance of international customary law can be a flexible and responsive mode of law-making in a changing world; and one that may be necessary to preserve international legal order. In essence, two requirements are needed for a rule of international customary law to be recognised: first, the material facts of the alleged customary rule must be found in *state practice*; and, secondly, states must subjectively believe that such practice is binding (*opinio juris*).

General international customary rules ought normally to be uniform and consistent in relation to both the above requirements, although a rigid prescription of these requirements should be avoided. The context and nature of the customary rule may give a different emphasis as to how these requirements are viewed. In domestic legal systems, the *duration* of an alleged custom is often of importance.[22] In international law, customs can appear instantly. For example, the customary rule about state sovereignty over air space appeared around the time of the First World War and the rule of non-sovereignty of space appeared at the time the first satellites were being launched in the 1950s and 1960s (Haanappel 2003).

In theory, all states can participate in the formation of international customary law. However, the influence and power of particular nations on specific issues may mean that an individual state's contribution to international discussion on certain issues will lead the direction of international law-making on those issues. For example, the United Kingdom, a powerful maritime nation in the 19th century, had a key influence on the formation of the international law of the sea, and prize law. Russia and the United States had a crucial influence on the formation of space law.

However, matters affecting human rights generally, and children's rights in particular, are unlikely to be viewed explicitly in this way. The core ethic of human rights law is the recognition of the dignity of an individual person irrespective of his or her national identity. In principle, it would seem ironic if only the economically powerful nations had a significant influence in designing the structure of international human rights law. On the other hand, the post-war emergence of the United Nations system and the Universal Declaration of Human Rights (UDHR) of 1948 can be seen as international architecture heavily influenced by the victor nations of the Second World War. As one commentator puts it: 'scholars should not jump too quickly to the conclusion ... that altruism must motivate the establishment of morally attractive international norms' (Moravcsik 2000: 48). It would be difficult, and ethnocentric, to assert that there might be a principled basis for certain nations to claim some special distinctive role or superior moral

22 One of the tests to identify custom as a recognised source of English law is famously whether it has been so regarded since 'time immemorial', the latter being a reference to 3 September 1189, the date of the coronation of King Richard I (Ward and Akhtar 2011).

authority in relation to forming legal standards that are relevant specifically to children's rights.

On the other hand, to ignore the influence of power relations embedded in the international community in this field would be naïve. The drafting process of a multilateral treaty is ultimately a diplomatic one not immune from the influence of power politics. The way in which such instruments are perceived and acted upon (or not acted upon) after they subsequently emerge into the body of international law is also a process often more driven by the shape of international relations than as a result of applying principles from the legal text of an international instrument.

As we have seen, the first requirement for a rule to have the status of customary law is to show a *state practice*. The state practice must be uniform and consistent with the alleged rule of customary law, and a range of materials may evidence this. For example, the state's official publications, diplomatic exchanges, resolutions made by the General Assembly of the United Nations, drafts produced by the International Law Commission and the cumulative practice of international organisations may be good evidence of customary law.

Some states have produced extensive digests and yearbooks containing their own state practices relevant to the international community which have particular authority; for example, the *British Yearbook of International Law* (Lowe and Crawford 2012), and the *Digest of US Practice in International Law* (Guymon 2012). The domestic law of a state may, in certain circumstances, be evidence of a state practice. Ultimately, the identification of state practice which may form the basis of customary law is a somewhat circular exercise.

The requirement to establish *opinio juris* involves a subjective belief by a state that its practice is binding. As might be expected, a high threshold is required to prove it. Objections by other states may interrupt the legitimising process of custom formation. It is difficult to be prescriptive about this process; sometimes state protests may themselves contain the seeds of a new customary rule. Two customary rules may coexist for a while side by side. For example, in the 1960s some countries used the customary three-mile rule, that is, national rights were limited to waters extending from the coast to three nautical miles (the 'cannon shot' rule). Others used the customary 12-mile rule that had developed in the post-war period onwards as nations laid claim to mineral resources in order to protect fishing and to enforce pollution control in their territorial waters.[23]

An important feature of rules of international customary law is that they will be binding on *all* states unless a state has objected to it from the start. In some states, including the United Kingdom, international customary law may be regarded as being automatically incorporated into domestic law according to the 'incorporation doctrine' (section 2.3). It can therefore be very important from both a

---

23 Maritime international customary rules have been codified in the UN Convention on the Law of the Sea, opened for signature 10 December 1982, 1833 UNTS 3 (entered into force 16 November 1994).

national and an international perspective to determine whether an international rule has become part of customary law.

The relationship and status of treaties and customary law has been a difficult issue in international law discourse. Historically, custom preceded the more modern liking for formal treaty-making. On the other hand, treaties, although often desired because they promised greater certainty, often include some codification of existing customary law. However, where a treaty has effectively codified a part of customary law, the treaty provision has not necessarily substituted the customary source of law.

The ICJ (see section 2.4.1.1) held in the *Nicaragua Case*[24] that a customary rule about a state's right of self-defence had not been superseded by a provision of the United Nations Charter (1945):[25] these two sources of law coexisted. In the context of international child law, for example, it is arguable that international customary law protects the child against sexual, economic and other forms of exploitation analogous to slavery, similar to the protection offered in some of the articles relating to such exploitation contained in the CRC (Van Bueren 1998).

2.2.3 General principles of law recognised by civilised nations

The international legal order will inevitably have significant gaps where it may appear there is no law, or where the law is silent on a particular matter. Where there is no treaty or customary law rule, case law may well fill some of these gaps. However, in the international legal system there is often a lack of case law in particular areas, either because the subject has not been litigated or because there is no court-like forum that forms part of the international arrangements at issue. This is so in relation to the operation of the CRC, a treaty which does not have an international court forum comparable to the ICJ.

However, an accepted standard of international law is that every international situation is, as a matter of law, capable of being determined (Shaw 2008: 99). One of the functions, therefore, of the 'general principles of law' in the context of Article 38 of the Statute of the International Court of Justice is to fill such gaps where necessary. The provenance and content of these general principles are contested by scholars, but it is thought that they may include legal principles that are common to a large number of domestic law systems. However, it is much more difficult precisely to identify these principles, and indeed some commentators regard them as a sub-category of either treaties or custom, rather than a discrete but limited source of law. On one view, general principles tend to be preconditions for the

---

24 *Nicaragua v United States (Military and Paramilitary Activities in and against Nicaragua) (Judgment)* [1986] ICJ Rep 14.

25 'Nothing in the present Charter shall impair the inherent right of individual or collective self-defence if an armed attack occurs against a Member of the United Nations, until the Security Council has taken measures necessary to maintain international peace and security. ...' Charter of the United Nations and Statute of the International Court of Justice, concluded 26 June 1945, 1 UNTS XVI (entered into force 23 October 1945) art 51.

operation and efficiency of the international legal system as a whole. For example, the key general principle that international agreements are binding and must be carried out in good faith (*pacta sunt servanda*) is a presupposition without which the whole of treaty law would lack the key quality of legal obligation.

Similarly, 'equity' and 'equitable principles' are often regarded as part of the 'general principles' of international law. There is also the fundamental principle of 'good faith' in the UN Charter, which provides that 'all Members, in order to ensure to all of them the rights and benefits resulting from membership, shall fulfil in good faith the obligations assumed by them in accordance with the present Charter'.[26]

Again, principles of equity and good faith can be viewed as preconditions for a well ordered international legal order. A leading British authority (Shaw 2008: 109) on international law concludes:

> Although generalised principles or concepts that may be termed community value-judgments inform and pervade the political and therefore the legal orders in the broadest sense, they do not themselves constitute as such binding legal norms. This can only happen if they have been accepted as legal norms by the international community through the mechanisms and techniques of international law creation. Nevertheless, 'elementary principles of humanity' may lie at the base of such norms and help justify their existence in the broadest sense, and may indeed perform a valuable role in endowing such norms with an additional force within the system.

In practice, the appeal to the so-called 'general principles of law' may derive either from domestic law analogies or from international law. However, the extraction of principles from domestic law will need to be at a sufficient level of generality to come within the formulation in Article 38(1)(c) of the Statute of the International Court of Justice. The ICJ and its predecessor, the Permanent Court of International Justice (PCIJ), have managed on occasion to extract general principles from domestic legal systems.[27]

2.2.4 *Judicial decisions and publicists' writings*

Article 38 of the Statute of the International Court of Justice appears to establish a hierarchy of sources; judicial decisions and the writings of publicists are said to be a 'subsidiary' means for the determination of rules of law. There is no binding doctrine of precedent in international law. Even the decisions of the ICJ are

---

26 Charter of the United Nations and Statute of the International Court of Justice, concluded 26 June 1945, 1 UNTS XVI (entered into force 23 October 1945) art 2(2).

27 For example *Factory at Chorzów (Germany v Poland) (Merits)* [1928] PCIJ Ser A No 17, 29. It is thought one of the most significant general principles is that of good faith: see *Nuclear Tests (New Zealand v France) (Judgment)* [1974] ICJ Rep 457, 473.

expressly stated to have no binding force except as between the parties and in relation to the case in hand.[28]

Nevertheless, some of these cases do have considerable influence and authority. The intellectual content of some decisions of the ICJ and PCIJ have found their way subsequently into the text of treaties. In any event, court decisions may provide useful interpretations of existing treaty provisions. An example is the *Boll* case,[29] a rare child law case heard by the ICJ, which had to consider various provisions of the Hague Convention on Guardianship[30] (1902) (see further section 2.4.1.1).

The phrase 'judicial decisions' in Article 38 also includes international arbitration awards and the rulings of national courts. Supreme Court decisions in federal states, for example, may be considered when examining the issue of border disputes. In some areas, certainly in the past, writers have had a key influence on the formation of the law. Shaw (2008: 112) comments that authorities such as Gentili, Grotius, Pufendorf, Bynkershoek and Vattel 'were the supreme authorities in the sixteenth to eighteenth centuries and determined the scope, form and content of international law'. Their influence has waned, in part because of the proliferation of treaty law.[31]

Although the historical importance to international law of the writings of jurists as a source in its own right has declined, the leading textbooks are routinely consulted by states, courts and international organisations, perhaps more so than in the past given the increased growth in international law instruments and their increasing significance in international affairs.

2.2.5   *Hierarchy of sources and* jus cogens

If there is a hierarchy of sources in international law, then one can say that judicial decisions and juristic writings are given a 'subsidiary' role under the terms of Article 38 of the Statute of the International Court of Justice. The 'general principles of law' appear to function as a limited supplement to custom and treaty. The priority order between custom and treaty is generally that the later in time will have priority. However, there are some rules of international law that are regarded as so fundamental that the usual relationship between custom and treaty

---

28 Statute of the International Court of Justice art 59.

29 *Application of the Convention of 1902 Governing the Guardianship of Infants (Netherlands v Sweden) (Judgment)* [1958] ICJ Rep 55 (aka the *Boll* case).

30 Hague Conference on Private International Law, Hague Convention on the Settlement of Guardianship of Minors, concluded 12 June 1902 (entered into force 30 July 1904, replaced by the Hague Convention on Jurisdiction, Applicable Law, Recognition, Enforcement and Co-operation in respect of Parental Responsibility and Measures for the Protection of Children, concluded 19 October 1996 (entered into force 1 January 2002).

31 The United Nations Treaty Series (UNTS) (December 1946–March 2010) collection contains over 200,000 treaties and related subsequent actions, published in hard copy in over 2660 volumes.

will be disrupted. The theoretical basis is that there are some obligations that each state has towards the international community as a whole, for example, outlawing aggression, genocide, prohibition of torture, protection from slavery and racial discrimination. The Vienna Convention on the Law of Treaties provides that a treaty will be void if it 'conflicts with a peremptory norm of general international law'.[32]

The rule, known as *jus cogens* (compelling law), also applies to customary rules. Such a peremptory norm cannot be derogated from by local custom. In short, such norms are binding on all nations; they cannot be derogated from, nor can they be usurped by treaty provision. In the context of child law, this is an important issue. An argument can be made that the CRC contains norms of the character fulfilling the requirements of *jus cogens*. Van Bueren (1994a: 55–56), for example, argues by analogy that the sexual and economic exploitation of children is comparable to slavery and should therefore be recognised as a 'peremptory norm of general international law', capable of overriding conflicting treaty provision and binding nations that have not ratified the treaties that provide protection against such exploitation of children.

2.2.6 'Soft law'

Although not a formal source of law, 'soft law' is a term often used to describe non-binding international instruments or documents. These are often called 'guidelines', 'principles', 'declarations', 'codes of practice' or 'recommendations', but the legal status of such an instrument is determined by the intention of states parties to create legal relationships rather than the instrument's title. Some of these instruments/documents may be part of, or lead up to, a treaty negotiating process; others may impact on the practice of states leading to the creation of international customary law.

The main advantage of soft law is that it provides states with a flexible means to indicate areas of policy agreement without the full commitment of treaty law. The organic growth of soft law in relation to particular policy areas can be seen as a testing ground for conversion at a later stage into a fully-fledged legal norm in the form of a treaty or customary law.

International soft law has been particularly prevalent in the areas of international economic and environmental law, although the increasing volume and range of soft law has been observed in the human rights arena too; for example, the UN Declaration on the Rights of Indigenous Peoples (2007).[33] However, the definition and analytical coherence of the term 'soft law' remains controversial in international legal scholarship. Guzman and Meyer (2010: 173) conclude:

---

32 Opened for signature 23 May 1969, 1155 UNTS 331 (entered into force 27 January 1980) art 53.
33 UNGA Res 61/295, UN Doc A/Res/61/295 (13 September 2007).

... soft law is best understood as a continuum, or spectrum, running between fully binding treaties and fully political positions. Viewed in this way, soft law is something that dims in importance as the commitments of states get weaker, eventually disappearing altogether.

2.3   The relationship between domestic and international law

The details of the relationship between domestic and international legal orders are complex: see further Shaw (2008: 129–94). There are two debates to consider: first, a debate concerning 'monist' and 'dualist' doctrines of international law; and, secondly, a debate about the 'transformation' and 'incorporation' doctrines of international law.

As regards the first debate, the older, monist doctrine asserts that domestic and international law are part of a single, integral legal order and, if there is a conflict between the two, international law ('the law of nations') should prevail. The dualist doctrine, by contrast, asserts that the two systems exist separately; they do not affect each other, and it therefore follows that neither system prevails over the other.

The two systems have different fundamental concerns. International law, it is argued, is primarily about the legal relationships *between* states, whereas domestic law is mainly concerned with the horizontal legal relationships between citizens and the vertical relationships between the sovereign state and its citizens. A third strand of thought, a modification of the dualist doctrine, has emerged, which acknowledges the separate realms of domestic and international law and concludes that there is therefore little conflict of obligation possible between the two systems.

A state's practice on a particular issue may well be in breach of its obligations under international law. This will be a matter for remedial action, if there is any available, in the international community. However, any 'conflicting' domestic legislation of a sovereign state will remain supreme unless specifically repealed in response to international 'naming and shaming' and other pressures. In fact, the practice of legislatures and the courts is sometimes thought to be a more reliable way to understand the relationship between domestic and international law.

The second area of contention, concerning the doctrines of transformation and incorporation, focuses on the practical problems of how domestic courts should deal with international legal standards. The doctrine of transformation (which is based on a 'dualist' understanding of the separate realms of domestic and international law) asserts that domestic law will not be able fully to digest rules of international law unless there has been an explicit (transformative) act of adoption. This will be achieved according to the constitutional machinery appropriate for the nation concerned.

In the United Kingdom, for example, it will be by the passage of an Act of Parliament. By contrast, the doctrine of incorporation (based on a 'monist' understanding of the unity of domestic and international law) holds that international law is automatically part of domestic law without the need for a constitutional ratification procedure. However, it should be noted immediately that the doctrine of incorporation is only to be applied to international customary law.

The position with international treaties is treated differently. A lengthy case law development, dating back to the 18th century, has produced an acceptance of the doctrine of incorporation (of international customary law) in English common law. The landmark case was *Trendtex Trading Corp v Central Bank of Nigeria*.[34] The Court of Appeal confirmed that the incorporation doctrine was the correct one and that international law did not know a rule of *stare decisis* (binding precedent). The domestic courts could implement changes in international customary law without waiting for any binding case precedents to be overturned in the Supreme Court.

Later cases have reaffirmed that '[c]ustomary international law is part of the common law'.[35] However, the certainty in choice of doctrine does nothing to resolve the problem that domestic courts may still have in identifying clearly what the relevant international customary rule is.

In dualist nations treaties are not incorporated automatically within the domestic legal system. In the United Kingdom, for example, the constitutional position is that, although the executive authority (the government ministers on behalf of the Crown) signs and ratifies international treaties,[36] which then will have effect within international law, there is an additional need for the legislature (Parliament) to produce an Act, before that treaty will have binding legal effect recognised by the domestic courts.

Depending on the government's political will on the matter, and the terms stated in the treaty to be met for it to enter into force, a long period of time might expire between international ratification and domestic enactment. For example, the UK Government was one of the first countries to sign (4 November 1950) and ratify (8 March 1951) the European Convention on Human Rights.[37] Although this Convention came into force in *international law* in 1953, the British courts only started to apply the Convention directly in the UK, by virtue of domestic legislation, nearly half a century later.[38] As will be seen in Chapter 3, the CRC

---

34 [1977] QB 529.

35 *R v Bow Street Metropolitan Stipendiary Magistrate, ex p Pinochet Ugarte (No 3)* [2000] 1 AC 147, 276 (HL).

36 This executive power is not entirely without parliamentary oversight. A constitutional convention arose from 1924 – the 'Ponsonby' rule – which required that most international treaties should be laid before Parliament for 21 days before ratification. This was placed on a statutory footing by the Constitutional Reform and Governance Act 2010, which has further strengthened Parliament's scrutiny role. The government must now lay most treaties subject to ratification before Parliament for 21 sitting days before it can ratify them. If either House objects, the government must give reasons why it wants to ratify before it can proceed, but the House of Commons can block ratification indefinitely (Thorp 2011).

37 European Convention for the Protection of Human Rights and Fundamental Freedoms, opened for signature 4 November 1950, 213 UNTS 221 (entered into force 3 September 1953).

38 The Human Rights Act 1998, which came into force on 2 October 2000.

was signed and ratified by the UK Government in 1989, but it has not yet been enacted through Parliament and therefore does not have binding legal effect in UK courts.[39]

However, an unincorporated international treaty does usually have some, albeit limited, significance in domestic law. Under English law, for example, a rule of statutory interpretation has developed to assist with possible conflicts between unincorporated international treaty provisions and domestic legislation. The rule presumes that Parliament could not, at least without express words, have legislated contrary to the state's international obligations.[40]

However, this presumption can be relied upon only in cases of ambiguity, not in cases where the statute offers a discretion. On the other hand, some cases have been more proactive in pointing to an unincorporated treaty provision to resolve a gap in domestic law.[41] However, this approach to utilising unincorporated treaties as an 'aid to construction' in statutory interpretation in the United Kingdom falls a long way short of allowing international law properly to enter the body of domestic law.

2.4   International organisations and institutions

The following sections contain some basic information about the main international organisations and institutions, in particular those that are connected to international children's rights. The references in this section should provide the reader with signposts to more specialist reading if required. Section 2.4.1 deals generally with the UN system, section 2.4.2 with the Hague Conference on Private International Law, and section 2.4.3 with the International Criminal Court. The international human rights charter and treaty bodies within the United Nations system are dealt with in more detail in section 2.5.

2.4.1   The United Nations (UN)[42]

The United Nations was established on 24 October 1945 by 51 nations in response to the Second World War, to preserve peace through international cooperation and collective security. UN membership is now global: all 193 states are members of the UN. The membership of the UN is divided into five (informal)

---

39 It is interesting to note, however, the gathering political pressures to incorporate the CRC in the United Kingdom. A Children's Rights Bill [HL Bill 8] contained provisions that would incorporate the CRC on much the same basis as the Human Rights Act 1998 incorporated the ECHR. The Bill was a Private Member's Bill moved by Baroness Joan Walmsley and received a first reading in the House of Lords on 19 November 2009, to coincide with the 20th anniversary of the adoption of the CRC.

40 *Garland v British Rail Engineering Ltd* [1983] 2 AC 751; *R v Secretary of State for the Home Department, ex p Brind* [1991] 1 AC 696.

41 *Derbyshire County Council v Times Newspapers Ltd* [1992] QB 770, 830.

42 See generally Weiss and Daws (eds) (2007).

groups for the purposes of nominating candidates for election to UN organs and subsidiary bodies: African (54), Asian (including the Middle East) (55), Eastern European (21), Latin American and Caribbean (33), and Western European and others (WEOG) (30). Membership of the UN involves accepting the obligations of the UN Charter[43] (1945), a treaty that sets out some principles of international relations. The UN Charter provided for six principal organs:[44]

- the General Assembly
- the Security Council
- the Economic and Social Council
- the Trusteeship Council
- the International Court of Justice (ICJ)
- the Secretariat.

In fact, there are now only five active organs. The Trusteeship Council (Wilde 2007) suspended operations on 1 November 1994.[45] All of the principal organs are based at the UN headquarters in New York, other than the ICJ which is located at The Hague in the Netherlands.

The General Assembly, established under the UN Charter,[46] is the main deliberative and policy-making organ of the UN and is made up of representatives of all (193) member states. In essence, this is the UN's debating chamber. Peterson (2007: 97) identifies two key functions: 'a forum for deliberation among member governments providing collective legitimation (or de-legitimation) of norms, rules, and actions; and a provider of some administrative oversight of the UN system'. It provides a unique forum for multilateral discussion of all the international issues covered by the Charter. It meets in regular session from September to December each year, and thereafter as required. Each member state in the Assembly, however powerful, has one vote. Votes taken on certain key issues, such as recommendations on peace and security and the election of Security Council members, require a two-thirds majority of member states. Other questions are decided by simple majority. In recent years there has been an effort to achieve consensus without the need to make decisions by way of a formal vote in order to strengthen the legitimacy of the Assembly's decisions.

The landmark Millennium Declaration[47] was adopted by the Assembly in 2000 and reflected the member states' commitment to create a new global partnership and to attain specific goals to attain peace, security and disarmament in addition

---

43 Charter of the United Nations and Statute of the International Court of Justice, concluded 26 June 1945, 1 UNTS XVI (entered into force 23 October 1945).

44 ibid art 2. An overview of the UN system is set out in a useful chart available at http://www.un.org/en/aboutun/structure/org_chart.shtml (accessed 12 February 2013).

45 It was originally established to provide international supervision of 11 Trust Territories. All of these territories have now achieved independence or self-government.

46 Chapter IV arts 9–22.

47 UNGA Res 55/2 (8 September 2000) UN Doc A/RES/55/2, adopted without a vote.

to development and eradicating poverty, safeguarding human rights and promoting the rule of law, protecting our common environment, meeting the special needs of Africa and strengthening the United Nations.

Some of these have time-bound targets, with a deadline of 2015, and have become known as the 'Millennium Development Goals' (MDGs). With the close of the general debate, the Assembly allocates items among its six main committees. The committees then prepare and present draft proposals and decisions for consideration at a plenary meeting of the Assembly. The six main committees[48] and the Secretariat carry the General Assembly's work forward when it is not in session.

The General Assembly is also authorised to establish 'subsidiary organs' as deemed necessary. This includes a number of boards, commissions, committees, councils, panels and working groups; an example is the UN Human Rights Council (UNHRC) established in 2006.[49] The UNHRC is elected by and reports to the Assembly and its 'special procedures' (section 2.5.1.1) are overseen by the Third Committee (the Social, Humanitarian and Cultural Committee). A number of programmes, funds and other bodies, for example the United Nations Children's Fund (UNICEF) and the Office of the High Commissioner for Human Rights (OHCHR), report directly to the General Assembly.

The Third Committee interacts with various special rapporteurs, independent experts and chairpersons of working groups of the UNHRC. It discusses the advancement of women, the protection of children, indigenous issues, the treatment of refugees, the promotion of fundamental freedoms through the elimination of racism and racial discrimination, and the promotion of the right to self-determination. This Committee also addresses important social development questions such as issues related to youth, family, ageing, persons with disabilities, crime prevention, criminal justice and drug control.

The General Assembly's *resolutions* are not strictly binding in international law, but they may have great moral authority, particularly where there is a unanimous resolution, or a resolution is passed consensually without the need for a vote. Nevertheless, they remain recommendatory in nature, except for decisions on internal matters, and 'over time the substance of certain resolutions may become accepted as reflecting customary international law' (Aust 2010: 190).

The Security Council[50] has the onerous task of maintaining international peace and security and convenes when necessary. It is organised so as to be able to function continuously; a representative of each of its members must be present at all times at UN Headquarters. There are five permanent Council members (known

---

48 First Committee (Disarmament and International Security); Second Committee (Economic and Financial); Third Committee (Social, Humanitarian and Cultural); Fourth Committee (Special Political and Decolonization); Fifth Committee (Administrative and Budgetary); and Sixth Committee (Legal).
49 The United Nations Human Rights Council (UNHRC) is the successor body to the United Nations Commission on Human Rights (UNCHR).
50 Charter of the United Nations, Chapter V arts 23–32.

as the 'P-5'): China, the Russian Federation, the United Kingdom, France and the United States, 'chosen on the basis of power politics in 1945' (Shaw 2008: 1206). There are also an additional 10 members elected by the General Assembly for periods of two years. In practice, the non-permanent membership is distributed according to the five regional groups: Africa (3), Asia (2), Eastern Europe (1), Latin America and the Caribbean (2) and WEOG (2).

Decisions of the Council, other than procedural matters, require nine votes and the absence of a veto by any of the five permanent members. It has been declared that the issue of whether a matter was procedural or not was itself subject to a veto.[51] The Council attempts to resolve disputes peacefully and in some cases will itself undertake investigation and mediation. The Council has frequently issued cease-fire directives and it also sends United Nations peacekeeping forces to troubled areas, often to keep opposing forces apart and to facilitate peaceful settlements (Malone 2007).

The Council can impose economic sanctions and trade and arms embargoes, and has authorised the use of collective military action to ensure its decisions are carried out. A recalcitrant member state may be suspended from exercising the rights of UN membership by the General Assembly on the recommendation of the Council, and a persistent violator of the principles of the Charter may be expelled from the United Nations by the Assembly on the Council's recommendation.

The Presidency of the Council rotates monthly, according to the listing of its member states. The Council has a number of subsidiary bodies, including the Counter-Terrorism Committee, established by Council resolutions[52] following the attack on the twin towers of the World Trade Center in New York City on 11 September 2001.

The Economic and Social Council[53] (ECOSOC) has a remit under Article 62 of the UN Charter in two broad areas: economic and social matters, and human rights. It also coordinates the work of the UN's 'specialized agencies' (see below). It has a potentially important role of interaction with non-government organisations (NGOs), acting as their main 'portal of entry' to the UN system, and has an oversight role in relation to an array of subsidiary bodies including the functional and regional commissions. Its decisions and resolutions are not binding on member states nor even the specialised agencies, indicative of its powerlessness (Rosenthal 2007). It has 54 member governments elected by the General Assembly for overlapping periods of three years. Seats on ECOSOC are allotted according to the five regional groupings: Africa (14), Asia (11), Eastern Europe (6), Latin America and the Caribbean (10) and WEOG (13).

51 'This "double-veto" constitutes a formidable barrier. Subsequent practice has interpreted the phrase "concurring votes of the permanent members" in Article 27 in such a way as to permit abstentions. Accordingly, permanent members may abstain with regard to a resolution of the Security Council without being deemed to have exercised their veto against it' (Shaw 2008: 1207).
52 UNSC Res 1373 [on threats to international peace and security caused by terrorist acts] (28 September 2001) UN Doc S/RES/1373.
53 Charter of the United Nations, Chapter X arts 61–72.

ECOSOC holds several short sessions and preparatory meetings with members of civil society throughout the year. It holds a four-week substantive session in July, alternating between New York and Geneva. This is organised in five segments (High-level, Coordination, Operational Activities, Humanitarian Affairs and General). A ministerial declaration is generally adopted on the theme of the High-level Segment, which provides policy guidance and recommendations for action.

ECOSOC has a number of functional and regional commissions and standing committees and expert bodies that report to it including, for example,[54] the Economic Commission for Africa. At the 2005 World Summit, heads of state and government mandated ECOSOC to hold annual Ministerial Reviews and a biennial Development Cooperation Forum. The objective of the former was to assess progress in achieving internationally agreed development goals. The objective of the latter was to enhance the coherence and effectiveness of activities of different development partners.

ECOSOC has generally been regarded as of decreasing importance in the UN system, in part because of the ambiguities surrounding its relationship with the General Assembly. ECOSOC has 'principal organ' status under the UN Charter, although the UN function of international economic and social cooperation is 'vested in the General Assembly and, under the authority of the General Assembly, in the Economic and Social Council'.[55]

This raises 'the vexing problem of the respective responsibilities' of the General Assembly and ECOSOC (Rosenthal 2007: 138). The reviews that have taken place to assess possible reform initiatives of ECOSOC have varying emphases on its global policy review and institutional coordination roles. Rosenthal (2007: 140) concluded:

> A close reading of the Charter suggests that ECOSOC was never intended to be the center of global policy coordination. Rather, the main powers emerging from World War II preferred to concentrate global policymaking in organizations that reflected their weight in world affairs. The right to exert a veto in the Security Council provided such a UN mechanism in the area of peace and security, while in the area of economic policymaking the weighted voting arrangements at the Bretton Woods institutions made the Word Bank and the IMF far more attractive alternatives to the UN General Assembly and ECOSOC, where each sovereign state has one vote.

One significant alteration to ECOSOC's balance of responsibilities has been the General Assembly's decision in 2006[56] to replace the UN Commission on Human

---

54 Also, the Commission on Human Rights, which came to an end in 2006.
55 Charter of the United Nations art 60.
56 UNGA Res 60/251 (15 March 2006) UN Doc A/RES/60/251. A recorded vote on this resolution was requested: adopted by 170 votes; against 4 (Israel, Marshall Islands, Palau and the USA); abstentions 3 (Belarus, Islamic Republic of Iran, Bolivarian Republic of Venezuela).

Rights (UNCHR) with the UN Human Rights Council (UNHRC), transferring this important oversight from ECOSOC to the General Assembly. However, the iteration of reform proposals and plans to strengthen ECOSOC[57] have not yet produced the coherence and clarifications that is required.

The ICJ,[58] sometimes referred to as the 'World Court', consists of 15 judges elected by the General Assembly and the Security Council; they sit for a renewable term of nine years. The ICJ decides claims between states, but the states' participation in this process is voluntary. It should be noted that the ICJ has no criminal jurisdiction nor is it a court of appeal. The ICJ also provides Advisory Opinions to the General Assembly and the Security Council. See further section 2.4.1.1 below.

The Secretariat[59] is headed by the Secretary-General of the UN,[60] currently Ban Ki-moon (Republic of Korea), the eighth Secretary-General,[61] who took office on 1 January 2007 and was unanimously re-elected on 21 June 2011 by the General Assembly on the recommendation of the Security Council and will continue to serve until 31 December 2016. The Secretariat conducts the administrative work of the UN, as directed by the other organs of the United Nations. It derives from the concept of an international civil service developed during the period of the League of Nations (1920–1946).

The Secretariat has some 40,000 staff members around the world.[62] There are UN offices at the headquarters in New York, and also in a number of other locations. Two important themes can be identified throughout the life of the Secretariat: 'a battle over its independent nature and an almost constant restructuring accompanied by calls for its reform' (Jonah 2007: 160). The UN Charter specifically provides that the Secretary-General and the staff of the Secretariat 'shall not seek or receive instructions from any government or from any other authority external to the Organization' and that each member state must respect the 'exclusively international character of the responsibilities of the Secretary-General and the staff and not to seek to influence them in the discharge of their responsibilities'.[63]

---

57 ESC Res 212/30 'Role of the Economic and Social Council in the integrated and coordinated implementation of and follow-up to the outcomes of the major United Nations conferences and summits, in the light of relevant General Assembly resolutions, including resolution 61/16' (27 July 2012) UN Doc E/RES/2012/30.

58 Charter of the United Nations, Chapter XIV arts 92–96.

59 Charter of the United Nations, Chapter XV arts 97–101.

60 See generally Newman, E. (2007) 'Secretary-General', Chapter 10 in Weiss, T.G. and Daws, S. (eds) (2007) *The Oxford Handbook on the United Nations*, Oxford: Oxford University Press 175–92.

61 Kofi A. Annan (Ghana) 1997–2006; Boutros Boutros-Ghali (Egypt) 1992–1996; Javier Perez de Cuellar (Peru) 1982–1991; Kurt Waldheim (Austria) 1972–1981; U Thant (Myanmar) 1961–1971; Dag Hammarskjöld (Sweden) 1953–1961; and Trygve Lie (Norway)1946–1953.

62 As at 30 June 2012, the total number of the staff of the Secretariat was 42,887, comprising all categories of staff recruited both internationally and locally; UNGA, 'Composition of the Secretariat: staff demographics, Report of the Secretary-General' (28 August 2012) UN Doc A/67/329 para 7.

63 Charter of the United Nations art 100.

The principal organs of the United Nations are also linked to the 'specialised agencies' through cooperative agreements. The specialised agencies are established by inter-governmental agreement and have 'relationship agreements' with the UN, and are linked to the coordinating machinery of ECOSOC.[64] There are currently 17 such agencies.[65] The oldest of these agencies is the International Labour Organization (ILO); see section 2.4.1.4. Many of the specialised agencies have developed methods to ensure that their decisions are practically binding on their members (Shaw 2008: 1285). The specialised agencies, together with the UN and its principal organs, are sometimes known collectively as the 'UN family' or the 'UN system'.

The work of the United Nations in establishing the UDHR in 1948 and the two International Covenants (the ICCPR and the ICESCR) in 1966, collectively referred to as the International Bill of Human Rights has already been outlined in Chapter 1. In recent years, the United Nations has changed its focus from providing international legal 'standard setting' to ensuring that human rights standards are implemented.

The Office of the United Nations High Commissioner for Human Rights (OHCHR) was created in 1993 as part of a package of wider reforms to the United Nations. The OHCHR is a subsidiary body of the UN's Secretariat. It supports the work of the various human rights mechanisms such as the UNHRC and the core treaty bodies (eg the Committee on the Rights of the Child). It also coordinates UN human rights education and public information activities. The High Commissioner has the rank of Under-Secretary and reports to the Secretary-General of the United Nations and to the General Assembly. The OHCHR seeks to prevent violations of human rights and works with governments to further the observance of human rights standards. The UN's system for human rights protection is explored in further detail in section 2.5 below.

The importance of the United Nations for the development of children's rights was underlined in a 'Special Session on Children' of the General Assembly held in May 2002.[66] It was the first session devoted exclusively to children and the first to include children as official delegates. The aim of the session was to review progress

---

64 See Charter of the United Nations arts 57 and 63.
65 Food and Agriculture Organization (FAO); International Atomic Energy Agency (IAEA); International Civil Aviation Organization (ICAO); International Fund for Agricultural Development (IFAD); International Labour Organization (ILO); International Maritime Organization (IMO); International Monetary Fund (IMF); International Telecommunications Union (ITU); United Nations Educational, Scientific and Cultural Organization (UNESCO); United Nations Industrial Development Organization (UNIDO); Universal Postal Union (UPU); World Bank (WB); World Food Programme (WFP); World Health Organization (WHO); World Intellectual Property Organization (WIPO); World Meteorological Organization (WMO); World Tourism Organization (WTO).
66 See the archived materials of this Session at http://www.unicef.org/specialsession/ (accessed 19 February 2013).

since the World Summit for Children[67] in 1990 and to revitalise commitment to children's rights. The document later derived from this special session, 'A World Fit for Children', was adopted by a resolution of the General Assembly,[68] and included a (non-binding) declaration that reaffirmed a commitment to promoting and protecting the rights of children and to a number of principles and objectives aimed at eradicating child poverty, discrimination, poor education, protection from harm, exploitation, disease and war.

'A World Fit for Children' also contained a detailed plan of action that recognised that chronic poverty remained the 'single biggest obstacle' to meeting children's needs and protecting their rights. It recognised that poverty hit children hardest and its eradication should be a central aim of development activities 'because it strikes at the very roots of their potential for development – their growing bodies and minds'.[69]

2.4.1.1 The International Court of Justice (ICJ)

The ICJ, the successor body to the Permanent Court of International Justice (PCIJ) (1922–1946), is the principal judicial organ of the United Nations. It is located at The Hague in the Netherlands. The Statute of the International Court of Justice (annexed to, and an integral part of, the UN Charter[70]) is the main constitutional document constituting and regulating the Court. The General Assembly and Security Council elect the 15 judges of the ICJ to a nine-year term of office. The Court cannot have more than one judge of each nationality and these judges must have the relevant qualifications for high judicial office in their respective countries. A judge of the nationality of a party to a case before the Court retains the right to sit on that case, and a states party to a case without a national judge of the Court may designate a judge ad hoc. Consequently, in some cases there may be as many as 17 judges sitting. The President and the Vice-President of the Court[71] are elected by the Members of the Court every three years by secret ballot.

The Court has two main roles: to hear and decide contentious cases between states, and to give advisory opinions on legal questions referred to it by authorised international bodies. As regards contentious cases, it is only states parties that may appear before the Court, which is only competent to hear a case if the states concerned have accepted its jurisdiction. Consent to jurisdiction may be given:

---

67 World Summit for Children, United Nations, New York (29–30 September 1990) http://www.un.org/geninfo/bp/child.html (accessed 16 October 2013).
68 UNGA Res S-27/2 (10 May 2002) UN Doc A/RES/S-27/2.
69 ibid para 18.
70 Charter of the United Nations and Statute of the International Court of Justice, concluded 26 June 1945, 1 UNTS XVI (entered into force 23 October 1945) Chapter XIV arts 92–96.
71 The current President is Judge Peter Tomka (Slovakia) and the current Vice-President is Judge Bernardo Sepúlveda-Amor (Mexico), both elected on 6 February 2012.

(i)   generally in advance
(ii)   by treaty with respect to a defined class of cases
(iii) by special agreement in relation to a dispute that has already arisen or
(iv)   by ad hoc consent.

Although there is an underlying principle of consent of the parties, the Court's jurisdiction has been described as 'quasi-compulsory' in cases (i) and (ii) above (Crawford and Grant 2007: 195). The Court's procedure is defined in its Statute and in essence includes a written and an oral stage, after which the Court deliberates in private and then delivers its judgment in public. The Court is competent to appoint individuals or bodies to provide an expert opinion or carry out an inquiry. There is no appeal from the judgment of the ICJ. Failure to comply with a judgment may result in the other party having recourse to the Security Council.

The first case entered in the General List of the Court was submitted on 22 May 1947.[72] From 1947 to 2011, there have been a total of 153 cases entered in the General List.[73] These have concerned a number of issues, including territorial sovereignty, land and marine boundary disputes, diplomatic relations, hostage taking and the right of asylum. The Court has gone through periods of inactivity; for example, from 1965 to 1985 relatively few cases were brought. The Court's cases expanded in volume and breadth in the 1980s and 1990s from a focus on land and maritime boundary disputes to military and paramilitary activities, compensation for the environmental effects of mining operations, diplomatic immunities and international criminal law.

There is, however, only one judgment to date directly relevant to children, and that concerned the issue of guardianship: see the *Boll* case (1958) below. This also remains the only case in which a Hague Convention was the principal subject of interpretation by a court with worldwide jurisdiction.

---

72 See *Corfu Channel Case (UK v Albania) (Merits)* [1949] ICJ Rep 4.
73 Comprising 127 'contentious' cases and 26 'advisory' proceedings. See http://www.icj-cij.org/docket/index.php?p1=3&p2=2 (accessed 16 October 2013).

Case study 2.1

Application of the Convention of 1902 Governing the Guardianship of Infants (Netherlands v Sweden) (Judgment) [1958] ICJ Rep 55 (the 'Boll case')[74]

Facts: A Dutch girl, Marie Elizabeth Boll, was the child of a Dutch seaman and his deceased Swedish wife. She had lived in Sweden with her mother before her mother's death, but only had Dutch nationality. On her mother's death the Dutch authorities assigned guardianship under their procedures. However, the Swedish authorities overrode this and placed her under their protective upbringing regime on the basis of her continuing residence in Sweden with her maternal grandparents. The Netherlands claimed that the Swedish measure of protective upbringing was incompatible with the obligations under the Hague Convention of 1902.[75] Under this Convention the application of the national law of the child was expressly extended to both the person and the property of the child. On the facts, this would have led to the child being handed over to a Dutch guardian.

Held: The ICJ construed the concept of guardianship narrowly. It held that the Convention of 1902 did not cover the social purpose of the Swedish protective upbringing regime; therefore, there was no failure by Sweden to observe its obligations under this Convention and the Netherlands' claim was rejected (by twelve votes to four).

Commentary: In effect, this decision 'allowed a state to void a guardianship established by another state with presumed jurisdiction by adopting a domestic public law measure voiding it of content' (Dyer 1997: 631). The Hague Conference responded to correct the result in *Boll* by drafting a further Convention in 1961,[76] which recognised a new concept: 'measures directed to the protection of [the child's] person or property', a notion sufficiently broad to cover both a state's private law measures and public care orders. The Convention of 1961 focused on the 'interests of the child' as the basis upon which the state of the child's nationality could override measures taken by another state (usually the state of the child's 'habitual residence').

---

74 See the *Boll* case (n 25).

75 Hague Conference on Private International Law, Hague Convention on the Settlement of Guardianship of Minors, concluded 12 June 1902 (entered into force 30 July 1904, replaced by the Hague Convention on Jurisdiction, Applicable Law, Recognition, Enforcement and Co-operation in respect of Parental Responsibility and Measures for the Protection of Children, concluded 19 October 1996 (entered into force 1 January 2002).

76 Hague Conference on Private International Law, Hague Convention concerning the powers of authorities and the law applicable in respect of the protection of infants, concluded 5 October 1961 (entered into force 4 February 1969).

This emphasis upon the interest of the child, a concept that appeared only for emergency measures in the 1902 Convention, reflected the intervening shift of attitudes that had been internationally expressed in the 1924 Declaration of the Rights of the Child and in the 1959 United Nations Declaration of the Rights of the Child. This was a recognition at the international level of a shift taking place in the domestic laws of many countries, from an emphasis on paternal or parental authority towards an emphasis on protecting the child, even from the child's parents. This concept foreshadowed the ideas reflected in the later 1989 Convention on the Rights of the Child, that a child should be viewed as a subject of rights and not merely as an object of rights or of protective action (Dyer 1997: 633).

The ICJ's function to provide advisory opinions is available only to international organisations. The UN Charter provides that it is only the General Assembly or the Security Council that may request advisory opinions of the Court. Other organs of the United Nations and the 'specialised agencies' authorised by the General Assembly may also request advisory opinions on legal questions within the scope of their activities,[77] although more often it is the General Assembly that requests advisory opinions. In one case,[78] the Court held that the request from the World Health Organization (WHO) did not fall within the remit of the WHO and refused jurisdiction.

There have been suggestions that the power to request advisory opinions could be given to the Secretary-General and to states parties and national courts (Schwebel 1984, 1988). The Court has made it clear that it will not decline a request for an advisory opinion on the basis only that the legal questions at issue also implicate political issues.[79]

In principle, the Court's advisory opinions are not binding in character, but there is provision to agree in advance that the advisory opinion will be binding. The Court has processed 26 advisory opinion proceedings since 1946, concerning, for example: the conditions of admission of a state to membership in the United Nations; reparation for injuries suffered in the service of the United Nations; the international status of South West Africa (Namibia); certain expenses of the United Nations; certain judgments rendered by the United Nations administrative tribunal; Western Sahara; questions relating to the privileges and immunities of human rights rapporteurs; the legality of the threat or use of nuclear weapons; and the legal consequences of the construction of a wall in the Israeli-occupied Palestinian territory. In general, it would seem that the ICJ 'is now playing a

---

77 Charter of the United Nations art 96.
78 *Legality of the Use by a State of Nuclear Weapons in Armed Conflict*, Advisory Opinion of 8 July 1996 [1996] ICJ Reports 226.
79 ibid 233–34; *Legal Consequences of the Construction of a Wall in the Occupied Palestinian Territory*, Advisory Opinion of 9 July 2004 [1994] ICJ Rep 136 and 155 (para 41).

more central role within the international legal system than thought possible two decades ago' (Shaw 2008: 1114).

2.4.1.2   The United Nations Children's Fund (UNICEF)[80]

The United Nations Children's Fund was created by the General Assembly on 11 December 1946 to provide emergency food and healthcare for children in countries that had been devastated by the Second World War. In 1953, UNICEF became a permanent part of the UN system and its name was shortened (from the original 'United Nations International Children's Emergency Fund'), but it has continued to be known by the popular acronym based on the old name.

UNICEF's 36-strong executive board is elected by ECOSOC to guide its work. Members are elected for three-year terms and the board regularly makes reports to ECOSOC. UNICEF has a strong presence in most countries. In the past nearly seven decades its role has evolved into broader development work to tackle poverty in order to meet the needs of children. The organisation was awarded the Nobel Peace Prize in 1965. In the 1980s there was a policy focus on addressing child mortality rates that was implemented by simple, low cost, primary health care activities to tackle the range of infections prevalent in early childhood.[81]

UNICEF also participated in the late 1980s in the establishment of the CRC. The CRC is fundamental to UNICEF's mission, which shifted in the 1990s from the promotion of the child's survival and development to supporting children's rights under the CRC. This approach broadened UNICEF's operation and 'has led the organization to address some of the most difficult issues of our times, such as children in armed conflict, child labor, and sexual exploitation of children' (Rios-Kohn 1998: 191). UNICEF has, it is argued, 'taken steps to integrate the principles of the CRC into all aspects of its activities' (Oestreich 1998: 184). This rights-based approach remains a key element of UNICEF's mission, although it is not without criticism in so far as this focus may detract from its child survival and mortality work (Horton 2004).

Its humanitarian work was also strengthened by the Core Commitments for Children in Humanitarian Action (UNICEF 2010), a global framework for humanitarian action for children undertaken by UNICEF and its partners. In all its activities UNICEF's approach prioritises children who are most vulnerable and in greatest need. In recent years, 'a renewed emphasis on equity for children has become a cornerstone of the organization's programme, policy and advocacy work' (Mullerbeck and Anthony 2011). More recently, UNICEF has produced a flagship annual publication entitled *The State of the World's Children*,[82] which focuses

---

80 See generally Black (1986, 1996) for a history of UNICEF http://www.unicef.org/about/history/index_publications.html (accessed 16 October 2013).

81 The techniques deployed were known as 'GOBI': 'G' for growth monitoring, 'O' for oral rehydration therapy, 'B' for breastfeeding and 'I' for immunisation.

82 See http://www.unicef.org/sowc/ (accessed 25 February 2013).

on a particular issue in detail, for example, children in an urban world (UNICEF 2012) and children with disabilities (UNICEF 2013).

There are a number of national committees that raise funds for UNICEF. Each country office initiates a five-year programme in collaboration with the host government, and focuses on practical ways in which to achieve the rights of children and women in accordance with the principles laid down in the CRC and the UN's Convention on the Elimination of All Forms of Discrimination against Women (1979).[83]

A situation report is produced at the beginning of each programme cycle. The overall policy on children is made at the UN headquarters. UNICEF helps to provide humanitarian aid in times of civil commotion and war, supplying food, safe water, medicine and shelter. It has also advanced the idea of 'children as zones of peace' and 'corridors of peace' to help protect children where there is armed conflict. On 1 May 2010, Anthony Lake became the sixth Executive Director of the United Nations Children's Fund.[84]

2.4.1.3   The International Law Commission (ILC)

When the United Nations was established, there was little support from those framing the UN Charter to give the United Nations direct law-making powers. However, there was support for a power to undertake studies and make recommendations for 'encouraging the progressive development of international law and its codification'.[85] The General Assembly established the ILC for this purpose in 1947, along with a Statute of the International Law Commission.[86] The ILC meets annually and is composed of 34 members elected by the General Assembly for five-year terms; members act as individuals and not as state representatives. The members serve in an individual capacity, reflecting their expertise, rather than as mandated government representatives. The topics for their work are sometimes referred to them by the General Assembly or ECOSOC, or requested either by a government, an inter-governmental organisation or a UN agency, and they are also initiated by the ILC itself.

It is provided that the ILC 'shall concern itself primarily with public international law, but is not precluded from entering the field of private international law'.[87] In fact, it has predominantly dealt with public international law matters. The Statute of the International Law Commission also makes a distinction between its two main tasks. 'Progressive development' means 'the preparation of

---

83 Opened for signature 1 March 1980, 1249 UNTS 13 (entered into force 3 September 1981).
84 See http://www.unicef.org/media/media_53427.html (accessed 25 February 2013) for a short biography.
85 Charter of the United Nations art 3(1).
86 UNGA A-RES-174(II) (21 November 1947). Amended on 12 December 1950, 3 December 1955 and 18 November 1981.
87 Statute of the International Law Commission art 1(2).

draft conventions on subjects which have not yet been regulated by international law or in regard to which the law has not yet been sufficiently developed in the practice of states. 'Codification' means 'the more precise formulation and systematization of rules of international law in fields where there already has been extensive State practice precedent and doctrine'.[88]

The ILC's work has resulted in a number of treaties that have made a significant contribution to the international legal order; for example, the Convention on the High Seas (1958),[89] the Vienna Convention on Diplomatic Relations (1961)[90] and the Vienna Convention on the Law of Treaties (1969).[91] It has also produced some significant 'soft law' instruments; for example, the Draft Articles on the Responsibility of States for Internationally Wrongful Acts (2001)[92] and the Guide to Practice on Reservations to Treaties (2011).[93]

Once a topic has been identified, a special rapporteur is usually appointed by the Commission, who will analyse it and report back to the Commission. States will have an opportunity to comment on the Commission's progress and their report will be further debated by the Sixth Committee (legal). Draft Articles are then generally submitted in final form to the General Assembly with a recommendation that it convenes a diplomatic conference to adopt the draft articles as a convention.

However, there are a number of questions (McCrae 2012) arising about the present and future practice of the ILC: are codification and progressive development separate or interrelated enterprises; what are the selection criteria and the evidence base for the analyses of the various topics under consideration; what is the appropriate relationship between the ILC and states and other international actors; can the Commission deal with politically controversial issues; and should the outcome of ILC work be formalised as draft articles ready for treaty-making or should it generate more soft law instruments?

A general criticism that is emerging (McCrae 2012) is that the days of major codification, the core of the Commission's work in the past, may be over, thus highlighting the current lack of a clearly defined role for the ILC. On the other hand, a shift to progressive development will bring the ILC into a more politicised environment rather than an expert forum.

---

88 Statute of the International Law Commission art 15.
89 Opened for signature 29 April 1958, 450 UNTS 11 (entered into force 30 September 1962).
90 Opened for signature 18 April 1961, 500 UNTS 95 (entered into force 24 April 1964).
91 Opened for signature 23 May 1969, 1155 UNTS 331 (entered into force 27 January 1980).
92 International Law Commission, *Draft Articles on Responsibility of States for Internationally Wrongful Acts* (November 2001), Supplement No 10 (A/56/10), chp.IV.E.1 http://www.unhcr.org/refworld/docid/3ddb8f804.html (accessed 26 February 2013).
93 International Law Commission, *Report on the Work of its Sixty-third Session*, UN GAOR, 66th Session, Supp No 10, UN Doc A/66/10 (2011), para 75. The report will appear in *Yearbook of the International Law Commission, 2011*, vol II Pt Two.

2.4.1.4 The International Labour Organization (ILO)[94]

The 'specialised agencies' of the UN[95] are a privileged and integral part of the UN system. The ILO is of particular interest to international child lawyers as one of its mainstream concerns is the problem of child labour (see Chapter 4). The ILO became the first 'specialised agency' of the UN system in 1946. It was originally founded in 1919 and is the only surviving creation of the Treaty of Versailles (1919) that established the League of Nations.

Its principal task is to establish international labour standards in the field of employment rights. It also provides technical assistance, for example, in the fields of employment policy, labour law and industrial relations, working conditions and labour statistics. Its general aims and purpose were set out in the Declaration of Philadelphia (1944) and this document is now annexed to the ILO Constitution (1946).[96] The ILO has a unique tripartite structure: workers' and employers' organisations participate as equal partners, along with governments, in its principal organs. The tripartite structure is reflected in all three of its main bodies; the International Labour Conference, the Governing Body and the International Labour Office.

There are three principal elements to the ILO's work. First, the ILO adopts a range of international labour standards ('ILO Conventions' and 'ILO Recommendations') for implementation by the ILO's member states. These conventions and recommendations contain guidelines on child labour, protection of women workers, hours of work, labour inspection, vocational guidance and training, social security protection, workers' housing, occupational health and safety, conditions of work at sea and the protection of migrant workers. They also encompass basic human rights, including: freedom of association; collective bargaining; the abolition of forced labour; the elimination of discrimination in employment; and the promotion of full employment.

At the time of writing, the ILO had adopted 189 Conventions and 202 Recommendations. Eight of these conventions have been identified by the ILO as 'fundamental',[97] and in 1995 the ILO started a campaign aimed at achieving universal ratification of these conventions. Secondly, it provides a programme of technical cooperation in conjunction with the United Nations Development Programme and other agencies to assist developing nations. Finally, international labour standard-setting and technical cooperation is further enhanced by an extensive research, training, education and publications programme.

94 See generally Kott and Droux (2013).
95 See n 65 above for the full list.
96 The General Conference of the International Labour Organization, Declaration concerning the aims and purposes of the International Labour Organisation ('Declaration of Philadelphia'), 26th session (10 May 1944) Philadelphia, § I. International Labour Organization, Constitution of the International Labour Organisation (ILO) (1 April 1919). Adopted by the Peace Conference in April 1919, the Constitution became Part XIII of the Treaty of Versailles (1919).
97 See ch 4 n 48 for citation of the 'fundamental' ILO Conventions.

The ILO operates a significant enforcement procedure. The ILO Constitution requires member states to make annual reports on the measures they have taken to implement the conventions they have adopted. Such reports are closely scrutinised by a committee of experts, which may follow up issues with the relevant governments. There is also a developed complaints system available to member states: see further details in sections 4.2.5 and 4.2.6.

The member states of the ILO (currently 185) meet in Geneva at the International Labour Conference in June of each year. Two government representatives and one worker delegate and one employer delegate represent each member state. Delegations are usually headed by Cabinet-rank ministers, but individual delegates can vote freely, even against their own delegation.

The conference plays a key role in discussing and adopting international labour standards. It elects the Governing Body and adopts the budget. The Governing Body is the executive council; it consists of 28 government, 14 worker and 14 employer member representatives, and 66 deputy members. Ten of the government seats are permanently held by states of chief industrial importance,[98] and representatives of the remaining government seats are elected at the conference every three years. It meets three times a year in Geneva. It sets the agenda for the ILO's policy and presents the programme and budget for approval by the conference. It will also elect a Director-General for a five-year term to lead the International Labour Office.[99] This body is the ILO's permanent secretariat and carries out the work of the organisation under the scrutiny of the Governing Body. The Office employs some 2700 officials from more than 150 nations at its Geneva headquarters and in 40 field offices. In addition, some 900 experts undertake missions in all regions of the world under the programme of technical cooperation.

2.4.2   *The Hague Conference on Private International Law*

The Hague Conference on Private International Law (Hague Conference) is *not* part of the UN system; its origins predate the formation of the League of Nations in 1919. The Hague Conference is an intergovernmental organisation whose main purpose is 'to work for the progressive unification of the rules of private international law'.[100] Relationships of a personal, family or commercial nature between individuals and companies in more than one country have become increasingly common in the modern world. One main function of the Hague Conference is to resolve the differences that may occur between the various legal systems involved through the formulation and adoption of 'private international law' rules. The Hague Conference has also developed its role as a centre for international judicial

---

98 Brazil, China, France, Germany, India, Italy, Japan, the Russian Federation, the United Kingdom and the United States.

99 Guy Ryder CBE (born Liverpool, UK on 3 January 1956) was elected the 10th Director General of the ILO in October 2012.

100 Statute of the Hague Convention on Private International Law (1955) art 1.

and administrative cooperation in the area of private law, especially in the fields of protection of the family and children, civil procedure and commercial law.

The first session of the Hague Conference was convened in 1893 by the Netherlands Government. Six sessions were held prior to the Second World War and the seventh session, held in 1951, saw the introduction of a Statute of the Hague Conference on Private International Law,[101] which made the Hague Conference a permanent inter-governmental organisation. There were, at the time of writing, 75 members of the Hague Conference comprised of 74 member states and one Regional Economic Integration Organisation (the European Union).

In 1980, the Conference opened its doors to non-member states, where the subject matter of the convention at issue indicated this was appropriate. This decision was taken with international trade law in mind, but there has been an increasing tendency for non-member states[102] both to participate in proceedings and to ratify Hague Conference Conventions across the whole range of subject matter (Van Loon 2000: 231).

The work of the Hague Conference has been to draw up multilateral conventions over a number of private international law fields, including conflict of law issues, the recognition of companies, jurisdiction and foreign judgments, and international judicial and administrative cooperation. Hague Conference activities are organised by a secretariat, the 'Permanent Bureau', headed by a Secretary-General. The Permanent Bureau's main role is to make the necessary preparations for the plenary sessions and for the Special Commissions. The Permanent Bureau will undertake some of the preliminary research on a convention or treaty and then refer it to a Special Commission made up of government experts. The drafts are then discussed and adopted at the plenary session. These sessions meet roughly every four years and additional 'Extraordinary Sessions' are convened on an ad hoc basis.

The Standing Government Committee of Private International Law formally sets the agenda for the plenary session under the Statute. However, more direct influence by Member States has evolved so that recommendations are made by the Special Commissions and then to the plenary sessions. At the plenary session each member state has one vote, and non-member states, invited to participate on an equal footing, also have a vote. By tradition, the President of the plenary session has always been the person leading the Netherlands delegation, reflecting its historical origins. The Conference has adopted 39 conventions since 1951.

Special Commissions are also used frequently to monitor the operation of particular conventions. This has occurred, for example, in relation to the conventions

101 The Statute was adopted during the 7th Session of the Hague Conference on Private International Law on 31 October 1951 and entered into force on 15 July 1955. Amendments were adopted during the 20th Session on 30 June 2005 (Final Act, C), approved by members on 30 September 2006 and entered into force on 1 January 2007.

102 At the time of writing, there were additionally 68 non-member states which had signed, ratified or acceded to one or more Hague Conventions.

aimed at child protection.[103] The Hague Conference has also been active in its outreach activities. It has organised international judicial seminars, for example, on child custody and the international protection of children.

The Hague Conference has increasingly become a centre for international judicial and administrative cooperation in the area of private law, especially in the fields of protection of the family and children, of civil procedure and commercial law. There are several modern Hague Conventions that have been particularly influential in the development of international child law and have been very successful Hague Conventions in their own right. These are the Hague Conventions on: the Civil Aspects of International Child Abduction (1980) (see Chapter 5) and the Protection of Children and Cooperation in respect of Intercountry Adoption (1993) (see Chapter 6).[104]

As the globalisation of human rights standard-setting increases, there arises a need to ensure the complementarity of Hague Conventions with other international legal regimes. One commentator observes that in relation, for example, to the Hague Child Abduction Convention and Intercountry Adoption Convention, the CRC 'provides the general framework', while the Hague Conventions 'implement the framework's principles, and provide coordination of the diversity of legal systems' (Van Loon 2011: 184).

2.4.3   The International Criminal Court

The International Criminal Court (ICC) began operating on 1 July 2002 following international discussions initiated by the General Assembly and established by the Rome Statute of the International Criminal Court (1998) (Rome Statute).[105] Its official seat is in The Hague but its proceedings may take place anywhere. It is the first permanent international court charged with trying those who commit the most serious crimes under international law, that is, 'crimes against humanity', 'war crimes' and 'genocide'.[106] It may in the future exercise jurisdiction over the crime of 'aggression', once a definition of this crime has been agreed by states parties and an amendment to the Rome Statute is made.[107] It should be noted

---

103   For example, *Conclusions and Recommendations of Part I and Part II of the Special Commission on the practical operation of the 1980 Child Abduction Convention and the 1996 Child Protection Convention* (April 2012, Hague Conference).

104   Other relevant Hague Conventions are: Convention on Jurisdiction, Applicable Law, Recognition, Enforcement and Cooperation in Respect of Parental Responsibility and Measures for the Protection of Children, concluded 19 October 1996 (entered into force 1 January 2002); Convention on the International Recovery of Child Support and Other Forms of Family Maintenance, concluded 23 November 2007 (entered into force 1 January 2013); Protocol on the Law Applicable to Maintenance Obligations, concluded 23 November 2007 (entered into force 1 August 2013).

105   Rome Statute of the International Criminal Court, opened for signature 17 July 1998, 2187 UNTS 90 (entered into force 1 July 2002).

106   Closely defined in the Rome Statute arts 6, 7 and 8.

107   See Rome Statute art 5(1)(d) and (2).

that it does not have a *general* criminal jurisdiction; it does not, for example, have jurisdiction over terrorism or drug trafficking.

The ICC is *not* part of the UN system. It is functionally independent of the UN in terms of personnel and financing, but some meetings of the ICC governing body, the Assembly of States Parties to the Rome Statute, are held at the UN. There is an agreement between the ICC and the United Nations that governs how the two institutions work with each other.[108] Although at the time of writing 122 countries are parties to the Rome Statute,[109] its authority is weakened by the absence from membership of China, India, Russia and the United States.[110] There have also been criticisms of the ICC relating to its power to assume jurisdiction over the nationals of non-states parties without those states' consent, in particular where the nationals are military personnel (Akande 2004).

The Court comprises four organs: the Presidency, the judicial Divisions, the Office of the Prosecutor, and the Registry. The Presidency consists of three judges of the Court elected by their fellow judges for a three-year term. The President and two Vice-Presidents of the Court are responsible for its overall administration. The judicial Divisions consist of 18 judges in three Divisions: Pre-trial, Trial and Appeals. The Office of the Prosecutor has responsibility for receiving referrals and information on crimes within the Court's jurisdiction and for conducting investigations and prosecutions before the Court. The Registry is responsible for the non-judicial administration of the Court. The Registrar, who is elected by the judges for a term of five years, performs his or her functions under the authority of the President of the Court.

There are three routes available to the prosecutor to undertake an investigation into a 'situation':

(a) on the basis of a referral from any state party;
(b) a referral from the UN's Security Council; and
(c) by the Prosecutor's own motion (*proprio motu*) on the basis of information received from individuals or organizations.[111]

Under routes (a) and (b) the Court can exercise jurisdiction only if: (i) the State on whose territory the crime was committed; or (ii) the State of the nationality of the accused person, is a States party to the Rome Statute. If neither is a States party, either can voluntarily accept the Court's jurisdiction.[112] The jurisdiction of the

---

108 International Criminal Court, *Negotiated Relationship Agreement between the International Criminal Court and the United Nations*, Doc No ICC-ASP/3/Res.1 (entry into force 22 July 2004).
109 Of these, 34 are African states, 18 are Asia-Pacific states, 18 are from Eastern Europe, 27 are from Latin American and Caribbean states and 25 are from Western European and other states.
110 The Russian Federation and the United States both signed the Rome Statute, but the United States expressly clarified later that it did not intend to ratify this treaty.
111 Rome Statute arts 13 and 15.
112 ibid art 12.

Court is also constrained by a 'complementarity' rule. The Court will determine a case is inadmissible where:

(a) The case is being investigated or prosecuted by a State which has jurisdiction over it, unless the State is unwilling or unable genuinely to carry out the investigation or prosecution;

(b) The case has been investigated by a state which has jurisdiction over it and the state has decided not to prosecute the person concerned, unless the decision resulted from the unwillingness or inability of the state genuinely to prosecute;

(c) The person concerned has already been tried for conduct which is the subject of the complaint, ... ;

(d) The case is not of sufficient gravity to justify further action by the Court.[113]

It should be noted, however, that a state must have incorporated in its domestic legislation the crimes envisaged in the Rome Statute in order to rely on the complementarity principle.

To date, eight 'situations' have been brought before the International Criminal Court. Uganda, the Democratic Republic of the Congo and the Central African Republic have referred situations occurring on their territories to the Court. In addition, the Security Council has referred the situation in Darfur, Sudan and the situation in Libya (both non-state parties). The Court granted the prosecutor authorisation to open an investigation *proprio motu* (on one's own motion/initiative) in the situations of Kenya in 2010 and in Côte d'Ivoire in 2011.

In addition, the Office of the Prosecutor is currently conducting preliminary examinations in a number of situations including Afghanistan, Georgia, Guinea, Colombia, Honduras, Korea and Nigeria. There were, at the time of writing, 21 cases before the Court.[114] The ICC's first trial to be brought to a judgment concerned the Congolese militia leader, Lubanga. On 10 July 2012, he was sentenced to a total period of 14 years of imprisonment for the war crime of enlisting and conscripting children under the age of 15 years into armed forces. At the time of writing his appeal against conviction and sentence was pending. See Case study 8.1 in Chapter 8 for further details.

2.5   Human rights protection

The overview of the development of human rights protection in Chapter 1 provides some detail about the introduction of the Universal Declaration of Human Rights (UDHR) (1948) and the two International Covenants (1966) (section 1.2.1),

---

113   Rome Statute art 17.
114   These 21 cases concerned the situations in: Uganda (1 case); Democratic Republic of the Congo (6); Darfur, Sudan (5); Central African Republic (1); Kenya (3); Libya (1); Côte d'Ivoire (3); Mali (1).

dealing respectively with (civil and political) and (economic, social and cultural) rights. The UDHR, made by resolution of the General Assembly, is not strictly binding in international law. However, it is generally treated as having entered into international customary law. The UDHR and the two (binding) Covenants are often referred to collectively as the International Bill of Human Rights.[115] It is thought to have three main elements: a declaration of principles (UDHR), a Convention (the two International Covenants of 1966 and their Optional Protocols) and the means of implementation: for example, periodic reports, technical assistance, global studies and the appointment of a High Commissioner for Human Rights (Hobbins 2001: 38–39).

The International Bill of Human Rights laid the modern foundation of international human rights law, and its provisions have found their way into the written constitutions of a number of states and subsequent human rights treaties. There have also been further UN treaties dealing with particular subject areas of human rights concerns, for example, racial discrimination, discrimination against women, the prevention of torture, the protection of migrant workers, enforced disappearances, the rights of persons with disabilities and the rights of the child.

2.5.1 Global protection: UN machinery

There are two types of body generally within the UN system of global protection that promote and protect human rights: first, those created under the UN Charter; and, secondly, those established by international human rights treaties. 'Charter bodies' are established under provisions of the UN Charter, or by bodies which themselves are created by the UN Charter. They are the political UN human rights institutions, made up of representatives of governments. The 'treaty bodies' are 'the quasi-judicial arm of UN human rights supervision' (Joseph and Kyriakakis (2010: 5) established under one of the international human rights conventions (see Table 2.1 below).

Most of these entities receive administrative support and coordination from the Office of the High Commissioner for Human Rights (OHCHR), a subsidiary body of the UN's Secretariat. The interrelationship between the range of human rights and the need for the United Nations to treat human rights pervasively within all its activities was recognised in the Vienna Declaration and Programme of Action adopted by the General Assembly in 1993,[116] following a World Conference on Human Rights in the same year. This Declaration emphasised that all human rights were universal, indivisible and interrelated; and it called for, inter alia, the creation of the OHCHR to spotlight and coordinate

---

115 See further 'The International Bill of Human Rights' *Fact Sheet No 2 (Rev.1)* Geneva, United Nations http://www.ohchr.org/Documents/Publications/FactSheet2Rev.1en.pdf (accessed 17 October 2013).

116 UNGA, *Vienna Declaration and Programme of Action*, UN Doc A/CONF.157/23 (12 July 1993). Endorsed by General Assembly resolution: UNGA Res 48/121, UN Doc A/RES/48/121 (20 December 1993).

human rights activities. The OHCHR was established some months later, and the first incumbent took office in 1994.

The OHCHR is based at the Palais Wilson in Geneva and the UN headquarters in New York City. The idea was to have a centre with strong moral authority to lead the human rights movement and to enhance the UN's ability to implement human rights standards. The OHCHR has forged links with non-government organisations (NGOs), academic institutions and others to promote human rights education, in addition to its involvement in preventative work. One of the aims of the OHCHR is to assist in *mainstreaming* human rights thinking throughout the UN system. The OHCHR is broadly tasked with a liaison role between all the human rights bodies within the UN and beyond.

The OHCHR acts as the principal focal point of human rights research, education, public information, and advocacy activities in the United Nations system. It also provides assistance to governments and others, in the areas, for example, of administration of justice, legislative reform and electoral process, to help implement international human rights standards on the ground. It works with governments, civil society, national human rights institutions and other international bodies to promote and protect human rights.

It undertakes three principal functional activities: standard-setting, monitoring, and implementation on the ground. It offers substantive and secretariat support to the different United Nations human rights bodies as they discharge their standard-setting and monitoring duties. The OHCHR, for example, serves as the Secretariat of the key 'charter body', the UN Human Rights Council (UNHRC) (see below). It also supports the work of 'special procedures' – including special rapporteurs, independent experts and working groups – appointed by UNHRC to monitor human rights in different countries or in relation to specific issues. OHCHR also supports the core human rights 'treaty bodies'.

Finally, the OHCHR works towards the implementation of international human rights standards on the ground through greater country engagement and its field presences. OHCHR employs around 1000 staff, based in Geneva and New York and in 12 country offices and 12 regional offices around the world, including a workforce of some 235 international human rights officers serving in UN peace missions. The High Commissioner is currently Navanethem Pillay.[117] She took up the post on 1 September 2008; her mandate has been renewed for two years beginning on 1 September 2012. It has been observed that the High Commissioner is called upon to fulfil somewhat contradictory roles – 'moral leadership, political sensitivity, and bureaucratic-managerial duties' (Ramcharan 2007: 452).

---

117 Previous High Commissioners were: Ms Louise Arbour, Canada, 2004–2008; Mr Bertrand Ramcharan (Acting High Commissioner), August 2003–July 2004); Mr Sergio Vieira de Mello, Brazil, 2002–2003; Mrs Mary Robinson, Ireland, 1997–2002; Mr José Ayala-Lasso, Ecuador, 1994–1997.

It should not be forgotten that the United Nations system provides, from time to time, a world stage upon which the message of human rights protection generally and children's rights in particular can be communicated with a powerful impact on a global audience.

Case study 2.2

United Nations: Youth Assembly on 'Malala Day' in New York on 12 July 2013
Pakistani schoolgirl Malala Yousafzai marked her 16th birthday by delivering a speech at the UN headquarters as part of her campaign to ensure free compulsory education for every child.

Malala's speech:
Honourable UN Secretary General Mr Ban Ki-moon, respected president of the General Assembly Vuk Jeremic, honourable UN envoy for global education Mr Gordon Brown, respected elders and my dear brothers and sisters: Assalamu alaikum.

Today is it an honour for me to be speaking again after a long time. Being here with such honourable people is a great moment in my life and it is an honour for me that today I am wearing a shawl of the late Benazir Bhutto. I don't know where to begin my speech. I don't know what people would be expecting me to say, but first of all thank you to God for whom we all are equal and thank you to every person who has prayed for my fast recovery and new life. I cannot believe how much love people have shown me. I have received thousands of good-wish cards and gifts from all over the world. Thank you to all of them. Thank you to the children whose innocent words encouraged me. Thank you to my elders whose prayers strengthened me. I would like to thank my nurses, doctors and the staff of the hospitals in Pakistan and the UK and the UAE government who have helped me to get better and recover my strength.

I fully support UN Secretary General Ban Ki-moon in his Global Education First Initiative and the work of UN Special Envoy for Global Education Gordon Brown and the respectful president of the UN General Assembly Vuk Jeremic. I thank them for the leadership they continue to give. They continue to inspire all of us to action. Dear brothers and sisters, do remember one thing: Malala Day is not my day. Today is the day of every woman, every boy and every girl who have raised their voice for their rights.

There are hundreds of human rights activists and social workers who are not only speaking for their rights, but who are struggling to achieve their goal of peace, education and equality. Thousands of people have been killed by the terrorists and millions have been injured. I am just one of them. So here I stand, one girl among many. I speak not for myself, but so those without a voice can be heard. Those who have fought for their rights. Their right to live in peace. Their right to be treated with dignity. Their right to equality of opportunity. Their right to be educated.

Dear friends, on 9 October 2012, the Taliban shot me on the left side of my forehead. They shot my friends, too. They thought that the bullets would silence us, but they failed. And out of that silence came thousands of voices. The terrorists thought they would change my aims and stop my ambitions. But nothing changed in my life except this: weakness, fear and hopelessness died. Strength, power and courage was born. I am the same Malala. My ambitions are the same. My hopes are the same. And my dreams are the same. Dear sisters and brothers, I am not against anyone. Neither am I here to speak in terms of personal revenge against the Taliban or any other terrorist group. I am here to speak for the right of education for every child. I want education for the sons and daughters of the Taliban and all the terrorists and extremists. I do not even hate the Talib who shot me.

Even if there was a gun in my hand and he was standing in front of me, I would not shoot him. This is the compassion I have learned from Mohamed, the prophet of mercy, Jesus Christ and Lord Buddha. This is the legacy of change I have inherited from Martin Luther King, Nelson Mandela and Mohammed Ali Jinnah.

This is the philosophy of nonviolence that I have learned from Gandhi, Bacha Khan and Mother Teresa. And this is the forgiveness that I have learned from my father and from my mother. This is what my soul is telling me: be peaceful and love everyone.

Dear sisters and brothers, we realise the importance of light when we see darkness. We realise the importance of our voice when we are silenced. In the same way, when we were in Swat, the north of Pakistan, we realised the importance of pens and books when we saw the guns. The wise saying, 'The pen is mightier than the sword'. It is true. The extremists are afraid of books and pens. The power of education frightens them. They are afraid of women. The power of the voice of women frightens them. This is why they killed 14 innocent students in the recent attack in Quetta. And that is why they kill female teachers.

That is why they are blasting schools every day because they were and they are afraid of change and equality that we will bring to our society. And I remember that there was a boy in our school who was asked by a journalist: 'Why are the Taliban against education?' He answered very simply by pointing to his book, he said: 'A Talib doesn't know what is written inside this book'.

They think that God is a tiny, little conservative being who would point guns at people's heads just for going to school. These terrorists are misusing the name of Islam for their own personal benefit. Pakistan is a peace-loving, democratic country. Pashtuns want education for their daughters and sons. Islam is a religion of peace, humanity and brotherhood. Islam says it's not only each child's right to get education, rather it is their duty and responsibility. Peace is a necessity for education. In many parts of the world, especially Pakistan and Afghanistan, terrorism, war and conflicts stop children from going to schools. We are really tired of these wars. Women and children are suffering in many ways in many parts of the world.

In India, innocent and poor children are victims of child labour. Many schools have been destroyed in Nigeria. People in Afghanistan have been affected by extremism. Young girls have to do domestic child labour and are forced to get married at an early age. Poverty, ignorance, injustice, racism and the deprivation of basic rights are the main problems, faced by both men and women.

Today, I am focusing on women's rights and girls' education because they are suffering the most. There was a time when women activists asked men to stand up for their rights. But this time we will do it by ourselves. I am not telling men to step away from speaking for women's rights, but I am focusing on women to be independent and fight for themselves. So dear sisters and brothers, now it's time to speak up. So today, we call upon the world leaders to change their strategic policies in favour of peace and prosperity. We call upon the world leaders that all of these deals must protect women and children's rights. A deal that goes against the rights of women is unacceptable.

We call upon all governments to ensure free, compulsory education all over the world for every child. We call upon all the governments to fight against terrorism and violence. To protect children from brutality and harm. We call upon the developed nations to support the expansion of education opportunities for girls in the developing world. We call upon all communities to be tolerant, to reject prejudice based on caste, creed, sect, colour, religion or agenda to ensure freedom and equality for women so they can flourish. We cannot all succeed when half of us are held back. We call upon our sisters around the world to be brave, to embrace the strength within themselves and realise their full potential.

Dear brothers and sisters, we want schools and education for every child's bright future. We will continue our journey to our destination of peace and education. No one can stop us. We will speak up for our rights and we will bring change to our voice. We believe in the power and the strength of our words. Our words can change the whole world because we are all together, united for the cause of education. And if we want to achieve our goal, then let us empower ourselves with the weapon of knowledge and let us shield ourselves with unity and togetherness.

Dear brothers and sisters, we must not forget that millions of people are suffering from poverty and injustice and ignorance. We must not forget that

> millions of children are out of their schools. We must not forget that our
> sisters and brothers are waiting for a bright, peaceful future.
> So let us wage a glorious struggle against illiteracy, poverty and terrorism,
> let us pick up our books and our pens, they are the most powerful weapons.
> One child, one teacher, one book and one pen can change the world.
> Education is the only solution. Education first. Thank you.

2.5.1.1 Charter bodies: the United Nations Humans Rights Council (UNHRC)

Two of the UN's 'principal organs' have a wide mandate in relation to human rights. The General Assembly may 'initiate studies and make recommendations ... assisting in the realization of human rights and fundamental freedoms for all without distinction as to race, sex, language, or religion'.[118] All the UN human rights bodies report back to the General Assembly. It can make (non-binding) resolutions or declarations. ECOSOC is also tasked with a human rights mandate; it 'may make recommendations for the purpose of promoting respect for, and observance of, human rights and fundamental freedoms for all'.[119]

ECOSOC 'effectively delegated its human rights functions to the Commission on Human Rights' (UNCHR) in 1946 (Joseph and Kyriakakis 2010: 6). Most of the UN human rights documents were drafted by the UNCHR up until 2006, when it was replaced with the United Nations Human Rights Council (UNHRC). In addition to its standard-setting it also laid the foundations for the development of complaints mechanisms and 'special procedures',[120] including country-specific mandates. However, its credibility waned:

> A number of key problems were widely recognised. Cynical manipulation of
> the [UN]CHR's mechanisms by Member States in order to avoid scrutiny
> and possible public censure or to score political points against other States,
> the increasing 'politicisation' of the CHR and in particular the selectivity
> reflected in the choice of States singled out for country-specific measures,
> and a number of high-profile elections to the CHR of States with particularly
> poor human rights records.
>
> (Joseph and Kyriakakis 2010: 9)

---

118 Charter of the United Nations art 13(1).
119 Charter of the United Nations art 62(2).
120 Despite an earlier resolution by ECOSOC in 1947 that UNCHR had 'no power to take any action in regard to any complaints concerning human rights' (ECOSOC Res 75 (V)), the Commission came under pressure from petitions from South Africa objecting to the apartheid regime. It departed from previous practice, and established in 1965 an ad hoc working group of experts to investigate the situation of human rights in Southern Africa (UNCHR resolution 2 (XXIII)). The ad hoc working group can be considered as the first 'special procedure' of the UNCHR.

The United Nations Human Rights Council (UNHRC) was established in 2006[121] and is the successor body to the UNCHR but, unlike its predecessor (which was a sub-commission of ECOSOC), it has a higher status as a direct subsidiary body of the General Assembly. The UNHRC is now the principal Charter body with responsibility for human rights, and comprises 47 member states elected for a term of three years by secret ballot by an absolute majority of the General Assembly. There is provision for periodic reviews of membership with the possibility of suspension for any state accused of systematic human rights violations.[122] The 47 seats are distributed among the UN's five regional groups: Africa (13); Asia (13); Eastern Europe (6); Latin America and the Caribbean (8); and Western Europe and others (7). The Council meets in regular session three times annually and in special session as needed, and reports to the General Assembly.

In September 2007 an Advisory Committee was established[123] (replacing the Sub-Commission on the Promotion and Protection of Human Rights, a part of the former UNCHR regime), which provides expert advice and serves as the UNHRC's think tank. The Advisory Committee has 18 members: Africa (5); Asia (5); Latin America and Caribbean (3); Western Europe and others (3); and Eastern Europe (2). The expert nature of the Advisory Committee ought in principle to act 'as an important counter-balance to the political machinations that necessarily take place in the Council', although regrettably it does not have the powers of own initiative that the Sub-Commission had (Joseph and Kyriakakis 2010: 15).

There is also a complaints procedure, established in 2007, that allows individuals and organisations to bring complaints about human rights violations to the attention of the UNHRC. It has a wide mandate to 'to address consistent patterns of gross and reliably attested violations of all human rights and all fundamental freedoms occurring in any part of the world and under any circumstances'.[124] The procedure retains its confidential nature, with a view to enhancing cooperation with the state concerned. A 'Working Group on Communications', consisting of five independent experts (serving for three-year terms) and representative of the five regions, make determinations as to whether a complaint deserves investigation. If it does, the complaint is passed to the 'Working Group on Situations', which again consists of five members (for a term of one year) representative of the five regions.[125] This group then reports to the UNHRC and makes recommendations about the course of action to be taken.

'Special procedures' is the general name given to the mechanisms established by the UNHRC's predecessor body to address either specific country situations or thematic issues. They involve independent human rights experts with mandates

121 UNGA Res 60/251, UN Doc A/RES/60/251 (15 March 2006). See n 56 above for the voting record on this resolution.
122 ibid paras 7–9.
123 *Institution-building of the United Nations Human Rights Council* HRC Res 5/1, 5th session, UN Doc A/ HRC/RES/5/1 (18 June 2007) [65–84].
124 ibid [85].
125 ibid [91–99].

to report and advise on human rights from a thematic or country-specific perspective. These have been retained in a similar form by the UNHRC, despite fears that the new structure would limit the independence and methods of special procedures. As of 1 October 2013 there were 37 thematic and 14 country mandates.

Special procedures report annually to the Human Rights Council; the majority of the mandates also report to the General Assembly. Their tasks are defined in the resolutions creating or extending their mandates. Special procedures consist of either an individual (a 'Special Rapporteur' or an 'Independent Expert') or a working group consisting of a member from each of the five regional groupings, who are appointed by the UNHRC and serve in their personal capacity. Mandate holders undertaking country visits typically send a letter to the state requesting cooperation with a visit. Some countries have issued 'standing invitations' indicating that they are, in principle, prepared to receive a visit from any special procedures mandate holder.[126] The UNHRC adopted a resolution in 2007 containing a Code of Conduct for special procedures mandate holders.[127]

In 2011, the UNHRC undertook a review of its work and functioning.[128] The review reaffirmed and strengthened essential principles, such as the obligation of states to cooperate with special procedures. Member states also confirmed their strong opposition to reprisals against persons cooperating with United Nations human rights mechanisms.

As part of the UNHRC's institution-building efforts in 2007, it also committed to undertaking a 'Universal Periodic Review' (UPR) to assess human rights situations in all the UN member states in four-year cycles.[129] This is an innovative procedure designed to be a cooperative, non-confrontational and non-political process. The stated objectives of the review are:

(a) The improvement of the human rights situation on the ground;

(b) The fulfilment of the State's human rights obligations and commitments and assessment of positive developments and challenges faced by the State;

(c) The enhancement of the State's capacity and of technical assistance, in consultation with, and with the consent of, the State concerned;

(d) The sharing of best practice among States and other stakeholders;

(e) Support for cooperation in the promotion and protection of human rights;

---

126 As of 3 September 2013, 95 states had extended standing invitations to the special procedures.

127 *Code of Conduct for Special Procedures Mandate-holders of the Human Rights Council*, HRC Res 5/2, 5th session, UN Doc A/HRC/RES/5/2 (18 June 2007).

128 *Review of the work and functioning of the Human Rights Council*, HRC Res 16/21, 16th session, UN Doc A/HRC/RES/16/21 (12 April 2011).

129 *Institution-building of the United Nations Human Rights Council*, HRC Res 5/1, 5th session, UN Doc A/HRC/RES/5/1 (18 June 2007) [1–38].

(f) The encouragement of full cooperation and engagement with the Council, other human rights bodies and the Office of the United Nations High Commissioner for Human Rights.[130]

The records of states are assessed against the standards contained in the UN Charter, the UDHR, any human rights instrument to which the state is a party, any voluntary commitments and any applicable humanitarian law. The utility of this new procedure remains contentious. UPR has been viewed as the remedy for the problems of the (discredited) UNCHR, in particular the problem of 'politicisation' of that body (Gaer 2007). It remains to be seen whether it will produce substantive outcomes in terms of human rights implementation, or whether it will have 'no consequences beyond embarrassment' in terms of the implementation of the review recommendations (Komanovics 2012).

2.5.1.2 UN human rights treaty bodies[131]

In addition to the 'Charter' bodies, there are also a number of human rights 'treaty bodies'. There are currently 10 such bodies established under their respective treaties[132] and tasked with monitoring the implementation of the principal human rights treaties. These are set out in Table 2.1 below. The treaty bodies carry out various functions in accordance with the provisions in the treaties that established them. They have three main functions:

(i)   the consideration of States parties' reports
(ii) issuing 'General Comments' and organising thematic discussion
(iii) the consideration of complaints ('communications').

The OHCHR makes efforts to coordinate the work of the various treaty bodies where necessary, and there is also an annual meeting of the chairpersons of the treaty bodies. This provides a forum for members of the 10 human rights treaty bodies to discuss their work, share best practice and consider ways to enhance the effectiveness of the treaty body system as a whole.

When a state has ratified one of these treaties it is obliged to implement the provisions of the treaty, including an obligation to submit periodic reports to the relevant treaty body reporting on how the treaty rights have been implemented.[133] For example, states parties to the CRC are obliged to produce an 'initial' report

---

130 *Institution-building of the United Nations Human Rights Council*, HRC Res 5/1, 5th session, UN Doc A/ HRC/RES/5/1 (18 June 2007) [4].
131 See generally Office of the High Commissioner for Human Rights (2012).
132 The exception is the Committee on Economic, Social and Cultural Rights, which was set up under the authority of an ECOSOC resolution: see ECOSO Res 1985/17 (28 May 1985).
133 The exception is the Subcommittee on Prevention of Torture etc (SPT), as the Optional Protocol of the Convention against Torture does not contain any reporting requirement.

Table 2.1 International Human Rights Treaty Bodies

Committee	Cttee Abbrev	Monitoring Treaty
Committee on the Elimination of Racial Discrimination	CERD	International Convention on the Elimination of All Forms of Racial Discrimination (1965)
Human Rights Committee	CCPR	International Covenant on Civil and Political Rights (1966)
Committee on Economic, Social and Cultural Rights	CESCR	International Covenant on Economic, Social and Cultural Rights (1966)
Committee on the Elimination of Discrimination Against Women	CEDAW	Convention on the Elimination of all forms of Discrimination against Women (1979)
Committee Against Torture	CAT	Convention against Torture and Other Cruel, Inhuman or Degrading Treatment (1984)
Committee on the Rights of the Child	CRC	Convention on the Rights of the Child (1989)
Committee on Migrant Workers	CMW	International Convention on the Protection of the Rights of all Migrant Workers and Members of their Families (1990)
Subcommittee on Prevention of Torture and other Cruel, Inhuman or Degrading Treatment or Punishment	SPT	Optional Protocol of the Convention against Torture (2002)
Committee on the Right of Persons with Disabilities	CRPD	International Convention on the Rights of Persons with Disabilities (2006)
Committee on Enforced Disappearances	CED	International Convention for the Protection of All Persons from Enforced Disappearance (2006)

after two years from ratification and then every five years.[134] Following problems of delay, both by states parties to produce their reports and by the Committees to process state reports expeditiously, there are now revised reporting requirements.[135] Two documents are presented by states parties to the treaty bodies for scrutiny: a 'core document' containing background information and information relating to provisions across a number of treaties; and a 'treaty-specific document' dealing with information customised to the state's obligations under a specific treaty.

The treaty bodies also benefit from the information that often accompanies these reporting cycles from national human rights institutions (NHRIs), national and international civil society organisations, and other UN intergovernmental

134 CRC art 44(1).
135 *Compilation of Guidelines on the Form and Content of Reports to be Submitted by States Parties to the International Human Rights Treaties*, UN Doc HRI/GEN/2/Rev.5 (29 May 2008).

Table 2.2 International Human Rights Treaty Bodies: communication/complaints procedures

Cttee	Treaty	Inter-state	Individual	Inquiry
CERD	*International Convention on the Elimination of all forms of Racial Discrimination (1965)*	Yes art 11–13	Yes art 14	No
HRCttee	*International Covenant on Civil and Political Rights (1966)*	Yes art 41–3	Yes 1st Optional Protocol	No
CESCR	*International Covenant on Economic, Social and Cultural Rights (1966)*	Yes Optional Protocol art 10	Yes Optional Protocol	Yes Optional Protocol art 11
CEDAW	*Convention on the Elimination of all forms of Discrimination against Women (1979)*	No	Yes Optional Protocol	Yes Optional Protocol art 8
CAT	*Convention against Torture and Other Cruel, Inhuman or Degrading Treatment (1984)*	Yes art 21	Yes art 22	Yes art 20
CRC	*Convention on the Rights of the Child (1989)*	Yes* 3rd Optional Protocol art 12	Yes* 3rd Optional Protocol art 5	Yes* 3rd Optional Protocol arts 13–14
CMW	*International Convention on the Protection of the Rights of all Migrant Workers and Members of their Families (1990)*	Yes* art 76	Yes* art 77	No
CRPD	*International Convention on the Rights of Persons with Disabilities (2006)*	No	Yes Optional Protocol art 1	Yes Optional Protocol art 6
CED	*International Convention for the Protection of all persons from Enforced Disappearance (2006)*	Yes art 32	Yes art 31	Yes art 33

(*) = procedure not yet entered into force

organisations, in addition to professional groups and academic institutions. There are some variations across the treaty bodies in the procedure governing the consideration of reports but in essence they enter into a written and oral dialogue with the state party delegation, culminating in the treaty body publishing its 'concluding observations' on the states party's report.

The jurisprudence of each treaty is also assisted by the 'General Comments' that each treaty body may issue.[136] These are published interpretations of the content of human rights provisions on thematic issues or methods of work.

136 For example, the Committee on the Rights of the Child has issued 17 General Comments. See http://www2.ohchr.org/english/bodies/crc/comments.htm (accessed 29 May 2013).

The competence of the treaty bodies includes a range of available 'communications procedures' (complaints). See Table 2.2 above. Most of the treaty bodies[137] now have an 'individual complaints' procedure and can, under certain conditions, receive petitions (aka 'communications') from individuals alleging that their rights have been violated. The decisions and recommendations of the treaty bodies made in response to such complaints are quasi-judicial in nature and may be regarded as a form of authoritative jurisprudence in relation to the interpretation of the treaties.

Some of the treaty bodies[138] also have provisions for 'inter-state complaints' where one states party may, under certain conditions, complain about violations of the treaty rights by another states party. It should be noted however, that no *inter-state communication* under these procedures to date has been made. Most of the treaty bodies[139] have, additionally, a procedure for investigating 'inquiry complaints', where they receive reliable information about *grave or systemic* violations of rights by a states party. For further details of the communication/complaints procedures available under the Convention on the Rights of the Child, see section 3.6.3.

---

137 CCPR, CERD, CAT, CEDAW, CRPD and CED all have individual communication procedures that have entered into force. The CRC, CMW and CESCR have individual communication procedures, but these three have not yet entered into force.

138 CCPR, CERD and CAT all have inter-state communication procedures in force. CED, CRC and CMW have such procedures but they have not yet entered into force. CEDAW, CRPD, and CESCR do not have an inter-state communication procedure.

139 CESCR, CAT, CEDAW, CRPD, CED. The CRC also has an inquiry procedure.

Chapter 3

The UN Convention on the Rights of the Child

3.1 Introduction

The United Nations Convention on the Rights of the Child (1989) (Convention)[1] is in many ways distinctive amongst international treaties and unique in terms of international law generally. It was produced after a lengthy drafting process that started in 1978. The participation of non-governmental organisations (NGOs) in both the drafting process and the reporting mechanism set up under the Convention is also significant. Another remarkable feature has been the way in which states have been eager to sign and ratify the Convention. On the first day the Convention was opened for signature (26 January 1990), no less than 61 states parties signed, something of a record for an international treaty: see Figure 3.1 below. The Convention entered into force in international law on 2 September 1990. A remarkable feature of the Convention is quite simply the near-global ratification it has received. There are currently 193 parties to the Convention; only Somalia and the United States remain to ratify it (see section 3.3). Detrick (1999: 721), who has provided a detailed and authoritative annotation of each of the substantive articles of the Convention, concluded:

> While the Convention on the Rights of the Child may not be the last – or complete – word on children's rights, it is the first universal instrument of a legally binding nature to comprehensively address those rights. As such, it forms a universal benchmark on the rights of the child – a benchmark against which all future claims for evolution will and must be answered.

The Convention contains not only civil and political rights but also social, economic and cultural rights. International law discourse used to refer to these as, 'first-' and 'second-generation' rights respectively. Lately, these labels have been dropped in deference to an increasing recognition that there should be no hierarchy of human rights, and that such rights are indivisible and interdependent. The Convention is the first, comprehensive, rights-based international treaty

---

1 Opened for signature 20 November 1989, 1577 UNTS 3 (entered into force 2 September 1990).

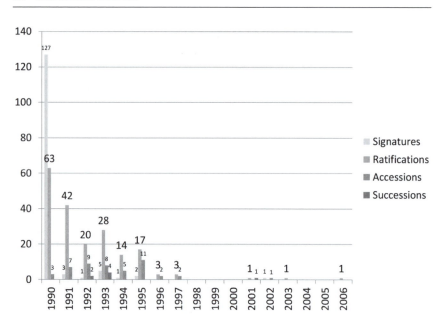

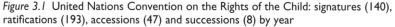

Figure 3.1 United Nations Convention on the Rights of the Child: signatures (140), ratifications (193), accessions (47) and successions (8) by year

Source: The data is taken from the status table of the Convention, Committee on the Rights of the Child website. The figures given for 'ratifications', in the larger font, add up to 193. The combination of figures for signatures, accessions and successions adds up to 195; two more than the total ratifications because both the USA and Somalia *signed* the Convention but have not followed through with ratification.

specifically constructed to protect and enhance the position of children. It marks a step-change in the international law of children's rights. Prior to this treaty, the international community had begun to recognise the child at least as a legitimate 'object' of international law. The Convention goes further and recognises the child as a more active 'subject' of international law who can be a holder of rights and participate in important decision making.

The Convention is a good example of the 'globalisation' process as applied in the international legal realm; it signals the worldwide convergence of normative legal standards. In its relatively short existence, it has established itself as the central international instrument on children's rights and has influenced the operation of international, regional and domestic law and policy. It can be reasonably claimed that the appearance of the Convention justifies the study of 'international child law' as a discrete subject in its own right. The Convention does more than establish an authoritative text of children's rights; it has also provided the international community with a powerful vehicle to institute programmes of action and shape policy initiatives to further advance their practical implementation. However, as will be seen, the Convention, along with the machinery it has established and the way in which it has been received by the international community, has not been immune from various defects and weaknesses.

3.2 Background and history

The Declaration of the Rights of the Child (1924),[2] emanating from the old League of Nations, was in fact the first human rights document approved by an inter-governmental institution and preceded the Universal Declaration of Human Rights (1948)[3] itself by 24 years. The Declaration of 1924 was merely a non-binding resolution of the League of Nations, although it carried significant moral force. It was reaffirmed by the League of Nations in 1934. The General Assembly of the United Nations unanimously adopted a new text of the Declaration of the Rights of the Child (1959),[4] containing 10 major principles. This document did not have international legal binding force either, but its *unanimous* adoption by the General Assembly enhanced its authority. The language used in the text of the Declaration of 1959 reflects the conception of a child as more than merely a passive recipient of international humanitarian aid, but rather as an active partici-pant in the enjoyment of human rights and freedoms.

However, the states that accepted the Declaration of 1959 also opposed the cre-ation of a legally binding treaty on the subject of children's rights. Interest in such a treaty was not to arise until 20 years later when the General Assembly proclaimed 1979 as the 'International Year of the Child'. In 1978, Poland submitted a draft text for a Convention on the Rights of the Child. Various states took the view that the Polish text merely replicated the Declaration of 1959 and did not provide an adequate update given the changes in social, economic and cultural development that had occurred in the previous two decades. Furthermore, it was thought that the revision of the 1959 principles was worded too vaguely for a Convention that was now intended to be legally binding. In 1979, the United Nations Commission on Human Rights (UNCHR)[5] organised an open-ended working group to review and expand the original Polish text. Any of the states that were then represented in the UNCHR could participate; other UN members could send observers and con-tribute from the floor, and inter-governmental organisations could also contribute. NGOs could also send observers but with no absolute right to speak, but their requests to take the floor were rarely refused (Detrick 1999). In order to encourage state ratification of the treaty, the working group adopted a principle of consensus

---

2 League of Nations, *Official Journal*, Special Supplement No 23, Records of the Fifth Assembly (Geneva, 1924) 177.

3 UN General Assembly, Universal Declaration of Human Rights (10 December 1948) 217 A (III).

4 General Assembly, Declaration of the Rights of the Child, 14th session, UN Doc A/RES/1386 (XIV) (20 November 1959).

5 The United Nations Commission on Human Rights (UNCHR) was abolished and replaced by the United Nations Human Rights Council (UNHRC) in 2006, in part because the former body had been discredited for including countries with poor human rights records: see further section 2.5.1.1. The UNHRC has 47 states members (October 2013).

working, so that no votes were taken during the course of the Convention's draft-ing. A report was issued on each of the working group's sessions and discussed by UNCHR, and in turn through the Economic and Social Council (ECOSOC) and by the General Assembly (section 2.4.1). The working group held 11 sessions between 1979 and 1988. The industrialised countries were over-represented in the drafting process, giving rise to criticisms that the Convention was a 'northern' oriented document. However, there were active contributions from some of the developing countries, in particular Algeria, Argentina, Senegal and Venezuela, and in 1988 there was a 'sudden last minute surge of delegates from the South, many from States with Islamic law' (Cantwell 1992: 23). The general thaw in East–West relations in the mid-1980s made a significant difference to the atmosphere of debate in these working group sessions. In the early 1980s, the delegations working on the drafts of the Convention and the Convention against Torture were work-ing, literally, along the corridor from each other, and on occasion the delegations traded concessions in their respective groups.

> The NGOs' contributions were in many respects remarkable. It is generally acknowledged in the international community that the NGOs had a direct and indirect impact on [the CRC], that is, without parallel in the history of drafting international instruments (Cantwell 1992: 24).

The ad hoc group of NGOs was able to identify no less than 13 substan-tive Articles for which they claimed primary responsibility, and a further similar number of Articles to which they had a less direct but nevertheless important input. Although every clause of the Convention was fully debated, Cantwell (1992: 26) has identified four key areas of principal controversy that occurred during the drafting process:

i.   the definition of the minimum age of the child (Article 1)
ii.   freedom of religion (Article 14)
iii. adoption (Article 21) and
iv.   the age at which children should be permitted to participate in armed conflict (Article 38).

The working group finally adopted a text in December 1988 and it was then trans-mitted to the General Assembly for approval and adoption through the UNCHR and ECOSOC. After 10 years of negotiation the Convention emerged, its word-ing clearly influenced by the Universal Declaration of Human Rights (1948) and the two International Covenants (1966) (these three documents, also known as the International Bill of Human Rights). The UN General Assembly unanimously adopted the Convention on the Rights of the Child on 20 November 1989. It was opened for signature on 26 January 1990. The Convention entered into force on 2 September 1990.[6]

---

6 Thirty days after the deposit of the 20th instrument of ratification or accession: see CRC art
   49(1). The difference between ratification and accession (as regards the CRC) is that those initially

There are at least two elements that go towards the explanation of how children's issues emerged at the top of the international agenda in the 1990s (Black 1996): first, the movement for children's rights, culminating in the Convention in 1989 (section 1.2.1.3); and, secondly, the child survival campaign resulting in the World Summit for Children in 1990. The latter was concerned mainly with health and other issues relating to children. In September 1990, a large gathering of world leaders; 71 heads of state and 88 other senior officials, mostly at ministerial level, assembled at the United Nations headquarters in New York. The summit adopted a Declaration on the Survival, Protection and Development of Children and a Plan of Action for Implementing the Declaration in the 1990s.[7] The Declaration and Plan of Action contained a number of targets for improving both the survival of children and their opportunities for positive growth and development. These included: the reduction of infant and under-five child mortality, the reduction of maternal mortality, the reduction of severe and moderate malnutrition among under-five children, universal access to safe drinking water, greater food supply and sanitary means of sewage disposal, universal access to basic education, the completion of primary education, the reduction of the adult illiteracy rate, and the improved protection of children in difficult circumstances. These targets have been revisited by the international community in the form of the 'Millennium Development Goals' (MDGs) (2000).

3.3   Failure to ratify the Convention on the Rights of the Child

The United States, Somalia and the Republic of South Sudan remain the only countries that have not ratified the Convention. It should, however, be noted that both the USA and Somalia are signatories to the Convention.[8] The act of signature is not without some legal effect.

Where signature is subject to ratification, acceptance, or approval, signature does not establish consent to be bound. However, signature qualifies the signatory state to proceed to ratification, acceptance, or approval and creates an obligation of good faith to refrain from acts calculated to frustrate the objects of the treaty (Crawford 2012: 372).

Article 18 of the Vienna Convention on the Law of Treaties (1969)[9] provides that states are bound not to do anything that would defeat the object and purpose of the relevant treaty until the state has made its intention *not* to ratify clear. In the case of Somalia, there has been no ratification to date as the combined effects

'signing' must *ratify*, whereas states that have *not* signed *accede*. The act of signature does not bind the party to ratify, although in practice this does usually follow. However, the act of signature on its own is not without legal effect. Such a state is bound not to do anything that would defeat the object and purpose of the relevant treaty until the state has made its intention not to ratify clear: see the Vienna Convention on the Law of Treaties (1969) art 18.

7 See http://www.unicef.org/wsc/declare.htm (accessed 21 May 2013).

8 The USA on 16 February 1995 and Somalia on 9 May 2002.

9 Opened for signature 23 May 1969, 1155 UNTS 331 (entered into force 27 January 1980).

of civil war since 1991 and successive waves of further inter-clan tensions have in effect produced a failed state that has lacked the governmental infrastructure of public institutions and sufficient stability to maintain diplomatic activity and contribute to international relations in the normal way. In August 2012, the Federal Government of Somalia, the first permanent central government in the country since the start of the civil war, was formed along with a new constitution and Parliament. The state is currently undergoing intense reconstruction, and is attracting increasing international support at the time of writing. There is support from a number of NGOs within Somalia for children's rights generally and from time to time the various governmental authorities in Somalia have made statements of intention to ratify the Convention,[10] although such statements have, to date, been symbolic gestures only.

On 9 July 2011, the Republic of South Sudan became a member nation of the UN, and children's rights are supported in the Constitution. As a newly constituted state, it has not yet signed or ratified the Convention, although the predecessor state of Sudan, from which it has seceded, was and remains a contracting state. While there remain conflicts with northern Sudan in the border regions where oil reserves are located, South Sudan is not able to provide education and healthcare for children. It is thought that South Sudan is unlikely to ratify the Convention 'until the conflict is resolved and oil revenues are secure'.[11]

The failure of the United States to ratify the Convention is a more significant weakness, given its global power and influence. President Clinton decided that the United States would sign the Convention but that, in sending it to the Senate for their 'advice and consent' to ratification, he would 'ask for a number of reservations and understandings ... [to] protect the rights of the various states under the nation's federal system of government and maintain the country's ability to use existing tools of the criminal justice system in appropriate cases'.[12] Madeleine Albright, acting as the US delegate to the United Nations, signed the Convention on behalf of the United States on 16 February 1995.

To an extent, the failure of the USA to ratify the Convention reflects the general policy of US foreign relations to strike up *bilateral* relations with other countries rather than participate at the *multilateral* level. This approach has had an enduring impact on the USA's disconnection generally from the UN human rights system. As one commentator put it, the failure to ratify the Convention 'is just one example of the United States' inability to marshal the United Nations convention system and place it in the service of U.S. foreign policy' (Engle 2011: 800).

---

10 For example, the statement made by the Somali Government in November 2009: see http://news.bbc.co.uk/1/hi/8370357.stm (accessed 22 May 2013).

11 See http://unchildrights.blogspot.co.uk/2010/05/corporal-punishment-banned-in-southern.html (accessed 24 May 2013).

12 Press Release, The White House, 'White House Statement on U.S. Decision to Sign UN Convention on Rights of the Child' (10 February 1995).

Rutkow and Lozman (2006) usefully explain the USA's failure to ratify the Convention in terms of four areas of concern: sovereignty, federalism, reproductive and family planning, and parental rights. In terms of sovereignty, the United States has often been very cautious about agreeing to international human rights treaties; for example, the International Convention on the Elimination of All Forms of Racial Discrimination[13] (1965) was only ratified by the USA 28 years after being signed by President Lyndon B. Johnson.[14] In essence, there are some structural and constitutional difficulties that have posed obstacles to US ratification (Kilbourne 1998), although increasingly commentators argue that such obstacles are either misconceived or have been superseded by subsequent developments. The concern about federalism is based on the fact that family law matters generally fall within the competence of the state legislatures rather than the Federal government,[15] so there are fears that ratification would federalise an area of law traditionally within the states' competence. Under Article VI of the US Constitution (the 'supremacy clause'),[16] an international treaty ratified by the United States should be applied as part of the 'law of the land'; that is, it would be binding in state and federal courts. In principle, therefore, such ratification would result in American courts being able to cite provisions of the Convention. However, in recent times, when the Senate has given its consent to the ratification of human rights treaties, it has often included a declaration that the rights-guarantee provisions are not 'self-executing' (Quigley 2002).

The lower courts have relied on these declarations as depriving litigants of the right to rely on the guarantee provisions. However, it has been pointed out that: 'This Senate practice, and the deference given by courts, remain controversial. No court has yet explained in constitutional terms how a Senate declaration of non-self-execution acquires the force of law (Quigley 2002).

Even if there were elements of the Convention that were 'self-executing', that is, automatically given domestic effect, the United States could deploy reservations to avoid their applicability (Engle 2011: 814). One particular sticking point has been the conflict between the 'right to life' in the Convention and the existence of the death penalty applicable to under-18-year-olds in some states in the USA. However, the US Supreme Court in 2005 abolished juvenile executions.[17] There have also been concerns about reproductive and family planning matters, mainly

13 Opened for signature 7 March 1966, 660 UNTS 195 (entered into force 4 January 1969).
14 Signed by USA on 28 September 1966, ratified on 21 October 1994.
15 The Tenth Amendment to the US Constitution; 'The powers not delegated to the United States by the Constitution, nor prohibited by it to the States, are reserved to the States respectively, or to the people'. This restricts the federal government's authority to legislate in this area.
16 'This Constitution, and the Laws of the United States which shall be made in Pursuance thereof; and all Treaties made, or which shall be made, under the Authority of the United States, shall be the supreme Law of the Land; and the Judges in every State shall be bound thereby, any Thing in the Constitution or Laws of any State to the Contrary notwithstanding': US Constitution 1787 art VI cl 2.
17 *Roper v. Simmons*, 543 U.S. 551 (2005).

on the basis of religious beliefs and that the Convention does not expressly offer protection of the foetus (Smolin 2006). The identification of the beginning of childhood proved problematic in drafting the Convention, and the combination of the text of Article 1 and the ninth preambular paragraph[18] in effect provides an opportunity for States parties to interpret the Convention as providing legal protection either from the moment of live birth or from conception, as the case may be.

The failure to ratify can also be explained by reference to certain objections in principle, in particular the issue of how far 'children's rights' might threaten 'parental rights'. It has been thought also that the inclusion of economic rights in the Convention might be inconsistent with American concepts of the limits of government. Finally, there are political and social factors to consider, particularly the influence of 'moral rearmament' groups that have often been prompted to resistance in particular by the emphasis in the Convention on children's participation rights (Rutkow and Lozman 2006: 165).

The influence of the Convention in the USA has been significant despite its failure to ratify to the extent that, arguably, 'the CRC is seen by U.S. courts as codifying customary international law, or at least as evidence of customary international law' (Engle 2011: 794). It is a matter of regret generally in the international community that the United States, although it signed the Convention in 1995, has still failed to transmit it to the US Senate for ratification, particularly in the light of its active interest and participation in the original drafting process and its support and ratification of the two substantive Optional Protocols (section 3.6) to the Convention. The USA will remain outside the deliberations of the international Committee until it ratifies. It has also been an important strand to US foreign policy to encourage human rights observance in other states, a policy made more difficult by its own delays in ratifying such instruments. The emergence of the Obama administration gave some early hope to reformers that the United States might eventually ratify the Convention. When President Obama was on the campaign trail preceding his first term of office, he responded to questions about US ratification thus:

> It's important that the United States return to its position as a respected global leader and promoter of Human Rights. It's embarrassing to find ourselves in the company of Somalia, a lawless land. I will review this and other treaties and ensure that the United States resumes its global leadership in Human Rights.
>
> (20 October 2008, Presidential Youth Debate, Walden University, USA)[19]

---

18 CRC preamble §9: 'Bearing in mind that, as indicated in the *Declaration of the Rights of the Child*, "the child, by reason of his physical and mental immaturity, needs special safeguards and care, including appropriate legal protection, before as well as after birth"'.

19 For text see http://www.youthdebate2008.org/debate-transcript (accessed 24 May 2013).

Indeed, there is a vigorous campaign group[20] in the United States that, at the time of writing, continues to advocate US ratification of the Convention.

3.4   The Committee on the Rights of the Child

The Convention provides for the establishment of a specialist Committee, the purpose of which is to examine the progress made by states in achieving the realisation of the obligations established under the Convention.[21] There was originally a Committee of 10 child law and policy experts elected by the states parties. The membership of the Committee was increased to 18 by an amendment to the Convention that came into force in 2003. Members of the Committee serve in their 'personal capacity' as experts; they do not hold a representative mandate from their respective countries. Each member is an independent expert of 'high moral standing and recognised competence in the field'. Nevertheless, an equitable geographical distribution and representation of the principal legal systems is taken into consideration in their selection.[22]

The Committee has a small permanent secretariat at the Office of the High Commissioner for Human Rights (OHCHR) in Geneva. Its primary function is to receive and comment upon the states parties' periodic country reports. It meets in Geneva for three sessions each year, normally in January, May and September. The Committee held its 1st session in October 1991.[23]

The Committee publishes its interpretation of the content of human rights provisions in the form of General Comments. As with the General Comments emanating from the other international human rights treaty bodies, these are increasingly taken to contain authoritative interpretation of the relevant Convention. Indeed, at least in relation to the key Human Rights Committee (which monitors the International Covenant on Civil and Political Rights (1966)), General Comments that receive wide support 'may be regarded as a secondary source of international law' (Aust 2010: 233). Table 3.1 below sets out the General Comments that the Committee have issued up to the end of 2013.

General Comments are also specifically referred to as relevant sources, which must be taken into account when states parties are preparing their periodic reports to the Committee.[24] The Committee also holds, in accordance with its rules of

---

20 'The Campaign for US Ratification of the CRC' http://www.childrightscampaign.org/ (accessed 24 May 2013).
21 CRC art 43.
22 ibid art 43(2).
23 At the time of writing, the Committee was in its 64th session (16 September–4 October 2013).
24 See *Treaty-specific guidelines regarding the form and content of periodic reports to be submitted by States parties under article 44, paragraph 1 (b), of the Convention on the Rights of the Child*, CRC/C/58/Rev.2 (23 November 2010) paras 13, 21, 27, 30, 32, 36, 38 and 40.

Table 3.1 General Comments of the Committee on the Rights of the Child

No	Title	Reference	Date
1	The aims of education	CRC/GC/2001/1	17 April 2001
2	The role of independent human rights institutions	CRC/GC/2002/2	15 November 2002
3	HIV/AIDS and the rights of the child	CRC/GC/2003/3	17 March 2003
4	Adolescent Health	CRC/GC/2003/4	01 July 2003
5	General measures of implementation for the Convention on the Rights of the Child	CRC/GC/2003/5	03 October 2003
6	Treatment of unaccompanied and separated children outside their country of origin	CRC/GC/2005/6 Rev.1	01 September 2005
7	Implementing child rights in early childhood	CRC/C/GC/7/ Rev.1	20 September 2006
8	The right of the child to protection from corporal punishment and other cruel or degrading forms of punishment	CRC/C/GC/8	02 March 2007
9	The rights of children with disabilities	CRC/C/GC/9	27 February 2007
10	Children's rights in Juvenile Justice	CRC/C/GC/10	25 April 2013
11	Indigenous children and their rights under the Convention	CRC/C/GC/11	12 January 2009
12	The right of the child to be heard	CRC/C/GC/12	20 July 2009
13	The right of the child to freedom from all forms of violence	CRC/C/GC/13	18 April 2011
14	The right of the child to have his or her best interests taken as a primary consideration (art 3 para 1)	CRC/C/GC/14	29 May 2013
15	The right of the child to the enjoyment of the highest attainable standard of health (art 24)	CRC/C/GC/15	17 April 2013
16	On State obligations regarding the impact of the business sector on children's rights	CRC/C/GC/16	17 April 2013
17	The right of the child to rest, leisure, play, recreational activities, cultural life and the arts	CRC/C/GC/17	17 April 2013

Note: See the Committee's website for an up-to-date account of the General Comments: http://www2.ohchr.org/english/bodies/crc/comments.htm (accessed 31 May 2013).

procedure,[25] a 'Day of General Discussion' on a thematic issue in its September session. These used to be held every year, but at its 61st session (17 September–5 October 2012) it resolved to hold general discussion days on a biennial basis.[26] These are public meetings open to representatives of states parties, UN agencies and bodies, NGOs, national human rights institutions, professional groups, academics, youth groups and other interested parties. The Committee sometimes chooses to develop a General Comment from an article, provision or theme that has been discussed earlier in one of its 'Days of General Discussion'.

The Committee also, from time to time, adopts Recommendations which, in recent years, have been referred to as Decisions.[27] Of the 10 Recommendations issued to date, seven are concerned with procedural matters relating to the reporting process. For example, Decision No 10[28] requests the General Assembly to provide appropriate financial support to enable it to work in two chambers at pre-sessional working group meetings due to take place in 2012 and at a session in 2013.

Although, as detailed below, the reporting process is the central activity of the Committee, it should not be thought that members of the Committee do not contribute outside of the formal sessions. Members regularly engage in numerous activities, eg conferences, seminars, lectures and courses, and may be involved in 'the follow-up to the Committee's Concluding Observations in a number of countries upon invitation from States, civil society organizations and the United Nations Children's Fund (UNICEF)'.[29] The Committee has also been active in the process initiated by the OHCHR in 2009 on strengthening the treaty body system.[30]

25 Committee on the Rights of the Child, *Rules of Procedure*, CRC/C/4/Rev.3 (16 April 201); Provisional rules of procedure were adopted at the Committee's first session and revised subsequently at its 33rd, 55th and 62nd sessions. See http://daccess-dds-ny.un.org/doc/UNDOC/GEN/G13/426/87/PDF/G1342687.pdf?OpenElement (accessed 5 June 2013). Rule 79 states that: 'In order to enhance a deeper understanding of the content and implications of the Convention, the Committee may devote one or more meetings of its regular sessions to a general discussion on one specific article of the Convention or related subject'.

26 The next 'Day of General Discussion' on the issue of 'Media, Social Networks and the Rights of the Child' takes place in September 2014 during the 67th session of the Committee; the 2016 day of general discussion will take place during the 73rd session on the theme: 'Access to justice and effective remedies to child rights violations' at the Palais des Nations.

27 See http://www2.ohchr.org/english/bodies/crc/decisions.htm#8 (accessed 31 May 2013). This book will refer to the first six issued as Recommendations and the seventh and subsequent ones as Decisions.

28 'Decision of the Committee on the Rights of the Child to request approval from the General Assembly at its 66th session to work in two chambers once per year', Decision No 10, Committee on the Rights of the Child (11 February 2011).

29 General Assembly, *Report of the Committee on the Rights of the Child*, A/67/41 (21 June 2012) para 16.

30 ibid para 17. The Committee was 'the first treaty body to endorse as a whole the Dublin II outcome document'.

3.5   The reporting process under the Convention

The Committee normally holds three regular sessions lasting for two or three weeks in and around January, May and September each year. In addition, a pre-sessional working group meeting is convened, lasting one week, following each of the plenary sessions. The sessions of the Committee are held at the United Nations Office at Geneva.

The legal framework for the reporting process is contained in Articles 43–45 of the Convention and in the Committee's Rules of Procedure[31] that have been established under Article 43(8) of the Convention. The Secretary-General provides the necessary staff and administrative facilities to service the work of the Committee. There is a primary legal duty for states parties to submit reports to the Committee both on the measures they have adopted to give effect to the Convention and on the progress made on the enjoyment of those rights.[32] The 'initial report' must be submitted within two years of the date the Convention entered into force for that state and thereafter a periodic report must be made every five years. The Convention emphasises that these reports should contain 'sufficient' information to provide the Committee with a 'comprehensive' understanding of its implementation of the Convention, but need not repeat basic data in subsequent periodic reporting cycles. As at May 2013, the Committee had received 580 reports pursuant to Article 44 of the Convention, including 197 initial, 153 second periodic, 112 third periodic, 99 fourth periodic and 19 fifth periodic reports.[33]

The guidelines for states parties on producing the 'initial report'[34] make it clear that such reports shall 'contain sufficient information to provide the Committee with a comprehensive understanding of the implementation of the Convention in the country concerned', and provides 'an important occasion for conducting a comprehensive review of the various measures undertaken to harmonize national law and policy with the Convention and to monitor progress'.[35] These guidelines and practice have also established nine groupings (referred to as 'clusters') under which states parties are expected to provide relevant information in both their initial and subsequent periodic reports. These are:

i.   General measures of implementation
ii.   Definition of the child
iii. General principles
iv.   Civil rights and freedoms

31 Committee on the Rights of the Child, *Rules of Procedure*, CRC/C/4/Rev.3 (16 April 2013).
32 CRC art 44.
33 *States parties to the Convention on the Rights of the Child and its two Optional Protocols and related status of submission of reports: Note by the Secretary-General*, CRC/C/63/2, Committee on the Rights of the Child (17 May 2013) para 3.
34 *General Guidelines regarding the form and content of initial reports to be submitted by States parties under Article 44, paragraph 1(a), of the Convention*, CRC/C/5 (30 October 1991).
35 ibid paras 2 and 3.

v.   Family environment and alternative family care
vi.   Violence against children
vii. Disability, basic health and welfare
viii. Education, leisure and cultural activities
ix.   Special protection measures.

The guidelines on periodic reports[36] have now developed according to harmonised guidelines on reporting to the international human rights treaty bodies.[37] States parties' reports are now constituted in two parts: a 'common core' document, and a document that specifically relates to the implementation of the Convention and its Optional Protocols (known as a 'treaty-specific report').[38] The combination of both of these documents constitutes the full report under the Convention.[39]

The common core document contains general statistical and other information about the reporting state, the general framework of human rights, including information on non-discrimination, equality and remedies.[40] This general information should not normally be repeated in the treaty-specific report, although the Committee can request that the common core document is updated.[41]

The treaty-specific report[42] should make specific reference to the previous recommendations of the Committee and include details on how the recommendations have been addressed in practice along with an account of obstacles encountered and any measures envisaged to overcome such obstacles.[43] Furthermore, it should contain information specific to the implementation of the Convention and its Optional Protocols including 'information of a more analytical nature on how laws, legal systems, jurisprudence, the institutional framework, policies and programmes impact on children within the jurisdiction of the State party'.[44] The guidelines emphasise that:

> While statistical information should be included in the common core document, the treaty-specific report should include specific data and statistics, disaggregated according to age, sex and other relevant criteria, which are pertinent to the implementation of the provisions of the Convention and the

36 *Treaty-specific guidelines regarding the form and content of periodic reports to be submitted by States parties under article 44, paragraph 1 (b), of the Convention on the Rights of the Child*, CRC/C/58/Rev.2 (23 November 2010).

37 HRI/GEN/2/Rev.6.

38 *Treaty-specific guidelines regarding the form and content of periodic reports to be submitted by States parties under article 44, paragraph 1 (b), of the Convention on the Rights of the Child*, CRC/C/58/Rev.2 (23 November 2010) para 5.

39 See 'Periodicity and Format of Reports – to supersede previous related decisions', Decision No 9, 55th session, Committee on the Rights of the Child (1 October 2010).

40 ibid para 7. The common core document should not exceed 60–80 pages.

41 ibid para 8.

42 ibid para 11 The treaty-specific report should be limited to 60 pages.

43 ibid para 12.

44 ibid para 13.

Optional Protocols. States parties should include statistical data as indicated in the annex to the present reporting guidelines.

(*Treaty-specific guidelines*, CRC/C/58/Rev.2 (23 November 2010) para 14)

The treaty-specific report also provides information organised according to the various clusters of rights, identified above, indicating the 'progress and challenges in achieving full respect for the provisions of the Convention and Optional Protocols'. Information on actions taken to implement the recommendations from previous Concluding Observations of the Committee as they relate to each cluster is particularly welcome.[45]

As stated earlier in this chapter, one of the distinctive features of the Convention machinery is that NGOs have had a more intense impact, as compared with other international human rights treaty bodies, both at the stage of drafting the Convention and their input into the reporting and monitoring activity of the Committee. The Committee has acknowledged the key role of the coalition of NGOs in supporting the reporting process.[46] Additional guidelines for the participation of NGOs and individual experts in the pre-sessional working group of the Committee make it clear that the reference to 'other competent bodies' in the Convention[47] includes NGOs; they announce that this Convention is 'the only international human rights treaty that expressly gives NGOs a role in monitoring its implementation'.[48] Requests by national, regional and international NGOs (INGOs) to participate should be submitted to the Committee through its secretariat at least two months prior to the pre-sessional working group. Based on the written information received, the Committee then selects NGOs to participate in the pre-sessional working group meeting (which is closed to the public). Detailed guidance on NGO submissions is provided by the NGO Group (NGO Group for the Convention on the Rights of the Child 2006). This Group was established in 1983 to influence the drafting of the Convention. The NGO Group is now known as Child Rights Connect and its website indicates the group's reach is currently made up of a registered network of 86 national and international NGOs committed to children's rights. Child Rights Connect holds special ECOSOC consultative status at the United Nations, and its core mission is 'to facilitate the promotion, implementation and monitoring of the Convention on the Rights of the Child'.[49]

---

45 ibid para 17.
46 See Committee on the Rights of the Child, General Comment No 5: *General measures of implementation for the Convention on the Rights of the Child*, CRC/GC/2003/5 para 59.
47 '(a) ... The Committee may invite the specialized agencies, the United Nations Children's Fund and other competent bodies as it may consider appropriate to provide expert advice on the implementation of the Convention in areas falling within the scope of their respective mandates...' CRC art 45(a). See also Detrick (1992: 25).
48 See 'Guidelines for the participation of partners (NGOs and individual experts) in the pre-sessional working group of the Committee on the Rights of the Child', *Report on the 22nd session*, CRC/C/90 (7 December 1999) Annex VIII para 1.
49 See Child Rights Connect http://www.childrightsnet.org/NGOGroup/ (accessed 6 June 2013).

There is nothing in the Convention itself to indicate any consequence or sanction for the non-submission of reports. The Committee's Rules of Procedure state that non-submission will result in the Committee sending to the states party 'a reminder concerning the submission of such report or additional information and undertake any other efforts in a spirit of dialogue between the State concerned and the Committee', and if the party remains recalcitrant the Committee can report this to the General Assembly.[50]

Currently, around nine states parties are invited to submit reports to be considered at each its regular plenary sessions. Priority is given to the examination of *initial* reports and the Committee will take into account the criterion of the chronological order of submissions. A states party's report will first be sent to the Secretariat of the Committee at the Office of the High Commissioner for Human Rights (OHCHR) in Geneva. The Committee will examine it at the next available session and currently attempts to examine reports within one year of receipt. Following receipt of the country report, the Committee will seek written information from other sources, such as NGOs National Human Rights Institutions (NHRIs) and inter-governmental organisations. This information is then reviewed during the Committee's pre-sessional working group. This is a *private* session composed of Committee members, where an initial review of the states party's report is carried out. NGOs and inter-governmental organisation representatives may be invited to attend the pre-sessional working group. The working group will then prepare a 'list of issues' that is submitted to the states party, to indicate the areas which the Committee considers to be priorities for discussion. States parties are requested to respond to these questions in writing, prior to the plenary session, which currently usually takes place within around seven months of the pre-sessional meeting.

During the plenary session, which (in contrast to the pre-sessional working group meeting) is held in *public*, the Committee examines the country report in the presence of the government representatives, who are invited to respond to the questions and comments made by Committee members. The Committee recommends that representatives of the government who are directly involved at the national level with the implementation of the Convention be present for the examination of the report. If the states party delegation has genuine participation and responsibility for strategy relating to children's rights the dialogue generated at the session is more likely to have impact on the formulation of policy and implementation activity.

The Committee devotes one day (two meetings of three hours each) to its public examination of states parties' reports and will usually appoint two Committee members to act as 'country rapporteurs' and lead the discussion with the states party delegation. Journalists are free to attend, in addition to NGO representatives and any interested individual. The order of play of the session procedure is described as follows:

50 *Rules of Procedure* (n 25) r 71.

After a brief introductory statement by the head of delegation the interactive dialogue starts. The Chairperson of the Committee will request the country rapporteur(s) to provide a brief overview of the state of child rights in the concerned State party. Thereafter the Chairperson will invite the Committee members to ask questions or make comments on the first cluster of rights, and the delegation may respond. The discussion moves step by step through the next group of issues identified in the reporting guidelines.

Towards the end of the discussion, the country rapporteurs summarize their observations on the report and the discussion itself and may also make suggestions and recommendations. Lastly, the State delegation is invited to make a final statement.

('Working Methods', Committee's website http://www2.ohchr.org/
english/bodies/crc/workingmethods.htm (accessed 7 June 2013))

After this dialogue, the Committee prepares, in a closed meeting at the end of the session, its Concluding Observations, which summarise the main points of discussion and pinpoint the key issues requiring further action and follow-up by the states party. It usually takes between two and three hours for its discussion of each set of Concluding Observations. Concluding Observations usually contain the following elements: an introduction; positive aspects including the progress achieved; factors impeding implementation; main subjects for concern; suggestions and recommendations addressed to the states party. The Concluding Observations are made public on the last day of a Committee session during the adoption of the session report. It is assumed that the concerns indicated in the Committee's Concluding Observations will be addressed in the country's next periodic report. All the relevant documentation of the reporting process is available from the Committee's website. For the purposes of maintaining an up-to-date register of the status of states parties' submission of reports and the adoption of related Concluding Observations, the Committee regularly issues a document that contains information on the exceptional measures taken to address late or non-reporting states parties.[51]

The throughput of states party reports has been around the same level for a number of years. Table 3.2 below shows the number of report examinations brought to a Concluding Observation in each of the sessions planned to take place in 2014 and 2015 respectively.

In earlier years the total number each year discloses a similar pattern.[52]

There is also a comparable reporting regime to the reporting process under the main Convention in relation to the obligations imposed by the Optional Protocol to the Convention on the Rights of the Child on the Sale of Children,

---

51 See for example: *States parties to the Convention on the Rights of the Child and its two Optional Protocols and related status of submission of reports: Note by the Secretary-General*, CRC/C/63/2, Committee on the Rights of the Child (17 May 2013).

52 2008: 30; 2009: 29; 2010: 54; 2011: 30; 2012: 35; 2013: 34.

Table 3.2 Number of state reports considered by the Committee on the Rights of the Child in 2014 and 2015, under the Convention and the two substantive Optional Protocols

Session No.	Month	CRC	OPSC	OPAC	Sub-totals
		Year 2014			
65th session	January	6	2	4	12
66th session	May	5	3	3	11
67th session	September	5	2	3	10
Total 2014					33
		Year 2015			
68th session	January	11	4	5	20
69th session	May	6	2	4	12
70th session	September	6	2	2	10
Total 2015					42

Child Prostitution and Child Pornography[53] (OPSC), and the Optional Protocol to the Convention on the Rights of the Child on the Involvement of Children in Armed Conflict[54] (OPAC). It is required that each states party must submit an initial report within two years following the entry into force for that states party, providing information on the measures it has taken to implement the provisions of the Protocol(s). Following the submission of this 'comprehensive' initial report, states parties are then obliged to submit any further information with respect to the implementation of the Protocol(s), in the periodic reports submitted to the Committee in accordance with Article 44 of the main Convention. States parties to the Optional Protocol(s) who are *not* parties to the main Convention (eg the USA) must submit subsequent reports every five years. The two sets of guidelines for OPSC[55] and OPAC[56] set out the categories of information requested from states parties. These obviously differ in their detail, but they share the following generic categories: general measures of implementation; prevention; prohibition; protection; international assistance and cooperation. These guidelines are aptly summarised by the NGO Group:

> The guidelines ... request States parties to provide information on progress and obstacles encountered in fulfilling obligations under the Protocols,

53 25 May 2000, 2171 UNTS 227 (entered into force 18 January 2002) art 12.

54 25 May 2000, 2173 UNTS 222 (entered into force 12 February 2002) art 8.

55 *Revised Guidelines Regarding Initial Reports to be Submitted by States parties under Article 12, Paragraph 1, of the Optional Protocol to the Convention on the Rights of the Child on the Sale of Children, Child Prostitution and Child Pornography*, CRC/C/OPSC/2 (3 November 2006).

56 *Revised Guidelines Regarding Initial Reports to be Submitted by States parties under Article 8, Paragraph 1, of the Optional Protocol to the Convention on the Rights of the Child on Involvement of Children in Armed Conflict*, CRC/C/OPAC/2 (19 October 2007).

budget allocation, and detailed disaggregated statistical data. Reports should also provide information on legal status, coordination, dissemination and awareness-raising and whether, and in what ways, the implementation of the Protocols are in line with the general principles of the Convention. It should also provide information on the involvement of non-governmental organizations in the preparation of the report.

(NGO Group for the Convention on the Rights of the Child 2006: 6)

The Committee issued a Recommendation in 2005 on the consideration of reports under the two Optional Protocols.[57] The procedures for reporting under the main Convention apply to the examination of country reports on the Optional Protocols. If a states party submits reports under both Optional Protocols at the same time, they will be considered at the next session of the Committee and given a maximum of six hours to consider both reports. If a states party only submits its report under OPSC it will receive a half-day slot at the next available session. However, where a states party only submits its report under OPAC, the Committee will not automatically examine it, except where it determines that the states party is 'facing or had recently faced serious difficulties in respecting and implementing [OPAC]'.[58] Other states parties are given the option of oral examination with a government delegation, or a technical review (a closed meeting), and the latter will take place in private without any governmental delegation present. As at May 2013, the Committee had processed 98 initial reports and one second periodic report under OPAC, and 83 initial reports and one second periodic report under OPSC.[59]

A significant weakness of the Committee, as with some of the other international human rights treaty bodies, has been the delays in managing the states party reporting process. This is all the more serious in the context of the Committee's work because, as explained earlier, the reporting process remains the core sanctioning mechanism available under the Convention, at least until such time as the communications procedure under the third Optional Protocol (section 3.6) comes into force. The problem of delay is twofold. First, there has been delay by the Committee itself in managing the reporting process. Secondly, there have been delays by some states parties in producing their initial and periodic reports. The Committee has made some efforts to manage the reporting process more efficiently. In January 2000, it increased its workload to examine 27 reports per year, compared to the 18 per annum previously. Several of the Committee's

57 'Consideration of reports under the two Optional Protocols of the Convention on the Rights of the Child', Recommendation No 8, Committee on the Rights of the Child, *Report on the Thirty-Ninth Session*, CRC/C/150 (21 December 2005).

58 ibid r 3(a).

59 *States parties to the Convention on the Rights of the Child and its two Optional Protocols and related status of submission of reports: Note by the Secretary-General*, CRC/C/63/2, Committee on the Rights of the Child (17 May 2013) para 6.

Recommendations[60] to date have been concerned with trying to address the delays experienced in the reporting cycle. In January 2002, the Committee recommended a system of 'combined reports' for states where the reporting cycle had been delayed. In May 2002, the Committee recommended that reports should not be too lengthy and should focus more on key developments and progress in actual implementation. In January 2003, the Committee added an additional rule requiring a combined second and third report where the second periodic report was due between one and two years following the dialogue with the Committee about its initial report. In September 2003, a Recommendation acknowledged that there was a two-year delay between the submission of reports and consideration by the Committee, and noted there were 13 initial reports and around 100 second periodic reports overdue.[61] It also acknowledged the extra workload caused by the reporting procedures under the two (substantive) Optional Protocols that would be expected from January 2004. The Committee proposed to work in two chambers in order to clear a target of 48 reports a year rather than 27 as previously.[62] However, it can be seen from Table 3.2 (above) that, nearly a decade later, this target had not been achieved (though in 2010 there were a total of 54 reports). The number of report examinations brought to Concluding Observations by the Committee, despite these organisational reforms, has averaged only 35.9 per annum in the six years from 2008. In 2010, the Committee continued its practice to allow states parties whose reports have been delayed to submit *combined* periodic reports and that, in compliance with the adoption of the Harmonized Treaty Specific Guidelines,[63] future states party reports should not exceed 60 pages. Finally, the Committee adopted another Decision in 2011 requesting approval from the General Assembly to work in two chambers in one of its three sessions every year. The request in 2004, implemented in 2006, to work in two chambers had resulted in clearing the backlog of reports awaiting review. However, '[w]hen the Committee resumed single-chamber sessions, a backlog again began to accumulate'. In 2008, the Committee requested a further four two-chamber sessions and three were approved and held in 2010 (which led to the highest number of reports processed to date of 54 in that year). However, Decision No 10 notes that since the last double-chamber sessions in October 2010, 'the backlog has again begun to increase and currently stands at approximately 90 reports'.[64] The Committee concluded that it would require one of its three annual sessions to be held in two chambers every year. The Committee, sitting in two

---

60 Recommendation No 3 (2002); Recommendation No 4 (2002); Recommendation No 5 (2003), Recommendation No 6 (2003); Decision No 8 (2005); Decision No 9 (2010); Decision No 10 (2011).
61 Recommendation No 5 (2003).
62 Recommendation No 6 (2003).
63 CRC/C/58/Rev.2.
64 'Decision of the Committee on the Rights of the Child to request approval from the General Assembly at its sixtysixth session to work in two chambers once per year', Decision No 10, Committee on the Rights of the Child (11 February 2011).

parallel chambers, each consisting of nine members would, the Committee calculated, increase the number of reports to be examined from 10 to 18 during one annual session, resulting in an annual increase from 30 to 38 reports a year.[65]

The twofold problem of delay – prevarication in the submission of country reports, and the Committee's own inability to process work expeditiously – remains a significant challenge in the Committee's work. If this problem of delay in the reporting process is not successfully managed, the impact is likely to be corrosive of the underlying aims of the Convention, and the resulting demoralisation within the international community may threaten the legitimacy of this type of international human rights instrument.

In addition to managing the periodic reporting cycle, the Committee must also submit reports about its own activities every two years to the General Assembly through ECOSOC.[66] These biennial reports[67] provide an update on the organisation and activities of the Committee, the submission of reports, membership and officers of the Committee, and some analysis of the overall progress achieved in the period under review. The Committee may also recommend to the General Assembly that the Secretary-General undertakes on its behalf a study on a specific issue relating to children's rights.[68]

In addition, there is a requirement under the recent Optional Protocol to the UN Convention on the Rights of the Child on a Communications Procedure[69] (OPIC) for the Committee to include in its report to the General Assembly a summary of its activities under that Protocol.[70] A further provision of the Convention requires the Committee to submit to specialised agencies, UNICEF and 'other competent bodies' any reports from states parties 'that contain a request, or indicate a need, for technical advice or assistance, along with the Committee's observations and suggestions, if any, on these requests or indications'.[71] The Committee decided in one of its sessions in 1993 that, when appropriate, it would indicate the possible need for technical assistance in is Concluding Observations on states parties' reports.[72]

Finally, the Committee is also empowered to make 'suggestions and general recommendations' based on the information received via the reporting process[73] and transmit these to any states party concerned.

---

65 ibid.
66 CRC art 44(5). The *Rules of Procedure* r 68 (n 18), add that the Committee may also 'submit such other reports as it considers appropriate'.
67 See for example: *Report of the Committee on the Rights of the Child*, A/67/41, General Assembly (21 June 2012).
68 CRC art 45(c).
69 28 February 2012, UN Doc A/RES/66/138 (not yet in force).
70 ibid; OPIC art 16.
71 CRC art 45(b).
72 Implementation Handbook at 656, citing Committee on the Rights of the Child, 3rd session, CRC/C/16 (January 1993) paras 139–45.
73 CRC art 45(d).

3.6   The optional protocols

There are now three Optional Protocols to the Convention:

(i)   the Optional Protocol to the Convention on the Rights of the Child on the Sale of Children, Child Prostitution and Child Pornography (OPSC)[74]

(ii)   the Optional Protocol to the Convention on the Rights of the Child on the Involvement of Children in Armed Conflict (OPAC)[75] and

(iii)   the Optional Protocol to the Convention on the Rights of the Child on a Communications Procedure (OPIC).[76]

It should be noted that an Optional Protocol is *not* an amendment to the text of a UN Convention. It is an *addition* to the main Convention on any topic relevant in the original treaty. Such Protocols are 'optional' as states may not wish to have the burden of additional duties to those in the main Convention that they have already ratified. In this text we shall refer to the OPSC and the OPAC as the two 'substantive' Optional Protocols, whereas the OPIC provides a 'procedural' process. As will be seen, the text of the OPIC establishes three procedures enabling complaints to be addressed to the Committee in relation to the violation of children's rights containing in the main Convention and/or either of the two substantive Optional Protocols. The OPIC entered into force three months after the deposit of the tenth ratification or accession, on 14 April 2014.[77] The reporting regime applicable to the two substantive Optional Protocols has been referred to above. As the third Optional Protocol (OPIC) is essentially a procedural instrument there is no country reporting system as such, but there is a requirement for the Committee to include a summary of its activities under the OPIC in its biennial report to the General Assembly.[78]

It should also be observed that the USA, which has conspicuously failed to ratify the main Convention to date, nevertheless *has* ratified both of the two substantive Optional Protocols. The following sections provide an overview of each Optional Protocol. The OPAC and the OPSC are discussed in further detail in Chapters 7 and 8 respectively.

---

74 25 May 2000, 2171 UNTS 227 (entered into force 18 January 2002). The OPSC had 120 signatories and 166 ratifications as at 15 February 2014.

75 25 May 2000, 2173 UNTS 222 (entered into force 12 February 2002). The OPAC had 129 signatories and 154 ratifications as at 15 February 2014.

76 28 February 2012, UN Doc A/RES/66/138 (entered into force 14 April 2014). The OPIC had 45 signatories and 10 ratifications as at 15 February 2014.

77 ibid. OPIC art 19(1).

78 OPIC art 16; CRC art 44(5).

3.6.1   Optional Protocol to the Convention on the Rights of the Child on the Sale of Children, Child Prostitution and Child Pornography (OPSC)[79]

The overall aim of the OPSC is to better achieve the implementation of various provisions in the Convention[80] relating to the prevention of a range of sexual and economic forms of exploitation. There was particular concern about the practice of 'sex tourism', the vulnerability of the girl child and the growing availability of child pornography on the internet and other social media. The drafting of the OPSC was prompted by an increasing international concern[81] about the traffic in children for the purposes of the sale of children, child prostitution and child pornography. The OPSC was developed in parallel with the Protocol to Prevent, Suppress and Punish Trafficking in Persons, Especially Women and Children[82] that supplements the UN Convention against Transnational Organized Crime.[83] In short, the OPSC was drafted in order to ensure the criminalisation of certain behaviours and better to provide for the protection of child victims. The 'sale of children', 'child prostitution' and 'child pornography' are given definitions in the OPSC, and states parties are enjoined to 'prohibit' such activities.[84] In particular, each state party must ensure 'as a minimum' that these activities, so defined, are 'fully covered under its criminal or penal law, whether such offences are committed domestically or transnationally or on an individual or organized basis'.[85] The OPSC also contains a general provision ensuring that nothing in the Protocol will affect any element of either domestic or international law that may be 'more conducive to the realization of the rights of the child'.[86] States parties are obliged to take necessary measures to establish jurisdiction over such defined offences, when the offences are committed in its territory, or when the offender or victim is a national of that state.[87] The OPSC also deems these offences to be included as extraditable offences in any extradition treaties between states parties.[88] States parties are further enjoined to provide measures of assistance with one another in respect of the Protocol offences including obtaining evidence at their disposal.[89] International cooperation is also supported in the OPSC by

---

79 25 May 2000, 2171 UNTS 227 (entered into force 18 January 2002). OPSC had 120 signatories and 166 ratifications as at 15 February 2014.

80 The preamble to OPSC refers to CRC arts 1, 11, 21, 32–36.

81 The preamble to OPSC refers to the International Conference on Combating Child Pornography on the Internet (Vienna, 1999); and, a programme of action and Declaration adopted at the World Congress against Commercial Sexual Exploitation of Child (Stockholm, 1996).

82 15 November 2000, 2237 UNTS 319 (entered into force 25 December 2003).

83 15 November 2000, 2225 UNTS 209 (entered into force 29 September 2003).

84 OPSC arts 1 and 2.

85 ibid art 3(1).

86 ibid art 11. Comparable provisions also appear in CRC art 41 and OPAC art 5.

87 OPSC art 4.

88 ibid art 5.

89 ibid art 6. States parties are additionally obliged, subject to their national law, to take measures to provide for the seizure and confiscation of certain goods and proceeds relating to the Protocol

provisions encouraging states parties to strengthen their cooperation around relevant multilateral, regional and bilateral arrangements, and between their own authorities and NGOs, INGOs and international organisations.[90]

The OPSC also establishes a set of legal normative standards to guide states parties in adopting measures to protect the rights and interests of *child victims*.[91] This ensures, inter alia, that the 'best interests of the child shall be a primary consideration' in their treatment by the criminal justice system.[92] The protection of child victims and witnesses was also given more detailed attention in Guidelines proposed by the International Bureau of Children's Rights[93] and adopted by ECOSOC in 2005.[94] The focus in the OPSC on the protection of child victims is further strengthened by obligations on states parties to take all feasible measures to ensure assisting such victims, including 'their full social reintegration and their full physical recovery', and that they have access to adequate procedures to seek compensation.[95] A country reporting regime,[96] comparable to the one under the main Convention, is also established under the OPSC, as discussed above.

It is interesting to note, however, that the proposal for an OPSC was not actively supported by the Committee, unlike its support for the OPAC. Hodgkin and Newell (2007: 669) provide the following explanation:

> It was felt that the issues were already addressed within the Convention, that they should not be seen in isolation but holistically within the broad range of children's human rights, and that energies should rather be put into strengthening the implementation of existing rights than into the creation of new instruments. Nonetheless the desire for more detailed state responsibilities to tackle these forms of child abuse, particularly as regards the prosecution and extradition of "sex tourists", ultimately ensured the Optional Protocol's adoption.

offences and to take measures aimed at closing premises used to commit such offences (CRC art 7).

90 OPSC art 10. The promotion of international cooperation is formulated explicitly 'to address the root causes, such as poverty and underdevelopment' contributing to children's exploitation; see ibid art 10(3).

91 Or 'child survivors', the term preferred by NGOs.

92 OPSC art 8.

93 An international non-governmental organisation, based in Montreal, Canada, established in 1994. It was given consultative status with ECOSOC in 2005: see http://www.ibcr.org/eng/home.html (accessed 12 June 2013).

94 ECOSOC 'Guidelines on Justice in Matters involving Child Victims and Witnesses of Crime', Res 2005/20 (22 July 2005).

95 OPSC art 9.

96 ibid art 12.

3.6.2   Optional Protocol to the Convention on the Rights of the Child on the Involvement of Children in Armed Conflict (OPAC)[97]

The age at which children should be permitted to participate in armed conflict, as stated earlier in this chapter, was one of four key issues that were the subject of controversy during the drafting of the Convention. Article 38 of the Convention obliges states parties: to respect the rules of international humanitarian law relevant to children; to take all feasible measures to ensure that persons under *15 years of age* do not 'take a direct part in hostilities'; to refrain from recruiting persons under the age of 15 years into their armed forces; and, to protect the civilian population in armed conflicts, including taking feasible measures to protect children affected by armed conflict. A proposal for a Protocol to strengthen this provision was proposed in the Committee's first 'Day of General Discussion' in 1992.[98] The OPAC was prompted by the international community's concern about 'the harmful and widespread impact of armed conflict on children and the long-term consequences it has for durable peace, security and development'.[99] Given the basic definition of a child in the Convention of an individual below the age of 18 years, it is not surprising that there was international discomfort with the age limitation of the protection in Article 38 to only those under 15 years of age. However, some consistency was achieved with the inclusion of the definition of the war crime of conscripting or enlisting children, again under the age of 15 years, or using them to participate actively in hostilities (in both inter- and intra-state conflicts), in the text of the Rome Statute of the International Criminal Court (1998).[100] Nevertheless, setting the threshold at *18 years* gained in popularity, and, as the preamble to the OPAC notes, the 26th International Conference of the Red Cross and Red Crescent recommended in 1995 that 'parties to conflict take every feasible step to ensure that children below the age of 18 years do not take part in hostilities'.[101]

Reflecting a paradigm shift in the global pattern of armed conflicts from inter-state conflicts to a preponderance of intra-state conflicts, the OPAC also contains a more explicit recognition of the need to expand the coverage of international law to not only recruitment into the state's armed forces, but also recruitment by non-state militias into 'armed groups distinct from the armed forces of a State, and recognizing the responsibility of those who recruit, train and use children in

---

97 25 May 2000, 2173 UNTS 222 (entered into force 12 February 2002). The OPAC had 129 signatories and 154 ratifications as at 15 February 2014.

98 Committee on the Rights of the Child, *Report of the second session*, CRC/C/10 (19 October 1992) para 75(e) http://www2.ohchr.org/english/bodies/crc/docs/discussion/conflict.pdf (accessed 25 June 2013).

99 OPAC preamble §3.

100 Opened for signature 17 July 1998, 2187 UNTS 90 (entered into force 1 July 2002) arts 8(2)(b) (xxvi) and 8(2)(e)(vii).

101 OPAC preamble §9.

this regard'.[102] In addition, it also recognises the need to strengthen international cooperation in the implementation of the Protocol as well as the 'physical and psychosocial rehabilitation and social reintegration of children who are victims of armed conflict'.[103]

The OPAC requires states parties to take 'all feasible measures' to ensure that members of their *armed forces* under the age of 18 years 'do not take a direct part in hostilities',[104] and must ensure that those under 18 years of age 'are not compulsorily recruited into their armed forces'.[105] A key provision requires states parties to raise the minimum age for voluntary recruitment into their national armed forces from 15 years as required by the Convention, by means of a declaration to be made upon ratification or accession, setting out a raised minimum age for these purposes, in addition to 'a description of the safeguards it has adopted to ensure that such recruitment is not forced or coerced'. A number of minimum standards relating to these safeguards are set out in this provision.[106] Many states made declarations asserting that 18 is the state's minimum age for either voluntary recruitment or conscription, thus complying with the position taken by the Committee and some states parties that failed to reach a consensus in the drafting process. However, there are other states that have specified minimum ages of 16 years (eg United Kingdom, Canada, India), or 17 years (eg USA, Australia, France, Germany, Israel, New Zealand): see Hodgkin and Newell (2007: 662) for a list of minimum ages for recruitment.

By contrast, the OPAC requires that *armed groups* (as distinct from state-sponsored *armed forces*) 'should not, under any circumstances, recruit or use in hostilities persons under the age of 18 years'. States parties are obliged to take all feasible measures to prevent such recruitment or use, including the criminalisation of such practices.[107] The OPAC also contains a provision clarifying that the Protocol is without prejudice to any provisions in domestic, international or humanitarian law that may be 'more conducive to the realization of the rights of the child'.[108] In addition to a general duty placed on states parties to 'take all necessary legal, administrative and other measures to ensure the effective implementation and enforcement' of the OPAC, they are also obliged to take all feasible measures 'to ensure that persons within their jurisdiction recruited or used in hostilities' contrary to the Protocol 'are demobilized or otherwise released from

---

102 ibid §11.

103 ibid §17. OPAC art 7 obliges states parties to cooperate with each other in the implementation of the Protocol.

104 ibid art 1.

105 ibid art 2.

106 ibid art 3 and see also CRC. There is an exception prescribed from the requirement to raise the minimum age in relation to 'schools operated by or under the control of the armed forces of the States parties': see ibid art 3(5). Some of the states parties' declarations indicate that children may be enrolled in military schools earlier than the prescribed minimum age.

107 ibid art 4.

108 ibid art 5. Comparable provisions also appear in CRC art 41 and OPSC art 11.

service' and to provide such persons with 'appropriate assistance for their physical and psychological recovery and their social reintegration'.[109] A country reporting regime,[110] comparable to the one under the main Convention, is also established under the OPAC, discussed above.

Many stakeholders in the working group drafting the Protocol wanted protection of all under-18-year-olds from any involvement in hostilities, direct or indirect, and any recruitment into the armed forces, irrespective of whether this was conscription or voluntary. However, as Hodgkin and Newell (2007: 660) comment:

> The resulting text is a compromise which does improve the protection offered by Article 38 of the Convention, but falls short of the clear standards sought by the Committee on the Rights of the Child, many States parties and many non-governmental organizations concerned with children's rights.

3.6.3 Optional Protocol to the Convention on the Rights of the Child on a Communications Procedure (OPIC)[111]

Prior to the appearance of the OPIC in 2012, it was the case that the Convention on the Rights of the Child was the only international human rights treaty that did not have a communication/complaints procedure attached to it. Part of the explanation for the absence of a complaints procedure in the Convention 'has been attributed to the NGO Ad Hoc Group's insistence during the CRC negotiations on a positive atmosphere for implementation' (Türkelli and Vandenhole 2012). NGOs started to campaign vigorously in 2007 for a communications procedure, a process helped considerably by the adoption of communication procedures by other treaty bodies.

A particular turning point was the adoption of the Optional Protocol of the International Covenant on Economic, Social and Cultural Rights (OP-ICESCR) in 2008.[112] Thereafter, it became more difficult to sustain objections to the *justiciability* of economic, social and cultural rights.[113] The Human Rights Council (HRC) established an open-ended working group (OEWG) in 2009.[114] It would appear that, as with the main Convention, the NGOs had a significant

---

109 ibid art 6(1) and (3).

110 ibid art 8.

111 28 February 2012, UN Doc A/RES/66/138 (not yet in force). The OPIC had 45 signatories and 10 ratifications as at 15 February 2014.

112 10 December 2008, UN Doc A/RES/63/117 (entered into force 5 May 2013). This Protocol had 45 signatories and 12 parties as at 15 February 2014.

113 Human Rights Council, *Report of the open-ended working group to explore the possibility of elaborating an optional protocol to the Convention on the Rights of the Child to provide a communications procedure*, 1st session report, UN Doc A/HRC/13/43 (21 January 2010, adopted 18 December 2009) [28] (OEWG 2010).

114 Human Rights Council, UN Doc A/HRC/11/L.3 (12 June 2009).

influence on international agenda-setting in this context (Türkelli, Vandenhole and Vandenbogaerde 2013; Buck and Wabwile 2013). During the OEWG discussions, some thought that the new Protocol ought not to merely duplicate the communications procedure texts drawn from other human rights treaty bodies; the new Protocol should reflect child-sensitive procedures in compliance with the principles and policy of the main Convention.[115] Amongst a number of arguments offered for its elaboration, the first session report of the OEWG records that: it would have potential to provide a remedy where the national system fails; it would develop a jurisprudence and contribute to the interpretation of the Convention; and, there would be no interference with national jurisdictions as it would require the exhaustion of domestic remedies. The report also notes that the procedure would 'give content to the right to be heard' and would be 'a child sensitive mechanism'.[116] The Chairperson-Rapporteur of the OEWG noted that 'the effectiveness of the procedure would depend to a large extent on its accessibility by children'.[117] The report of the second session of the OEWG[118] was adopted on 16 February 2011 and contains a record of the detailed consideration given to the revised drafts. A further HRC resolution adopting the final text and recommending adoption by the General Assembly followed on 17 June 2011.[119] The text was adopted by the General Assembly on 19 December 2011[120] and opened for signature on 28 February 2012.[121] The Rules of Procedure appeared in April 2013.[122]

The OPIC establishes three complaints procedures:

- individual communications
- inquiry procedure and
- inter-state communications.

The OPIC and the OPIC Rules of Procedure set out some general principles and methods of work that apply to all three procedures.[123] The Committee, in fulfilling its functions under the OPIC, shall be guided by the 'best interests' principle and also have regard to the rights and views of the child(ren). It must also take appropriate measures to ensure that children are 'not subject to improper pres-

---

115 OEWG 2010 (n 113).

116 ibid [31].

117 Drahoslav Štefánek (Slovakia): OEWG 2010 [40].

118 Human Rights Council, *Report of the open-ended working group on an optional protocol to the Convention on the Rights of the Child to provide a communications procedure*, second session report, UN Doc A/HRC/17/36 (25 May 2011, adopted 16 February 2011) (OEWG 2011).

119 Human Rights Council, UN doc A/HRC/RES/17/18 (14 July 2011, adopted 17 June 2011).

120 General Assembly, UN Doc A/RES/66/138 (27 January 2012, adopted 19 December 2011).

121 Twenty states signed OP3-CRC on the date of the signing ceremony. There are, at the time of writing, 36 signatories and 6 ratifications to the OPIC.

122 *Rules of procedure under the Optional Protocol to the Convention on the Rights of the Child on a communications procedure*, CRC/C/62/3 (8 April 2013) (OPIC Rules of Procedure).

123 ibid rr 1–11.

sure or inducement' by those acting on their behalf.[124] There is also a general 'principle of expeditiousness' that applies to the Committee's handling of communications and it must also encourage the parties to avoid unnecessary delays.[125] In order to reduce the risk that complainants may suffer repercussions from their initiation of a communication, their identity shall not be revealed publicly without their express consent.[126] The protection measures established in the OPIC that oblige states parties to take appropriate steps to ensure that individuals are not subject to such negative repercussions are further supported in the OPIC Rules of Procedure, which specify that in the event of a states party's failure to comply in this regard, the Committee may request the states party to take appropriate measures 'urgently to stop the breach reported' and submit written responses to the Committee.[127] As regards methods of work, the Secretary-General is obliged to maintain permanent records of violations under all three procedures, and this information must be made available to any member of the Committee.[128] The Committee may also consult with independent experts, at its own initiative, or at the request of any of the parties.[129]

3.6.3.1   Individual Communications

Individual communications may be submitted 'by or on behalf of an individual or group of individuals' within a states party, claiming to be victims by that states party of any of the rights (to which the state is a party) in the main Convention, the OPSC and the OPAC. Where a communication is submitted *on behalf of* an individual or group of individuals, this must be with their consent 'unless the author can justify acting on their behalf without such consent'.[130] The Committee also has a power, following receipt of the communication and prior to determination on the merits, to request that the states party take 'interim measures as may be necessary in exceptional circumstances to avoid possible irreparable damage' to the victim(s) of the alleged violation.[131] Complaints must meet certain admissibility requirements before they are determined by the Committee, in particular, that the same matter has not already been examined by the Committee or has or is being examined under another international procedure, and that 'all domestic remedies have not been exhausted' unless 'the application of remedies is unreasonably prolonged or unlikely to bring effective relief'.[132] The OPIC Rules of Procedure envisage a dedicated working group to deal with admissibil-

---

124 See OPIC art 2 and OPIC Rules of Procedure r 1.
125 OPIC Rules of Procedure r 2.
126 ibid r 3; and OPIC art 4.
127 OPIC Rules of Procedure r 4.
128 ibid r 5.
129 ibid r 10.
130 OPIC art 5.
131 ibid art 6.
132 See ibid art 7(d) and (e).

ity determinations and transmit their recommendations for determination by the Committee.[133] The Committee must bring the communication *confidentially* to the attention of the states party concerned as soon as possible, and the latter must submit a written response within six months.[134] Rather than proceeding to a merits hearing, the complaint can be dealt with, and the case closed, by means of a 'friendly settlement' reached under the auspices of the Committee.[135] The friendly settlement procedure is confidential … If the complaint goes to a merits determination by the Committee this will be held in a closed meeting and the Committee must transmit its views on the communication and recommendations without delay to the parties concerned.[136] The OPIC Rules of Procedure make it clear that the Committee can, in effect, hold oral hearings inviting the complaint and/or alleged victim(s) and representatives of the states party.[137] The principle of confidentiality is further supported in the OPIC Rules of Procedure, which establishes a presumption that all the working documents 'shall be confidential unless the Committee decides otherwise'.[138] Furthermore, the names of complainants and victims of a communication shall not be published in an inadmissibility or merits decision, or a decision closing its consideration following a friendly settlement, except where express consent is forthcoming. However, subject to the requirements to obtain express consent of individuals concerned, the complainant or the states party is free to make public any submission or information bearing on the proceedings.[139] Following receipt of the Committee's views and recommendations, the states party must submit a written response 'including information on any action taken and envisaged' as soon as possible and within six months.[140]

3.6.3.2   Inquiry procedure

States parties may declare upon signature or ratification of the OPIC that they are opting out of the inquiry procedure.[141] Many delegations in the OEWG sessions supported an opt-out facility as it would promote wider acceptance of the Protocol.[142] The procedure obliges the Committee, upon receipt of 'reliable information indicating grave or systematic violations' by a states party of rights set forth in the Convention or either of the two substantive Optional Protocols, to invite the states party to cooperate in an inquiry, conducted by one or more of

---

133   Rules of Procedure r 20.
134   OPIC art 8.
135   ibid art 9.
136   ibid art 10.
137   Rules of Procedure r 19.
138   ibid r 29.
139   ibid.
140   OPIC art 11.
141   ibid art 13(7). Such states parties may at any time withdraw the declaration to opt out of the inquiry procedure: ibid art 13(8).
142   OEWG 2011 [86].

the Committee members.[143] In the case of such 'reliable information' it may 'on its own initiative' commence an inquiry.[144] The inquiry shall be conducted confidentially and may include a visit to the states party territory.[145] The Committee may designate one or more of its members to conduct an inquiry and report back to the Committee.[146] It would seem that the member(s) conducting the inquiry will have liberty 'to determine their own methods of work'.[147] The principle of confidentiality is further supported in the OPIC Rules of Procedure, which protects all documents and proceedings of the Committee relating to the inquiry, and provides that meetings will be closed.[148] The Committee must transmit its findings to the states party together with any comments or recommendations, and the states party is obliged to respond with its observations within six months of receiving the Committee's findings. The Committee may then, if necessary, follow-up by inviting the states party to inform it of the measures taken and envisaged in response to the inquiry, and also request further information in the states party's subsequent reports under the main Convention or either of the two substantive Optional Protocols.[149]

3.6.3.3   Inter-state communications

This procedure is initiated where one states party claims that another states party is not fulfilling its obligations under the main Convention and/or either of the two substantive Optional Protocols.[150] By contrast to the *opt-out* provision of the inquiry procedure discussed above, the inter-state communications procedure requires states parties to *opt in* by making a declaration 'at any time' recognising the competence of the Committee in this respect.[151] Furthermore, *both* states parties must have made such opt-in declarations for the Committee to have competence to consider the case.[152] Like the individual communications procedure, the inter-state communications procedure also has provision for the states parties to arrive at a 'friendly solution' of the matter by availing themselves of the Committee's good offices.[153] The OPIC Rules of Procedure expands on this latter point by providing that the Committee may establish 'an ad hoc conciliation

---

143 OPIC art 13.
144 OPIC Rules of Procedure r 31.
145 OPIC art 13(2) and (3). On visits to the states party territory, see further OPIC Rules of Procedure rr 38 and 39.
146 OPIC Rules of Procedure r 36(1).
147 ibid r 36(3).
148 ibid r 33.
149 OPIC art 14.
150 ibid art 12(1).
151 Of the 10 states parties that had ratified OPIC, at the time of writing, four (Albania, Germany, Portugal and Slovakia) had opted in to the inter-state communication procedure.
152 OPIC art 12(2); OPIC Rules of Procedure r 45.
153 OPIC art 12(3).

commission' to deal with the case.[154] The Rules envisage two outcome documents arising from this procedure. First, if a 'friendly solution' is reached, then the Committee will adopt a report confined to 'a brief statement of the facts and of the solution reached'. Secondly, if such a solution cannot be reached, then a more fulsome report by the Committee is envisaged, including its own views on the matter along with the written submissions by each party.[155]

It should be noted that this procedure, although it has precedents in the international law relating to other international human rights treaties, nevertheless has 'an uninspiring track record' (Buck and Wabwile 2013: 216), as the mechanism has never been used in practice in relation to the other UN human rights treaty bodies.[156] The underlying risks of this procedure being captured and politicised by more general inter-state rivalries are obvious, and may account for states' unwillingness to subscribe to the procedure, a consideration, which no doubt led to the insertion of the opt-in facility in order to forestall wholesale rejection of the Protocol by states.

3.7   The implementation of the Convention on the Rights of the Child

The Committee's Guidelines on how to prepare 'initial'[157] and 'periodic' state reports[158] group the provisions of the Convention into nine thematic clusters and request responses using this structure. This approach reflects the Convention's holistic perspective of children's rights, an approach that is consistent with the general human rights law principle that such rights are indivisible and inter-related, and that equal importance should be attached to each and every right.

There is a detailed account of the legal provenance of each article of the Convention given in Detrick (1999). In the following sections (3.7.1–3.7.9), however, an account of each of these nine 'clusters', as defined in the Guidelines, is given with reference to the interactions between the states parties and the Committee in the reporting process.

In this section, all the Committee's Concluding Observations on reports submitted under Article 44 of the Convention in the 61st, 62nd and 63rd sessions[159] have been reviewed to prepare a summary and illustrative examples of the points

---

154 OPIC Rules of Procedure r 47.

155 ibid r 49.

156 OEWG 2011 (n 118) [89]. However, they have been used under the European Convention for the Protection of Human Rights and Fundamental Freedoms, opened for signature 4 November 1950, 213 UNTS 221 (entered into force 3 September 1953).

157 *General Guidelines regarding the form and content of initial reports to be submitted by States parties under Article 44, paragraph 1(a), of the Convention,* CRC/C/5 (30 October 1991).

158 *Treaty-specific guidelines regarding the form and content of periodic reports to be submitted by States parties under article 44, paragraph 1 (b), of the Convention on the Rights of the Child,* CRC/C/58/Rev.2 (23 November 2010).

159 61st session – 17 September to 5 October 2012; 62nd session – 14 January to 1 February 2013; 63rd session – 27 May to 14 June 2013.

discussed under each theme. It is hoped that this will enable the reader to obtain an understanding not only of the standard-setting achieved by the text of the Convention, but also of the way in which it is actually being implemented in practice across a wide range of countries.

3.7.1   General measures of implementation: Articles 4, 42 and 44(6)

These Convention articles contain strongly worded provisions emphasising states parties' duties to *implement* and *disseminate* the principles and provisions of the Convention. Article 4 of the Convention obliges states parties to 'undertake all appropriate legislative, administrative, and other measures for the implementation of the rights recognized' in the Convention. However, the text of Article 4 also makes it clear that with regard to *economic, social and cultural rights*, the states parties' obligation to action implementation measures shall be undertaken 'to the maximum extent of their available resources and, where needed, within the framework of international co-operation'. Article 42 obliges states parties to 'make the principles and provisions of the Convention widely known, by appropriate and active means, to adults and children alike'. Article 44(6) places a duty on states parties to 'make their reports widely available to the public in their own countries'. The Committee has set out useful advice to states parties in its General Comment No 5[160] in 2003 on how these obligations can be pursued. It commends the development of a comprehensive and rights-based strategy built on the framework of the Convention. The Committee takes the view that economic, social and cultural rights, as well as civil and political rights, 'must be regarded as justiciable'.[161]

The 'general measures' cluster in the Committee's Concluding Observation usually opens with a commentary on the extent to which its recommendations and concerns in the previous reporting round have been addressed. The Committee will usually be able to find specific areas from the previous reporting cycle which it considers the states party has not sufficiently addressed. For example, it urged Austria to attend particularly to the withdrawal of reservations, coordination, non-discrimination and juvenile justice.[162]

Clearly, the assessment of the extent to which specifically 'legislative' measures have contributed towards successful implementation of the Convention is a significant task that is performed in the reporting process. The Committee will

---

160 Committee on the Rights of the Child, General Comment No 5: *General measures of implementation of the Convention on the Rights of the Child (arts 4, 42 and 44 para 6)* 34th session, CRC/GC/2003/5 (27 November 2003).

161 ibid [25].

162 CRC/C/AUT/CO/3-4 (5 October 2012) [7]. Similarly, the Committee noted with regret that recommendations from their concluding observations of Albania's initial report 'had not been sufficiently implemented, particularly those related to non-discrimination, abuse and neglect, children deprived of a family environment, children with disabilities and juvenile justice'. CRC/C/ALB/CO/2-4 (5 October 2012) [8].

welcome countries that proactively amend their national laws[163] or even their constitutions[164] to accommodate the legal standards set out in the Convention. For example, the Committee welcomed a new Children's Law in Liberia, although remained concerned that there were still inconsistencies between the new Law and existing legislation and some customary laws were inconsistent with the Convention, particularly relating to the minimum age of marriage, adoption and juvenile justice.[165] Austria was praised for its enactment of a Federal Constitution Law on the Rights of Children (2011), but the Committee noted its concern that the Law did not include all the rights in the Convention.[166] Equally, the Committee will express concern, for example in respect of Andorra, where it found an 'absence of specific legislation dedicated to child protection covering basic provisions of the Convention'.[167] Where laws have been drafted, their completion may have simply been delayed, sometimes for several years.[168] The Committee can frequently be seen to encourage states parties to bring their domestic law into conformity with the Convention and to strengthen their efforts towards formal recognition of it in domestic law, and will express concern where the Convention is not directly applicable by courts and cited in court judgments.[169] There are often challenges with countries that have a federal/state constitutional structure in receiving the Convention into their domestic systems in ways that are acceptable to the Committee and which avoid disparate application of the Convention, depending on whether this occurs within the federal, state or district levels of government jurisdiction. The Committee found, for example, that an absence of overall national legislation in Canada's federal system had resulted in fragmentation and inconsistencies in the implementation of children's rights and recommended that the states party find 'the appropriate constitutional path' to resolve matters.[170] Equally, the Committee will be concerned where a country, for example the Republic of Guinea, has a plural legal system which includes customary law and 'results in discrimination particularly against girls and encourages harmful practices'.[171] Domestic customary law is often viewed by the Committee as an obstacle to the implementation of the Convention.[172]

---

163 For example the Committee noted that Albania had adopted the Law on the Protection of the Rights of the Child on 4 November 2010, but was concerned about 'about the generally weak capacity of the State party to effectively implement child-related laws': CRC/C/ALB/CO/2-4 (5 October 2012) [9].

164 Guyana established a 'Rights of the Child Commission' following its revision of the constitution: CRC/C/GUY/CO/2-4 (5 February 2013) [18].

165 CRC/C/LBR/CO/2-4 (5 October 2012) [10].

166 ibid.

167 CRC/C/AND/CO/2 (9 October 2012) [9].

168 For example in Armenia: CRC/C/ARM/CO/3-4 (14 June 2013) [8].

169 CRC/C/UZB/CO/3-4 (14 June 2013) [8].

170 CRC/C/CAN/CO/3-4 (5 October 2012) [10–11].

171 CRC/C/GIN/CO/2 (30 January 2013) [11].

172 For example in Guinea-Bissau: CRC/C/GNB/CO/2-4 (14 June 2013) [10].

However, the Committee will go much further than a mere paper audit of child-friendly legislation. It will want to see that the legislation in question has a substantial impact in the real world. Regrettably, implementation is often measured by some states according to a rather narrow focus on the compatibility of its municipal legal system with Convention standards. Some countries have incorporated the Convention into their domestic laws, but the relationship between municipal and international law is often a subtle one. France's *Cour de Cassation*, for example, has recognised the direct applicability of the Convention to domestic law, and the *Conseil d'État* followed suit, but the Committee had to express concern that only a limited number of provisions of the Convention were recognised to have such direct effect.[173]

There were, at the time of writing, around 60 states parties that had current declarations and/or reservations on ratifying the Convention. The Committee routinely urges states to withdraw reservations; for example, it recommended that Canada should promptly withdraw its reservation to Article 37(c).[174] Over the years, many reservations have been withdrawn, for example, all four of the UK's reservations made upon ratification have now been withdrawn.[175] The facility to make reservations is often a useful diplomatic tool to persuade countries to ratify an international instrument. However, there are some limits to making them. Any reservation that is against the 'object and purpose' of the Convention would not be allowed,[176] and even if such reservations were not expressly prohibited in the Convention, they would be prohibited under the Vienna Convention on the Law of Treaties (1969).[177] The Committee has been concerned that some reservations plainly breach the Convention 'by suggesting, for example, that respect for the Convention is limited by the State's existing Constitution or legislation, including in some cases religious law'.[178]

The Committee rarely misses an opportunity to stress the need for countries that lack a national policy and strategy on children to develop and adopt these 'detailing a clear vision with strategies, objectives and specific benchmarks and indicators to address children's interest and concerns'.[179] It also encourages states to mainstream children's rights across all relevant sectors. In its quest to encourage states parties to develop comprehensive national policies, the

---

173   CRC/C/FRA/CO/4 (11 June 2009) [10].

174   'The Government of Canada accepts the general principles of article 37 (c) of the Convention, but reserves the right not to detain children separately from adults where this is not appropriate or feasible' CRC/C/CAN/CO/3-4 (5 October 2012) [9].

175   These reservations concerned: children's hearings in Scotland, younger workers, nationality and immigration issues, and child detention. They were withdrawn in respectively: 1997, 1999, 2008 and 2008. See Buck (2011: 99–102) for details of the UK's reservations.

176   CRC art 51(2).

177   Opened for signature 23 May 1969, 1155 UNTS 331 (entered into force 27 January 1980).

178   Committee on the Rights of the Child, General Comment No 5: *General measures of implementation of the Convention on the Rights of the Child (arts 4, 42 and 44 para 6)* 34th session, CRC/GC/2003/5 (27 November 2003) [15].

179   CRC/C/AND/CO/2 (9 October 2012) [12].

Committee emphasises the need for coordination and collaboration by different government entities and the clear identification of the lead government Ministry in managing a coordinated response. For example, it noted concern about the coordination in Albania of a 'multitude of actors' and lack of coherence between existing child rights institutions.[180] The Committee was also concerned that 'multiple ministries and other government bodies' were working 'without a common plan of action on children' in Andorra.[181] In Austria, there was no specific body at Federal and Länder levels with a clear mandate to coordinate.[182] Some countries have complex political and administrative structures that pose challenges for uniform application at a national level.[183] Even where there is an identifiable lead agency, the Committee will often find that it lacks sufficient authority or resources to meet an overall coordination role.[184] The Committee has pointed out that the decentralisation of government power does not in any way reduce states parties' direct responsibility to fulfil their responsibilities. Equally, such decentralisation or devolution may require safeguards to protect groups from discrimination. The Committee has encouraged states to adopt a continuous process of 'child impact assessment' and evaluation to be built into the policy-making process itself.

The requirement in the Convention for states parties to commit the 'maximum extent' of their available resources in pursuit of economic, cultural and social rights, under Article 4 is given further elaboration in one of the Committee's 'Days of General Discussion'. This makes it clear that states parties are expected to ensure that domestic adjudicating bodies are able 'to give full justiciability to economic, social and cultural rights of children'.[185] It also favours a principle of 'progressive realisation'[186] of these rights, a principle that imposes 'an immediate obligation to undertake targeted measures to move as expeditiously and effectively as possible towards the full realization of economic, social and cultural rights of children'.[187] In parallel with this principle, the Committee also takes the view that states parties are, at the least, obliged to satisfy a 'core minimum content' of such rights.[188] To that end, the Committee encourages states parties to consider legislating a specific proportion of public expenditure to be allocated to children and to make children a priority in budgetary allocations and consider using

---

180 CRC/C/ALB/CO/2-4 (5 October 2012) [13].
181 CRC/C/AND/CO/2 (9 October 2012) [13].
182 CRC/C/AUT/CO/3-4 (5 October 2012) [14].
183 For example, in Bosnia Herzegovina, there are two Entities and ten Cantons and administrative Districts: CRC/C/BIH/CO/2-4 (5 October 2012) [9, 11, 14].
184 For example CRC/C/GUY/CO/2-4 (5 February 2013) [12].
185 'Day of General Discussion' on *Resources for the Rights of the Child – Responsibility of States* in Committee on the Rights of the Child, *Report on the 46th session*, CRC/C/46/3 (22 April 2008) [42–95] http://www2.ohchr.org/english/bodies/crc/discussion2013.htm (accessed 26 June 2013).
186 A principle first developed by the Committee on Economic, Social and Cultural Rights.
187 'Day of General Discussion' on *Resources for the Rights of the Child – Responsibility of States* [47].
188 ibid [49]. This also makes reference to the Committee on Economic, Social and Cultural Rights' statement on the *Maximum of Available Resources*, UN Doc E/C.12.2007/1 (10 May 2007).

rights-based monitoring and analysis in addition to child impact assessments on how investments in any sector may serve children's best interests.[189] As with other matters, but especially in relation to questions about resources, the Committee will often apply higher standards and expectations of more affluent countries.[190] The Committee has noted that some states 'have claimed it is not possible to analyse national budgets in this way. But others have done it and publish annual "children's budgets"'.[191] The Committee is likely to make criticisms where it perceives budgetary allocations are inadequate For example, in relation to Albania, the Committee was concerned 'that the proportion of the budget allocated to areas of direct relevance to children has decreased over the reporting period, and that the state party relies excessively on civil society and international donors' and, additionally, the 'high level of corruption in the state party contributes to divert resources that could enhance the implementation of the rights of the child'.[192] The Committee identifies states parties where it considers that corruption remains pervasive as clearly this will impact on resource allocation processes.[193] Where data is available, discriminatory allocation is sometimes exposed. For example, the Committee noted with concern that the average spending per child in Israel in Arab areas was estimated to be more than a third lower than in Jewish localities.[194] In keeping with the 'Day of General Discussion' on resources, the Committee will pinpoint where there are weaknesses; for example, where there is no adequate tracking, monitoring and evaluation system for the allocations. For example, the Committee noted, in relation to Andorra, its concern about a lack of a specific budget allocated for implementation, the absence of a single mechanism to track such allocation, and a lack of strategic budgetary lines for children in vulnerable groups.[195] It focused its concern on Liberia's 'heavy dependency on donor funding of the social sectors benefiting children' as unsustainable,[196] and on the absence of a child's rights perspective in Slovenia's budgeting process.[197]

---

189 'Day of General Discussion' on *Resources for the Rights of the Child – Responsibility of States* [23, 30].

190 In relation to Canada, it observed: 'Bearing in mind that the State party is one of the most affluent economies of the world and that it invests sizeable amounts of resources in child-related programmes, the Committee notes that the State party does not use a child-specific approach for budget planning and allocation in the national and provinces/territories level budgets, thus making it practically impossible to identify, monitor, report and evaluate the impact of investments in children and the overall application of the Convention in budgetary terms': CRC/C/CAN/CO/3-4 (5 October 2012) [16].

191 General Comment No 5: *General measures of implementation of the Convention on the Rights of the Child* [51].

192 CRC/C/ALB/CO/2-4 (5 October 2012) [15].

193 See also CRC/C/LBR/CO/2-4 (5 October 2012) [18] and CRC/C/GIN/CO/2 (30 January 2013) [19], where the Committee was 'concerned that corruption remains pervasive in the State party'. The Committee was 'gravely concerned' about the severity and pervasiveness of corruption in Uzbekistan: CRC/C/UZB/CO/3-4 (14 June 2013) [14].

194 CRC/C/ISR/CO/2-4 (14 June 2013) [13].

195 CRC/C/AND/CO/2 (9 October 2012) [15].

196 CRC/C/LBR/CO/2-4 (5 October 2012) [16].

197 CRC/C/SVN/CO/3-4 (14 June 2013) [14].

The Committee has acknowledged that the obligations of the Convention, although placed on states parties, in practice stretch beyond state institutions and services and require the cooperation of civil society and the family. It urges governments to give NGOs non-directive support and develop sound links with them, and will often comment on the quality of cooperation with civil society organisations.[198] On occasion it may report 'deep concern', for example in relation to Rwanda, 'over reported threats, harassment, intimidation and arrests of human rights defenders'.[199] The Committee has also stressed that Article 4 requires *international* cooperation and urges states to meet internationally agreed targets. For example, it noted with concern Canada's record of achieving overseas development assistance with only 0.33 per cent of gross national income for 2010–11 compared with the recommended aid target of 0.7 per cent.[200]

The Committee often points out the need for states to collect reliable statistical data, appropriately disaggregated,[201] to enable the identification of discrimination and other disparities in realising children's rights.[202] It regularly requests data that identifies ethnic groups, age profiles, gender, street children, Roma children, refugee and asylum-seeker children, and encourages the development of nationally applicable and robust statistical indicators. The Committee often has to point out the need for some countries to establish a comprehensive data collection system.[203] Even where countries have established national statistics institutions that collect data on a regular basis, the Committee will pinpoint areas where the statistics are weak, for example, in Austria, where it took the view that data relating to migrant children, refugee and asylum-seeking children and other children in vulnerable situations was insufficiently disaggregated.[204]

While approving governments' self-monitoring and evaluation, the Committee also regards the *independent* monitoring of progress as essential. It encourages this, in particular, by recommending the establishment of independent human rights institutions. The Committee issued General Comment No 2 on this subject and it 'considers the establishment of such bodies to fall within the commitment made by states parties upon ratification to ensure the implementation of the Convention

---

198 See for example its criticisms of Israel's treatment of NGOs operating in the Occupied Palestinian Territory: CRC/C/ISR/CO/2-4 (14 June 2013) [17]; and the limited resources allocated to NGOs in Slovenia, CRC/C/SVN/CO/3-4 (14 June 2013) [14].

199 CRC/C/RWA/CO/3-4 (14 June 2013) [19].

200 CRC/C/CAN/CO/3-4 (5 October 2012) [18–19].

201 For example 'Data should include all children up to the age of 18 years, be disaggregated, inter alia, by age, sex, urban/rural area, ethnicity and socio-economic background to facilitate analysis on the situation of all children. CRC/C/ALB/CO/2-4 (5 October 2012) [18].

202 Committee on the Rights of the Child, General Comment No 5: *General measures of implementation of the Convention on the Rights of the Child (arts 4, 42 and 44(6))* 34th session, CRC/GC/2003/5 (27 November 2003) [12].

203 For example CRC/C/AND/CO/2 (9 October 2012) [17–18].

204 CRC/C/AUT/CO/3-4 (5 October 2012) [18].

and advance the universal realization of children's rights'.[205] However, such independent institutions should be seen as complementary to government structures; governments ought not merely to delegate their monitoring functions to them. The Committee typically recommends the establishment of a Children's Commissioner or Ombudsman where there is none. Some states parties do not have a functional independent national human rights institution.[206] Where there is a general national human rights institution it may lack an explicit mandate to investigate children's complaints,[207] or simply lack the required human and financial resources to operate successfully.[208] The Committee generally raises criticisms where it perceives that the body in question falls below the standard of independence as indicated in General Comment No 2[209] and the 'Paris Principles'.[210] More recently, it has expressed concern with states parties, such as Slovenia, whose Ombudsman Office was only credited with a 'B' status by the International Coordinating Committee of National Institutions for the Promotion and Protection of Human Rights.[211]

The duties to disseminate and publicise the Convention in Articles 42 and 44(6) are especially important. These duties often require relevant language translations for minority or indigenous groups, and programmes of rights awareness through mass media, professional training, school and other educational curricula. The Committee notes some of the positive efforts made; for example, an initiative to raise awareness of the Convention through the 'Day of the Namibian Child', or the efforts of countries such as Austria to disseminate via the internet.[212] The involvement of NGOs and children in such advocacy campaigns has

205 Committee on the Rights of the Child, General Comment No 2: *The role of independent national human rights institutions in the promotion and protection of the rights of the child*, 32nd session, CRC/GC/2002/2 (15 November 2002) [1].

206 For example the Republic of Guinea: CRC/C/GIN/CO/2 (30 January 2013) [23].

207 CRC/C/LBR/CO/2-4 (5 October 2012) [22].

208 CRC/C/RWA/CO/3-4 (14 June 2013) [17].

209 Committee on the Rights of the Child, General Comment No 2: *The role of independent national human rights institutions in the promotion and protection of the rights of the child*, 32nd session, CRC/GC/2002/2 (15 November 2002).

210 General Assembly, 'Principles Relating to the Status of Independent National Human Rights Institutions', RES/48/134 (20 December 1993) (Paris Principles).

211 CRC/C/SVN/CO/3-4 (14 June 2013) [18]. The International Coordinating Committee of National Institutions for the Promotion and Protection of Human Rights (ICC) is a representative body of national human rights institutions established in 1993 and aims to assist in establishing and strengthening independent and effective National Human Rights Institutions (NHRIs), which meet the international standards set out in the Paris Principles. One of its key functions is to provide accreditation of an 'A' status to NHRIs which comply fully with the Paris Principles. These are eligible to become voting members of the ICC and to hold governance positions. NHRIs which only partially comply with the Paris Principles – and which have been granted 'B status' by the ICC Bureau – can participate in meetings of the ICC but are not eligible to vote or to hold governance positions.

212 See respectively: CRC/C/NAM/CO/2-3 (16 October 2012) [22]; CRC/C/AUT/CO/3-4 (5 October 2012) [20].

become a hallmark of such activity. Indeed, the Committee has concluded that: '[o]ne of the satisfying results of the adoption and almost universal ratification of the Convention has been the development at the national level of a wide variety of new child-focused and child-sensitive bodies, structures and activities'.[213] However, the reporting process is still revealing low levels of awareness of the Convention; for example, the Committee notes, as regards Albania, the 'limited measures taken by the State party to promote awareness of the Convention and the fact that the States party's report was not shared with the media and/or the public at large'.[214] The Committee has commented on the low levels of public awareness in Niue, though praises efforts there to translate the states party's report into local languages and distribute it to the public.[215] In general, there do appear to be better reports emerging about the public's awareness of the Convention, at least in some countries. For example, in the UK's combined 3rd/4th periodic report to the Committee, it is stated that, in an online children's survey commissioned by the Department for Children, Schools and the Family, about 70 per cent of respondents reported some awareness of the Convention.[216]

The Committee frequently recommends that all professional groups working for and with children receive adequate and systematic training,[217] in particular law enforcement officials, teachers, health workers, social workers, religious leaders and those working in alternative care. The Committee also recommends states parties to take into account the principles contained in the World Programme for Human Rights Education[218] in designing their policies and strategies.[219]

The Committee issued General Comment No 16[220] in 2013 regarding the impact of the business sector on children's rights. This establishes that states parties are not relieved of their general obligations under the Convention 'when their functions are delegated or outsourced to a private business or non-profit organization' and a state will be in breach of its obligations 'where it fails to respect, protect and fulfil children's rights in relation to business activities and operations that impact on children.[221] The Committee has called, for example, for a clear regulatory framework to be established in Namibia in relation to mining and uranium-producing industries to ensure that their activities, involving high

---

213 Committee on the Rights of the Child, General Comment No 5: *General measures of implementation of the Convention on the Rights of the Child (arts 4, 42 and 44para 6)* 34th session, CRC/GC/2003/5 (27 November 2003) [9].

214 CRC/C/ALB/CO/2-4 (5 October 2012) [21].

215 CRC/C/NIU/CO/1 (29 January 2013) [18].

216 CRC/C/GBR/4 (25 February 2008) [61].

217 For example CRC/C/ALB/CO/2-4 (5 October 2012) [24]; CRC/C/AND/CO/2 (9 October 2012) [21].

218 The World Programme was established by the General Assembly's resolution 59/113 (10 December 2004). OHCHR provides global coordination of the World Programme.

219 CRC/C/GIN/CO/2 (30 January 2013) [28].

220 Committee on the Rights of the Child, General Comment No 16: *State obligations regarding the impact of the business sector on children's rights*, 62nd session, CRC/C/GC/16 (17 April 2013).

221 ibid [25].

levels of radioactive toxicity and pollution, do not affect human rights or endanger the environment.[222] Similarly, concerns about a lack of a regulatory framework were expressed about the steel industry and private security services operating in Bosnia and Herzegovina,[223] and the risks of sexual exploitation associated with the tourism industry in Malta.[224] The Committee will recommend that the states party adopts an effective corporate responsibility model.[225]

3.7.2   Definition of the child: Article 1

Article 1
For the purposes of the present Convention, a child means every human being below the age of eighteen years unless under the law applicable to the child, majority is attained earlier.

The issue of the definition of a child was a crucial and contentious part of the negotiations in the original drafting of the Convention (Cantwell 1992: 26). Article 1 was essentially a compromise: it sets the international legal definition of a child as a person below 18 years, but subject to the proviso that a domestic law that sets legal majority at an earlier age will not be compromised. In its General Comment No 4, the Committee underlined that:

> … adolescents up to 18 years old are holders of all the rights enshrined in the Convention; they are entitled to special protection measures, and, according to their evolving capacities, they can progressively exercise their rights (art 5).[226]

The Human Rights Committee has also stated that protective ages must not be set 'unreasonably low', and that in any case a states party cannot absolve itself under the International Covenant on Civil and Political Rights (1966) (ICCPR)[227] from obligations to children under 18 years old, even if they have reached the age of majority under domestic law.[228]

In some countries an age lower than 18 years is used to define the child. For example, in Namibia, the Constitution defines 'child' as anyone under the age of

---

222   CRC/C/NAM/CO/2-3 (16 October 2012) [26–27].
223   CRC/C/BIH/CO/2-4 (5 October 2012) [27–28]. Similarly, the steel and rubber industries in Liberia, where children were engaged in hazardous work to meet companies' production quotas: CRC/C/LBR/CO/2-4 (5 October 2012) [29].
224   CRC/C/MLT/CO/2 (5 February 2013) [24–25].
225   CRC/C/GUY/CO/2-4 (5 February 2013) [23].
226   Committee on the Rights of the Child, General Comment No 4: *Adolescent health and development in the context of the Convention on the Rights of the Child*, CRC/GC/2003/4 (1 July 2003) [1].
227   International Covenant on Civil and Political Rights, opened for signature 16 December 1966, 999 UNTS 171 (entered into force 23 March 1976).
228   Human Rights Committee, General Comment No 17: *Rights of the child (art 24)*, UN Doc HRI/GEN/1/Rev.8 (4 July 1989) [4].

16 years.[229] Where the general legal majority age is lower than 18, the Committee encourages states parties to raise it to 18 years where possible. In some countries there is no clearly defined age of majority.[230]

In many countries the general age of majority is 18 years, for example, in Norway, Germany, Italy, China and the United Kingdom. However, such countries will also have specific legislation that offers legal capacity in particular areas. However, the setting of the upper age limit of 18 years for the definition of a child remains an important target for some countries, particularly those that, like India, still have problems with the prevalence of child marriages and child labour.

In some countries there is no uniform definition of the child in the laws and policies of the country. The Committee observed, for example, that in Malta there were numerous areas of legislation where the states party did not provide for children above the age of 16 years 'resulting in a de facto definition of the child being a person under 16 years of age'.[231] There may also be, for example, conflicting legal minimum ages of children for marriage according to whether civil law or sharia law applies.[232] There are often inconsistencies in the definition of a child at federal, provincial and territorial levels between secular and sharia law.[233] The Committee was concerned that Israel had raised the age of majority in military courts from 16 to 18 years but this had not been applied in practice. It recommended that those living in the Occupied Palestinian Territory should be regarded as children up to the age of 18 and thus would have the full protection of the Convention, particularly those provisions relating to juvenile justice.[234]

In its General Comment No 4 the following observations aptly summarise the objections to early marriage and the Committee's recommendations to address this issue.

> The Committee is concerned that early marriage and pregnancy are significant factors in health problems related to sexual and reproductive health, including HIV/AIDS. Both the legal minimum age and actual age of marriage, particularly for girls, are still very low in several States parties. There are also non-health-related concerns: children who marry, especially girls, are often obliged to leave the education system and are marginalized from social activities. Further, in some States parties married children are legally considered adults, even if they are under 18, depriving them of all the special protection measures they are entitled under the Convention. The Committee strongly recommends that States parties review and, where necessary, reform their legislation and practice to increase the minimum age for marriage with and without parental consent to 18 years, for both girls and boys. The

229 CRC/C/NAM/CO/2-3 (16 October 2012) [27].
230 For example, in Niue: CRC/C/NIU/CO/1 (29 January 2013) [22].
231 CRC/C/MLT/CO/2 (5 February 2013) [26].
232 CRC/C/BGD/CO/4 (26 June 2009) [30].
233 CRC/C/PAK/CO/3-4 (15 October 2009) (CO Pakistan 2009) [26].
234 CRC/C/ISR/CO/2-4 (14 June 2013) [19–20].

Committee on the Elimination of Discrimination against Women has made a similar recommendation (general comment No. 21 of 1994).[235]

There are still some countries, for example Liberia, where early and forced marriages continue to be widely practised.[236] The Committee characteristically comments unfavourably about the existence of low and/or discriminatory age rules in relation to marriage. In Malta, for example, it was concerned that the age of marriage was set at 16 years.[237] It noted that in Guinea, although the minimum legal age had been fixed at 18 for both boys and girls the Children's Code there allowed marriage under the age of 18 where the individuals' parents or legal guardians consented.[238] It noted its concern with the low minimum marriage age of 16 (and 14 years with permission of a judge) in Andorra.[239] The Committee also noted with concern that, in Niue, the minimum age for marriage for girls was 15 years.[240] Even where the minimum age of marriage has been set at 18 years, this may not necessarily apply to 'customary' marriages.[241] The Committee has addressed the prevention of early marriage according to the custom and practice in some countries by recommending awareness-raising campaigns to be led by traditional leaders in the country concerned.[242]

The differential definitions of legal majority within a country can often deprive older children of essential services and care. For example, in Kyrgyzstan, assistance to families with children with HIV/AIDS has been provided only to children under the age of 16, and children aged 16 and over have been transferred to adult psychiatric care.[243]

Article 40(3)(a) of the Convention provides that:

States parties shall seek to promote the establishment of laws, procedures, authorities and institutions specifically applicable to children alleged as, accused of, or recognised as having infringed the penal law, and, in particular:

The establishment of a minimum age below which children shall be presumed not to have the capacity to infringe the penal law.

---

235 Committee on the Rights of the Child, General Comment No 4: *Adolescent health and development in the context of the Convention on the Rights of the Child*, CRC/GC/2003/4 (1 July 2003) [20]. See also Committee on the Elimination of Discrimination against Women, General Recommendation No 21: *Equality in marriage and family relations*, HRI/GEN/1/Rev.8 (1994) [36].

236 CRC/C/LBR/CO/2-4 (5 October 2012) [31].

237 CRC/C/MLT/CO/2 (5 February 2013) [26].

238 CRC/C/GIN/CO/2 (30 January 2013) [33–34].

239 CRC/C/AND/CO/2 (9 October 2012) [22].

240 CRC/C/NIU/CO/1 (29 January 2013) [22].

241 CRC/C/NAM/CO/2-3 (16 October 2012) [28–29]; CRC/C/LBR/CO/2-4 (5 October 2012) [31].

242 For example in Malawi: CRC/C/MWI/CO/2 (27 March 2009) [27].

243 CRC/C/15/Add.244 (3 November 2004) [24].

In the Committee's General Comment No 10 in 2007 it observes:

The minimum age of criminal responsibility
The reports submitted by States parties show the existence of a wide range of minimum ages of criminal responsibility. They range from a very low level of age 7 or 8 to the commendable high level of age 14 or 16. Quite a few States parties use two minimum ages of criminal responsibility. Children in conflict with the law who at the time of the commission of the crime are at or above the lower minimum age but below the higher minimum age are assumed to be criminally responsible only if they have the required maturity in that regard. The assessment of this maturity is left to the court/judge, often without the requirement of involving a psychological expert, and results in practice in the use of the lower minimum age in cases of serious crimes. The system of two minimum ages is often not only confusing, but leaves much to the discretion of the court/judge and may result in discriminatory practices. In the light of this wide range of minimum ages for criminal responsibility the Committee feels that there is a need to provide the States parties with clear guidance and recommendations regarding the minimum age of criminal responsibility.[244]

There is also a comparable recognition in the United Nations Standard Minimum Rules for the Administration of Juvenile Justice (Beijing Rules), that the minimum age of criminal responsibility should not be fixed at too low an age level, bearing in mind the facts of emotional, mental and intellectual maturity.[245] Article 40(3) of the Convention requires states parties to promote a minimum age (unspecified) below which children will be presumed to lack capacity to break penal law. Children above the minimum age but below 18 years can be charged but the criminal justice process must be in full compliance with the Convention and General Comment No 10. The minimum age of criminal responsibility ought not to be fixed at 'too low an age level, bearing in mind the facts of emotional, mental and intellectual maturity'.[246] The General Comment concludes that 'a minimum age of criminal responsibility below the age of 12 years is considered by the Committee not to be internationally acceptable', and states parties are encouraged to increase this minimum age threshold to higher levels over time.[247] However, there are still diverse rules relating to the age of criminal responsibility across different countries. In the United Kingdom, for example, the age of criminal responsibility in England, Wales and Northern Ireland is 10 years old.

244 Committee on the Rights of the Child, General Comment No 10: *Children's rights in juvenile justice*, CRC/C/GC/10 (25 April 2007) [30].
245 The United Nations Standard Minimum Rules for the Administration of Juvenile Justice (Beijing Rules), General Assembly, 96th plen. UN Doc A/RES/40/33 (29 November 1985) r 4.
246 Committee on the Rights of the Child, General Comment No 10: *Children's rights in juvenile justice*, CRC/C/GC/10 (25 April 2007) [32].
247 ibid [32].

In Scotland, the age of criminal responsibility has been raised from eight to the internationally acceptable (minimum) standard of 12 years.[248] The Committee recommended in 2008[249] that the UK should raise the minimum age of criminal responsibility in accordance with General Comment No 10.

It is of greater difficulty to determine when childhood *begins*. Van Bueren (1994: 33) notes that states 'hold such fundamentally conflicting views when childhood begins that they cannot be reconciled simply by the device of a treaty'. She concludes that there is no universally agreed point of time when childhood begins, but it would appear that international law protects the beginning of childhood, at least from the moment of a live birth. States are not prevented from extending their definition of childhood to include periods in the womb, but such protection cannot be read into customary international law or into treaty provisions that protect the right to life. The combination of the text of Article 1 and a preambular paragraph of the Convention[250] in effect provides an opportunity for states parties to interpret the Convention as providing legal protection either from the moment of live birth or from conception, as the case may be. The Implementation Handbook explains the key point from the drafting history of the Convention:

> The preambular statement [...] caused difficulties within the Working Group that drafted the Convention. In order to reach consensus, the Group agreed that a statement should be placed in the *travaux préparatoires* to the effect that 'In adopting this preambular paragraph, the Working Group does not intend to prejudice the interpretation of Article 1 or any other provision of the Convention by States parties' (E/CN.4/1989/48 8–15; Detrick [1992] at 110).
>
> (Newell and Hodgkin 2007: 2)

Some states have registered a number of reservations or declarations in order to clarify their country's position in relation to this question. For example, the United Kingdom has made an interpretative declaration in respect of Article 1.[251] However, other countries, for example Argentina, have specifically appealed to the (ninth) preambular paragraph of the Convention and the (third) preambular paragraph of the Declaration of the Rights of the Child (1959) in support of the contention that the Convention confers rights on the human foetus.

---

248 See respectively: Crime and Disorder Act 1998 s 34; Criminal Justice (Northern Ireland) Order 1998 s 3; and Criminal Justice and Licensing (Scotland) Act 2010 s 52.
249 CRC/C/GBR/CO/4 (20 October 2008) [78].
250 CRC preamble §9. See n 18 above.
251 'The United Kingdom interprets the Convention as applicable only following a live birth.'

3.7.3   General principles: Articles 2, 3, 6 and 12

These are the foundational principles of the Convention. Article 2 (non-discrimination principle), Article 3 (best interests principle), Article 6 (right to life, survival and development) and Article 12 (participation rights according to evolving capacities) are fundamental to an understanding of the Convention. States parties are expected to provide information not only in respect of these general principles but also, pervasively, in relation to how these principles may impact on the implementation of other specific rights contained in the Convention.

3.7.3.1   The non-discrimination principle

Article 2
1. States parties shall respect and ensure the rights set forth in the present Convention to each child within their jurisdiction without discrimination of any kind, irrespective of the child's or his or her parent's or legal guardian's race, colour, sex, language, religion, political or other opinion, national, ethnic or social origin, property, disability, birth or other status.
2. States parties shall take all appropriate measures to ensure that the child is protected against all forms of discrimination or punishment on the basis of the status, activities, expressed opinions, or beliefs of the child's parents, legal guardians, or family members.

The grounds for discrimination in Article 2 of the Convention are similar to those contained in ICCPR[252] and ICESCR,[253] with the addition of 'ethnic … origin' and 'disability'. There is no definition of 'discrimination' within the text of the Convention, nor is there a dedicated General Comment on the non-discrimination principle. However, it is clear from General Comment No 5 that an *active approach* to implementation is envisaged. The non-discrimination obligation requires states actively to identify individual children and groups of children, the recognition and realisation of whose rights may demand special measures. For example, the Committee highlights, in particular, the need for data collection to be disaggregated to enable discrimination or potential discrimination to be identified. Addressing discrimination may require changes in legislation, administration and resource allocation, as well as educational measures to change attitudes. It should be emphasised that the application of the non-discrimination principle of equal access to rights does not mean identical treatment. A General Comment by the Human Rights Committee has underlined the importance of

---

252 International Covenant on Civil and Political Rights, opened for signature 16 December 1966, 999 UNTS 171 (entered into force 23 March 1976) art 2.

253 International Covenant on Economic, Social and Cultural Rights, opened for signature 16 December 1966, 993 UNTS 3 (entered into force 3 January 1976) art 2.

taking special measures in order to diminish or eliminate conditions that cause discrimination.[254]

The language of Article 2 further supports this active approach to the non-discrimination principle. The obligation to 'ensure' goes beyond the obligation to 'respect' and implies an affirmative obligation on states to take the necessary measures to enable individuals to enjoy and exercise the relevant rights (Alston 1992: 5). This approach has been confirmed recently in General Comment No 14 relating to the 'best interests principle'.

> The right to non-discrimination is not a passive obligation, prohibiting all forms of discrimination in the enjoyment of rights under the Convention, but also requires appropriate proactive measures taken by the State to ensure effective equal opportunities for all children to enjoy the rights under the Convention. This may require positive measures aimed at redressing a situation of real inequality.[255]

The non-discrimination principle applies in conjunction with all the substantive rights in the Convention, but does not provide an *independent* right to freedom from discrimination (Detrick 1999: 72). The words 'birth or other status' cover discrimination in relation to children born out of wedlock. The prohibition of discrimination does not of course 'outlaw the legitimate differentiation between children in implementation – for example to respect the "evolving capacities" of children' (Hodgkin and Newell 2007: 26).

The fundamental nature of the principle of non-discrimination is recognised by some states parties (eg Mauritania and Chad)[256] by incorporating the principle into their Constitutions. Of course, this does not necessarily provide sufficient protection. In Mauritania, for example, the constitutional protection has not been sufficient to prevent discrimination against children living in slavery or of slave descent, or children living in poverty.[257] The Committee has expressed deep concern where there is no explicit prohibition of discrimination in the Constitution, as in Niue, for example.[258] The Committee noted with regret that certain provisions in Liberia's Constitution restricted the granting of citizenship to children born in the state party on the basis of colour or racial origin,[259] and called for a revision of these provisions. The Committee considers that legislative measures play a decisive role in addressing discrimination. It criticises states parties where

254 Human Rights Committee, General Comment No 18: *Non-discrimination*, 37th session (10 November 1989) [5].
255 Committee on the Rights of the Child, General Comment No 14: *The right of the child to have his or her best interests taken as a primary consideration (art 3 para 1)*, CRC/C/GC/14 (29 May 2013) [41].
256 CRC/C/TCD/CO/2 (12 February 2009) [30].
257 CRC/C/MRT/CO/2 (17 June 2009) [29].
258 CRC/C/NIU/CO/1 (29 January 2013) [24].
259 CRC/C/LBR/CO/2-4 (5 October 2012) [41].

non-discrimination is not expressly guaranteed under their Basic Laws, as in Israel, which had adopted numerous discriminatory laws affecting 'primarily Palestinian children in all aspects of their life'.[260] On occasion, the reporting process to the Committee has identified sex-selective abortion practices and recommends their prohibition, for example, in Armenia.[261]

There have been moves to facilitate the assimilation of the legal status of legitimate and illegitimate children, although in some countries discrimination against children born out of wedlock persists.[262] One extreme example of discrimination in relation to illegitimate children can found in Rwanda, where the Committee expressed concern at the stigma and discrimination of persons who were born as a result of rape during the genocide that took place there in 1994.[263]

Roma children are frequently the recipients of discriminatory attitudes and practices. The Committee expressed its concern, for example, in relation to Slovenia's 'persistent discrimination against Roma children in all stages of their lives, with no effective remedies for acts of discrimination committed by public and private actors'. In addition, it noted with disapproval that the legislative protection that did exist only applied to autochthonous but not non-autochthonous Roma populations.[264]

The Committee has observed discrimination in some states parties applied to migrant children. For example, in relation to Malta, it was 'deeply concerned about serious instances of discrimination against children in irregular migration situations'.[265] The state reports to the Committee often expose the persistence of discrimination in relation, particularly, to the 'girl child'. The Committee held a 'Day of General Discussion' on this subject.[266] This emphasised that the Convention on the Rights of the Child and the Convention on the Elimination of All Forms of Discrimination against Women[267] needed to be regarded as mutually reinforcing and complementary instruments. Furthermore:

> Within the larger movement for the realisation of women's rights, history had clearly shown that it was essential to focus on the girl child in order to break down the cycle of harmful traditions and prejudices against women. Only through a comprehensive strategy to promote and protect the rights of girls,

---

260 CRC/C/ISR/CO/2-4 (14 June 2013) [21].
261 CRC/C/ARM/CO/3-4 (14 June 2013) [18–19].
262 For example CRC/C/QAT/CO/2 (14 October 2009) [25–26].
263 CRC/C/RWA/CO/3-4 (14 June 2013) [21]. See generally http://www.unitedhumanrights. org/genocide/genocide_in_rwanda.htm (accessed 8 July 2013).
264 CRC/C/SVN/CO/3-4 (14 June 2013) [24]. See also CRC/C/ALB/CO/2-4 (5 October 2012) [28].
265 CRC/C/MLT/CO/2 (5 February 2013) [28].
266 Committee on the Rights of the Child, 'Day of General Discussion' on *The Girl Child*, Report on the eighth session, CRC/C/38 (27 January 1995) [275–99].
267 Convention on the Elimination of All Forms of Discrimination against Women, opened for signature 18 December 1979, 1249 UNTS 13 (entered into force 3 September 1981).

starting with the younger generation, would it be possible to build a shared and lasting approach ...[268]

Discrimination is often directed against the girl child, and this usually reflects more fundamental discriminatory attitudes on gender within a state. For example, the Committee referred to 'the persistence of adverse and traditional attitudes and norms' in relation to Guinea,[269] and concern about 'the existing patriarchal attitudes, practices and stereotypes that discriminate against girls' in Andorra.[270] Such pervasive gender discrimination has drawn strong criticism from the Committee, for example, in the case of Pakistan.[271] The Committee's Concluding Observations continue to identify evidence of multiple, gender-based discrimination in relation to the girl child; for example, in Guinea-Bissau, practices such as female genital mutilation and cutting (FGM/C) and child marriage.[272] As the Committee observed in its 'Day of General Discussion':

> There was a need to ensure that a woman's life cycle would not become a vicious cycle, where the evolution from childhood to adulthood would be blighted by fatalism and a sense of inferiority. Only through the active involvement of girls, who are at the root of the life cycle, would it be possible to initiate a movement for change and betterment.[273]

The Committee has frequent cause to express its concern about discrimination against children belonging to particular minority ethnic groups within a state. For example, it noted concern at 'the prevalence of discrimination against Amerindian children in Guyana.[274] On occasion, the Committee has observed 'serious and widespread' racial discrimination, for example in relation to Bosnia and Herzegovina,[275] and 'manifestations of Neo-Nazism, racism, xenophobia and related intolerance towards migrant communities, refugees, asylum seekers and persons of certain ethnic backgrounds' in Austria.[276] It also noted concerns in relation to Sweden about discrimination and racist attitudes towards children of ethnic minorities, refugee and asylum-seeking children and children belonging to migrant families.[277] The Committee responds to these various concerns with a range of possible recommendations. These often include urging the country in

268 ibid [284].
269 CRC/C/GIN/CO/2 (30 January 2013) [36].
270 CRC/C/AND/CO/2 (9 October 2012) [24].
271 CRC/C/PAK/CO/3-4 (15 October 2009) [28].
272 CRC/C/GNB/CO/2-4 (14 June 2013) [24].
273 Committee on the Rights of the Child,' Day of General Discussion' on *The Girl Child*, Report on the eighth session, CRC/C/38 (27 January 1995) [285].
274 CRC/C/GUY/CO/2-4 (5 February 2013) [24].
275 CRC/C/BIH/CO/3-4 (5 October 2012) [29].
276 CRC/C/AUT/CO/3-4 (5 October 2012) [24].
277 CRC/C/SWE/CO/4 (12 June 2009) [25].

question to ensure that its domestic legislation is Convention-compliant, to adopt awareness-raising campaigns and to embark upon training programmes with the relevant professionals.

The Committee has, in recent years, given much attention to the plight of indigenous children (see generally Chapter 9). It has held a 'Day of General Discussion'[278] and also issued General Comment No 11[279] on this topic. The Committee is concerned that 'indigenous children enjoy all of their rights equally and without discrimination, including equal access to culturally appropriate services including health, education, social services, housing, potable water and sanitation'.[280] It has observed 'widespread discrimination against children from indigenous communities' in, for example, Namibia.[281] It has also noted with concern the 'significant overrepresentation of Aboriginal and African-Canadian children in the criminal justice system and out-of-home care in respect of Canada'.[282]

As regards discrimination against children with disabilities, it should be noted that the Convention was the first international human rights treaty to contain a specific reference to 'disability' and Article 23 is exclusively dedicated to the rights and needs of children with disabilities. The Committee also issued General Comment No 9 on this topic.

> [T]he Committee on the Rights of the Child ... has paid sustained and particular attention to disability based discrimination while other human rights treaty bodies have paid attention to disability based discrimination under 'other status' in the context of Articles on non-discrimination of their relevant Convention.[283]

General Comment No 9 recommends that states parties should take the following measures to combat discrimination against disabled children:

(a) Include explicitly disability as a forbidden ground for discrimination in constitutional provisions on non-discrimination and/or include specific prohibition of discrimination on the ground of disability in specific anti-discrimination laws or legal provisions.

(b) Provide for effective remedies in case of violations of the rights of children with disabilities, and ensure that those remedies are easily

---

278 Committee on the Rights of the Child, 'Day of General Discussion' on *The Rights of Indigenous Children*, Report on the 34th session, CRC/C/GC/11 (3 October 2003).

279 Committee on the Rights of the Child, General Comment No 11: *Indigenous children and their rights under the Convention*, 50th session, CRC/C/GC/11 (12 February 2009).

280 Committee on the Rights of the Child, 'Day of General Discussion' on *The Rights of Indigenous Children*, Report on the 34th session, CRC/C/GC/11 (3 October 2003) [9].

281 CRC/C/NAM/CO/2-3 (16 October 2012) [30].

282 CRC/C/CAN/CO/3-4 (5 October 2012) [32].

283 Committee on the Rights of the Child, General Comment No 9: *The rights of children with disabilities*, 43rd session, CRC/C/GC/9 (27 February 2007) [2].

accessible to children with disabilities and their parents and/or others caring for the child.

(c) Conduct awareness-raising and educational campaigns targeting the public at large and specific groups of professionals with a view to preventing and eliminating de facto discrimination against children with disabilities.[284]

The Committee regularly expresses its concern about the harassment and stigmatisation of children with disabilities in some states parties, for example, in Liberia.[285] As pointed out by Hodgkin and Newell (2007: 29):

... the barrier [to the full enjoyment of rights] is not the disability itself but rather a combination of social, cultural, attitudinal and physical obstacles which children with disabilities encounter in their daily lives. The strategy for promoting their rights is therefore to take the necessary action to remove these barriers.

The way in which the principle of non-discrimination applies in the context of education rights is given some detailed treatment in General Comment No 1.

Discrimination on the basis of any of the grounds ... offends the human dignity of the child and is capable of undermining or even destroying the capacity of the child to benefit from educational opportunities. ... To take an extreme example, gender discrimination can be reinforced by practices such as a curriculum which is inconsistent with the principles of gender equality, by arrangements which limit the benefits girls can obtain from the educational opportunities offered, and by unsafe or unfriendly environments which discourage girls' participation. Discrimination against children with disabilities is also pervasive in many formal educational systems and in a great many informal educational settings, including in the home. Children with HIV/AIDS are also heavily discriminated against in both settings. All such discriminatory practices are in direct contradiction with the requirements in Article 29(1)(a) that education be directed to the development of the child's personality, talents and mental and physical abilities to their fullest potential.[286]

The Committee routinely draws states parties' attention to the principles of the Declaration and Programme of Action (Durban Declaration 2001), in addition

---

284 ibid [9].

285 CRC/C/LBR/CO/2-4 (5 October 2012) [33].

286 Committee on the Rights of the Child, General Comment No 1: *Article 29(1) – The Aims of Education*, 26th session, CRC/GC/2001/1 (17 April 2001) [10].

to the outcome document[287] adopted at the 2009 Durban Review Conference. The Committee typically welcomes warmly the establishment of a national body with responsibility to remedy problems of discrimination, particularly where it has the power to receive individual complaints, for example, the Haute Autorité de Lutte contre Discriminations et pour l'Égalité in France.[288] The Committee has criticised the so-called 'two-schools-under-one-roof' and the mono-ethnic schools policy in Bosnia and Herzegovina, and called for an immediate end to such educational segregation by ethnicity.[289]

3.7.3.2   The best interests principle

Article 3
1. In all actions concerning children, whether undertaken by public or private social welfare institutions, courts of law, administrative authorities or legislative bodies, the best interests of the child shall be a primary consideration.

This principle first appeared, at the international level, in principles 2 and 7 of the Declaration of the Rights of the Child (1959).[290] The principle has appeared in various forms in different countries and over a range of international legal instruments. For example, one objective of the Hague Convention on Protection of Children and Co-operation in respect of Intercountry Adoption[291] is: 'to establish safeguards to ensure that inter-country adoptions take place in the best interests of the child and with respect for his or her fundamental rights as recognised in international law'.[292] In addition to its appearance in Article 3, the 'best interests' principle is also referred to elsewhere in the Convention and in all three Optional Protocols.[293]

The principle has been controversial, not least because of the difficulties in pinpointing its core meaning and implementation with any intellectual precision. One persistent criticism of the best interests principle is that any one country's construction of its normative meaning will 'enable cultural considerations to be

---

287 UN Office of the High Commissioner for Human Rights, *Outcome document of the Durban Review Conference* (24 April 2009) http://www.refworld.org/docid/49f584682.html (accessed 9 July 2013).

288 CRC/C/FRA/CO/4 (11 June 2009) [28].

289 CRC/C/BIH/CO/3-4 [29–30].

290 General Assembly, Declaration of the Rights of the Child, 14th session, UN Doc A/RES/1386 (XIV) (20 November 1959). Principle 2 of the Declaration of 1959 provides the stronger legal threshold, that is, 'the best interests of the child shall be the paramount consideration' in contrast to the 'primary consideration' in the Convention. It has sometimes been argued that the 'paramountcy' standard should be the basic rule in international child law.

291 Hague Conference on Private International Law, concluded 29 May 1993 (entered into force 1 May 1995).

292 ibid art 1(a). See ch 6.

293 See CRC arts 9(1)(3), 18(1), 20(1), 21, 37(c) and 42(b)(iii); OPSC preamble art 8; OPAC preamble arts 2 and 3; OPIC preamble arts 2 and 3(2).

smuggled by states into their implementation of the rights recognised in the CRC' (Detrick 1999: 89). In addition to its referencing in earlier General Comments, the Committee issued General Comment No 14[294] in 2013, which is dedicated to interpreting and analysing the best interests principle contained in Article 3(1).[295] The appearance of this General Comment has, to an extent, provided an answer to the criticisms of 'vagueness' that have been levelled against it. General Comment No 14 makes it clear that: '[t]he concept of the child's best interests is aimed at ensuring both the full and effective enjoyment of all the rights recognized in the Convention and the holistic development of the child'.[296] Furthermore, the Committee asserts that it is a 'threefold concept':

(a) *A substantive right*: The right of the child to have his or her best interests assessed and taken as a primary consideration when different interests are being considered in order to reach a decision on the issue at stake, and the guarantee that this right will be implemented whenever a decision is to be made concerning a child, a group of identified or unidentified children or children in general. Article 3, paragraph 1, creates an intrinsic obligation for States, is directly applicable (self-executing) and can be invoked before a court.

(b) *A fundamental, interpretative legal principle*: If a legal provision is open to more than one interpretation, the interpretation which most effectively serves the child's best interests should be chosen. The rights enshrined in the Convention and its Optional Protocols provide the framework for interpretation.

(c) *A rule of procedure*: Whenever a decision is to be made that will affect a specific child, an identified group of children or children in general, the decision-making process must include an evaluation of the possible impact (positive or negative) of the decision on the child or children concerned. Assessing and determining the best interests of the child require procedural guarantees. Furthermore, the justification of a decision must show that the right has been explicitly taken into account. In this regard, States parties shall explain how the right has been respected in the decision, that is, what has been considered to be in the child's best interests; what criteria it is based on; and how the child's interests have been weighed against other considerations, be they broad issues of policy or individual cases.[297]

---

294 Committee on the Rights of the Child, General Comment No 14: *The right of the child to have his or her best interests taken as a primary consideration (art 3, para 1)*, CRC/C/GC/14 (29 May 2013).

295 General Comment No 14 does not deal with arts 3(2) and (3). A commentary on these provisions can be found in Hodgkin and Newell (2007: 40–42).

296 ibid para 4.

297 ibid para 6.

In addition, General Comment No 14 identifies three different types of obligations for states parties.[298] First, they must ensure that the child's best interests are appropriately integrated and applied in every action taken by public institutions. Secondly, states parties must ensure that all judicial and administrative decisions and policies and legislation concerning children demonstrate that the child's best interests have been a primary consideration. Finally, states parties must ensure that the child's interest have been equally attended to as a primary consideration in decisions and actions taken by the private sector. In order to ensure compliance, General Comment No 14 advises that states parties should undertake a number of 'implementation measures', for example, reviewing and amending domestic legislation and other sources of law so as to incorporate Article 3(1).[299] The 'actions' referred to in Article 3(1) 'does not only include decisions, but also all acts, conduct, proposals, services, procedures and other measures' and also omissions and failures to take action.[300] It is also clear that the best interests principle should be applied 'to children not only as individuals, but also in general or as a group'.[301] General Comment No 14 also makes an attempt to define 'the best interests of the child'. It states that the concept is 'flexible and adaptable' to the specific situation of children, and its content can be best clarified, in making both individual and collective assessments, on a 'case-by-case basis'.[302] However, the General Comment also implies a warning deriving from the inherent flexibility of the concept:

> [I]t may also leave room for manipulation; the concept of the child's best interests has been abused by Governments and other State authorities to justify racist policies, for example; by parents to defend their own interests in custody disputes; by professionals who could not be bothered, and who dismiss the assessment of the child's best interests as irrelevant or unimportant.[303]

The expression 'a primary consideration' means 'that the child's best interests may not be considered on the same level as all other considerations'.[304] Inevitably, children's interests will need to be weighed against other interests, although 'a larger weight must be attached to what serves the child best'.[305]

> Viewing the best interests of the child as 'primary' requires a consciousness about the place that children's interests must occupy in all actions and a

298 ibid para 14.
299 ibid para 15(a) and see also sub-paras (b) – (h).
300 ibid paras 17 and 18.
301 ibid para 23.
302 ibid para 32.
303 ibid para 34.
304 ibid para 37.
305 ibid para 39.

willingness to give priority to those interests in all circumstances, but especially when an action has an undeniable impact on the children concerned.[306]

General Comment No 14 contains a detailed account of the approach that should be taken to the *assessment* and *determination* of a child's best interests and the necessary *procedural safeguards* required to guarantee its implementation. As regards assessment, it recommends in particular that decision-makers 'draw up a non-exhaustive and non-hierarchical list of elements that could be included in a best-interests assessment',[307] and sets out (seven) elements to take into account.[308] These are: the child's views; the child's identity; preservation of the family environment and maintaining relations; care, protection and safety of the child; situations of vulnerability; the child's right to health; and the child's right to education. Of course, '[n]ot all the elements will be relevant to every case, and different elements can be used in different ways in different cases', and such elements 'may be in conflict when considering a specific case and its circumstances'.[309] As regards procedural safeguards, the Committee suggests that states parties and others pay special attention to a list of (seven) safeguards/guarantees: the right of the child to express his or her own views; the establishment of facts; time perception; qualified professionals; legal representation; legal reasoning; mechanisms to review or revise decisions; and child-rights impact assessment (CRIA).[310] This is a welcome prompt for states parties that the Committee has had cause to criticise on the basis of 'the absence of guidelines and procedures for ensuring that the [best interests principle] is applied continuously throughout the State party's policies, legislation and programmes'.[311]

The fundamental nature of the best interests principle has encouraged some countries to include the principle in their constitutions, although of course this is never a guarantee that the principle is actually fully integrated with the country's national laws or policies.[312] On occasion, the Committee will recommend that the principle ought to be included in a state's constitution.[313] The Committee, in its Concluding Observations, frequently has cause to comment on the failure of states parties to incorporate the best interests principle fully in major pieces of legislation and/or in key policies, programmes and decision-making processes.[314] Weaker legal formulations of the principle, for example, the 'legitimate interests' of the

---

306 ibid para 40.
307 ibid para 50.
308 ibid paras 52–79.
309 ibid paras 80 and 81.
310 ibid paras 89–99.
311 CRC/C/GUY/CO/2-4 (5 February 2013) [26].
312 CRC/C/NAM/CO/2-3 (16 October 2012) [32]; CRC/C/AUT/CO/3-4 (5 October 2012) [26].
313 For example in Slovenia: CRC/C/SVN/CO/3-4 (14 June 2013) [29].
314 See for example CRC/C/ALB/CO/2-4 (5 October 2012) [29]; CRC/C/AND/CO/2 (9 October 2012) [26]; CRC/C/GIN/CO/2 (30 January 2013) [38].

child, are likely to be criticised by the Committee as falling below the expected standard.[315] However, the Committee's Concluding Observations also record successful amendment to national legal regimes by, not only revisions of national legislation, but revisions brought about by the superior national or constitutional courts. For example, Israel was commended for its Supreme Court rulings in 2006 and 2008,[316] which revoked decisions of the Sharia and Rabbinical courts granting custody of children to their father without taking into account consideration of the children's best interests.[317] The French *Cour de cassation* aligned its jurisprudence with that of the *Conseil d'État* in acknowledging the direct applicability of Article 3(1) in 2009.[318]

Sometimes the Committee's Concluding Observations show that the best interests principle has been poorly applied or not applied at all in respect of particular groups of children. For example, in Bosnia and Herzegovina the principle was 'not adequately applied in situations concerning children deprived of a family environment'.[319] Similarly, there was an inadequate application of the principle in courts and social work centres in such cases in Slovenia.[320] In Sweden, the best interests of asylum-seeker and migrant children were not taken sufficiently into account in asylum processes;[321] similarly in Canada the principle was 'not appropriately applied' in asylum-seeking, refugee and/or immigration detention situations.[322]

The Committee's Concluding Observations also provide some evidence of the negative perceptions of the best interests principle that may be present in some states parties. One of the (eight) 'implementation measures' set out in General Comment No 14 specifically identifies:

> (h) Combating all negative attitudes and perceptions which impede the full realization of the right of the child to have his or her best interests assessed and taken as a primary consideration, through communication programmes involving mass media and social networks as well as children, in order to have children recognized as rights holders.[323]

For example, the Committee expressed its concern about 'the general societal perception in [Liberia] that best interests of adults should prevail over those of the

---

315 For example in Uzbekistan and Armenia: CRC/C/UZB/CO/3-4 (14 June 2013) [22]; CRC/C/ARM/CO/3-4 (14 June 2013) [20].

316 HCJ 1129/06 *Anonymous et al v The Shari'a' Court of Appeals et al* (5 June 2006); HCJ 1073/05 *Anonymous et al v The High Rabbinical Court et al* (25 June 2008).

317 CRC/C/ISR/CO/2-4 (14 June 2013) [23].

318 CRC/C/FRA/CO/4 (11 June 2009) [35].

319 CRC/C/BIH/CO/3-4 (5 October 2012) [31].

320 CRC/C/SVN/CO/3-4 (14 June 2013) [28].

321 CRC/C/SWE/CO/4 (12 June 2009) [27].

322 CRC/C/CAN/CO/3-4 (5 October 2012) [34]. Similar criticisms were made in CRC/C/MLT/CO/2 (5 February 2013) [30] and CRC/C/SVN/CO/3-4 (14 June 2013) [28].

323 General Comment No 14 para 15(h).

child',[324] and it noted with concern that, in Niue, 'interests of families, communities or adults often prevail over the best interests of the chid as is the case notably concerning teenage pregnancy'.[325]

As mentioned above, one of the (seven) procedural safeguards contained in General Comment No 14 is the 'child-rights impact assessment' (CRIA). The need for child impact assessment and evaluation was first advocated in an earlier General Comment.[326] What is envisaged is a 'continuous process' of CRIA, which should be designed to 'predict the impact of any proposed policy, legislation, regulation, budget or other administrative decision which affect children and the enjoyment of their rights ...'.[327]

CRIA needs to be built into government processes at all levels and as early as possible in the development of policy and other general measures in order to ensure good governance for children's rights. Different methodologies and practices may be developed when undertaking CRIA. At a minimum, states must use the Convention and its Optional Protocols as a framework, in particular ensuring that the assessments are underpinned by the general principles and have special regard for the differentiated impact of the measure(s) under consideration on children.[328]

Israel was commended for their adoption of a Law that provides for CRIA in new legislation.[329]

3.7.3.3   The right to life, survival and development

Article 6

1. States parties recognize that every child has the inherent right to life.
2. States parties shall ensure to the maximum extent possible the survival and development of the child.

The right to life, like its counterpart in the ICCPR,[330] is the only right in the Convention described as an 'inherent' right. Indeed, some commentators take the view that this is one of the 'peremptory norms of general international law', in other words, the *jus cogens* rule comes into play (see section 2.2.5). The right to life differs, however, from its counterpart in other major human rights treaties, as it additionally requires States to ensure 'to the maximum extent possible' the child's

---

324 CRC/C/LBR/CO/2-4 (5 October 2012) [35].

325 CRC/C/NIU/CO/1 (29 January 2013) [26].

326 Committee on the Rights of the Child, General Comment No 5: *General measures of implementation of the Convention on the Rights of the Child (arts 4, 42 and 44(6))* 34th session, CRC/GC/2003/5 (27 November 2003) [45–47].

327 General Comment No 14 paras 35 and 99.

328 ibid para 99.

329 CRC/C/ISR/CO/2-4 (14 June 2013) [23].

330 'Every human being has the inherent right to life. This right shall be protected by law. No one shall be arbitrarily deprived of his life', ICCPR art 6(1).

'survival and development'. These were seen as complementary elements, implying, for example, the need for state measures to reduce infant mortality. Given the difficulties experienced in the drafting process to arrive at a satisfactory definition of the child (see section 3.7.2), it is not surprising that a few countries have made declarations or reservations to ensure that the interpretation of Article 6 will not conflict with national abortion and family planning legislation. For example, China's reservation[331] aims to protect its 'one child' policy. Luxembourg, Tunisia and France have made declarations ensuring that Article 6 does not interfere with their abortion legislation.[332]

The Committee has not yet issued a General Comment on this general principle, in part perhaps because the Human Rights Committee has already developed a jurisprudence around the earlier, comparable provision in ICCPR. It issued a General Comment in 1982 that stated:

> ... [T]he [Human Rights] Committee has noted that the right to life has been too often narrowly interpreted. The expression 'inherent right to life' cannot properly be understood in a restrictive manner, and the protection of this right requires that States adopt positive measures. In this connection, the Committee considers that it would be desirable for States parties to take all possible measures to reduce infant mortality and to increase life expectancy, especially in adopting measures to eliminate malnutrition and epidemics.[333]

However, Article 6 has been referenced in some of the Committee on the Rights of the Child's General Comments. For example, in General Comment No 7, the following paragraph appears:

> [10]. *Right to life, survival and development.* Article 6 refers to the child's inherent right to life and States parties' obligation to ensure, to the maximum extent possible, the survival and development of the child. States parties are

---

331 '[T]he People's Republic of China shall fulfil its obligations provided by Article 6 of the Convention under the prerequisite that the Convention accords with the provisions of Article 25 concerning family planning of the Constitution of the People's Republic of China and in conformity with the provisions of Article 2 of the Law of Minor Children of the People's Republic of China.'

332 'The Government of Luxembourg declares that Article 6 of the present Convention presents no obstacle to implementation of the provisions of Luxembourg legislation concerning sex information, the prevention of back-street abortion and the regulation of pregnancy termination.' 'The Government of the Republic of Tunisia declares that the Preamble to and the provisions of the Convention, in particular Article 6, shall not be interpreted in such a way as to impede the application of Tunisian legislation concerning voluntary termination of pregnancy.' 'The Government of the French Republic declares that this Convention, particularly Article 6, cannot be interpreted as constituting any obstacle to the implementation of the provisions of French legislation relating to the voluntary interruption of pregnancy.'

333 Human Rights Committee, General Comment No 6: *Article 6 (Right to life)*, 16th session, HRI/GEN/1/Rev.8 (1982) [5].

urged to take all possible measures to improve perinatal care for mothers and babies, reduce infant and child mortality, and create conditions that promote the well-being of all young children during this critical phase of their lives. Malnutrition and preventable diseases continue to be major obstacles to realizing rights in early childhood. Ensuring survival and physical health are priorities, but States parties are reminded that Article 6 encompasses all aspects of development, and that a young child's health and psychosocial well-being are in many respects interdependent. Both may be put at risk by adverse living conditions, neglect, insensitive or abusive treatment and restricted opportunities for realizing human potential. [...] The Committee reminds States parties (and others concerned) that the right to survival and development can only be implemented in a holistic manner, through the enforcement of all the other provisions of the Convention [...].[334]

The specific threat to children's lives presented by HIV/AIDS is highlighted in the Committee's General Comment No 3.

State obligation to realize the right to life, survival and development also highlights the need to give careful attention to sexuality as well as to the behaviours and lifestyles of children, even if they do not conform with what society determines to be acceptable under prevailing cultural norms for a particular age group. In this regard, the female child is often subject to harmful traditional practices, such as early and/or forced marriage, which violate her rights and make her more vulnerable to HIV infection, including because such practices often interrupt access to education and information.[335]

The Committee will often express its most 'grave', 'deep' or 'serious' concern in relation to the loss of children's lives resulting from military conflicts. For example, in its Concluding Observation on Israel:

[T]he Committee reiterates its deepest concern that children on both sides of the conflict continue to be killed and injured, children living in the OPT [Occupied Palestinian Territory] being disproportionately represented among the victims. The Committee expresses serious concerns that hundreds of Palestinian children have been killed and thousands injured over the reporting period as a result of the State party military operations, especially in Gaza where the State party proceeded to air and naval strikes on densely

---

334 Committee on the Rights of the Child, General Comment No 7: *Implementing child rights in early childhood*, CRC/C/GC/7/Rev.1 (20 September 2006) [10].

335 Committee on the Rights of the Child, General Comment No 3: *HIV/AIDS and the rights of the child*, CRC/GC/2003/3 (17 March 2003) [11].

populated areas with a significant presence of children, thus disregarding the principles of proportionality and distinction.[336]

As regards the Republic of Congo, the Committee was 'gravely concerned that children's right to life, survival and development are violated as a consequence of being the most vulnerable of victims in hostilities.[337]

The Committee has expressed its concern with a number of Article 6 issues in its examination of states party reports, for example, the high neonatal and infant mortality rates and child malnutrition in some states.[338] The objective assessment of neonatal mortality is usually carried out in accordance with an internationally recognised World Health Organization (WHO) definition of a live birth. The Committee criticised Uzbekistan, which had adopted an inconsistent definition.[339] Preventable domestic accidents also caused large number of deaths in the Republic of Guinea.[340] Traffic accidents too have remained a major cause of fatal injuries of children and young people in some states.[341]

The Committee has expressed 'grave concern at the abandonment of newborn children (or "baby-dumping") and infanticide in [Namibia], often resulting from the high number of teenage pregnancies, child rape and inadequate access to sexual and reproductive health care and information'.[342] The Committee has expressed concern about the 'still widespread and increasing problem of honour killings' affecting children'.[343] An earlier General Comment noted the problem of honour killings and the need for states parties to 'take all effective measures to eliminate all acts and activities which threaten the right to life of adolescents, including honour killings'.[344] In a similar vein, it has expressed concern about 'the persistence of "blood feuds" [in Albania] resulting from the application of customary law known as "Kanun" and in particular the killing of children ...', [345] and the Committee 'remains seriously concerned at the persistence of ritualistic killings of children [in Liberia]'.[346] On occasion, extreme instances of ritual killing has been identified. The Committee noted, in relation to Guinea-Bissau, '... with deep

---

336 CRC/C/ISR/CO/2-4 (14 June 2013) [25]. The Committee recommended, inter alia, ceasing the construction of the Wall in OPT and fully lifting the Gaza Blockade to allow the entry of housing construction materials for Palestinian families.

337 CRC/C/COD/CO/2 (10 February 2009) [33].

338 CRC/C/GIN/CO/2 (30 January 2013) [40].

339 CRC/C/UZB/CO/3-4 (14 June 2013) [24].

340 ibid.

341 CRC/C/SVN/CO/3-4 (14 June 2013) [30].

342 CRC/C/NAM/CO/2-3 (16 October 2012) [34].

343 CRC/C/PAK/CO/3-4 (15 October 2009) [37].

344 Committee on the Rights of the Child, General Comment No 4: *Adolescent health and development in the context of the Convention on the Rights of the Child*, CRC/GC/2003/4 (1 July 2003) [24].

345 CRC/C/ALB/CO/2-4 (5 October 2012) [31].

346 CRC/C/LBR/CO/2-4 (5 October 2012) [37].

concern the reported cases of ritual murder of albinos, children with disabilities, twins and other children who were accused of practising witchcraft'.[347]

3.7.3.4   The right to express views and participate in decisions

Article 12

1. States parties shall assure to the child who is capable of forming his or her own views the right to express those views freely in all matters affecting the child, the views of the child being given due weight in accordance with the age and maturity of the child.

2. For this purpose, the child shall in particular be provided the opportunity to be heard in any judicial and administrative proceedings affecting the child, either directly, or through a representative or an appropriate body, in a manner consistent with the procedural rules of national law.

One of the continuing concerns for children's rights advocacy has been the extent to which important decisions are made about children without children's own participation. This Article is one of the four general principles of the Convention identified by the Committee. When read together with Articles 5 and 13, it reflects a move away from merely identifying what decisions children are *not* competent to take, to the consideration of how children *can* participate. Its importance has been underlined by the Committee's production of recommendations following a 'Day of General Discussion',[348] which are now contained in General Comment No 12,[349] which provides a comprehensive legal analysis of Article 12.

As regards the first paragraph of Article 12, General Comment No 12 points out that the phrase 'shall assure' in Article 12 'is a legal term of special strength, which leaves no leeway for state parties' discretion'.[350] The phrase 'capable of forming his or her own views' is a phrase that 'should not be seen as a limitation, but rather as an obligation for States parties to assess the capacity of the child to form an autonomous opinion to the greatest extent possible'.[351] Furthermore, as regards the phrase 'to express those views freely':

> 22. [..] 'Freely' means that the child can express her or his views without pressure and can choose whether or not she or he wants to exercise her or his right to be heard. 'Freely' also means that the child must not be manipulated or subjected to undue influence or pressure. 'Freely' is further intrinsically

347 CRC/C/GNB/CO/2-4 (14 June 2013) [28].

348 Committee on the Rights of the Child, 'Day of General Discussion' on the *Right of the child to be heard*, Report on the 43rd session, CRC/C/43/3 (16 July 2007) [980–1041].

349 Committee on the Rights of the Child, General Comment No 12: *The right of the child to be heard*, CRC/C/GC/12 (20 July 2009).

350 ibid para 19.

351 ibid para 20. Furthermore, states parties should presume that a child has such capacity.

related to the child's 'own' perspective: the child has the right to express her or his own views and not the views of others.

23. States parties must ensure conditions for expressing views that account for the child's individual and social situation and an environment in which the child feels respected and secure when freely expressing her or his opinions.[352]

It is also clear that the phrase 'in all matters affecting the child' should be 'respected and understood broadly'.[353] Furthermore, '[A]rticle 12 stipulates that simply listening to the child is insufficient; the views of the child have to be seriously considered when the child is capable of forming his or her own views'.[354]

As regards the second paragraph of Article 12:

> The Committee emphasises that this provision applies to all relevant judicial proceedings affecting the child, without limitation, including, for example, separation of parents, custody, care and adoption, children in conflict with the law, child victims of physical or psychological violence, sexual abuse or other crimes, health care, social security, unaccompanied children, asylum-seeking and refugee children, and victims of armed conflict and other emergencies. Typical administrative proceedings include, for example, decisions about children's education, health, environment, living conditions, or protection. Both kinds of proceedings may involve alternative dispute mechanisms such as mediation and arbitration.[355]

General Comment No 12 sets out five steps that can be taken to implement the child's right to be heard. First, the need for *preparation*, for example, the need for decision-makers to ensure that the child is informed about their right to express views and the option of communicating directly or through a representative. Secondly, the context of the *hearing* needs to be enabling and encouraging. Thirdly, the need for developing good practice in the *assessment of the capacity of the child*. Fourthly, *information about the weight given to the views of the child (feedback)* needs to be provided to ensure that the child's views have been heard and taken seriously. Finally, legislation is required to provide *complaints, remedies and redress* routes for children whose rights to be heard have been disregarded or violated.[356]

The General Comment also outlines how Article 12 relates to other important provisions of the Convention, and examines the implementation of the child's right to be heard in different settings and situations. It concludes that states parties should avoid tokenistic approaches to the implementation of this Article.

---

352 ibid paras 22–23.
353 ibid paras 26–27.
354 ibid para 28.
355 ibid para 32.
356 ibid paras 41–47.

Children's *participation*[357] should be understood as a process, not as a one-off event. The General Comment recommends that all processes in which children are heard and participate must conform to a number of benchmarks.[358] They must be given accessible information about their right to express their views freely, how this participation will take place and its scope, purpose and potential impact. This should be a voluntary process and children's views should be treated with respect. The issues on which children have a right to express their views must be of real relevance to their lives; children should be enabled to address issues they themselves identify as relevant. Environments and working methods should be adapted to accommodate children's evolving capacities. Participation should be inclusive, encouraging opportunities for marginalised children to be involved. Adults need support and training to facilitate children's participation. In certain situations, expression of views may expose children to risks and every precaution should be made to minimise any harmful risks. There is a need for accountability. Any research or consultative process involving children should provide some evaluation and follow-up in order to inform children how their views have been interpreted and used and, where necessary, provide opportunities for children to challenge and influence the analysis of findings.

The Committee's Concluding Observations on states parties' reports reflect some of the practical ways in which the child's right to be heard is being taken forward and, in some cases, the limitations on its progress. For example, the Committee has generally welcomed the creation of Youth or Children's Parliaments (in Albania, Liberia, Guinea, Guyana and Guinea-Bissau)[359] as an obvious indicator of progress in the democratisation of children's voices, although on further analysis some of these new institutions lack resources and are insufficiently consulted and heard.[360] In some states lower voting ages have been adopted. For example, Austria lowered its voting age from 18 to 16 years in 2007.[361]

As with the other general principles of the Convention, the Committee will commend states parties, for example Austria,[362] that have placed the rights

---

357 'A widespread practice has emerged in recent years, which has been broadly conceptualized as "participation", although this term itself does not appear in the text of Article 12. This term has evolved and is now widely used to describe ongoing processes, which include information-sharing and dialogue between children and adults based on mutual respect, and in which children can learn how their views and those of adults are taken into account and shape the outcome of such processes' ibid para 3.

358 General Comment No 12 paras 134(a)–(i).

359 CRC/C/ALB/CO/2-4 (5 October 2012) [33]: CRC/C/LBR/CO/2-4 (5 October 2012) [39]; CRC/C/GIN/CO/2 (30 January 2013) [42]; CRC/C/GUY/CO/2-4 (5 February 2013) [26]; CRC/C/GNB/CO/2-4 (14 June 2013) [30].

360 For example the Children's Parliaments in Guinea, Armenia and Slovenia: CRC/C/GIN/CO/2 (30 January 2013) [42]; CRC/C/ARM/CO/3-4 (14 June 2013) [22]; CRC/C/SVN/CO/3-4 (14 June 2013) [32].

361 CRC/C/AUT/CO/3-4 (5 October 2012) [28].

362 CRC/C/AUT/CO/3-4 (5 October 2012) [28].

contained in Article 12 into their own constitutional or ordinary legislative regimes. However, all too often the Committee has to report that, for example in Bosnia and Herzegovina, '[a]ctual implementation of legislation recognizing the rights of children to express their views in decisions affecting them, including relevant legal proceedings is rarely undertaken and is not systematically monitored by social workers and courts'.[363] The Committee will also be critical of states parties that have not passed laws or regulations establishing explicitly the child's right to be heard in any judicial and administrative proceedings affecting him or her.[364] Where a states party has passed laws purporting to incorporate the child's freedom of expression the Committee will comment where it detects that the national laws fall short of international standards.[365] The Committee will also welcome developments in the states parties' superior courts that signal adoption of children's participation rights. For example, it welcomed Canada's Yukon Supreme Court decision in 2010,[366] which determined that all children have the right to be heard in custody cases.[367]

The Committee's overall task, as indicated in General Comment No 12,[368] to build a 'culture of respect' for children's views, is undoubtedly a challenging one. One key obstacle identified in its Concluding Observations is the prevalence of traditional and societal attitudes that appear to limit children in freely expressing their views in schools, communities and within the family. For example, the Committee found, in relation to Albania, that 'certain traditional and cultural attitudes might limit the full implementation of Article 12 [...] and that children generally feel that their views are not taken into account in schools in alternative care institutions and at home'.[369] While undoubtedly some states parties are making better progress in developing a culture of respect for children's views, there are intransigent obstacles in others. For example, the Committee had cause to note its concern, in relation to Rwanda, 'that mechanisms for facilitating meaningful and empowered participation of children with disabilities, without parental care or from marginalized communities [...] in legislative, policy and programme development processes which impact on them, are almost non-existent'.

It is interesting to note that the General Comment states that 'in most societies around the world, implementation of [Article 12] continues to be impeded by many long-standing practices and attitudes, as well as political and economic

---

363   CRC/C/BIH/CO/3-4 (5 October 2012) [33].
364   CRC/C/NIU/CO/1 (29 January 2013) [28].
365   For example in Uzbekistan: CRC/C/UZB/CO/3-4 (14 June 2013) [26].
366   *B.J.G.* v. *D.L.G.*, 2010 YKSC 44.
367   CRC/C/CAN/CO/3-4 (5 October 2012) [36].
368   General Comment No 12 para 136.
369   CRC/C/ALB/CO/2-4 (5 October 2012) [33]. A similar comment was made in relation to Guinea where it was also noted that 'in the reality, very few children are heard in the official decisions': CRC/C/GIN/CO/2 (30 January 2013) [42]. See also CRC/C/GUY/CO/2-4 (5 February 2013) [28], where the Committee reiterated concerns about 'socio-cultural attitudes and traditions continuing to limit children from freely expressing their views in schools, courts and within the family'.

barriers'.[370] The General Comment acknowledges that the comprehensive fulfilment of the obligations required by Article 12 is likely to be a challenge for many states parties:

> Achieving meaningful opportunities for the implementation of Article 12 will necessitate dismantling the legal, political, economic, social and cultural barriers that currently impede children's opportunity to be heard and their access to participation in all matters affecting them. It requires a preparedness to challenge assumptions about children's capacities, and to encourage the development of environments in which children can build and demonstrate capacities. It also requires a commitment to resources and training.[371]

3.7.4   Civil rights and freedoms: Articles 7, 8, 13–17, 28(2) and 37(a)

During the drafting process of the Convention, there was a general move to incorporate provisions from the ICCPR (Detrick 1992: 233). The US delegation had proposed a single provision to include a child's right to civil and political freedoms, in particular a right to privacy (now Article 16), a right to freedom of association (now Article 15) and the right to freedom of expression (now Article 13). The US delegation stated that children not only had the right to expect certain benefits from governments but they also had civil and political rights to protect them from abusive actions by governments. The consensus view during the drafting process had been that children should have broadly the same civil and political rights as applied to adults, other than the right to vote. However, the identity rights contained in Article 7, which first appeared in the Declaration of the Rights of the Child (1959),[372] were a novel addition in a major human rights treaty. The duty on states parties to ensure that systems are in place for the registration of every child at or immediately after birth is also a key provision.

3.7.4.1   Birth registration and identity rights (Articles 7 and 8)

> *Article 7*[373]
> 1. The child shall be registered immediately after birth and shall have the right from birth to a name, the right to acquire a nationality and. as far as possible, the right to know and be cared for by his or her parents.

The existence of an enduring and robust birth registration system is a necessary precondition to the formulation of child policy and planning; a reliable

370 General Comment No 12 para 4.
371 ibid para 135.
372 'The child shall be entitled from his birth to a name and a nationality': Declaration of the Rights of the Child of 1959, Principle 3.
373 See generally Hodgkin and Newell (2007: 97–112) for a detailed analysis of art 7.

and accurate demographic profile will be a valuable tool in national planning. Furthermore, where a child remains unregistered it is easier to abduct, sell or induce that child into prostitution, and a child may become stateless as a result of non-registration and consequently prevented from accessing health, education and other social services.

Registration is the state's first official acknowledgement of the child's existence; it represents recognition of each child's individual importance to the state and of the child's status under the law. Where children are not registered, they are likely to be less visible, and sometimes less valued. Children who are not registered often belong to groups who suffer from other forms of discrimination (Hodgkin and Newell 2007: 98).

In a 'Day of General Discussion' held in 2004, the Committee recommended to states parties:

> ... to undertake all necessary measures to ensure that all children are regis-
> tered at birth, inter alia, by using mobile registration units and make birth
> registration free of charge. The Committee also reminds states parties of
> the importance of facilitating late registration of birth, and to ensure that
> children, despite being not yet registered, have equal access to health care,
> education and other social services.[374]

Article 7 resonates with the text of Article 24(2) and (3) of the ICCPR,[375] and also contains an additional right 'to know and be cared for by his or her parents'. The Human Rights Committee issued a General Comment on Article 24 of ICCPR,[376] which states that the right to be registered immediately after birth and to have a name is of special importance in relation to children born out of wedlock; and that '[t]he main purpose of the obligation to register children after birth is to reduce the danger of abduction, sale of or traffic in children, or of other types of treatment'. Special attention was also needed in relation to the child's right to acquire a nationality in order to prevent a child becoming stateless.

During the reporting process, the Committee will often encourage states parties to enshrine their birth registration systems into legislation; for example, it welcomed Guyana's new law on universal birth registration, although it remained

---

374 Committee on the Rights of the Child, 'Day of General Discussion' on *Implementing Child Rights in Early Childhood*, Report on the 37th session, CRC/C/143 (12 January 2005) [532–63 at 547].

375 '1. Every child shall have, without any discrimination as to race, colour, sex, language, religion, national or social origin, property or birth, the right to such measures of protection as are required by his status as a minor, on the part of his family, society and the State.
2. Every child shall be registered immediately after birth and shall have a name.
3. Every child has the right to acquire a nationality'. ICCPR art 24.

376 Human Rights Committee, General Comment No 17: *Rights of the child (Article 24)*, 35th session (7 April 1989) [7–8].

concerned that children in the hinterland/remote areas experienced difficulties in obtaining a birth certificate.[377] As Hodgkin and Newell comment (2007: 101):

> [T]he Convention does not specify what must be registered, other rights (to name and nationality, to know parentage, family and identity) imply that registration ought, as a minimum, to include:
>
> - the child's name at birth,
> - the child's sex,
> - the child's date of birth,
> - where the child was born,
> - the parents' names and addresses,
> - the parents' nationality status.

The Committee welcomes states parties' efforts to improve national systems of birth registration. For example, it commended Bosnia and Herzegovina[378] on its endorsement of the *Zagreb Declaration* of 2011,[379] which aims to address civil documentation and registration gaps in South Eastern Europe. The Committee welcomed Liberia's efforts to pilot universal, free birth registration in several countries. Equally, the Committee will commonly express concern in relation to countries where there is a poor registration system. For example, despite some progress in Liberia, the Committee remained concerned at the very low rate (7 per cent) of birth registration and the regional and gender disparities along with low levels of public awareness of its importance.[380] The Committee noted with concern, as regards Rwanda, that 'only 63 per cent of the children were registered with civil authorities and less than 7 per cent had birth certificates in 2010'.[381] In some countries, birth registration is almost universal, for example in Canada, although the Committee expressed concern that 'some children have been deprived of their identity due to the illegal removal of the father's name on original birth certificates by government authorities, especially in cases of unwed parents'.[382]

It would appear that, in some countries, the progress in birth registration seems to have gone into reverse. For example, the Committee was 'deeply concerned' that in Guinea-Bissau birth registration declined from 39 per cent in 2006 to 24 per cent in 2010, and that 61 per cent of children under five years of age were not registered.[383]

---

377 CRC/C/GUY/CO/2-4 (5 February 2013) [30].
378 CRC/C/BIH/CO/3-4 (5 October 2012) [35].
379 UN High Commissioner for Refugees, *Zagreb Declaration* (27 October 2011 http://www.refworld. org/docid/4fa2193e2.html (accessed 1 August 2013).
380 CRC/C/LBR/CO/2-4 (5 October 2012) [43].
381 CRC/C/RWA/CO/3-4 (14 June 2013) [25].
382 CRC/C/CAN/CO/3-4 (5 October 2012) [38].
383 CRC/C/GNB/CO/2-4 (14 June 2013) [32]. See also reports of the decreasing rates of birth registration in the Democratic Republic of Congo and Niger: CRC/C/COD/CO/2 (10 February 2009) [35] and CRC/C/NER/CO/2 (18 June 2009) [35] respectively.

The Committee has been tireless in its encouragement of *free* birth registration. It criticises those states parties, for example Albania and Uzbekistan, where birth registration is not free.[384] In some countries, such as Bosnia and Herzegovina, it is free if the birth occurs in a hospital but not free outside of hospitals.[385] Administrative and criminal provisions are sometimes configured in a manner that deters parents from registering births. For example, the Committee recommended, in relation to Rwanda, that it ought to remove penalties of imprisonment (for failure to register within the first 45 days) and all legal and procedural barriers that impede birth registration.[386]

The adoption of mobile registration units, particularly in rural areas, and the establishment of national electronic birth registration databases are encouraged where necessary. For example, the Committee welcomed Namibia's progress in developing birth registration through a national mobile registration campaign in 2009 and 2010, although it remained concerned that only two-thirds of Namibia's children under the age of five years have birth certificates and registration is particularly low in rural areas. Furthermore, the legal framework for birth registration was criticised as containing restrictive requirements to present civic documentation further limiting the accessibility of the registration system.[387] Similarly, it welcomed numerous measures introduced in Guinea to increase birth registration rates but remained concerned that only one-third of children are registered at birth.[388]

There are often particular concerns about birth registration of minority groups and indigenous children, as greater proportions of such children remain unregistered and therefore are also at a high risk of becoming stateless. The Committee urges that states parties with indigenous populations should take special measures to ensure a robust, equitable and free-of-charge birth registration system.[389] There are frequently problems in the registration of Roma children due to a lack of translation/interpretation services, a lack of public awareness of the importance of registration and the doubtful immigration status of some Roma parents, in for example, Bosnia and Herzegovina, which can often prevent the authorities from registering their children.[390] In Israel, the ban on granting citizenship to children born of an Israeli parent and a parent from the OPT, the decision to stop processing residency applications for Palestinian children since 2000 and 'the arbitrary revocation of residency and identity of those living in East Jerusalem' have

---

384 CRC/C/ALB/CO/2-4 (5 October 2012) [36]; CRC/C/UZB/CO/3-4 (14 June 2013) [28–29].
385 CRC/C/BIH/CO/3-4 (5 October 2012) [35].
386 CRC/C/RWA/CO/3-4 (14 June 2013) [25–26].
387 CRC/C/NAM/CO/2-3 (16 October 2012) [36].
388 CRC/C/GIN/CO/2 (30 January 2013) [44].
389 Committee on the Rights of the Child, General Comment No 11: *Indigenous children and their rights under the Convention*, CRC/C/GC/11 (12 February 2009) [41–45].
390 CRC/C/BIH/CO/3-4 (5 October 2012) [35].

resulted in 'thousands of unregistered Palestinian children excluded from access to health services, education and any other type of social benefit'.[391]

Children's rights from birth to a 'name and to acquire nationality' are of course prejudiced where the states party withholds granting citizenship on a discriminatory basis.[392] The Committee noted with concern that, in Niue, regulations allowed a parent to change a child's name without his or her consent up to the age of 21 years.[393] The text of Article 7 also contains the child's right to know and be cared for by his or her 'parents'. This latter term is perhaps contentious in terms of its scope. The Committee certainly interprets this to include the child's right to know his or her *biological* parents. Some commentators argue for a much wider interpretation:

> [A] reasonable assumption is that, as far as the child's right to know his or her parents is concerned, the definition of "parents" includes genetic parents (for medical reasons alone this knowledge is of increasing importance to the child) *and* birth parents, that is the mother who gave birth and the father who claimed paternity through partnership with the mother at the time of birth (or whatever the social definition of father is within the culture: the point being that such social definitions are important to children in terms of their identity). In addition, a third category, the child's psychological parents – those who cared for the child for significant periods during infancy and childhood – should also logically be included since these persons too are intimately bound up in children's identity and thus their rights under Article 8.
>
> (Hodgkin and Newell 2007: 105–106)

Where national adoption systems include a mother's right to conceal her identity and remain anonymous, this is likely to be criticised.[394] Nevertheless, Luxembourg's reservation to Article 7 seems to contradict this interpretation:

> The Government of Luxembourg believes that Article 7 of the Convention presents no obstacle to the legal process in respect of anonymous births, which is deemed to be in the interest of the child, as provided under Article 3 of the Convention.[395]

Article 8 of the Convention provides that:

> 1. States parties undertake to respect the right of the child to preserve his or her identity, including nationality, name and family relations as recognized by law without unlawful interference.

---

391 CRC/C/ISR/CO/2-4 (14 June 2013) [29].
392 As in Liberia. CRC/C/LBR/CO/2-4 (5 October 2012) [41–42]. See p 132 above.
393 CRC/C/NIU/CO/1 (29 January 2013) [30].
394 CRC/C/FRA/CO/4 (11 June 2009) [43].
395 Committee on the Rights of the Child website http://www2.ohchr.org/english/bodies/crc/ (accessed 1 August 2013).

2. Where a child is illegally deprived of some or all of the elements of his or her identity, States Parties shall provide appropriate assistance and protection, with a view to re-establishing speedily his or her identity.

The drafting of Article 8 was originally proposed by Argentina (Detrick 1992: 292–93) and was prompted by the enforced disappearance of children and adults in that country under the previous military junta regime. The Committee commended the work done by Argentina's National Commission for the Right to an Identity to recover children who had disappeared during the military regime (1976–83) and noted that, out of an estimated 500 cases of disappearance of children, 73 had been found.[396] During the armed conflict in El Salvador (1980–92), more than 700 children had disappeared, of whom 250 had been traced by NGOs.[397] In 2006, the General Assembly adopted an International Convention for the Protection of All Persons from Enforced Disappearance.[398]

Article 8 protects three elements of a child's identity: nationality, name and family relations. A child's nationality may be derived from his or her parents' nationality. Consequently, laws that prohibit children from inheriting nationality from their parents might not be compliant with the Convention. Where a child's nationality is derived from residence, laws that prohibit the acquisition of nationality by means of lengthy periods of residence might also fall below the standard set in this article. The protection of a right to a name derives in part from an aversion to the dehumanising impact of ascribing numbers to the mass movements of refugees or migrants. Most countries have prescriptive rules for the registration of names and what names should be used. Many of these systems are uncontroversial and are aimed to protect, in particular, children born outside of marriage. Of necessity, parents are the most likely persons to decide a child's name, but arguably, this should not be an absolute right (Hodgkin and Newell 2007: 103):

> Domestic laws should have appropriate mechanisms to prevent registration of a name that might make a child an object of ridicule, bad luck or discrimination, as for example in Malawi's 'practice of derogatory names being assigned to some children such as children born out of wedlock', which the Committee recommended the government abolish.
>
> (Malawi CRC/C/15/Add.174 paras 31 and 32)

The element of identity relating to 'family relations' reflects a growing recognition of the importance of children's relationships not only with their immediate family but also with the wider family. The right to acquire a nationality and a

396 CRC/C/15/Add.187 (9 October 2002) [34].
397 CRC/C/15/Add.232 (30 June 2004) [31].
398 General Assembly, International Convention for the Protection of All Persons from Enforced Disappearance, opened for signature 20 December 2006, UN Doc A/RES/61/177 (entered into force 23 December 2010). This Convention had 93 signatories and 42 parties as at 15 February 2014.

name has important implications for the right to obtain a passport and the right to vote. In general, under international law, nationality rules fall within the domain of municipal law, a point emphasised in the United Arab Emirates' reservation to Article 7.[399] This has led to nations adopting different rules on nationality, and consequently there are persons who may fall between the various rules and become stateless. For example, the Committee expressed concern that Canada's laws placed significant limitations on acquiring citizenship for children born to Canadian parents abroad, and that this could in some circumstances lead to statelessness.[400] It noted with concern that Guinea-Bissau did not have any administrative policy designed to prevent statelessness and protect stateless children.[401] The Committee urges states parties to ratify relevant international instruments, in particular the UN Convention Relating to the Status of Stateless Persons (1954)[402] in order to address such problems.

Identity rights may also be damaged by adoption laws, such as in Israel, which allow hiding from a child the fact that he or she is adopted.[403] One practice in Austria, identified by the Committee as a violation of Articles 7 and 8, is anonymous abandonment through the use of 'baby flaps' or 'baby nests'. The Committee strongly urged the states party to end this practice and promote alternatives, for example, anonymous births at hospitals as a measure of last resort.[404]

3.7.4.2   The rights to freedom of expression, thought, conscience, religion, association, no interference with privacy and access to information (Articles 13–17)

The following commentary from the Manual of Human Rights Reporting (OHCHR 1997) provides an overview of these provisions:

> Articles 13 to 17 constitute an important chapter of the Convention which clearly indicates the need to envisage the child not simply as a vulnerable and weak human being, but also as an active subject of rights. … It is important to stress that these rights had already generally been recognized by previous international instruments to "every human being", thus also including children. The prevailing reality was however, and to a certain extent still is, that children, in view of their evolving maturity, are in practice not recognized as having the necessary capacity or competence to exercise them.
>
> (OHCHR 1997: 434–45)

---

399 'The United Arab Emirates is of the view that the acquisition of nationality is an internal matter and one that is regulated and whose terms and conditions are established by national legislation'.

400 CRC/C/CAN/CO/3-4 (5 October 2012) [40].

401 CRC/C/GIN/CO/2 (30 January 2013) [34].

402 UN Convention Relating to the Status of Stateless Persons, opened for signature 28 September 1954, 360 UNTS 117 (entered into force 6 June 1960).

403 CRC/C/ISR/CO/2-4 (14 June 2013) [31].

404 CRC/C/AUT/CO/3-4 (5 October 2012) [29–30].

These articles are, to an extent, a reflection of the desire during the drafting process of the Convention to ensure that existing rights in the ICCPR were explicitly applied to children. The Human Rights Committee confirmed in a General Comment that: 'as individuals, children benefit from all of the civil rights enunciated in the Covenant'.[405]

Article 13

1. The child shall have the right to freedom of expression; this right shall include freedom to seek, receive and impart information and ideas of all kinds, regardless of frontiers, either orally, in writing or in print, in the form of art, or through any other media of the child's choice.
2. The exercise of this right may be subject to certain restrictions, but these shall only be such as are provided by law and are necessary:

   (a) For respect of the rights or reputations of others; or
   (b) For the protection of national security or of public order (ordre public), or of public health or morals.

This Article is based on similar provisions in the International Bill of Human Rights.[406] During the drafting process the question of the parents' role in relation to the child's civil rights arose, and an earlier draft of Article 13 (Detrick 1992: 230) explicitly protected the child's right from limiting or otherwise affecting 'the authority, rights or responsibilities of a parent'. It was agreed that this would not be necessary because, 'while children might need direction and guidance from parents or guardians in the exercise of these rights, this does not affect the contents of the rights themselves' (Hodgkin and Newell 1997: 181). Parents' rights and responsibilities to provide appropriate direction and guidance, where consistent with 'the evolving capacities of the child', are protected instead by Article 5.

The Committee's Concluding Observations have raised a number of issues in recent years. For example, it expressed concern in relation to ethical rules issued by the education ministry in Uzbekistan for higher education establishments prohibiting students from publishing materials that were critical of schools or did not correspond to 'national values'. It was also concerned that a recently enacted Law on Information Security of Minors did not have adequate safeguards for freedom of expression.[407] Similarly, the Committee noted its concern in relation to the Republic of Korea that 'schools continue to prohibit the political activities of students' and their management committees 'preclude the participation of students' thus constraining children's rights of free expression.[408] Freedom of expression is often in jeopardy during periods of political and other crises in a states party.

405 Human Rights Committee, General Comment No 17: *Rights of the child (art 24)*, 35th session, Annex IV (7 April 1989) (173–75) [2].
406 See UDHR art 19 and ICCPR art 19.
407 CRC/C/UZB/CO/3-4 (14 June 2013) [30].
408 CRC/C/KOR/CO/3-4 (2 February 2012) [40].

For example, the Committee noted concern about reports of infringements on freedom of expression in Madagascar 'including attacks on journalists and closing down media outlets', together with reports that the population, particularly children, had very limited access to information through media.[409] The Committee also expressed its concern over reports that children were kept political prisoners in Myanmar (previously known as Burma) and their rights to freedom of expression and association were 'severely limited in practice'.[410] In the Syrian Arab Republic the Committee noted its particular concern 'at the arrest and incommunicado detention in March 2011 of a group of school children aged from 8 to 15 years accused of painting anti-Government graffiti on a schoolhouse wall'.[411] The Committee also raised concerns about Vietnam where it stated that 'all sources of information – and media in particular – are subject to Government control and do not allow for diversity'.[412]

Article 14
1. States parties shall respect the right of the child to freedom of thought, conscience and religion.
2. States parties shall respect the rights and duties of the parents and, when applicable, legal guardians, to provide direction to the child in the exercise of his or her right in a manner consistent with the evolving capacities of the child.
3. Freedom to manifest one's religion or beliefs may be subject only to such limitations as are prescribed by law and are necessary to protect public safety, order, health or morals, or the fundamental rights and freedoms of others.

The text of Article 14[413] protects the child's right to 'freedom of thought, conscience and religion'. Freedom of religion was one of the four principal areas of controversy in the drafting process of the Convention (Cantwell 1992). An earlier draft of Article 13 included 'the freedom to have or to adopt a religion ... of his choice'. It was pointed out that a child's right to *choose* a religion did not exist under Islamic law; it could only apply to adults.

This put the drafters in a delicate situation. What attitude was to be taken towards the elimination of a right of the child in the future Convention that was already conferred by a well established international human rights instrument

---

409 CRC/C/MD/G/CO/3-4 (8 March 2012) [35–36].
410 CRC/C/MMR/CO/3-4 (14 March 2012) [47].
411 CRC/C/SYR/CO/3-4 (8 February 2012) [46].
412 CRC/C/VNM/CO/3-4 (15 June 2012).
413 See UDHR art 18 and ICCPR art 18. '[ICCPR Article 18] protects theistic, non-theistic and atheistic beliefs, as well as the right not to profess any religion or belief': Human Rights Committee, General Comment No 22: *Article 18 (Freedom of thought, conscience or religion)*, 48th session, CCPR/C/21/Rev.1/Add.4 (30 July 1993) [2].

[the International Covenant on Civil and Political Rights, Article 18] without restriction as to the age of the beneficiary? Reluctantly, in the end, the proponents of retaining the full right agreed to drop all reference to choice, 'in the spirit of compromise' (Cantwell 1992: 26).

This uneasy compromise has not resolved all differences, and perhaps explains why more states parties have made reservations and declarations concerning Article 14 than any other Article. The Belgian government, for example, made an interpretative declaration that Article 14(1) 'implies also the freedom to choose his or her religion or belief'. Similarly, the Netherlands made a declaration that the Article 'shall include the freedom of a child to have or adopt a religion or belief of his or her choice as soon as the child is capable of making such choice in view of his or her age or maturity'. Whereas the Holy See declared that it 'interprets the Articles of the Convention in a way which safeguards the primary and inalienable rights of parents, in particular insofar as these rights concern education (Articles 13 and 28), religion (Article 14), association with others (Article 15) and privacy (Article 16)'. The Government of the Republic of Maldives made a reservation to Article 14(1) on the basis that 'the Constitution and the Laws of the Republic of Maldives stipulate that all Maldivians should be Muslims'. Nevertheless, most commentators (Hodgkin and Newell 2007: 188) would agree that:

> The wording of Article 14 and the Convention Articles identified as general principles certainly do not support the concept of children automatically following their parent's religion until the age of 18, although Article 8 (preservation of identity), Article 20 (preservation of religion when deprived of family environment), and Article 30 (right to practice religion in community with members of the child's group) support children's right to acquire their parents' religion.

The child's right to freedom of thought, conscience and religion has been challenged in the context of France's constitutional arrangements that require a strict separation of church and state (Eva 2006). French laws support a strictly secular public education system by prohibiting the wearing of religious signs or symbols in public schools, which have been a cause for concern for the Committee. The Committee's Concluding Observation on France in 2009 stated:

> The Committee notes that the States party has undertaken measures to attenuate the consequences of the Law No. 2004-228 of 15 March 2004 banning the wearing of 'signs or dress through which pupils ostensibly indicate which religion they profess in public, primary and secondary schools', including the establishment of a mediator in the national public education system. Nevertheless, the Committee endorses the concluding observations of CEDAW [the Committee on the Elimination of Discrimination against Women], that the ban should not lead to a denial of the right to education for any girl and their inclusion into all facets of the States party's society

(CEDAW/C/FRA/CO/6, para. 20), as well as those adopted by the Human Rights Committee noting that respect for a public culture of *laïcité* would not seem to require forbidding wearing such common religious symbols.

(CCPR/C/FRA/CO/4 para 23).[414]

In Pakistan, while there are constitutional provisions giving a right of minorities to profess and practise their religions freely, the Committee noted their concern that this was limited in practice and that citizens normally governed by secular law might sometimes be subject to sharia law. The Committee was also concerned about reports that non-Muslim students had been forced to complete Islamic studies.[415] The Committee noted as positive the fact that the Republic of Korea prohibited compulsory education in schools, but was concerned that 'in practice, private schools managed by religious institutions continue to restrict the freedom of religion of its students', and 'that current initiatives do not adequately facilitate an atmosphere conducive to religious diversity or sufficiently take into account the specific needs or constraints of children of particular religions, including with regard to their dietary requirements'.[416]

The Committee noted that the constitution of Uzbekistan enshrined the right to freedom of thought, conscience and religion, but was concerned that in practice 'only mainstream religions are permitted, such as approved Muslim, Jewish, and Christian denominations while unregistered religious activities, which are frequently those of minorities, are subject to criminal and/or administrative sanctions resulting in a curtailment of the right of the child'.[417] The Committee also noted concern regarding the 'restricted conditions for professing another religion than Islam' in Algerian law and 'the attacks and violence against religious minorities'.[418]

As regards Myanmar, the Committee was concerned in particular about reports 'that some children are placed in Buddhist monasteries and converted to Buddhism without their parents' knowledge or consent and that the Government seeks to induce members of the Naga ethnic group, including children ... to convert to Buddhism'.[419]

Article 15

1. States parties recognize the rights of the child to freedom of association and to freedom of peaceful assembly.
2. No restrictions may be placed on the exercise of these rights other than those imposed in conformity with the law and which are necessary in a democratic society in the interests of national security or public safety,

---

414 CRC/C/FRA/CO/4 (11 June 2009) [45].
415 CRC/C/PAK/CO/3-4 (15 October 2009) [43].
416 CRC/C/KOR/CO/3-4 (2 February 2012) [38].
417 CRC/C/UZB/CO/3-4 (14 June 2013) [32].
418 CRC/C/DZ/A/CO/3-4 (18 July 2012) [41].
419 CRC/C/MMR/CO/3-4 (14 March 2012) [45].

> public order (ordre public), the protection of public health or morals or the protection of the rights and freedoms of others.

The Committee encourages states parties, as with other civil rights, to incorporate this Article within their own legislation. It has acknowledged positively, in a 'Day of General Discussion', the increasing number of youth-led organisations in states.[420] Although these rights are based upon the texts of the International Bill of Human Rights[421] it would seem that Article 15 remains relatively undeveloped in the context of children's rights.

It should be noted that, in general, the law concerning contracts and administration of organisations may pose obstacles for children below the age of majority or the age of legal capacity acting as directors or trustees of public associations. It seems that few countries have as yet explored this from the perspective of the full implementation of Article 15 (Hodgkin and Newell 2007: 198).

The Committee has expressed concern over the use in some countries of high-frequency ultrasound (mosquito devices), flash ball devices and taser guns at public demonstrations and elsewhere.[422] The Committee observed, in relation to Vietnam, that although children had the 'formal possibility to form associations' in practice this was 'severely restricted'.[423] The Committee takes note where there are improvements in ensuring freedom of association, for example, in Turkey where a law allowed children over the age of 15 years to establish children's associations 'with the written permission of their legal guardians'.[424] As regards Myanmar, the Committee was concerned that 'little space has been created for children to assemble or form associations outside the framework of Government-controlled NGOs'.[425] Finally, the Committee reiterated its concern that in certain states and territories of Australia police could remove children and young people who assemble peacefully in groups and recommended that the states party should consider alternatives to police and criminalisation to address any problems of peaceful assembly and review its legislation.[426]

Article 16

1 No child shall be subjected to arbitrary or unlawful interference with his or her privacy, family, home or correspondence, nor to unlawful attacks on his or her honour and reputation.

2. The child has the right to the protection of the law against such interference or attacks.

---

420 Committee on the Rights of the Child, 'Day of General Discussion' on the *Right of the child to be heard*, Report on the 43rd session, CRC/C/43/3 (16 July 2007) [1016].
421 See UDHR art 20 and ICCPR arts 21–22.
422 CRC/C/FRA/CO/4 (11 June 2009) [47].
423 CRC/C/VNM/CO/3-4 (15 June 2012) [41].
424 CRC/C/TUR/CO/2-3 (20 July 2012) [38].
425 CRC/C/MMR/CO/3-4 (14 March 2012) [47].
426 CRC/C/AUS/CO/4 (28 August 2012) [39–40].

The wording of this right is based on the texts contained in the International Bill of Human Rights.[427] The Human Rights Committee issued a General Comment on the right as formulated in Article 17 of ICCPR.[428] This states, as regards the term 'privacy':

> As all persons live in society, the protection of privacy is necessarily relative. However, the competent public authorities should only be able to call for such information relating to an individual's private life the knowledge of which is essential in the interests of society as understood under the Covenant. Accordingly, the Committee recommends that States should indicate in their reports the laws and regulations that govern authorized interferences with private life.[429]

Article 16 of the Convention on the Rights of the Child has figured in an increasing amount of adverse commentary by the Committee on the relationship between the media, privacy and children. For example, with regard to Bosnia and Herzegovina, while commending the state for including the right to privacy in its Constitution, it also raised concerns about the 'frequent instances of unethical and unprofessional conduct by journalists publishing personal details of children and youth who are victims or perpetrators of offences'.[430] The Committee also noted its concern in relation to Austria about cases of violations of privacy rights in the news reporting of criminal proceedings involving child victims and/or child perpetrators in TV, radio and other media. Of increasing concern is the misuse of social media and its impact on children:

> [The Committee] is seriously concerned about instances of humiliation, insult, 'cyber mobbing' and grooming of children via internet or mobile phones. The Committee is also concerned that the dangers and risks of the internet are not sufficiently discussed at school, and that parents and teachers are often unaware of the legal consequences in case of misuse of electronic media by children.[431]

The Committee was concerned about the 'lack of effective regulation on media' to protect children from harmful content and ensure their right to privacy in Andorra.[432] It has also had cause to comment on the insufficient respect given to

---

427 UDHR art 12, ICCPR art 17.
428 Human Rights Committee, General Comment No 16: *Article 17 (Right to Privacy), the Right to Respect of Privacy, Family, Home and Correspondence, and Protection of Honour and Reputation*, 32nd session (8 April 1988) [7].
429 ibid [7].
430 CRC/C/BIH/CO/3-4 (5 October 2012) [37].
431 CRC/C/AUT/CO/3-4 (5 October 2012) [31].
432 CRC/C/AND/CO/2 (9 October 2012) [28].

children's privacy in Uzbekistan in relation to children's personal effects and correspondence in alternative care and juvenile justice facilities.[433]

The General Comment issued by the Human Rights Committee states that:

> The gathering and holding of personal information on computers, data banks and other devices, whether by public authorities or private individuals or bodies, must be regulated by law.
>
> Effective measures have to be taken by States to ensure that information concerning a person's private life does not reach the hands of persons who are not authorized by law to receive, process and use it, and is never used for purposes incompatible with the Covenant. In order to have the most effective protection of his private life, every individual should have the right to ascertain in an intelligible form, whether, and if so, what personal data is stored in automatic data files, and for what purposes. Every individual should also be able to ascertain which public authorities or private individuals or bodies control or may control their files. If such files contain incorrect personal data or have been collected or processed contrary to the provisions of the law, every individual should have the right to request rectification or elimination.[434]

The Committee has expressed its concern about the proliferation of databases in which personal data of children are gathered, stocked and used for a lengthy period, and that parents cannot oppose and/or are not informed of the registration of their children's data.[435] The Committee will want to ensure that such databases are lawfully regulated with clear aims, that the information cannot reach unauthorised recipients and that there are suitable rights of access by children and their parents to such data.

3.7.4.3 Access to appropriate information (Article 17)

Article 17 (first paragraph)
States parties recognize the important function performed by the mass media and shall ensure that the child has access to information and material from a diversity of national and international sources, especially those aimed at the promotion of his or her social, spiritual and moral well-being and physical and mental health. ...

---

433 CRC/C/UZB/CO/3-4 (14 June 2013) [34].

434 Human Rights Committee, General Comment No 16: *Article 17 (Right to Privacy), the Right to Respect of Privacy, Family, Home and Correspondence, and Protection of Honour and Reputation*, 32nd session (8 April 1988) [10].

435 CRC/C/FRA/CO/4 (11 June 2009) [50].

To this end, the Article sets out five strategies to deliver these aims (Article 17(a) – (e)). The original draft of this Article had been formulated in negative language, providing protection for children from the mass media, but was eventually reworked in more positive terms and acknowledged the educational role of mass media (Detrick 1992: 279). It has been stated that Article 17 'addresses in an innovative way the important area of the role of mass media, and of information in general, in the realization of children's rights' (OHCHR 1997: 439).

The Committee held a 'Day of General Discussion' in 1996 that explored the relationship of the child with media,[436] and made 12 specific recommendations largely focusing on ways in which children's participation, portrayal and education in the media could be improved, state support to media for children and encouraging agreements with media companies to protect children from harmful influences.

The Committee's Concluding Observations provide examples of children's access to appropriate (and inappropriate) information. For example, the Committee was prompted to voice its concern about violent and pornographic material that children were exposed to on TV, the internet and other media in Azerbaijan.[437] It was concerned that, in relation to Albania, 'inappropriate movies are routinely broadcasted during hours when children can be expected to watch television whereas quality educative programmes are rare'.[438] The Committee noted its concern that Turkey, in the course of trying to protect children, 'has put in place extensive restrictions on children's access to information on the internet'. It took the view that Turkey's reservations to Article 17 'can hamper the production and dissemination of children's books and serve as an obstacle to children's access to appropriate information'.[439] The Committee was concerned that reporting in Thailand's media was such that 'children's identity can often be established through related information provided by the media such as family names, addresses and photographs' especially in sensitive cases of child abuse and exploitation and under the juvenile justice system.[440] The Committee also registered its concern about 'the very limited access of children to internet, new technologies and appropriate information' in Myanmar.[441] The Committee, in its observations on the Cook Islands, noted its 'particular concern' that the absence of protection of privacy in law and in practice 'has extremely serious implications on child victims of sexual abuse and their families who often decide not to report sexual assault cases to the authorities'.[442] The Committee recommended that Australia, 'consider enacting comprehensive national legislation enshrining the

---

436 Committee on the Rights of the Child, 'Day of General Discussion' on *The Child and the Media*, Report on the 13th session, CRC/C/15/Add.65 (7 October 1996) [242–57].
437 CRC/C/AZE/CO/3-4 (12 March 2012) [43].
438 CRC/C/ALB/CO/2-4 (5 October 2012) [37].
439 CRC/C/TUR/CO/2-3 (20 July 2012) [40].
440 CRC/C/THA/CO/3-4 (17 February 2013) [45].
441 CRC/C/MMR/CO/3-4 (14 March 2012) [49].
442 CRC/C/COK/CO/1 (22 February 2012) [33].

right to privacy', and further, that it ought to abolish legislation that allowed the publication of child offender details.[443]

3.7.5   Family environment and alternative care: Articles 5, 18(1), (2), 9–11, 19–21, 25, 27(4) and 39

This cluster of rights relates to the integrity of the family unit and the way in which the state intervenes both to support families and to provide alternative care where the family environment has failed to function properly. The framework of the Convention provides that *parents* (or, as the case may be, legal guardians) will have 'the primary responsibility for the upbringing and development of the child' and the best interests of the child will be 'their basic concern'.[444] The state's responsibilities will generally be to give parents appropriate assistance to perform their child-rearing responsibilities and to 'ensure the development of institutions, facilities and services for the care of children'.[445] The important relationship between the respective obligations of states parties and parents/other carers in relation to children's exercise of rights is set out in the following key Article of the Convention.

> *Article 5*
> States Parties shall respect the responsibilities, rights and duties of parents or, where applicable, the members of the extended family or community as pro-vided for by local custom, legal guardians or other persons legally responsible for the child, to provide, in a manner consistent with the evolving capacities of the child, appropriate direction and guidance in the exercise by the child of the rights recognized in the present Convention.

The primacy of the family unit is further supported in the Convention by the principle that the state must ensure the non-separation of children from their parents against their will 'except when competent authorities subject to judicial review determine, in accordance with applicable law and procedures, that such separation is necessary for the best interests of the child'.[446] A child who is sepa-rated from his or her parents has a right 'to maintain personal relations and direct contact with both parents on a regular basis, except if it is contrary to the child's best interests'.[447] States are under a further obligation to deal with cases of family reunification, 'in a positive, humane and expeditious manner', where for example the child or parents have applied to enter or leave the state,[448] and a child whose parents reside in different states has the right to maintain on a regular basis 'direct

443   CRC/C/AUS/CO/4 (28 August 2012) [41–42].
444   CRC art 18(1).
445   ibid art 18(2).
446   ibid art 9(1).
447   ibid art 9(2).
448   ibid art 10(1).

contact with both parents'.[449] States are also obliged to 'take measures to combat the illicit transfer and non-return of children abroad'.[450] States parties are also obliged to 'take all appropriate measures to secure the recovery of maintenance for the child from the parents or other persons having financial responsibility for the child, both within the state party and from abroad'.[451]

Where a child is 'temporarily or permanently deprived of his or her family environment' the Convention provides that the child will be 'entitled to special protection and assistance provided by the State'.[452] In particular, states are obliged to 'ensure alternative care for such a child' in accordance with their national laws.[453] This could include, 'foster placement, *kafalah* of Islamic law, adoption or if necessary placement in suitable institutions for the care of children'.[454] A child who has been placed by the competent authorities in foster care or in other protective arrangements has a right 'to a periodic review of the treatment provided … and all other circumstances relevant to his or her placement'.[455] If adoption is the chosen route for a particular states party, the Convention provides that the state must ensure that 'the best interests of the child shall be the paramount consideration'.[456] This is a stronger legal formulation than the general 'best interests' principle in Article 3(1), where it is formulated as 'a primary consideration'. The Convention further provides that adoptions must be authorised by the competent authorities that will determine whether the adoption is permissible according to applicable law and procedure.[457] States are also obliged to recognise that inter-country adoption may also be an appropriate alternative care solution for a child who cannot be adopted, fostered or placed in any suitable manner in the child's country of origin.[458] Article 19 obliges states parties to protect children from all forms of violence, including sexual abuse'. This provision is discussed in more detail in section 3.7.6.1 below.

Some of the relevant standards within this cluster of rights have been given further focus by the Committee's Decision No 7[459] adopted in 2004, which recognised, inter alia, the frequency with which its Concluding Observations addressed

---

449 ibid art 10(2).
450 ibid art 11(1).
451 ibid art 27(4).
452 ibid art 20(1).
453 ibid art 20(2).
454 ibid art 20(3). 'Placing children in *Kafalah* is similar to adoption, but not necessarily with the severing of family ties, the transference of inheritance rights, or the change of the child's family name. Traditional Muslim law does not appear to allow formal adoption because it refuses to accept the legal fiction which an adoption creates, namely that an adopted child can become equal to a blood relative of the adopting father' (Pearl and Menski 1998: 408).
455 ibid art 25.
456 ibid art 21.
457 ibid art 21(a).
458 ibid art 21(b).
459 Committee on the Rights of the Child, Decision No 7: *Children without parental care*, 37th session, CRC/C/143 (12 January 2005) 4–5.

'serious difficulties regarding the provision of care for children in informal or formal fostering, including kinship care and adoption, or in residential facilities, often recommending the strengthening and regular monitoring of alternative care measures'.[460] The Committee has also convened a 'Day of General Discussion' on the subject of children without parental care adopted in 2005.[461] This confirmed that 'the family, as the fundamental group of society, is the natural environment for the survival, protection and development of the child', and the need for states parties to develop 'a comprehensive national policy on families and children which supports and strengthens families'.[462] It noted however that in many states parties 'the number of children separated from their parents and placed in alternative care is increasing and at a high level. It is concerned that these placements are not always a measure of last resort and therefore not in the best interests of the child'.[463] Interestingly, the Committee raised the question whether a 'new paradigm' was needed to replace the traditional institutional model of children's out-of-home placement and to challenge 'the deep-rooted ideology behind the institutional model' by, for example, establishing smaller specialised units within institutions.[464] The Committee also emphasised its approval of a 'principle of individualization' in this field:

> Every child is unique and the separation from parents and the placement into out-of-home care should always be looked at case by case. There is no one solution which fits all situations. The individualization of solutions means more tailored solutions based on the actual situation of the child, including her/his personal, family and social situation. This provides better opportunities for the assessment of the child's long-term development and it respects the principle of the best interests of the child, e.g. what are the actual needs of the child, how to keep a close relationship with the biological family.[465]

A key theme underlying the Committee's Concluding Observations on this cluster of rights is the appropriate balance to be struck between the state's obligations and family responsibilities for children (see section 1.1.4). In some countries there is evidence that the family unit has been fundamentally and structurally weakened, often as a result of civil strife, war, HIV/AIDS and poverty. The Committee noted with concern in the 'Day of General Discussion' that these factors resulted in a significant number of children being orphaned, or otherwise separated from their parents.[466] For example, in Rwanda the Committee was 'deeply concerned'

---

460 ibid 4.
461 Committee on the Rights of the Child, 'Day of General Discussion' on *Children without parental care*, Report on the 40th session, CRC/C/153 (17 March 2006) [636–89].
462 ibid [644–45].
463 ibid [654].
464 ibid [660–61].
465 ibid [667].
466 ibid [687].

that as a result of the genocide in 1994, one-third of children in Rwanda had been orphaned.[467] Twenty-eight per cent of Namibian children under the age of 18 are orphans and/or vulnerable, 34 per cent do not live with one of the parents, and only 26 per cent of all children live with both parents.[468] The Committee also noted at the 'Day of General Discussion' that 'precise guidance available to states working to meet their obligations with respect to suitable alternative care remains partial and limited', and it recommended that 'a set of international standards for the protection and alternative care of children without parental care' be developed for the General Assembly to consider.[469] Detailed Guidelines for the Alternative Care of Children were adopted by a General Assembly resolution celebrating the 20th anniversary of the Convention.[470] The Guidelines set out 'desirable orientations for policy and practice', and seek in particular:

(a) To support efforts to keep children in, or return them to, the care of their family or, failing this, to find another appropriate and permanent solution, including adoption and *kafala* of Islamic law;

(b) To ensure that, while such permanent solutions are being sought, or in cases where they are not possible or are not in the best interests of the child, the most suitable forms of alternative care are identified and provided, under conditions that promote the child's full and harmonious development;

(c) To assist and encourage Governments to better implement their responsibilities and obligations in these respects, bearing in mind the economic, social and cultural conditions prevailing in each state; and

(d) To guide policies, decisions and activities of all concerned with social protection and child welfare in both the public and the private sectors, including civil society.[471]

3.7.5.1   Family environment

The Committee welcomes states parties' efforts to strengthen family environments through investment in education, health and social services. The Committee will, for example, support efforts to develop early childhood care facilities in support of parents' child-rearing responsibilities, and it welcomes state support of foster care services in lieu of institutional care.[472] The Committee has raised concerns in relation to some countries about 'the insufficient resources and measures to enhance the capacities of parents, especially teenage parents, for the performance of their

467   CRC/C/15/Add.234 (1 July 2004) [40].
468   CRC/C/NAM/CO/2-3 (16 October 2012) [47].
469   Committee on the Rights of the Child, 'Day of General Discussion' on *Children without parental care*, Report on the 40th session, CRC/C/153 (17 March 2006) [687–88].
470   General Assembly, *Guidelines for the Alternative Care for Children*, 64th session, UN Doc A/RES/64/142 (24 February 2010).
471   ibid [2].
472   For example in Malta: CRC/C/MLT/CO/2 (5 February 2013) [43–46].

child-rearing responsibilities'.[473] The Committee was concerned, in relation to Albania, where it identified a 'lack of parent counselling programmers to support parents in caring for their children', in particular where the parents and/or the children were disabled.[474] It will be concerned where, as in Bosnia and Herzegovina, a simple lack of financial resources is accepted as a reason to separate children from their families and placing them in institutional care.[475] The Committee noted its concern in relation to Armenia, where child protection at the local level appeared 'to a large extent by volunteers without necessary qualifications and training'.[476]

The particular context pertaining to the state under scrutiny may impact dramatically on issues relating to the family environment. For example, in Rwanda, the Committee noted that the states party had 'one of the highest proportions of child-headed households in the world as a result of the 1994 genocide and HIV/AIDS'.[477] The Committee urges states to provide more assistance to families in some disadvantaged communities in crisis situations due to poverty and other factors. For example, it raised concerns in relation to Canada, about the number of pregnant girls and teenage mothers who drop out of school.[478]

In some states, there are no alternative care institutions available. For example, in Niue the Committee noted that it is the 'extended family system that provides solidarity in case parents cannot fulfil their responsibilities', and the state party 'depends exclusively on the extended families for the alternative care of children'.[479] The particular ways in which parental responsibility is exercised (Articles 5, 18(1) and (2)) is a persistent subject of commentary by the Committee. It has expressed 'serious concern' in relation to the Civil Code in Guinea, which contains family law provisions 'that discriminate against women and girls and reinforce discriminatory social practices'; on divorce, a woman only has custody of her children up to the age of seven. The Committee urged the states party to 'take prompt measures to ensure that mothers and fathers equally share the legal responsibility for their children in accordance with Article 18(1) of the Convention'.[480]

In Albania, the Committee noted that in the northern areas of the country 'mothers are not allowed to maintain contact with their children when they live on their own or go back to their original families following divorce or death of their spouse due to the application of the 'Kanun'.[481]

---

473 For example in Liberia: CRC/C/LBR/CO/2-4 (5 October 2012) [54].
474 CRC/C/ALB/CO/2-4 (5 October 2012) [52].
475 CRC/C/BIH/CO/3-4 (5 October 2012) [49].
476 CRC/C/ARM/CO/3-4 (14 June 2013) [29].
477 CRC/C/RWA/CO/3-4 (14 June 2013) [36].
478 CRC/C/CAN/CO/3-4 (5 October 2012) [53].
479 CRC/C/NIU/CO/1 (29 January 2013) [47].
480 CRC/C/GIN/CO/2 (30 January 2013) [61–62].
481 CRC/C/ALB/CO/2-4 (5 October 2012) [52]. The *Kanun* is a set of traditional Albanian Laws, originally oral but produced in written form in the 20th century.

The limited degree to which fathers take parental responsibility for their children is sometimes a cause for concern, particularly where the Committee has identified, for example in Guyana, a 'widespread phenomenon of absentee or transient fathers' based on 'deeply rooted social and cultural factors influencing fathers to neglect their parental responsibilities'.[482] The states' obligations regarding the recovery of maintenance under section 27(4) of the Convention has also been found wanting in some countries, for example in Slovenia, where the Committee was concerned about 'the persistence of lengthy legal proceedings which create sustained uncertainty for the child, and the continuing backlog of family cases in courts'.[483] The Committee will also comment on states parties where there is an insufficient enforcement of maintenance decisions as required by Article 27(4), particularly where the parent has emigrated abroad.[484]

When supporting children in their own family environments fails, then the options for alternative, out-of-home care will need to be explored. The Committee's examination of alternative care options frequently raises a number of difficulties, not least that the maintenance of suitable family-type alternative care, for example, well-run national fostering services, ultimately requires the commitment of significant resources. The Committee comments adversely in circumstances, such as in Bosnia and Herzegovina, where social work and family centres have limited financial, technical and human resources, and will recommend that these issues are addressed.[485] The lack of any comprehensive, funded system of foster care frequently results in 'low standards of care', inadequate support for children leaving care and tends to discourage 'reunification of children with biological parents even where this may be a viable option'.[486] Israel has also come under much criticism from the Committee for its 'severe restrictions on family reunification' contrary to Articles 9 and 10 of the Convention:

> The Committee is particularly concerned about the state party's decision to stop processing residency applications for Palestinian children since 2000 and to revoke the residency status of Palestinians living in East Jerusalem. The Committee notes with deep concern that even children who have lost one of their parents are prevented from reuniting with their surviving parent in the West Bank.[487]

The Guidelines recognise that 'residential care facilities and family-based care complement each other in meeting the needs of children' but where such large residential (institutions) facilities remain, 'alternatives should be developed in

---

482 CRC/C/GUY/CO/2-4 (5 February 2013) [39].
483 CRC/C/SVN/CO/3-4 (14 June 2013) [46].
484 CRC/C/ALB/CO/2-4 (5 October 2012) [52].
485 CRC/C/BIH/CO/3-4 (5 October 2012) [46–47].
486 CRC/C/BIH/CO/3-4 (5 October 2012) [48].
487 CRC/C/ISR/CO/2-4 (14 June 2013) [49].

the context of an overall deinstitutionalization strategy'.[488] Over the years the Committee has noted in relation to several countries that an increasing number of children are being placed in institutional care. For example, it noted with concern in relation to Guyana,[489] the increasing number of such placements, particularly in relation to children of single-parent families and the lack of safeguards and procedures to ensure that institutional care is genuinely used as 'a measure of last resort', as suggested in the Guidelines for the Alternative Care of Children.[490] The Committee has made similar comments in relation to Armenia,[491] where it recommended that children should not be placed in institutional care for financial reasons only.[492] As regards Canada, the Committee was 'deeply concerned' about the high number of children in alternative care and 'at the frequent removal of children from their families as a first resort in cases of neglect or financial hardship or disability'.[493] Institutional care was also identified by the Committee in relation to Uzbekistan, as the 'predominant means' rather than a measure of last resort, and placements were a result of 'socio-economic hardship, divorce, abandonment, and/or lack of family support services'.[494] The Committee was concerned that as the majority of the institutional care population consisted of children with disabilities, this was a strong indicator that 'there are inadequate support measures for children with disabilities to live with their families'.[495] The Committee noted, as regards Israel, that 'only a small proportion of children are placed in foster care compared to those placed in residential institutions'.[496] In addition to the problems identified with some states parties' institutional care arrangements, particularly the prevalence of physical, sexual and emotional abuse, some countries, for example Rwanda, have been criticised for being over-reliant on NGOs to provide such care institutions, rather than the state party developing its own.[497] The Committee has also noted, for example in relation to Austria,[498] that no adequate statistical data is available about institutional care or family-type alternative care, contrary to the advice given in the Guidelines for the Alternative Care of Children.[499] Conditions can be notoriously poor and damaging within institutional care settings, a situation that is often not helped by the administrative

488 General Assembly, *Guidelines for the Alternative Care for Children*, 64th session, UN Doc A/RES/64/142 (24 February 2010) [23].
489 CRC/C/GUY/CO/2-4 (5 February 2013) [41].
490 General Assembly, *Guidelines for the Alternative Care for Children*, 64th session, UN Doc A/RES/64/142 (24 February 2010) [14].
491 CRC/C/ARM/CO/3-4 (14 June 2013) [29–32].
492 CRC/C/ARM/CO/3-4 (14 June 2013) [30].
493 CRC/C/CAN/CO/3-4 (5 October 2012) [55].
494 CRC/C/UZB/CO/3-4 (14 June 2013) [47].
495 ibid [45].
496 CRC/C/ISR/CO/2-4 (14 June 2013) [47].
497 CRC/C/RWA/CO/3-4 (14 June 2013) [39].
498 CRC/C/AUT/CO/3-4 (5 October 2012) [40].
499 General Assembly, *Guidelines for the Alternative Care for Children*, 64th session, UN Doc A/RES/64/142 (24 February 2010) [69].

arrangements. For example, in Albania, the Committee noted that the organisation of institutions by age groups resulted in 'frequent moves of children, the disruption of their relations with staff and children and the separation from their own siblings'. Furthermore, children had to leave care at the age of 15 years without any support from the state.[500]

3.7.5.2 Adoption

Article 21

States parties that recognize and/or permit the system of adoption shall ensure that the best interests of the child shall be the paramount consideration and they shall:

(a) Ensure that the adoption of a child is authorized only by competent authorities who determine, in accordance with applicable law and procedures and on the basis of all pertinent and reliable information, that the adoption is permissible in view of the child's status concerning parents, relatives and legal guardians and that, if required, the persons concerned have given their informed consent to the adoption on the basis of such counselling as may be necessary;

(b) Recognize that inter-country adoption may be considered as an alternative means of child's care, if the child cannot be placed in a foster or an adoptive family or cannot in any suitable manner be cared for in the child's country of origin;

(c) Ensure that the child concerned by inter-country adoption enjoys safeguards and standards equivalent to those existing in the case of national adoption;

(d) Take all appropriate measures to ensure that, in inter-country adoption, the placement does not result in improper financial gain for those involved in it;

(e) Promote, where appropriate, the objectives of the present Article by concluding bilateral or multilateral arrangements or agreements, and endeavour, within this framework, to ensure that the placement of the child in another country is carried out by competent authorities or organs.

In essence, Article 21 establishes the stronger legal formulation of a *paramountcy principle* with regard to the consideration of children's best interests, and also sets out a series of (five) safeguards. Inter-country adoption is recognised as a potential option of alternative care in Article 21(b) subject to an important 'subsidiarity principle', that is, it is acceptable only where suitable arrangements cannot be made in the child's country of origin: see further Chapter 6. The requirement that, in matters of adoption, the best interests of the child must be 'the

---

500 CRC/C/ALB/CO/2-4 (5 October 2012) [52].

paramount' (in contradistinction to 'a primary') consideration is commented on in the Implementation Handbook:

> The provision establishes that no other interests, whether economic, political, state security or those of the adopters, should take precedence over, or be considered equal to, the child's.
>
> ...
>
> The paramountcy principle should be clearly stated in law. Any regulation that fetters the principle could lead to a breach of the Convention – for example inflexible rules about the adopters, such as the setting of age limits, or about the child, for example requiring a lengthy period before an abandoned child can be adopted.
>
> (Hodgkin and Newell 2007: 295)

Article 21 was one of the four principal issues of controversy in the drafting of the Convention identified by Cantwell (1992: 26). Since the Western notion of adoption – the full severing of the legal relationship between parent and child – is not recognised under Islamic law, the aim was to ensure that the text did not compel the Islamic states to recognise or establish systems of adoption. However, new thinking on adoption had already emerged in the form of a Declaration[501] approved by the General Assembly in 1986.

This Declaration contained a number of fundamental principles that deserved inclusion in the Convention, and indeed translated the new thinking on inter-country adoption in particular, whereby emphasis was to be placed on guaranteeing the protection of the children concerned rather than on facilitating the process. The revised text of Article 21 took due account of all these questions (Cantwell 1992: 26).

Inter-country adoption (see further Chapter 6) was given finer international focus several years after the Declaration with the adoption of the Hague Convention on Protection of Children and Co-operation in respect of Intercountry Adoption (1993).[502] The Committee, consistently with Article 21(e) of the Convention, promotes the adoption of such treaties by states parties. For example, while acknowledging that the number of such adoptions were low in Guyana and Bosnia and Herzegovina, the Committee was nevertheless concerned that safeguards were inadequate, and recommended that these states parties acceded to the Hague Convention.[503] Similarly, with respect to Namibia, the Committee recommended

---

501 Declaration on Social and Legal Principles relating to the Protection and Welfare of Children, with special reference to Foster Placement and Adoption, Nationally and Internationally. General Assembly, 95th plenary meeting, UN Doc A/RES/41/85 (3 December 1986).

502 Hague Conference on Private International Law, Hague Convention on Protection of Children and Co-operation in respect of Intercountry Adoption, concluded 29 May 1993 (entered into force 1 May 1995).

503 CRC/C/GUY/CO/2-4 (5 February 2013) [43–44]; CRC/C/BIH/CO/3-4 (5 October 2012) [51].

the states party to expedite the ratification of the Hague Convention.[504] As the Committee has observed with concern, in relation to Austria, 'the current normative framework is insufficient to ensure the rights and best interests of children in cases of inter-country adoptions when children come from countries that have not ratified the Hague Convention'.[505] Where a states party has ratified the Hague Convention, the Committee is keen to evaluate the extent to which it has adopted implementing regulations or established necessary structures and mechanisms to implement it, a point that it found lacking in the case of Rwanda.[506]

Article 21 of the Convention, together with a number of other international instruments, is aimed at providing a more orderly regulation of adoption, particularly inter-country adoption, in order to protect children from a range of exploitative behaviours that can surround these transactions. The Committee took note, for example, of the existence of customary adoption, for example, *tama taute* in Niue,[507] and recommended that the state party introduce adequate measures to ensure the registration and monitoring of all adopted children, particularly under these customary arrangements. The regulation of adoptions generally, envisaged in Article 21(a), enables the Committee to assess the overall picture of domestic and inter-country adoption laws and procedures. For example, as regards the former, it expressed concern in relation to Albania, in particular about 'the considerable delays by the institutions to declare a child abandoned and by the judges to conduct adoption proceedings, as a result of which children are kept for years in orphanages although biological parents have released the child and new parents have been found'. The Committee was additionally concerned that the views of children under the age of 10 years were not given due weight, and there was no legal obligation in the Family Code to inform and provide counsel to biological parents.[508] The Committee comments on the potential gaps between the standards set in the Convention and states parties' adoption law and procedure. For example, with respect to Bosnia and Herzegovina, it was concerned that its adoption legislation was not in full conformity with the Convention and there were 'discrepancies in adoption legislation amongst its Entities and territories, resulting in legislative ambiguity and protection gaps'.[509] One particular concern was '[t]he upper age limit of five years for children in the Republika Srpska, resulting in most children there not being eligible for adoption'.[510] Similar issues relating to the

---

504 CRC/C/NAM/CO/2-3 (16 October 2012) [50]. See also, CRC/C/LBR/CO/2-4 (5 October 2012) [59]. The Hague Convention on Intercountry Adoption had 93 ratifications at the time of writing.

505 CRC/C/AUT/CO/3-4 (5 October 2012) [42].

506 CRC/C/RWA/CO/3-4 (14 June 2013) [49].

507 CRC/C/NIU/CO/1 (29 January 2013) [51–52]. *Tama taute* is a custom whereby a child is raised by other members of the extended family, ie a form of informal adoption.

508 CRC/C/ALB/CO/2-4 (5 October 2012) [56].

509 CRC/C/BIH/CO/3-4 (5 October 2012) [50].

510 ibid.

variations in domestic adoption legislation, policy and practice set by each of the provinces and territories in Canada were noted with concern by the Committee.

The Committee has expressed concern where a states party does not provide for a specific body to monitor, particularly inter-country adoptions. This was the case in relation to Andorra, where the Committee recommended that the states party entrust a monitoring and data-collecting role, including post-adoption monitoring, to a specific body and ensure that the principle of the best interests of the child was considered.[511] The Committee was, in respect of Namibia, 'deeply concerned that domestic and intercountry adoptions take place unofficially through unauthorized private channels, and without any oversight by the states party'. It recommended again that the states party establish a specific body with a monitoring and data-collection role.[512] Similarly, the Committee was 'highly concerned' with respect to Liberia about 'the persistence of informal domestic adoption and inter-country adoption in the states party where in many cases parents' informed consent is not provided'.[513] As regards Armenia, although the Committee welcomed its ratification of the Hague Convention and its recent adoption laws, it raised a number of concerns about their implementation, for example, '[c]riteria for selection of adoptive parents are too formal and are based on material conditions of potential parents and not on the parenting skills'.[514]

3.7.6   Violence against children: Articles 19, 37(a), 34 and 39

3.7.6.1   Freedom of the child from all forms of violence

Article 19

1. States parties shall take all appropriate legislative, administrative, social and educational measures to protect the child from all forms of physical or mental violence, injury or abuse, neglect or negligent treatment, maltreatment or exploitation, including sexual abuse, while in the care of parent(s), legal guardian(s) or any other person who has the care of the child.

2. Such protective measures should, as appropriate, include effective procedures for the establishment of social programmes to provide necessary support for the child and for those who have the care of the child, as well as for other forms of prevention and for identification, reporting, referral, investigation, treatment and follow-up of instances of child maltreatment described heretofore, and, as appropriate, for judicial involvement.

---

511 CRC/C/AND/CO/2 (9 October 2012) [37–38].
512 CRC/C/NAM/CO/2-3 (16 October 2012) [49–50].
513 CRC/C/LBR/CO/2-4 (5 October 2012) [58].
514 CRC/C/ARM/CO/3-4 (14 June 2013) [33].

Article 19 has been given further focus in General Comment No 13[515] issued in 2011, with the stated rationale that 'the extent and intensity of violence exerted on children is alarming'.[516] The link between Article 19 and OPSC is also recognised by the Committee, but 'the Committee holds that Article 19 forms the core provision for discussion and strategies to address and eliminate all forms of violence in the context of the Convention more broadly'.[517] This General Comment contains, inter alia, a detailed legal analysis of the text of Article 19. For example, it explains the phrase 'all forms of' thus:

> *No exceptions.* The Committee has consistently maintained the position that all forms of violence against children, however light, are unacceptable. "All forms of physical or mental violence" does not leave room for any level of legalized violence against children. Frequency, severity of harm and intent to harm are not prerequisites for the definitions of violence. States parties may refer to such factors in intervention strategies in order to allow proportional responses in the best interests of the child, but definitions must in no way erode the child's absolute right to human dignity and physical and psychological integrity by describing some forms of violence as legally and/or socially acceptable.[518]

The Committee has frequently referenced the UN Study on Violence against Children, led by Professor Paulo Sergio Pinheiro, in its Concluding Observations.[519] This study has been influential in guiding strategy and policy in this field, and in particular it was stated that the study 'should mark a turning point — an end to adult justification of violence against children, whether accepted as "tradition" or disguised as "discipline"'.[520] The study addressed violence against children in five settings: the family, schools, alternative care institutions and detention facilities, places where children work and communities. It called for urgent action to prevent and respond to all forms of violence and presented a set of strategic recommendations. In addition, it suggested the appointment of a Special Representative of the Secretary General on Violence against Children (SRSG), which was realised by a General Assembly resolution in 2008.[521] The SRSG reports directly to the UN Secretary General, and collaborates closely with a wide range of partners, within and beyond the UN system.[522]

---

515 Committee on the Rights of the Child, General Comment No 13: *The right of the child to freedom from all forms of violence*, CRC/C/GC/13 (18 April 2011).
516 ibid [2].
517 ibid [7].
518 ibid [17].
519 For example CRC/C/AND/CO/2 (9 October 2012) [36].
520 General Assembly, *Rights of the Child: Note by the Secretary-General, Study on Violence against Children*, UN Doc A/61/299 (29 August 2006) [2].
521 General Assembly, *Rights of the Child*: Resolution, UN Doc A/RES/62/141 (22 February 2008).
522 See generally http://srsg.violenceagainstchildren.org (accessed 26 September 2013).

From the basis of the material contained in General Comment No 13, the UN Study and the activities of the SRSG, the Committee characteristically proceeds to a number of recommendations in this field. For example, in relation to Albania, it recommended that the states party: develop a comprehensive national strategy to prevent and address all forms of violence against children; adopt a national coordinating framework to address these issues; pay particular attention to the gender dimension of violence; and, cooperate with the SRSG on violence against children and other relevant United Nations institutions.[523] The Committee will sometimes pinpoint particular areas of concern in this field. It raised concern, for example in relation to Canada, about girls in vulnerable situations, including Aboriginal, African Canadian children and those with disabilities, and recommended that the states party 'ensure that the factors contributing to the high levels of violence among Aboriginal women and girls are well understood and addressed in national and province/territory plans'.[524] Another recurrent theme identified by the Committee is, for example in relation to Liberia, 'the high level of impunity enjoyed by perpetrators of violence against children, against whom mostly social measures rather than prosecutions are applied'.[525] Equally, the Committee will often raise concerns, for example in relation to Guinea, about the low rate of reporting cases of violence against women and children 'because of the taboo surrounding abuse – especially of a sexual nature – and by fear of being further stigmatized'.[526] The Committee will on occasion recommend that the states party establish a three-digit, toll-free helpline staffed with trained personnel, available to children, and promote awareness of how children can access the helpline.[527]

3.7.6.2   The right not to be subjected to torture or other cruel, inhuman or degrading treatment or punishment: in particular, corporal punishment (Article 37(a))

Article 37(a)
States parties shall ensure that:
No child shall be subjected to torture or other cruel, inhuman or degrading treatment or punishment. Neither capital punishment nor life imprisonment without possibility of release shall be imposed for offences committed by persons below eighteen years of age;
...

---

523 For example CRC/C/ALB/CO/2-4 (5 October 2012) [49]. See also CRC/C/AND/CO/2 (9 October 2012) [36]: CRC/C/AUT/CO/3-4 (5 October 2012) [39]; CRC/C/GUY/CO/2-4 (5 February 2013) [38]; CRC/C/ARM/CO/3-4 (14 June 2013) [26], which repeats, almost verbatim, the same language.
524 CRC/C/CAN/CO/3-4 (5 October 2012) [46–47].
525 CRC/C/LBR/CO/2-4 (5 October 2012) [47].
526 CRC/C/GIN/CO/2 (30 January 2013) [57].
527 For example CRC/C/NIU/CO/1 (29 January 2013) [49]; CRC/C/UZB/CO/3-4 (14 June 2013) [44].

This Article resonates with similar provision in the International Bill of Human Rights.[528] A 'Day of General Discussion' held in 2000,[529] recommended, inter alia, that:

> States parties review all relevant legislation to ensure that all forms of violence against children, however light, are prohibited, including the use of torture, or cruel, inhuman or degrading treatment (such as flogging, corporal punishment or other violent measures), for punishment or disciplining within the child justice system, or in any other context. The Committee recommends that such legislation incorporate appropriate sanctions for violations and the provision of rehabilitation for victims.[530]

Protection from corporal punishment has also been the subject of a dedicated General Comment No 8,[531] which contains a useful analysis of the child's right not to be tortured or suffer cruel, inhuman or degrading treatment including corporal punishment in a variety of settings: for example, at school, in the family, in alternative care and in justice institutions. The General Comment acknowledges that there is 'widespread acceptance or tolerance of corporal punishment of children' and its elimination is not only mandated under the Convention but 'is also a key strategy for reducing and preventing all forms of violence in societies'.[532] The General Comment further notes that the elimination of violent and humiliating punishment of children has been reflected in the views of some of the other international human rights treaty bodies,[533] and regional human rights mechanisms.[534] As regards the core meaning of Article 37(a):

> The Committee defines 'corporal' or 'physical' punishment as any punishment in which physical force is used and intended to cause some degree of pain or discomfort, however light. Most involves hitting ('smacking', slapping, spanking') children, with the hand or with an implement – a whip, stick, belt, shoe, wooden spoon, etc. But it can also involve, for example, kicking, shaking or throwing children, scratching, pinching, biting, pulling hair or boxing

---

528 See UDHR art 5 and ICCPR art 7.

529 Committee on the Rights of the Child 'Day of General Discussion' on *Violence against Children*, Report on the 25th session, CRC/C/97 (22 September 2000), Annex IV; and Report on the 25th session, CRC/C/100 (14 November 2000), [666–88].

530 CRC/C/100 (14 November 2000), [688, sub-para 8].

531 Committee on the Rights of the Child, General Comment No 8: *The right of the child to protection from corporal punishment and other cruel or degrading forms of punishment (arts 19; 28, para 2; and 37, inter alia)*, CRC/C/GC/8 (2 March 2007).

532 ibid [3].

533 ibid [22]. Specifically, the Human Rights Committee, the Committee on Economic, Social and Cultural Rights and the Committee against Torture.

534 See the references to the European Court of Human Rights decisions, an Advisory Opinion of the Inter-American Court of Human Rights, and a decision on an individual communication to the African Commission on Human and People's Rights, in General Comment No 8: *The right of the child to protection from corporal punishment and other cruel or degrading forms of punishment* [23–25].

ears, forcing children to stay in uncomfortable positions, burning, scalding or forced ingestion (for example, washing children's mouths out with soap or forcing them to swallow hot spices). In the view of the Committee, corporal punishment is invariably degrading. In addition, there are other non-physical forms of punishment that are also cruel and degrading and thus incompatible with the Convention. These include, for example, punishment which belittles, humiliates, denigrates, scapegoats, threatens, scares or ridicules the child.[535]

The General Comment clarifies that the rejection of violence 'is not in any sense rejecting the positive concept of discipline'.[536] The Committee also make the distinction between the use of force to punish and the (legitimate) use of force motivated by the need to protect a child from harm.[537] It further underlines that the wording of Article 19 makes it clear that *legislative* and other measures are required to fulfil states' obligation to protect children from all forms of violence. The Committee notes that provisions such as the long-standing (common law) defence of 'lawful', 'reasonable' or 'moderate' chastisement or the 'right of correction' in French law should be removed.[538] The General Comment notes that, given the pervasive traditional acceptance of corporal punishment, 'simply repealing authorization of corporal punishment and any existing defences is not enough'; explicit prohibition in civil and criminal law, in sectoral legislation and in professional codes of ethics and guidance is also required.[539] Implementation will require a range of awareness-raising, guidance and training.[540] The General Comment further emphasises the need for systematic monitoring by states parties through the development of appropriate indicators and reliable data collection.[541] There is also a 'Global Initiative to End All Corporal Punishment of Children',[542] launched in April 2001, which aims to speed the end of corporal punishment of children across the world. It currently records that (as at February 2014) there were 35 states with full prohibition of corporal punishment in their laws.

General Comment No 8 is frequently cited in the Committee's Concluding Observations. The Committee will routinely urge states parties to enact legislation that explicitly prohibits all forms of corporal punishment in the family, schools, alternative care settings and penal institutions.[543] Sometimes, countries will make corporal punishment prohibited in schools while it remains lawful in the home and

---

535 General Comment No 8: *The right of the child to protection from corporal punishment and other cruel or degrading forms of punishment* [11].

536 ibid [13].

537 ibid [15].

538 ibid [31].

539 ibid [34–35].

540 ibid [38].

541 ibid [50].

542 See http://www.endcorporalpunishment.org/ (accessed 8 August 2013).

543 For example in Andorra: CRC/C/AND/CO/2 (9 October 2012) [31].

alternative care settings.[544] The Committee will positively support national legislation or case law development that prohibits corporal punishment and will deplore the continuance of the 'reasonable chastisement' defence, where it occurs.[545] The Concluding Observations reveal many countries that continue 'to lack legislation explicitly prohibiting corporal punishment in all settings'.[546] Even where countries have made serious efforts to eliminate corporal punishment from institutional settings, the Committee will comment adversely where 'corporal punishment in the home remains widespread in the State party'.[547] The reports reveal evidence of the persistence of traditional views about disciplining children. For example, in Niue, the Committee was concerned 'that corporal punishment is still commonly practiced in schools and in the home and that violent punishment, mockery, ridicule, public humiliation and verbal abuse of children are widely accepted as valid forms of discipline'.[548] In some countries, for example, in Rwanda, where parents had a 'right of correction' under its Civil Code, the Committee was 'gravely concerned' that 'the use of corporal punishment is considered appropriate in education and is still widespread in all settings, including families and school.[549] The Committee's Concluding Observations provide plenty of examples of violations: for example, in Albania, by public officials and the police in pre-trial detention centres, in prisons and in care institutions;[550] or in Guinea where the Committee expressed 'deep concern' about children detained in police stations who are subjected to ill treatment or torture 'in order to confess the commission of an offence'.[551] The Committee was, in relation to Uzbekistan: 'gravely concerned' about continued reports of torture and ill-treatment being routinely used in investigations, including persons under the age of 18 years; and 'deeply concerned' about the use of solitary cells as punishment in juvenile prisons; and 'seriously concerned' about the frequent use of forced labour as a form of punishment for children in government institutions such as schools and orphanages.[552] There are often concerns expressed, particularly in relation to 'closed institutions', such as some care homes identified in Armenia.[553]

The Committee has also expressed its deep concern about the plight of Palestinian children in the OPT, in particular the 'reported practice of torture

544 CRC/C/GNB/CO/2-4 (14 June 2013) [36].
545 For example in Namibia and Canada: CRC/C/NAM/CO/2-3 (16 October 2012) [38]; CRC/C/CAN/CO/3-4 (5 October 2012) [45].
546 For example in Malta: CRC/C/MLT/CO/2 (5 February 2013) [36].
547 CRC/C/BIH/CO/3-4 (5 October 2012) [39].
548 CRC/C/NIU/CO/1 (29 January 2013) [34].
549 CRC/C/RWA/CO/3-4 (14 June 2013) [27].
550 CRC/C/ALB/CO/2-4 (5 October 2012) [39]. The Committee was also 'deeply concerned' about information on ill-treatment of juveniles in detention in relation to the arrests following a demonstration on 21 January 2011.
551 CRC/C/GIN/CO/2 (30 January 2013) [46]. This report also states that: '[s]ome religious interpretations wrongly prescribe whipping as being an integral part of learning the Koran' [48].
552 CRC/C/UZB/CO/3-4 (14 June 2013) [38].
553 CRC/C/ARM/CO/3-4 (14 June 2013) [24–25].

and ill-treatment of Palestinian children arrested, prosecuted and detained by the military and the police' and Israel's failure to end these practices despite the concerns expressed by a range of treaty bodies, special procedures mandate holders and others.[554] Indeed, the situation in the OPT was thought by the Committee to be of a sufficient gravity to justify the '[l]aunch without delay [of] an independent inquiry into all alleged cases of torture and ill-treatment of Palestinian children'.[555]

The Committee was 'highly alarmed by the frequent incidence of corporal punishment, including extreme physical violence suffered by children at school and in the home' in Liberia.[556] In line with General Comment No 8, the Committee will recommend the strengthening and expansion of awareness-raising campaigns 'to promote positive and alternative forms of discipline and respect for children's rights, with the involvement of children'.[557]

3.7.6.3 Sexual exploitation and abuse (Article 34)

Article 34

States parties undertake to protect the child from all forms of sexual exploitation and sexual abuse. For these purposes, states parties shall in particular take all appropriate national, bilateral and multilateral measures to prevent:

(a) The inducement or coercion of a child to engage in any unlawful sexual activity;

(b) The exploitative use of children in prostitution or other unlawful sexual practices;

(c) The exploitative use of children in pornographic performances and materials.

The Committee characteristically advises states parties to implement appropriate policies and programmes in accordance with the Declaration and Agenda for Action and the Global Commitment adopted at the 1996, 2001 and 2008 World Congresses against Commercial Sexual Exploitation of Children (see Chapter 7). The Committee examines carefully states parties' criminal/penal codes to ensure compliance with the Convention in this area. For example, in Albania children between the age of 14 and 18 years are only protected 'if there is violence and girls only up to the age of puberty, causing the Committee to recommend a revision of its legislation to protect all children up to the age of 18 years.[558] In Niue, the rape of boy children is not legally prohibited, and punishment for sexually abusing children was very low: a maximum three years imprisonment for sexual intercourse

---

554 CRC/C/ISR/CO/2-4 (14 June 2013) [35].
555 ibid [36].
556 CRC/C/LBR/CO/2-4 (5 October 2012) [45].
557 For example, in Austria: CRC/C/AUT/CO/3-4 (5 October 2012) [34].
558 CRC/C/ALB/CO/2-4 (5 October 2012) [45–46].

with girls between 12–15 years.[559] The Committee raised concerns in relation to Slovenia about its 'limited definition of violence against children in national legislation [which] does not explicitly refer to sexual violence'.[560]

The Committee raised concerns, in relation to Austria, about insufficient measures to encourage child victims to report instances of violence, abuse and neglect, in particular in alternative care institutions.[561] As regards Canada, the Committee welcomed its efforts to combat sexual exploitation of children on the internet, but remained concerned that insufficient action had been taken against other forms of sexual exploitation, and was 'gravely concerned' about cases of 'Aboriginal girls who were victims of child prostitution and have gone missing or were murdered and have not been fully investigated with the perpetrators going unpunished'.[562] The Committee was also 'gravely concerned', in relation to Liberia, that child rape and sexual offences were among 'the most commonly reported crimes in the State party'; a high number of cases were settled out of court 'due to the pressure of the families of alleged perpetrators'; and, there were 'corrupt practices of judicial officials, and a 'lack of sufficient investigative and forensic capacity remains a challenge'.[563] A similar pattern of sexual exploitation and abuse arises across a number of states parties. In Namibia, for example, the Committee was 'gravely concerned' about the high incidence of child rape, low prosecution rates for crimes of sexual violence against children and 'the pervasiveness of extra-judicial settlements, leading to impunity for perpetrators'.[564] The Committee was also concerned, in relation to Guinea, about 'the shortcomings in the relevant legislation in particular that sexual violence is considered as an offense against morality as opposed to a crime against the person', and 'the prevailing culture of corruption and impunity in this field'.[565] Impunity in this area is a common theme in the periodic reports. For example, the Committee noted, in relation to Niue, that 'perpetrators of child sexual abuse are almost never brought to justice'.[566] There are concerns also, as in relation to Malta, about the adequacy of 'mechanisms for ensuring the detection, investigation and prosecution of perpetrators of child exploitation and abuse'.[567] The Committee will welcome states parties that raise the age of sexual consent; for example, from 13 to 16 years in Guyana.[568] The Committee will characteristically recommend that the states party: conduct a national study on sexual abuse of children to determine root causes and assess its scale; strengthen its legislation; develop a long-term societal behaviour change

559 CRC/C/NIU/CO/1 (29 January 2013) [38].
560 CRC/C/SVN/CO/3-4 (14 June 2013) [41].
561 CRC/C/AUT/CO/3-4 (5 October 2012) [35].
562 CRC/C/CAN/CO/3-4 (5 October 2012) [48].
563 CRC/C/LBR/CO/2-4 (5 October 2012) [49].
564 CRC/C/NAM/CO/2-3 (16 October 2012) [40].
565 CRC/C/GIN/CO/2 (30 January 2013) [52].
566 CRC/C/NIU/CO/1 (29 January 2013) [38].
567 CRC/C/MLT/CO/2 (5 February 2013) [40].
568 CRC/C/GUY/CO/2-4 (5 February 2013) [36].

campaign to reduce sexual abuse and its acceptability; address harmful cultural practices involving child abuse and exploitation; ensure mandatory reporting of child sex abuse; ensure it has programmes and policies for the prevention, recovery and reintegration of child victims in accordance with the outcome documents adopted at the 1996, 2001 and 2008 World Congresses against Sexual Exploitation of Children.[569]

A number of 'harmful practices' are often commented upon under this heading by the Committee: for example the persistence of practices of early marriage in Rwanda, Namibia and Armenia;[570] forced child marriages in Guinea-Bissau, Canada and Slovenia;[571] female genital mutilation (FGM) in Austria, Liberia, Guinea and Guinea-Bissau;[572] and levirate and sororate marriage in Guinea.[573] The Committee also comments frequently on the nature and level of child abuse and neglect prevalent within both family and alternative care settings. This may involve criticisms of a states party's legislative regime,[574] high levels of abuse and neglect revealed by national survey work,[575] the limited access to services for abused children, the high level of impunity enjoyed by perpetrators of violence against children,[576] and low levels of reporting and prosecution of child abuse and neglect.[577]

3.7.6.4   Recovery and reintegration of child victims

Article 39

States parties shall take all appropriate measures to promote physical and psychological recovery and social reintegration of a child victim of: any form of neglect, exploitation, or abuse; torture or any other form of cruel, inhuman or degrading treatment or punishment; or armed conflicts. Such recovery and reintegration shall take place in an environment which fosters the health, self-respect and dignity of the child.

One corollary of the obligations in Article 19 (section 3.7.6.1) is the further duty placed on states parties contained in Article 39. The Committee has indicated

---

569 CRC/C/GUY/CO/2-4 (5 February 2013) [37].
570 CRC/C/RWA/CO/3-4 (14 June 2013) [31]; CRC/C/NAM/CO/2-3 (16 October 2012) [42];
      CRC/C/ARM/CO/3-4 (14 June 2013) [27].
571 CRC/C/CAN/CO/3-4 (5 October 2012) [50]; CRC/C/GNB/CO/2-4 (14 June 2013) [41];
      CRC/C/SVN/CO/3-4 (14 June 2013) [43].
572 CRC/C/AUT/CO/3-4 (5 October 2012) [37]; CRC/C/LBR/CO/2-4 (5 October 2012) [49];
      CRC/C/GIN/CO/2 (30 January 2013) [54]; CRC/C/GNB/CO/2-4 (14 June 2013) [43].
573 CRC/C/GIN/CO/2 (30 January 2013) [55]. Sororate marriage is where a husband engages in
      marriage or sexual relations with the sister of his wife, usually after the death of his wife, or once
      his wife has proven infertile. Levirate marriage is where a man is obligated to marry his brother's
      widow, and the widow is obligated to marry her deceased husband's brother.
574 CRC/C/BIH/CO/2-4 (5 October 2012) [41–43].
575 CRC/C/CAN/CO/3-4 (5 October 2012) [46].
576 CRC/C/LBR/CO/2-4 (5 October 2012) [47].
577 CRC/C/GIN/CO/2 (30 January 2013) [50].

that 'the wording of Article 39 requires consideration of a wide range of potential child victims' (Hodgkin and Newell 2007: 590). Following its 'Day of General Discussion' on state violence against children,[578] the Committee made various recommendations on the rehabilitation of child victims. These included encouraging the existing 'United Nations human rights mechanisms with a mandate to consider individual complaints concerning violations of human rights to identify ways to respond more effectively to individual complaints concerning violence against children';[579] a recommendation that may perhaps be revisited with renewed interest by the Committee when OPIC enters into force (Buck and Wabwile 2013). It also recommended that states parties review all relevant legislation to prohibit 'all forms of violence against children, however light', and that such legislation ought to 'incorporate appropriate sanctions for violations and the provision of rehabilitation for victims', and to 'ensure that children under 18, who are in need of protection are not considered as offenders' but are dealt with under child protection mechanisms.[580] OPSC also contains a provision that obliges states parties to 'take all feasible measures with the aim of ensuring all appropriate assistance to victims of [the Protocol] offences, including their full social reintegration and their full physical and psychological recovery' and states must 'promote international cooperation to assist child victims in their physical and psychological recovery, social reintegration and repatriation'.[581] OPAC contains a reference in its Preamble to the need for 'the physical and psychosocial rehabilitation and social reintegration of children who are victims of armed conflict' and the Protocol obliges states parties to provide, 'when necessary … all appropriate assistance for their physical and psychological recovery and their social reintegration'.[582]

3.7.7 Disability, basic health and welfare: Articles 6, 18(3), 23, 24, 26, 27(1), (2) and (3), and 33

Article 6 of the Convention (the right to life, survival and development) has been discussed above (section 3.7.3.3). Article 23 establishes rights relating to disabled children.

> *Article 23(1)*
> 1. States Parties recognize that a mentally or physically disabled child should enjoy a full and decent life, in conditions which ensure dignity, promote self-reliance and facilitate the child's active participation in the community.
> …

---

578 Committee on the Rights of the Child, 'Day of General Discussion' on *State Violence against Children*, Report on the 25th session, CRC/C/97 (22 September 2000) [666–88].
579 ibid [688(4)].
580 ibid [688(8–9)].
581 OPSC arts 9(3), 10(2).
582 OPAC, preamble §17; art 6(3).

Article 24 sets out the child's right to health.

Article 24(1)
1. States Parties recognize the right of the child to the enjoyment of the highest attainable standard of health and to facilities for the treatment of illness and rehabilitation of health. States Parties shall strive to ensure that no child is deprived of his or her right of access to such health care services.

The child's enjoyment of health facilities is complemented by the obligation on states parties to take 'all appropriate measures to ensure that children of working parents have the right to benefit from child-care services and facilities for which they are eligible' in Article 18(3). A further important right of the child is the right to an adequate standard of living.

Article 27(1)
1. States Parties recognize the right of every child to a standard of living adequate for the child's physical, mental, spiritual, moral and social development.

Related to this right is the right of every child 'to benefit from social security, including social insurance' in Article 26. Finally, further protection is offered in Article 33.

Article 33
States Parties shall take all appropriate measures, including legislative, administrative, social and educational measures, to protect children from the illicit use of narcotic drugs and psychotropic substances as defined in the relevant international treaties, and to prevent the use of children in the illicit production and trafficking of such substances.

Under this cluster of rights there has been an accretion of 'soft law' instruments (section 2.2.6) to guide states parties in their focus in reporting to the Committee on these issues. States parties are requested to take into account a number of relevant General Comments of the Committee:

- General Comment No 3 on HIV/AIDS[583]
- General Comment No 4 on adolescent health[584]
- General Comment No 9 on the rights of children with disabilities[585]
- General Comment No 15 on the right to health.[586]

---

583 Committee on the Rights of the Child, General Comment No 3: *HIV/AIDS and the rights of the child*, CRC/GC/2003/3 (17 March 2003).
584 Committee on the Rights of the Child, General Comment No 4: *Adolescent health and development in the context of the Convention on the Rights of the Child*, CRC/GC/2003/4 (1 July 2003).
585 Committee on the Rights of the Child, General Comment No 9: *The rights of children with disabilities*, 43rd session, CRC/C/GC/9 (27 February 2007).
586 Committee on the Rights of the Child, General Comment No 15: *The right of the child to the enjoyment of the highest attainable standard of health (art 24)*, 62nd session, CRC/C/GC/15 (17 April 2013).

3.7.7.1   Children with disabilities

The Committee has noted the historical exclusion of disabled children from participation in 'normal' childhood activities and the fact that 'their plight rarely figured
high on the national or international agenda, and they tended to remain invisible'
in a 'Day of General Discussion' held in 1997,[587] which recommended, inter
alia, that the Committee consider the possibility of drafting a General Comment
on disabled children.[588] General Comment No 9 appeared in 2006.[589] In the
same year the United Nations also produced a new Convention on the Rights
of Persons with Disabilities (2006),[590] along with an Optional Protocol[591] that
will allow the Committee on the Rights of Persons with Disabilities (CRPD) 'to
receive and consider communications from or on behalf of individuals or groups
of individuals subject to its jurisdiction who claim to be victims of a violation by
that States party of the provisions of the Convention'.[592] One of the eight general
principles of the Convention on the Rights of Persons with Disabilities is '[r]espect
for the evolving capacities of children with disabilities and respect for the right of
children with disabilities to preserve their identities'.[593] There is also a discrete
provision in the Convention on the Rights of Persons with Disabilities relating to
children with disabilities that complements Article 23 of the Convention on the
Rights of the Child:

> *Children with disabilities*
> 1. States parties shall take all necessary measures to ensure the full enjoyment
> by children with disabilities of all human rights and fundamental freedoms on
> an equal basis with other children.
> 2. In all actions concerning children with disabilities, the best interests of the
> child shall be a primary consideration.
> 3. States parties shall ensure that children with disabilities have the right to
> express their views freely on all matters affecting them, their views being
> given due weight in accordance with their age and maturity, on an equal basis

---

587   Committee on the Rights of the Child, 'Day of General Discussion' on *The Rights of Children
  with Disabilities*, Report on the 16th session, CRC/C/69 (26 November 1997) [310–38 at 312].
588   ibid [338].
589   Committee on the Rights of the Child, General Comment No 9: *The rights of children with disabilities*, 43rd session, CRC/C/GC/9 (27 February 2007).
590   Convention on the Rights of Persons with Disabilities, opened for signature 13 December 2006,
  2514 UNTS 3 (entered into force 3 May 2008). This Convention had 141 parties at the time of
  writing (February 2014).
591   Optional Protocol to the Convention on the Rights of Persons with Disabilities, opened for signature 13 December 2006, UN Doc A/61/611 (entered into force 3 May 2008). This Optional
  Protocol had 79 parties at the time of writing (February 2014).
592   ibid art 1.
593   UN Convention on the Rights of Persons with Disabilities art 3(h).

with other children, and to be provided with disability and age-appropriate assistance to realise that right.[594]

As stated in General Comment No 9:

> The Committee, in reviewing State party reports, has accumulated a wealth of information on the status of children with disabilities worldwide and found that in the overwhelming majority of countries some recommendations had to be made specifically to address the situation of children with disabilities.[595]

As regards the barriers to the full enjoyment of the rights in the Convention experienced by children with disabilities, the Committee emphasised that 'the barrier is not the disability itself but rather a combination of social, cultural, attitudinal and physical obstacles which children with disabilities encounter in their daily lives'.[596] In some states the built environment itself can pose challenges for children with disabilities. For example, in Bosnia and Herzegovina, the Committee noted with concern a 'persistence of architectural and physical barriers in public areas, including schools'.[597] In Austria, the Committee noted with concern 'the limited accessibility of their physical environment'.[598] Cultural barriers are often indicated by a 'high level of stigmatization of children with disabilities', as identified by the Committee in relation to Liberia,[599] or similarly, the '[w]idespread social prejudice and stigma against children with disabilities' identified in relation to Uzbekistan.[600] Sometimes the cultural barriers can be detected by reference to the language used in legislation and policy documents. For example, as regards Niue, the Committee disapproved of 'derogatory language identifying girls with disabilities as "idiots, imbeciles or of unsound mind"' in the relevant national legislation.[601] The Committee was also concerned that in Niue there were lower criminal sanctions for sexual crimes against children with disabilities and recommended that these were repealed.[602] The Committee will express concern about the situation of children with disabilities where most of them are being 'totally excluded from mainstream society', and are, for example in Albania, 'being kept isolated in their homes and live in situations of poverty with high risks of being ill-treated'.[603]

594 UN Convention on the Rights of Persons with Disabilities art 7.
595 Committee on the Rights of the Child, General Comment No 9: *The rights of children with disabilities*, 43rd session, CRC/C/GC/9 (27 February 2007) [3].
596 ibid [5].
597 CRC/C/BIH/CO/2-4 (5 October 2012) [52].
598 CRC/C/AUT/CO/3-4 (5 October 2012) [44].
599 CRC/C/LBR/CO/2-4 (5 October 2012) [60].
600 CRC/C/UZB/CO/3-4 (14 June 2013) [49].
601 CRC/C/NIU/CO/1 (29 January 2013) [53].
602 ibid [53–54].
603 CRC/C/ALB/CO/2-4 (5 October 2012) [58].

The Convention was the first international human rights treaty to refer explicitly in its non-discrimination principle (Article 2) to 'disability' as a discrete heading of discrimination (section 3.7.3.1). General Comment No 9 suggests that states parties, in their efforts to eliminate disability discrimination, should include explicitly disability as a forbidden ground in their Constitutional and/or their specific anti-discrimination laws; provide effective and accessible remedies; and, conduct awareness-raising and educational campaigns.[604] There are sometimes references in the Committee's Concluding Observation, for example, as in relation to Guyana, that '[s]ocietal discrimination against children with disabilities remains widespread'.[605] The Committee has noted with concern the lack of protection in, for example Guinea-Bissau, where it recommended that the states party needed to '[e]radicate impunity for abuse of children with disabilities'.[606] Discriminatory practice in relation to children with disabilities is frequently derived from multiple forms of discrimination, for example in Namibia the Committee noted concern in particular in relation to children with disabilities 'especially girls and those living in rural areas'.[607] Such discrimination is frequently a deeply rooted phenomenon. For example, the Committee was deeply concerned in relation to Rwanda, that children with disabilities were 'often discriminated due to cultural stigma and superstition'.[608]

During the reporting process, the Committee will recommend that states parties ratify the related international instruments referred to above, if they have not already done so.[609] It will of course welcome states parties' ratification of the Convention on the Rights of Persons with Disabilities (2006), for example by Bosnia and Herzegovina, but will also express its concern where 'no concrete steps have been taken to establish a clear legislative definition of disability' and the states party has failed to align its national and regional jurisdictions with these international standards.[610]

The Committee's Concluding Observations frequently refer to the need for the states party to take into account General Comment No 9 and the Standard Rules on the Equalization of Opportunities for Persons with Disabilities.[611] General Comment No 9 also emphasises the need to set up and develop robust mechanisms for data collection. It points out that 'this issue is often overlooked and not viewed as a priority'. It further notes the need to develop a widely accepted definition for disabilities 'that guarantees the inclusion of all children with disabili-

---

604 Committee on the Rights of the Child, General Comment No 9: *The rights of children with disabilities*, 43rd session, CRC/C/GC/9 (27 February 2007) [9].
605 CRC/C/GUY/CO/2-4 (5 February 2013) [45].
606 CRC/C/GNB/CO/2-4 (14 June 2013) [50–51].
607 CRC/C/NAM/CO/2-3 (16 October 2012) [51].
608 CRC/C/RWA/CO/3-4 (14 June 2013) [43].
609 CRC/C/GUY/CO/2-4 (5 February 2013) [45]
610 CRC/C/BIH/CO/2-4 (5 October 2012) [52].
611 General Assembly, *Standard rules on the equalization of opportunities for persons with disabilities*, A/RES/48/96, 48th session (20 December 1993).

ties so that children with disabilities may benefit from the special protection and programmes developed for them'.[612] The 'lack of detailed and disaggregated data hindering the state party formulating and taking effective measures to address the needs of children with disabilities' is a frequent refrain in the Committee's Concluding Observations.[613]

Access to education services is clearly also an important part of the overall objective to include children with disabilities into mainstream society and provide them with the skills and means to contribute economically as an adult. The Committee noted with concern situations such as in Guinea, where there was 'only one secondary school facility accessible to children with disabilities'.[614] It noted its concern, in relation to Albania, that '[m]ost children with disabilities are deprived from their right to education'.[615] It often has cause to remark on the need for inclusive education and training of teachers, for example in Liberia,[616] and the limitations on its provision, for example in Guyana, 'particularly for children with sensory, cognitive, and/or mental impairments, which leads to the majority of children with disabilities staying at home, resulting in isolation, stigmatisation and compromised access to employment opportunities and social services'.[617] Similarly, the Committee was concerned in relation to Bosnia and Herzegovina that '[i]nclusive education remain[s] severely limited, with the majority of children with disabilities staying at home or being segregated in special institutions/ schools', resulting in stigmatisation and compromised access to employment opportunities and social services.[618] In Israel, the Committee was concerned that the 'overwhelming majority of children with disabilities attend special schools or special classes in ordinary schools'.[619] In some states parties, for example Canada, '[t]here is great disparity among the different provinces and territories … in access to inclusive education, with education in several provinces and territories being mostly in segregated schools'.[620] Where there is a choice for a child with disabilities to attend a special school or an inclusive school, this decision may rest with the parents, which may conflict with the best interests of the child as the Committee found, for example, in relation to Austria and Israel.[621]

The Committee will also register its concern where it finds that a states party provides little in the way of support for families.[622] The Committee noted with concern, for example in relation to Bosnia and Herzegovina, that it had not

---

612 Committee on the Rights of the Child, General Comment No 9: *The rights of children with disabilities*, 43rd session, CRC/C/GC/9 (27 February 2007) [19].

613 CRC/C/GUY/CO/2-4 (5 February 2013) [45].

614 CRC/C/GIN/CO/2 (30 January 2013) [63].

615 CRC/C/ALB/CO/2-4 (5 October 2012) [58].

616 CRC/C/LBR/CO/2-4 (5 October 2012) [60].

617 CRC/C/GUY/CO/2-4 (5 February 2013) [45].

618 CRC/C/BIH/CO/2-4 (5 October 2012) [52].

619 CRC/C/ISR/CO/2-4 (14 June 2013) [51].

620 CRC/C/CAN/CO/3-4 (5 October 2012) [59].

621 CRC/C/AUT/CO/3-4 (5 October 2012) [44]; CRC/C/ISR/CO/2-4 (14 June 2013) [51].

622 CRC/C/LBR/CO/2-4 (5 October 2012) [60].

established a sufficient social services infrastructure 'necessary for addressing the needs of children with disabilities while allowing them to continue living with their families'.[623] The Committee will also be seriously concerned where it appears that there are a high number of children with disabilities in institutional care, as for example it found in relation to Austria and Armenia where the number of children with disabilities in children's homes was increasing 'due to lack of family support and alternative family and community based care options'.[624] The Committee recommended, for example in relation to Rwanda, that 'the placement of children with disabilities in institutions is used only as a measure of last resort, when it is absolutely necessary and in the best interests of the child'.[625]

3.7.7.2   Health and access to health services

General Comment No 15 explains further the normative content of the right to health in Article 24:

> The notion of 'the highest attainable standard of health' takes into account both the child's biological, social, cultural and economic preconditions and the State's available resources, supplemented by resources made available by other sources, including non-governmental organizations, the international community and the private sector.

Children's right to health contains a set of freedoms and entitlements. The freedoms, which are of increasing importance in accordance with growing capacity and maturity, include the right to control one's health and body, including sexual and reproductive freedom to make responsible choices. The entitlements include access to a range of facilities, goods, services and conditions that provide equality of opportunity for every child to enjoy the highest attainable standard of health.[626]

Child mortality rates have been a cause for deep concern by the Committee, and indeed the reduction of child mortality is one of the UN's 'millennium development goals' (MDGs).[627] There has been an overall improvement in child mortality figures, from 12.4 million in 1990 to 6.9 million in 2011. However, an increasing proportion of child deaths are in sub-Saharan Africa where one in nine children die before the age of five and in Southern Asia where one in 16 die before age five. Furthermore, although the overall under-five deaths figure is declining, the proportion that occurs during the first month after birth is

---

623   CRC/C/BIH/CO/2-4 (5 October 2012) [52].
624   CRC/C/AUT/CO/3-4 (5 October 2012) [44]; CRC/C/ARM/CO/3-4 (14 June 2013) [35].
625   CRC/C/RWA/CO/3-4 (14 June 2013) [44].
626   Committee on the Rights of the Child, General Comment No 15: *The right of the child to the enjoyment of the highest attainable standard of health (art 24)*, 62nd session, CRC/C/GC/15 (17 April 2013) [23–24].
627   'Target 4A: Reduce by two thirds, between 1990 and 2015, the under-five mortality rate' (MDG 4) http://www.un.org/millenniumgoals/childhealth.shtml (9 September 2013).

increasing.[628] The Committee has noted with concern high child mortality rates in a number of states parties.[629] On occasion, where the problem is particularly severe, the Committee will express its 'deep concern', for example in the case of Guinea-Bissau.[630] The Committee noted with regard to this states party that the high rate of child deaths was 'mostly due to preventable causes' (eg malaria, acute respiratory infections, diarrhoea and the vaccine-preventable diseases) and only 42 per cent of children under one year old had received all the required immunisations. The Committee noted with concern that the states party's annual budget allocation for health was below the MDG target of 15 per cent.[631] High maternal deaths are also a subject of concern to the Committee[632] and comprise another area targeted in the MDGs.[633]

Malnutrition accounts for many child deaths and a number of associated health problems, often exacerbated in remote or rural areas in the states party.[634] Guinea, for example, was reported to have a chronic malnutrition rate of 35 per cent.[635] In Niue, there were estimates of a deteriorating child death profile, and that the recruitment and retention of skilled health professionals was presenting a major challenge.[636] Malaria and tuberculosis continue to play a central role in the child mortality and morbidity rates in many countries.[637] In Liberia, for example, high levels were 'mainly attributable to malaria (67%), pneumonia (14%) and malnutrition (13%)'.[638] A key concern for the Committee will be to encourage states parties to '[d]evise and implement a strong primary health care system to cover the whole country'.[639] The Committee will often be eager to recommend that a states party (eg Guinea-Bissau) provides a 'continuum of care' for mothers, new-borns and children, including ante-natal care, training care at birth, and a package of infant and young child care.[640]

---

628 ibid.
629 CRC/C/GIN/CO/2 (30 January 2013) [65]; CRC/C/NIU/CO/1 (29 January 2013) [55]; CRC/C/GUY/CO/2-4 (5 February 2013) [47]; CRC/C/ALB/CO/2-4 (5 October 2012) [60].
630 CRC/C/GNB/CO/2-4 (14 June 2013) [52].
631 ibid.
632 See CRC/C/NAM/CO/2-3 (16 October 2012) [53]; CRC/C/GIN/CO/2 (30 January 2013) [65]; CRC/C/GUY/CO/2-4 (5 February 2013) [47]; CRC/C/UZB/CO/3-4 (14 June 2013) [51].
633 'Target 5A: Reduce by three quarters the maternal mortality ratio. Target 5B: Achieve universal access to reproductive health' (MDG 5) http://www.un.org/millenniumgoals/childhealth.shtml (9 September 2013).
634 CRC/C/ALB/CO/2-4 (5 October 2012) [60]; CRC/C/NAM/CO/2-3 (16 October 2012) [53]; CRC/C/RWA/CO/3-4 (14 June 2013) [46].
635 CRC/C/GIN/CO/2 (30 January 2013) [65].
636 CRC/C/NIU/CO/1 (29 January 2013) [55].
637 CRC/C/GIN/CO/2 (30 January 2013) [65]; CRC/C/GUY/CO/2-4 (5 February 2013) [47].
638 CRC/C/LBR/CO/2-4 (5 October 2012) [64].
639 CRC/C/LBR/CO/2-4 (5 October 2012) [63].
640 CRC/C/GNB/CO/2-4 (14 June 2013) [53].

In addition to the early childhood diseases there are also cases of environmental threats to children's health. For example, the Committee noted with concern, in relation to Albania, the 'impact on children's health of air pollution ... of contamination of drinking water with pesticides and bacteriological substances and of poor food quality'.[641] It also expressed concern, with regard to Bosnia and Herzegovina, about the detrimental health effects of the existing 15 depleted uranium contaminated sites which have led to substantial increases in the occurrence of cancer, particularly amongst children who continue to live at these sites'.[642]

The poverty, hunger and consequent mortality and health problems associated with developing economies may not be present in developed economies, at least not to the same extent. However, the Committee identifies a number of health issues that appear to be associated with the more advanced economy. With regard to Canada, for example, the Committee has noted with concern that despite the 'free and widespread access to high-quality healthcare', there is a 'high incidence of obesity among children'[643] and a 'lack of regulations on the production and marketing of fast foods and other unhealthy foods, especially as targeted at children'.[644] It also noted concern about suicide rates among young people, particularly youth belonging to the Aboriginal community, and the 'increasingly high rates of children diagnosed with behavioural problems and the over-medication of children without expressly examining root causes or providing parents and children with alternative support and therapy'.[645] The Committee also registered its concern, in relation to Austria, about 'the over-prescription of medication such as Ritalin for children with attention deficit and hyperactivity disorder'.[646]

The Committee may also provide more specialist advice and recommendations, for example, by referencing the recommendations of the Special Rapporteur on the human right to safe drinking water and sanitation in its Concluding Observations,[647] or advising the states party to seek suitable technical advice and assistance from, inter alia, UNICEF and the WHO.[648] On occasion, but less frequently, mental health services are the subject of the Committee's concern, not least because of the failure to collect reliable data on mental health issues.[649] For example, as regards Malta, the Committee noted it only had one special unit

641 CRC/C/ALB/CO/2-4 (5 October 2012) [60].
642 CRC/C/BIH/CO/2-4 (5 October 2012) [56].
643 See also, CRC/C/ARM/CO/3-4 (14 June 2013) [37] and CRC/C/SVN/CO/3-4 (14 June 2013) [52] which records a high level of obesity amongst under-fives in Armenia and Slovenia respectively.
644 CRC/C/CAN/CO/3-4 (5 October 2012) [63].
645 ibid [65].
646 CRC/C/AUT/CO/3-4 (5 October 2012) [46].
647 CRC/C/NAM/CO/2-3 (16 October 2012) [54], citing: Human Rights Council, *Report of the Special Rapporteur on the human right to safe drinking water and sanitation*, 21st session, UN Doc A/HRC/21/42/Add.3 (28 June 2012).
648 CRC/C/GNB/CO/2-4 (14 June 2013) [53].
649 CRC/C/NIU/CO/1 (29 January 2013) [57].

providing residential psychiatric care to children up to the age of 17 years.[650] The Committee's concerns also extend to high levels of suicides in some states parties among children, for example in Namibia, where the suicide rate among youth had increased in recent years.[651]

In some states parties, for example Albania, there is a 'pervasive practice of health workers and doctors asking for informal payments which prevents children from accessing health services'.[652] In Uzbekistan, although the states party's Constitution entitles citizens to free medical care, 'the collection of informal fees for consultations and treatment is prevalent and results in the majority of persons and families in socio-economically disadvantaged situations being precluded from health services'.[653] The Committee also noted with concern in relation to Armenia that, '[i]nformal (under the table) payments are common especially in hospital settings, which creates obstacles in accessing free medical care'.[654]

The issue of unequal access to health care and services often arises as a consequence of underlying discriminatory practice and is frequently a cause for the Committee's concern. For example, with regard to Bosnia and Herzegovina, the Committee noted that the 'large proportion of the Roma population remains deprived of health insurance'.[655] The Committee also had cause to regret, in relation to Israel, 'the unequal access to [health] services which mainly affects Bedouin and Arab children as well as children belonging to the Ethiopian Israeli community', and expresses 'deep concern' that the deteriorated situation of health and health services for children in the OPT ... [had] considerably worsened over the reporting period due to attacks on hospitals and clinics of Gaza'.[656]

3.7.7.3 Breastfeeding

The Committee urges states parties to encourage the exclusive breastfeeding of infants up to the age of six months, and sustain breastfeeding for two years or more as recommended by WHO.[657] States parties that fall below this standard[658] are urged to adopt legislation and monitor compliance based on the International Code of Marketing of Breast-milk Substitutes.[659] The Committee noted, in relation to

---

650 CRC/C/MLT/CO/2 (5 February 2013) [47].
651 CRC/C/NAM/CO/2-3 (16 October 2012) [53].
652 CRC/C/ALB/CO/2-4 (5 October 2012) [60].
653 CRC/C/UZB/CO/3-4 (14 June 2013) [51].
654 CRC/C/ARM/CO/3-4 (14 June 2013) [37].
655 CRC/C/BIH/CO/2-4 (5 October 2012) [54].
656 CRC/C/ISR/CO/2-4 (14 June 2013) [53].
657 World Health Organisation & UNICEF (2003) *The Global Strategy for Infant and Young Child Feeding*, Geneva: WHO http://www.who.int/nutrition/publications/infantfeeding/9241562218/en/index.html (accessed 10 September 2013).
658 See for example CRC/C/NAM/CO/2-3 (16 October 2012) [61].
659 World Health Organization (1981) *International Code of Marketing of Breast-milk Substitutes*, Geneva: WHO http://www.who.int/nutrition/publications/code_english.pdf (accessed 9 September 2013).

Namibia for example, its deep concern that 'only 5.7 per cent of all mothers continue to exclusively breastfeed until their child is 4 to 5 months old and only 1 per cent of all mothers continue to breastfeed until their child is 6 to 8 months old', and that the states party lacked national legislation and policies to effectively enforce the International Code of Marketing of Breast-milk Substitutes.[660] In some countries, for example Armenia, the Committee has noted its concern about 'the aggressive marketing practices of infant food companies and distributors and the weak enforcement of laws that regulate infant food marketing'.[661] Even where the International Code has been adopted, in Canada for example, the state party had not integrated it into its regulatory framework and 'as a result, formula companies have routinely violated the Code and related World Health Assembly resolutions with impunity'.[662] Supporting the International Code also requires support of maternity leave for adequate periods of time, combined with facilities at work for breastfeeding mothers. The Committee noted concern, in relation to Niue, that mothers had to go back to work after three months.[663] The Committee will also encourage states parties to develop hospitals that are 'Baby Friendly Hospital Initiative' accredited.[664]

3.7.7.4   Adolescent health

General Comment No 4 sets out a useful description of the challenges posed by adolescence in the context of the Convention rights:

> Adolescence is a period characterized by rapid physical, cognitive and social changes, including sexual and reproductive maturation; the gradual building up of the capacity to assume adult behaviours and roles involving new responsibilities requiring new knowledge and skills. While adolescents are in general a healthy population group, adolescence also poses new challenges to health and development owing to their relative vulnerability and pressure from society, including peers, to adopt risky health behaviour. These challenges include developing an individual identity and dealing with one's sexuality. The dynamic transition period to adulthood is also generally a period of positive changes, prompted by the significant capacity of adolescents to learn rapidly, to experience new and diverse situations, to develop and use critical thinking, to familiarize themselves with freedom, to be creative and to socialize.[665]

---

660   CRC/C/NAM/CO/2-3 (16 October 2012) [61].
661   CRC/C/ARM/CO/3-4 (14 June 2013) [41].
662   CRC/C/CAN/CO/3-4 (5 October 2012) [61].
663   CRC/C/NIU/CO/1 (29 January 2013) [61].
664   A worldwide programme of WHO and UNICEF established in 1992. See http://www.unicef. org.uk/babyfriendly/ (accessed 10 September 2013), and CRC/C/GUY/CO/2-4 (5 February 2013) [53–55].
665   Committee on the Rights of the Child, General Comment No 4: *Adolescent health and development in the context of the Convention on the Rights of the Child*, CRC/GC/2003/4 (1 July 2003) [2].

In some countries, the nature and extent of adolescent health problems are not well understood, and the Committee will characteristically advise that a comprehensive study is made as a basis for the formulation of adolescent health policies and practices. The Committee will encourage states parties to develop appropriate data collection mechanisms and '[w]here appropriate, adolescents should participate in the analysis to ensure that the information is understood and utilized in an adolescent-sensitive way'.[666] It noted concern, in relation to Guinea, about 'the absence of comprehensive information on key health issues affecting adolescent[s], including teenage pregnancy, substance abuse (including alcohol and drugs), HIV/AIDS and sexually transmitted diseases (STDs) and non-communicable diseases (NCD)'.[667] The Committee noted its concern, in the case of Malta for example, about the prevalence of unplanned adolescent pregnancies and was 'gravely concerned that abortion is illegal in all cases and with no exception under the law of the state party and that girls and women who choose to undergo abortion are subject to imprisonment'.[668] The Committee was concerned, in relation to Guyana, about the lack of sex and reproductive education on the education syllabus of the states party, and the 'the stigma, discrimination and resulting hindrance to services and education that pregnant adolescents and adolescent mothers are frequently subjected to'.[669] The Committee was also concerned, with regard to Bosnia and Herzegovina, about alcohol, tobacco and illegal drug consumption, which remained 'widespread among adolescents in the State party'. It recommended, inter alia, that the states party 'consider prohibiting all forms of advertisements promoting alcohol and tobacco products in the media and/or information commonly accessed by children'.[670] It noted similar concerns, in relation to Austria, about 'the high rate of alcohol, tobacco, cannabis and other illicit substance abuse, as well as depression and obesity, among children in the State party'.[671] The Committee will characteristically recommend a number of measures, usually referenced in General Comment No 4: for example, the provision of access to adolescent-sensitive and confidential counselling and care services, which also include access to contraceptive services; awareness programmes on the consequences of substance abuse, particularly alcohol, tobacco and drugs;[672] and the promotion of healthy life-style education at schools and other children institutions, including information on reproductive health and services.[673] In General

---

666 General Comment No 4 [13].

667 CRC/C/GIN/CO/2 (30 January 2013) [67].

668 CRC/C/MLT/CO/2 (5 February 2013) [49]. See the Committee's reference to a 'punitive abortion law [in Andorra] that could lead adolescents to seek other alternative solutions in the neighbouring countries'; CRC/C/AND/CO/2 (9 October 2012) [41]. See also CRC/C/ NAM/CO/2-3 (16 October 2012) [57].

669 CRC/C/GUY/CO/2-4 (5 February 2013) [49].

670 CRC/C/BIH/CO/2-4 (5 October 2012) [58–59].

671 CRC/C/AUT/CO/3-4 (5 October 2012) [50].

672 CRC/C/GNB/CO/2-4 (14 June 2013) [55].

673 CRC/C/UZB/CO/3-4 (14 June 2013) [54].

Comment No 4, the Committee set out its concerns about the problems of mental health and suicide that some adolescents will be vulnerable to.

The Committee is also very concerned about the high rate of suicide among this age group. Mental disorders and psychosocial illness are relatively common among adolescents. In many countries symptoms such as depression, eating disorders and self-destructive behaviours, sometimes leading to self-inflicted injuries and suicide, are increasing. They may be related to, inter alia, violence, ill-treatment, abuse and neglect, including sexual abuse, unrealistically high expectations, and/ or bullying or hazing in and outside school. States parties should provide these adolescents with all the necessary services.[674]

The Committee has noted its concern, in relation to Israel for example, about 'the high rate of suicide and attempts at suicide among adolescents in the State party, especially among girls'.[675] It also recorded its concern that in Slovenia, 'suicide is the second major reason for mortality among children aged 10–14'.[676]

3.7.7.5 The prevalence of HIV/AIDS

The prevalence of HIV/AIDS has been a source of profound concern in many nations. General Comment No 3 provides a detailed commentary about this issue and its relevance in the context of the Convention. It is noted, for example, that:

Initially children were considered to be only marginally affected by the epidemic. However, the international community has discovered that, unfortunately, children are at the heart of the problem.[677]

In some countries the incidence of HIV/AIDS is high and overall awareness of the disease may be low. Low awareness may occur particularly in minority groups within a states party, for example, among Amerindian, socio-economically disadvantaged people in rural areas in Guyana.[678] In addition to recommending that states parties attend to the guidance in General Comment No 3, the Joint United Nations Programme on HIV/AIDS (UNAIDS) and OHCHR have produced the International Guidelines on HIV/AIDS and Human Rights (UNAIDS 2006). The formulation of these guidelines represented a culmination of a number of international, regional and national declarations and activities. Many of these confirmed that discrimination on the basis of actual or presumed HIV/AIDS status was prohibited by existing international human rights standards, and clarified that the term 'or other status' used in the non-discrimination clauses of such texts 'should be interpreted to include health status, such as HIV/AIDS' (UNAIDS 2006: 108).

---

674 General Comment No 4 [22].
675 CRC/C/ISR/CO/2-4 (14 June 2013) [55].
676 CRC/C/SVN/CO/3-4 (14 June 2013) [54].
677 Committee on the Rights of the Child, General Comment No 3: *HIV/AIDS and the rights of the child*, CRC/GC/2003/3 (17 March 2003) [2].
678 CRC/C/GUY/CO/2-4 (5 February 2013) [51]. In Armenia, there was low awareness especially among children in rural areas: CRC/C/ARM/CO/3-4 (14 June 2013) [39].

This, and other, human rights aspects of the HIV/AIDS pandemic have proved to be key elements in preventing a stigmatisation and marginalisation process that might otherwise prevent open access to health care services. The Committee has expressed concern, for example in relation to Albania, that children infected by HIV/AIDS 'are detected at a very late stage due to the lack of access to confidential voluntary testing and the deficiencies in the surveillance system'.[679] In Namibia, a requirement that children under 16 years had to obtain the consent of their parents or guardian to gain access to HIV/AIDS voluntary counselling and testing, was found by the Committee severely to restrict the right of children to information and health care.[680] The Committee commended the high level commitment to fight HIV/AIDS in Liberia, although remained concerned at unequal access to relevant health services and care.[681] In some countries, HIV/AIDS continues to be a culturally and religiously sensitive topic that poses challenges in terms of transmission channels, treatment and preventive measures. The Committee noted its concern, with regard to Uzbekistan for example, that 'there is no mandatory and comprehensive sex education in school curricula as it is considered to be "against national values"'.[682] High incidences of HIV and children orphaned by HIV have been reported, for example, in the Democratic Republic of Congo.[683] In some countries there is a very low coverage of antiretroviral treatment for the prevention of mother-to-child transmission, in others some progress has been recorded.[684] The human capacity constraints of trained health care workers with regard to children have been reported in Guinea-Bissau for example.[685] Finally, the Committee will frequently recommend, where the states party's record in coping with the pandemic is particularly inadequate, that it seeks technical assistance from, inter alia, UNAIDS, the United Nations Population Fund (UNFPA) and UNICEF.[686]

3.7.7.6   Standard of living

The child's right to an adequate standard of living under Article 27(1) is complemented by the recognition in Article 27(2) that parents have the *primary responsibility* to secure living conditions necessary for a child's development. States parties are in turn obliged to take appropriate measures to assist parents and others responsible for the child to implement this right, and 'in case of need provide material assistance and support programmes, particularly with regard to nutrition, clothing

---

679 CRC/C/ALB/CO/2-4 (5 October 2012) [64].
680 CRC/C/NAM/CO/2-3 (16 October 2012) [59].
681 CRC/C/LBR/CO/2-4 (5 October 2012) [68].
682 CRC/C/UZB/CO/3-4 (14 June 2013) [55].
683 CRC/C/COD/CO/2 (10 February 2009) [61].
684 For example, in Namibia: CRC/C/NAM/CO/2-3 (16 October 2012) [59].
685 CRC/C/GNB/CO/2-4 (14 June 2013) [56].
686 CRC/C/GUY/CO/2-4 (5 February 2013) [52]; CRC/C/LBR/CO/2-4 (5 October 2012) [69]; CRC/C/GNB/CO/2-4 (14 June 2013) [57]; CRC/C/UZB/CO/3-4 (14 June 2013) [56].

and housing'.[687] Child poverty is therefore a key concern. These provisions of the Convention resonate with some of the MDGs.[688] In particular, child poverty impacts frequently on marginalised and minority groups of children. For example, the Committee was concerned, in relation to Guinea, that 'structural and long-term investment measures to maintain families out of poverty are insufficient to reduce the high level of disparities in the quality and level of access to social services, with rural regions being in the most disadvantaged situation'.[689] Although some progress was noted in relation to Guyana over the past 20 years, the Committee was concerned 'that 36% of the population still live below the poverty line, with much higher rates of poverty in rural and Amerindian areas'.[690] Child poverty was also noted as a matter of concern about Roma families and families with children with disabilities in Albania.[691] The Committee also noted its concerns about unequal access to a range of services by Roma children in Slovenia.[692] As regards Liberia, the Committee was 'alarmed by the extremely high proportion of people living below the poverty line (80%) and in extreme poverty (48%)'.[693] The Committee noted with concern that, in Rwanda, 'up to 60 per cent of the State party's children live below the poverty line'.[694] In relation to Israel, the Committee remained 'deeply concerned' about the increasing poverty among Palestinian children and 'the serious violations of their right to an adequate standard of living resulting from the occupation of the Palestinian territories by the State'.[695]

Access to clean, potable drinking water and safe sanitation systems is also a good indicator of standards of living and health. The Committee was concerned, with respect to Guinea-Bissau, that 'about 44 per cent of the population of the state party has no access to safe drinking water, and 82 per cent has no access to adequate sanitation facilities, proportions that significantly increase in rural areas'.[696] In Israel, for example, the Committee noted their concern about the 'critical water shortage faced by Palestinian children and their families and by Bedouin children ... due to prohibitions of access to natural resources, restrictions on water utilization and destruction of water services'.[697]

---

687 CRC art 27(3).
688 Millennium Development Goal 1. Target 1.A: Halve, between 1990 and 2015, the proportion of people whose income is less than $1.25 a day. Target 1.B: Achieve full and productive employment and decent work for all, including women and young people. Target 1.C: Halve, between 1990 and 2015, the proportion of people who suffer from hunger.
689 CRC/C/GIN/CO/2 (30 January 2013) [71].
690 CRC/C/GUY/CO/2-4 (5 February 2013) [55].
691 CRC/C/ALB/CO/2-4 (5 October 2012) [66].
692 CRC/C/SVN/CO/3-4 (14 June 2013) [58].
693 CRC/C/LBR/CO/2-4 (5 October 2012) [70].
694 CRC/C/RWA/CO/3-4 (14 June 2013) [48].
695 CRC/C/ISR/CO/2-4 (14 June 2013) [59].
696 CRC/C/GNB/CO/2-4 (14 June 2013) [60].
697 CRC/C/ISR/CO/2-4 (14 June 2013) [59].

The Convention also obliges states parties to recognise 'for every child the right to benefit from social security, including social insurance'.[698] The Committee noted, for example in relation to Bosnia and Herzegovina, that although children did have a direct right to benefit this appeared to be limited to children only up to the age of 15 years and that 'a large proportion of children in the state party live below the poverty line'.[699] The Committee was also concerned, in relation to Armenia, that 'only 54.3% of extremely poor families and 4.1% of poor families benefit on a regular basis, due to the inadequate family benefit formula and lack of awareness of the existing government support'.[700]

3.7.8   Education, leisure and cultural activities: Articles 28, 29 and 31

Article 28(1)(a)

1. States Parties recognize the right of the child to education, and with a view to achieving this right progressively and on the basis of equal opportunity, they shall, in particular:

   (a) Make primary education compulsory and available free to all;

   ...

Article 29(1)(a)

1. States Parties agree that the education of the child shall be directed to:

   (a) The development of the child's personality, talents and mental and physical abilities to their fullest potential;

   ...

Article 31

1. States Parties recognize the right of the child to rest and leisure, to engage in play and recreational activities appropriate to the age of the child and to participate freely in cultural life and the arts.
2. States Parties shall respect and promote the right of the child to participate fully in cultural and artistic life and shall encourage the provision of appropriate and equal opportunities for cultural, artistic, recreational and leisure activity.

3.7.8.1   The right to education

The Convention's prescription for primary education in Article 28(1)(a) is also reflected in the MDGs.[701] The various aims of education, which states parties

---

698 CRC art 26(1).
699 CRC/C/BIH/CO/2-4 (5 October 2012) [60].
700 CRC/C/ARM/CO/3-4 (14 June 2013) [43].
701 Millennium Development Goal -Target 2.A: Ensure that, by 2015, children everywhere, boys and girls alike, will be able to complete a full course of primary schooling.

agree children should be directed to, are contained in Article 29(1)(a) to (e) and have been given a detailed commentary by the Committee in General Comment No 1.[702] The General Comment states that this provision is 'of far-reaching importance' and that the aims of education 'are all linked directly to the realization of the child's human dignity and rights'.[703] In particular, the General Comment states that:

> Article 29(1) not only adds to the right to education recognised in Article 28 a qualitative dimension which reflects the rights and inherent dignity of the child; it also insists upon the need for education to be child-centred, child-friendly and empowering, and it highlights the need for educational processes to be based upon the very principles it enunciates.[704]

While Article 28 adverts to matters of access to education, Article 29(1) provides a framework of substantive *values* in which the content of education can be firmly rooted. The General Comment notes that education policies and programmes all too often seem to miss the elements embodied in Article 29(1).[705] Furthermore, this provision serves to highlight, in the context of the Convention, the following dimensions:

- the indispensable *interconnected nature* of the Convention's provisions
- the *importance of the process* by which the right to education is to be promoted
- the individual and subject right to a specific *quality of education*
- a *holistic and balanced approach* to education
- The need for education to be *designed to reflect a range of specific ethical values* enshrined in the Convention and
- the vital role of appropriate educational opportunities in *promoting all other human rights* and the understanding of their indivisibility.[706]

The Committee also urges states parties to consider and understand the critical importance of education and implementing children's rights specifically in *early childhood*. General Comment No 7[707] arose from the Committee's experience of reviewing states parties' reports, where it identified that 'very little information had been offered about early childhood'.[708] Finally, the Committee has further

---

702   Committee on the Rights of the Child, General Comment No 1: *Article 29(1) – The Aims of Education*, 26th session, CRC/GC/2001/1 (17 April 2001).

703   ibid [1].

704   ibid [2].

705   ibid [3].

706   ibid [6–14].

707   Committee on the Rights of the Child, General Comment No 7: *Implementing child rights in early childhood*, CRC/C/GC/7/Rev.1 (20 September 2006).

708   ibid [1].

considered, in a 'Day of General Discussion',[709] how the right to education should be viewed in 'emergency situations'.[710] It concurred with the general principle that the right to education should be upheld 'as a priority and an integral component of humanitarian relief response in emergency situations'.[711]

The Committee's Concluding Observations often identifies failures by states parties to allocate sufficient resources to education. For example, in Albania only 3.2 per cent of GDP was devoted to education.[712] As regards Guinea, the Committee was concerned 'at the limited budgetary allocations to that sector and that one third of children remain completely deprived of access to education'.[713]

In Liberia, the Committee found that 90 per cent of the primary education budget was spent on salaries and wages and 'the overall education budget highly skewed towards tertiary education'.[714] Sometimes, concerns are specifically raised in relation to *early* childhood. For example, in Austria, the Committee was concerned about 'a lack of State-funded early childhood care facilities for children under 5'.[715] The Committee was concerned, in relation to Canada, that 'despite the State party's significant resources, there has been a lack of funding directed towards the improvement of early childhood development'.[716] The Committee was concerned in relation to Bosnia and Herzegovina, about the 'rate of children attending pre-school education remaining at a low of 9%'.[717] On occasion, the Committee has cause to welcome the 'achievement of almost universal primary education' by a states party, for example, by Guyana.[718] In other states parties, primary school enrolment generally may be low. For example, in Liberia, the Committee found that primary school enrolment stood at only 37 per cent 'of which only one-third complete the primary school'.[719] These barriers to access education result in a number of difficulties in delivering the rights envisaged in the Convention. In Albania for example, only 10 per cent of all children between one and three years old have access to pre-school education, furthermore, the educational system there was found to be 'seriously affected by corruption'.[720] The

---

709 Committee on the Rights of the Child, 'Day of General Discussion' on *The Right of the Child to Education in Emergency Situations*, Report on the 49th session, CRC/C/49/3 (3 October 2008, 25 February 2010) [37–94].

710 '[D]efined as all situations in which anthropogenic [man-made] or natural disasters destroy, within a short period of time, the usual conditions of life, care and education facilities for children' ibid [61].

711 Committee on the Rights of the Child, 'Day of General Discussion' on *The Right of the Child to Education in Emergency Situations* (n 709) [63].

712 CRC/C/ALB/CO/2-4 (5 October 2012) [70].

713 CRC/C/GIN/CO/2 (30 January 2013) [73].

714 CRC/C/LBR/CO/2-4 (5 October 2012) [72].

715 CRC/C/AUT/CO/3-4 (5 October 2012) [52].

716 CRC/C/CAN/CO/3-4 (5 October 2012) [71].

717 CRC/C/BIH/CO/2-4 (5 October 2012) [62].

718 CRC/C/GUY/CO/2-4 (5 February 2013) [57].

719 CRC/C/LBR/CO/2-4 (5 October 2012) [72].

720 ibid [70].

corrosive effects of corruption in this context can be seen elsewhere. For example, the Committee found, in relation to Uzbekistan, that '[c]orruption continues to negatively affect the quality of education with grades and degrees being frequently purchased and informal fees resulting in compromised access to education, particularly for children in socio-economically disadvantaged situations'.[721]

Access to education is also often made difficult, for example in Namibia, by disparities between urban and rural areas and by an 'insufficient number of well-trained teaching staff, and poor school infrastructure and children's limited access to school materials and textbooks'.[722] Some states parties, such as Namibia, are also encouraged to 'eliminate all types of hidden or additional fees in the school system'.[723] The Committee has raised concerns, with regard to Bosnia and Herzegovina, about the 'lack of free textbooks and free transportation to and from school in the majority of primary and secondary schools, exacerbating the difficulties in accessing education for children from low-income families and contributing to the low, 31%, rate of secondary education completion'.[724] Access to education can also be seriously jeopardised by hidden costs. For example, in Liberia the Committee was concerned about '[h]idden school fees despite the existence of a free-of-charge education right'.[725] Similarly, the Committee noted with concern that, in relation to Rwanda, there were '[h]idden education fees that prevent children from accessing education, especially children living in poverty and children in vulnerable situations'.[726]

The built environment of education can also be a significant obstacle. The Committee noted, for example, that in Niue, schools had not been refurbished for a long time due to lack of resources and 'as a result school buildings and facilities remain old and in poor conditions'.[727] In Israel, the Committee found 'a state of disrepair of school infrastructure in all the OPT which have led Palestinian children to be deprived of education or to attend classes in tents or caravans in unsuitable and overcrowded conditions'.[728]

Discriminatory practice in the provision of education will also be criticised by the Committee. It found, in relation to Israel for example, that 'Jewish and Arab children continue to be educated in segregated school systems'.[729] In Slovenia, 'Roma children are rarely enrolled in pre-school educational institutions'.[730]

721 CRC/C/UZB/CO/3-4 (14 June 2013) [59].
722 CRC/C/NAM/CO/2-3 (16 October 2012) [63].
723 ibid [64].
724 CRC/C/BIH/CO/2-4 (5 October 2012) [62].
725 CRC/C/LBR/CO/2-4 (5 October 2012) [72].
726 CRC/C/RWA/CO/3-4 (14 June 2013) [52].
727 CRC/C/NIU/CO/1 (29 January 2013) [63].
728 CRC/C/ISR/CO/2-4 (14 June 2013) [63].
729 ibid [61].
730 CRC/C/SVN/CO/3-4 (14 June 2013) [60].

General Comment No 1 notes that Article 29(1) can also be seen as 'a foundation stone for the various programmes of human rights education' called for by the World Conference on Human Rights, held in Vienna in 1993.[731]

> Human rights education should provide information on the content of human rights treaties. But children should also learn about human rights by seeing human rights standards implemented in practice, whether at home, in school, or within the community. Human rights education should be a comprehensive, life-long process and start with the reflection of human rights values in the daily life and experiences of children.[732]

The Committee has urged some states parties, for example Bosnia and Herzegovina,[733] to develop national plans of action for human rights education as recommended in the framework of the World Programme for Human Rights Education.[734] The Committee, as regards Slovenia, was concerned 'that NGOs have the main responsibility for carrying out human rights education at schools'.[735]

3.7.8.2   The right to rest, leisure, play, recreational activities, cultural life and the arts: Article 31

The importance of play and recreation for children was referred to in the Declaration of the Rights of the Child (1959).[736] The Convention on the Rights of the Child contains a more detailed provision (see above). During the drafting process the German and Japanese delegates doubted whether it was advisable to proclaim a universal right of the child to rest and leisure. The German representative 'indicated his preference for dealing with the issue in the context of the provision against economic and social exploitation' (Detrick 1992: 416). Nevertheless, the text of Article 31 was agreed and no country has entered a reservation in relation to this Article. The Committee's Concluding Observations have to date contained little commentary on this provision. Occasionally, the Committee records that facilities for such activities are somewhat limited and sometimes not really integrated in community and urban development planning.[737] In some

---

731 See http://www.ohchr.org/EN/ABOUTUS/Pages/ViennaWC.aspx (accessed 17 September 2013).

732 Committee on the Rights of the Child, General Comment No 1: *Article 29(1) – The Aims of Education*, 26th session, CRC/GC/2001/1 (17 April 2001) [15].

733 CRC/C/BIH/CO/2-4 (5 October 2012) [65].

734 General Assembly, 59th session, UN Doc A/RES/59/113 (10 December 2004).

735 CRC/C/SVN/CO/3-4 (14 June 2013) [62].

736 'The child shall have full opportunity for play and recreation, which should be directed to the same purposes as education; society and the public authorities shall endeavour to promote the enjoyment of this right': General Assembly, Declaration of the Rights of the Child, 14th session, UN Doc A/RES/1386 (XIV) (20 November 1959) Principle 7(3).

737 CRC/C/BOL/CO/4 (2 October 2009) [69].

countries, the Committee has observed a decrease in, for example, playground space for children[738] and a need to increase such playground spaces.[739] Some of the Committee's observations simply do not make any mention of Article 31 issues at all.

It had been noted in General Comment No 7 in 2006 that 'insufficient attention has been given by states parties and others to the implementation of the provisions of Article 31'.[740] General Comment No 7 attempted to highlight the importance of these rights in the context of early childhood.

> Play is one of the most distinctive features of early childhood. Through play, children both enjoy and challenge their current capacities, whether they are playing alone or with others. The value of creative play and exploratory learning is widely recognized in early childhood education. Yet realizing the right to rest, leisure and play is often hindered by a shortage of opportunities for young children to meet, play and interact in child-centred, secure, supportive, stimulating and stress-free environments.[741]

The poor recognition by states parties of the rights contained in Article 31 prompted the Committee to issue General Comment No 17[742] in 2013, focusing specifically and in detail on this Article. This General Comment notes that, where states do invest in this area: 'it is in the provision of structured and organized activities, but equally important is the need to create time and space for children to engage in spontaneous play, recreation and creativity'.[743] It also refers to a number of 'profound changes' in the world that impact upon children's opportunities to enjoy these rights, for example a global increase in urbanisation and violence.[744] General Comment No 17 contains a detailed legal analysis of the text of Article 31. For example, it delineates the concepts of 'rest', 'leisure', 'play', 'recreational activities' and 'cultural life and the arts'. But it goes much further than textual analysis and also supplies a detailed commentary addressing the creation of the context for the realisation of Article 31, for example, the growing role of electronic media.

Information and communication technologies are emerging as a central dimension of children's daily reality. Today, children move seamlessly between offline and online environments. These platforms offer huge benefits – educationally,

---

738 CRC/C/FRA/CO/4 (11 June 2009) [82].

739 CRC/C/ROM/CO/4 (12 June 2009) [78].

740 Committee on the Rights of the Child, General Comment No 7: *Implementing child rights in early childhood*, CRC/C/GC/7/Rev.1 (20 September 2006) [34].

741 ibid.

742 Committee on the Rights of the Child, General Comment No 17: *The right of the child to rest, leisure, play, recreational activities, cultural life and the arts (art 31)*, 62nd session, CRC/C/GC/17 (17 April 2013).

743 ibid [2].

744 ibid [4].

socially and culturally – and states are encouraged to take all necessary measures to ensure equality of opportunity for all children to experience those benefits. Access to the internet and social media is central to the realisation of Article 31 rights in the globalised environment.[745]

It is possible that the appearance of General Comment No 17 may in the future stimulate a more engaged implementation of children's rights to play and leisure by some states parties and perhaps also more intense scrutiny by the Committee of this important provision of the Convention.

3.7.9 Special protection measures: Articles 22, 30, 32–36, 37(b)–(d), 38–40

Under this cluster of rights, states parties are requested in the reporting guidelines[746] to provide relevant information on the following matters:

i.   *Asylum-seeking and refugee children (Article 22).*This heading deals with children outside their country of origin seeking refugee protection, unaccompanied asylum-seeking children, internally displaced children, migrant children and children affected by migration;

ii.   *Children belonging to a minority or an indigenous group (Article 30).*

iii. *Children in situations of exploitation (Articles 32–36).* This heading can be broken down into the following categories:
   a.   Economic exploitation, including child labour (art 32)
   b.   Use of children in the illicit production and trafficking of narcotic drugs and psychotropic substances (art 33)
   c.   Sexual exploitation and sexual abuse (art 34)
   d.   Sale, trafficking and abduction (art 35) and
   e.   Other forms of exploitation (art 36).

iv.   *Children in street situations.*

v.   *Children in armed conflicts (Articles 38 & 39)*, including physical and psychological recovery and social reintegration;

vi.   *Children in conflict with the law, victims and witnesses.* This heading can be broken down into the following two categories:
   a.   The administration of juvenile justice (art 40)
   b.   Children deprived of their liberty, and measures to ensure that any arrest, detention or imprisonment of a child shall be used a measures of last resort and for the shortest appropriate time and that legal and other assistance is promptly provided (art 37 (b)–(d)).

---

745 ibid [45].

746 Treaty-specific guidelines regarding the form and content of periodic reports to be submitted by States parties under art 44, para 1 (b), of the Convention on the Rights of the Child, CRC/C/58/Rev.2 (23 November 2010).

The following sub-sections below follow this categorisation.

3.7.9.1   Asylum-seeking and refugee children (Article 22)

Article 22(1)

1. States parties shall take appropriate measures to ensure that a child who is seeking refugee status or who is considered a refugee in accordance with applicable international or domestic law and procedures shall, whether unaccompanied or accompanied by his or her parents or by any other person, receive appropriate protection and humanitarian assistance in the enjoyment of applicable rights set forth in the present Convention and in other international human rights or humanitarian instruments to which the said States are Parties.

In this context, 'other international … instruments' refers to, inter alia: the Convention relating to the Status of Refugees[747] (1951) and its Protocol[748] (1967) – these two provide the international definition of 'refugee'; the Convention relating to the Status of Stateless Persons[749] (1954) and the Convention on the Reduction of Statelessness[750] (1961). A Handbook[751] produced by the Office of the United Nations High Commissioner for Refugees (UNHCR) is widely regarded as an authoritative interpretation of international refugee law.[752] The Committee will remind states parties that they need to conform to these standards, and/or ensure that they ratify these various instruments.[753] Article 22(2) of the Convention further obliges states parties to provide as they consider appropriate 'co-operation' in the efforts of the UN and other intergovernmental and non-governmental organisations to protect and assist such children, including family tracing to obtain the necessary information for reunification. States parties are requested to take into account the Committee's General Comment No 6 issued in 2005 on aspects of this

---

747 Convention relating to the Status of Refugees, opened for signature 28 July 1951, 189 UNTS 137 (entered into force 22 April 1954).

748 Protocol relating to the Status of Refugees, opened for signature 31 January 1967, 606 UNTS 267 (entered into force 4 October 1967).

749 Convention relating to the Status of Stateless Persons, opened for signature 28 September 1954, 360 UNTS 117 (entered into force 6 June 1960).

750 Convention on the Reduction of Statelessness, opened for signature, 989 UNTS 175 (entered into force 13 December 1975).

751 UNHCR, Handbook and Guidelines on Procedures and Criteria for Determining Refugee Status under the 1951 Convention and the 1967 Protocol Relating to the Status of Refugees, December 2011, HCR/1P/4/ENG/REV. 3. Available at: http://www.refworld.org/docid/4f33c8d92. html (accessed 18 September 2013).

752 See also UNHCR Summary Note: *UNHCR's Strategy and Activities Concerning Refugee Children* (October 2005) http://www.refworld.org/docid/439841784.html (accessed 18 September 2013).

753 See CRC/C/ARM/CO/3-4 (14 June 2013) [47]; CRC/C/UZB/CO/3-4 (14 June 2013) [62]; and CRC/C/RWA/CO/3-4 (14 June 2013) [58].

Article.[754] The general objectives of this detailed General Comment were: to draw attention to the particularly vulnerable situation of unaccompanied and separated children; to outline the challenges faced by states parties and other actors in ensuring that such children are able to access and enjoy their rights; and, to provide guidance on the protection, care and proper treatment of unaccompanied and separated children based on the entire legal framework provided by the Convention. An increasing number of children are engaged in an asylum-seeking or refugee situation, prompted by a number of factors; for example, persecution of the child or the parents, armed conflicts, trafficking, and the search for better opportunities. There are a number of protection gaps, including the greater risks for such children of sexual exploitation, military recruitment, child labour and detention. They often face discrimination and may be denied access to food, shelter, housing, health services and education. They may also find difficulty in accessing appropriate identification, registration and similar documentation. They may be denied entry to or detained by border or immigration officials. In other cases they may be admitted but are denied access to asylum procedures or their asylum claims may have been handled inappropriately.[755] There has also been a 'Day of General Discussion' in 2012 on the subject of children and international migration.[756]

The Committee's scrutiny of country reports under this heading provides a wide range of observations, often critical, about the impact of states parties' immigration and asylum-seeking policies. For example, it expressed concern that immigrants to Albania were routinely detained and deported back to their countries of origin 'without having had access to legal procedures to determine their best interests, or to specialized services and assistance of a legal guardian'.[757] It recommended, inter alia, that the Border Police should not detain unaccompanied minors and in this regard to seek technical assistance from the UNHCR. The Committee was also 'deeply concerned', in relation to Canada, 'about the frequent detention of asylum-seeking children it being done without consideration for the best interests of the child'.[758] Child detention without proper safeguards is often identified as a consequence of states parties' approaches to immigration. The Committee was 'deeply concerned', for example, that foreigners on Maltese territory without rights of entry, transit or residence, 'are subject to mandatory immigration detention until removal from Malta is carried out, resulting in the detention of children pending age determination'.[759] The Committee was prompted to recommend that Malta should '[r]efrain from criminalising children in irregular migration

---

754 Committee on the Rights of the Child, General Comment No 6: *Treatment of Unaccompanied and Separated Children Outside their Country of Origin*, 39th session, CRC/GC/2005/6 (1 September 2005).

755 ibid [1–4].

756 Committee on the Rights of the Child, 'Day of General Discussion' on *The Rights of all Children in the Context of International Migration* http://www2.ohchr.org/english/bodies/crc/discussion2012.htm (accessed 18 September 2013).

757 CRC/C/ALB/CO/2-4 (5 October 2012) [72].

758 CRC/C/CAN/CO/3-4 (5 October 2012) [73].

759 CRC/C/MLT/CO/2 (5 February 2013) [57].

situations for their or their parent's migration status and expeditiously and completely cease the detention of children in irregular migration situations', and also should improve and expedite its age assessment process.[760] The report of the 'Day of General Discussion' contains a strongly worded paragraph condemning child detention in this context:

> Children should not be criminalized or subject to punitive measures because of their or their parents' migration status. The detention of a child because of their or their parent's migration status constitutes a child rights violation and always contravenes the principle of the best interests of the child. In this light, States should expeditiously and completely cease the detention of children on the basis of their immigration status.[761]

Domestic laws can conflict badly with the Convention framework protecting asylum-seeking, refugee children and children of migrant workers. For example, the Committee expressed concern about the 'Anti-Infiltration Law' enacted in Israel in 2012, which allowed for 'the prolonged detention of children, including child victims of exploitation, torture and trafficking who migrate illegally to the state party'.[762] As with other areas of the Convention, this heading also attracts critical comments by the Committee about the failures, for example in Guinea, to collect disaggregated statistical information on refugee children.[763] In some countries, for example Andorra, there is also 'a lack of domestic legislation on asylum seekers and refugees, and in particular at the absence of measures to protect unaccompanied and refugee children'.[764] In Liberia, the Committee found that the states party allowed refugees into its territory and there was 'no mechanism to provide protection and assistance to refugee children, in particular unaccompanied and separated children seeking asylum'.[765] In other countries, there are long-standing migrant reception centres/camps that can pose difficult challenges. For example, the Committee noted their concern, in relation to Bosnia and Herzegovina, about the '[p]ersisting inadequacies in living conditions for Roma and minority returnee children, as well as IDP [Internally Displaced Person] children living in collective centres that continue to exist although the conflict ended sixteen years ago'.[766]

In conformity with the Convention that obliges states parties to provide assistance to parents and legal guardians, and entitles children 'temporarily or

---

760 ibid [58].

761 Committee on the Rights of the Child, 'Day of General Discussion' on *The Rights of all Children in the Context of International Migration* http://www2.ohchr.org/english/bodies/crc/discussion2012. htm (accessed 18 September 2013) [78].

762 CRC/C/ISR/CO/2-4 (14 June 2013) [69].

763 CRC/C/GIN/CO/2 (30 January 2013) [75].

764 CRC/C/AND/CO/2 (9 October 2012) [43].

765 CRC/C/LBR/CO/2-4 (5 October 2012) [74].

766 CRC/C/BIH/CO/2-4 (5 October 2012) [66].

permanently deprived of his or her family environment' to 'special protection and assistance provided by the State',[767] General Comment No 6 makes it clear that states are required to 'secure proper representation of an unaccompanied or separated child's best interests' and therefore 'States should appoint a guardian or adviser as soon as the unaccompanied or separated child is identified and maintain such guardianship arrangements until the child has either reached the age of majority or has permanently left the territory and/or jurisdiction of the State'.[768] In Austria,[769] the Committee found that unaccompanied children were not so provided, and furthermore that age determination methods in the state party may not be in conformity with General Comment No 6.[770] Similarly, as regards Slovenia, the Committee noted with concern that '[u]naccompanied minors are not assigned legal guardians immediately after entering the State party'.[771] The Committee will also examine evidence relating to children where one or more parents are employed as migrants in other states. As stated in the 'Day of General Discussion':

> Policies, programmes and measures to protect children from poverty and social exclusion must include children in the context of migration, regardless of their status, in particular those left behind in countries of origin and those born to migrant parents in countries of destination. The capacity of national social protection systems to prevent and address all situations of vulnerability directly or indirectly related to migration should be strengthened ...[772]

As regards Uzbekistan, the Committee noted concern that there were 'substantial numbers of children with one or both parents employed as migrant workers in other States, subjecting them to situations of particular vulnerability and with no special protection measures'.[773]

---

767 CRC arts 18(2) and 20(1).
768 Committee on the Rights of the Child, General Comment No 6: *Treatment of Unaccompanied and Separated Children Outside their Country of Origin*, 39th session, CRC/GC/2005/6 (1 September 2005) [33].
769 CRC/C/AUT/CO/3-4 (5 October 2012) [54].
770 Committee on the Rights of the Child, General Comment No 6: *Treatment of Unaccompanied and Separated Children Outside their Country of Origin*, 39th session, CRC/GC/2005/6 (1 September 2005) [31(i)].
771 CRC/C/SVN/CO/3-4 (14 June 2013) [66].
772 Committee on the Rights of the Child, Day of General Discussion on *The Rights of all Children in the Context of International Migration* (28 September 2012) [88] http://www2.ohchr.org/english/bodies/crc/docs/discussion2012/2012CRC_DGD-Childrens_Rights_InternationalMigration.pdf (accessed 30 October 2013).
773 CRC/C/UZB/CO/3-4 (14 June 2013) [63].

3.7.9.2 Children belonging to a minority or an indigenous group (Article 30)

Article 30

In those States in which ethnic, religious or linguistic minorities or persons of indigenous origin exist, a child belonging to such a minority or who is indigenous shall not be denied the right, in community with other members of his or her group, to enjoy his or her own culture, to profess and practise his or her own religion, or to use his or her own language.

This provision is nearly identical to the ICCPR, Article 27, but it has the addition to the stated minorities of 'persons of indigenous origin'. The negative formulation of 'a child ... shall not be denied the right', despite some suggestions during the drafting process that it should be changed to a more positive obligation, 'a child ... shall have the right ...', was nevertheless retained in the final text of Article 30. In part this was because the Convention Working Group did not want to pre-empt other international discussions of indigenous rights and how these could be framed in international law (Detrick 1999: 408–414). As noted in the Implementation Handbook:

> Article 30 emanated from a proposal by a non-governmental organisation called the Four Directions Council, supported by Mexico, to dedicate an Article of the Convention to the rights of indigenous children. The drafting Working Group quickly agreed that this should embrace the rights of all minority children and concluded that it would not be helpful to introduce wording which departed from that of the International Covenant on Civil and Political Rights. (E/CN.4/1986/39 at 13; Detrick [1992] at 408.
>
> (Hodgkin and Newell 2007: 456)

It is therefore instructive to look to General Comment No 23,[774] issued by the Human Rights Committee on this comparable provision, albeit without benefit of the indigeneity element. That General Comment provides, inter alia, that irrespective of the negative language used in the text of Article 27, it nevertheless does recognise the existence of a 'right' and consequently 'a State party is under an obligation to ensure that the existence and the exercise of this right are protected against their denial or violation'.[775]

The Committee reaffirmed its commitment to 'promote and protect the human rights of indigenous children by addressing more systematically the situation of indigenous children under all relevant provisions and principles of the Convention when periodically reviewing State party reports' in its recommendations arising from a 'Day of General Discussion' in 2003 on the rights of

---

774 Human Rights Committee, General Comment No 23: *Article 27 (Rights of Minorities)*, CCPR/C/21/Rev.1/Add.5 (8 April 1994).

775 ibid [6.1].

indigenous children.[776] A more comprehensive international instrument addressing the rights of *indigenous persons* generally appeared in the form of the United Nations Declaration on the Rights of Indigenous Peoples (2007).[777] The position of indigenous children's rights is given further detailed treatment in Chapter 9. Canada made a clear 'statement of understanding' about Article 30 on joining the Convention on the Rights of the Child.

> It is the understanding of the Government of Canada that, in matters relating to aboriginal peoples of Canada, the fulfilment of its responsibilities under Article 4 of the Convention must take into account the provisions of Article 30. In particular, in assessing what measures are appropriate to implement the rights recognized in the Convention for aboriginal children, due regard must be paid to not denying their right, in community with other members of their group, to enjoy their own culture, to profess and practice their own religion and to use their own language.[778]

France, however, has made a reservation disapplying Article 30 in the light of a provision of the Constitution of the French Republic.[779] However, the Committee took the view that 'equality before the law' may be insufficient to ensure equal enjoyment of rights by minority and indigenous groups in France's overseas departments and territories.[780] Venezuela takes the position, in its interpretative declaration, that Article 30 'must be interpreted as a case in which Article 2 of the Convention [the principle of non-discrimination] applies'.

The Committee's Concluding Observations comment on children belonging to minority groups under this heading, and also under the non-discrimination principle in Article 2 (section 3.7.3.1) and other provisions of the Convention. The Committee has referenced, in relation to Albania for example, the 'weak implementation of the various programmes and strategies for Roma [children] due mainly to inadequate allocation of resources and the insufficient coordination between institutions involved at central and local levels'.[781] The Committee was also concerned that Egyptians were not recognised as a minority group in Albania and Egyptian children therefore remained unprotected in that states party.[782] The Committee further comment upon the disparities between children belonging

776 Committee on the Rights of the Child, 'Day of General Discussion' on *The rights of indigenous children*, Report on the 34th session, CRC/C/133 (3 October 2003) [624(2)].
777 General Assembly, United Nations Declaration on the Rights of Indigenous Peoples, 61st session, UN Doc A/RES/61/295 (2 October 2007).
778 See http://treaties.un.org/Pages/ViewDetails.aspx?src=TREATY&mtdsg_no=IV-11&chapter =4&lang=en (accessed 21 September 2013).
779 Article 2 of the French Constitution provides a guarantee of 'equality before the law to all citizens without distinction on the basis of origin, race or religion'. The implication was that art 30, by virtue of its selection of minority/indigenous group children was itself discriminatory.
780 CRC/C/FRA/CO/4 (11 June 2009) [101].
781 CRC/C/ALB/CO/2-4 (5 October 2012) [76].
782 ibid [76].

to minority groups, particularly Roma children, and children of the majority population in Slovenia.[783] As regards Rwanda, the Committee was 'seriously troubled' by the states party's lack of recognition of the existence of certain minority and indigenous people, including the Batwa community. It was 'deeply concerned' that Batwa children 'continue to experience severe marginalization and discrimination as many live in extreme poverty and lack access to basic services'. In particular, the Committee raised concerns, inter alia, that 'Batwa communities, including children, have been forcibly displaced from their ancestral forest lands without consent or compensation and deprived of their traditional livelihoods'.[784]

3.7.9.3 Children in situations of exploitation (Articles 32–36)

ECONOMIC EXPLOITATION, INCLUDING CHILD LABOUR (ART 32)

Article 32(1)
1. States parties recognize the right of the child to be protected from economic exploitation and from performing any work that is likely to be hazardous or to interfere with the child's education, or to be harmful to the child's health or physical, mental, spiritual, moral or social development.

...

Article 32(2) further provides a general duty on states parties to take all legislative and other measures to ensure the implementation of these obligations, and in particular: to provide for a minimum age for admission to employment; to provide for the regulation of hours and conditions of employment; and, to provide appropriate penalties or other sanctions to ensure effective enforcement. Exploitative child labour is not only regulated by the Convention, but is also addressed by a number of International Labour Organisation (ILO) Conventions: the Minimum Age Convention (1973),[785] the Elimination of the Worst Forms of Child Labour Convention (1999)[786] and the Decent Work for Domestic Workers Convention (2011).[787] The subject of child labour is dealt with in further detail in Chapter 4. The Committee held a 'Day of General Discussion' on the economic exploitation of the child in October 1993.

The discussion made clear the need for a comprehensive and concerted action for prevention, protection and rehabilitation. The need to strengthen preventive actions was stressed and education was referred to in that regard as an essential

---

783 CRC/C/SVN/CO/3-4 (14 June 2013) [68].
784 CRC/C/RWA/CO/3-4 (14 June 2013) [56].
785 International Labour Organization, Minimum Age Convention, ILO Convention No 138 (26 June 1973).
786 International Labour Organization, Worst Forms of Child Labour Convention, ILO Convention No 182 (17 June 1999).
787 This instrument obliges states parties to commit to 'the effective abolition of child labour': International Labour Organization, Convention Concerning Decent Work for Domestic Workers, ILO Convention No 189 (16 June 2011), PR No 15A art 3(2)(c).

tool. Recommendations were also made in the field of the protection of the rights of the child, including the establishment of an ombudsperson who might intervene and assist the child victim of economic exploitation. The important role of recovery and social reintegration of child victims of any form of economic exploitation was recognised. At all levels of action, effective coordination was recognized as an essential aspect to achieve progress, both at the national and the international level.[788]

The Committee adopted the recommendations referred to above at its fifth session in January 1994, including 'the establishment of a national mechanism for coordinating policies and monitoring the implementation of the Convention on the Rights of the Child, having specific competence in the area of protection from economic exploitation'.[789] The economic exploitation of children appears in many forms in the periodic report to the Committee, and may involve, for example in Albania, children in 'hazardous occupations, such as agriculture, domestic work and illegal activities'.[790] It may take obvious forms, such as forced labour in the cotton industry in Uzbekistan.[791] It also covers practices, such as exist in Bosnia and Herzegovina, of forced child begging, where, as the Committee observed, there was 'no systematic approach to address this issue' and it was not recognised in the states party's criminal code.[792] Child begging was also identified by the Committee, in relation to Slovenia, as an 'allegedly growing phenomenon', in addition to 'the involvement of children from vulnerable populations, particularly Roma, in forced illegal activities such as theft and sale of illegal drugs'.[793] 'Child labour' is also a contested concept and states parties often struggle, as in Guyana, to provide an adequate legislative definition and clarity in their policies, 'particularly with regards to domestic work and work for family businesses and farms where large numbers of children are economically active'.[794]

A frequent contributing factor to economic exploitation, particularly child labour, is the absence of, or weakness in, a labour inspectorate system. In Albania, for example, this facilitated a grave incident affecting a large number of children in March 2008 'where they were illegally working to dismantle ammunition'.[795] The Committee welcomes efforts by states parties to provide legislation consistent with international labour standards and also point out protection gaps in domestic legal regimes. For example, it identified that Andorra's legislation 'does not comprehensively address the situation of children employed in the family context,

---

788 Committee on the Rights of the Child, 'Day of General Discussion' on *The Economic Exploitation of the Child*, Report on the 4th session, CRC/C/20 (25 October 1993) [186–96 at 194].
789 Committee on the Rights of the Child, Report on the 5th session, CRC/C/24 (January 1994) [176–77].
790 CRC/C/ALB/CO/2-4 (5 October 2012) [78].
791 CRC/C/UZB/CO/3-4 (14 June 2013) [65].
792 CRC/C/BIH/CO/2-4 (5 October 2012) [70].
793 CRC/C/SVN/CO/3-4 (14 June 2013) [69].
794 CRC/C/GUY/CO/2-4 (5 February 2013) [59].
795 ibid.

in particular to ensure that such employment or working hours do not interfere with children's right to education', nor did it provide a satisfactory definition of 'light work'.[796] The latter is frequently a challenging area of concern. In Austria, for example, the Committee found that 'the law lacks a precise definition of light work and that after-school work of children, in particular in family businesses, is not monitored effectively'.[797] The Committee recommended that the states party provide a legal definition 'with a view to ensuring that children are not deprived of their right to rest and leisure and to engage in play after they have completed their daily schooling'.[798] The Committee was 'alarmed', in relation to Liberia, about 'the prevalence and level of child labour in almost all sectors of the economy, including hazardous work' that resulted 'in two thirds of children not enrolled in schools'.[799] One of the pervasive difficulties in addressing child labour is that it occurs frequently in the informal sector and in rural areas, often far removed from any official monitoring, as noted by the Committee in relation to Namibia.[800] The Committee was also concerned, with regards to Armenia, about the 'significant numbers of children ... dropping out of schools to work in informal sectors such as agriculture, car service, construction and gathering of waste metal and family businesses'.[801] The Committee also observed with concern that, in relation to Namibia, there was an 'inconsistency between the minimum age for employment in the Labour Act, which is 14 years of age, and the age of completing education, which is 16 years'.[802] Even where the minimum employment age has been adjusted to correspond with the minimum age of completing education, as in Malta, the Committee noted its concern 'that the regulations do not apply to occasional and short-term work which is frequently taken up by adolescents in, inter alia, hotels, catering, food and beverage establishments or domestic work during the school holidays'.[803] The Committee was also concerned, in relation to Guinea, about the large number of children involved in labour activities, including the informal sector, in agriculture, in the fishing industries and in domestic labour, including '[g]irls as young as 5 years who perform domestic labour, carry heavy loads, are often not paid for their work and subject to emotional, physical and sexual abuse.[804]

As with other areas of Convention rights, the Committee is often concerned, for example in relation to Canada, 'that data on child labour is not systematically collected in all provinces and territories'.[805] The Committee recommended,

---

796 CRC/C/AND/CO/2 (9 October 2012) [47].
797 CRC/C/AUT/CO/3-4 (5 October 2012) [58].
798 ibid [59].
799 CRC/C/LBR/CO/2-4 (5 October 2012) [78].
800 CRC/C/NAM/CO/2-3 (16 October 2012) [67].
801 CRC/C/ARM/CO/3-4 (14 June 2013) [49].
802 CRC/C/NAM/CO/2-3 (16 October 2012) [67].
803 CRC/C/MLT/CO/2 (5 February 2013) [59].
804 CRC/C/GIN/CO/2 (30 January 2013) [79].
805 CRC/C/CAN/CO/3-4 (5 October 2012) [79].

inter alia, that the state should '[t]ake steps to establish a unified mechanism for systematic data collection on incidences of hazardous child labour and working conditions, disaggregated by age, sex, geographical location and socio-economic background as a form of public accountability for protection of the rights of children'.[806]

Economic exploitation can also be enhanced as a result of the prevalence of practices – widespread in Guinea-Bissau – of giving away children to other family members or acquaintances that can supposedly provide better conditions and education for the children. The Committee was concerned about this practice (known as *meninos de criação*) and their resulting vulnerabilities.[807]

USE OF CHILDREN IN THE ILLICIT PRODUCTION AND TRAFFICKING OF NARCOTIC DRUGS AND PSYCHOTROPIC SUBSTANCES (ART 33)

Article 33
States parties shall take all appropriate measures, including legislative, administrative, social and educational measures, to protect children from the illicit use of narcotic drugs and psychotropic substances as defined in the relevant international treaties, and to prevent the use of children in the illicit production and trafficking of such substances.

The principal international treaties relevant to this provision are: the Single Convention on Narcotic Drugs (1961) as amended by a Protocol (1972),[808] and the Convention on Psychotropic Substances (1971).[809] Alcohol, tobacco and solvents are not controlled by international treaties but their use may be 'illicit'.

In the post-war decades, children's involvement in illicit drugs was not a significant concern so the issue did not figure in the declarations and conventions of that era. Today, drug abuse by children and young people is causing alarm worldwide because such abuse threatens both the child's development and nations' prosperity and social order (Hodgkin and Newell 2007: 504).

As the authors of the Implementation Handbook make clear: '[t]he problem of drug abuse by children is peculiarly alarming to the adult world because we cannot accurately map it and we do not know how best to tackle it: simply making its production and sale illegal is clearly not enough' (Hodgkin and Newell 2007: 506).

---

806 CRC/C/CAN/CO/3-4 (5 October 2012) [80].
807 CRC/C/GNB/CO/2-4 (14 June 2013) [65].
808 Single Convention on Narcotic Drugs (1961) as amended by the Protocol amending the Single Convention on Narcotic Drugs (1961) 976 UNTS 105 (entered into force 8 August 1975).
809 Convention on Psychotropic Substances, opened for signature 21 February 1971, 1019 UNTS 175 (entered into force 16 August 1976).

SEXUAL EXPLOITATION AND SEXUAL ABUSE (ART 34)

Sexual exploitation and abuse (Article 34) is discussed in section 3.7.6.3 above, and is also dealt with in further detail in Chapter 7.

SALE, TRAFFICKING AND ABDUCTION (ART 35)

Article 35
States parties shall take all appropriate national, bilateral and multilateral measures to prevent the abduction of, the sale of or traffic in children for any purpose or in any form.

The problem of trafficking and the sale of children has become a global one, and has attracted increasing international attention. Two UN Special Rapporteur mandates have evolved in this area. First, the UNCHR resolved to have a Special Rapporteur on the sale of children, child prostitution and child pornography in 1990.[810] Secondly, a Special Rapporteur on trafficking in persons, especially in women and children was established by the UNCHR in 2004[811] and an Optional Protocol to the Convention on the Rights of the Child on the Sale of Children, Child Prostitution and Child Pornography (OPSC) entered into force in 2002: see further Chapter 7. One example of a 'multilateral measure' referred to in Article 35, has been the Multilateral Cooperation Agreement to Combat Trafficking in Persons (2005), and the Joint Plan of Action against Trafficking in Persons, Especially Women and Children, in the West and Central African region.[812] An earlier draft of Article 35 had initially been combined with the text of Article 34 (sexual exploitation and abuse), but delegates eventually agreed there should be two separate Articles:

> [t]he problem of the sale or traffic of children was wider in scope than that of sexual exploitation and children were subjected to sale or traffic for many reasons: economic exploitation, sexual exploitation and sexual abuse, as well as for reasons of adoption or labour.
>
> (Detrick 1992: 430)

The Implementation Handbook describes Article 35 as a 'failsafe' or 'safety net' provision, which is reinforced by OPSC (Hodgkin and Newell 2007: 531). The

---

810 UN Commission on Human Rights, Resolution 1990/68 (7 March 1990). See also http://www. ohchr.org/en/issues/children/pages/childrenindex.aspx (accessed 30 September 2013).

811 UN Commission on Human Rights, Report on the 60th Session, Supplement No 3 (23 April 2004), E/CN.4/2004/127; E/2004/23 at 330. See also http://www2.ohchr.org/english/ issues/trafficking/ (accessed 30 September 2013).

812 These and other measures can be found in the UN's *Toolkit to Combat Trafficking in Persons*, http:// www.unodc.org/unodc/en/human-trafficking/2008/electronic-toolkit/electronic-toolkit-to-combat-trafficking-in-persons---index.html (accessed 30 September 2013).

obvious elements of criminality associated with these activities make it a difficult subject on which to gather reliable data or analysis. The Committee characteristically recommends the establishment of strong monitoring mechanisms and supporting programmes and information campaigns to prevent trafficking. The Committee will, as in other areas of its Concluding Observations, welcome states parties' efforts to combat the sale, trafficking and abduction of children, for example by adopting national action plans, incorporating awareness-raising programmes in school curricula and establishing a database for the victims of trafficking.[813] It will identify states that it considers are a source,[814] transit[815] or destination[816] country (or some combination of these) for children subjected to sex trafficking and forced labour (including forced begging). Trafficking may occur within states or across borders. For example, the Committee was 'deeply concerned' that children in Namibia were trafficked within the country 'for employment in agriculture, road construction, vending and commercial sex work, and that children from other countries are trafficked to the State party for livestock and child-minding work'. It was also concerned, in relation to Guinea-Bissau, about 'trafficking for sexual exploitation inside and outside the country'.[817] In addition, it noted concern about the absence of human trafficking legislation or prosecutions in that country.[818] Particularly vulnerable groups of children, for example girls of Roma ethnicity in Slovenia and Bosnia and Herzegovina, are often of concern to the Committee in this context.[819] The impunity of perpetrators of human trafficking has been attributed by the Committee, in relation to Liberia, to 'the high levels of corruption' in that state. Moreover, it expressed concern about 'reports claiming that orphanages and adoption agencies are used as hubs for child trafficking in the State party'.[820] In Austria, the Committee was concerned 'that child victims of prostitution are sometimes treated as offenders rather than victims in the State party and are imposed administrative fines'.[821] Trafficking is an area that the Committee often identifies as characterised, as in Canada for example, by 'the weak capacity of law enforcement organizations to identify and subsequently protect child victims of trafficking and the low number of investigations and prosecutions in this respect'.[822]

---

813 For example CRC/C/ALB/CO/2-4 (5 October 2012) [82].

814 ibid; CRC/C/GIN/CO/2 (30 January 2013) [83]; CRC/C/MLT/CO/2 (5 February 2013) [61]; CRC/C/SVN/CO/3-4 (14 June 2013) [71].

815 For example CRC/C/GIN/CO/2 (30 January 2013) [83]: CRC/C/SVN/CO/3-4 (14 June 2013) [71].

816 For example CRC/C/GIN/CO/2 (30 January 2013) [83]; CRC/C/MLT/CO/2 (5 February 2013) [61]; CRC/C/SVN/CO/3-4 (14 June 2013) [71].

817 CRC/C/GNB/CO/2-4 (14 June 2013) [66].

818 CRC/C/NAM/CO/2-3 (16 October 2012) [71].

819 CRC/C/SVN/CO/3-4 (14 June 2013) [71]; CRC/C/BIH/CO/2-4 (5 October 2012) [72].

820 CRC/C/LBR/CO/2-4 (5 October 2012) [82].

821 CRC/C/AUT/CO/3-4 (5 October 2012) [64].

822 CRC/C/CAN/CO/3-4 (5 October 2012) [81].

Article 36
States parties shall protect the child against all other forms of exploitation prejudicial to any aspects of the child's welfare.

The Implementation Handbook states that 'Article 36 was introduced to ensure that the "social" exploitation of children was recognized, along with their sexual and economic exploitation, although examples of what was meant by social exploitation were not provided' (Hodgkin and Newell 2007: 543). They offer several forms of exploitation not addressed under other Articles: eg the exploitation of gifted children, children used in criminal activities, the exploitation of children in political activities (for example in violent demonstrations), the exploitation of children by the media and the exploitation of children by researchers or for the purposes of medical or scientific experimentation (Hodgkin and Newell 2007: 543–44).

3.7.9.4   Children in street situations

Children living and working on the street are obviously in a vulnerable situation and may be prime targets for organised child- and drug-trafficking operations, susceptible to abuse, and may be charged with the crime of vagrancy and generally treated like offenders rather than victims. In some countries, for example in Bosnia and Herzegovina, forced child-begging is a dominant form of child exploitation. The Committee noted that although some local measures had been taken there was 'no systematic approach to address this issue'.[823] There are reports of large numbers of street children in some countries, although the data is often incomplete.[824] The Committee registered its 'deepest concern' about the high number of such children in, for example, Albania where street children 'are subjected to the worst forms of exploitation, including begging in the street, extreme marginalization, homelessness and are at risk of becoming victims of trafficking and sexual exploitation'.[825] In Liberia, the Committee was highly concerned at the large number of street children 'including former child combatants, internally displaced children, children who have been sent by their parents for better opportunities and end up being used for vending on [the] streets, or children who fled orphanages and other residential care'.[826] The Committee frequently urges states parties to undertake a systematic assessment of the situation of street children in order to obtain a better understanding of root causes.[827] The Committee will

---

823   CRC/C/BIH/CO/2-4 (5 October 2012) [70].
824   For example CRC/C/GIN/CO/2 (30 January 2013) [81]; CRC/C/UZB/CO/3-4 (14 June 2013) [67].
825   CRC/C/ALB/CO/2-4 (5 October 2012) [80].
826   CRC/C/LBR/CO/2-4 (5 October 2012) [80].
827   CRC/C/GIN/CO/2 (30 January 2013) [82].

recommend, for example in Namibia, that states parties offer effective alternatives to the institutionalisation of street children and facilitate reunification of children with their families where possible and taking into account the best interests of the child.[828]

3.7.9.5 Children in armed conflicts (Articles 38 and 39)

Article 38

1. States parties undertake to respect and to ensure respect for rules of international humanitarian law applicable to them in armed conflicts which are relevant to the child.
2. States parties shall take all feasible measures to ensure that persons who have not attained the age of fifteen years do not take a direct part in hostilities.
3. States parties shall refrain from recruiting any person who has not attained the age of fifteen years into their armed forces. In recruiting among those persons who have attained the age of fifteen years but who have not attained the age of eighteen years, States parties shall endeavour to give priority to those who are oldest.
4. In accordance with their obligations under international humanitarian law to protect the civilian population in armed conflicts, States parties shall take all feasible measures to ensure protection and care of children who are affected by an armed conflict.

Article 39

States parties shall take all appropriate measures to promote physical and psychological recovery and social reintegration of a child victim of: any form of neglect, exploitation, or abuse; torture or any other form of cruel, inhuman or degrading treatment or punishment; or armed conflicts. Such recovery and reintegration shall take place in an environment which fosters the health, self-respect and dignity of the child.

The age at which children should be able to participate in armed conflicts was one of the four areas of controversy in the drafting history of the Convention (Cantwell 1992: 26). To an extent and because of the unsatisfactory compromises reached in relation to the drafting of Article 38, there remained an appetite within the international community to campaign for an Optional Protocol to raise the age to 18 years and provide more comprehensive protection in this area. Further international recognition of the criminality of conscripting or enlisting children under the age of 15 into national armed forces and non-state militias arrived with the Rome Statute of the International Criminal Court (1998).[829] The Optional

---

828 CRC/C/NAM/CO/2-3 (16 October 2012) [70].
829 Opened for signature 17 July 1998, 2187 UNTS 90 (entered into force 1 July 2002).

Protocol to the Convention on the Rights of the Child on the involvement of children in armed conflict (OPAC)[830] followed in 2000 (section 3.6.2). The subject of children's involvement in armed conflict is given more detailed treatment in Chapter 8.

In some countries, for example Niger, the minimum age for voluntary or compulsory recruitment is not specified in law, and children as young as 13 years old can enrol in military schools and be taught basic handling of firearms.[831] Similarly, in Bosnia and Herzegovina, the recruitment and use in armed conflict of persons under the age of 18 years 'is not explicitly prohibited nor criminalized in State and Entity level legislation'.[832] As regards Liberia, the Committee observed with concern that 'armed actors along the borders continue to recruit children into their ranks and that the State party has not taken any actions to redress the situation'.[833] The Committee raised its concern in relation to Austria that 'students from age 14 are trained on the use of small arms at the Vienna military academy'.[834] It recommended that 'the State party ensure that the education of child cadets at military academies is free from any form of arms training and military drill and consistent with the aims of education, as recognized in Article 29 of the Convention and in general comment No. 1'.[835] The Committee noted with concern, in relation to Canada, that 'recruitment strategies may in fact actively target Aboriginal youth and are conducted at high school premises'.[836] The Committee expressed its 'deep concern', in relation to Guinea, that between 2000 and 2001: 'thousands of young people, including children as young as 13 were recruited into militias known as "Young Volunteers", operating under the Ministry of Defense to participate in counter-attacks against Liberia'; only a small minority followed the demobilisation process in 2004; and that 'a large number of former child soldiers lived, without any support, in the country's forests'.[837] As regards Israel, the Committee expressed 'deep concern' about 'the continuous use of Palestinian children as human shields and informants', and that 'the soldiers convicted for having forced at gunpoint a nine-year old child to search bags suspected of containing explosives only received a suspended sentence of three months and were demoted'.[838]

The Committee has made some interesting observations in relation to the case of Omar Khadr, a Canadian citizen who was the first person since the Second World War to be prosecuted in a military commission for war crimes committed while still a minor. He was captured by American forces in Afghanistan in 2002 (when he was 15 years and 10 months old), and detained at Guantanamo Bay

---

830 25 May 2000, 2173 UNTS 222 (entered into force 12 February 2002).
831 CRC/C/NER/CO/2 (18 June 2009) [68].
832 CRC/C/BIH/CO/2-4 (5 October 2012) [68].
833 CRC/C/LBR/CO/2-4 (5 October 2012) [76].
834 CRC/C/AUT/CO/3-4 (5 October 2012) [56].
835 CRC/C/AUT/CO/3-4 (5 October 2012) [57].
836 CRC/C/CAN/CO/3-4 (5 October 2012) [75].
837 CRC/C/GIN/CO/2 (30 January 2013) [77].
838 CRC/C/ISR/CO/2-4 (14 June 2013) [71].

detention camp in Cuba. His father had been a close family friend of the late ter-rorist leader Osama bin Laden, and had been accused of being a fundraiser for al-Qaida. Omar pleaded guilty in October 2010 in a diplomatic (United States and Canada) plea agreement to murder and providing support for terrorist activi-ties. He accepted an 8-year sentence, with the possibility of a transfer to Canada after at least one year to serve the remainder of the sentence there. On September 29, 2012 Khadr was repatriated to Canada. Under Canadian law he was eligible for parole in mid-2013. The Committee welcomed his return to the custody of the state party:

> However, the Committee is concerned that as a former child soldier, Omar Kadr has not been accorded the rights and appropriate treatment under the Convention. In particular, the Committee is concerned that he experi-enced grave violations of his human rights, which the Canadian Supreme Court[839] recognized, including his maltreatment during his years of deten-tion in Guantanamo, and that he has not been afforded appropriate redress and remedies for such violations.[840]

The Committee urged the states party, inter alia, to 'promptly provide a rehabili-tation program for Omar Kadr that is consistent with the Paris Principles for the rehabilitation of former child soldiers'.[841]

3.7.9.6   Children in conflict with the law, victims and witnesses (Articles 37(b)–(d) and 40)

The Committee has devoted a 'Day of General Discussion'[842] (1995), a Recommendation[843] (1999) and General Comment No 10[844] (2007) to the admin-istration of juvenile justice. In the record of the 'Day of General Discussion', it was stated:

> The experience of the Committee has shown that the administration of juve-nile justice is of practical concern in all regions of the world and in relation to all legal systems. The challenging and innovative philosophy arising from the Convention on the Rights of the Child and other United Nations standards adopted in the field ... predicates a child-oriented system that recognises the

---

839 *Canada (Prime Minister) v Khadr*, 2010 SCC 3, [2010] 1 SCR 44.

840 CRC/C/CAN/CO/3-4 (5 October 2012) [77].

841 CRC/C/CAN/CO/3-4 (5 October 2012) [78].

842 Committee on the Rights of the Child, 'Day of General Discussion' on *The administration of juvenile justice*, Report on the 10th session, CRC/C/46 (18 December 1995) [203–38].

843 Committee on the Rights of the Child, Recommendation No 2: *The administration of juvenile justice*, Report on the 22nd session, CRC/C/90 (7 December 1999) 3–4.

844 Committee on the Rights of the Child, General Comment No 10: *Children's rights in juvenile justice*, CRC/C/GC/10 (25 April 2007).

child as a subject of fundamental rights and freedoms and ensures that all actions concerning him or her are guided by the best interests of the child as a primary consideration.[845]

The Recommendation recalls 'that since the beginning of its work, the administration of juvenile justice has received consistent and systematic attention from the Committee' and notes that the Committee's juvenile justice standards 'are in many instances not reflected in national legislation or practice, giving cause for serious concern'.[846] The Committee emphasises in the General Comment that its objectives are to develop and implement a *comprehensive* juvenile justice policy; an approach that should not be limited by the implementation of just Articles 37 and 40, but will also take into account the 'general principles' and other relevant provisions of the Convention, in addition to promoting the integration in national juvenile justice policy of a range of existing international standards. Particular examples of these latter 'soft law' instruments are referred to in the General Comment.[847] They are:

- United Nations Standard Minimum Rules for the Administration of Juvenile Justice (Beijing Rules)[848]
- United Nations Guidelines for the Prevention of Juvenile Delinquency (Riyadh Guidelines)[849] and
- United Nations Rules for the Protection of Juveniles Deprived of their Liberty (Havana Rules).[850]

The Committee additionally recommends to states parties that they take account of the Vienna Guidelines for Action on Children in the Criminal Justice System,[851] and the United Nations Rules for the Protection of Juveniles Deprived of their Liberty.[852]

845 Committee on the Rights of the Child, 'Day of General Discussion' on *The administration of juvenile justice*, Report on the 10th session, CRC/C/46 (18 December 1995) [206].
846 Committee on the Rights of the Child, Recommendation No 2: *The administration of juvenile justice*, Report on the 22nd session, CRC/C/90 (7 December 1999) 3–4.
847 Committee on the Rights of the Child, General Comment No 10: *Children's rights in juvenile justice*, CRC/C/GC/10 (25 April 2007) [4].
848 General Assembly, *United Nations Standard Minimum Rules for the Administration of Juvenile Justice* (Beijing Rules): resolution adopted by the General Assembly, UN Doc A/RES/40/33 (29 November 1985).
849 General Assembly, *United Nations Guidelines for the Prevention of Juvenile Delinquency* (Riyadh Guidelines): resolution adopted by the General Assembly, UN Doc A/RES/45/112 (14 December 1990).
850 General Assembly, *United Nations Rules for the Protection of Juveniles Deprived of Their Liberty* (Havana Rules): resolution adopted by the General Assembly, UN Doc A/RES/45/113 (14 December 1990).
851 Economic and Social Council, *Administration of juvenile justice*, ECOSOC resolution, UN Doc E/1997/30 (21 July 1997) 85–86.
852 General Assembly, *United Nations Rules for the Protection of Juveniles Deprived of Their Liberty*: resolution adopted by the General Assembly, UN Doc A/RES/45/113 (14 December 1990).

CHILDREN DEPRIVED OF THEIR LIBERTY, AND MEASURES TO ENSURE THAT ANY ARREST, DETENTION OR IMPRISONMENT OF A CHILD SHALL BE USED AS MEASURES OF LAST RESORT AND FOR THE SHORTEST APPROPRIATE TIME AND THAT LEGAL AND OTHER ASSISTANCE IS PROMPTLY PROVIDED (ART 37 (B)–(D))

The Committee will be concerned where children are subjected to pre-trial detention without the necessary safeguards. For example, it found in relation to Albania, cases of 'children being held 48 hours in police stations, interrogated in inappropriate rooms, without the assistance of a lawyer, subjected to ill treatment from the police and their inmates and detained in cells together with adults', and where '70 percent of convicted juveniles will have spent their sentence in detention while awaiting their trial'.[853] Similarly, in Liberia the Committee found an 'extensive use of lengthy pre-trial detention for children; lack of due process; and extremely poor detention conditions'.[854] In Austria, the Committee was concerned that the 'maximum length of pre-trial detention for juveniles is one year'.[855] In such cases, the Committee will recommend that such detention must be only used as a measure of last resort and for the shortest period time in compliance with Article 37(b), and reviewed on a regular basis with a view to withdrawing it.[856] The Committee is further concerned by the treatment of children while in detention. For example, in relation to Canada, it observed that there was an 'excessive use of force, including the use of tasers, by law enforcement officers and personnel in detention centers against children during the arrest stage and in detention'.[857] Similarly, the Committee observed, in relation to Guinea-Bissau, 'ill-treatment of children in custody by police, including in pre-trial detention, and the absence of penal procedural rules during their trial'.[858] As regards Uzbekistan, the Committee noted with concern 'reports of children in conflict with the law being subject to torture during interrogations and detention'.[859] The Committee provided a robust critique of Israel's treatment of Palestinian children in this context:

> The Committee is … concerned that the State party fully disregarded the recommendations it made in 2002 and 2010 in relation to arrest and detention of Palestinian children and their detention conditions and has continued to deny all these guarantees and safeguards to children living in the OPT [Occupied Palestinian Territory] who remain subject to military orders. The Committee is gravely concerned that an estimated 7000 Palestinian children aged from 12 to 17 years, but sometimes as young as nine years, have been

853 CRC/C/ALB/CO/2-4 (5 October 2012) [84].
854 ibid.
855 CRC/C/AUT/CO/3-4 (5 October 2012) [66].
856 ibid [85]. See also: CRC/C/AUT/CO/3-4 (5 October 2012) [67]; CRC/C/GIN/CO/2 (30 January 2013) [85].
857 CRC/C/CAN/CO/3-4 (5 October 2012) [85(d)].
858 CRC/C/GNB/CO/2-4 (14 June 2013) [68].
859 CRC/C/UZB/CO/3-4 (14 June 2013) [69].

arrested, interrogated and detained by the State party's army over the reporting period (an average of two children per day), this number having increased by 73 per cent since September 2011, as observed by the United Nations Secretary General (A/67/372 para 28).[860]

THE ADMINISTRATION OF JUVENILE JUSTICE (ART 40)

Article 40

1. States parties recognize the right of every child alleged as, accused of, or recognized as having infringed the penal law to be treated in a manner consistent with the promotion of the child's sense of dignity and worth, which reinforces the child's respect for the human rights and fundamental freedoms of others and which takes into account the child's age and the desirability of promoting the child's reintegration and the child's assuming a constructive role in society.

Article 40(2) additionally specifies particular guarantees to the child alleged as, or accused of, having infringed the penal law, including the presumption of innocence and the right to be informed promptly and directly of the charges against them. Article 40(3) obliges states parties to promote the establishment of laws, procedures, authorities and institutions 'specifically applicable to children' in conflict with penal law, and in particular to establish a minimum age of criminal responsibility. States are also obliged to seek measures other than judicial proceedings for such children. Article 40(4) stipulates that there should be a variety of dispositions (for example, foster care) as alternatives to 'institutional care'.

The Committee will be concerned where it identifies that a states party, for example Bosnia and Herzegovina, lacks significant *alternatives* to 'institutional care', thus failing to comply with Article 40(4).[861] It raised concerns in relation to Guinea, where '[d]eprivation of liberty is the most common sentence for children in conflict with the law, including for children as young as 13 years old'.[862] In Malta, the Committee found that there were 'inadequate alternatives to deprivation of liberty and diversion possibilities, to avoid the prejudicial effects of deprivation of liberty'.[863] The guidance in Article 37(c) relating to the desired separation of children from adults in detention and prison facilities is often a cause of concern by the Committee. For example, in relation to Namibia, it was concerned by the lack of special detention facilities for children, both boys and girls, children being incarcerated with adults, and the poor conditions of detention, including in prisons'.[864] The Committee recommends, for example in relation to Canada, that

860 CRC/C/ISR/CO/2-4 (14 June 2013) [73].
861 CRC/C/BIH/CO/2-4 (5 October 2012) [76].
862 CRC/C/GIN/CO/2 (30 January 2013) [85].
863 CRC/C/MLT/CO/2 (5 February 2013) [65].
864 CRC/C/NAM/CO/2-3 (16 October 2012) [73].

states parties should ensure that boys and girls are held separately from each other and 'that girls are monitored by female prison guards so as to better protect girls from the risk of sexual exploitation'.[865]

The Committee has frequently criticised the low age of criminal responsibility (section 3.7.2) existing in some states. For example, in Namibia the minimum age of criminal responsibility (seven years of age) was regarded by the Committee as 'unacceptably low'.[866] The Committee was concerned that in Malta it has remained at nine years of age.[867] Similarly, in Niue it was 'as low as 10 years', and the Committee recommended that 'an internationally accepted age and, under no circumstances, under 12 years' should be adopted.[868] The Committee will note, with appreciation, where the age of criminal responsibility has been raised, for example to 18 years in Andorra.[869] The Committee will also be concerned where a states party appears to have no specialised courts, customised to the needs of children, contrary to Article 40(3) of the Convention, as for example in relation to Liberia.[870] In some countries, the juvenile justice system may not have been established at all, or be at a very early stage of development. In Niue for example, the Committee recognised that, although the number of juvenile crimes and offenders was small, it remained 'deeply concerned' that '[a] juvenile justice system is not yet put in place, particularly in the court proceedings, no qualified public defender is available for young offenders, and judges and police officers are not given proper training to effectively deal with juvenile offenders and children victims in a child-sensitive manner'.[871] In Uzbekistan, the Committee was concerned that '[t]he State party continues to have no holistic juvenile justice system and its laws on juvenile justice are fragmented'.[872] Similarly, in Armenia, the Committee found that there was 'no holistic juvenile justice system, including juvenile courts and comprehensive law on juvenile justice, with provisions for diversion mechanisms and efficient alternatives to the formal justice system'.[873] As regards Rwanda, the Committee regretted that despite its previous recommendations the state party had not established independent children's courts.[874]

The Committee will also focus its attention on the protection of child victims and witnesses of crime. It found, for example in Namibia, that there was a lack of adequate mechanisms to protect such victims/witnesses of sexual abuse

865 CRC/C/CAN/CO/3-4 (5 October 2012) [86]. See also CRC/C/UZB/CO/3-4 (14 June 2013) [69].
866 CRC/C/NAM/CO/2-3 (16 October 2012) [73].
867 CRC/C/MLT/CO/2 (5 February 2013) [65].
868 CRC/C/NIU/CO/1 (29 January 2013) [69–70]. The minimum age of criminal responsibility was also 10 years of age in Guyana, and a criminal majority age of 17 years (rather than 18); CRC/C/GUY/CO/2-4 (5 February 2013) [61].
869 CRC/C/AND/CO/2 (9 October 2012) [50].
870 CRC/C/LBR/CO/2-4 (5 October 2012) [84].
871 CRC/C/NIU/CO/1 (29 January 2013) [69].
872 CRC/C/UZB/CO/3-4 (14 June 2013) [69].
873 CRC/C/ARM/CO/3-4 (14 June 2013) [51].
874 CRC/C/RWA/CO/3-4 (14 June 2013) [62].

during legal proceedings.[875] In Guyana, the Committee found that 'there are no child witness support and protection programmes for guiding child victims and safeguarding and facilitating their situation in complaints, interrogation and testimony processes'.[876] The Committee will typically recommend[877] in this field that the states party should fully take into account the United Nations Guidelines on Justice in Matters Involving Child Victims and Witnesses of Crime,[878] and provide the necessary protection required in those Guidelines.

Finally, the Committee will typically recommend, particularly in relation to states parties whom it considers to have a poor record on juvenile justice standards, that the states party seek technical assistance in this area from the United Nations Interagency Panel on Juvenile Justice and its members, including the United Nations Office on Drugs and Crime (UNODC), UNICEF, OHCHR and NGOs and make use of the tools developed by the Interagency Panel.[879]

875 CRC/C/NAM/CO/2-3 (16 October 2012) [75].

876 CRC/C/GUY/CO/2-4 (5 February 2013) [63].

877 For example CRC/C/GIN/CO/2 (30 January 2013) [87]; CRC/C/NIU/CO/1 (29 January 2013) [71]; CRC/C/GUY/CO/2-4 (5 February 2013) [64]; CRC/C/ARM/CO/3-4 (14 June 2013) [54]; and CRC/C/RWA/CO/3-4 (14 June 2013) [64].

878 Economic and Social Council, *Guidelines on Justice in Matters Involving Child Victims and Witnesses of Crime*, ECOSOC resolution, UN Doc E/RES/2005/20 (22 July 2005).

879 For example CRC/C/LBR/CO/2-4 (5 October 2012) [85]; CRC/C/NIU/CO/1 (29 January 2013) [70]; CRC/C/GUY/CO/2-4 (5 February 2013) [62]; and CRC/C/UZB/CO/3-4 (14 June 2013) [71].

Chapter 4

Child labour

4.1 The phenomenon of child labour

The complexity of the phenomenon of child labour is widely acknowledged. It can be viewed as an economic, structural, governmental, moral and ethical issue, including human rights concerns (Abernethie 1998: 83). The pervasive process of globalisation has enabled a more intense international focus on the problem, and has also added to the complexities in debates surrounding it (Muntarbhorn 1998: 255). Child labour involves not only concerns about children's welfare and development but also considerations of effects on macroeconomic and labour markets.

Furthermore, the different economic, developmental, humanitarian and moral grounds that might justify the elimination of child labour sometimes conflict with each other. For example, the elimination of child labour from factories could lead to an increase in adult employment and wage rates, but might also negatively affect children's welfare if there are no adequate schools available and the children's only remaining option is to undertake more hazardous work in the 'informal sector' of the economy (Anker 2000: 264).

In addition, the image of child labour is too often portrayed as a phenomenon principally relevant to the *developing* countries, whereas there is evidence of child labour in industrialised Europe, the United States and other *developed* nations (Selby 2008; Kilkelly 2003). In the field of child labour, one needs particularly to be aware of the different perceptions of childhood in northern and southern countries respectively. Arguably, the ethnocentrism of industrialised countries inappropriately dominates the international discourse on children's rights (Boyden 1997). The following sub-sections discuss the key elements of the phenomenon of child labour.

4.1.1 Difficulties of definition and types of child labour

The concept of 'child labour' tends to conjure up several stereotypes that are not always helpful in properly identifying the nature of the problem. One such image is of children working in terrible conditions in sweatshops in India in the carpet or garment industries, or in the firecracker or matches industries in China. Another such image focuses on exploitation in export-related jobs and sex tourism.

However, the reality is that most child labourers in the world are employed in the agriculture sector. The International Labour Organization (ILO) estimates that there are 168 million children worldwide who are child labourers, that is, almost 11 per cent of the child population as a whole. Of these, 98 million, ie 59 per cent of all child labourers, are working in the agriculture sector (ILO 2013: 3, 7).

It has been estimated that exploitation in export-related jobs accounts for a quite small proportion of the total number of child labourers, and that commercial sexual exploitation of children is dominated by local rather than foreign customers. There are also believed to be a large number of children working in the 'informal economy', in other words children doing work outside of a country's formal employment sector. Such work may be exploitative, for example, where children are working long hours under bad conditions in family-run enterprises or in illegal activities within an organised crime environment.

However, work in the informal sector may also be beneficial to an individual child, depending on the context; for example, work delivering newspapers, babysitting or gardening (Selby 2008: 170). Some studies have identified quite positive attitudes by children themselves towards 'light work' and helping out in the family and home environment (Ochaíta and others 2000: 31).

It should be clear that, for the purposes of imposing a legal regime to reduce child labour or eliminate it entirely, we need to define more precisely what 'child labour' should mean for these purposes. The task of defining child labour has been much discussed and contested, precisely because there are many different views about what type of work or work characteristics are consistent with a child's welfare and development and what types are not, or indeed may have deleterious consequences.

It is now generally accepted, and also reflected in the international legal regime, that a distinction must be drawn between work that children do, either at home within the family or for an external employer, which may be *beneficial* and contribute to their development and wellbeing, and 'child labour' that can be said to be *exploitative*. This begs the question of what practices can be regarded as 'exploitative' for these purposes. Exploitation is a somewhat value-laden term that is difficult to define objectively (Anker 2000: 260–61). But of course not all forms of child labour are exploitative, and in some settings child work may be an 'integral part of the socialization process' (Alston 1989: 36). There is clearly a need to view the work that children do as lying on a continuum between dangerous and exploitative work on the one hand and beneficial work on the other.

> We can speak of dangerous and exploitative work when it has the following characteristics: it is carried out full-time at too early an age; the working day is excessively long; it is carried out in inadequate conditions; it is not sufficiently well-paid; it involves excessive responsibility; it undermines the child's dignity and self-esteem. On the other hand, beneficial work is defined as that which promotes or stimulates the child's integral development – physical, cognitive and social – without interfering in his/her scholastic or recreational activity

or rest. This type of work contributes to children's socialisation, offering them the opportunity to carry out certain tasks that provide them with feelings of competence and independence that are fundamental to the proper development of their self-concept and self-esteem.

(Ochaíta and others 2000: 19–20)

It is now widely accepted that the dividing line between exploitative/dangerous and beneficial child work is identified by an examination of how such work impacts on a child's development. The Convention on the Rights of the Child[1] obliges states parties to 'recognize the right of the child to be protected from economic exploitation and from performing any work that is likely to be hazardous or to interfere with the child's education (see Case study 4.1 below), or to be harmful to the child's health or physical, mental, spiritual, moral or social development'[2] (section 3.7.9.3).

Governments and economists responsible for collecting national statistics may have a rather narrower definition of child labour where they define it initially as 'employment'. This might capture those with a 'contract of employment' and also those recognised as 'self-employed', but could miss a range of others engaged in exploitative work.

The definition of 'economic' used by the UN's System of National Accounts (SNA) is formulated in broader terms relating to the content and productive nature of the work; so gathering fuel for household use would come within the SNA definition, even though it often occurs outside a market context, and such children would be classed as child labourers. On the other hand, burning fuel in the process of cooking a meal would not be classified as economic and many would say this was a case of a child being engaged in household 'chores', a delineation that typically has gender consequences (Dorman 2008).

The ILO (section 2.4.1.4) currently uses three categories: 'children in employment', 'child labour' and 'hazardous work', for the purpose of constructing their global statistics. Its definitions are reproduced below:

> *Children in employment* are those engaged in any economic activity for at least one hour during the reference period. Economic activity covers all market production and certain types of non-market production (principally the production of goods and services for own use). It includes forms of work in both the formal and informal economies; inside and outside family settings; work for pay or profit (in cash or in kind, part-time or full-time), or as a domestic worker outside the child's own household for an employer (with or without pay). ...

---

1 Convention on the Rights of the Child, opened for signature 20 November 1989, 1577 UNTS 3 (entered into force 2 September 1990).
2 CRC art 32.

Children in child labour are a subset of *children in employment*. They include those in the worst forms of child labour and children in employment below the minimum age, excluding children in permissible light work, if applicable. Child labour is therefore a narrower concept than 'children in employment'; child labour excludes those children who are working only a few hours a week in permitted light work and those above the minimum age whose work is not classified as a worst form of child labour, including 'hazardous work' in particular.

Hazardous work by children is defined as any activity or occupation that, by its nature or type, has or leads to adverse effects on the child's safety, health and moral development. In general, hazardous work may include night work and long hours of work; exposure to physical, psychological or sexual abuse; work underground, under water, at dangerous heights or in confined spaces; work with dangerous machinery, equipment and tools, or which involves the manual handling or transport of heavy loads; and work in an unhealthy environment which may, for example, expose children [to] hazardous substances, agents or processes, or to temperatures, noise levels, or vibrations damaging their health.

(ILO 2013: 16)

However, there is no universally accepted definition of 'child labour'. The phrase is used in public discourse to refer to 'child time in activities that are somehow harmful to the child' (Edmonds 2008). Economists think in terms of 'opportunity costs' to determine what might be 'harmful', that is, what activities would the child participate in if s/he was *not* working, and on balance would these be more beneficial? In other words, 'harmful' could be understood as implying the child would be made better off by not participating in the activity.

According to Edmonds, who reviewed a large number of academic papers and reports on this problem, this definition of child labour creates 'the problem of the counterfactual', that is, it is impossible to know what such children would be doing in the absence of work (Edmonds 2008: 1). He argues that this problem is implicitly recognised in the ILO Convention concerning the Prohibition and Immediate Action for the Elimination of the Worst Forms of Child Labour (1999, Worst Forms of Child Labour Convention),[3] where hazardous work and other *worst forms* of child labour are identified on the basis of job characteristics. He concludes that the international definition of child labour needs to be based on the key ILO Conventions and defined on the basis of a list of job attributes and work characteristics that can be tracked; for example, total hours worked, numbers of children working in certain industries (manufacturing, mining and quarrying, hotels and restaurants, private residences other than that of the child's family)

---

3 International Labour Organization, Worst Forms of Child Labour Convention, ILO Convention No 182 (17 June 1999).

and certain working conditions (streets, at night or pre-dawn, low lighting, lack of ventilation, operating machinery or powered tools) (Edmonds 2008: 38).

A further problem with efforts to define child labour is that the pattern of child labour is frequently *intermittent*; for example, it may occur intensely in rural communities around harvest time (see Case Study 4.1 below). Many children may move from school into work and back again several times; some children attend school and also work and these patterns may vary considerably over time. In one study, using longitudinal data from Brazil, where the authors tracked the employment patterns of thousands of children aged 10–16 during four months of their lives in the 1980s and 1990s, it was concluded that 'intermittent employment is a crucial characteristic of child labour which must be recognised to capture levels of child employment adequately and identify child workers (Levison and others 2007: 245). Such problems of definition also pose difficulties in attempting to construct credible measurements of the extent of child labour (see section 4.1.6).

4.1.2   Identifying the causes of child labour

The complexity of the phenomenon of child labour is particularly apparent in analyses of its *causes*. Some commentators have attempted to produce typologies of causation, deploying categories which range from the dynamics of the family unit through to the school system, the labour situation of adults and, finally, macrosystemic elements such as prevailing cultural attitudes towards childhood, economic and social policies and existing legislation (Ochaíta and others 2000: 16–17). The income from child labour may reflect a family's strategy simply to subsist. A key feature of child labour is that it is not only *caused* by structural economic, educational and social disadvantage, but it also *contributes* to the maintenance of such inequalities:

> Child labour is often regarded as a consequence of poverty. By depriving the child of education and an opportunity for development to her or his full potential, child labour is also a cause of perpetuating poverty to the next generation.
>
> It is necessary to break the vicious cycle with a strong political will and comprehensive set of practical measures, supported by solid legal framework.
>
> (Noguchi 2010: 533)

The research literature (Dorman 2008) is replete with discussion of the linkage with poverty and the lack of education and health services. In low-income countries, child labour tends to decline with increases in gross per capita domestic product (GDP) (Betcherman and others 2004: 12–13).

The ILO has estimated the incidence of child labour against different levels of national income, grouping countries into four categories according to their national income per capita (GNI). As can be seen from Table 4.1 below, the incidence of child labour decreases with the level of national income.

Table 4.1 Global child labour by level of national income, 2012

National income	Total number of children ('000)	Child labour ('000)	%
Total	**1,585,566**	**167,956**	**10.6**
Low income	330,257	74,394	22.5
Lower middle income	902,174	81,306	9.0
Upper middle income	197,977	12,256	6.2
High income	155,159	na	na

Source: IPEC 2013 [2.7, Table 13]

The increasing recognition of child labour located within a poverty matrix indicates much about the remedial strategies to tackle the problem, that is, strategies which integrate anti-poverty and wider development goals (Cooper 1997: 429). The way in which the matrix of poverty, educational disadvantage and child labour are linked by both cause and effect prompted the ILO to announce a decade ago that:

> We have surely reached a moment in history where the absolute number of child labourers, and the proportion of a country's children who are subject to child labour, particularly to its worst forms, should become key indicators of economic and social development.
>
> (ILO 2002 para 63)

The role of education is a key component in any discussion about the causes of child labour; '[c]hild labour can be defined as a form of denial of the right to education' (Humbert 2009: 33). There is, perhaps unsurprisingly, a lot of evidence confirming the adverse impact of child labour on educational attainment (Betcherman and others 2004: 13). In a study on Bangladesh it was observed that children from poorer households who had little access to secondary education became engaged in a range of economic activity, some of which was hazardous (Masum 2002: 266).

Another commentator argues, in relation to child domestic workers in Ghana, that '[i]f governments can ensure that all children have access to a free compulsory universal basic education … the problem of girl child labour will be drastically reduced' (Tetteh 2011: 230). In developing countries, it is estimated that one in five children (aged 6–11) is not in school; that is, more than 100 million children in total. Children drop out of school often because of poor teaching and learning conditions and they are predominantly poor, rural and disproportionately female (Betcherman and others 2004: 17). If the states parties' obligations under the Convention on the Rights of the Child to make primary education compulsory and available free for all (section 3.7.8.1),[4] and the MDG goal to strengthen universal

---

4 CRC art 28(1)(a).

primary education are to be achieved, then it follows that child labour will necessarily diminish. The persistence of child labour in any country is clearly a significant obstacle to achieving universal education (Betcherman and others 2004: 2).

It is also thought that school attendance will both prevent child labour from occurring and have the potential to rehabilitate rescued child labourers and ensure their social reintegration. It would seem that '[a]dvances in the right to education therefore cannot but go hand in hand with the elimination of child labour' (Noguchi 2002: 362). However, developing nations have often been reluctant to invest in universal education on the basis of the large costs involved, and that poor families rely upon their children's income. Such arguments appear unsatisfactory when one considers the historical evidence, which suggests a range of factors contributing to the introduction of universal education. Japan introduced compulsory education in 1872 and North and South Korea, Taiwan and China introduced compulsory education shortly after the Second World War; all at a time when per capita incomes in those countries were low and poverty widespread. Nevertheless, in one country after another the phased extension of the age of compulsory education accompanied further restrictions on the employment of children (Weiner 1994: 128).

However, it should not be thought that the causative factors underlying child labour follow the same pattern in every country. A reasonable assumption in relation to the United Kingdom, the first industrialised nation, might be that child labour is intimately linked with the process of industrialisation. However, that assertion is belied by the widespread incidence of child labour in India, where the majority of child labourers are employed in small-scale enterprises and in agriculture (Weiner 1994: 122). The pervasiveness and durability of the causative mix of factors leading to child labour in any one country is explained better by detailed investigation of the national profile.

This, at least, should enable the disposal of several myths that have grown up around the child labour issue, for example, that children's 'nimble fingers' enable them to handle more efficiently tasks such as producing knots in the weaving of carpets, picking tea leaves and packing matches. A detailed study surveying the gem, brassware, glass, pottery and lock industries in India refutes a number of these claims (Burra 1995). Given the causative significance of poverty to the existence and extent of child labour, it is tempting to conclude that any remedial strategy (see section 4.3) should prioritise the eradication of poverty. The problem is that such policies take many years, sometimes several generations, to make significant development gains.

The UN Commission on Human Rights[5] (UNCHR) stated long ago that '[p]overty is often the main cause of child labour, but generations of children should not be condemned, until poverty is overcome, to exploitation' (UNCHR 1993: para 2). Human rights advocates are in agreement with this point:

---

5 Replaced in 2006 by the United Nations Human Rights Council (UNHRC). See section 2.5.1.1.

To argue that the enormous problem of poverty must be solved first and that the problem of child labor should be addressed gradually is antithetical to the inherent logic of human rights.

(Silk and Makonnen 2003: 368)

However, the reduction of educational disadvantage and poverty cannot be a complete answer to the problem of child labour. There have been significant efforts in India to reduce poverty and strengthen education. However, one study observes that '[n]otwithstanding these economic successes, the number of children working in India has not decreased significantly and may have even increased', and that it is important that the Indian Government stops thinking in terms of child labour being a problem simply associated with poverty (Agarwal 2004: 665, 713).

Some empirical research shows that the relationship between poverty and child labour is weaker than is often believed (Betcherman and others 2004: 3). Indeed, the causative strength of poverty and lack of education weakens when we consider the persistence of child labour within the developed nations. In Europe, it seems likely that a significant number of children, rather than being motivated by family survival strategies typical in developing nations, are more motivated by the desire to obtain 'supplementary income necessary to meet their consumer desires and the demands of peer pressure' (Kilkelly 2003: 347).

4.1.3 The extent and location of exploitative child labour

The ILO's global report on child labour announced optimistically in 2006 that 'a future without child labour is at last within reach' (ILO 2006: 1). The claim was principally based on the identification of a significant fall (11.2 per cent) in the number of children in child labour from 245.5 million in 2000 to 218 million in 2004. Furthermore, within this figure the number of children in 'hazardous work' had fallen even more steeply (26.1 per cent) from 170.5 million in 2000 to 126 million in 2004.[6] Improvements in these figures have continued in recent years. The comparable figures for 2008 and 2012 (see Table 4.2 below) show a fall (22 per cent) from 215 million children in child labour in 2008 to 168 million in 2012, and a fall (26 per cent) from 115 million to 85 million in the same period in relation to hazardous work.

Of the total number of 168 million child labourers in 2012, there were 99.8 million (59 per cent) boys compared to 68.2 million (41 per cent) girls (IPEC 2013: 10). The incidence of child labour across the five regions in Table 4.3 below shows the Asia and Pacific region has the *largest number* (77.7 million) of child labourers, followed by Sub-Saharan Africa (59 million), Latin America and the Caribbean (12.5 million) and the Middle East and North African region (MENA) (9.2 million).[7]

---

6 See the second edition of this book, Table 4.2 at 173.
7 'Other regions' includes the Middle East and North Africa (MENA), the developed countries and the former transition economies of Eastern Europe and Asia.

Table 4.2 Global estimates of number of children (age 5–17) in child labour and hazardous work, 2008 and 2012

(2008 – 2012)	Child population		Child labour		Hazardous work	
Year	2008	2012	2008	2012	2008	2012
('000s)	1,586,288	1,585,566	215,269	167,956	115,314	85,344
% change	na	-0.0004	na	-22	na	-26

Source: extracted from IPEC 2013, Table 6, p 9.

Table 4.3 Regional estimates of child labour, 5–17 years old, 2012

Region	Child population		Child labour	
	2008	2012	2008	2012
World	1,586,288	1,585,566	215,269	167,956
Asia and the Pacific	853,895	835,334	113,607	77,723
Latin America and the Caribbean	141,043	142,693	14,125	12,505
Sub-Saharan Africa	257,108	275,397	65,064	59,031
Other regions	334,242	332,143	22,473	18,697
of which MENA	–	110,411	–	9,244

Source: IPEC 2013: Table 9, p 11.

Table 4.4 Regional estimates of children in hazardous work, 5–17 years old, 2012

Region	Total children ('000)	Hazardous work ('000)	Incidence rate (%)
World	1,585,566	85,344	5.4
Asia and the Pacific	835,334	33,860	4.1
Latin America and the Caribbean	142,693	9,638	6.8
Sub-Saharan Africa	275,397	28,767	10.4
Other regions	332,143	13,078	3.9
of which MENA	110,411	5,224	4.7

Source: IPEC 2013: Table 11, p 14.

In *relative* terms, Sub-Saharan Africa ranks highest. Around 21 per cent of its total child population was in child labour in 2012. In 2012, 85.3 million children were in hazardous work (Table 4.4 below). They constituted almost half of those in child labour (50.8 per cent) and about one-third of children in employment (32.3 per cent).

The incidence of hazardous work increases with age; it is 2.2 per cent among children 5 to 11 years old (18.5 million), 5.3 per cent among teenagers 12 to 14

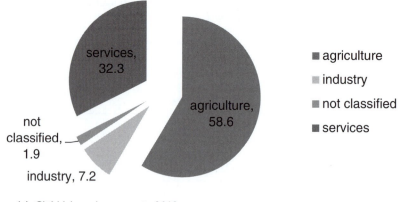

Figure 4.1 Child labour by sector in 2012
Source: IPEC 2013: Chart 9, p 16.

years old (19.3 million) and 13.0 per cent among adolescents 15 to 17 years old (47.5 million).

The sectoral distribution of child labour is usually presented by the ILO in terms of three generic sectors: agriculture, services and industry. Agriculture consists primarily of work on smallholder family farms, although it also extends to activities such as livestock production, fishing and aquaculture. See also Case Study 4.1 below concerning the use of child labour in the cotton fields in Uzbekistan.

The service sub-sectors of most relevance for child labour include hotels and restaurants, wholesale and retail trade (commerce); maintenance and repair of motor vehicles; transport; other community, social and personal service activities; and domestic work. The industry sub-sectors of most relevance for child labour include construction, mining and manufacturing (ILO 2013). Globally, child labour is concentrated in agriculture (Figure 4.1 below) and includes over 98 million children in absolute terms.

In relative terms, there has been a net increase of child labour in the services sector from 2008 to 2012, from 25.6 to 32.3 per cent. According to the new estimates, there were some 11.5 million child labourers in domestic work (included in the 'services' category) in 2012.

Although the widely held assumption that exploitative child labour occurs mostly in the developing world is borne out by the ILO estimates, it should not be thought that the occurrence of child labour in developed countries is insignificant (Dorman 2001). Indeed, even where the employment of children is lawful, such work may be injurious (O'Donnell and White 1999). Furthermore, relatively effective labour regulatory systems in the developed countries are unlikely to identify or exert much influence over children who are involved in informal or illegal work, outside the scope of health and safety legislation and hidden from national monitoring systems (Kilkelly 2003: 347).

The ILO has observed that in Europe there has always been a relatively large number of children working for pay, in seasonal activities, street trades, small workshops or in a home work setting. There is a similar pattern in the United States, where 'the growth of the service sector, the rapid increase in the supply of part-time jobs and the search for a more flexible workforce have contributed to the expansion of the child labour market' (ILO 1996: para 13).

The global headline estimates and profiles of child labour produced by the ILO and other international institutions can also mask the nature of child labour experienced in individual countries. In a study of Bangladesh, for example, it was found that 63.5 per cent of child labourers worked unpaid in family enterprises and that waged employment accounted for only 8.5 per cent of total child employment (Masum 2002: 237). In a study in the United States, a high proportion of children, often from ethnic minorities and immigrant groups, were identified as working in agriculture (Davidson 2001: 206–07). Unfortunately, the variety of studies using different methodologies and statistical categories does not make the task of comparing one country's performance with another any easier.

4.1.4   Cultural relativism and child labour

The general problem of 'cultural relativism' was discussed in section 1.3 and, as already noted at the beginning of this chapter, some commentators have argued that the ethnocentrism of industrialised countries inappropriately dominates the international discourse on children's rights (Boyden 1997). The issues touching upon cultural relativism in the child labour field are particularly poignant. Indeed, some regard for the differing perspectives of developing, non-industrialised countries has been built into the ILO constitution.[8]

Some of the earlier policy thinking about child labour was dominated by the idea that the ultimate goal should be to remove all children from work completely and that children's best interests would be served by freeing them to enjoy a childhood in caring family environments. This approach then became discredited on the basis that it depended on a northern country ideal of childhood and led to caution by southern countries to open dialogue with northern donors and development agencies on the issue of child labour (Crawford S 2000). In southern countries, children's work is more likely to be considered an acceptable element of family survival strategy. In some studies, it is argued that the reality and need for children to work should be acknowledged, and therefore the design of education systems should try to accommodate the working child (Dachi and Garrett 2003: 11).

The basic differences in the underlining perceptions of childhood in northern/developed/industrialised countries on the one hand, and southern/developing/non-industrialised countries on the other, has provided ongoing obstacles to the

---

8 International Labour Organization, Constitution of the International Labour Organisation (ILO) (1 April 1919) art 19(3).

reception of the international legal regime. However, although there may be credible arguments that minimum age rules are driven by the ethnocentric concerns of the developed nations, it is less easy to maintain such criticisms in relation to the desire to eliminate the worst forms of child labour. As one commentator notes: 'it is important not to confuse the argument that some types of employment may be acceptable with cultural relativist arguments that exploitative or harmful child labour may be tolerable because of cultural differences' (Selby 2008: 171).

4.1.5   Covert nature of child labour

It is widely accepted that a dominant and characteristic feature of child labour is that it frequently occurs covertly and in the so-called 'informal sector', for example, family-based enterprises outside of state regulatory regimes. In some countries the proportion of children in the informal economy is very high. In Bangladesh it has been reported that the informal segment within the private sector accounted for 94 per cent of total child employment (Masum 2002: 237). In one study on Africa it was noted that less than 10 per cent of the population was employed by the formal sector (Bonnet 1993: 381). In another study relating to Pakistan, it was observed that most child labourers work unpaid in the home and the government has no way to keep track of them; less than half of all children attend school, and there is no way to monitor the children (Johnson 1999: 170).

The covert forms of child labour in the informal sector will often be outside the remit and/or practical reach of regulatory labour inspectorates. For example, in Lesotho's and Portugal's thriving shoe industries and in the Philippine garment industry 'entire families work at home, making inspection nearly impossible' (Davidson 2001: 220).

It is difficult to collect reliable data on child labour that is carried out covertly and/or in the informal sector of an economy. It does seem likely, however, that gender is an important element to help explain national child labour profiles. For example, in a study relating to Turkey it is reported that it is traditionally expected that a young woman remains chaste if she is unmarried, and consequently it is thought best to keep young females within the domestic setting to protect her and the honour of the family (Bakirci 2002: 56). These kinds of societal attitudes will often be responsible for a disproportionate number of girls being engaged in home-based, domestic settings for a range of child labour activities.

4.1.6   Measuring the extent of child labour

The definitional problems discussed in section 4.1.1 and the clandestine nature of much of the informal economy discussed in section 4.1.5 make the task of measuring its incidence much harder. However, despite the conceptual, technical and infrastructural obstacles to establishing reliable statistical profiles of child labour, the estimates do at least prompt attention to the size of the problem as a legitimate concern for the international community. The literature reviewing statistical work shows that the scale of the problem is often *underestimated* because of the covert nature of child labour. Nevertheless, international organisations, national governments and non-governmental organisations (NGOs) all have their own agendas and no doubt headline figures are often deployed for 'advocacy' purposes (Invernizzi and Milne 2002).

In addition, national efforts to collect relevant data in the formal sector are variable and use different methodologies. The landscape of child labour is often fast-moving and 'intermittent' (Levison and others 2007) and difficult to capture. While human rights advocates may have an interest in *overestimation* to focus public discussion, national governments may have an interest in *underestimating* the extent of the problem; consequently, it is unsurprising that official statistics may be underestimating the real size of the problem (Bakirci 2002: 55).

In *developing* countries there may be the additional problem of a lack of governmental infrastructure to support accurate statistical survey activity. However, it should not be assumed that there are no significant defects in the data relating to *developed* countries. It has been observed that many of the European Member States have insufficiently effective systems of data collection and there remains an overwhelming lack of such data in Europe (Kilkelly 2003: 326, 346).

The ILO and the Committee on the Rights of the Child have been aware for some time of the need for more reliable and appropriately calibrated statistical estimates in order better to inform the policy-making process at the global, regional, national and local levels. Indeed, there is a requirement in the Worst Forms of Child Labour Recommendation No 190[9] (1999) on ILO member states to compile and maintain detailed statistical data.[10]

There have been attempts, since the 'International Year of the Child' in 1979, to collate reliable global statistics on the extent of child labour disaggregated by age, gender, region, formal/informal economy, economic sector, type of work and other criteria. The different estimates made by the ILO, other international bodies and NGOs prompted one commentator to observe that: '[t]hese divergences reflect the difficulty of obtaining any sort of precise figures in relation to a practice which is generally ignored by official statistics' (Alston 1989: 36).

In 1998, a unit within the ILO's 'International Programme on the Elimination of Child Labour' (IPEC) (see section 4.2.5), the 'Statistical Information and Monitoring Programme on Child Labour' (SIMPOC), was established to provide

---

9 R190 Worst Forms of Child Labour Recommendation 1999 (No 190), Recommendation concerning the prohibition and immediate action for the elimination of the worst forms of child labour. Adoption: Geneva, 87th ILC session (17 June 1999). ILO Recommendations are not binding in international law, 'but are frequently found by governments, by national parliaments, by employers' and workers' organisations and other interested groups to be a useful checklist of actions that may be taken to give effect to the obligations entered into by ratification of a Convention' (ILO 2002a: 35).

10 R190 Worst Forms of Child Labour Recommendation para 5(1).

more sophisticated estimates. It has been argued by one observer that several estimates are needed to represent the different types of work and their location along the exploitative/beneficial continuum of child labour (Anker 2000: 265).

The first integrated study of the economic costs and benefits of eliminating child labour throughout the developing and transitional countries was undertaken by the ILO in 2004 (ILO 2004). A general programme of action was developed and (hypothetically) applied in each country under examination, estimations being made of the costs and benefits from eliminating child labour. Estimates were made of the two principal benefits: first, the benefits of improved productivity and earning capacity resulting from greater education; and, secondly, the benefits of reduced illness and injuries, owing to the elimination of the worst forms of child labour.

The study found that the total economic benefits resulting from the elimination of child labour over the period 2000–2020 would be US$5,106.3 billion, whereas the total economic costs would be US$760.3 billion. In other words, there would be a total net economic benefit of US$4,346.1 billion. The study concluded that the 'single most import result is that the elimination of child labour and its replacement by universal education is estimated to yield enormous economic benefits' (ILO 2004: 4).

4.2   International legal protection of child labour

Child labour, a term that was first coined in Britain during the 19th century (Humbert 2009: 27), became increasingly a matter of concern as the Industrial Revolution in Europe advanced. Legislation regulating safety and other labour standards in factories and elsewhere arose as a result of these developments and were prompted by the pressures brought to bear by vigorous trade union movements.

The ILO Conventions, discussed in the following paragraphs, first made their appearance in 1919. International concern was focused on child labour by a major international campaign run by the Anti-slavery Society for the Protection of Human Rights in 1975, and in 1980 the United Nations appointed a Special Rapporteur, Mr Abdelwahab Bouhdiba, whose report provided further impetus for international action (Bouhdiba 1982).[11]

There are three main international instruments to consider, which in combination form the core of international legal standards in this area:

---

11 The Committee on the Rights of the Child noted that this report needed to be updated. Committee on the Rights of the Child, 'Day of General Discussion' on *The Economic Exploitation of the Child*, Report on the 4th session, CRC/C/20 (25 October 1993) [186–96 at 190].

i.   the Minimum Age Convention of 1973[12]
ii.   various Articles of the Convention on the Rights of the Child 1989[13] and
iii.   the Worst Forms of Child Labour Convention of 1999.[14]

Arguably, these three Conventions reflect competing notions of childhood and the role of children's work. It is argued that the Minimum Age Convention reflects traditional and northern-country ethnocentric ideas about children and work, and that it treats children as helpless victims needing adults to intervene on their behalf and does not give children any participation rights. The Convention on the Rights of the Child, on the other hand, reflects albeit a Euro-American view of more active children requiring adult partnership, rather than imposed super-vision. Finally, the Worst Forms of Child Labour Convention reflects 'a more democratic model better structured to accommodate diversity while focusing on a realistic social objective against which progress can be monitored' (Myers 2001: 45–53).

One commentator identifies *four stages* in the development of the international legal protection of child labour (Smolin 2000: 943). First, there were five specific areas of work identified for minimum age regulation between 1919 and 1932 in ILO Conventions.[15] The standards of these old Conventions were low com-pared with contemporary ones. There were broad exemptions for work in a family business and domestic work within a family performed by family members. The abolition of child labour was not specifically identified as an ultimate goal, and the minimum age set for admission to employment was generally 14 years (but with younger ages permitted for India and Japan).

However, these Conventions began a process of recognition, in an increasingly competitive and industrialised world, that all nations had to move in the same direction in reducing child labour. This was seen as necessary because, putting aside any humanitarian or welfare argument, countries needed to maintain fair and economic positions in the context of an increasingly competitive and global economy. A second wave of ILO Conventions raised the minimum age from 14 up to 15 years.[16]

---

12 International Labour Organization, Minimum Age Convention, ILO Convention No 138 (26 June 1973).
13 UN General Assembly, Convention on the Rights of the Child, opened for signature 20 November 1989, 1577 UNTS 3 (entered into force 2 September 1990).
14 International Labour Organization, Worst Forms of Child Labour Convention, ILO Convention No 182 (17 June 1999).
15 Minimum Age (Industry) Convention of 1919 (No 5); Minimum Age (Sea) Convention of 1920 (No 7); Minimum Age (Agriculture) Convention of 1921 (No 10); Minimum Age (Trimmers and Stokers) Convention of 1921 (No 15); and Minimum Age (Non-Industrial Employment) Convention of 1932 (No 33).
16 Minimum Age (Sea) Convention (Revised) of 1936 (No 58); Minimum Age (Industry) Convention (Revised) of 1937 (No 59); and, Minimum Age (Non-industrial Employment) Convention (Revised) of 1937 (No 60).

There were also attempts to regulate certain hazardous forms of employment.[17] However, the absence of any principle to *abolish* child labour remained. A third stage saw a process of consolidation of the existing Conventions in the form of the Minimum Age Convention, which would gradually replace the 10 previous, more specific ILO Conventions. Smolin's fourth stage of development started in the 1990s and continues to the present day (Smolin 2000: 945). This period is characterised by efforts to *mainstream* the issue of child labour within the core business of the ILO and other international institutions.

The following sections deal with the three principal international instruments in addition to a further section on 'other international instruments'. The broader roles of the Convention on the Rights of the Child and the Committee on the Rights of the Child were dealt with in Chapter 3, but in this chapter we also look at the wider role of the ILO (section 4.2.5) as a key international actor in formulating, establishing and monitoring international labour standards.

4.2.1   The Minimum Age Convention of 1973

The Minimum Age Convention[18] was adopted by the International Labour Conference on 26 June 1973 and entered into force on 19 June 1976. The overall aim of the Minimum Age Convention was expressed in terms of the *abolition* of child labour and each of the ILO's member states[19] is under an obligation 'to pursue a national policy designed to ensure the effective abolition of child labour and to raise progressively the minimum age for admission to employment or work to a level with the fullest physical and mental development of young persons'.[20]

Some commentators argue that this Convention reflects ethnocentric, northern-country ideas about children and work (Myers 2001: 47). Indeed, it has been argued that one of the effects of the Minimum Age Convention, in relation to the developing countries, has been that child work below a certain age is not regulated and may be criminalised, with the consequence that such children are subsequently pressurised into the worst forms of child labour (Calitz 2013).

The overall intention was that it should apply throughout all spheres of economic activity, replacing the previous ILO Conventions applicable to limited economic sectors. However, the Convention did not supply much guidance as to the contents of such 'national policy'.[21] The phrase 'employment or work' is significant in that it encompasses child labour performed irrespective of whether

---

17 Minimum Age (Fishermen) Convention of 1959 (No 112) and Minimum Age (Underground Work) Convention of 1965 (No 123).

18 International Labour Organization, Minimum Age Convention, ILO Convention No 138 (26 June 1973). This Convention had 166 parties (22 February 2014).

19 There were 185 member states of the ILO as at 22 February 2014.

20 Minimum Age Convention of 1973 art 1.

21 There is some guidance on 'national policy' in: R146 Minimum Age Recommendation 1973 (No 146), Recommendation concerning Minimum Age for Admission to Employment. Adoption: Geneva, 58th ILC session (26 June 1973) para 5.

there is a contract of employment; it will include the self-employed working under contracts for services in addition to those working in family arrangements without any formal legal status (Creighton 1997: 372).

The core obligation placed on each member state is to declare upon ratification a minimum age for admission to employment.[22] Further declarations may raise the specified age. The general rule is that the minimum age must not be less than that for completion of compulsory education, and in any event not less than 15 years, although there is a concession for developing countries to specify a minimum age of 14 years.[23]

Although it is necessary to achieve a suitable nexus between compulsory education and the minimum permissible age for work, compliance with this provision, according to the ILO's Committee of Experts on the Application of Conventions and Recommendations (CEACR), further requires appropriate restrictions on work undertaken outside school hours. In order to provide states with some flexibility according to their national profiles, the Minimum Age Convention contains a number of permissible departures from the declared minimum age contained in Articles 4 to 7. One of the criticisms levelled against the Convention has been its lack of flexibility. To an extent, this criticism has been strengthened by a lack of awareness and low take-up of the various departures from the prescribed obligations contained in it.

First, Article 4 allows the state's 'competent authority', after consultation with employers and workers, to exclude from the application of the Convention 'limited categories of employment or work in respect of which special and substantial problems of application arise'. There is no specification within the Convention as to which 'categories' might be excluded. The omission was deliberate, in order to allow national authorities a wide measure of discretion to apply the Convention appropriately to its own national profile; possible exclusions discussed during the Convention's preparatory stages included employment in family undertakings, domestic service in private households, homework and other work outside the supervision and control of employers (Creighton 1997: 374).

Each member state ratifying the Convention must list such excepted categories in its first report to the ILO and give reasons for such exclusions.[24] Implicitly, the range of exclusions cannot be extended subsequently to the submission of the first report. There was some concern that this prescription might be too rigid and/or might lead countries to produce an expanded list of exclusions in the first report (Creighton 1997: 375). However, this does not appear to have occurred. Indeed, it would appear that member states' lack of awareness about this and other 'flexibility' clauses contributed to the slow pace of its ratification (Creighton 1997: 375).

22 Minimum Age Convention of 1973 art 2(1).
23 Minimum Age Convention of 1973 art 2(3) and (4). See also R146 Minimum Age Recommendation 1973 (No 146) para 7.
24 Minimum Age Convention of 1973 art 4(2).

Secondly, under Article 5, there is also a generic concession to member states 'whose economy and administrative facilities are insufficiently developed' (ie developing countries), which are 'initially' allowed to 'limit the scope of application' of the Convention. Where a member state does so limit its application, it must append a declaration to its ratification specifying 'the branches of economic activity or types of undertakings' to which it will apply the Convention.[25] However, as a minimum protective requirement the Convention will always be applicable to the following activities:

> ... mining and quarrying; manufacturing; construction; electricity, gas and water; sanitary services; transport, storage and communication; and plantations and other agricultural undertakings mainly producing for commercial purposes, but excluding family and small-scale holdings producing for local consumption and not regularly employing hired workers.
>
> (Minimum Age Convention art 5(3))

Thirdly, Article 6 provides that the Convention does not apply to work done by children and young persons in schools or in other training institutions where this is an integral part of a course of education or training for which a school or training institution is responsible, or a training programme in an undertaking approved by the competent authority, or a programme of guidance to facilitate occupation choice or training.

It is also inapplicable to work done in undertakings by persons of 14 years or more as part of an apprenticeship or similar arrangement. Care must be taken that a 'training' relationship should not be used as a subterfuge to enable an employer to put children to work who are under the legal minimum age. The ILO Recommendation therefore provides that measures should be taken 'to safeguard and supervise the conditions in which children and young persons undergo vocational orientation and training within undertakings, training institutions and schools for vocational or technical education and to formulate standards for their protection and development'.[26]

Fourthly, Article 7 provides that 'light work' may be authorised by national laws in relation to children aged 13–15 years on two conditions: first, it must be 'not likely to be harmful to their health or development'; and, secondly, it must be 'not such as to prejudice their attendance at school, their participation in vocational orientation or training programmes ... or their capacity to benefit from the instruction received'. National laws may also permit the employment of persons who are at least 15 years old but have not completed their compulsory schooling.

25 Minimum Age Convention of 1973 art 5(2).
26 R146 Minimum Age Recommendation 1973 (No 146), Recommendation concerning Minimum Age for Admission to Employment. Adoption: Geneva, 58th ILC session (26 June 1973) para 12(2).

Developing countries are given further concessions to the general rule on light work by allowing them to specify 12 instead of 13 years and 14 instead of 15 years.[27] Where national laws or regulations do permit light work, the competent authority must prescribe 'the number of hours during which and the conditions in which such employment or work may be undertaken'.[28]

In 2009, the CEACR issued a 'general observation' on the concept of 'light work' contained in the Minimum Age Convention on the basis that 'the need to determine the types of light work that are authorised and the related conditions are often poorly understood by States parties and therefore likely to give rise to abuse'.[29] The general observation[30] notes that the Convention's 'preparatory work'[31] showed that differences of views had emerged during the drafting process, but the drafting committee did adopt Article 7 on the basis that it 'attempts to combine the measure of flexibility necessary to permit the wide application of the Convention (especially in view of its general scope) with the restrictions necessary to ensure adequate protection'.[32]

It is noted that a large number of countries have determined the age of admission to light work and, in particular, that in countries that have specified a minimum age for admission to employment or work of 15 or 16 years, the age from which employment on light work may be authorised has been set at 13 years, while in those countries which have determined a minimum age for admission to employment of 14 years, the age for admission to light work is 12 years.

Furthermore, in respect of certain countries that had not determined an age of admission, it was observed that 'in the great majority of these cases, this is because they have not regulated employment in these types of work'. As regards Article 7(3), it was observed that only a few countries had determined the types of light work and established the hours of work and other conditions that could be undertaken. The general observation notes that the types of light work most frequently determined by member states were as follows:

> (1) agricultural work, such as the preparation of seeds and crops, the maintenance of crops without the use of insecticides or herbicides, the harvesting of fruit, vegetables or flowers, picking and sorting in farms and herding;

---

27 Minimum Age Convention of 1973 art 7(4).

28 ibid art 7(3).

29 Committee of Experts on the Application of Conventions and Recommendations (CEACR), *General Report of the Committee of Experts on the Application of Conventions and Recommendations 2009*, International Labour Conference, 98th session, Geneva: International Labour Office at 34.

30 CEACR, *General Observation concerning Convention No 138*, International Labour Conference, ILOLEX document no 052009138 (2009) Geneva: International Labour Office.

31 International Labour Conference (ILC), 57th Session (1972) Report IV(2) 39–43; and ILC, 58th Session (1973) Report IV(2) 19–21.

32 CEACR, *General Observation concerning Convention No 138*, International Labour Conference, ILOLEX document no 052009138 (2009) Geneva: International Labour Office.

(2) forestry work and landscaping, including the planting of bushes and the maintenance of public gardens, without the use of insecticides or herbicides;

(3) domestic work, such as kitchen help, household help or looking after children; and

(4) the distribution of mail, newspapers, periodicals or publicity.[33]

The Committee further noted that some countries had laid down the hours of work for light work, that is, between two and four-and-a-half hours a day and between 10 and 25 hours a week. Certain countries have established that the time spent in school and on light work shall not exceed seven hours a day, while others prohibit light work during school term time. Furthermore, certain countries prohibit night work (between 8 pm and 6 am) and work on Sundays and public holidays, while others provide for annual leave of up to four weeks a year.

Article 8 of the Minimum Age Convention provides a general concession to the prohibition of work for children below the declared minimum age under Article 2, which the competent authority can grant by permit 'in individual cases' and 'for such purposes as participation in artistic performances'. Such permits will limit 'the number of hours during which and prescribe the conditions in which employment or work is allowed'.[34]

The five 'flexibility' clauses (Articles 4–8) discussed earlier all provide for concessions to the general rule of a minimum age of not less than the age of completion of compulsory education, or in any event 15 years (or 14 years for developing countries). However, Article 3 provides that the minimum age for admission to employment or work 'which by its nature or the circumstances in which it is carried out is likely to jeopardise health, safety or morals of young persons' must not be less than 18 years.[35] Although this appears to establish a prescriptive standard more demanding than the general obligation in Article 2, the types of employment or work which are referred to in Article 3 must be determined again 'by national laws or regulations or by the competent authority' after consultation.[36]

In determining the types of employment or work to which Article 3 applies, 'full account should be taken of relevant international labour standards, such as those concerning dangerous substances, agents or processes (including ionising radiations), the lifting of heavy weights and underground work' and the list of types

33 ibid.

34 Minimum Age Convention of 1973 art 8(2).

35 ibid art 3(1). Furthermore, 'Where the minimum age for admission to types of employment or work which are likely to jeopardise the health, safety or morals of young persons is still below 18 years, immediate steps should be taken to raise it to that level': R146 Minimum Age Recommendation 1973 (No 146), Recommendation concerning Minimum Age for Admission to Employment. Adoption: Geneva, 58th ILC session (26 June 1973) para 9.

36 ibid art 3(2).

of such employment or work 'should be re-examined periodically and revised as necessary'.[37]

Furthermore, such national laws may authorise employment from the age of 16 years, 'on condition that the health, safety and morals of the young persons concerned are fully protected'.[38] As regards enforcement, Article 9 provides that 'all necessary measures, including the provision of appropriate penalties' must be taken by the competent authority to ensure the 'effective enforcement' of the Convention. National laws or regulations or the competent authority shall define 'the persons responsible for compliance with the provisions giving effect to the Convention',[39] and they will also prescribe the 'registers or other documents' that must be kept and made available by employers of persons whom he employs and who are less than 18 years.[40]

The guidance on enforcement given in the Minimum Age Recommendation emphasises the strengthening of labour inspection, and the inspectors' close coordination and cooperation with the services responsible for the education, training, welfare and guidance of children and young persons. It also states that special attention should be paid to the enforcement of provisions concerning employment in hazardous types of employment or work; and to the prevention of the employment or work of children and young persons during the hours when instruction is available.

Measures to facilitate the verification of ages should include the maintenance of an effective system of birth registration,[41] and a requirement that employers keep and make available registers or other documents not only of children and young persons employed by them but also of those receiving vocational orientation or training in their undertakings.[42] Finally, Article 10 provides for the revision of the 10 previous ILO Conventions on minimum age-setting in various industries.

Despite the merits of the Minimum Age Convention, some commentators have concluded that it did not 'constitute an adequate response' to the problem of abusive child labour (Creighton 1997: 386). Creighton (1997: 387) identified a number of problems, for example, a lack of flexibility:

> [A]rticle 7 proceeds on the assumption that employment or work for children under thirteen is to be impermissible in all circumstances. This means that

---

37 R146 Minimum Age Recommendation 1973 (No 146), Recommendation concerning Minimum Age for Admission to Employment. Adoption: Geneva, 58th ILC session (26 June 1973) para 10.

38 Minimum Age Convention of 1973 art 3(3).

39 ibid art 9(2).

40 ibid art 9(3).

41 For birth registration and identity rights in the Convention on the Rights of the Child see section 3.7.4.1.

42 R146 Minimum Age Recommendation 1973 (No 146), Recommendation concerning Minimum Age for Admission to Employment. Adoption: Geneva, 58th ILC session (26 June 1973) paras 14–16.

it is not acceptable in terms of the Convention for a twelve-year-old to work on a morning or evening newspaper route, or for an eleven-year-old to wash cars or weed a neighbour's garden on a Saturday afternoon. Furthermore, since the Convention applies to employment or work, it would be necessary to regulate unpaid work by children or young people on a family farm or in a family restaurant.

Developing countries have had difficulties in complying with the Convention as it is premised on the assumption that child labour should be entirely eliminated, which is simply not a practical proposition for many countries. The Convention also fails to articulate clear national priorities. Much is left to the discretion of member states, without sufficient guidance on setting priorities for national action. A growing awareness has developed that the process of eliminating child labour must be an *incremental* one and strategies should be fully integrated with other measures to promote economic and educational development and protect employment standards (Creighton 1997: 396).

It is not only the developing countries that had have difficulty with the Minimum Age Convention; the United States and New Zealand have not ratified this Convention. As regards New Zealand, one commentator observes that there is little hard information available about child labour and the national census no longer collects information about the employment of children and children are invisible to the tax system (Roth 2010).

The Minimum Age Convention of 1973 was a significant advance over previous efforts, but it failed in its first two decades of existence to attract sufficient ratifications to deliver the intended reforms effectively. Indeed, it is difficult to say that there was any real coherence in international standards on child labour prior to the late 1990s. By 1996, only 49 of the member states had ratified it. The Asian countries and other developing nations were conspicuously absent from the list of ratifying countries during this period.

At the time of the adoption of the Worst Forms of Child Labour Convention of 1999, the Minimum Age Convention of 1973 had attracted only 76 ratifications. The success of the Worst Forms of Child Labour Convention prompted further ratifications to the Minimum Age Convention. Two years after the coming into force of the former (in November 2002), the ratifications to the Minimum Age Convention rose to 121. As at 22 February 2014 there were 166 parties to this Convention.

An important contributory factor to the increasing international attention to child labour, following the Minimum Age Convention, has been the combination of the ILO's focus on international labour standards with the recognition of their importance within the post-war human rights and children's rights agendas. The arrival of the rights-based approach of the Convention on the Rights of the Child (1989) has reinforced and helped to transform the ILO's older approaches to labour standards, first commenced in 1919.

4.2.2   The UN Convention on the Rights of the Child and Child Labour

In the 1980s and 1990s there was further recognition of the rights of children at the international level, reflected in particular by the introduction of the Convention on the Rights of the Child in 1989 (see generally Chapter 3). There are a number of provisions of this Convention[43] that, it can be claimed, provide a framework of rights relevant to child labour. The Convention on the Rights of the Child has tended to produce standards of a broad general nature, as compared with those adopted by the ILO, which contain a more detailed and precise set of standards (Alston 1989: 37). In particular, Article 32 (protection from economic exploitation and child labour) contains some core obligations in this area, and indeed was the subject of one of the Committee on the Rights of the Child's first 'Days of General Discussion'[44] (section 3.7.9.3).

The original proposal of the text of Article 32 during the drafting process of the Convention specifically placed duties on states parties to set a minimum age for admission to employment of 15 years, comparable with Article 2 of the Minimum Age Convention of 1973. However, that proposal was not adopted and instead the phrase 'work' was used in the text to cover both work within the employment relationship and work falling outside of that relationship (Detrick 1992: 418–19). The Committee on the Rights of the Child has generally avoided expressing an opinion about the merits or otherwise of the linkage between international trade and labour standards (section 4.3.3). It continues to refer to the ILO Conventions as the key framework in assessing national situations of child labour (Doek 2003: 243).

It is tempting also to draw comparisons between the effectiveness of the reporting processes undertaken by the Committee on the Rights of the Child (section 3.5) and by the ILO in the field of child labour. Some commentators take the view that the UN supervisory regime is 'less rigorous and comprehensive than that of the ILO' (Creighton 1997: 369). Kilkelly (2003: 324) notes that many of the reports submitted to the Committee on the Rights of the Child 'fail to address the issue of economic exploitation of children under Article 32 in a complete manner, or at all'. Others view the Convention on the Rights of the Child and the ILO Conventions, and their respective monitoring procedures, as increasingly operating in a more helpful complementary manner to each other (Noguchi 2002: 357, 368).

However, in the 1990s there was an increasing urgency within the international community around child labour issues. This was prompted to some extent by the recognition that the process of globalisation was exposing more intense competitive behaviour which, it was feared, could generate more child labour rather than reduce it. Governments attending the ILO Conference in Geneva in June 1996

---

43 CRC arts 11, 34, 35 and 38.

44 Committee on the Rights of the Child, 'Day of General Discussion' on *The Economic Exploitation of the Child*, Report on the 4th session, CRC/C/20 (25 October 1993) [186–96].

agreed that there was a pressing need to proceed immediately with the prohibition of the most intolerable features of child labour. The Committee on the Rights of the Child also lent its support to the ILO's new project to establish a Convention aimed at the *worst forms* of child labour, and made observations on the drafts of the new ILO Convention (Noguchi 2002: 365) discussed in the next section.

4.2.3   Elimination of the Worst Forms of Child Labour Convention of 1999

The decision of the ILO's Governing Body in March 1996 to place 'intolerable' forms of child labour on the Conference agenda for 1998 reflected the frustrations with the apparent failures of the ILO's efforts to gather support for the Minimum Age Convention of 1973 (section 4.2.1). The disappointment with the slow ratification rate in relation to this Convention encouraged the international community to design a new Convention that was more narrowly focused in order that it could match the areas of concern where there was more obviously an emerging global consensus (Davidson 2001: 203).

The ILO also adopted in June 1998 a landmark 'soft law' instrument, the Declaration on Fundamental Principles and Rights at Work and its Follow-up,[45] in which the International Labour Conference declared that all member states should respect principles concerning four 'fundamental rights', including the elimination of child labour. The Worst Forms of Child Labour Convention of 1999[46] came into force on 19 November 2000. Since 2002, the UN's 'World Day against Child Labour' has been celebrated on 12 June of each year, marking the date of adoption in 1999 of this landmark ILO Convention. Each year a different theme is selected for the World Day.[47]

The Worst Forms of Child Labour Convention is distinctive in that it was the only ILO Convention to have been unanimously adopted by the tripartite representation of member states, and it has had the best record in the ILO's history for rapid ratification. It had been ratified by 130 states within two and a half years from its adoption; at the time of writing there were 178 ratifications.

It should be noted that the Worst Forms of Child Labour Convention does not revise or replace the Minimum Age Convention. The latter remains the foundation for international action to abolish child labour, whereas the Worst Forms of Child Labour Convention supplements and highlights this underlying aim by setting out standards to eliminate and prohibit the *worst forms* of child labour.

---

45 See http://www.ilo.org/declaration/lang--en/index.htm (2 November 2013).

46 International Labour Organization, Prohibition and Immediate Action for the Elimination of the Worst Forms of Child Labour Convention, ILO Convention No 182 (17 June 1999). This Convention had 178 states parties as at 22 February 2014.

47 For example the exploitation of girls in child labour (2009); the goal of ending child labour (2010); children in hazardous work (2011); and child labourers in domestic work (2013). See http://www.ilo.org/ipec/Campaignandadvocacy/wdacl/lang--en/index.htm (accessed 2 November 2013).

However, the policy aims of the Worst Forms of Child Labour Convention were not to produce just another ILO Convention to fill gaps in protection. There was a more ambitious aim to adopt an instrument that would 'pack a real punch and be capable of encouraging real impact' (Crawford S 2000: 5). The adoption of the Worst Forms of Child Labour Convention can also be seen as a part of the process of mainstreaming child labour in the ILO's activities (Smolin 2000: 945; Noguchi 2002: 362).

A key innovative feature of the Worst Forms of Child Labour Convention was to focus on areas where strong international agreement clearly existed, that is, the elimination of the worst forms of child labour that had been generally recognised as intolerable. This has had the effect of extending the policy areas of concern through the explicit inclusion of such (criminal) matters as prostitution, pornography and drug trafficking. These distinctive features of the Worst Forms of Child Labour Convention have resulted in its iconic presence in the international legal regime to eliminate child labour. Much of the commentary reflects the optimism that this Convention is both more analytically sound and has a better chance of making a real difference (Betcherman and others 2004: 29).

The preambular paragraphs of the Worst Forms of Child Labour Convention make it clear that the intention was to complement the Minimum Age Convention, not only by ensuring the elimination of the worst forms of child labour but also by providing for children's 'rehabilitation and social integration', a duty resonant with Article 39 of the Convention on the Rights of the Child (section 3.7.6.4). It is also interesting to note the clear recognition of poverty as the root cause of child labour and that, according to the text, the solution indicated lies in 'sustained economic growth'.

The preambular paragraphs also 'recall' the text of the Convention on the Rights of the Child and the ILO's landmark Declaration on Fundamental Principles and Rights at Work and its Follow-up (see section 4.2.5), adopted by the International Labour Conference in June 1998. The ILO's Governing Body identified the Worst Forms of Child Labour Convention as one of eight Conventions[48] that it regards as being *fundamental* to people's rights at work, irrespective of the level of development of individual states.

The core duty contained in the Worst Forms of Child Labour Convention is stark. Nothing less than 'immediate and effective measures' are required from member states to secure the results of both the 'prohibition' and 'elimination' of

---

48 The eight 'fundamental' Conventions are: Forced Labour Convention of 1930 (No 29) (177 parties); Freedom of Association and Protection of the Right to Organise Convention of 1948 (No 87) (152 parties); Right to Organise and Collective Bargaining Convention of 1949 (No 98) (163 parties); Equal Remuneration Convention of 1951 (No 100) (171 parties); Abolition of Forced Labour Convention of 1957 (No 105) (174 parties); Discrimination (Employment and Occupation) Convention of 1958 (No 111) (172 parties); Minimum Age Convention of 1973 (No 138) (166 parties); and the Worst Forms of Child Labour Convention of 1999 (No 182) (178 parties) (figures as at 22 February 2014).

the worst forms of child labour 'as a matter of urgency'.[49] This does not mean that a state is violating the Convention if the worst forms are not immediately erased. The duty requires immediate 'measures', not necessarily 'results'. For example, this may mean the adoption of appropriate legislation and regulation that will, in the future, ensure the prohibition and elimination of child labour. The definition of a child is taken as applying to all persons under the age of 18 years.[50]

This does not imply, however, a comprehensive ban on work for all persons under 18 years of age. The general minimum age for work is usually lower than 18 (section 4.2.1) and such work is legitimate provided it does not fall foul of the criteria defining the worst forms of child labour. It should be noted that the Worst Forms of Child Labour Convention does not make any exception to the 18 years limit. However, it should be remembered that not all countries have an adequate system of birth registration (section 3.7.4.1).

The international community found some difficulty in arriving at a definition of the 'worst forms of child labour'. There was the need to identify the common denominator of what a majority of states would find to be intolerable. There was also a need for a formulation that would provide a reasonable fit with national laws, in particular in relation to prostitution and the armed forces. Article 3 of the Worst Forms of Child Labour Convention defines the meaning of 'worst forms of child labour', which comprises:

> (a) all forms of slavery or practices similar to slavery, such as the sale and trafficking of children, debt bondage and serfdom and forced or compulsory labour, including forced or compulsory recruitment of children for use in armed conflict;
> (b) the use, procuring or offering of a child for prostitution, for the production of pornography or for pornographic performances;
> (c) the use, procuring or offering of a child for illicit activities, in particular for the production and trafficking of drugs as defined in the relevant international treaties;
> (d) work which, by its nature or the circumstances in which it is carried out, is likely to harm the health, safety or morals of children.

The first three categories provide unqualified protection, while the last, (d), is necessarily more elusive and is left for further definition by the national authorities. The first three categories are often referred to as the 'intolerable forms of child labour' and the more elusive category (d) as 'hazardous work'. It should be noted that category (a) conspicuously falls short of an outright ban on the use of children as soldiers in armed conflict; it only applies where recruitment is 'forced or compulsory'. It has been said that this was one of the most controversial aspects

49 Worst Forms of Child Labour Convention of 1999 art 1.
50 ibid art 2.

of the drafting negotiations and that the United States blocked a proposal that would have produced broader prohibition of child soldiers (Davidson 2001: 217).

Controversy about this provision was perhaps unsurprising, given the similar controversy experienced in relation to the drafting of Article 38 of the Convention on the Rights of the Child (section 3.7.9.5). This category includes a list of forbidden practices, such as 'debt bondage':

> Bonded labour is considered to be a temporary form of slavery, where an individual pays off a debt with his or her own work, and where he or she is not free to leave the work place or change the employer. Half of these bonded labourers, approximately 5.7 million, are estimated to be children.
>
> (Molfenter 2011: 261)

A further difficult issue in the drafting negotiations was the approach to be taken to 'hazardous work'. Worker representatives at the ILO wanted a specific list of hazardous work conditions (eg work underground, at dangerous heights or in confined spaces), thus removing discretion from governments to regulate such work. Most government representatives preferred a more flexible approach, which permitted them to take into account circumstances in their countries that would make work more or less hazardous. A compromise was reached, allowing the discretion of member states to determine what constitutes hazardous work, and there was an understanding between employer and worker members that Article 3(d) did not encompass situations where children work on their parents' family farms (Dennis 1999: 945). The repeated use of the word 'work' (rather than 'employment') in Articles 2 and 3 ensures that the definition of the worst forms of child labour does not have any link with the existence of a contractual employment relationship or production for commercial or trading purposes (Noguchi 2002: 360).

The Worst Forms of Child Labour Convention can therefore be applied to employment and work in both the formal and the informal sectors and in family settings where there is no commercial/trading product. The wording of Article 3 differs from that of Article 3(1) of the Minimum Age Convention, which only deals with employment or work which 'is likely to jeopardise the health, safety or morals of young persons'. A state that has ratified the Minimum Age Convention will still have to determine a list of hazardous work for the purposes of the Worst Forms of Child Labour Convention. In practice, the lists may be identical but they need not be so, given the different aims of these two Conventions.

In earlier ILO Conventions, 'domestic' work had been expressly excluded from the protected areas. However, it is thought that domestic work is implicitly included in all categories contained in Article 3. The literature on child labour consistently cites domestic work and the informal economy as areas where child labour is prevalent (Scullion 2013). However, there are difficult distinctions between child labour that ought to be prohibited and that ought to be regarded as legitimate precisely in this area. There is a qualitative difference between situations where children 'give a "helping hand" in their own home' and '"child domestic labour" where children perform domestic tasks in the home of a third party or "employer" under exploitative conditions' (IPEC 2004: 1).

Crawford observes that there are a number of 'hidden' forms of child labour that have not been fully drawn out in the text of Article 3 (Crawford S 2000: 12–13). The precise boundaries of meaning in the 'hazardous work' category in Article 3(d) are left to be determined at the national level after consultation, and in particular taking into account the guidance on hazardous work laid down in an ILO Recommendation.[51] The Recommendation provides some detailed criteria for identifying the types of work referred to in category (d).[52] It specifically provides that this category of work should be positively authorised by a state in respect of children aged 16 years or more, but only after due consultation with workers and employers and subject to the safeguards regarding children's health, safety, morals and sufficient training.

The requirement for competent authorities to identify such work[53] was added in an amendment and was intended to ensure that countries positively investigated the existence of such practices, rather than merely going through a hypothetical definitional exercise. The duties to identify the various categories of child labour are also to be periodically reviewed and monitored by states.[54] This will enable them to retain some flexibility in updating their lists of prohibited child labour in a changing industrial environment.

Each member state is under a duty to take all necessary measures to ensure the effective implementation of the Worst Forms of Child Labour Convention.[55] The Recommendation provides, in particular, that member states should compile '[d]etailed information and statistical data on the nature and extent of child labour' as 'a basis for determining priorities for national action'.[56] In addition, each member state must, after consultation with employers' and workers' organisations, 'establish or designate appropriate mechanisms to monitor the implementation' of the Convention.[57]

This is again reinforced by the Recommendation, which urges member states to ensure coordination between the national competent authorities, to cooperate with any international efforts and to identify responsible persons in the event of non-compliance with national provisions.[58] Most importantly, member states 'shall design and implement programmes of action to eliminate as a priority

---

51 R190 Worst Forms of Child Labour Recommendation 1999 (No 190), Recommendation concerning the prohibition and immediate action for the elimination of the worst forms of child labour. Adoption: Geneva, 87th ILC session (17 June 1999).

52 ibid para 4.

53 Worst Forms of Child Labour Convention of 1999 art 4(2).

54 ibid art 4(3).

55 ibid art 7(1).

56 R190 Worst Forms of Child Labour Recommendation 1999 (No 190) para 5(1).

57 Worst Forms of Child Labour Convention of 1999 art 5.

58 R190 Worst Forms of Child Labour Recommendation 1999 (No 190) paras 8–11.

the worst forms of child labour'.[59] This is given some practical substance in the Recommendation, which states that such programmes should aim at the identification and prevention of the worst forms of child labour, giving due attention to vulnerable groups of children.[60]

Each member state has a mandatory duty to take all necessary measures to ensure the effective implementation of the Worst Forms of Child Labour Convention, including penal or other sanctions.[61] The guidance provided by the Recommendation indicates that member states should designate three categories as criminal offences (practices similar to slavery, child prostitution and other illicit activities).[62] This list is in fact identical to the wording of the first three categories of the Worst Forms of Child Labour Convention (Articles 3(a)–(c)), with the addition of the regulation of 'firearms'.

Additionally, the Recommendation advises that, where appropriate, member states should provide criminal penalties for violations of any national provisions prohibiting and eliminating the hazardous work referred to in Article 3(d). It also suggests the 'special supervision of enterprises which have used the worst forms of child labour, and, in cases of persistent violation, consideration of temporary or permanent revoking of permits to operate'.[63] If a member state has additionally ratified the Forced Labour Convention of 1930,[64] then the protection offered there against illegal compulsory labour would already be punishable as a criminal offence.[65] The Recommendation reinforces the provisions of the Worst Forms of Child Labour Convention and urges cooperation with international efforts by exchanging information concerning such criminal offences.[66]

The centrality of education in any strategy to eliminate child labour is confirmed in Article 7(2), which obliges member states, in taking effective and time-bound measures, to take into account 'the importance of education in eliminating child labour'. IPEC has developed a number of 'time-bound' programmes (section 4.2.5) to reflect the commitment contained in Article 7(2). One of the listed measures under this provision is to 'ensure access to free basic education, and, wherever possible and appropriate, vocational training, for all children removed

---

59 Worst Forms of Child Labour Convention of 1999 art 6(1).
60 R190 Worst Forms of Child Labour Recommendation 1999 (No 190) para 2.
61 Worst Forms of Child Labour Convention of 1999 art 7(1).
62 R190 Worst Forms of Child Labour Recommendation 1999 (No 190) para 12.
63 R190 Worst Forms of Child Labour Recommendation 1999 (No 190) paras 13 and 14.
64 C029 Forced Labour Convention of 1930 (No 29), Convention concerning Forced or Compulsory Labour (entry into force: 1 May 1932). Adoption: Geneva, 14th ILC session (28 June 1930).
65 'The illegal exaction of forced or compulsory labour shall be punishable as a penal offence, and it shall be an obligation on any Member ratifying this Convention to ensure that the penalties imposed by law are really adequate and are strictly enforced': Forced Labour Convention of 1930 art 29.
66 R190 Worst Forms of Child Labour Recommendation 1999 (No 190) para 11.

from the worst forms of child labour'.[67] The relationship between exploitative labour and education was another key issue in the drafting negotiations:

> Some governments, including the United States, as well as all worker members, wanted the Convention to cover work that systematically prevents a child from taking advantage of available or compulsory education. Other delegations opposed this formulation, asserting that lack of access to education was fundamentally different from the other abuses targeted by the Convention and that its inclusion would harm the prospects for ratification.
>
> (Dennis 1999: 946)

There were also some discussions about the meaning of 'basic education'; some interpretations in other international instruments correlate this phrase with primary education. Dennis notes that the worker and employer members clarified the record with their understanding that a broader meaning should be given, that is, 'basic education means primary education plus one year (ie, eight or nine years of schooling), such education being based on curriculum and not age' (Dennis 1999: 946).

It should be noted that the aim of Article 7(2)(c) is to provide rehabilitation and reintegration of children who have been 'removed' from the worst forms of child labour, which is a provision that resonates with the general duty in the Convention on the Rights of the Child (Article 39) on states parties to achieve the recovery and social reintegration of a child victim of any form of neglect, exploitation or abuse. The Recommendation further encourages 'adopting appropriate measures to improve the educational infrastructure and the training of teachers to meet the needs of boys and girls'.[68]

The growing acknowledgement that the problem of child labour was indeed a global one requiring action at the international level is reflected in the text of Article 8, which obliges member states to 'take appropriate steps to assist one another' in giving effect to the Convention 'through enhanced international co-operation and/or assistance including support for social and economic development, poverty eradication programmes and universal education'. The Recommendation indicates various measures on which states may cooperate, such as mutual legal assistance and technical assistance, including the exchange of information.[69]

In the drafting negotiations, the worker and employer members, together with governments of most developing countries, had sought an amendment that would have committed governments to 'enhanced international cooperation and assistance, including support for social and economic development'. Some governments, however, felt this might create a legal obligation to increase financial contributions to other states or ILO child labour programmes. The ILO Deputy

---

67 Worst Forms of Child Labour Convention of 1999 art 7(2)(c).
68 R190 Worst Forms of Child Labour Recommendation 1999 (No 190) para 15(j).
69 R190 Worst Forms of Child Labour Recommendation 1999 (No 190) para 16(b) and (c).

Legal Adviser confirmed that the final text did not create any legal obligations concerning the nature or amount of any cooperation or assistance (Dennis 1999: 947).

There seems little doubt that the arrival of the Worst Forms of Child Labour Convention of 1999 marked a new confidence in the growing coherence and influence of a worldwide movement to progress international labour standards.[70] The campaign work of the ILO and NGOs that occurred before, during and after the adoption of the Worst Forms of Child Labour Convention has been very successful, certainly if success is measured by the fast rate of ratification. The optimistic environment that appears to have existed around the introduction of this Convention has also been significant in terms of providing international donors with some assurance about the strength of international support, which has helped to increase funding for ILO campaigns against child labour. One commentator has observed that this shows 'a recognition that, for an issue like child labour, changing people's perception and way of thinking is not an auxiliary action of public information but itself a substantive measure to tackle the phenomenon effectively and from its roots' (Noguchi 2002: 365).

More recently, a Global Child Labour Conference was held in The Hague in May 2010, organised by the Ministry of Social Affairs and Employment of the Netherlands in close collaboration with the ILO.[71] Over 500 representatives from 97 countries around the world participated. The Conference adopted a 'roadmap' (ILO 2010a) for achieving the elimination of the worst forms of child labour by 2016. A further Global Child Labour Conference was hosted by Brazil with the ILO in October 2013 in order to measure the progress made towards the goal of 2016.[72]

4.2.4   Other international instruments relating to child labour

A further ILO Convention on domestic workers was adopted in 2011.[73] The Domestic Workers Convention of 2011 requires that states parties commit to,

---

70 One commentator remarked: 'Before it had even arrived, the U.S. Senate had taken the unusual step of adopting, by a 98–1 roll-call vote, a sense-of-the-Senate amendment to the Foreign Relations Authorization Act that commended the ILO Member States for negotiating this "historic convention" and "called for the U.S. to continue to work with all foreign nations and international organizations to put an end to abusive and exploitative child labour". Early ratification by the United States should encourage other states to follow suit' (Dennis 1999: 948).

71 See The Hague Global Child Labour Conference, *Towards a world without child labour – Mapping the road to 2016* (10–11 May 2010, The Hague, The Netherlands). http://www.ilo.org/ipec/Campaignandadvocacy/GlobalChildLabourConference/lang--en/index.htm (accessed 13 October 2013).

72 III Global Conference on Child Labour – Brasilia (8–10 October 2013) *Towards a child labour-free world*. See http://www.ilo.org/ipec/Campaignandadvocacy/BrasiliaConference/lang--en/index.htm (accessed 13 October 2013).

73 C189 Domestic Workers Convention of 2011 (No 189), Convention concerning decent work for domestic workers (entry into force: 5 September 2013). Adoption: Geneva, 100th ILC session (16 June 2011). This Convention had 12 parties as at 22 February 2014.

inter alia, 'the elimination of all forms of forced or compulsory labour' and 'the effective abolition of child labour'.[74] In addition, member states must set a minimum age for domestic workers consistent with the Minimum Age Convention and the Worst Forms of Child Labour Convention, which must be 'not lower than that established by national laws and regulations for workers generally'. Member states are further obliged to take measures 'to ensure that work performed by domestic workers who are under the age of 18 and above the minimum age of employment does not deprive them of compulsory education, or interfere with opportunities to participate in further education or vocational training'.[75]

There are a number of UN international instruments relevant to eliminating child labour. The Supplementary Convention on the Abolition of Slavery, the Slave Trade and Institutions and Practices Similar to Slavery of 1956[76] provides that states parties 'shall take all practicable and necessary legislative and other measures to bring about progressively and as soon as possible the complete abolition or abandonment' of a number of listed institutions and practices, 'whether or not they are covered by the definition of slavery contained in Article 1 of the Slavery Convention [of 1926]'. The four types of servile status are: (a) debt bondage; (b) serfdom; (c) forced marriage; and (d) child exploitation:

> Any institution or practice whereby a child or young person under the age of 18 years, is delivered by either or both of his natural parents or by his guardian to another person, whether for reward or not, with a view to the exploitation of the child or young person or of his labour.[77]

The kind of practice which the drafting committee had in mind underlying this provision is well illustrated by the following extract from the proceedings of an ad hoc committee on slavery in 1951:

> The Committee next turned to the practice, particularly prevalent in the Far East, which in some localities is known as 'mui tsai'. This involves the sale of a child's working capacity and usually takes the form of the transfer of a small child, usually a girl, for employment as a domestic servant by means of an adoption procedure, sometimes fraudulent. The custom has been known to exist under other names in other regions of the world, including parts of Africa. The Committee recognised that in many cases an element of servitude may not be involved. Often the parents of the child affect such a transfer in what they believe to be the best interests of the child. The Committee therefore felt that a status or condition of servitude existed only when the

---

74 ibid art 3(2)(b) and (c).

75 ibid art 4(1) and (2).

76 Supplementary Convention on the Abolition of Slavery, the Slave Trade and Institutions and Practices Similar to Slavery of 1956, opened for signature 7 September 1956, 266 UNTS 3 (entered into force 20 April 1957).

77 ibid art 1(d).

conditions of the transfer were such as to permit the exploitation of the child regardless of its welfare.[78]

A few years later, the following 'principle' was drafted in the (non-binding) Declaration of the Rights of the Child (1959):

> The child shall be protected against all forms of neglect, cruelty and exploitation. He shall not be the subject of traffic, in any form.
>
> The child shall not be admitted to employment before an appropriate minimum age; he shall in no case be caused or permitted to engage in any occupation or employment which would prejudice his health or education, or interfere with his physical, mental or moral development.[79]

The International Covenant on Civil and Political Rights (ICCPR) (1966) carries the following provision:

> 1. Every child shall have, without any discrimination as to race, colour, sex, language, religion, national or social origin, property or birth, the right to such measures of protection as are required by his status as a minor, on the part of his family, society and the State.[80]

In addition, the International Covenant on Economic, Social and Cultural Rights (ICESCR) 1966 carries the following provision:

> Special measures of protection and assistance should be taken on behalf of all children and young persons without any discrimination for reasons of parentage or other conditions. Children and young persons should be protected from economic and social exploitation. Their employment in work harmful to their morals or health or dangerous to life or likely to hamper their normal development should be punishable by law. States should also set age limits below which the paid employment of child labour should be prohibited and punishable by law.[81]

---

78 Economic and Social Council, *Report of the Ad Hoc Committee on Slavery*, 2nd session UN Doc E/1988, E/AC33/13 (4 May 1951) 2. Cited in Allain (2008: 305).

79 General Assembly, *Declaration of the Rights of the Child*, 14th session, UN Doc A/RES/1386 (XIV) (20 November 1959) principle 9.

80 International Covenant on Civil and Political Rights, opened for signature 16 December 1966, 999 UNTS 171 (entered into force 23 March 1976) art 24(1). At the time of writing it had 167 parties.

81 International Covenant on Economic, Social and Cultural Rights, opened for signature 16 December 1966, 993 UNTS 3 (entered into force 3 January 1976) art 10(3). At the time of writing it had 161 parties.

These various provisions, combined with the relevant provisions of the Convention on the Rights of the Child, the Minimum Age Convention and the Worst Forms of Child Labour Convention, comprise a fairly comprehensive international legal regime addressing the economic exploitation of children in the employment/work context. The ILO's role as a leader within the international community in this field is explored further in the next section.

4.2.5   The wider role of the International Labour Organization (ILO)

The ILO has been the most important and long-standing inter-governmental organisation in the field of international labour standards generally and of child labour in particular. The International Labour Conference adopted the Minimum Age (Industry) Convention of 1919[82] at its very first session. The current 185 member states of the ILO include the membership of the United States of America, with which the ILO has had an erratic relationship. The USA did not join the ILO until 1934; it withdrew its membership in 1934 and rejoined in 1980.

The ILO's structure, and the way in which its standards are formulated and monitored, are grounded in *tripartism*, that is, the involvement of government, worker and employer representation (aka 'social partners'). This provides several advantages, in that in particular the ILO is uniquely positioned to monitor and report on child labour violations; the workers' groups provide access to data on current labour conditions and the employers' and government representatives 'lend it legitimacy with both private and public actors' (Ho 2006: 342).

The ILO has also forged partnerships with other international organisations better to facilitate its work of establishing international labour standards and meeting the challenges of child labour, for example, with the international human rights treaty bodies, including the Committee on the Rights of the Child, with UNICEF and with the World Bank (Betcherman and others 2004: 30).

Although other international organisations and NGOs have taken an interest in child labour issues – for example, the UNHRC,[83] UNICEF (1997), the International Organization of Employers, the Anti-slavery Society and the International Confederation of Free Trade Unions – the ILO 'has always considered itself to have a special mandate in this area' (Creighton 1997: 366). The ILO has played a central role in producing international standards of protection. NGOs do not have a formal role in the preparation of new ILO standards, but 'in

---

82 C005 Minimum Age (Industry) Convention of 1919 (No 5), Convention Fixing the Minimum Age for Admission of Children to Industrial Employment (entry into force: 13 June 1921). Adoption: Washington, 1st ILC session (28 November 1919).

83 See for example UN Commission on Human Rights (UNCHR) *Programme of Action for the Elimination of the Exploitation of Child Labour*, E/CN.4/RES/1993/79, Geneva: Office of the United Nations High Commissioner for Human Rights.

practice NGOs do have opportunities to make a contribution' (Blagbrough 1997: 126).

In many ways the policy trends that have informed the ILO's activities are punctuated by three 'soft law' instruments (section 2.2.6). First, there was the Declaration of Philadelphia concerning the aims and purposes of the International Labour Organization, issued on 10 May 1944. This reaffirms the fundamental principles on which the organisation is based, in particular, that:

(a) labour is not a commodity;
(b) freedom of expression and of association are essential to sustained progress;
(c) poverty anywhere constitutes a danger to prosperity everywhere;
(d) the war against want requires to be carried on with unrelenting vigor within each nation, and by continuous and concerted international effort in which the representatives of workers and employers, enjoying equal status with those of governments, join with them in free discussion and democratic decision with a view to the promotion of the common welfare.[84]

The Declaration of Philadelphia also observes that 'lasting peace can be established only if it is based on social justice' and affirms that 'all human beings, irrespective of race, creed or sex, have the right to pursue both their material well-being and their spiritual development in conditions of freedom and dignity, of economic security and equal opportunity'.[85] However, there is little in the way of specific provision relating to children, and it is certainly not couched in the language of children's rights. Amongst the world programmes to which the ILO declares its commitment is the 'provision for child welfare and maternity protection'.[86]

The ILO continued to produce a number of Conventions in the post-war period through to the 1960s and 1970s. There was a shift away from 'standard-setting' in the international community in the early 1980s to public awareness campaigns (Cordova 1993) and, at the beginning of the 1990s, an emphasis on 'technical assistance' to member states (ILO 1996: para 99). The appropriate balance between 'hard' and 'soft' law in international legal protection and their integration with practical programmes of assistance became an issue attracting greater attention.

---

84 The General Conference of the International Labour Organization, Declaration concerning the aims and purposes of the International Labour Organisation (Declaration of Philadelphia), 26th session (10 May 1944) Philadelphia § I. The Declaration of Philadelphia has now been annexed to the ILO's constitution. See International Labour Organization, Constitution of the International Labour Organisation (ILO) (1 April 1919), adopted by the Peace Conference in April 1919, the ILO constitution became Part XIII of the Treaty of Versailles (1919).
85 Declaration of Philadelphia of 1944 § II(a).
86 ibid § III(h).

Secondly, in June 1998, the ILO adopted the soft law instrument, the Declaration on Fundamental Principles and Rights at Work and its Follow-up,[87] an instrument which, inter alia:

> Declares that all Members, even if they have not ratified the Conventions in question, have an obligation arising from the very fact of membership in the Organization to respect, to promote and to realize, in good faith and in accordance with the Constitution, the principles concerning the fundamental rights which are the subject of those Conventions, namely:
> (a) freedom of association and the effective recognition of the right to collective bargaining;
> (b) the elimination of all forms of forced or compulsory labour;
> (c) the effective abolition of child labour; and
> (d) the elimination of discrimination in respect of employment and occupation.[88]

The ILO's Director-General annually prepares a 'global report' on one of these fundamental rights, thus providing a four-year periodic cycle of reporting on each. There have been three global reports on child labour at the time of writing (ILO 2002; ILO 2006; and ILO 2010).

The Declaration on Fundamental Principles and Rights at Work and its Follow-up of 1998 has been an important landmark in the history of the ILO. Although it is a 'soft law' instrument, its authority is enhanced by the fact that it was unanimously agreed by ILO member states. Arguably, the Declaration provided the necessary flexibility required in an increasingly globalised world. Such core labour rights could be better universalised and reach further afield through the development of such principles.

Alston (2004: 518–21) provides a robust critique of this approach, noting that the Declaration marks a new normative hierarchy whereby the four core labour standards are privileged at the expense of the ILO's careful construction of 'rights' in the various ILO Conventions over many years. Replying to these criticisms, Langille (2005) argues that these core labour standards are conceptually coherent and in fact *support* the existing international labour regime rather than undermine it. The ILO's first global report on child labour concluded with an action plan resting on three 'pillars':

- The first pillar is to reinforce the work of IPEC.
- The second pillar is to mainstream the abolition of child labour more actively across other ILO programmes and strengthen cross-sectoral collaboration and policy integration to this end.

---

87 ILO Declaration on Fundamental Principles and Rights at Work and its Follow-up. Adopted by the International Labour Conference at its 86th session, Geneva (18 June 1998) (Annex revised 15 June 2010).
88 ibid art 3.

- The third pillar is to forge closer partnerships with employers' and workers' organizations, as well as with other institutions and groups that share the goal of abolishing child labour.

(ILO 2002: 118–19)

The ILO's second global report in 2006 set out an action plan that is built upon the three-pillar approach, and it concluded optimistically that the elimination of the worst forms of child labour was within reach and set a goal to achieve this by 2016 (ILO 2006: 83–90). In its third quadrennial global report in 2010, the ILO observed more cautiously that the goal to eliminate the worst forms of child labour by 2016 appeared to be slipping away:

> There are clear signs of progress but also disconcerting gaps in the global response. As things are today, the pace of progress is not fast enough to achieve the 2016 target. A flagging in the worldwide movement, a certain "child labour fatigue", must be prevented.

(ILO 2010: xiii)

The report identified that 'the critical fight against child labour has to be won in South Asia, where the greatest numbers of child labourers are to be found' (ILO 2010: xv).

4.2.6   ILO reporting, representation and complaints procedures

The ILO has a unique supervisory mechanism that provides two types of international monitoring: regular supervision and ad hoc procedures (Noguchi 2002: 366). The system is based on the ILO constitution,[89] so separate Conventions do not contain dedicated provisions on reporting and monitoring as they do in relation to, for example, the Convention on the Rights of the Child (section 3.5). The ILO relies (usually) on public shaming through documentation in ILO reports, together with technical expertise and financial assistance to promote compliance (Ho 2006: 341).

4.2.6.1   Regular supervision and reporting

Regular supervision is provided under Article 22 of the ILO's constitution. Each member state ratifying an ILO Convention agrees to make an annual report to the International Labour Office on the measures it has taken to give effect to the Conventions it has ratified. The Governing Body decides the form and content of such reports. They are then examined by the Committee of Experts on the

---

89 International Labour Organization, Constitution of the International Labour Organisation (ILO) (1 April 1919). Adopted by the Peace Conference in April 1919, the constitution became Part XIII of the Treaty of Versailles (1919).

Application of Conventions and Recommendations (CEACR). The Director-General must present summaries of the reports so received before the next conference.[90]

The reports, when submitted to the conference, are then discussed by a tripartite committee. In practice, reports are submitted every two years for the so-called 'fundamental'[91] and 'priority' Conventions,[92] and every five years for other Conventions, unless the CEACR requests them sooner. Since 2003, reports have been submitted according to Conventions grouped by subject matter. Governments are required to provide relevant legislation, statistics and documentation necessary for the full examination of their reports. Where a government has not satisfactorily provided such information, CEACR will write requesting it.

Although, in certain respects, there are distinct merits to the system of reporting under the Convention on the Rights of the Child (section 3.5), the ILO reporting procedures can be seen to have some advantages. There is, for example, an opportunity for a technical analysis by independent experts (the CEACR) in addition to an examination by the tripartite bodies of the ILO (that is, governments, workers and employer representatives). Like the Convention on the Rights of the Child system, there is regular monitoring on the basis of country reports and responses to reports, but there is also the opportunity under the ILO machinery for the use of ad hoc procedures in cases of severe violations. The Declaration on Fundamental Principles and Rights at Work and its Follow-up of 1998 provides for a system for gathering information from countries that have not yet ratified the relevant fundamental Conventions through annual reports.[93]

The CEACR produces two types of commentary on the application of the Conventions: *observations* and *direct requests*. 'Individual observations' contain comments on fundamental questions raised by the application of a particular Convention by a particular government, and these are reproduced in the

---

90 International Labour Organization, *Constitution of the International Labour Organisation* (ILO) (1 April 1919) arts 22 and 23.

91 See n 48 above for the eight 'fundamental' ILO Conventions.

92 The ILO's Governing Body designated four Conventions as 'priority' instruments. Since 2008 these Conventions are now referred to as 'Governance Conventions'. They are: C081 Labour Inspection Convention of 1947 (No 81), Convention concerning Labour Inspection in Industry and Commerce (entry into force: 7 April 1950) Adoption: Geneva, 30th ILC session (11 July 1947); C122 Employment Policy Convention of 1964 (No 122), Convention concerning Employment Policy (entry into force: 15 July 1966) Adoption: Geneva, 48th ILC session (9 July 1964); C129 Labour Inspection (Agriculture) Convention of 1969 (No 129), Convention concerning Labour Inspection in Agriculture (entry into force: 19 January 1972) Adoption: Geneva, 53rd ILC session (25 June 1969); C144 Tripartite Consultation (International Labour Standards) Convention of 1976 (No 144), Convention concerning Tripartite Consultations to Promote the Implementation of International Labour Standards (entry into force: 16 May 1978) Adoption: Geneva, 61st ILC session (21 June 1976).

93 ILO Declaration on Fundamental Principles and Rights at Work and its Follow-up. Adopted by the International Labour Conference at its 86th session, Geneva (18 June 1998) (Annex revised 15 June 2010) § IIA(1) and (2).

Committee's annual report[94]. Occasionally, it also produces a 'general observation' on one of the Conventions. For example, in 2009 the CEACR issued a 'general observation'[95] on the concept of 'light work' in the Minimum Age Convention (section 4.2.1). 'Direct requests' usually relate to more technical questions or questions of lesser importance and are not published in the report, but are communicated directly to the governments concerned.

4.2.6.2   Ad hoc procedures

Where there are acute problems or persistent non-observance of a ratified Convention, the ILO Constitution provides for ad hoc procedures.[96] As the ILO depends heavily on a principle of voluntarism by member states, these procedures are not invoked routinely. There are two types of procedure to consider: 'representation' and 'complaints' procedures. There are two 'representation' procedures available.

First, representations can be made, by either an industrial association of employers or workers, that any of the member states 'has failed to secure in any respect the effective observance within its jurisdiction of any Convention to which it is a party'. The Governing Body may then communicate this representation to the government concerned and invite it to make a statement. If either the government fails to make a statement in response, or the Governing Body does not deem its response satisfactory, then the latter may publish the representation and the statement, if any, made in reply to it.[97]

Secondly, there is a 'reference' procedure[98] available for member states where another member has failed to respond to ILO standard-setting. A member state, when ratifying a Convention or a Recommendation, is under an obligation[99] to bring the measure 'before the authority or authorities within whose competence the matter lies, for the enactment of legislation or other action' within one year from the adoption of the measure or, in exceptional circumstances, 18 months.

There is, additionally, a 'complaint' procedure[100] available. Member states have a right to file a complaint with the International Labour Office if they are not satisfied that any other member is securing the effective observance of any Convention that both have ratified. The Governing Body has a discretion to

---

94 For example International Labour Conference, *General Report of the Committee of Experts on the Application of Conventions and Recommendations 2009*, ninety-eighth session, Geneva: International Labour Office.

95 International Labour Conference, *General Observation concerning Convention No 138*, ninety-eighth session, Committee of Experts on the Application of Conventions and Recommendations, Geneva: International Labour Office.

96 International Labour Organization, Constitution of the International Labour Organisation (ILO) (1 April 1919) arts 24 and 26.

97 ibid arts 24 and 25.

98 ibid art 30.

99 ibid art 19(5)(b) and 19(6)(b).

100 ibid arts 26–28.

request a statement from the government in question. If there is no satisfactory reply, or the Governing Body does not think it necessary to request one, it may appoint a Commission of Inquiry to consider the complaint and report. After full consideration of the complaint, the Commission must prepare a report setting out its findings of facts and such recommendations it may have as to the steps to be taken to meet the complaint and their timing. The Director-General must then communicate the report to the Governing Body and to each of the governments concerned in the complaint and arrange for its publication. Each of the governments must respond within three months, stating to the Director-General whether it accepts the recommendations contained in the Commission's report. If not, the governments may indicate that they propose to refer the complaint on to the International Court of Justice (ICJ) (section 2.4.1.1). The ICJ's decisions with regard to a complaint shall be final and 'may affirm, vary or reverse any of the findings or recommendations of the Commission of Inquiry, if any'.[101]

The ILO has reserved the use of Commissions of Inquiry for really grave and persistent violations of the international labour standards.[102] For example, the Commission's report on Myanmar in 1998[103] detailed the widespread and systematic use of forced labour in that country and a broad pattern of violation of fundamental human rights by the military government. The ruling military regime had used the civilian population (including women and children) as an unlimited pool of labourers to build and maintain a number of projects in construction, agriculture, and in hotels and other infrastructure projects (Sarkin and Pietschmann 2003). A member state failing to carry out the recommendations of a Commission of Inquiry or a decision of the ICJ[104] will be vulnerable to the Governing Body recommending 'such action as it may deem wise and expedient to secure compliance therewith' to the conference.

The involvement of the ILO's 'social partners' in initiating ad hoc procedures and examining a case of representation is significant:

> They [the social partners] have a power to channel concerns of civil society into the mechanism of international standards. In the above-mentioned

101 International Labour Organization, Constitution of the International Labour Organisation (ILO) (1 April 1919) arts 29, 31 and 32.

102 An example is the Commission of Inquiry set up in March 1997 following a complaint lodged by 25 worker delegates to the 83rd Session of the International Labour Conference in June 1996, to examine the application of the Forced Labour Convention of 1930 in Myanmar: see n103 below. This situation also resulted in the unprecedented invocation of art 33 of the ILO Constitution, which provides certain enforcement powers.

103 ILO Commission of Inquiry, *Forced Labour in Myanmar (Burma)*, report of the Commission of Inquiry under art 26 of the Constitution of the International Labour Organization to examine the observance by Myanmar of the Forced Labour Convention 1930 (No 29) (2 July 1998) Geneva: International Labour Office. http://www.ilo.org/public/english/standards/relm/gb/docs/gb273/myanmar.htm#Part I (accessed 13 October 2013).

104 International Labour Organization, Constitution of the International Labour Organisation (ILO) (1 April 1919) arts 33 and 34.

regular supervision, workers and employers organizations are very much encouraged to submit their comments and observations on the government's reports.

(Noguchi 2002: 367)

4.3   Progressing the elimination of exploitative child labour

This section discusses how the global movement to eliminate child labour can best move forward. The rapid ratification of the Worst Forms of Child Labour Convention of 1999 and the substantial amounts of donor funding that have supported IPEC are encouraging developments, although there remain a few conspicuous omissions to the ratification list of this Convention and the Minimum Age Convention of 1973.[105] It has been recognised that a holistic approach to the elimination of child labour is required to address the multi-faceted nature of the problem; its complexity is certainly no excuse for inaction. As one commentator remarked:

> The indivisibility and interdependence of all human rights, which is the lynchpin of the United Nations approach, is perhaps nowhere more evident tha[n] in the quest for solutions to the problem of the exploitation of child labour.
>
> (Alston 1989: 39)

Most commentators prefer an integrated strategy to tackle the elimination of child labour (Masum 2002). Earlier commentaries have remarked on the unwillingness of governments to acknowledge the existence or at least the extent of child labour within jurisdictions, and indeed official acknowledgement is a prerequisite in seeking international, technical or financial assistance (Alston 1989: 38). However, there are no uniform, pre-packaged solutions in this field. CEACR noted long ago that the uneven incidence of child labour within countries required detailed investigation followed by pilot programmes to determine the most effective measures.[106]

It is clear that the elimination of child labour will involve legislative, judicial and administrative interventions, but these are only one element of measures taken at the national level. Equally, the adoption of inappropriately tough legislation may make such practices go underground. Furthermore, a prerequisite for any credible programme to tackle child labour requires detailed and specific information;

---

105 At the time of writing there were 19 ILO member states (including the USA) that had *not* ratified the Minimum Age Convention of 1973, and seven member states that had not ratified the Worst Forms of Child Labour Convention of 1999. Five parties had not ratified *either* Convention: India, Marshall Islands, Palau, Somalia and Tuvalu.

106 CEACR, *General Survey by the Committee of Experts on the Application of Conventions and Recommendations: Minimum Age*, International Labour Conference, 67th session, Report III, pt 4B (1981) Geneva: International Labour Office at 407.

there is a continuing need for studies to provide robust analysis and policy prescriptions (Alston 1989: 40–6).

4.3.1 Child labour in international law: assessing the role of law and the enforceability problem

Much of public international law is vulnerable to the criticism that it lacks 'teeth', but that is often because inappropriate expectations are made of the extent to which it can deliver progress, particularly in relation to complex social, economic and cultural problems such as child labour. It should not be thought that the existence of law to eliminate child labour is *necessarily* the best form of intervention. The decline in child labour in the industrialised countries between 1880 and 1920 'is thought to be due to both economic and legal reasons, with the former predominating' (Betcherman and others 2004: 25).

It should also be remembered that international law has evolved alongside a deep history that supports the autonomy and equality of state sovereignty, which has comprised 'the basic constitutional doctrine of the law of nations' (Crawford 2012: 289). The principles of the sovereign equality of all state members of the UN and non-intervention in domestic jurisdictions are enshrined in the Charter of the United Nations.[107]

It has been said that the lack of enforceability of Conventions often reflects concern in the drafting process about the preservation of state sovereignty (Silk and Makonnen 2003: 363; Selby 2008: 175). Furthermore, international human rights instruments are the result of political consensus within the international community; they 'reflect what governments and interest groups could agree on, not necessarily what experts believe should be done' (Betcherman and others 2004: 5).

However, despite such limitations, these instruments do provide important standards from which national policy and benchmarks to assess policy interventions can be derived. In considering the *enforceability* dimension to the three key international instruments discussed in this chapter, it should not be forgotten that ultimately they rely heavily on national efforts. For example, it is particularly important that appropriate national systems of labour inspection are established, particularly given children's powerlessness in many work situations (Alston 1989: 44).

As we have seen (section 4.1.4), the dilemma between universal standard-setting and cultural relativity is a poignant one in relation to child labour. Northern countries tend to articulate children's rights against a background idea of childhood as a biologically driven natural phenomenon 'characterized by physical and mental growth stages that are everywhere roughly the same' (Myers 2001: 40). This dominant view of childhood tends to keep children separated off from adulthood and discourages participation in adult concerns, particularly the economic

---

107 Charter of the United Nations and Statute of the International Court of Justice, concluded 26 June 1945, 1 UNTS XVI (entered into force 23 October 1945) art 2(1) and (7).

maintenance of the family. On the other hand, southern societies stress collective family unity and solidarity and accept a much greater degree of participation and contribution to the economic maintenance of the family.

The problem of delay in the reporting processes of many international mechanisms also appears in the ILO machinery. Some commentators have observed that the dilemma in this area is that there are (now) strong legal norms but weak enforcement mechanisms, a process which has in turn contributed to a rise in private action to prevent child labour (Silk and Makonnen 2003: 359). Silk and Makonnen offer a useful model of the evolution of human rights enforcement to consider.

The identification of human rights abuses leads to the setting of strong international legal standards, but with weak institutions and processes of enforcement; this in turn leads to a range of NGO and IGO interventions of a non-law enforcement character aiming to achieve compliance with the established normative standards. Finally, aspects of these private initiatives may in turn be incorporated into effective, enforceable national and international law (Silk and Makonnen 2003: 369).

4.3.2   Partnership and coordination

It is widely accepted that the implementation of human rights standards generally will benefit greatly from well planned partnerships between governments and NGOs. It has been said that NGOs may be able to be more robustly abolitionist in their stance towards child labour than official international institutions, which are always dependent on political compromise and diplomacy (Silk and Makonnen 2003: 369). They have certainly undertaken some very successful anti-sweatshop campaigns in the 1990s, for example. NGOs are often able to strike clearer, principled aims and objectives.

The increasing focus on the NGO contribution is derived, to an extent, from the growing recognition of the limitations of standard-setting. Most commentators agree that the complexity and multi-faceted nature of child labour in particular requires national governments to strike such constructive partnerships. The development of NGO action around child labour issues has involved the emergence of, for example, voluntary codes of corporate conduct. Indeed, some of the independent monitoring schemes evolved in this way have been criticised by organised labour as a 'privatisation of law enforcement', undermining the traditional protections for workers of collective bargaining (Silk and Makonnen 2003: 365). The increasing need for partnerships with NGOs and IGOs also assumes there will be successful coordination between these bodies to achieve the desired synergies.

In the past there have certainly been criticisms that the ILO has carried 'virtually singlehandedly' the burden of international efforts in relation to the elimination of child labour (Alston 1989: 48). There is greater coordination now, and other bodies such as UNICEF, the UN Development Programme (UNDP) and the Food and Agriculture Organization (FAO) have more input in this field than they used to.

However, it is not only coordination between the relevant international and other bodies concerned that is required. There is also a need to coordinate the policy approaches taken, particularly in relation to education at the national level. The role of education (section 4.1.2) is central to debates about child labour, both causatively and consequentially. With regard to developing countries, where it seems likely that the worst forms of child labour will persist for longer, it is important to construct an approach that is integrated with wider development policies available to improve social conditions (Selby 2008: 178).

The research literature relating to child labour raises interesting questions about the potential role of, and partnership with, the business community in assisting with efforts to eliminate child labour. Hassel (2008), for example, argues that in the last decade, and prompted by the ILO Declaration on Fundamental Principles and Rights at Work and its Follow-up of 1998, there has been a fundamental change of approach by business and governments towards global labour and social issues. International labour law has moved away from ILO Conventions towards the principles of 'core labour standards'. This has in effect led to an indirect pattern of self-regulation.

Indeed, it is argued that the proliferation of corporate codes and a variety of company-based independent monitoring schemes indicate 'an apparent shift from reliance on public international measures to private action' (Silk and Makonnen 2003: 363). Furthermore, the adoption by the ILO of this 'soft law' approach fits better into the wider debate of linking trade with labour standards (Hassel 2008: 237).

4.3.3   Linking trade and labour standards

The frustrations with the defects in the international legal regime have opened up another front for action at the international level: the linkage of the issue of child labour with international trade regulation (Cooper 1997: 420). Supporters of the trade–labour linkage have relied on competition and human rights arguments. The competition-based argument is that countries with lower labour standards generally have lower production costs, which offer them a competitive trade advantage. Consequently, there may be a 'race to the bottom', that is, a lowering of labour standards to remain competitive.

The human rights argument is simply that by imposing the linkage the international community is protecting individuals against the violation of core labour standards (including the abolition of child labour). The counter-argument relies on the theory of protectionism: in effect, that trade–labour linkage would allow developed countries to protect their interests by preventing less developed nations from exploiting their lower wage cost advantages and that would slow economic growth, further worsening the child labour problem (Ho 2006: 343). However, the protectionist argument is not as credible if applied to the worst forms of child labour. Nevertheless, there are those that do not see trade sanctions as a primary remedy for eliminating child labour. As one commentator observes: '[c]ountries with large, affluent populations of consumers will always have more leverage both in adopting sanctions against countries and deflecting them against themselves' (Cullen 1999: 25). Trade–labour linkage supporters have argued either for a stronger enforcement mechanism within the ILO, such as trade sanctions or the addition of a labour clause in the World Trade Organization (WTO) agreements.

Some argue the need to integrate child labour elimination into national economic regulation. Various organisations have advocated the need to link trade and labour standards. For example, the International Confederation of Free Trade Unions has advocated the prohibition of imports of any goods produced with exploitative child labour. In essence, the proposition to have a 'social clause' inserted into WTO and other trade agreements, will involve an obligation by parties to the agreement to respect labour standards, including the elimination of child labour, and recognition that the obligation can be enforced with trade sanctions.

The advocacy to establish trade–labour linkages has met with fierce resistance, mainly on the basis that such a linkage could be seen as a disguised form of protectionism and an attempt to undermine the competitive advantage of developing countries (Cooper 1997: 421). National trade boycotts have had a mixed reception. When a Bill that would ban entry of any goods into the United States manufactured with the use of child labour was introduced into Congress by Senator Harkin in 1993, employers in Bangladesh laid off tens of thousands of children. Subsequent UNICEF studies showed that none of these children returned to school (Cooper 1997: 423), although in the aftermath of international pressure there were a number of improvements achieved (English 1997: 439).

Child labour legislation in India prescribed fines for employers and made the employment of children more costly, but this caused the wages of children to drop, 'causing either more children in the household to work or those already working to work more hours' (Betcherman and others 2004: 27). Simplistic measures such as dismissal of child labourers without any effort to rehabilitate and reintegrate them into the community should be avoided (Muntarbhorn 1998: 305). Consumer boycotts can be effective, but there is a need for such campaigns to be a part of a comprehensive strategy to avoid such negative consequences. Labelling campaigns can be useful to assure consumers that products have been manufactured without child labour.[108]

There has also been some imaginative collaboration between multinational corporations and their local suppliers, in combination with international organisations, to eliminate child labour in a specific industrial sector. For example,

---

108 For example, the *Rugmark* system established in 1994. Rugmark International is an international NGO working to end illegal child labour in the handmade rug industry and to offer educational opportunities to children in India and Nepal. Rugmark was replaced by *Good Weave* on all rugs certified as from August 2009.

international concerns over the widespread use of children to hand-stitch footballs persuaded the Sialkot region in Pakistan to sign a memorandum of understanding with the ILO, UNICEF and Save the Children–UK in Atlanta in 1997 (Johnson 1999). This started a unique programme in Pakistan, coordinated by IPEC. However, it would seem, for the present at least, that the option of persuading the World Trade Organization (WTO) to embrace a social clause is not available. The WTO rejected in principle the formulation of a trade–labour link at the Singapore Ministerial Conference in 1997[109] and has in effect moved the discussion back to the ILO and has refused to consider any sort of trade–labour linkage since 1997 (Ho 2006: 344).

Equally, the ILO has been averse to pursuing the link as it 'is concerned to protect its institutional legitimacy which is founded on tripartism and voluntarism' (Cullen 1999: 29). As the options that might have been possible via WTO and ILO action appear to be closing, Ho argues that a *nationalised* trade–labour linkage would provide better enforcement against child labour violations, rather than trying to create a strong *international* system (Ho 2006: 349). The argument is that the system of child labour regulation could be best accommodated by focusing on the ILO facilitating a nationalisation of the international movement to abolish child labour (Ho 2006: 338).

The basic idea is that developed countries, such as the United States, could create unilateral or bilateral trade agreements through which trade benefits or sanctions are not determined by individual countries but by ILO findings. Humbert (2009: 375) argues forcefully that 'trade measures should complement the existing ILO and UN implementation systems for the prohibition of child labour'.

The case study below contains the Committee on the Rights of the Child's 'Conducting Observations' on Uzbekistan's periodic report in 2013 in relation to 'economic exploitation'. The background to the Committee's comments about Uzbekistan's important and lucrative cotton industry is that some Western clothes retailers had threatened to boycott Uzbekistan if it did not stop using schoolchildren to pick the cotton harvest. Although the Uzbeks had officially banned the use of child labour, it appeared that they had reneged on their promise with children as young as 11 or 12 working in the fields.[110]

109 Ministerial Conference of the World Trade Organization, Singapore Ministerial Declaration, adopted 13 December 1996, 36 ILM 218 (1997).

110 See: 'Uzbek cotton fields still using child labour', Russian Qobi (11 November 2009), BBC News website: http://news.bbc.co.uk/1/hi/world/asia-pacific/8340630.stm (accessed 22 February 2014).

Case study 4.1

Concluding observations on the combined third and fourth periodic reports of Uzbekistan, adopted by the Committee at its 63rd session (27 May–14 June 2013)
CRC/C/UZB/CO/3-4 (14 June 2013) paras 65–66

Economic exploitation, including child labour
65. The Committee welcomes the State party's ratification of ILO Conventions No 138 concerning Minimum Age for Admission to Employment and No 182 concerning the Prohibition and Immediate Action for the Elimination of the Worst Forms of Child Labour, as well as its efforts to address the forced labour of children in the cotton industry. The Committee also appreciates that the State party's legislation is in principle compliant with international standards. However, the Committee remains gravely concerned about:

(a) The lack of mechanisms for effectively enforcing the permanent prohibition of child labour, particularly in the context of the cotton industry;
(b) The continued involvement of children above the age of 16 years in forced labour in the cotton industry; and,
(c) The lack of positive responses to the recommendation contained in the observations issued in 2011 by the Committee of Experts on the Application of Conventions and Recommendations of the International Labour Organisation (ILO) to accept a high-level tripartite mission and avail itself to ILO technical assistance.

66. The Committee urges the State party to:

(a) Undertake all necessary monitoring and enforcement measures for ensuring the full compliance of its labour and employment situation with the Convention and international standards, in practice and throughout its territory, with particular emphasis on the cotton industry and any situations of informal and/or unregulated employment;
(b) Ensure that for children above the age of 16 involved in labour, that their involvement is based on genuine free choice and subject to adequate safeguards based on the Convention and international standards;
(c) Implement the recommendations of the Committee of Experts on the Application of Conventions and Recommendations of the International Labour Organisation (ILO) and accept a high-level tripartite mission and avail itself to ILO technical assistance; and,
(d) Consider ratifying ILO Convention No 189 (2011) concerning Decent Work for Domestic Workers.

Chapter 5

International parental child abduction

5.1   International parental child abduction[1]

The act of removing children from their usual abode to another country and in the context of a parental dispute will almost inevitably be damaging to the welfare of those children. A child is likely to feel uprooted from a familiar environment, especially in circumstances where the child loses contact with friends and relatives. The move may disrupt not only the child's relationships but also his or her education and general sense of security, particularly if such a move is conducted in the context of a parental dispute. In a US review of the research literature on parental child abduction, it was concluded:

> The research on parental abduction indicates that these incidents can be highly traumatic for both children and left-behind parents and that the longer the period of separation, the more damaging the impact is for the child and the left-behind parent. Parental abduction is a crime in all 50 States and the District of Columbia. However, for a variety of reasons, the criminal justice system's response to these cases has historically been inadequate and sporadic. Improved education—for law enforcement personnel, prosecutors, and the public-at-large—is needed to ensure a quicker and more effective response to the children and families affected by these crimes.
>
> (Chiancone 2001)

In a study undertaken in the United Kingdom, involving interviews with 30 adults and 10 children, it was concluded that 'abduction and its effects linger for many years after the ending of the abduction' and 'the lack of contact between parents and children during the period of the abduction is a source of immense continuing anxiety for those concerned, many years after the abduction' (Freeman 2006: 46). Further research on the long-term effectiveness of mediation (section 5.5 below) in cases of international parental child abduction informed by interviews with 52

---

1 See generally Lowe and others (2004, 2014) and Schuz (2013).

adults and involving 46 children also revealed evidence of severe health effects in relation to both the *left-behind* and *taking parents* involved (Buck 2012: 65, 70).

In many national jurisdictions child abduction is regarded as a sufficiently serious matter to require the protection of the criminal law. For example, the English common law developed a criminal law offence of 'kidnapping', defined by the House of Lords as the taking or carrying away of one person by another, by force or by fraud, without the consent of the person taken or carried away and without lawful excuse.[2] Furthermore, the Child Abduction Act 1984 provides that 'a person connected with a child under the age of 16 commits an offence if he takes or sends the child out of the United Kingdom without the appropriate consent'. The maximum penalty for a conviction is seven years' imprisonment.[3]

Parental child abduction convictions are not numerous in the UK because, unlike the offence of child abduction by strangers, no prosecution for this offence can be instituted except by or with the consent of the Director of Public Prosecutions.[4] Child abductions by strangers will usually be covered by the national criminal code relevant to the country in which the abduction took place (Newiss and Fairbrother 2004).

There are also various provisions in the UN Convention on the Rights of the Child (1989)[5] and the Optional Protocol on the Rights of the Child on the Sale of Children, Child Prostitution and Child Pornography (OPSC 2000)[6] relevant to those scenarios. The latter, for example, is intended both to strengthen the international criminalisation of such practices and provide welfare protection for child victims (Buck 2008).

Some national jurisdictions also provide civil regulation of child abduction carried out within their own borders. In the United Kingdom, for example, the Family Law Act 1986 provides for common jurisdictional rules to apply and a set of rules for the mutual recognition and enforcement of custody orders in each territory of the United Kingdom. However, 'once a child has been removed from the United Kingdom, parental abduction is usually treated as a civil matter'.[7]

The focus of this chapter is on the private international law aspects of the parental/carer abduction of the child and, in particular, the operation of the Hague Convention on the Civil Aspects of International Child Abduction of 1980 (Hague Convention).[8] However, before analysing this set of rules, it is worth considering for a moment the social phenomenon of international parental child

---

2 *R v D* [1984] AC 778 at 800.

3 Child Abduction Act 1984 ss 1, 2 and 4(1).

4 ibid s 4(2).

5 Opened for signature 20 November 1989, 1577 UNTS 3 (entered into force 2 September 1990).

6 Opened for signature 25 May 2000, 2171 UNTS 227 (entered into force 18 January 2002).

7 See the International Child Abduction and Contact (ICACU) website http://www.justice.gov.uk/protecting-the-vulnerable/official-solicitor/international-child-abduction-and-contact-unit (accessed 7 January 2013).

8 Hague Conference on Private International Law, concluded 25 October 1980 (entered into force 1 December 1983).

abduction. What are the underlying causes? Are there any distinctive character-istics of those parents who abduct children? What kind of dysfunctional family scenario is likely to result in abduction? Are men more likely to abduct children than women? Are babies and infants more likely to be abducted than older chil-dren? There is some empirical evidence available to address these questions, but it is a changing and incomplete picture.

When the Hague Convention was being prepared in the 1970s the paradigm case was that of the father taking the child abroad and possibly attempting to conceal his own and the child's whereabouts from the left-behind mother. He may have been motivated by bitter feelings generated by a deteriorating relationship with the mother, and he may have been frustrated by restrictions on his access. He may have lost legal custody of the child(ren). However, even the few surveys that were available in the 1990s challenged this stereotype (Beaumont and McEleavy 1999: 9–10). The statistical evidence on international parental abduction has not yet been fully developed, although the work of Lowe and others (1999, 2006, 2011(a)(b)(c)) has influenced the Hague Conference to develop its own statistical database.[9]

Lowe (2011a: paras 27–30) estimated that (in 2008) there was a maximum of 2460 Hague Convention applications globally, comprising 2080 return (85 per cent) and 380 access (15 per cent) applications. Combining both incoming and outgoing applications, some central authorities of the states parties had higher workloads than others. The USA handled the most (598) applications, followed by England & Wales (466), Germany (383), Mexico (272) and Italy (238), and some central authorities handled no applications at all in 2008.

With regard to return applications, it is at least now clear that the stereotype of a non-custodial father removing or retaining his children does not reflect the reality of proceedings made under the Hague Convention. Lowe estimated that, in 2008, 69 per cent of taking persons were the mothers of the children involved, 28 per cent were fathers and the remaining 3 per cent involved grandparents, institutions or other relatives (Lowe 2011a: para 42). Overall, 72 per cent of taking persons were the child's primary or joint primary carer (Lowe 2011a: para 47).

It should not be assumed that the taking person will necessarily take the child to his or her own country, although most did. In 2008, 60 per cent of taking persons took the children to a state of which they were a national (Lowe 2011a: para 50). There was an average of 1.38 children for each return application, and the average age of a child involved was 6.4 years (Lowe 2011a: paras 56, 60). The outcomes of return applications in 2008 are set out in Table 5.1 below.

The emerging picture of international parental abduction is that, although the absolute number of abductions remains relatively modest, there has been a

9 On 28 September 2007 an electronic statistical database, INCASTAT, was launched, which generates the annual statistical forms covering return and access applications relating to the Hague Convention of 1980; it also produces statistical charts. INCASTAT is available only to the central authorities designated under the 1980 Child Abduction Convention.

Table 5.1 Outcomes of return applications in 2008 under the Hague Convention

Outcome	Frequency	Percentage (%)
Rejection	85	5
Voluntary return	366	19
Judicial return by consent order	124	7
Judicial return not by consent	280	15
Judicial return consent unknown	104	5
Judicial refusal	286	15
Access ordered	41	2
Access agreed	21	1
Other agreement	25	1
Pending	154	8
Withdrawn	337	18
Other	63	3
Different outcomes for different children	11	1
More than one outcome	4	<1
Total	**1901**	**≈100**

Source: Lowe 2011a: 20.

steady increase in the three decades since the Hague Convention was concluded. It would appear that the number is rising as the process of globalisation provides more opportunities for international marriages or partnerships to take place. Motivations to abduct vary from parents wanting to force reconciliation with the left-behind parent, to having a desire to blame or punish the left-behind parent, or to protect the child from a parent who is perceived to abuse or neglect the child (Chiancone 2001).

One possible explanation for parental child abduction lies in the impact of reformed custody laws. The international legal recognition of the child's right to contact with both parents under the Convention on the Rights of the Child[10] has increasingly been observed (section 3.7.5). Part of the explanation may also lie in the increasing number of persons who marry or cohabit with a person of a different nationality. When the relationship fails there may well be pressures on the couple to return to their respective countries of habitual residence. It may appear to be the obvious course of action for the primary carer to return home with the children.

5.2   Introduction to the international legal instruments

There are four international instruments considered here in relation to international parental child abduction: the Convention on the Rights of the Child (Articles 9–11); the European Convention on Recognition and Enforcement of

10 CRC art 9(1) and (3).

Decisions Concerning Custody of Children and on Restoration of Custody of Children (1980, European Convention of 1980);[11] Council Regulation (EC) No 2201/2003 (Revised Brussels II Regulation);[12] and the Hague Convention on Child Abduction of 1980. The first three are dealt with, in outline only, in the following three sections. This Chapter focuses mainly on the Hague Convention on Child Abduction of 1980, which is dealt with in more depth in section 5.3 below.

5.2.1 UN Convention on the Rights of the Child

Article 9(1) of the Convention on the Rights of the Child provides that:

> States Parties shall ensure that a child shall not be separated from his or her parents against their will, except when competent authorities subject to judicial review determine, in accordance with applicable law and procedures, that such separation is necessary for the best interests of the child.

Furthermore, states parties are obliged to 'respect the right of the child who is separated from one or both parents to maintain personal relations and direct contact with both parents on a regular basis, except if it is contrary to the child's best interests'.[13] This latter provision resonates with, and was in part based upon, the recognition given in the Hague Convention on Child Abduction to the maintenance of relations between children and both parents, in particular where the parents are of different nationalities (Detrick 1999: 194). Article 10(2) provides that '[a] child whose parents reside in different States shall have the right to maintain on a regular basis, save in exceptional circumstances personal relations and direct contacts with both parents'.

Article 11 of the Convention on the Rights of the Child is, according to Hodgkin and Newell (2007: 143), 'primarily concerned with parental abductions or retentions'. It further obliges states parties to 'take measures to combat the illicit transfer and non-return of children abroad' and, to this end, they must promote the conclusion of bilateral or multilateral agreements,[14] which is taken to be principally a reference to the Hague Convention on Child Abduction. The reference to the 'illicit transfer and non-return of children abroad' is, according to Detrick (1999: 201), a reference to international child abduction by a parent: '[i]t is to be distinguished from the specific form of exploitation of children which is referred to in Article 35 as the "abduction of children"'.

---

11 European Convention on Recognition and Enforcement of Decisions concerning Custody of Children and on Restoration of Custody of Children, opened for signature 20 May 1980, CETS No 105 (entered into force 1 September 1983).

12 Council Regulation (EC) No 2201/2003 of 27 November 2003 concerning jurisdiction and the recognition and enforcement of judgments in matrimonial matters and the matters of parental responsibility, repealing Regulation (EC) No 1347/2000 [2003] OJ L338/1–29.

13 CRC art 9(3).

14 CRC art 11(1) and (2).

In summary, Articles 9 to 11 of the Convention on the Rights of the Child provide a legal framework that emphasises the child's right to maintain personal relations with his or her parents in circumstances including where a parental abduction or retention has occurred. States are obliged to combat the problem of international parental child abduction, mainly by ratifying and implementing relevant international instruments such as the Hague Convention on Child Abduction. However, as will be seen, the Hague Convention does little to maintain the child-centred focus of Articles 9 to 11.

It should also be noted that the Convention on the Rights of the Child has in recent years started to have a more pervasive influence over the way in which Hague Convention cases are dealt with; a process that has been advanced in particular by the case law emanating from the European Court of Human Rights (ECtHR) (Schuz 2013). Recent ECtHR cases[15] have emphasised that the European Convention on Human Rights (ECHR) cannot be interpreted in a vacuum. According to Article 31(3)(c) of the Vienna Convention on the Law of Treaties (1969), any relevant rules of international law applicable to the contracting states parties must be taken into account. Furthermore, the positive obligations that Article 8 of the ECHR impose on states with respect to reuniting parents with their children must therefore be interpreted in the light of the Convention on the Rights of the Child and the Hague Convention of 1980.

5.2.2   European Convention on Recognition and Enforcement of Decisions Concerning Custody of Children and on Restoration of Custody of Children of 1980

The European Convention of 1980,[16] as its name suggests, is concerned with the enforcement and recognition of custody orders and decisions relating to access. Consequently, and in contrast to the Hague Convention of 1980, it requires that there is a custody or access 'order' in existence as a necessary precondition for invoking its jurisdiction. The European Convention of 1980 requires that each contracting state must establish an administrative body, the 'Central Authority', which will collate and send information to the appropriate agencies and, if necessary, initiate legal proceedings. For example, the Central Authority for England and Wales under both the European Convention of 1980 and the Hague Convention of 1980 is the Lord Chancellor, who delegates the duties of the Central Authority to the International Child Abduction and Contact Unit (ICACU), which is based in the Office of the Official Solicitor and Public Trustee.

---

15 For example *Neulinger and Shuruk v Switzerland* (Application No 41615/07), Grand Chamber (6 July 2010); (2012) 54 EHRR 31, HC/E/ 1323; and *Šneersone and Kampanella v Italy* Application No 14737/09 (12 July 2011).

16 European Convention on Recognition and Enforcement of Decisions concerning Custody of Children and on Restoration of Custody of Children, opened for signature 20 May 1980, CETS No 105 (entered into force 1 September 1983). As at 22 February 2014, 37 of the 47 member states of the Council of Europe had ratified or acceded to this Convention.

ICACU is also the designated Central Authority under the Revised Brussels II Regulation (section 5.2.3).

The underlying assumption behind each Convention is that a peremptory return of the child to the *status quo ante* will ultimately be in the child's best interests. The European Convention of 1980 can be used to assist in finding the whereabouts of a child and/or securing the recognition or enforcement of a custody order. If an application is made within six months of abduction, it is likely that the restoration of custody will be immediate on establishing the facts of an unlawful removal. An application outside of this time limit, however, will have to satisfy further conditions.

There are some limited circumstances in which an application under the European Convention of 1980 may be the better remedy. First, if the application is made within six months, a return order will be virtually mandatory.[17] Secondly, there are some advantages where the main dispute concerns the enforcement of an *access* order. It would appear that, of the contracting states which have ratified both Conventions,[18] much more use is made of the Hague Convention of 1980, where applications for the return of children are founded on the concept of a breach of custody rights, rather than the registration and recognition of custody decisions in the receiving state (Official Solicitor 1997: para 11).

5.2.3　The Revised Brussels II Regulation of 2003

Under the Revised Brussels II Regulation[19] since 1 March 2005, abductions and the enforcement of orders for contact or access within the European Union (other than Denmark) have been governed by the Hague Convention of 1980 as modified by the EU instrument with regard to intra-EU parental child abductions. The Regulation has introduced a more streamlined process for dealing with parental abductions within Europe. The details of how this Regulation interacts with the Hague Convention are quite complex.

As will be discussed in the next section, the Hague Convention of 1980 in essence establishes a peremptory return order procedure whereby an abducted or retained child under the age of 16 will be returned by the court in the country to which the child has been removed (the requested state, or the state of refuge) to the country of the child's habitual residence (the requesting state). The underlying policy presumption is that most child welfare and custody or access issues will be determined in the requesting state following an order of return from the state of refuge.

---

17 European Convention of 1980 art 8.

18 At the time of writing, all 37 states that had ratified or acceded to the European Convention of 1980 (except Andora, Liechtenstein and Moldova) were also parties to the Hague Convention on Child Abduction of 1980.

19 Council Regulation (EC) No 2201/2003 of 27 November 2003 concerning jurisdiction and the recognition and enforcement of judgments in matrimonial matters and matters of parental responsibility, repealing Regulation (EC) No 1347/2000 [2003] OJ L338/1–29.

There are some limited discretionary 'exceptions' or 'defences' (section 5.3.3) built into Hague proceedings to resist the usual outcome of a return order. If one or more of those exceptions are made out in the proceedings, then as a matter of discretion the court is at liberty to make a 'non-return order', that is, authorising the child to *remain* in the country of refuge (the requested state). The original proposal of the European Commission for an EU Regulation in this area would have replaced entirely the Hague machinery and provided a new legal regime for intra-EU child abductions that would have reduced the courts' jurisdiction in the country of refuge to an even more limited facility to make provisional holding orders only, without any possibility of making a permanent 'non-return order'. In the negotiations leading up to the making of the Regulation, this proposal was very controversial and it was eventually agreed in essence to retain the Hague Convention machinery, subject to more minor adjustments.

The overriding policy of the legal regime under the Regulation is to strengthen the existing machinery of peremptory return orders under the Hague Convention. There are four key points to note:

i.   Preservation of jurisdiction of the courts of the country of the child's habitual residence (the 'requesting State')
ii.   Presumption of child's right to be heard in proceedings
iii.   Court in the country of refuge (the 'requested State') cannot make a non-return order on basis of 'grave risk of harm' where adequate protective arrangements would exist for the child after return
iv.   Where a non-return order has been made in the country of refuge, the left-behind parent may still litigate the issue of residence/custody on its merits in the requesting State, and this will override the decision of the court in the country of refuge.

First, the Regulation does aim to prevent the jurisdiction of the child's country of habitual residence being changed by an abduction event. Article 10 of the Regulation provides that the courts of the child's country of habitual residence shall retain their jurisdiction until the child has acquired habitual residence in another member state. This protects the right of the court of the country of the child's habitual residence to hear any custody dispute except in specified circumstances.

Secondly, Article 11(2) of the Regulation establishes a presumption supporting the child's participation rights in proceedings. Where a court in the country of refuge is considering making either a return order or a non-return order under the Hague Convention: 'it shall be ensured that the child is given the opportunity to be heard during the proceedings unless this appears inappropriate having regard to his or her age or degree of maturity'.

The House of Lords determined in *Re D (A Child) (Abduction: Rights of Custody)*[20] that this provision will apply, not only when one or more of the 'defences' is raised

20 [2006] UKHL 51, [2007] 1 AC 619.

but in every Hague return application reaching the court. Baroness Hale observed that the introduction of the Regulation would lead to children being heard more frequently in Hague Convention proceedings than before. Interestingly, in the same case, the court held that the obligation to hear the child would also apply in non-intra-EU Hague Convention cases because of the developing influence of the participation rights contained in Article 12 of the Convention on the Rights of the Child.[21] Also, the Regulation provides the parent requesting a return (the left-behind parent) to be given an opportunity to be heard in non-return order cases. The details of how these rights are secured in national courts is left to national law and consequently the procedures for hearing the child will vary between member states.

In some jurisdictions the judge will hear the child directly; in others there may be exclusive reliance on written documentation. In England and Wales, the Court of Appeal has made it clear that the child must be heard in return proceedings under the Regulation.[22] Since the drafting of the Hague Convention of 1980 there has been an increased recognition of children's 'agency', which has led to increased European support for the further development of children's legal procedural rights (Lamont 2008). This can be seen in recital 33 of the preamble to the Regulation, which references Article 24 (rights of the child) of the Charter of Fundamental Rights of the European Union.[23] To some extent this strengthening of children's participation rights in this context may conflict with the dominant theme of the Regulation to reinforce the Hague Convention return order machinery.

Thirdly, the Regulation provides that '[a] court cannot refuse to return a child on the basis of Article 13b [the "grave risk of harm" defence] of the 1980 Hague Convention if it is established that adequate arrangements have been made to secure the protection of the child after his or her return'.[24] This provision in effect constrains the court's discretion to make a non-return order on the basis of a perceived grave risk of harm to the child if returned to the requesting state in circumstances where adequate protective arrangements are available in that state. All the other 'defences' in the Hague Convention machinery are left untouched by the Regulation.

Fourthly, even where a non-return order has been made[25] in the requested state, or where the removal or retention has not been found to be 'wrongful', the left-behind parent may still litigate the issue of residence on its merits in the requesting state. In other words, the requesting state in such circumstances retains

---

21 The Court of Appeal approved the seeking of the views of children of sufficient age and maturity as a principle of universal application *in Re M (A Child) (Abduction: Child's Objections to Return)* [2007] EWCA Civ 260, [2007] 2 FLR 72.

22 *Re F (Abduction: Child's Wishes)* [2007] EWCA Civ 468.

23 Council of the European Union, Charter of Fundamental Rights of the European Union (2007/C 303/01) (14 December 2007).

24 Council Regulation (EC) No 2201/2003 art 11(4).

25 The 'non-return order' or 'refusal order' must be made under one of the limbs of art 13 of the Hague Convention (but not under arts 12(2) or 20).

control over custody issues and the children's ultimate return to that state. The court in the country of refuge that made a non-return order will, in effect, be overridden by the court in the requesting state if it chooses to issue a return order following a merits review.[26]

In summary, although the Regulation enhances the procedure for hearing the child's views, it also reinforces the policy of peremptory return of the child to the country of the child's habitual residence, by supporting the preservation of jurisdiction by requesting states and their ability to override the requested state's non-return order(s). Arguably, the interaction of these two elements has not been well thought out. Further strengthening of the return policy may result in the tendency that a child's views are accorded little weight. For example, in *JPC v SLW and SMW (Abduction)*,[27] a 14 year old's cogent objection was not enough to prevent the operation of the return mechanism.

A number of commentators have questioned the value and purpose of Article 11(2) of the Regulation (McEleavy 2005; Lowe 2007; Lamont 2008; Schultz 2008). Indeed, given the predominance of female taking parents, and the EU policy of 'gender mainstreaming', that is, including gender concerns into the formation of EU law, it has been argued that the gendered nature of child abduction was insufficiently addressed in the development of the Regulation (Lamont 2011).

5.3 The Hague Convention on the civil aspects of international child abduction (1980)

The Hague Convention of 1980[28] puts contracting states under an obligation to take appropriate measures to implement the Convention's primary objectives: to secure the prompt return of children 'wrongfully removed to or retained in any contracting state' and to ensure that rights of custody and access are respected.[29] States must use 'the most expeditious procedures available'[30] to achieve these objectives. The assumption is that the main remedy in the Convention of a speedy return order will be appropriate to all the main participants involved in international child abduction. It will act as a deterrent to would-be abductors. It will reduce the harm done to the children and it will protect the rights of the left-behind parent. The Supreme Court of Canada commented on the aims of the Convention:

---

26 Council Regulation (EC) No 2201/2003 art 11(6)–(8). See generally the first reported English case on the Regulation: *Re A (Custody Decision after Maltese Non-Return Order)* [2006] EWHC 3397 (Fam), [2007] 1 FLR 1923.

27 [2007] EWHC 1349 (Fam), [2007] 2 FLR 900.

28 Hague Conference on Private International Law, Convention on the civil aspects of international child abduction, concluded 25 October 1980 (entered into force 1 December 1983). There were 91 contracting states to this convention at the time of writing.

29 ibid art 1.

30 ibid art 2.

The automatic return procedure implemented by the Act [in Canada implementing the Hague Convention] is ultimately intended to deter the abduction of children by depriving fugitive parents of any possibility of having their custody of the children recognized in the country of refuge and thereby legitimizing the situation for which they are responsible. To that end, the Act favours the restoration of the status quo as soon as possible after the removal of the child by enabling one party to force the other to submit to the jurisdiction of the court of the child's habitual place of residence for the purpose of arguing the merits of any custody issue. The Act, like the Convention, presumes that the interests of children who have been wrongfully removed are ordinarily better served by immediately repatriating them to their original jurisdiction, where the merits of custody should have been determined before their removal. Once that determination has been made, the Convention and the Act give full effect thereto by protecting custody rights through the mandatory return process. ...

Thus, the Convention and the Act represent a compromise between the flexibility derived from reviewing each situation on its merits and the effectiveness needed to deter international child abduction, which depends in particular on the rapidity of the return procedure.[31]

It should be noted that a Convention application can be activated only in relation to a child that has not attained the age of 16 years.[32]

Delay in a child abduction situation can, of course, have very serious and permanent consequences for the relationship between the child and the left-behind parent (Freeman M 2003, 2006). Speed is therefore an important element to the structure of the Convention,[33] and this is reinforced by an implicit duty[34] on the relevant judicial or administrative authorities of each contracting state to reach a decision within six weeks of the date of commencement of proceedings. The reality of expedition in Hague proceedings is different. In *Chafin v. Chafin* the Supreme Court of the United States of America observed that:

Cases in American courts often take over two years from filing to resolution; for a six-year-old such as E. C., that is one-third of her lifetime. Expedition will help minimize the extent to which uncertainty adds to the challenges confronting both parents and child.[35]

It should also be noted that, in keeping with the practice of the Hague Conference on Private International Law, an explanatory report was produced on the Hague

---

31　*W.(V.) v. S.(D.)*, (1996) 2 SCR 108, (1996) 134 DLR 4th 481m, HC/E/CA 17.

32　Convention on the civil aspects of international child abduction art 4.

33　ibid art 11.

34　ibid art 11(2). There is a concrete obligation to reach a decision under the Revised Brussels II Regulation art 11(3).

35　*Chafin v. Chafin*, 133 S. Ct. 1017, 185 L. Ed. 2d 1 (2013); HC/E/US 1206.

Convention of 1980 (Pérez-Vera 1980). Such explanatory reports have an especially persuasive status when the courts are trying to interpret the Convention's provisions (section 2.2.1). Indeed, the essential aims of the explanatory report relating to the Hague Convention of 1980 are described as follows:

> On the one hand, it must throw into relief, as accurately as possible, the principles which form the basis of the Convention and, wherever necessary, the development of those ideas which led to such principles being chosen from amongst existing options. … This final Report must also fulfil another purpose, viz to supply those who have to apply the Convention with a detailed commentary on its provision.
>
> (Pérez-Vera 1980: paras 5–6)

Thus the Pérez-Vera report on this Convention remains an authoritative source of interpretative material. For example, the following extract indicates that an implicit aim of the Convention is to ensure that consideration of any issue around the custody of the children should occur in the state where the children had their habitual residence prior to the removal or retention:

> In a final attempt to clarify the objects of the Convention, it would be advisable to underline the fact that, as is shown particularly in the provisions of Article 1, the Convention does not seek to regulate the problem of the award of custody rights. On this matter, the Convention rests implicitly upon the principle that any debate on the merits of the question, *i.e.* of custody rights, should take place before the competent authorities in the State where the child had its habitual residence prior to its removal; this applies as much to a removal which occurred prior to any decision on custody being taken – as to a removal in breach of a pre-existing custody decision.
>
> (Pérez-Vera 1980: para 19)

The structure of the Hague Convention of 1980 (see Figure 5.1) can be summarised as follows. First, it defines what is meant by a 'wrongful' removal or retention. Secondly, if the facts fit this definition then an immediate duty arises for the court in the country of refuge to make a return order. The child is returned to the country from which he or she has been removed to uphold the position as it was before the removal or retention. Further disputes about the child will then have to be addressed in domestic proceedings in the child's country of habitual residence. The full force of the duty to order a peremptory return will last for 12 months from the date of removal or retention.[36]

Thirdly, after the 12 month period has elapsed there is a proviso which permits the court to refuse to order a return if it considers that the child is sufficiently

---

36 This is one of the reasons why the Hague Convention of 1980 is preferred over the European Convention of 1980, where the active time period is only six months.

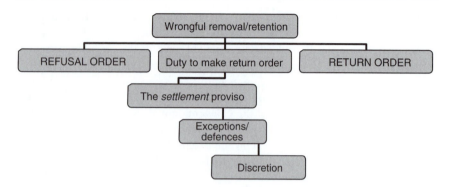

Figure 5.1 Structure of the Hague Convention of 1980

settled in his or her new environment to justify a departure from the underlying duty to return. Fourthly, the duty to return may also be refused if one or more of the 'exceptions', sometimes referred to as 'defences', applies.

Finally, even if one or more of these exceptions/defences are made out, the court will still have a *discretion* to make the return order if it sees fit. It can choose to exercise its discretion in favour of the taking parent and refuse to make a return order (a non-return order), or in favour of the left-behind parent by making the return order. The following sections examine these elements in further detail.

Finally, it should be noted that there is now a considerable body of case law in many jurisdictions of the states that are parties to the Hague Convention of 1980. In order to encourage a consistent interpretation of the Convention, the Permanent Bureau of the Hague Conference established in 1999 the International Child Abduction Database (INCADAT), which contains all the leading decisions.[37] The cases cited in this chapter end with the INCADAT citation where available.

5.3.1 *Wrongful removal or retention*

The Hague Convention of 1980 defines what is to be considered a wrongful removal or retention:

Article 3
The removal or the retention of a child is to be considered wrongful where –

a) it is in breach of rights of custody attributed to a person, an institution or any other body, either jointly or alone, under the law of the State in

---

37 See http://www.incadat.com/index.cfm?act=text.text&lng=1 (accessed 8 November 2013).

which the child was habitually resident immediately before the removal or retention; and

b) at the time of removal or retention those rights were actually exercised, either jointly or alone, or would have been so exercised but for the removal or retention.

The rights of custody mentioned in sub-paragraph a) above, may arise in particular by operation of law or by reason of a judicial or administrative decision, or by reason of an agreement having legal effect under the law of that State.[38]

The applicant who is seeking a return order under the Hague Convention has the evidential burden of showing that there has been a wrongful removal or retention. It should be noted that the inclusion of the notion of a wrongful *retention* ensures that a much wider number of situations are covered than would otherwise be the case. A typical retention might involve a child leaving his or her country of habitual residence with the agreement of person(s) having custody rights for a defined period of time (eg for a holiday or visitation period).

Where a child is not returned on the expiry of an agreed period and in breach of the left-behind parent's custody rights, there is a wrongful retention, and this may occur earlier than the agreed period if the abducting parent has formed such an intention at an earlier time. Consequently, the Hague Convention is sufficiently broad to cover cases where the wrongful retention is identified as occurring sometime after an initial (and lawful) *removal* takes place. It can be seen from the text of Article 3 that whether a removal or retention is 'wrongful' will depend largely upon the consideration of two key legal concepts: 'rights of custody' and 'habitual residence', which are discussed in the following sections.

5.3.1.1   Rights of custody

'Rights of custody' are defined non-exhaustively in Article 5(a) of the Convention to include 'rights relating to the care of the person of the child and, in particular, the right to determine the child's place of residence'.[39] The relevant law to determine whether rights of custody exist will be the law of the country of the child's habitual residence immediately before the removal/retention.[40] The final paragraph of Article 3 (above) indicates three ways in which rights of custody *may* arise. The concept of 'operation of law' includes rights of custody that are recognised in the internal law of the relevant domestic jurisdiction.[41]

---

38 Hague Convention of 1980 art 3.

39 ibid art 5(a).

40 ibid art 3(a).

41 '[C]ustody *ex lege* can be based either on the internal law of the State of the child's habitual residence, or on the law designated by the conflict rules of that State' (Pérez-Vera 1980: para 68).

Custody rights arising 'by reason of a judicial or administrative decision', according to Pérez-Vera, requires a wide interpretation and 'embraces any decision or part of a decision (judicial or administrative) on a child's custody and, on the other hand, that these decisions may have been issued by the courts of the State of the child's habitual residence as well as by the courts of a third country' (Pérez-Vera 1980: para 69). Finally, rights of custody may arise 'by reason of an agreement having legal effect under the law of that State'. This includes '[i]n principle, the agreements in question may be simple private transactions between the parties concerning the custody of their children' (Pérez-Vera 1980: para 70). It is again a broad category that in principle will include all custody arrangements that are not specifically prohibited by law.

Even if rights of custody cannot be identified as belonging in either of the above three categories, the notion of 'inchoate' rights of custody has been developed. This provides a way in which persons who have been actual carers of the children in question but who lack formally recognised forms of legal custody may nevertheless be able to be regarded as having rights of custody for Convention purposes. Such 'inchoate' rights of custody were first identified in an English decision in 1994,[42] and have been followed subsequently in that jurisdiction.[43]

In some jurisdictions the concept has attracted support; for example, in New Zealand.[44] However, the notion was rejected by the Irish Supreme Court in *H.I. v M.G.*,[45] a position that was upheld by the Court of Justice of the European Union.[46] Several jurisdictions have accepted that the doctrine of *patria potestas* ('power of a father'), which still exists in many Spanish speaking jurisdictions, may also give rise to Convention rights of custody.[47]

It is perhaps unsurprising that the developing interpretation of 'rights of custody' under the Convention has been generally broadened. The adoption of a narrower, formalist approach would have excluded many meritorious applications for a return order. Indeed, most contracting states have now accepted that a person's mere right of veto over the removal of the child amounts to a right of custody for Convention purposes.[48] There was some division of opinion in the Federal Courts of Appeal in the USA until the Supreme Court decision of *Abbott v Abbott*,[49] which endorsed the international standard.

---

42 *Re B (A Minor) (Abduction)* [1994] 2 FLR 249; HC/E/UKe 4.

43 For example *Re G (Child Abduction) (Unmarried Father: Rights of Custody)* [2002] EWHC 2219 (Fam), [2002] All ER (D) 79 (November), [2003] 1 FLR 252; HC/E/UKe 506.

44 *Anderson v Paterson* [2002] NZFLR 641; HC/E/NZ 471.

45 *H.I. v M.G.* [1999] 2 ILRM 1, [2000] 1 IR 110; HC/E/IE 284.

46 Case C–400/10 PPU *J. McB. v L.E.*; HC/E/ 1104, (5 October 2010).

47 *Whallon v. Lynn*, 230 F.3d 450 (1st Cir. October 27, 2000); HC/E/USf 388.

48 For example *Re D (A Child) (Abduction: Rights of Custody)* [2006] UKHL 51, [2007] 1 AC 619; HC/E/UKe 880.

49 *Abbot v. Abbott*, 130 S. Ct. 1983 (2010); HC/E/USf 1029.

This position has also been confirmed by the European Court of Human Rights (ECtHR) in *Neulinger and Shuruk v Switzerland*.[50] However, where a person merely has a right to object to a removal and apply to a court to prevent such removal, several jurisdictions have held that this falls short of a right of veto and does not rank as a right of custody for Convention purposes.[51] This position has also been confirmed by the Court of Justice of the European Union.[52]

A further element of the definition of 'wrongful removal or retention' is the requirement contained in Article 3(b) (see above). The purpose of this provision is to ensure that applications for return orders cannot be initiated by persons whose custody rights have gone 'stale'; for example, where a person has in effect abandoned all responsibility in relation to a child. This will generally occur through a failure actively to engage with the child over a significant period of time. There needs to be at least some evidence of the actual exercise of the custody rights in question to fulfil the legal requirements of a 'wrongful removal or retention'. In practice, however, it is unusual for this element of the definition to be a live issue in the overwhelming majority of cases. The desire on the part of the left-behind parent to make an application in the first place is generally prompted by having some form of active participation in the child's life prior to the occurrence of a removal or retention:

> This condition, by defining the scope of the Convention, requires that the applicant provide only some preliminary evidence that he actually took physical care of the child, a fact which normally will be relatively easy to demonstrate. Besides, the informal nature of this requirement is highlighted in Article 8 which simply includes, in sub-paragraph (c), 'the grounds on which the applicant's claim for return of the child is based', amongst the facts which it requires to be contained in applications to the Central Authorities.
>
> (Pérez-Vera 1980: para 73)

It should also be noted that the rights of custody contained in Article 3(a) (see above) must be 'attributed to a person, an institution or any other body'. Article 8 repeats this formula to identify eligible applicants for a return order under the Convention. Parents seek the majority of return applications, but the drafting is wide enough to enable applications from public law bodies that have 'rights of custody' to apply; two examples drawn from the case law include a licensed adoption agency in Texas[53] and an Irish court.[54]

50 *Neulinger and Shuruk v Switzerland* (Application No 41615/07, Grand Chamber (6 July 2010); HC/E/ 1323.
51 Canada: *W.(V.) v. S.(D.)*, 134 DLR 4th 481 (1996); HC/E/CA17; Ireland: *W.P.P. v S.R.W.* [2001] ILRM 371, HC/E/IE 271; UK: *Re V.-B. (Abduction: Custody Rights)* [1999] 2 FLR 192; HC/E/UKe 261.
52 Case C–400/10 PPU *J. McB. v L.E.*, HC/E/ 1104 (5 October 2010).
53 *Re JS (Private International Adoption)* [2000] 2 FLR 638.
54 *Re H (A Minor) (Abduction: Rights of Custody)* [2002] 2 AC 291.

5.3.1.2   Article 15 declarations

Article 15

The judicial or administrative authorities of a Contracting State may, prior to the making of an order for the return of the child, request that the applicant obtain from the authorities of the State of the habitual residence of the child a decision or other determination that the removal or retention was wrongful within the meaning of Article 3 of the Convention, where such a decision or determination may be obtained in that State. The Central Authorities of the Contracting States shall so far as practicable assist applicants to obtain such a decision or determination.

This article allows, as a matter of discretion, a request by the court or administrative authority of the country of refuge that the applicant (the left-behind parent) obtain a determination from the authorities of the state of the habitual residence of the child on the question whether the removal or retention was 'wrongful'. The House of Lords (United Kingdom: England & Wales) held[55] that where such a declaration was sought, then the ruling of the foreign court as to the content of the rights held by the applicant must be treated as conclusive, save in exceptional cases; for example, where the ruling has been obtained by fraud or in breach of the rules of natural justice.

It was also noted that recourse to an Article 15 declaration would lead to delay and therefore the procedure should be used selectively; a balance had to be struck between acting on too little information and over-zealous examination. The underlying problem with Article 15 declarations would appear to be that they tend to trespass on the development of a number of 'autonomous' Convention concepts:

> Common law jurisdictions are divided as to the role to be played by the Article 15 mechanism, in particular whether the court in the child's State of habitual residence should make a finding as to the wrongfulness of the removal or retention, or, whether it should limit its decision to the extent to which the applicant possesses custody rights under its own law. This division cannot be dissociated from the autonomous nature of custody rights for Convention purposes as well as that of 'wrongfulness' i.e. when rights of custody are to be deemed to have been breached.[56]

In some jurisdictions the view is that the court in the country of the child's habitual residence should constrain its consideration to matters of national law but not

---

55   *Re D (A Child) (Abduction: Rights of Custody)* [2006] UKHL 51, [2007] 1 AC 619; HC/E/UKe 880.
56   McEleavy, P. and Fiorini, A., *Case law analysis*, INCADAT, Hague Conference on Private International Law http://www.incadat.com/index.cfm?act=analysis.show&sl=3&lng=1 (accessed 23 October 2013).

move into the consideration of whether a removal was 'wrongful' or not. The courts in the state of refuge should undertake that function using its assessment of the autonomous law of the Convention.[57]

5.3.1.3 Habitual residence

'Habitual residence' is a key concept within the definition of a wrongful removal or retention contained in Article 3 (see above). The identification of the country in which a child was habitually resident prior to a removal or retention is important in two respects. First, it locates the relevant jurisdiction to be examined in order to determine whether the left-behind parent has any 'rights of custody' (or can rely on the rights of custody vested in a court or other body) in the relevant domestic law. Secondly, the jurisdiction of the Hague Convention of 1980 will apply only 'to any child who was habitually resident in a Contracting State immediately before any breach of custody or access rights'.[58]

The underlying notion of habitual residence is that a child should be returned to the country where he or she has the most obvious connection prior to a wrongful removal or retention. This reflects the philosophy of the Convention to place the parties back into the position they were in prior to the alleged wrongful removal or retention (*status quo ante*) and to prevent and deter parents from taking the unilateral action implied by a removal or retention. The country of the child's habitual residence is a logical and practical starting point. It is certainly a more appropriate and practical connecting factor between a child and a sovereign state than the abstract legal concepts of 'domicile' or 'nationality'.

The concept of habitual residence is not defined in the Convention; it is left to be determined as a question of fact. This allows some flexibility for the courts and central authorities to come to practical solutions across the range of cases presented. However, such flexibility has also brought difficulties in arriving at consistent interpretations across the diverse jurisdictions of the contracting states. There has been an increasing volume of case law emerging from many of these domestic jurisdictions (Beaumont and McEleavy 1999: 88–113; Schuz 2001, 2001a).[59]

This is perhaps unsurprising since, if a taking parent can establish that the country of refuge has in fact become the country of the child's 'habitual residence', then the left-behind parent will not be able to access the Convention's jurisdiction at all.[60] One of the problems is that some jurisdictions have favoured the decision on habitual residence being led by a *factual* enquiry: how long had the child lived in the country in question? Others have placed more emphasis on the identification of an *intentionality* element: is there a settled purpose habitually to reside in the

---

57 *Fairfax v Ireton* [2009] NZFLR 433 (NZ CA); HC/E/NZ 1018.
58 Hague Convention of 1980 art 4.
59 A search for cases on the INCADAT database raising the issue of 'habitual residence' identified 624 such cases across the contracting states since 1990. See http://www.incadat.com/index.cfm?act=search.detailed&sl=2&lng=1n (accessed 24 October 2013).
60 Hague Convention of 1980 art 4.

country in question? It is beyond the remit of this book to provide a comprehensive coverage of the voluminous case law across many jurisdictions in this area, but the following commentary provided on the Hague Conference INCADAT case analysis website pages provides a useful and authoritative signpost to the underlying difficulties of interpretation:

> There is a lack of uniformity as to whether in determining habitual residence the emphasis should be exclusively on the child, with regard paid to the intentions of the child's care givers, or primarily on the intentions of the care givers. At least partly as a result, habitual residence may appear a very flexible connecting factor in some Contracting States yet much more rigid and reflective of long term residence in others.
>
> Any assessment of the interpretation of habitual residence is further complicated by the fact that cases focusing on the concept may concern very different factual situations. For example habitual residence may arise for consideration following a permanent relocation, or a more tentative move, albeit one which is open-ended or potentially open-ended, or indeed the move may be for a clearly defined period of time.[61]

A situation involving 'a more tentative' move, at least in the first instance, was addressed in a case from the High Court of New Zealand.

Case study 5.1

High Court of New Zealand
***RCL v APBL* [2012] NZHC 1292; HC/E/NZ 1231 (J W Gendall J)**
Judgment 11 June 2012

Facts:
[1] This is an appeal against a decision of District Court Judge S J Coyle in the Family Court at Queenstown (heard at Alexandra) ordering that the two children of the appellant and respondent be returned to the United Kingdom pursuant to s 105 of the Care of Children Act 2004 (the Act) and the Hague Convention.

Background

[2] The parties (to be described as mother and father) are the parents of two boys born in the United Kingdom on 31 May 2006 and 4 November 2007. They were aged five and four at the time of the hearing in the Family Court. The parents were originally from New Zealand and moved to live in

61 McEleavy and Fiorini (n 56).

the United Kingdom in mid 2001, and were married in August 2002. The marriage broke down and the parties were divorced on 23 March 2010.

[3] On 14 May 2010, the parents, in the course of mediation, reached an agreement relating to custody and care of the children in the United Kingdom, but as part of which agreed that the mother could make a trip to New Zealand via South Africa from August 2010, to return to the United Kingdom in March 2011. It was agreed that then the children would be in the care of each of the parents on a shared and equal basis. Consequently, on 28 August 2010, the mother left the United Kingdom with the children and arrived in New Zealand.

[4] Within three weeks, the mother advised the father that she would not be returning to the United Kingdom. The father did not agree to the children staying in New Zealand. The mother naturally wished the children to remain with her, but she indicated to the father that he could come to New Zealand and collect the children to return to the United Kingdom. She believed it was unlikely that he would come (although this was not actually stated until the proceedings were well in train). So although there was a wish the children remain in New Zealand, the mother did not say that she would refuse to yield them up and appeared to accept that the children could be collected by their father in March 2011.

[5] The father's position was that, through emails and other communications, the mother had led him to believe that he could travel to New Zealand to collect the children in March 2011 as had been agreed. The father, on 1 December 2010, said:

... I still struggle to come to grips with the fact that you were taking the boys to NZ for a 6 month holiday and within a month of getting to NZ you decided to stay, even though the agreement at mediation was for this not to happen. Whilst not legally binding, I took your word on the fact that you would be back and also that we had set up co-parenting arrangements which we both wanted and you seemed genuinely happy with.

[6] And on 2 December 2010:

Clearly very upset and angry that you have in effect abducted my children away from me ...

[7] Later, on 9 January 2011, the mother and father had a further electronic communication in which they agreed that the children could remain in New Zealand until the youngest boy was due to start school – he turn[ed] five on 4 November 2012. So the father's understanding was that the children

would remain living in New Zealand for some time until November 2012. Thereafter they would live and go to school in the United Kingdom and practical childcare arrangements would be looked at or 'revisited'. The father and his partner travelled to New Zealand in late February/early March 2011 to see the children.

[8] On 29 May 2011, the mother and the children went from New Zealand to the United Kingdom for an 18 day holiday, intended to be until 16 June 2011. In his judgment, the subject of appeal, Judge Coyle said:

What is unclear is why [the father] did not, with the children in the jurisdiction of United Kingdom Courts, apply for an order preventing [the boys] being removed from the United Kingdom at that point in time. The reality, however, is that he did not.

[9] One explanation might be that the father believed there was an agreement that the children would be returned to the United Kingdom in November 2012.

[10] At about 4pm on Sunday, 12 June 2011, the mother and father met at a café and she then informed him that she would not be returning the children to the United Kingdom in November 2012, or ever, and the children would live with her thereafter in New Zealand. The mother left the United Kingdom with the children on their return flight to New Zealand on Thursday, 16 June 2011. The father sought legal advice and made an application to the United Kingdom Central Authority for return of the children on 31 August 2011.

[11] On 14 November 2011, the father's application for return of the children to the United Kingdom was filed in the Family Court in Queenstown.

Held:
Conclusion
[122] For the foregoing reasons, the appeal fails. I agree with Judge Coyle that the children must be returned. In summary:
The children's habitual residence is in the United Kingdom and this has not changed.
The parents agreed that the children could be removed to New Zealand for a limited period from August 2010 to March 2011.
That agreement was varied to extend the period in New Zealand until November 2012.
The mother, when in the United Kingdom on holiday with the children, unequivocally repudiated the agreement.
The father never accepted that repudiation.

The anticipatory breach of the agreement by the mother entitled the father to cancel it.

The removal of the children on 16 June 2011 after they had been temporarily in the United Kingdom was wrongful removal given the mother's anticipatory breach.

The father did not thereafter consent to, or acquiesce in, the children's continued residence in New Zealand.

Judge Coyle was correct in his decision on the basis of the case as argued in the Family Court. Although the case as argued on appeal differs, it nevertheless fails upon full reconsideration.

[123] The appeal is dismissed. The children are to be returned to the United Kingdom as directed by Judge Coyle.

[124] The father is entitled to costs if the mother is not legally aided. Counsel may submit memoranda as to that fact, and quantum.

The analysis of the 'habitual residence' issue in the same case is instructive.

The unilateral purpose of one parent cannot change the habitual residence of a child, because to hold otherwise will go against the policy of the Hague Convention and provide encouragement for abduction and retention. But a very lengthy period of residence, even in such a situation, might eventually change a child's habitual residence. A length of stay in the country to which a child is taken is a factor to take into account, but only one factor, with the purpose of the stay and strength of ties to the existing state also to be taken into account. Even in cases where residence in another state is intended to be for a limited, defined period, followed by return to an existing habitual residence, that will not automatically lead to a finding that habitual residence remains in the old state. ... [I]t will depend on the circumstances of the particular case.[62]

The court made it clear that 'the enquiry into habitual residence had to be a broad factual enquiry, with the notion being free from technical rules which might produce rigidity and inconsistencies'.[63]

Similar complexities can be seen at work in *A v A (Children: Habitual Residence)* from the Supreme Court (United Kingdom: England & Wales).[64] In this case, there was a thorough review of the case law on habitual residence and the Court concluded with eight key points:

---

62 *RCL v APBL* [2012] NZHC 1292; HC/E/NZ 1231 [95].
63 ibid [99].
64 *A v A (Children: Habitual Residence)* [2013] UKSC 60; HC/E/UKe 1233.

- [H]abitual residence is a question of fact and not a legal concept such as domicile. There is no legal rule akin to that whereby a child automatically takes the domicile of his parents.
- Habitual residence for the purpose of the Brussels IIa Regulation must be interpreted consistently with the concept in the 1980 Hague Child Abduction Convention and the Family Law Act 1986.
- The test adopted by the European Court is 'the place which reflects some degree of integration by the child in a social and family environment' in the country concerned.
- It is now unlikely that the latter test would produce any different results from that hitherto adopted in the English courts under the 1986 Act and the Hague Child Abduction Convention.
- [T]he test adopted by the European Court is preferable to that earlier adopted by the English courts, being focused on the situation of the child, with the purposes and intentions of the parents being merely one of the relevant factors. The test derived from *R v Barnet London Borough Council, ex p Shah*[64a] should be abandoned when deciding the habitual residence of a child.
- The social and family environment of an infant or young child is shared with those (whether parents or others) upon whom [the child] is dependent. Hence it is necessary to assess the integration of that person or persons in the social and family environment of the country concerned.
- The essentially factual and individual nature of the inquiry into habitual residence should not be glossed with legal concepts which would produce a different result from that which the factual inquiry would produce.
- [I]t is possible that a child may have no country of habitual residence at a particular point in time.

5.3.2   The duty to make a return order

Once the applicant (left-behind person) has met the evidential burden of showing that there was a 'wrongful removal or retention' within the meaning of Article 3, a duty to return the child arises:

Article 12
Where a child has been wrongfully removed or retained in terms of Article 3 and, at the date of the commencement of the proceedings before the judicial or administrative authority of the Contracting State where the child is, a period of less than 1 year has elapsed from the date of the wrongful removal or retention, the authority concerned shall order the return of the child forthwith.

The judicial or administrative authority, even where the proceedings have been commenced after the expiration of the period of 1 year referred to in

64a [1983] 2 A.C. 309.

the preceding paragraph, shall also order the return of the child, unless it is demonstrated that the child is now settled in its new environment.

Where the judicial or administrative authority in the requested State has reason to believe that the child has been taken to another State, it may stay the proceedings or dismiss the application for the return of the child.

This Article 'forms an essential part of the Convention, specifying as it does those situations in which the judicial or administrative authorities of the State where the child is located are obliged to order its return' (Pérez-Vera 1980: para 106). There are two cases to consider: where a period of less than one year has elapsed since the wrongful removal/retention and up to the commencement of proceedings; and where a period of one year or more has elapsed within this timeframe. It can be noted that the duty set out in the first case in Article 12§1 emphasises the peremptory nature of the return order procedure; the return must be made 'forthwith'.

In the second case, Article 12§2 ensures that the duty to return still remains where the taking person and child have been in the country of refuge for a period of one year or more, subject to a finding that the child 'is now settled in its new environment'. The evidential burden to demonstrate such settlement will rest on the taking person to resist a return order. For ease of reference this route to avoid a return is referred to in this chapter as the 'settlement exception'. There are also other exceptions to the underlying duty to return. Most of these appear in Article 13 and there is also an exception contained in Article 20. These are explained in the following sections and, by way of introduction, Table 5.2 below indicates the proportion of cases that have relied on one or more of the various exceptions in litigation across all the contracting states.

In addition, Table 5.2 includes cases where there was no wrongful removal/retention on the basis of either a finding that the child was not habitually resident in the requesting state or that the applicant left-behind parent had no rights of custody. The data is derived from Lowe's statistical survey in respect of 269 applications in 2008, where the information was available. In 48 of these applications there was more than one reason given for judicial refusal (121 reasons in total). The combined reasons for judicial refusal are set out in Table 5.2.

Comparing these results with his previous surveys for 1999 and 2003, he concludes:

> Although in broad terms there is a common pattern for the reasons for refusal over the three surveys and, in particular, the most common successfully invoked exception has always been Article 13(1) b), there is a marked increase in refusals based on Article 13(1) b) in 2008. The second most common reason for refusal in 2008 was the child's objections, the third was a finding that the child was not habitually resident in the requesting State and the fourth was Article 12.
>
> (Lowe 2011a: 29)

Table 5.2 Reasons for judicial refusal

Reasons for refusal	Frequency	Percentage (%)
Child not habitually resident in requesting state	53	15
Applicant no rights of custody	28	8
Art 12	46	13
Art 13(1) a) not exercising rights of custody	23	7
Art 13(1) a) consent	16	5
Art 13(1) a) acquiescence	17	5
Art 13(1) b) grave risk	91	27
Child's objections	58	17
Art 20	2	1
Other	8	2
Total	**342**	**100**

Source: Lowe 2011a: 30.[65]

5.3.3   Exceptions from the duty to make a return order

The following sub-sections include an outline of the various 'exceptions' to the underlying duty to make a return order. These are:

- the 'settlement' exception – Article 12§2
- not exercising custody rights at time of removal/retention – Article 13§1(a)
- consent to removal/retention – Article 13§1(a)
- acquiescence to removal/retention – Article 13§1(a)
- grave risk of harm to child – Article 13§1(b)
- child objects to return – Article 13§2
- not permitted by human rights protection of the requested State – Article 20.

The exceptions founded on Article 13 are sometimes also referred to in the case law as 'defences'.

5.3.3.1   The settlement exception

Article 12§2 (see above) provides a limited exception to the return order in circumstances where the applicant left-behind person can demonstrate 'the child is now settled in its new environment'. As with several other areas of case law in respect of the Hague Convention of 1980, there have been divergent approaches to this provision across the contracting states:

A uniform interpretation has not emerged with regard to the concept of settlement; in particular whether it should be construed literally or rather in accordance with the policy objectives of the Convention. In jurisdictions

---

65 Lowe points out that 'what is recorded here are actual refusals and does not reflect the number of applications in which these exceptions had been argued unsuccessfully (2011a: 28).

favouring the latter approach the burden of proof on the abducting parent is clearly greater and the exception is more difficult to establish.[66]

In earlier cases there had been some debate whether settlement prompted an obligation not to return, or simply provided a discretion not to order a return. This matter was resolved in favour of the latter position by the House of Lords (United Kingdom: England & Wales) in *Re M (Children) (Abduction: Rights of Custody)*.[67] It can also be seen that where a taking person has deliberately concealed the whereabouts of the child, it would be inequitable if that provided an unjustified advantage in terms of the expiry of the one-year period. On the other hand, an automatic deduction of any period of time during which there was deliberate concealment might not provide the required flexibility for the court.

The Court of Appeal (United Kingdom: England & Wales) approached the matter in *Cannon v Cannon*[68] by examining more intensely the necessary elements of settlement in concealment cases. Lord Justice Thorpe concluded:

> 61. I would unhesitatingly uphold the well-recognised construction of the concept of settlement in Article 12(2): it is not enough to regard only the physical characteristics of settlement. Equal regard must be paid to the emotional and psychological elements. In cases of concealment and subterfuge the burden of demonstrating the necessary elements of emotional and psychological settlement is much increased. The judges in the Family Division should not apply a rigid rule of disregard but they should look critically at any alleged settlement that is built on concealment and deceit especially if the defendant is a fugitive from criminal justice.
>
> 62. Even if settlement is established on the facts the court retains a residual discretion to order a return under the Convention. The discretion is specifically conferred by Article 18. But for Article 18 I would have been inclined to have infer the existence of a discretion under Article 12, although I recognise the power of the contrary arguments.[69]

5.3.3.2   Approach to Article 13 exceptions/defences

Article 13
Notwithstanding the provisions of the preceding Article, the judicial or administrative authority of the requested State is not bound to order the return of the child if the person, institution or other body which opposes its return establishes that –

---

66 McEleavy and Fiorini (n 56).
67 [2007] UKHL 55, [2008] 1 AC 1288; HC/E/UKe 937.
68 [2004] EWCA Civ 1330, [2005] 1 FLR 169, [2005] 1 WLR 32.
69 *Cannon v Cannon* [2004] EWCA Civ 1330, [2005] 1 FLR 169; HC/E/UKe 598, [61–2].

a) the person, institution or other body having the care of the person of the child was not actually exercising the custody rights at the time of removal or retention, or had consented to or subsequently acquiesced in the removal or retention; or

b) there is a grave risk that his or her return would expose the child to physical or psychological harm or otherwise place the child in an intolerable situation.

The judicial or administrative authority may also refuse to order the return of the child if it finds that the child objects to being returned and has attained an age and degree of maturity at which it is appropriate to take account of its views.

In considering the circumstances referred to in this Article, the judicial and administrative authorities shall take into account the information relating to the social background of the child provided by the Central Authority or other competent authority of the child's habitual residence.

The drafters of the Convention envisaged that any routes to mitigate the inevitability of a return order should be narrowly construed: 'they are to be interpreted in a restrictive fashion if the Convention is not to become a dead letter', and furthermore, 'a systematic invocation of the said exceptions … would lead to the collapse of the whole structure of the Convention by depriving it of the spirit of mutual confidence which is its inspiration' (Pérez-Vera 1980, para 34).

However, as authoritative commentators on the case law have previously observed, 'a desire to give effect to the primary goal of promoting return and thereby preventing an over-exploitation of the exceptions, had led to an additional test of exceptionality being added to the exceptions'.[70] This additional test of exceptionality was laid to rest by the House of Lords (United Kingdom: England & Wales) in *Re M (Children) (Abduction: Rights of Custody)* by Baroness Hale:

> I have no doubt at all that it is wrong to import any test of exceptionality into the exercise of discretion under the Hague Convention. The circumstances in which return may be refused are themselves exceptions to the general rule. That in itself is sufficient exceptionality. It is neither necessary nor desirable to import an additional gloss into the Convention.[71]

As with the 'settlement exception' (section 5.3.3.1), the evidential burden of proof to establish one or more of the Article 13 exceptions to achieve a non-return order rests with the person opposing the return order, i.e. the taking person. Even if one or more of the exceptions in Article 13 has been made out, the court will still need to consider whether it nevertheless has available an overriding discretion to go

---

70 McEleavy and Fiorini (n 56).

71 *Re M (Children) (Abduction: Rights of Custody)* [2007] UKHL 55, [2008] 1 AC 1288; HC/E/ UKe 937 [40].

ahead with a return order rather than a non-return order. Again, there are differences of approach by various contracting states on this issue and it is dealt with in further detail in section 5.3.4.

5.3.3.3   Failure to exercise custody rights

One of the objectives of the Convention is that a person should not be able to rely on a breach of rights of custody that have, in fact, been overtaken by subsequent events, or have gone stale. As can be seen from Table 5.1 above, judicial refusals are rarely based on this exception:

> The Convention includes no definition of 'actual exercise' of custody, but this provision expressly refers to the care of the child. Thus, if the text of this provision is compared with that of Article 5 which contains a definition of custody rights, it can be seen that custody is exercised effectively when the custodian is concerned with the care of the child's person, even if, for perfectly valid reasons (illness, education, etc.) in a particular case, the child and its guardian do not live together. It follows from this that the question of whether custody is actually exercised or not must be determined by the individual judge, according to the circumstances of each particular case.
>
> (Pérez-Vera 1980: para 115)

It will be recalled that the failure to exercise custody rights is also an integral element to the way in which the Convention defines a wrongful removal or retention within the meaning of Article 3 (section 5.3.1.1). A distinction in the meaning of the failure actually to exercise rights of custody as it appears in Articles 3 and 12 was made in a High Court (Family Division) case (United Kingdom: England & Wales):

> Article 13(a) refers to rights of custody which are not being actually exercised by the person who has the care of the person of the child: this contrasts with Article 3 which refers to rights of custody generally. The Article 13(a) defence in this context is thus limited to the situation in which the child's actual caretaker is not actually taking care of him. This is a much narrower situation, and plainly does not apply in the instant case.[72]

It is perhaps unsurprising, given the underlying central policy theme to support the return order procedure, that in many jurisdictions there has been some generosity in viewing even the applicant's limited engagement with a child as sufficient to rank as an exercise of rights of custody for the purpose of Article 13(a).

---

72 *Re W (Abduction: Procedure)* [1995] 1 FLR 878; HC/E/UKe 37.

The Supreme Court of Ireland has held[73] that a father's imprisonment did not divest him of his rights of custody under the Convention. The court referred to other situations where a parent might have a low-level input to the routine care of a child: for example, where a parent was disabled, incapacitated, or in a job which necessitated long absences from home. On the facts, his children had visited him in prison and he had taken a sufficient interest to obtain a prohibited steps order. However, differences in approach remain across the contracting states. Some have made it clear that what is required is quite clear and unequivocal evidence of abandonment in order to establish a failure to exercise custody rights; others set the threshold somewhat lower.[74]

5.3.3.4 The consent exception

Earlier case law had considered whether the issue of consent was better understood in terms of the concept of wrongful removal/retention as defined in Article 3 rather than in Article 13(a). However, it would appear that the majority view now is that it can be better understood exclusively within Article 13(a).[75] Equally, previous case law that determined only clear and compelling evidence of consent in writing[76] would suffice, appears to have been overtaken with a more practical and fact-specific understanding of consent.[77]

For example, the Austrian Supreme Court[78] has observed that consent may be implicit but it must refer to a permanent change of residence and can be evidenced by a statement or derived from a set of circumstances. The key point was the nature of the taking person's understanding of the left-behind person. It would appear that both consent and acquiescence are ultimately questions of fact to be determined on their merits in each case.

5.3.3.5 Acquiescence

It would seem that the practical distinction between *consent* and *acquiescence* is one of timing (Ranton 2009: 20). Consent will generally predate the removal or retention, whereas acquiescence occurs after such removal or retention. Earlier case law identified different approaches for 'active' and 'passive' acquiescence, but the House of Lords (United Kingdom: England & Wales) in *Re H (Abduction: Acquiescence)*[79] stressed that the key question was whether the subjective state of

---

73 [2000] 3 IR 390.
74 Compare the cases of *O v O* 2002 SC 430; HC/E/UKs 507 and *S v S* 2003 SLT 344; HC/E/UKs 577.
75 For example in Australia: *Director-General, Department of Child Safety v Stratford* [2005] Fam CA 1115; HC/E/UKe 830.
76 *Re W (Abduction: Procedure)* [1995] 1 FLR 878; HC/E/UKe 37.
77 See for example *Re K (Abduction: Consent)* [1997] 2 FLR 212; HC/E/UKe 55.
78 1Ob256/09t, Oberster Gerichtshof; HC/E/AT 1049.
79 [1998] AC 72.

mind of the left-behind parent constituted acquiescence. The only departure from this would be where any words or actions of the left-behind parent unequivocally showed, and led the abducting parent to believe, that the left-behind parent would not assert his or her right to summary return; then the court would be likely to hold that the left-behind parent had acquiesced.

The cases also indicate that where the parties are merely undertaking negotiations with each other about where the child is to live, such negotiations will not amount to 'acquiescence'.[80] To take the opposite view would have undermined the support provided by the Hague Convention of 1980 to achieving voluntary settlement where possible.[81]

5.3.3.6   Grave risk of harm/intolerable situation

As can be seen from Table 5.1 above, this exception/defence is the most frequently litigated exception in Hague proceedings. It is therefore important that the scope of behaviours it may cover appropriately reflects the underlying philosophy of the Hague Convention of 1980 and achieves an appropriate balance between the provision of a robust return order procedure while taking into account children's interests in individual cases that might justify a departure from the standard process.

Inevitably, different contracting states have taken differing approaches to identifying the precise nature and scope of the exception. The statistical surveys undertaken under the auspices of the Hague Conference have indicated, in respect of the last survey of data relating to 2008, that globally: 'the large majority (72%) of taking persons were the "primary carer" of the child' (Lowe 2011a: 6). In such cases there are likely to be stronger child welfare justifications for a non-return order than cases where the taking person has not had a primary carer role.

Some contracting states will only accept the grave risk defence in genuinely atypical situations. In other states, there are indications of a more liberal approach. For example, in the United States, one commentator found from a study of 47 published US state and federal court opinions involving the Convention and allegations of domestic violence perpetrated by the left-behind parent that US courts were reluctant to employ the provisions under the Convention that could prevent children from being returned to the mother's batterer (Vesneski, Lindhorst and Edleson 2011).

The European Court of Human Rights (ECtHR) has moved from the former to the latter position in its analysis of the issue. The most recent stance is represented in the more child-centric case of *Neulinger and Shuruk v Switzerland*. This case concerned a child born in Israel in 2003 to a Swiss mother and an Israeli father. The father had joined a religious sect and the custody of the child had been withdrawn from him on account of the atmosphere of fear that he had created in the family

---

80 For example *Re I (Abduction: Acquiescence)* [1999] 1 FLR 778.
81 Hague Convention of 1980 art 7(c).

home. The mother secretly took the child to Switzerland in June 2005 and the father filed his return petition a year later. The first instance court in Switzerland found a grave risk of harm and refused to order a return of the child to Israel. This was confirmed on appeal, but in August 2007 the Swiss Federal Court ordered a return, finding no basis for the grave risk exception to be upheld. The mother and child petitioned the ECtHR in September 2007. Interim measures were applied not to return the child. On 8 January 2009, the ECtHR ruled by a 4 to 3 majority, that there had not been a breach of the mother and child's right to family life under Article 8 of the European Convention on Human Rights (ECHR).[82] The applicants requested in March 2009 that the case be referred to the Grand Chamber of the ECtHR. The Grand Chamber gave judgment on 6 July 2010,[83] holding by 16 to 1 that, if the return order were enforced, there would be a violation of the mother and child's right to family life under Article 8 of the ECHR. The ECtHR held, inter alia, that Article 8 of the ECHR required that a child's return could not be ordered mechanically whenever the Hague Convention of 1980 was applicable, and that what was in the child's best interest had to be assessed in each case. The Court held that:

> 138 It follows from art 8 [ECHR] that a child's return cannot be ordered automatically or mechanically when the Hague Convention is applicable. The child's best interests, from a personal development perspective, will depend on a variety of individual circumstances, in particular his age and level of maturity, the presence or absence of his parents and his environment and experiences. For that reason, those best interests must be assessed in each individual case. That task is primarily one for the domestic authorities, which often have the benefit of direct contact with the persons concerned. To that end they enjoy a certain margin of appreciation, which remains subject, however, to a European supervision whereby the Court reviews under the Convention the decisions that those authorities have taken in the exercise of that power.
>
> 139 In addition, the Court must ensure that the decision-making process leading to the adoption of the impugned measures by the domestic court was fair and allowed those concerned to present their case fully. To that end the Court must ascertain whether the domestic courts conducted an in-depth examination of the entire family situation and of a whole series of factors, in particular of a factual, emotional, psychological, material and medical nature, and made a balanced and reasonable assessment of the respective interests of each person, with a constant concern for determining what the best solution would be for the abducted child in the context of an application for his return to his country of origin.[84]

82 *Neulinger and Shuruk v Switzerland* (Application No 41615/07), Grand Chamber (6 July 2010), (2012) 54 EHRR 31; HC/E/1323.
83 ibid.
84 ibid paras 138–9.

The judgment has prompted some controversy as the notion of a full-scale welfare inquiry to be applied when the exception is raised in the courts of the country of refuge arguably conflicts with the underlying policy of the Hague Convention of 1980 to have such issues debated in the courts of the *requesting* states. The apparent implication of *Neulinger* was that national courts should abandon their traditionally restrictive approach to the interpretation of the exceptions and instead should carry out an in-depth examination of the best interests of the child (Walker 2010; Paton 2012). Chamberland (2012) argues that the return of the child under the Hague Convention of 1980 should not be subordinate to a consideration of the best interests of the child.

Equally, it is important that the jurisdictions of the ECtHR and the ECJ are reasonably aligned in this field and do not travel along contrasting pathways (Walker and Beaumont 2011). The Supreme Court (United Kingdom: England & Wales) has also doubted the recommendation in *Neulinger* to conduct an extensive welfare enquiry. See Case Study 5.2 below.

Case study 5.2

In re S (A Child) (Abduction: Rights of Custody) [2012] UKSC 10, [2012] 2 AC 257

Facts: The Australian father and the British mother, who also had Australian citizenship, lived together unmarried in Australia. Their son was born and habitually resident there. In 2011 the mother returned to live in England, taking the son with her without the father's consent or the permission of an Australian court. The removal of the son was thus in breach of the father's custody rights under Australian law and was therefore wrongful for the purposes of Article 3 of the Hague Convention on the Civil Aspects of International Child Abduction (1980). The father issued proceedings in England under section 1(2) of the Child Abduction and Custody Act 1985 and Article 12 of the Convention for the immediate return of the son to Australia. The mother resisted the application in reliance on Article 13(b) of the Convention on the grounds that to order the son's immediate return would put him at grave risk of being placed in an intolerable situation. She did not give oral evidence before the judge but adduced written evidence, including emails and texts, to explain why her life with the father in Australia had become so intolerable that she had returned with the son to England. In doing so she made serious allegations against the father which she linked with medical evidence about the state of her psychological health while she had been in Australia. The father put forward by undertakings measures to protect the mother and the son if they returned to Australia. The judge concluded that the mother was genuinely convinced that she had been the victim of domestic abuse, that her anxieties were based on objective reality and that the protective measures offered by the father would not obviate the grave risk that, if returned to Australia, the son would be placed in an intolerable situation, and he accordingly refused to order the son's return. The Court of Appeal, holding that the crucial question for the judge was whether the mother's asserted risk, insecurities and anxieties were realistically and reasonably held in the face of the package of protective measures which could be put in place and declining to accept that the mother's subjective perception of risks on return leading to an intolerable situation for the child was a permissible ground for refusing a return order, allowed the father's appeal and ordered the son's return.

On the mother's appeal—

Held: Allowing the appeal, that the terms of Article 13(b) of the Hague Convention were plain, needing neither elaboration nor gloss; that the critical question, where on an application under Article 12 a defence under Article 13(b) was raised, was what would happen if, with the parent who had wrongfully removed him, the child were returned; that if the court concluded that, on return, that parent would suffer such anxieties that their effect on her mental health would create a situation which was intolerable for the child, the child should not be returned, and it mattered not whether those anxieties would be reasonable or unreasonable, although the extent to which there would, objectively, be good cause for such anxieties would nevertheless be relevant to the court's assessment of her mental state if the child were returned; that it was for the trial judge, whether or not he had received oral evidence, to make the judgment about the level of risk which Article 13(b) required, and an appellate court should not overturn his judgment unless, whether by reference to the law or to the evidence, it had not been open to the judge to make it; that, although the judge had not heard oral evidence, he had carefully studied the written evidence which revealed that several of the allegations made by the mother against the father were admitted or could not realistically be denied; that it had been open to the judge to decide that in the light of all the evidence the interim protective measures offered by the father did not obviate the grave risk to the son if he were returned to Australia; and that, accordingly, it had not been open to the Court of Appeal to substitute its contrary view for that of the judge (post, paras 6, 7, 27, 29, 31–2, 34, 35, 36).

In re J (A Child) (Custody Rights: Jurisdiction) [2006] 1 AC 80 (HL(E)) applied.
In re E (Children) (Abduction: Custody Appeal) [2012] 1 AC 144 (SC(E)) explained.

Per curiam: In the determination of an application under the Hague Convention for a summary order for a child's return to the state of his habitual residence it would be entirely inappropriate for the court to conduct an in-depth examination of the entire family situation and of factors of a factual, emotional, psychological, material and medical nature (post, paras 37, 38).

Dictum in *Neulinger and Shuruk v Switzerland* [2011] 1 FLR 122 para 39 (GC) doubted.

Decision of the Court of Appeal in *S v C* [2011] EWCA Civ 1385, [2012] 1 FCR 172 reversed.

It can be appreciated that, in general, some level of psychological harm is almost inevitable in the context of parental child abduction. However, something more than the expected level of harm is required, after all there must be a 'grave' risk, in other words, something very serious. One factor that may take a case into this higher level of risk is where the court is satisfied that an established pattern of domestic violence may have induced the removal or retention in the first place.[85] However, it must be remembered that the wording of Article 13(1)(b) requires the exposure of the *child* to physical or psychological harm. Domestic violence aimed at a *parent* will only be relevant to the extent that such action can be shown to be damaging to the child.

One category of case which has appeared in recent years concerns allegations of a grave risk of harm owing to the security situation pertaining in the country of the child's habitual residence. It would seem that it does not matter whether it is actually a state of war or terrorist activity, or some other civil commotion. What is important is to assess the actual level of risk of harm to the child from the available evidence. The argument was not accepted in an English Court of Appeal case[86] relating to an Israeli mother who had removed her child to England and argued that a return to Israel would expose her child to the difficult security situation there: see further (Schuz 2003). The House of Lords (United Kingdom: England & Wales) in *Re M (Children) (Abduction: Rights of Custody)* also rejected the argument that the moral and political climate in Zimbabwe meant that children generally would be at grave risk of psychological harm, or should not be expected to tolerate living there.[87]

One factor which could heighten the risk of harm is where the court is not satisfied that there are sufficient institutional protective arrangements in the country of the child's habitual residence.[88] As we have seen the Revised Brussels II Regulation (section 5.2.3) provides that, in intra-EU cases (other than ones involving Denmark), a court *cannot* refuse to return a child on the basis of the grave risk of harm exception if it is established that adequate arrangements have been

---

85 See *Sonderup v Tondelli* 2001 (1) SA 1171 (CC) (Constitutional Court of South Africa); *Walsh v. Walsh No. 99–1747* (1st Cir, July 25, 2000) (US Court of Appeals for the First Circuit).

86 See *Re S (A Child) (Abduction: Grave Risk of Harm)* [2002] EWCA Civ 908, [2002] 3 FCR 43; HC/E/UKe 469.

87 *Re M (Children) (Abduction: Rights of Custody)* [2007] UKHL 55, [2008] 1 AC 1288; HC/E UKe 937.

88 For example see *TB v JB (formerly JH) (Abduction: Grave Risk of Harm)* [2001] 2 FLR 515; *W v W* [2004] 2 FLR 499.

made to secure the protection of the child after return. Equally, in other Hague Convention cases it would appear that the discretion that is available to make a non-return order in the face of the exception having been established is also quite constrained (see section 5.3.4).

5.3.3.7   The child's objections

This exception is of particular interest in international child law as it touches upon the extent to which a child's 'autonomy rights' will be respected (section 1.2.1.2). The requirement is not only that a child 'objects' but also that the child 'has attained an age and degree of maturity at which it is appropriate to take account of its views'. The question of a child's maturity is a matter of fact in which the court is required to exercise its judgment on the basis of the available evidence. The key question is about maturity rather than merely chronological age.

Some of the cases have shown the practical difficulty of ordering a return in the face of a child who persistently objects to it.[89] The older the individual, the more likely that greater weight will be given to that child's views. Pérez-Vera (1980: para 30) concluded that 'it would be very difficult to accept that a child of, for example, 15 years of age, should be returned against its will'. However, the courts will be wary to exercise their discretion to refuse a return order where the evidence shows that a parent has heavily influenced and/or coached the child to adopt those objections.[90]

Although there are differences of approach across the contracting states in approaching this exception (McEleavy 2008), the majority do appear to accept that a mere preference for the state of refuge will not be sufficient. For example, in the Ontario Superior Court of Justice (Canada) in *Crnkovich v. Hortensius* the judge held, inter alia, that:

> [34] There has been considerable jurisprudence defining and commenting on the meaning and breadth of the verb 'objects'. In *R (A Minor) (Abduction), Re* [1992] 1 FLR 105 (Eng. C.A.), Bracewell J. said, "The word 'objects' imports a strength of feeling which goes far beyond the usual ascertainment of the wishes of the child in a custody dispute. The passage is oft quoted in cases dealing with this Article 13 issue.
>
> [35] To meet the 'objects' criteria, it must be shown that the child displayed a strong sense of disagreement to returning to the jurisdiction of his habitual residence. He must be adamant in expressing his objection. The objection cannot be ascertained by simply weighing the pros and cons of the two

89 For example in *Re HB (Abduction: Child's Objections) (No 2)* [1998] 1 FLR 564.
90 See *AQ v JQ* Outer House of the Court of Session (Scotland) (12 December 2001); HC/E/ UK 415.

competing jurisdictions, such as in a best interests analysis. It must be some-thing stronger than a mere expression of preference.[91]

As we have seen, Article 11(2) of the Revised Brussels II Regulation (section 5.2.3) establishes a presumption supporting the child's participation rights in proceed-ings. The House of Lords (United Kingdom: England &Wales) determined in *Re D (A Child) (Abduction: Rights of Custody)*[92] that this provision will apply in every Hague return application reaching the court, and Baroness Hale observed that this would lead generally to children being heard more frequently in Hague pro-ceedings. This would require more than the taking person presenting the child's views; separate representation of the child may also be required. In a subsequent House of Lords case, *Re M (Abduction: Zimbabwe)*,[93] it was pointed out that child objection and settlement cases (section 5.3.3.1) were very likely to be combined and the court must consider at the outset how best to hear the child's views.

Ordering separate representation would not be automatic, even in all child objections cases, but this might be more routinely ordered in settlement cases. The question for the directions judge would be 'whether separate representation of the child will add enough to the court's understanding of the issues that arise under the Hague Convention to justify the intrusion, the expense and the delay that may result'.[94] This exception also raises the issue of the extent to which the separate representation of children who object should be arranged (Boezaart 2013).

5.3.3.8   Article 20

Article 20
The return of the child under the provisions of Article 12 may be refused if this would not be permitted by the fundamental principles of the requested State relating to the protection of human rights and fundamental freedoms.[95]

This Article provides the court with an additional, but little used, discretion (see Table 5.1 above) to refuse a return order on the basis that otherwise the return of the child would breach the fundamental principles of human rights of the country of refuge. In the United Kingdom, Article 20 was not expressly incorporated in its domestic legislation, the Child Abduction and Custody Act 1985. It was thought that the violation of primary human rights was likely to be a breach of Article 13(1)(b) and therefore this Article would have been otiose. Baroness Hale observed

---

91 *Crnkovich v. Hortensius* [2009] WDFL 337, 62 RFL (6th) 351, 2008; HC/E/CA1028 at [34–35] (O'Connor J).
92 [2006] UKHL 51, [2007] 1 AC 619.
93 [2007] UKHL 55, [2008] 1 FLR 251.
94 ibid (Baroness Hale).
95 Hague Convention of 1980 art 20.

in *Re D (A Child) (Abduction: Rights of Custody)*[96] that Article 20 had in essence been given effect through the adoption of the Human Rights Act 1998.

The trend appears to be that this provision will be used only where there is an *obvious* conflict with fundamental principles of human rights. For example, Article 20 was considered by the full court of the Family Court of Australia in *Director-General, Department of Families, Youth and Community Care v Rhonda May Bennett*,[97] which noted that the regulation giving effect to Article 20 was extremely narrow and should only be invoked exceptionally where the return of a child would utterly 'shock the conscience' of the court or offend all notions of due process. It was held that the return of a child of Aboriginal or Torres Strait Islander heritage to a foreign country would not per se breach any fundamental principle in Australia relating to the protection of human rights and fundamental freedoms.

The few reported English cases that refer to Article 20 suggest a reluctance to use this provision to refuse a return order. In *NJC v NPC*,[98] the Inner House of the Court of Session (United Kingdom: Scotland) rejected a father's argument that the Convention proceedings had breached his right to a fair trial under Article 6 of the ECHR; he may not have been able to focus his submissions as a professional lawyer would, but he had had every opportunity to address the relevant issues.

In *Re M (Children) (Abduction: Rights of Custody)*[99] Baroness Hale declined to accept arguments based on Article 20 and the ECHR. She held that returning the children against their will would be a graver interference with their rights than failing to do so would be with the rights of the father. Calculating the proportionality of interfering with his rights against the proportionality of interfering with the rights of the mother and the children would lead to the same result.

In the *Nottinghamshire County Council v KB and KB*, a case from the Supreme Court of Ireland,[100] an interesting distinction is made between the Article 13 exceptions and Article 20. The latter, in its view, 'does not so much create an exception as recognise one'.[101] The Court's analysis of Article 20 is instructive:

> Article 20 does not ask whether the law, or even the constitutional law, of the requested state *differs* from that of the requesting State. If it did, it would be difficult to see how the Convention could function effectively. In such circumstances Article 20 might not merely prevent the return of children <u>from</u> Ireland, but might just as effectively inhibit the return of children <u>to</u> Ireland. The text of the Convention makes it clear however that this is <u>not</u> the test. The focus of Article 20 is not upon what occurs or may occur in the requesting State (in this case England). On the contrary it is what occurs in the

96 [2007] UKHL 55 [19], [2008] 1 AC 1288; HC/E/UKe 937.
97 [2000] Fam CA 253; HC/E/AU 275.
98 [2008] CSIH 34, 2008 SC 571.
99 [2007] UKHL 55 [19], [2008] 1 AC 1288; HC/E/UKe 937.
100 *Nottinghamshire County Council v KB and KB* [2011] IESC 48; HC/E/IE 1139.
101 ibid [21] (O'Donnell J).

requested State (the return) which is the focus for the Court of the requested State (in this case Ireland). The concept of "return" directs attention to at least two relevant matters. First, that the child has a prior connection with the State requesting the return (defined under the Convention as the State of habitual residence) to which he or she may be going back. Second, that a difference in the legal regime, and even a constitutional difference, will not itself suffice to trigger Article 20. The test is rather whether what is proposed or contemplated in the requesting State is something which departs so markedly from the essential scheme and order envisaged by the Constitution and is such a direct consequence of the Court's order that return is not permitted by the Constitution.[102]

5.3.4   Exercising discretion

Even if the taking person can demonstrate that one or more of the exceptions discussed in the previous sections applies on the facts, a non-return order will *not* be given *automatically*, but relies on the court's further consideration of whether to make a return order or not as a matter of its exercise of discretion. As with other areas of the Convention, different approaches to determining the nature of this discretion and the particular factors that may be taken into account and the extent to which they can be relied upon have varied across the contracting states. For example, the High Court of Australia has arguably undertaken a departure at times from the international consensus in its approach to some of the exceptions/defences and a tendency for the court to refuse to make return orders appeared (Kirby 2010).

There have been some differences in approach concerning the nature of the discretion applicable to the exceptions according to where the various discretions are located in the legal framework of the Convention. The settlement exception in Article 12(2) can be contrasted with the exceptions in Article 13. The latter Article *expressly* provides the competent authorities with discretion to make a return order, whereas the former does not.

The permissive language used in the Article 20 exception also expressly provides discretion. Furthermore, Article 18 appears as arguably a general discretionary default power available where other claims to appeal to an authoritative source of discretionary power run out. Article 18 provides that '[t]he provisions of this Chapter do not limit the power of a judicial or administrative authority to order the return of the child at any time':

> ... This provision ... underlines the non-exhaustive and complementary nature of the Convention. In fact, it authorizes the competent authorities to order the return of the child by invoking other provisions more favourable

102 ibid [54] (O'Donnell J).

to the attainment of this end. This may happen particularly in the situations envisaged in the [settlement exception].

(Pérez-Vera 1980: para 112)

Although earlier cases had based the discretion stage of determination on the text of Article 18, this approach was expressly rejected in *Re M (Children) (Abduction: Rights of Custody)*,[103] where it was pointed out that Article 18 did not confer any new power to order the return of a child under the Convention: it merely contemplated powers conferred by domestic law. The court retains its discretion to make a return order.

What has remained controversial in the developing case law and across the contracting states is the *approach* that may be taken towards applying these categories of discretion. In earlier cases there had been some debate whether the settlement exception prompted an obligation not to return, or simply provided discretion not to order a return. This matter was resolved in favour of the latter position by the House of Lords (United Kingdom: England & Wales) in *Re M (Children) (Abduction: Rights of Custody)*. This case provided a comprehensive review of the exercise of discretion with regard to the exceptions to a return order.

Case study 5.3

Re M (Children) (Abduction: Rights of Custody) [2007] UKHL 55, [2008] 1 AC 1288: HC/E/UKe 937

Facts: Two girls who were born in Zimbabwe to Zimbabwean parents lived there with their father after their parents separated early in 2001. In March 2005 they were brought secretly to England by their mother who claimed asylum. The asylum claim was refused in April 2005 but she and the children remained in England because of a moratorium on the return of failed asylum seekers to Zimbabwe. The girls were not happy in England at first and in September 2005 they contacted their father asking him to come and take them home. However, it was not until a year later that the father commenced proceedings under the Hague Convention on the Civil Aspects of International Child Abduction 1980, as scheduled to the Child Abduction and Custody Act 1985, for their return. The English central authority did not receive notification from the Zimbabwean central authority until January 2007 and proceedings were finally issued in May 2007, more than two years after the children had been removed. By that time the girls, who were then 13 and 10 years old, felt settled in their new home and did not want to return. The judge found that the children were indeed settled in England, and so he was under no duty to order their return

103 [2007] UKHL 55, [2008] 1 AC 1288; HC/E/UKe 937.

under Article 12 of the Convention; that they genuinely objected to being returned to Zimbabwe; and that they were of an age and maturity which made it appropriate for him to take account of their views under Article 13. However, he decided that the case was not exceptional and he thus declined to exercise his discretion to refuse to order the girls' immediate return. The Court of Appeal upheld his decision.

On appeal by the mother, with the girls intervening—

Held: (1) (Lord Rodger of Earlsferry dissenting) that once a child had become settled for the purposes of Article 12 the court still had a discretion to return him within the Convention procedures (post, paras 1–5, 30–31, 59).

(2) That when exercising the discretion under the Convention there were general policy considerations, such as the swift return of abducted children, comity between contracting states and the deterrence of abduction, which might be weighed against the interests of the child in the individual case; that the Convention discretion was at large and the court was entitled to take into account the various aspects of the Convention policy alongside the circumstances which gave the court a discretion in the first place, and the wider considerations of the child's rights and welfare; that the weight to be given to the Convention considerations and to the interests of the child would vary enormously, as would the extent to which it would be appropriate to investigate such other welfare considerations; that it did not necessarily follow that the Convention objectives should always be given any more weight than any other consideration; and that the further away one got from the speedy return envisaged by the Convention the less weighty those general Convention objectives must be, since the major objective of the Convention could not be met (post, paras 1–2, 7–8, 31–2, 38–9, 41–4, 47–8, 59).

In re J (A Child) (Custody Rights: Jurisdiction) [2006] 1 AC 80 (HL(E)) considered.

(3) That the circumstances in which the Convention itself provided that return might be refused were themselves exceptions to the general rule which amounted to sufficient exceptionality; that it was neither necessary nor desirable to import an additional gloss into the Convention; and that, accordingly, a judge did not need to find something exceptional in a case before he could refuse to order return under the Convention (post, paras 1–2, 8, 34–7, 40, 59).

Zaffino v Zaffino (Abduction: Children's Views) [2006] 1 FLR 410 (CA) and *Vigreux v Michel* [2006] 2 FLR 1180 (CA) disapproved.

(4) That in cases where the child objected to being returned the range of considerations might be even wider than those under the other exceptions to ordering immediate return; that taking account of a child's views did not

mean that those views would always be determinative or even presumptively so, but that was far from saying that a child's objections should only prevail in the most exceptional circumstances; and that the older the child was the greater the weight her objections were likely to carry (post, paras 1–2, 8, 46–7, 57, 59).

(5) Allowing the appeal, that, since the trial judge had erroneously regarded the case as needing to be exceptional before he should exercise his discretion to refuse return, it was open to the House to reach its own conclusion; that, having considered the facts and that the children felt fully settled in England and wanted to stay, the policy of the Convention could carry little weight; that the children should not be made to suffer for the sake of general deterrence of the evil of child abduction worldwide; and that, accordingly, the father's proceedings would be dismissed (post, paras 1–2, 8, 34–6, 49, 52, 54–6, 58–9).

Decision of the Court of Appeal [2007] EWCA Civ 992 reversed.

As regards the grave risk/intolerable exception, the Supreme Court (United Kingdom: England & Wales)[104] has held (see Case study 5.2) that although technically the establishment by a respondent of this exception confers upon the court only a discretion not to order the child's return, '[i]n reality, however, it is impossible to conceive of circumstances in which, once such a risk is found to exist, it would be a legitimate exercise of the discretion nevertheless to order the child's return'.

5.4   International parental abduction and non-convention countries

The Hague Convention of 1980 has been successful in many respects in securing the prompt return of children to the country of habitual residence prior to removal. An increasing number of states have ratified the Convention.[105] The level of judicial and administrative co-operation has grown and become more sophisticated with the advent, for example, of international judicial seminars where the details of the Convention's mechanics can be fully aired. However, there remains the very significant problem of resolving international parental abductions where the taking person chooses to go to a country that has not ratified the Convention. One commentator divides the states that have not become parties to the Hague Convention into two categories: those with a principled objection to the Convention such as some of the Islamic states; and those that do not have such a principled objection but have not yet ratified it such as India (Sharma and Viswanathan 2011).

104 *In re S (A Child) (Abduction: Rights of Custody)* [2012] UKSC 10, [2012] 2 AC 257 para 5.
105 At the time of writing 91 states had ratified the Hague Convention of 1980.

Where a taking person does remove a child to a country that has not ratified the Hague Convention of 1980 and/or where there is no relevant regional instrument, the court will need to consider and balance the interests of the child alongside the general international policy in this area; for example, the requirement under the Convention on the Rights of the Child to prevent the illicit transfer and non-return of children abroad[106] (section 5.2.1). In the absence of any amicable, voluntary solution between the taking and left-behind person, the latter must attempt to commence proceedings in the domestic courts of the country of refuge.

The Scottish Government's website contains the following caution:

> In some Islamic countries, non-Muslim mothers have very little chance of winning custody and return of your child may not be an option. The Foreign and Commonwealth Office can provide advice on the options available to you and practical information about the customs and laws of the foreign country.[107]

For countries that have already ratified the Hague Convention of 1980 the choice of approach has been between favouring a focus on the child's individual welfare or applying Convention case law analogously to non-convention countries. *In Re J (A Child) (Return to Foreign Jurisdiction: Convention Rights)*,[108] the House of Lords (United Kingdom: England & Wales) favoured a child-centric approach. See Case Study 5.4 below.

Case study 5.4

Re J (A child) (Return to foreign jurisdiction: Convention rights) [2005] UKHL 40, [2006] 1 AC 80; HC/E/UKe 801

Facts: The mother was born in the United Kingdom and had dual British and Saudi Arabian citizenship. She was raised largely in Saudi Arabia until the age of 16 when she was educated in Britain. After completing her education she returned to Saudi Arabia and married the father, a Saudi national, in accordance with Shariah law. Their child spent his early years in Saudi Arabia. In mid-2002 mother and child came to the United Kingdom and, with the father's consent, arranged to stay for a year while the mother studied for a master's degree. During the course of the year the marriage failed and the mother decided that she did not wish to return to Saudi Arabia. In May 2003 she presented a divorce petition in England and also applied to

---

106 CRC art 11(2).
107 Scottish Government website http://www.scotland.gov.uk/Topics/Justice/law/17867/fm-children-root/18533/13579/13588 (accessed 27 October 2013).
108 [2005] UKHL 40, [2006] 1 AC 80; HC/E/UKe 801.

the British Muslim authorities for a divorce under Shariah law. The father applied for a stay of the divorce proceedings so that the matter could be dealt with in Saudi Arabia according to Shariah law and a specific issue order, pursuant to section 8 of the Children Act 1989, that the child be summarily returned to Saudi Arabia. The judge refused to make the order. The decisive factor in his reasoning was that the father had raised, and then withdrawn, allegations against the mother which would, if raised before a Shariah court, have disastrous consequences for the mother and thereby seriously damage the child's interests. The Court of Appeal reversed the judge's decision on the ground that he had given that particular concern more weight than the evidence justified.

On appeal by the mother—

Held:

(1) allowing the appeal, that whether the father was likely to resurrect his allegations against the mother was a matter which depended on the judge's evaluation of the father's oral evidence, involving findings of credibility and primary fact with which an appeal court was not entitled to interfere; that once those findings had been made they became factors to be weighed in the balance in the exercise of the judge's discretion; that an appellate court was not entitled to interfere with the judge's discretion unless his decision was plainly wrong; that the Court of Appeal had not found that the judge's decision had been based on error; and that, accordingly, on that ground alone the appeal should be allowed (post, paras 1–4, 10–12, 46–8).

Piglowska v Piglowski [1999] 1 WLR 1360 (HL(E)) and *G v G (Minors: Custody Appeal) [1985] 1 WLR 647 (HL(E))* applied.

(2) That any court which was determining any question with respect to the upbringing of a child had a statutory duty to regard the welfare of the child as its paramount consideration; that the application of the welfare principle might be specifically excluded by statute as, for example, by the Child Abduction and Custody Act 1985, which gave effect in domestic law to the Hague Convention on the Civil Aspects of International Child Abduction; that a court did have power, in accordance with the welfare principle, to order the immediate return of a child to a foreign jurisdiction without conducting a full investigation of the merits; that, however, there was no warrant, either in statute or authority, for the principles of the Hague Convention to be extended or applied by analogy to countries which were not parties to it; that, where non-Convention countries were involved, a trial judge had to focus on the individual child in the particular circumstances of the case; that, if there was a genuine issue between the parents as to whether it was in the best interests of the child to live in the United Kingdom or elsewhere, it was a relevant factor that the courts of the non-Convention country to which he was to be returned had no choice but to do as the father wished so that the mother could not ask them to decide, with an open mind,

in which country the child would be better off living; that in such circumstances an English court would have to take into account whether it would be in the interests of the child to enable that dispute to be heard; and that, accordingly, in some cases, the absence of a jurisdiction to allow a child to be relocated against his father's wishes from the non-Convention country might be a decisive factor in refusing to order his summary return to that country (post, paras 1–4, 18, 20, 22, 25–6, 28–9, 39, 46–8).

In re B's Settlement [1940] Ch 54; *McKee v McKee [1951] AC 352 (PC)*; *J v C [1970] AC 668 (HL(E))* and *In re JA (Child Abduction: Non-Convention Country) [1998] 1 FLR 231 (CA) applied.*
Osman v Elasha [2000] Fam 62 (CA) disapproved.
Decision of the Court of Appeal [2004] EWCA Civ 417, [2004] 2 FLR 85 reversed.

There have also been attempts to provide 'soft law' solutions (section 2.2.6) to bridge the gap in international mechanisms. For example, both Pakistan and Egypt have not ratified the Hague Convention. A UK–Pakistan Protocol[109] was agreed between the President of the Family Division and the Hon Chief Justice of Pakistan in 2003 (see Freeman 2009). In essence, in a spirit of international judicial cooperation and assisted by a system of liaison judges, it was agreed in the Protocol that '[i]n normal circumstances the welfare of a child is best determined by the courts of the country of the child's habitual/ordinary residence' and that '... the judge of the court of the country to which the child has been removed shall not ordinarily exercise jurisdiction over the child, save in so far as it is necessary for the court to order the return of the child to the country of the child's habitual/ordinary residence'.[110]

Similarly, a (non-binding) arrangement between the UK and Egypt, known as the Cairo Declaration,[111] was concluded in 2005, comprising a number of agreed principles applying to cross-border cases. However, the Cairo Declaration does not appear to have been as successful as the UK–Pakistan Protocol. The Office of the Head of International Family Justice for England and Wales observed that: '[t]he Cairo Declaration has not borne the fruit that the Pakistan Protocol has and we do not anticipate this changing in the near future'.[112]

---

109 See http://www.reunite.org/edit/files/Library%20-%20International%20Regulations/UK-Pa kistan%20Protocol.pdf (accessed 27 October 2013).

110 ibid paras 1 and 2.

111 See http://www.reunite.org/edit/files/Library%20-%20International%20Regulations/Cairo %20Declaration.pdf (accessed 27 October 2013).

112 Office of the Head of International Family Justice for England and Wales, Annual Report (2012). See http://www.judiciary.gov.uk/Resources/JCO/Documents/Reports/international_family_ justice_2013.pdf (accessed 29 October 2013).

5.5   The use of mediation in international parental child abduction

The profile of the international regulation of parental child abduction would not be complete without some mention of the role that mediation is having on the process. Both the Hague Convention of 1980 and the Revised Brussels II Regulation contain strong messages for the parties to family disputes and professionals to facilitate agreement rather than relying solely on litigation to reach a resolution. The former instrument provides that:

> *Article 7*
> Central Authorities shall co-operate with each other and promote co-operation amongst the competent authorities in their respective States to secure the prompt return of children and to achieve the other objects of this Convention.
> In particular, either directly or through any intermediary, they shall take all appropriate measures –
> ...
> *c)* to secure the voluntary return of the child or to bring about an amicable resolution of the issues;
> ...

The latter instrument provides that:

> *Article 55*
> *Cooperation on cases specific to parental responsibility*
> The central authorities shall, upon request from a central authority of another Member State or from a holder of parental responsibility, cooperate on specific cases to achieve the purposes of this Regulation. To this end, they shall, acting directly or through public authorities or other bodies, take all appropriate steps in accordance with the law of that Member State in matters of personal data protection to:
> ...
> (e) facilitate agreement between holders of parental responsibility through mediation or other means, and facilitate cross-border cooperation to this end.

'Mediation' provides *one* process to facilitate agreement/amicable resolution as required in both instruments. Some states, for example, seek to encourage dispute resolution either before initiating court process or as a first step and such efforts can be effective too. Vigers (2011: 36, 38) identifies three broad models of mediation:

- a process within the State of refuge, designed by the State and using mediators trained in that State

- a bi-national co-mediation process where the scheme is constructed and operated across both States and usually one mediator trained or connected to each State and
- a 'mediation-based' approach whereby all relevant professionals view the application against the backdrop of mediation.

Vigers strongly prefers the first model (similar to the Reunite scheme in the UK) and argues that the ethos of the bi-national approach is 'flawed' and 'can be unduly onerous', although it may be 'a useful first-step as States experiment with developing Convention mediation', while the third model misses the point that mediation should be viewed as a discrete element of the general procedure for handling Convention applications and that some cases will not be suitable for mediation and will require court resolution.

In her examination of the additional added value to be had from Convention mediation, she notes that 'the demographic of child abduction has ... undergone a well-documented paradigm shift' (Vigers 2011: 63) from mainly taking fathers, to taking mothers. This has meant that the benefits of some of the practical outcomes of the Convention have been lost: a return to the country of the child's habitual residence will not generally be a return to the primary carer – more often it will be a return to the left-behind (and secondary carer) father.

Furthermore, subsequent litigation on the merits is likely to result in residence awarded to the taking (primary carer) mother who will then relocate with the child, thus 'subjecting the child to the disruption of three locations' (Vigers 2011: 63). Return orders may well lead to the separation from the primary carer. On the issue of whether mediation might add to the problem of delay, she argues that the evidence so far shows that a discrete specialist mediation scheme within the Convention framework can operate expeditiously and need not result in any undue delay.

Some empirical research has also been conducted to examine the long-term effectiveness of mediation in international parental child abduction in the Reunite[113] scheme in Leicester (UK) (Buck 2012). The study population consisted of those parents who had participated in mediation with Reunite between December 2003 and December 2009. In total, 52 individual parents agreed to be interviewed, and comprised 22 taking parents and 30 left-behind parents. These all concerned (except one case) 'incoming cases', that is, a taking parent coming from another country into the UK. The resulting analysis divided the cases into 29 'resolved cases', that is, where the Memorandum of Understanding (MoU) drafted following mediation had been reached quickly followed by a consent order in the courts; and 23 'unresolved cases', where the dispute was not agreed in mediation and had to be further referred back to the courts for an authoritative decision.

---

113 Reunite: International Child Abduction Centre is the principal NGO in the UK. See http://www.reunite.org/ (accessed 28 October 2013).

The overall message from the research was that mediation does have a significant role to play in the context of the legal process of Hague proceedings, but it needs to be used proportionately and with care, particularly with regard to devising a robust mechanism to select cases that might be suitable for mediation in the first place. The research found that the effects are durable in the sense that, at least for 'resolved cases' so defined, the agreed MoUs provided broadly a framework or template that shaped future family arrangements. However, in 'unresolved' cases the mediation attempt had very little or no impact on alleviating the families' difficulties and they opted for what often turned out to be lengthy repeated court appearances before their family arrangements could find a more settled resting point.

The Hague Conference has been proactive in supporting mediation schemes across the contracting states, and currently encourages these developments through 'soft law' techniques rather than advocating a new legally binding instrument to integrate mediation into Hague proceedings. It has produced a comprehensive 'Guide to Good Practice on Mediation'.[114]

5.6   Concluding remarks

A fundamental tension present in the Hague Convention of 1980 is that there is a persistent conflict between *collective* and *individual* rights. One can see that, in general, it will be in children's best interests collectively to have a decision on their future made by courts located in their countries of habitual residence. However, the children's rights agenda, considerably strengthened by the appearance of the Convention on the Rights of the Child in 1989, also prompts a focus on the best interests of the individual child. To an extent, the availability of the settlement exception (section 5.3.3.1), and the additional exceptions/defences in Article 13 (sections 5.3.3.2–5.3.3.7) and the possibility of an Article 20 (section 5.3.3.8) argument, all provide possible routes whereby the centre of gravity of a Convention case can be steered away from the underlying aim of peremptory return to the country of habitual residence and focus instead on the individual child's welfare interests in the country of refuge.

Nevertheless, the process of increasing international judicial cooperation and the holding of Special Commissions on the Convention has developed a recognisable way of dealing with these cases. The position of abductions to non-convention countries (section 5.4) remains a worrying concern, although the production of bilateral agreements such as the UK–Pakistan Protocol appears to be a beneficial development.

---

114 Guide to Good Practice: Mediation, Permanent Bureau of the Hague Conference on Private International Law (June 2012). See http://www.hcch.net/upload/guide28mediation_en.pdf (accessed 8 November 2013).

Chapter 6

Inter-country adoption

6.1 Introduction

Inter-country adoption is a subject that has seized much popular attention, and on occasion has attracted news headlines about celebrity adoptions. A storm of protest occurred when Madonna attempted to adopt an infant from an orphanage in Malawi (Mezmur 2008, 2009), and Angelina Jolie's adoption of an infant from Ethiopia has been said to have had a role to play in the increased number of adoptions from that country (Mezmur 2012: 51). In one respect, inter-country adoption is seen as an act which provides a loving and secure home to a child who faces an otherwise bleak future.

On the other hand, depictions of inter-country adoption include reports of child-trafficking, children being kidnapped, mothers relinquishing their children under dubious circumstances and comments that inter-country adoption is an exploitation of poor countries and impoverished inhabitants of those states by wealthier and more powerful nations. Inter-country adoption remains a controversial area that generates different views about its utility and necessity. There are complexities too around the question of what motivates states to engage with inter-country adoption and the effect of these motivations on the approach taken to the 'best interests' standard (Sargent 2009).

Inter-country adoption, or *international adoption*, as it is sometimes known, has occurred historically alongside various causes of population displacement and migration. For example, in the United Kingdom child migration was used for a number of policy aims unconnected with child welfare. It has been estimated that some 130,000 children were 'exported' to various parts of the former British Empire between around 1860 and 1930 in order to provide a cheap method to populate the colonies. Many were subjected to abuse and cruelty and brought up to believe they were orphans.

After the Second World War there were around 10,000 children who were sent off to Australia and New Zealand; the last batch went as recently as 1967 (Bean and Melville 1989). Many of these later cohorts of children were never placed in families and some found themselves in harsh conditions. The placements were arranged by reputable childcare agencies and the view at the time was that arranging for their migration was in their best interests. There was evidence, however, of exploitation and abuse in respect of these children. Given this background, a House of Commons committee urged 'extreme caution' when considering applications for inter-country adoption.

> Child migration was a bad and, in human terms, costly mistake. ... We have met many former child migrants who continue to suffer from emotional and psychological problems arising directly from this misguided social policy. ... Many child migrants were separated from siblings and lived in profound geographical and social isolation, which left them unable to prepare themselves effectively for integration into adult life and society at large.[1]

Warfare too has had its influence on child migration patterns. The United States, the biggest 'receiving State' of children for adoption from other countries, is reckoned to have experienced its first wave of such adoptions at the end of the Second World War, with children being adopted from war-torn Europe and Japan. A second wave began with the Korean War in the 1950s, where children who were orphaned or born as a result of liaisons with United States military personnel were adopted (Choy 2007). The appearance of inter-country adoption, at least in its modern form, is said to have started during and following the end of the Korean War in the 1950s (Hubinette 2006: 139).

In the United States, private, and often religious-based, agencies promoted the adoption of Korean children. The only rules on how inter-country adoption was to occur were those that were made by the agencies, with very little oversight from either the South Korean or the American governments. Agencies worked in tandem with the governments, but the privileging of private agencies has to an extent been introduced into the Hague Convention on Protection of Children and Co-operation in respect of Intercountry Adoption[2] (Hague Convention of 1993). One scholar comments on the occurrence of inter-country adoption in South Korea, the role of the agencies and government and the children who were sent to other countries:

> Of the many needy children, mixed-race children were most likely to be considered for homes abroad by the Korean government and private adoption agencies. Most mixed-race children were born to Korean women and U.S. soldiers stationed at U.S. bases in Korea during and after the war. The women who gave birth to mixed-race children were regarded as military prostitutes. Thus, those children bearing the stigma of their mothers' occupation are identified as a group of children who needed homes outside of Korea.

---

1 Select Committee on Health, *The Welfare of Former British Child Migrants*, 3rd Report, Select Committee on Health, 1997–98 session (23 July 1998) London: The Stationery Office 98.
2 Hague Conference on Private International Law, concluded 29 May 1993 (entered into force 1 May 1995).

In 1954, the South Korean government established the Child Placement Service ... to place biracial children in foreign adoption, particularly to their father's country, the United States.

(Kim 2007: 136)

A third wave occurred similarly as a result of the Vietnam War in the 1970s. A mass evacuation of children ('Operation Babylift') from South Vietnam to the USA and other countries was organised at the end of the Vietnam War from 3–26 April 1975, and many of these children were adopted. It is estimated that a total of 2547 orphans were processed under Operation Babylift and of these 602 went on to other countries, leaving a total of 1945 adopted in the United States.[3]

From the 1990s, substantial numbers of children started to be adopted internationally from countries such as Romania, the former Soviet Union and China, and the children displaced most recently by the wars in Afghanistan and Iraq continue to present challenges to the process of inter-country adoption (Richards 2013).

Finally, inter-country adoption is often appealed to as a solution for children orphaned as a result of natural disasters. For example, calls for such action followed the devastation caused by an earthquake in Haiti in early 2010, although some would caution against taking children away from their homeland, especially in times of crisis (Selman 2011).

6.1.1   Inter-country adoption: the statistics

As inter-country adoption operates across many countries and their respective family law and official statistics regimes are diverse, there have been difficulties in determining the global number of children involved in inter-country adoption. Selman's work on the statistics of inter-country adoption is the most authoritative. He estimates that there has been a global total of around 970,000 inter-country adoptions since 1948. In the most recent decade (2000 to 2010) there have been around 410,000 children adopted by citizens of 27 countries: 'the highest number for any decade' (Selman 2012: 4). See Table 6.1 below.

Table 6.1 shows the successive increases in inter-country adoptions in the decades following the Second World War.

Tables 6.2 and 6.3 below provide a more detailed profile of inter-country adoptions by receiving states and sending states respectively in the period 2003 to 2011.

The United States *received* the highest number of inter-country adoptions in the period (159,180), followed by Spain (34,661), Italy (31,749), France (31,136) and

---

3 United States Agency for International Development, *Operation Babylift Report* (Emergency Movement of Vietnamese and Cambodian Orphans for Intercountry Adoption, April–June 1975) Washington D.C. pp 1–2, 5, 6, 9–10, 11–12, 13–14.

Table 6.1 Estimated numbers of children adopted via inter-country adoption 1948–2010: total 970,000 adoptions

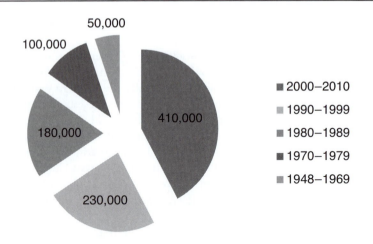

Source: Derived from Selman (2012: 4)

Table 6.2 Inter-country adoptions to 23 receiving states 2003–2011

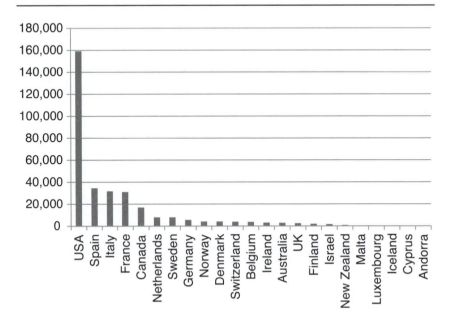

Source: Derived from Selman (2013: Table 1).

Table 6.3 15 countries sending most children for inter-country adoption to the 23 receiving states in Table 6.2 above: 2003–2011

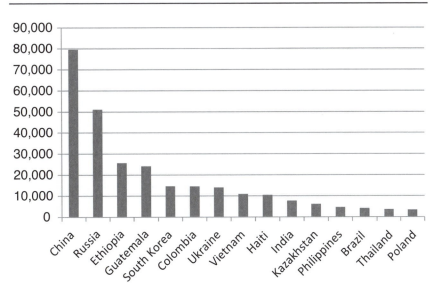

Source: Derived from Selman (2012, Table 2).

Canada (17,053). The lowest was Andorra (50). In total there were 324,641 inter-country adoptions in the period 2003 to 2011.

Table 6.3 above shows that, in the period, 2003–2011, China *sent* the most children for inter-country adoption (79,577), followed by Russia (51,142), Ethiopia (25,708) and Guatemala (24,138). The lowest number of these 15 countries was sent by Poland (3371).

Although the global figures since 1948 (Table 6.1 above) suggest an ever-increasing trend upwards in the number of inter-country adoptions, this is not necessarily so. Selman (2012: 2) comments on trends in recent years:

> The global number of intercountry adoptions peaked in 2004 after a steady rise in annual numbers from the early 1990s. Since then, annual numbers have decreased to the point that by 2008 the total was lower than it had been in 2001 … and by 2009 lower than it was in 1998 … During this time, the rise and fall was evident in most regions and countries. In 2009, however, things began to change, with more children going to European countries than to the United States – which had, until that time, accounted for about half of all international adoptions since the mid-1980s.

6.1.2 The sending and receiving countries

As Tables 6.2 and 6.3 above suggest, there are a number of countries that can be viewed as sending states and others that can be characterised as receiving states. However, over time these patterns do change and the bilateral relationships between a pair of sending and receiving states, eg the US and South Korea, France and Vietnam, come and go. Studies of inter-country adoption have tended to focus on the conditions prevalent in the *sending countries* that have generated the *supply* side of the adoption equation.

There is less research about the *demand* for inter-country adoptions from the *receiving countries*: 'Consequently, current scholarship in this area tends to perpetuate the understanding of intercountry adoption as a symptom of what is wrong with source [sending] countries' (Chen 2003). There is much controversy surrounding the practice of inter-country adoption, not least the impression that it is an act of international charity or 'rescue'. The perspective of children's rights, on the other hand, emphasises the 'best interests' of the child principle, now concretised in the Convention on the Rights of the Child (1989)[4] (section 3.7.3.2).

The power balance between the generally poorer sending countries and the richer receiving countries tends to emphasise the practice of inter-country adoption as primarily a means of addressing the interests and needs of the prospective adoptive parents in the receiving states and also reflects on the weaknesses of family care options within the sending states rather than maintaining the focus on the needs of the child.

The attraction of relatively high adoption fees in sending states, for example in China, can sustain the inter-country adoption market for much longer and out of proportion with the original demographic factors triggering these practices. The history of inter-country adoptions from South Korea is a good example. The original factors of war-related disruption to the population, giving rise to inter-country adoptions in the 1950s, are no longer relevant today. South Korea is now a relatively prosperous country with a low birth rate. It is a plausible argument, as in the Romanian case, that the continuation of inter-country adoption has in fact discouraged the proper development of internal children's services in South Korea (Sarri, Baik and Bombyk 1998).

6.2 The need for international legal regulation

6.2.1 The Hague Convention of 1965

International legal regulation of inter-country adoptions started with the appearance of the Hague Convention on Jurisdiction, Applicable Law and Recognition

---

4 Opened for signature 20 November 1989, 1577 UNTS 3 (entered into force 2 September 1990).

of Decrees Relating to Adoptions[5] (1965). The purpose of that Convention was seen by one contemporary commentator as 'mainly concerned with recognition [of decrees relating to adoption] and its key provision is found in Article 8 under which every adoption governed by this Convention and granted by an authority competent under it shall be recognised without further formality in all contracting states' (Unger 1965: 463). That there should be a Convention that dealt solely with international adoptions was found to need explanation:

> ... its scope is severely limited since, under Article 2(b), it will not apply in the ordinarily case where these parties are all nationals of the same state and are habitually resident in it. The machinery and conditions of recognition established by the Convention will therefore operate only in cases of what Article 6 describes as 'inter-country adoption'.
>
> (Unger 1965: 464)

This Convention was based on the European situation in the 1960s: that is, 'international adoptions spanning relatively short geographical distances and between countries with more or less comparable socio-economic, cultural and legal systems' (Van Loon, 1995). The Convention met with limited success and did not enter into force until 1978, by which time the social reality had changed with larger numbers of children from developing countries being adopted by families in the industrialised countries. The Convention was only ratified by three states (Austria, Switzerland and the United Kingdom), although it was subsequently denounced and ceased to have effect from 23 October 2008.

6.2.2 Adoption and the UN Convention on the Rights of the Child

A Special Commission (section 2.4.2) of the Hague Conference appointed by the Permanent Bureau in January 1988 again took up the subject of legal cooperation in relation to inter-country adoption. The emerging global phenomenon of inter-country adoption required a different approach 'with more emphasis on the need to define substantive safeguards and procedures for courts, administrative authorities and private intermediaries than on traditional rules of conflict of jurisdiction and of applicable law' (Van Loon 1995: 463).

The Hague Convention on the Civil Aspects of International Child Abduction[6] (1980) had set a useful precedent in moving away from legal standards that were constrained to sorting out rules of jurisdiction and choice of applicable law, to establishing standards that advanced practical measures for judicial and administrative cooperation. In addition, the UN Convention on the Rights of the

---

5 Hague Conference on Private International Law, concluded 15 November 1965 (entered into force on 23 October 1978; denounced and ceased to have effect on 23 October 2008).

6 Hague Conference on Private International Law, concluded 25 October 1980 (entered into force 1 December 1983).

Child acted as a source of inspiration during the negotiations for a new Hague Convention to regulate inter-country adoptions.

Article 21 of the Convention on the Rights of the Child had included, for the first time in international human rights law, principles of good adoption practice (Detrick 1999: 343). The text of Article 21 and some detailed commentary can be found in section 3.7.5.2. The duties in this Article only apply to states that 'recognise and/or permit the system of adoption', thus providing an escape clause for a number of Islamic countries that did not recognise the institution of adoption. Arguably, countries that did not recognise adoption but permitted children to leave and be adopted abroad come within the ambit of Article 21 (Van Bueren 1994: 102). If the wording left any doubt about the matter, a state could always lodge a reservation.[7]

Where the Article does apply, the standard required of states is to ensure that the best interests of the child shall be the *paramount* consideration. This Article recognises the principle that inter-country adoption may be considered as an alternative means of care for children, if the child cannot be cared for in the child's country of origin (the 'subsidiarity principle' – section 3.7.5.2). The *travaux préparatoires* reveal that inter-country adoption will only be regarded as a subsidiary means of care when all other possibilities are exhausted (Detrick 1999: 351). Furthermore, the safeguards and standards should be 'equivalent' to those existing in domestic adoptions and states should take all appropriate measures to prevent 'improper financial gain' from inter-country adoptions. The Hague Convention of 1993 specifies clearly that 'only costs and expenses including reasonable professional fees' may be charged or paid.[8]

Finally, Article 21 of the Convention on the Rights of the Child provides that these principles and standards should be promoted by 'concluding bilateral or multilateral arrangements or agreements' (such as the Hague Convention of 1993). This latter paragraph 'particularly reflects the concern of the drafters of the Convention on the Rights of the Child over the sale and trafficking of children for the purposes of intercountry adoption' (Detrick 1999: 354).

6.2.3　The Special Commission and the Hague Convention of 1993

A Hague Conference Special Commission (section 2.4.2) recommended that non-member states participate in the preparatory work on drafting a new Convention. The principle of participation by non-member states had been accepted by the 14th session of the Hague Conference in 1980. Around 70 states and 20 international organisations participated in the negotiations. The Hague Conference viewed the involvement of non-member states as indispensable, given that many

---

7　Reservations lodged by Islamic countries in respect of CRC art 21: Bangladesh, Brunei Darussalam, Jordan, Kuwait, Maldives, Oman, and the United Arab Emirates. Egypt withdrew its reservation on 31 July 2003, and the Syrian Arab Republic partially withdrew its reservation on 13 June 2012.

8　Hague Convention of 1993 art 32(2).

children subject to inter-country adoption arrangements originated from these 'sending' states.

There was a general acknowledgement of the inadequacy of existing international legal instruments to meet the perceived problems of inter-country adoption. In particular, it was recognised that there was a need to establish legally binding standards and a system of supervision to ensure observance. There was also a need to establish channels of communication and cooperation between authorities in countries of origin and in receiving states. In short, there was:

> [a] clear practical need for a multilateral instrument which would not, or not only, be a convention unifying private international law rules. As a matter of fact, it was felt that actual protection of children required the definition of certain substantive principles and the establishment of a legal framework of co-operation between authorities in the States of origin and in the receiving States.
>
> (Parra-Aranguren 1994: para 8)

Several meetings of the Special Commission took place from 1990 to 1992. Its report and a draft of the Convention were considered by the 17th session of the Hague Conference in May 1993. The Hague Convention on Protection of Children and Co-operation in respect of Intercountry Adoption[9] of 1993 was unanimously approved and concluded at the end of May 1993. The Hague Convention of 1993 was intended to provide solutions in a difficult and complex area in relation to both jurisdictional and substantive points of legal regulations:

> Intercountry adoption is legally complex. Rules of private substantive law governing adoption vary significantly from one country to another, which gives rise to problems of private international law such as questions of jurisdiction, applicable law and recognition of foreign adoptions. In many countries intercountry adoption is, in addition, subject to various provisions which override those rules of private international law, including laws requiring preliminary permission to adopt a child in intercountry cases, immigration laws and nationality laws. The Hague Convention on Intercountry Adoption aims to solve many of these problems. It is not a typical private international law convention. It does provide for a framework to solve problems of conflicts of jurisdiction and of applicable law. However, it also provides for substantive safeguards and procedures in respect of intercountry adoption, and judicial and administrative co-operation in matters of private law.
>
> (Detrick 1999: 355)

---

9 Hague Conference on Private International Law, concluded 29 May 1993 (entered into force 1 May 1995).

Finally, the Convention places a duty on the Secretary-General of the Hague Conference to 'convene a Special Commission' at regular intervals 'in order to review the practical operation of the Convention.[10]

This codifies the practice, evolved under other Hague Conventions requiring judicial and administrative cooperation, of holding periodic meetings of Special Commissions to undertake the review work:

> Article 42 ... takes into account the remarkable experience of other Hague Conventions, in particular the Child Abduction Convention, to express the idea that the Convention on intercountry adoption should not be an end in itself, but rather lay the groundwork for an ongoing review and amelioration of its application. Therefore, the Secretary-General of the Hague Conference on Private International Law shall, after the Convention enters into force, convene Special Commissions, at regular intervals, to review its operation – meetings that may be attended by all States Parties, together with Member States and other non-Member States that participated in the Seventeenth Session, as well as by international organisations, public and private, invited to participate.
>
> (Parra-Aranguren 1994: para 586)

There have been four Special Commissions examining the Hague Convention of 1993, in 1994, 2001, 2005 and 2010 respectively.[11] For example, the Special Commission of 2010 gave its general endorsement to a draft of the Guide to Good Practice No 2[12] concerning accredited bodies and authorised the Permanent Bureau to progress work on the drawing up of accreditation criteria. The Special Commission also made the following recommendations relating to inter-country adoptions in the wake of disasters:

Response to disaster situations

38. The Special Commission recognised that, in a disaster situation, efforts to reunite a displaced child with his or her parents or family members must

---

10 Hague Convention of 1993 art 42. Subsequent Hague Conventions have contained a similar provision. See Hague Conference on Private International Law, Convention on Jurisdiction, Applicable Law, Recognition, Enforcement and Co-operation in respect of Parental Responsibility and Measures for the Protection of Children, concluded 19 October 1996 (entered into force 1 January 2002); Hague Conference on Private International Law, Convention on the International Recovery of Child Support and Other Forms of Family Maintenance, concluded 23 November 2007 (entered into force 1 January 2013); and Hague Conference on Private International Law, Protocol on the Law Applicable to Maintenance Obligations, concluded 23 November 2007 (entered into force 1 August 2013).

11 See http://www.hcch.net/index_en.php?act=conventions.publications&dtid=2&cid=69 (accessed 10 November 2013).

12 Permanent Bureau of the Hague Conference on Private International Law, 'Guide to Good Practice No 2: Accreditation and Adoption Accredited Bodies, Bristol: Family Law' http://www.hcch.net/upload/adoguide2en.pdf (accessed 12 November 2013).

take priority. Premature and unregulated attempts to organise the adoption of such a child abroad should be avoided and resisted.

39. No new adoption applications should be considered in the period after the disaster or before the authorities in that State are in a position to apply the necessary safeguards.

40. The Special Commission also recognised the need for a common approach on the part of Central Authorities in dealing with such situations and for Central Authorities to discuss and review actions taken in response to, and lessons learned from, disaster situations.[13]

6.2.4   UNICEF's position

The United Nations Children's Fund (UNICEF) (section 2.4.1.2) released statements in October 2007 and July 2010 to clarify its position on the priority that should be accorded to inter-country adoption. The latter statement is reproduced below.

UNICEF's position on inter-country adoption
http://www.unicef.org/media/media_41918.html (accessed 9 November 2013)

Since the 1960s, there has been an increase in the number of inter-country adoptions. Concurrent with this trend, there have been growing international efforts to ensure that adoptions are carried out in a transparent, non-exploitative, legal manner to the benefit of the children and families concerned. In some cases, however, adoptions have not been carried out in ways that served the best interest of the children – when the requirements and procedures in place were insufficient to prevent unethical practices. Systemic weaknesses persist and enable the sale and abduction of children, coercion or manipulation of birth parents, falsification of documents and bribery.

The Convention on the Rights of the Child, which guides UNICEF's work, clearly states that every child has the right to grow up in a family environment, to know and be cared for by her or his own family, whenever possible. Recognising this, and the value and importance of families in children's lives, families needing assistance to care for their children have a right to receive it. When, despite this assistance, a child's family is unavailable, unable or unwilling to care for her/him, then appropriate and stable

---

13 Permanent Bureau of the Hague Conference on Private International Law, *Conclusions and Recommendations and Report of the Special Commission on the practical operation of the 1993 Hague Intercountry Adoption* Convention (17–25 June 2010), March 2011.

family-based solutions should be sought to enable the child to grow up in a loving, caring and supportive environment.

Inter-country adoption is among the range of stable care options. For individual children who cannot be cared for in a family setting in their country of origin, inter-country adoption may be the best permanent solution. UNICEF supports inter-country adoption, when pursued in conformity with the standards and principles of the 1993 Hague Convention on Protection of Children and Co-operation in Respect of Inter-country Adoptions – already ratified by more than 80 countries. This Convention is an important development for children, birth families and prospective foreign adopters. It sets out obligations for the authorities of countries from which children leave for adoption, and those that are receiving these children. The Convention is designed to ensure ethical and transparent processes. This international legislation gives paramount consideration to the best interests of the child and provides the framework for the practical application of the principles regarding inter-country adoption contained in the Convention on the Rights of the Child. These include ensuring that adoptions are authorised only by competent authorities, guided by informed consent of all concerned, that inter-country adoption enjoys the same safeguards and standards which apply in national adoptions, and that inter-country adoption does not result in improper financial gain for those involved in it. These provisions are meant first and foremost to protect children, but also have the positive effect of safeguarding the rights of their birth parents and providing assurance to prospective adoptive parents that their child has not been the subject of illegal practices.

The case of children separated from their families and communities during war or natural disasters merits special mention. Family tracing should be the first priority and inter-country adoption should only be envisaged for a child once these tracing efforts have proved fruitless, and stable in-country solutions are not available. This position is shared by UNICEF, UNHCR, the UN Committee on the Rights of the Child, the Hague Conference on Private International Law, the International Committee of the Red Cross, and international NGOs such as the Save the Children Alliance and International Social Service.

UNICEF offices around the world support the strengthening of child protection systems. We work with governments, UN partners and civil society to protect vulnerable families, to ensure that robust legal and policy frameworks are in place and to build capacity of the social welfare, justice and law enforcement sectors.

Most importantly, UNICEF focuses on preventing the underlying causes of child abuse, exploitation and violence.

(New York, 22 July 2010)

6.3   The Hague Convention on Intercountry Adoption of 1993[14]

There are, at the time of writing, 93 states[15] that have ratified or acceded to the Hague Convention of 1993. The Special Commission also drew up a (non-binding) Recommendation on the general principles to be applied when implementing the Convention specifically to refugee and other internationally displaced children.

HAGUE RECOMMENDATION ON REFUGEE CHILDREN (ADOPTED ON 21 OCTOBER 1994)

http://www.hcch.net/upload/recomm33refugee_en.pdf (accessed 9 November 2013)

Pursuant to the Decision of the Seventeenth Session of the Hague Conference on Private International Law, held at The Hague from 10 to 29 May 1993, to convene a Special Commission to study the specific questions concerning the application to refugee children and other internationally displaced children of the Hague Convention of 29 May 1993 on Protection of Children and Co-operation in Respect of Intercountry Adoption.

The Special Commission gathering at The Hague from 17 to 21 October 1994, in consultation with the Office of the United Nations High Commissioner for Refugees,

Adopts the following Recommendation –

RECOMMENDATION

Whereas the Hague Convention on Protection of Children and Co-operation in Respect of Intercountry Adoption was concluded at The Hague on 29 May 1993,

Considering that in the application of the Convention to refugee children and to children who are, as a result of disturbances in their countries, internationally displaced, account should be taken of their particularly vulnerable situation,

Recalling that according to the Preamble of the Convention each State should take as a matter of priority appropriate measures to enable the child to remain in the care of his or her family of origin, and that intercountry adoption may offer the advantage of a permanent family to a child for whom a suitable family cannot be found in his or her State,

---

14 Hague Conference on Private International Law, concluded 29 May 1993 (entered into force 1 May 1995).

15 Comprised of 60 member states of the Hague Conference and 31 non-member states. At the time of writing, three states had signed but not ratified/acceded to the Hague Convention of 1993: Republic of Korea (24 May 2013); Russian Federation (7 September 2000); Nepal (28 April 2009).

The Hague Conference on Private International Law recommends to the States which are, or become, Parties to the Convention that they take into consideration the following principles in applying the Convention with respect to refugee children and to children who are, as a result of disturbances in their countries, internationally displaced –

1 – For the application of Article 2, paragraph 1, of the Convention, a State shall not discriminate in any way in respect of these children in determining whether they are habitually resident in that State.

With respect to these children, the State of origin referred to in Article 2, paragraph 1, of the Convention, is the State where the child is residing after being displaced.

2 – The competent authorities of the State to which the child has been displaced shall take particular care to ensure that–

    a) before any intercountry adoption procedure is initiated,

        – all reasonable measures have been taken in order to trace and reunite the child with his or her parents or family members where the child is separated from them; and

        – the repatriation of the child to his or her country, for purposes of such reunion, would not be feasible or desirable, because of the fact that the child cannot receive appropriate care, or benefit from satisfactory protection, in that country;

    b) an intercountry adoption only takes place if

        – the consents referred to in Article 4(c) of the Convention have been obtained; and

        – the information about his or her identity, adoptability, background, social environment, family history, medical history including that of the child's family, the child's upbringing, his or her ethnic, religious and cultural origins, and any special needs of the child, has been collected in so far as is possible under the circumstances.

In carrying out the requirements of sub-paragraphs a) and b), these authorities will seek information from the international and national bodies, in particular the Office of the United Nations High Commissioner for Refugees, and will request their cooperation as needed.

3 – The competent authorities shall take particular care not to harm the well-being of persons still within the child's country, especially the child's family members, in obtaining and preserving the information collected in connection with paragraph 2, as well as to preserve the confidentiality of that information according to the Convention.

4 – The States shall facilitate the fulfilment, in respect to children referred to in this Recommendation, of the protection mandate of the United Nations High Commissioner for Refugees.

> The Hague Conference also recommends that each State take these principles and those of the Convention into account for adoptions creating a permanent parent-child relationship between, on the one hand, spouses or a person habitually resident in that State and, on the other hand, a refugee or internationally displaced child in the same State.

As regards the practical operation of the Hague Convention, the reader may want to consult the detail contained in the Guide to Good Practice No 1 issued by the Permanent Bureau of the Hague Conference in 2008.

> *The Implementation and Operation of the 1993 Hague Intercountry Adoption Convention: A Guide to Good Practice* is a project of post-Convention support initiated by the Permanent Bureau for the purpose of assisting States (whether or not already Contracting States) with the practical implementation of the Convention, in a manner which achieves the objects of the Convention, namely, the protection of children who are adopted internationally. It is the first such Guide for the 1993 Convention, and it identifies important matters related to planning, establishing and operating the legal and administrative framework to implement the Convention. It does not always claim to be a guide for best practices because some practices are necessarily different in different Contracting states.[16]

The following sub-sections outline the principal features of the Hague Convention of 1993.

6.3.1   The best interests of the child are paramount

The Hague Convention of 1993, as we have seen, was inspired by the UN Convention on the Rights of the Child (1989), and to an extent was conceived to build upon Article 21 of the earlier Convention (section 6.2.2), which prescribes that 'the best interests of the child shall be the *paramount* consideration' (my emphasis) for states parties' development and the operation of their adoption systems.

Where inter-country adoption is developed as an option within a national child care system, it should be ethical and child-centred. Consequently, the Hague Convention of 1993 provides certain rules to ensure that adoptions take place in the best interests of the child. It contains the best interests principle explicitly in relation to two key determinations made by the state of origin. First, the sending

---

16 Permanent Bureau of the Hague Conference on Private International Law, 'Guide to Good Practice No 1: The Implementation and Operation of the 1993 Hague Intercountry Adoption Convention, 2008, Bristol: Family Law [1] http://www.hcch.net/upload/adoguide_e.pdf (accessed 12 November 2013).

state must determine, after possibilities for placement of the child have been given due consideration, that an inter-country adoption is in the child's best interests.[17]

Secondly, the sending state must determine on the basis of the evaluation reports relating to the child and the prospective adoptive parents whether the envisaged match is in the best interests of the child.[18] Clearly, there may often be ambiguities around the process of identifying what is in an individual child's best interests, a dilemma that is arguably exemplified by perceptions of inter-country adoption as a form of 'rescue' (Davies 2011).

More broadly, the best interest principle is further supported by state obligations to:

- ensure the child is adoptable
- preserve information about the child and his/her parents
- evaluate thoroughly the prospective adoptive parents
- match the child with a suitable family
- impose additional safeguards where needed and
- implement the principle of subsidiarity (section 6.3.2).

A Hague Convention adoption will only apply in relation to persons under the age of 18 years at the time the agreements required are granted.[19] The age of 18 is consistent with the definition of the child to be found in the Convention on the Rights of the Child,[20] but the Hague Convention of 1993 is silent as to the age limit relevant to the question of whether a child is 'adoptable'. This is left to the applicable law determined by the conflict rules of each state.

For example, if the applicable law only permits adoption under a lower age, for example, 12 years old, then this must be respected (Parra-Aranguren 1994: para 96). The competent authorities of the state of origin must establish that the child is adoptable (under the relevant applicable law); it must determine that an inter-country adoption is 'in the child's best interests' after due consideration has been given to possibilities of placement within its own state.[21] The competent authorities of the receiving state must determine that the child is or will be authorised to enter and reside permanently in that state.[22]

Central authorities (or their delegate bodies) in both states of origin and receiving states are obliged to 'collect, preserve, and exchange information about the situation of the child and the prospective adoptive parents, so far as is necessary to complete the adoption'.[23]

---

17 Hague Convention of 1993 art 4(b).
18 ibid art 16(1)(d).
19 ibid art 3.
20 CRC art 1.
21 Hague Convention of 1993 art 4(a).
22 ibid art 5(c).
23 ibid art 9(a).

The competent authorities of contracting states are further obliged to 'ensure that information held by them concerning the child's origin, in particular information concerning the identity of his or her parents, as well as the medical history, is preserved' and that children or their representatives have access to such information under appropriate guidance.[24] In one study, the authors argue that 'preservation of a child's background is perceived to be in conflict with other interests of the child, such as gaining a position in her/his adoptive family equal to that of a biological child and being loved unconditionally (Lind and Johansson 2009: 235).

Prospective adoptive parents must apply to the central authority of their own state if they wish to adopt a child habitually resident in another contracting state.[25] The evaluation of prospective adoptive parents is undertaken by the competent authorities of the receiving state. They must be satisfied that 'the prospective adoptive parents are eligible and suited to adopt' and must have ensured that the prospective adoptive parents 'have been counselled as may be necessary'.[26]

The matching of the child with prospective adoptive parents is undertaken following an exchange of reports by the receiving state and the state of origin. Once the receiving state is satisfied that the applicants are eligible and suited to adopt, it is obliged to 'prepare a report including information about their identity, eligibility and suitability to adopt, background, family and medical history, social environment, reasons for adoption, ability to undertake an intercountry adoption, as well as the characteristics of the children for whom they would be qualified to care'.[27]

Once the state of origin is satisfied that the child is adoptable, it is also under a duty to 'prepare a report including information about his or her identity, adoptability, background, social environment, family history, medical history including that of the child's family, and any special needs of the child'.[28] In addition to this, it must ensure that due consideration has been given to 'the child's upbringing and to his or her ethnic, religious and cultural background' and ensure that the necessary consents have been obtained.[29] Then it will determine on the basis of the reports relating to the child and the prospective adoptive parents 'whether the envisaged placement is in the best interests of the child'.[30]

The central authority of the state of origin will transmit its report on the child back to the central authority of the receiving state, along with proof of any necessary consents and the reasons for the placement, 'taking care not to reveal the identity of the mother and father if, in the state of origin, these identities may not

24 ibid art 30.
25 ibid art 14.
26 ibid art 5(a) and (b).
27 ibid art 15(1).
28 ibid art 16(1)(a).
29 ibid art 16(1)(b) and (c).
30 ibid art 16(1)(d).

be disclosed'.[31] The necessary preconditions for a placement decision to occur in the state of origin are set out in Article 17. These are:

- that the prospective adoptive parents agree
- that the central authority of the receiving state has approved such a decision (where such approval is required under the law of that state or by the central authority of the state of origin)
- that the central authorities of both states have agreed that the adoption may proceed; and it has been determined that the prospective adoptive parents are 'eligible and suited to adopt' and
- that the child is or will be authorised to enter and reside permanently in the receiving state under Article 5.

Both the state of origin and the receiving state are obliged to ensure that all necessary steps are taken to obtain permission for the child to leave the state of origin and enter and reside permanently in the receiving state.[32]

The transfer of the child should take place 'in secure and appropriate circumstances' and if possible in the company of the adopters.[33] The central authorities are put under a continuing duty to monitor the progress of the transferred child, particularly where there is a probationary placement in the receiving state.[34] If the placement does not work out, it is provided that the central authority of the receiving state will take measures necessary to protect the child. This can include arranging for the return of the child to the sending state, withdrawal from the prospective adopters and placement in temporary care. It can also involve an arrangement of a new placement or alternative long-term care, after consultation with the sending state.[35]

In short, the sending state must verify compliance with four main conditions:

- the adoptability of the child
- respect for the subsidiarity principle
- the necessary consents of other persons than the child and
- the wishes, opinions or consent of the child.

Similarly, the receiving state has responsibility to verify that:

- the prospective adoptive parents are eligible and suited to adopt
- the prospective adoptive parents have been counselled as may be necessary and

---

31 ibid art 16(2).
32 ibid art 18.
33 ibid art 19(2).
34 ibid art 20.
35 ibid art 21.

- the child is or will be authorised to enter and reside permanently within its
territory.

To be 'eligible' to adopt means to fulfil all the legal conditions, according to
the applicable law. To be 'suited' to adopt means to satisfy the necessary socio-
psychological qualifications (Parra-Aranguren 1994: para 180).

6.3.2 Subsidiarity principle

This principle, as we have seen, was first recognised in relation to inter-country
adoption by the Convention on the Rights of the Child[36] (section 3.7.5.2). In the
context of the Hague Convention of 1993, the principle of subsidiarity means
that states recognise that generally children should be raised by their parents or
extended family where possible. If that is not possible other options of permanent
care in the state of origin should be explored.[37] It is only where the national solutions have been considered and found wanting should inter-country adoption be
explored, and then only if it is in the individual child's best interests.[38]

In general, institutional care should be considered as a last resort. Whether
inter-country adoption does in fact reduce the number of children remaining
in institutional care remains contentious. Chou and Browne (2008: 45–47) concluded that 'countries with high proportions of outgoing international adoptions
also had high numbers of young children in institutional care' and the evidence
did not support the proposition that inter-country adoption reduced the number
of children remaining in institutional care.[39]

6.3.3 Safeguards to protect children from abduction, sale and trafficking

One of the overall objectives of the Hague Convention is to establish safeguards
and thereby to 'prevent the abduction, the sale of, or traffic in children'[40] by:

- protecting birth families from exploitation and undue pressure
- ensuring only children in need of a family are adoptable and adopted
- preventing improper financial gain and corruption and
- regulating agencies and individuals involved in adoptions by accrediting
them in accordance with Convention standards.

The protection of birth families from exploitation and undue pressure is achieved
principally by the requirements that states of origin must meet to ensure that the

---

36 CRC art 21(b).
37 Hague Convention of 1993 preamble §2.
38 ibid art 4(b).
39 See also Gay y Blasco and others (2008) and Browne and Chou (2008).
40 Hague Convention of 1993 art 1(b).

necessary *consents*[41] have been given. The persons whose consent is necessary for adoption must have been 'counselled as may be necessary and duly informed of the effects of their consent, in particular whether or not an adoption will result in the termination of the legal relationship between the child and his or her family of origin'.[42] Such consents must be given: 'freely, in the required legal form, and expressed or evidenced in writing'; must not have been 'induced by payment or compensation of any kind'; and, the mother's consent (where required) must have been given *after* the birth of the child.[43]

Similarly, the competent authorities of the state of origin must ensure that, having regard to the child's age and degree of maturity, the *child* is counselled and informed of the effects of the adoption, consideration is given to the child's wishes and feelings and the child gives freely, in the required legal form, his or her own consent (where required) to the prospective adoption.[44]

In addition, the Convention lays down that there shall be no contact between the prospective adopters and the child's parents or any other person who has care of the child until the requirements of Articles 4(a)–(c) and 5(a) have been met, unless the adoption takes place within a family or is in compliance with the conditions established by the competent authority of the state of origin.[45] The aim of this provision is:

> [...] to prevent trafficking and any other kind of practices that may be contrary to the purposes of the Convention, in particular, to avoid the result whereby consents required for the granting of the adoption are induced by payment or compensation, which is expressly forbidden by Article 4, sub-paragraph(c)(3).
>
> (Parra-Aranguren 1994: para 495)

Such practices occurred in Romania and were known to have occurred in Latin America and Asia (Van Loon 1995: 467).

The Convention contains two Articles preventing improper financial gain and corruption:

Article 8
Central Authorities shall take, directly or through public authorities, all appropriate measures to prevent improper financial or other gain in connection

---

41 The draft version of the Convention additionally required that consents would be 'unconditional'. However, that would have precluded adoptions where consent had been conditional on placing a child in a family of the same religion. It was thought that there might be circumstances where the imposition of some conditions by the biological parents would be appropriate and permitted by the state of origin (Parra-Aranguren 1994: para 143).

42 Hague Convention of 1993 art 4(c)(i).

43 ibid art 4(c)(ii)–(iv).

44 ibid art 4(d).

45 ibid art 29.

with an adoption and to deter all practices contrary to the objects of the Convention.

Article 32
(1) No one shall derive improper financial or other gain from an activity related to an intercountry adoption.
(2) Only costs and expenses, including reasonable professional fees of persons involved in the adoption, may be charged or paid.
(3) The directors, administrators and employees of bodies involved in an adoption shall not receive remuneration which is unreasonably high in relation to services rendered.

Article 32 is designed to prevent *anyone* from deriving improper financial or other gain from an activity related to inter-country adoption. This also reflects the principle that has been established in the Convention on the Rights of the Child:[46]

> The importance of the matter had been strongly stressed in the Special Commission, where it was recalled 'the existing situation reveals that it is not only the intermediary bodies that are attracted by improper financial gain', because 'as it has sometimes happened, lawyers, notaries, public servants, even judges and university professors, have either requested or accepted excessive amounts of money or lavish gifts from prospective adoptive parents' (Report of the Special Commission, No 310).
>
> (Parra-Aranguren 1994: para 527)

The extent to which these provisions have been successful remains controversial:

> [I]n some ways a Hague-based intercountry adoption system could be even more vulnerable to child laundering schemes than the pre-Hague system. The Hague regime can appear to allocate the tasks of ensuring that children are truly orphans eligible for adoption to the sending country, despite the fact that many sending countries have significant problems with corruption, large-scale document fraud and inadequate legal, administrative, or governmental processes.
>
> (Smolin 2007: 54)

One of the safeguards provided by the Convention is the system of accreditation of agencies and individuals involved in inter-country adoptions. The Convention provides that '[a]ccreditation shall only be granted to and maintained by bodies demonstrating their competence to carry out properly the tasks with which they

---

46 CRC art 21(d).

may be entrusted'.[47] The Convention further provides certain minimum standards for accredited bodies:

Article 11
An accredited body shall —

a) pursue only non-profit objectives according to such conditions and within such limits as may be established by the competent authorities of the state of accreditation;
b) be directed and staffed by persons qualified by their ethical standards and by training or experience to work in the field of intercountry adoption; and
c) be subject to supervision by competent authorities of that state as to its composition, operation and financial situation.

Furthermore, a body accredited in one contracting state may act in another state 'only if the competent authorities of both States have authorised it to do so', and the names and addresses of the accredited bodies must be communicated by each state to the Permanent Bureau of the Hague Conference.[48]

6.3.4 Cooperation between states and within states

In order to ensure that the safeguards, discussed above, are respected, one of the Convention's overall objectives is 'to establish a system of co-operation among Contracting States'.[49] Article 7(1) confers a duty on central authorities to 'co-operate with each other and promote co-operation amongst the competent authorities in their States to protect children and to achieve the other objects of the Convention'. The central authorities must take directly all appropriate measures: (a) to provide information about their state laws and other general information; and (b) to keep each other informed about the operation of the Convention.[50]

Finally, a competent authority that detects any abuse, or serious risk of abuse, of the Convention is put under a duty immediately to inform the central authority of its state, and the latter is placed in a position of responsibility for ensuring appropriate measures are taken.

The cooperative framework is established by means of an agreed division of responsibilities. The Convention provides that both the state of origin[51] and the receiving state[52] must ensure that a number of preconditions are met before a Convention adoption can occur. These conditions therefore establish a set

---

47 Hague Convention of 1993 art 10.
48 ibid arts 12 and 13.
49 ibid art 1(b).
50 ibid art 7(2).
51 ibid art 4.
52 ibid art 5.

of minimum standards that must be adhered to. However, it remains open to each contracting state to impose additional (and higher) conditions. The general approach behind the Convention is that it 'should restrict itself to only regulating the essential issues of substantive law in relation to intercountry adoption, leaving all others to the applicable law' (Parra-Aranguren 1994: para 165).

6.3.5 Automatic recognition of adoption decisions

One of the overall objectives of the Convention is 'to secure the recognition in Contracting States of adoptions made in accordance with the Convention'.[53] A key achievement of the Hague Convention of 1993 has been its establishment of a system of automatic recognition of adoptions. The adoptions covered in the Hague Convention of 1993 are those 'which create a permanent parent-child relationship'.[54]

A tighter definition of 'adoption' was rejected on the basis that many states have systems of 'simple' or 'limited' adoption, that is, adoption that will not entirely *terminate* the legal relationship with the birth family and transfer *all* parental rights to the adoptive family. As a result, both simple and full adoptions that have been certified and made in accordance with Convention procedures, are recognised 'by operation of law' in all other contracting states.[55] Consequently, the status of the child is made more certain and it precludes the need for a procedure for recognition of orders, or readoption in the receiving state. This procedure therefore superseded:

> ... the [then] existing practice that an adoption already granted in the State of origin is to be made anew in the receiving State only in order to produce such effects, and also prevents a revision of the contents of the foreign adoption. For these reasons, it only requires a certification, made by the competent authorities of the State where the adoption took place, attesting that the Convention's rules were complied with and that the agreements under subparagraph (c) of Article 17 were given, specifying when and by whom.
>
> (Parra-Aranguren 1994: para 402)

Recognition of an adoption may be refused exceptionally by a contracting state on the grounds that the 'adoption is manifestly contrary to its public policy, taking into account the best interests of the child'.[56] It is understood that this exception is to be construed restrictively; otherwise the overall objective to secure recognition in contracting states would be undermined (Parra-Aranguren 1994: para 426).

---

53 ibid art 1(c).
54 ibid art 2(2).
55 ibid art 23.
56 ibid art 25.

The concept of 'recognition' of a Convention adoption is given finer focus by Article 26. This proved to be a difficult issue in the drafting process of the Convention. However, most participants were of the view that it would not be desirable to restrict the scope of the Convention to the type of adoption that terminates the legal relationship between the child and his or her birth family ('full' adoptions). All kinds of inter-country adoption ought to be covered.

The Convention defines (non-exhaustively) what such recognition will include:

> *Article 26(1)*
> The recognition of an adoption includes recognition of –
>
> (a) the legal parent-child relationship between the child and his or her adoptive parents;
> (b) parental responsibility of the adoptive parents for the child;
> (c) the termination of a pre-existing legal relationship between the child and his or her mother and father, if the adoption has this effect in the Contracting State where it was made.

Where an adoption has had the (usual) effect in (c) above, Article 26(2) provides that the adopted child shall enjoy, in the receiving state, equivalent rights to persons adopted under the purely internal law of the contracting state. Article 26(3) safeguards the application of any provision 'more favourable' to the child in force in the contracting state that recognises the adoption. Where an adoption granted in the state of origin does *not* have the effect of terminating completely a pre-existing legal parent-child relationship, for example, in the case of a 'simple' or 'limited' adoption, a 'conversion' procedure,[57] is available if the law of the receiving state so permits and subject to the grant of the necessary consents.[58]

6.3.6 Competent authorities, central authorities and accredited bodies

The Convention requires that only 'competent authorities' should perform Convention functions. Competent authorities may be:

- central authorities
- public authorities, including judicial or administrative authorities and
- accredited bodies.

The Convention provides for a system of central authorities in all contracting states and imposes certain general obligations on them, such as:

- cooperation with one another, for example, through the exchange of general information concerning intercountry adoption

---

57 ibid art 27.
58 However, it should be noted that the conversion procedure does not cover the case where the adoption is granted in the *receiving* state: see Parra-Aranguren (1994: para 477).

- the elimination of any obstacles to the application of the Convention (art 7(2)(b)) and
- a responsibility to deter all practices contrary to the objects of the Convention (art 8).

The Convention requires that contracting states 'designate a Central Authority' to discharge the duties imposed by the Convention.[59] The Convention provides that some functions need to be performed directly by the central authorities; for example, the duty to cooperate with each other and promote cooperation internally, and to provide certain types of information about the laws of the state and statistical information.[60]

However, other functions could be delegated; for example, the duty to prevent improper financial gain and other practices, and certain measures to preserve and exchange information, facilitate proceedings, promote adoption counselling, and provide general evaluation reports.[61] Consequently, the responsibilities assigned to the central authorities may be discharged, depending on the function in question, by other public authorities, accredited bodies, or even by non-accredited bodies or persons.

The appearance of 'accredited bodies' was a novelty and probably driven by the history of the US, the largest receiving state, that had privileged private agencies as intermediaries for inter-country adoption arrangements:

> It reflects the present reality that private organisations play an important role as intermediaries in the intercountry adoption process. Their role is recognised, but also defined and regulated by the Convention, in particular as to their competence, non-profit objectives and the need for supervision.
>
> (Van Loon 1995: 466)

Therefore, the central authorities are not the sole operators of the Convention. Cooperation may be obtained through other channels, as permitted by the law of each contracting state:

> This feature makes the present Convention different from the Hague Child Abduction Convention, where the Central Authority remains the unique institution responsible for compliance with the obligations imposed by the Convention. For this reason, it is more flexible and may bring about a factual decentralisation of the functions assigned to the Central Authority.
>
> (Parra-Aranguren 1994: para 225)

---

59 Hague Convention of 1993 art 6. See also the comparable provision in the Hague Convention on International Child Abduction of 1980 art 6.

60 Hague Convention of 1993 art 7.

61 ibid arts 8 and 9.

The Permanent Bureau of the Hague Conference has produced an extensive Guide to Good Practice on accreditation issues.[62] Indeed, one of the most contentious points about the Hague Convention of 1993 has been the provision in Article 22 permitting private persons and bodies to act as intermediaries in international adoptions. Article 22 deals with the difficult area of 'independent' or 'private' adoptions, that is, adoptions carried out by bodies other than 'accredited' ones. Although all applications have to be made to a central authority, another public authority or an accredited body, other bodies and persons may act as intermediaries, but only under certain conditions:

> [F]irstly, the Contracting State must have made a specific declaration to that effect; secondly, they must meet the requirements fixed by the Convention; thirdly, the names and addresses of these bodies and persons must be made known to the Secretariat of the Hague Conference; fourthly, the reports on the child and prospective adoptive parents should in all cases be prepared under the responsibility of the central authority or an accredited body; and finally, any State of origin may veto the activities of such other bodies or persons in the adoption process concerning its children.
>
> (Van Loon 1995: 467)

It is thought that this does provide scope for the intrusion of trafficking and sale of children into the inter-country adoption system, and there are concerns that this provision, potentially allowing untrained and possibly unsuitable persons a key role, cannot possibly promote the best interests of children (Sachlier 1993).

Arguably, the safeguarding role of the Convention is compromised by the 'Convention's implicit toleration of the involvement of so-called "approved (non-accredited) persons" at critical stages in the ICA [intercountry adoption] process' (Watkins 2012: 390). However, this matter remains contentious. One commentator argues that 'the Convention was designed to scrutinise independent adoptions, not to get rid of them' and that the Convention in fact strikes a fair balance between authoritative state regulation and a liberal environment for civil society and individuals (Hayes 2011: 316).

6.4   Hague Conference International Centre for Judicial Studies and Technical Assistance

The Hague Conference International Centre for Judicial Studies and Technical Assistance was established in 2006 at the Academy Building on the premises of the Peace Palace, as an integral part of the Permanent Bureau of the Hague

---

62 Permanent Bureau of the Hague Conference on Private International Law, *Guide to Good Practice No 2: Accreditation and Adoption Accredited Bodies*, Bristol: *Family Law* http://www.hcch.net/upload/adoguide2en.pdf (accessed 12 November 2013).

Conference on Private International Law.[63] The centre has been developed in response to the increase in cross-border movement of people: 'As an increasing number of States become Party to the Conventions, the need for implementation assistance expands in parallel'.[64] The centre provides administrative and logistical support to Convention-specific projects, as well as regional and other initiatives being undertaken and developed by the Permanent Bureau in consultation with its member states. There are three major themes of action:

(a) identifying weaknesses or needs in States/regions or where a Hague Convention is about to come into operation
(b) considering what the Hague Conference is able to offer itself and in co-operation with others (States Parties, Regional Bodies or NGOs) in the way of training and technical assistance and
(c) examining how to access any necessary funding.[65]

From time to time the centre has been instrumental in arranging fact-finding missions to places of particular interest in terms of inter-country adoption practice. Fact-finding missions have been undertaken in relation to Guatemala (2007),[66] Nepal (2009)[67] and Kazakhstan (2011).[68]

The case study below provides an extract from the report of the Kazakhstan mission and illustrates a number of contemporary issues concerning the operation of the Hague Convention of 1993. By way of background, it should be noted that Kazakhstan acceded to the Convention on 9 July 2010 and the Convention entered into force on 1 November 2011 in respect of this state. The 'Children Rights Protection Committee' of the Ministry of Education and Science (MOES) was designated as the central authority. Kazakhstan had had a system of private, independent adoptions in the past and, as a consequence, there had been serious problems with its inter-country adoption system, which had been assessed as quite unsafe by the International Social Service. That report (Boéchat and Cantwell 2007) identified various problems, in particular the money required by different

63 Hague Conference of Private International Law, *The Hague Conference International Centre for Judicial Studies and Technical Assistance: the intercountry adoption technical assistance programme* (November 2009) Permanent Bureau: The Hague, Netherlands.
64 ibid [1].
65 ibid [4].
66 Hague Conference of Private International Law, *Report of a Fact-Finding Mission to Guatemala in Relation to Intercountry Adoption* (26 February–9 March 2007), prepared by Ignacio Goicoechea, Liaison Legal Officer for Latin America with the assistance of Jennifer Degeling, Principal Legal Officer (May 2007) Permanent Bureau: The Hague, Netherlands.
67 Hague Conference of Private International Law, *Report of Mission to Nepal* (23–27 November 2009), Jennifer Degeling (4 February 2010) Permanent Bureau: The Hague, Netherlands.
68 Hague Conference of Private International Law, *Report of Mission to Kazakhstan* (9–12 May 2011), Jennifer Degeling and Laura Martínez-Mora (July 2011) Permanent Bureau: The Hague, Netherlands.

intermediaries in Kazakhstan, and the (false) categorisation of children as having special needs for the purposes of getting them into the inter-country adoption stream.

The Government of Kazakhstan requested UNICEF to help it achieve compliance with the Convention while setting up a new system to implement it. UNICEF then sent a request for technical assistance to the Permanent Bureau. The main objective of the Hague mission was to provide technical assistance to the Government of Kazakhstan (in particular to the Children Rights Protection Committee) by sharing the international experience from the states who are parties to the Convention and advising on development of policies, structures and capacities for the implementation of the Convention.

Case study 6.1

Extract from:
Hague Conference of Private International Law, *Report of Mission to Kazakhstan* **(9–12 May 2011), Jennifer Degeling and Laura Martínez-Mora (July 2011) Permanent Bureau: The Hague, Netherlands.**

5. GENERAL OBSERVATIONS

We were very pleased to see that the Central Authority leaders have good knowledge and understanding of 1993 Hague Adoption Convention and its requirements and have been using the *Guide to Good Practice No 1 on the Implementation and Operation of the 1993 Hague Adoption Convention (Guide to Good Practice No 1)* which has been translated into Russian. The Government seems committed to preparing for the effective implementation of the 1993 Hague Adoption Convention.

In addition they have a good understanding of the subsidiarity principle. This is reflected in the practice, as national adoptions are very developed and are reported as very high i.e. almost 80% of all adoptions.

However, there seems to be fragmented approach to child protection. The responsibilities are spread over a number of ministries and it seems that there is a lack of effective coordination as ministries are protecting their own territory and may not wish to be directed by a body at the level of the Committee.

It has to be noted that it was not possible to get any view of how things are working in the regions, and Astana is not representative of the rest of the country.

6. RECOMMENDATIONS

a. Elements of a safe system: Recommendation No 1 of 2010 Special Commission on the practical operation of the 1993 Hague Adoption Convention

We would like to draw the attention of the Government of Kazakhstan to the recommendations made during the 2010 Special Commission regarding the elements of a safe system of adoption. The following are essential features of a well regulated system:

a) effective application of Hague Convention procedures and safeguards including, as far as practicable, in relation to non-Convention adoptions;

b) independent and transparent procedures for determining adoptability and for making decisions on the placement of a child for adoption;

c) strict adherence to the requirements of free and informed consent to adoption;

d) strict accreditation and authorisation of agencies, and in accordance with criteria focusing on child protection;

e) adequate penalties and effective prosecution, through the appropriate public authorities, to suppress illegal activities;

f) properly trained judges, officials and other relevant actors;

g) prohibition on private and independent adoptions;

h) clear separation of intercountry adoption from contributions, donations and development aid;

i) regulated, reasonable and transparent fees and charges;

j) effective co-operation and communication between relevant authorities both nationally and internationally;

k) implementation of other relevant international instruments to which states are parties;

l) public awareness of the issues.

b. Revisions to the chapters on adoption of the Family Code

The Permanent Bureau recalls its offer of assistance to revise the amended version of the chapters related to adoption of the Family Code if it is translated into English.

c. Address the issue of fragmentation of functions and responsibilities

It is not easy to understand who is responsible for what in the child protection system. This fragmentation of functions and responsibilities can be very problematic. It is therefore recommended to address this issue and to try to concentrate functions and responsibilities more effectively.

d. Ensure effective co-ordination between national authorities and bodies – a Central Authority responsibility under art 7

The Central Authority has to promote cooperation amongst the competent authorities in Kazakhstan to protect children and to achieve the objectives of the 1993 Hague Adoption Convention (art 7). According to the 2007 ISS Report, regional authorities may have different approaches and the rate of intercountry adoptions may vary tremendously from region to region. As mentioned in the report, a coordinated national policy and assurance of good co-operation is needed.

e. Ensure all authorities and bodies are aware of the obligation of the protection of the best interests of child as the guiding principle in decision making
The protection of the best interest of the child should always be the primary consideration in all matters related to adoption. An adoption should only be made when it is in the child's best interests to do so. This has to be clear for all authorities and bodies involved.

f. Matching must be done by professionals
We understood that the modifications to the Family Code include a major and very important change: prospective adoptive parents will no longer be allowed to choose a child personally.

As it is said in the Guide to Good Practice No 1, the matching should not be done by the prospective adoptive parents, for example, parents should not visit an institution to pick out an appealing child or choose a child from photo lists. The matching should be assigned to a team and not be left to the responsibility of an individual; the team should be composed of child protection professionals trained in adoption policies and practices. They should preferably be specialists in psycho-social fields. Matching should not be done by computer alone even if an initial screening is made on criteria such as age, gender or special needs of the child. The final match should always be made by professionals and take into account the child's wishes and best interest.

g. Training and supervision for regional authorities and persons involved in child homes
All regional authorities and bodies involved in the adoption procedure should be trained on how to properly implement the 1993 Hague Adoption Convention and on the new legal framework when it will be approved. This should also include the personnel of children's homes.

New responsibilities should be explained properly and procedural manuals to implement the new legal framework properly should be written for staff of the Central Authority and others.

h. Proper regulation for the authorisation of foreign adoption bodies and limits on the number of foreign adoption accredited bodies in Kazakhstan

Kazakhstan should include in its new legislation proper regulation for the authorisation of foreign adoption bodies to work in the country. We understood that this is the intention and therefore some of our presentations during the mission focussed on this aspect.

It is also recommended that Kazakhstan limits the number of foreign adoption accredited bodies that it authorises to work in the country. This will help to prevent pressure. The number of adoption accredited bodies should be proportionate to the number of intercountry adoptions. In addition special attention should be given to selecting the best ones using ethical criteria (see *Draft Guide to Good Practice No 2 on Accreditation and Adoption Accredited Bodies*).[8]

i. Foreign adoption accredited bodies' representatives in Kazakhstan

It is recommended that foreign adoption accredited bodies have their own representatives in Kazakhstan who they will support, train, monitor and for whom they will be responsible. Therefore, it will no longer be needed to have "independent facilitators", as this task should be assumed by the adoption accredited bodies and their respective representatives. This will make it easier to ensure that adoption accredited bodies and their representatives follow the same standards (see Draft Guide to Good Practice No 2, chapter 7).

j. Financial issues

The ISS Report makes quite worrying statements regarding financial issues surrounding intercountry adoption in Kazakhstan, in particular the costs associated with agencies and facilitators. This issue was not raised in our public meetings. However, some interlocutors were also very concerned and told us that it was a widespread problem.

Contracting States and their respective Central Authority have a particular responsibility to regulate the cost of intercountry adoption by taking measures to prevent improper financial gain. It is reasonable to expect that payments will be necessary for both government and non-government services connected with intercountry adoptions. Both receiving States and States of origin are permitted to charge reasonable fees for services provided. The 1993 Hague Adoption Convention is concerned with achieving transparency in costs and fees as a means of preventing improper financial gain.

Regarding this point we recommend following all the recommendations set out in Chapter 5 of the Guide to Good Practice No 1. The modifications to the Family Code should include regulation of adoption financial issues. Costs and fees should be very transparent, accountable and clear. We also recommend that as a requirement for authorisation to work in Kazakhstan, all adoption accredited bodies publish their costs and charges on their website and on the website of the Central Authority of Kazakhstan.

k. Special Needs Children

Special needs children are usually not adopted domestically. Therefore, special campaigns should be carried out in order to promote their adoption in Kazakhstan. For instance, good campaigns have improved the rate of adoption of siblings and older children in States of origin.

The problem of categorising children as special needs children when they are not special needs, in order to put them in the intercountry adoptable stream more quickly, should be addressed. It is recommended that authorities ensure that medical reports are accurate.

6.5   Concluding remarks

Despite the attempts to provide better international legal regulation of intercountry adoption concerns remain about the success of the overall project of international adoptions. Smolin (2010: 493) comments:

> The Hague Convention was a response to the chaotic, corrupt, and abusive practices endemic to pre-Hague intercountry adoptions. The purpose of the Convention was to engender an orderly, ethical, intercountry adoption system free of child trafficking. Adoption advocates also saw the Hague Convention as providing a greater measure of legitimacy for intercountry adoption than exists under the Convention on the Rights of the Child. Seventeen years after the creation of the Hague Convention, the Convention thus far has failed to meet its goals. Child laundering scandals have continued to arise in the Hague era in sending countries such as Cambodia, Chad, China, Guatemala, Haiti, India, Liberia, Nepal, Samoa, and Vietnam. Many potential sending countries, particularly in Africa and Latin America, have decided to close themselves to all or almost all intercountry adoptions, in significant part based on concern over abusive practices. Years of determined cheerleading by the adoption community have failed to cleanse intercountry adoption from its associations with scandal, corruption, trafficking, and profiteering. The boom in intercountry adoption that accompanied the initial decade after the creation of the Hague Convention is now abating, with further declines anticipated. The legitimacy that intercountry adoption sought has been diminished by a sense of lawlessness, despite the extensive regulation and bureaucratic procedures which often accompany it.

Chapter 7

Sexual exploitation

7.1 Introduction

It has been remarked that an outside observer would believe that the issue of child sexual abuse and exploitation is a modern concept (Phoenix and Oerton 2005: 52), yet we know this is not true. The sexual abuse and exploitation of children has occurred for hundreds of years. However, it was not until the later years of the 20th century that the issue of child sexual exploitation began to be taken seriously at a policy level in many countries, and certainly not until the 1990s that it began to feature notably at an international level. This chapter analyses how international law seeks to prevent the sexual exploitation and abuse of children.

7.1.1 What is sexual exploitation?

The first issue is to identify what sexual exploitation is. A variety of terms can be used in this area, but the two most often used are 'sexual abuse' and 'sexual exploitation'. There is disagreement as to what these terms mean and whether they are interchangeable. Some authors believe that each term is the equivalent of the other (Kempe 1978: 382) and it will be seen later that the UN Convention on the Rights of the Child[1] does not differentiate between the terms: see the text of Article 34 in section 3.7.6.3.

However, some believe that a distinction can, and arguably should, be drawn. Van Bueren argues that abuse is the wider term and that 'all forms of exploitation are intrinsically abusive', although she then purports to draw a distinction between them by stating 'the distinguishing feature of sexual exploitation is that it generally involves notions of commercial gain' (Van Bueren 1994a: 52). Others would undoubtedly contest the argument that exploitation necessarily involves commercialisation, and Ost suggests that a more appropriate definition is 'a situation or context in which an individual takes unfair advantage of someone else for his own ends' (Ost 2009: 139). At the heart of this concept is Ost's belief, in the context of child pornography and child solicitation (and it is submitted that

---

1 Opened for signature 20 November 1989, 1577 UNTS 3 (entered into force 2 September 1990).

this applies equally to child prostitution and child trafficking), that exploitation involves an imbalance of power or abuse of a position of vulnerability (Ost 2009: 130). If Ost is correct, and it is submitted she is, then the commercial element sought by Van Bueren is unnecessary.

The natural meanings of the words 'exploitation' and 'abuse' would appear to confirm that there is a distinction between them and that exploitation is the wider term. A dictionary definition of 'exploit' is 'make use of unfairly; benefit unjustly from the work or actions of' something.[2] This supports the definition adopted by Ost, and it is submitted that reference to unfairness and unjustness also implicitly supports the notion of vulnerability, something particularly important in the context of the sexual exploitation of a child. Abuse is defined, inter alia, as 'treat with cruelty or violence; assault sexually; cruel and violent treatment'. Whilst there is undoubtedly some overlap, it would seem that sexual abuse could be considered to be the direct inappropriate sexual assault on a child, whereas exploitation includes those who do not directly assault the child but use the child sexually for their own (material) benefit.

Child sexual abuse and exploitation remain inherently secretive phenomena and this causes significant difficulties in estimating their prevalence in society (Johnson 2004: 462). This is particularly true at the international level. As will be seen, international law commonly tackles the commercial sexual exploitation of children and, indeed, it has been noted that prior to the appearance of the Convention on the Rights of the Child[3] in 1989 sexual abuse (rather than the exploitation of a child) never featured in international law (Van Bueren 1994: 46).

The focus on commercial sexual exploitation in international law is perhaps understandable as it has become a lucrative and global enterprise. A single child pornography website – 'Landslide Productions' – had receipts of US$1.4 million per month (Taylor and Quayle 2003: 5) and this was by no means the only commercial child pornography website. Trafficking is similarly lucrative and has become a modern-day slave trade. Whilst it has been acknowledged that, given the nature of the behaviour, it is difficult to be precise as to the number of persons trafficked for the purposes of sexual exploitation (Riiskjær and Gallagher 2008: 5), estimates range from 800,000 to 1.7 million[4] people per year (Riiskjær and Gallagher 2008: 6). It has been suggested that the trafficking of persons is now more profitable than the smuggling of drugs and arms (Kelly 2002: 13).

A child subject to sexual exploitation is not able to exercise free control over his or her activities. An adult can, in some situations, exercise a degree of choice over the activities that he or she participates in. Whilst the common perception of trafficking is based on coercion or abduction, it is clear that this is not necessarily

2 Concise Oxford English Dictionary.

3 Opened for signature 20 November 1989, 1577 UNTS 3 (entered into force 2 September 1990).

4 The higher figure comes from the International Labour Organisation (ILO) (see section 2.4.1.4), which estimates that 2.5 million people are trafficked each year but that one-third of these figures are for economic purposes rather than for sexual exploitation.

always the case, with some women choosing to migrate to work in the sex industry (Melrose and Barrett 2006: 114). Similarly, it can be said that some adults make the choice to enter the sex industry as a sex worker[5] or choose to be involved in pornography. However, even though some argue that adult women have the ability to make this choice – although it should be noted that such an argument is fiercely resisted by others who argue that the sex industry is about the subjugation of women – a child does not have this choice, nor is he or she equipped to make the choice.

A child has the right not to be sexually exploited. At the first 'World Congress against Commercial Sexual Exploitation of Children' in Stockholm (1996: 9), it was stated:

> The commercial sexual exploitation of children can result in serious, lifelong, even life threatening consequences for the physical, psychological, spiritual, moral and social development of children ...

The consequences for trafficking and prostitution include threats of violence (including threats to kill), pregnancy (including forcible terminations) and the acquisition of sexually transmitted diseases including AIDS. A premium can be charged for children and for not using condoms, the latter meaning that the risks are greater. The consequences of being involved in child pornography are similar. Where penetrative activity is being filmed the same risks above are present but, regardless of what type of pornography is filmed, it becomes a permanent record of the exploitation or abuse.

Research suggests that once an image has been placed on the internet it is almost impossible for it to be recovered as it is quickly downloaded, mirrored and disseminated (Taylor and Quayle 2003: 24). The impact on children of this is that they fear, for the rest of their lives, that the photograph will be seen by someone known to them who may believe that they were willingly involved in the activity rather than being exploited (Palmer 2005), potentially leading to psychological difficulties. It has been cogently argued that child pornography can amount to the revictimisation of a child who has been sexually assaulted (Taylor and Quayle 2003: 31).

There is an inherent power imbalance between the adult photographer and the child (Taylor and Quayle 2003: 4), and the status of a child as a 'minor' makes this exploitative. The same logic can be found with the other forms of commercial child sexual exploitation and it is this, together with the negative consequences of involvement, which requires action to be taken.

---

5 Collectives such as the International Union of Sex Workers (www.iusw.org) campaign for the right of adults to join a legalised sex work industry.

7.2   International action

Before turning to examine the principal international legislation that exists in this area it is worth pausing to note the bodies that have a mandate to combat child sexual exploitation.

7.2.1   Global bodies

The final decade of the 20th century led to the issue of child sexual abuse and exploitation beginning to feature at the international level. In the broader policy context, the United Nations and its agencies began to take seriously the issue of child sexual exploitation and they began to assist non-governmental organisations (NGOs) who sought to work directly with victims and agencies trying to combat the sexual exploitation of children.

Perhaps the most notable NGO to be set up was ECPAT ('Ending Child Prostitution and Trafficking')[6], an international organisation which was established in 1990 by a series of researchers. ECPAT quickly began to formalise and by 1996 it was acting in partnership with the United Nations. It remains an independent organisation (with its headquarters based in Bangkok, Thailand) but it has a close relationship with global, regional and local governments. At governmental level there are two bodies of particular note: the G8 and the United Nations.

7.2.1.1   G8

The G8 owes it origins to an economic summit in 1975 attended by the then five richest countries (France, Germany, Japan, the United Kingdom and the United States of America). By the end of the decade the group became the G-7, with the addition of Italy and Canada, but during the 1980s and 1990s the Soviet Union (and then Russia after the dissolution of the USSR) was invited to attend the meetings, which had begun to stray beyond mere economics and into more geopolitical issues.

In 1998 the group formally changed its name from the G-7 to the G8. In 2001 the G8 established the Lyon/Roma group, which was designed to tackle international crime. A sub-group of the Lyon/Roma group was specifically tasked to examine the issue of sexual exploitation, and by 2003 a strategy was created (G8 2003: paras 15–17). In 2009, following a global symposium on the issue of child pornography, the G8 issued a ministerial declaration on 30 May in Rome. This declaration reaffirmed the group's commitment to tackling child pornography, and stated:

---

6 Originally ECPAT meant 'Ending Child Prostitution in the Asian Territories': see http://www.ecpat.net.

Effective international cooperation would be achieved through a wider membership in multilateral task forces, sharing specialised software and closely coordinating on line undercover investigations and other international law enforcement operations.

(G8 2009: 6)

This was followed in 2013 by a ministerial declaration on combating child sexual abuse during conflicts, including the use of rape as a weapon and the use of children as sex slaves. The G8 reaffirmed that sexual violence in armed conflict could amount to a war crime and that the G8 accepted responsibility, in part, for ensuring that such crimes were prosecuted. The group also committed to assisting victims of armed conflict and working to provide more long-term support (G8 2013: 2).

These statements demonstrate how the G8 has evolved a policy role on tackling child sexual exploitation and, whilst it has not yet produced any treaties, its declaration arguably reaffirms the action that it has committed to in the various international instruments discussed in the following sections. However, it is important that these are not mere words. The G8 includes the four permanent members of the UN Security Council and so they have influence that should be used to tackle child sexual exploitation at an international policy level. It is also important that they themselves show leadership, something that does not always seem to occur (see the comments below in respect of the UN Special Rapporteur).

7.2.1.2   United Nations

The principal global player in this area is the United Nations. The final decades of the 20th century led to the issue of child sexual abuse and exploitation beginning to feature on the United Nations global agenda, particularly through the United Nations Children's Fund (UNICEF) (section 2.4.1.2), the United Nations Human Rights Council (UNHRC) (section 2.5.1.1) and the UN Economic and Social Council (ECOSOC) (section 2.4.1). The United Nations also works closely with national governments, regional groupings and NGOs to fund and operate programmes that are designed to provide real assistance to victims of child sexual exploitation.

The three most notable initiatives of the United Nations will all be discussed in this chapter. Two are legislative: the first is the Convention on the Rights of the Child of 1989, which is discussed throughout this book but is considered later in the specific context of the sexual exploitation of children; the second instrument is the Optional Protocol to the Convention on the Rights of the Child on the Sale of Children, Child Prostitution and Child Pornography of 2000[7] (OPSC) (section 3.6.1). This has quickly established itself as the leading instrument specifically designed to tackle forms of child sexual exploitation, and it will also be discussed later.

7   25 May 2000, 2171 UNTS 227 (entered into force 18 January 2002).

The third initiative is the establishment of the Special Rapporteur on the sale of children, child prostitution and child pornography.[8] Established in 1990, following a resolution of the UN Commission on Human Rights,[9] the mandate has been continuously renewed. The mandate[10] includes:

- to consider matters relating to the sale of children, child prostitution and child pornography
- to continue, through continuous and constructive dialogue with Governments, intergovernmental organisations and civil society ... the analysis of the root causes of the sale of children, child prostitution and child pornography; addressing all the contributing factors, especially the demand factor
- to identify and make concrete recommendations on preventing and combating new patterns of sale of children, child prostitution and child pornography
- to continue ... to promote comprehensive strategies and measures on the prevention of sale of children, child prostitution and child pornography.[11]

In order to discharge her mandate, the Special Rapporteur will visit a number of countries (Buck 2008: 169) in order to have policy-level discussions and consider how the states parties are discharging their obligations under the OPSC. The Special Rapporteur produces an annual report to the Human Rights Council (eg Maalla 2012), which in turn reports to the UN General Assembly.

Buck, whilst observing the valuable work that the Special Rapporteur performs, notes that a difficulty is that the office is under-resourced (Buck 2008: 170). This inspite of the fact that the mandate passed by the Human Rights Council requests the Secretary-General of the United Nations and the High Commissioner for Human Rights to 'provide all the human, technical and financial assistance' needed by the Special Rapporteur.[12] The under-resourcing of the office means that the Special Rapporteur is limited in the amount of research that can be commissioned and visits conducted. Ideally, it would be beneficial for there to be an 'Office of the Special Rapporteur' that would employ a (small) number of staff also to conduct visits and commission and interpret research. Instead, a single mandate holder is in place and, whilst her role is invaluable, it does mean that its use is somewhat limited.

8 See http://www.ohchr.org/en/issues/children/pages/childrenindex.aspx (accessed 14 October 2013). Previous mandate holders are Mr Vitit Muntarbhorn (1991–4), Ms Ofelia Calcetas-Santos (1994–2001) and Mr Juan Miguel Petit (2001–08). Ms Najat M'jid Maalla (Morocco) was appointed Special Rapporteur in May 2008.

9 UN Commission on Human Rights, resolution 1990/68 (7 March 1990). The mandate was renewed by: UN Human Rights Council, *Rights of the child: a holistic approach to the protection and promotion of the rights of children working and/or living on the street*: Resolution 16/12, UN Doc A/HRC/RES/16/12 (3 May 2011).

10 Human Rights Council, *Mandate of the Special Rapporteur on the sale of children, child prostitution and child pornography*, Resolution 7/13, 40th meeting (27 March 2008).

11 ibid para 2.

12 ibid para 5.

Another problem with the Special Rapporteur is the extent to which it can be said that countries cooperate with her office. Despite states being requested to cooperate with the Special Rapporteur it does not appear that this always occurs. For example, the last two reports have examined two important themes (child sexual exploitation following national disasters (Maalla 2011) and child sex tourism (Maalla 2012)). Both thematic reports involved evidence gathering. The Special Rapporteur sent a questionnaire to all (193) member states of the UN and yet only 23 states responded to the 2011 request (Maalla 2011:4) and 35 for the 2012 report (Maalla 2012:4).

Of this latter report – which concerned an issue of child sexual exploitation where citizens of developed countries are responsible for the majority of the abuse – it is notable that only two members of the G8 (Germany and Russia) responded, the other six members did not. This perhaps demonstrates a lack of support by leading countries in facilitating the work of the Special Rapporteur in discharging her mandate, something that is to be regretted. Developed countries, especially leading ones such as those belonging to the G8 or G20, should be setting an example and dismissing requests from the Special Rapporteur to identify an evidence base does not do this.

7.2.2 Regional bodies

It is not only global bodies that have a mandate to combat child sexual exploitation; some regional groupings also operate in this area. Regional mandates exist in part as a method of strengthening the work undertaken at global level but also to demonstrate a regional commitment to tackling this problem. The key difference between the global and regional mandates is that the regional ones, as their name suggests, ordinarily involve localised action. The mandate does demonstrate the political will to work towards combating child sexual exploitation.

Examples of regional instruments include the Organisation of African Unity's (OAU) African Charter on the Rights and Welfare of the Child[13] and the South Asian Association for Regional Co-operation (SAARC)[14] Convention on Preventing and Combating Trafficking in Women and Children for Prostitution[15] of 2002, which attempted to address one particular form of commercial sexual exploitation.

13 OAU, African Charter on the Rights and Welfare of the Child (11 July 1990) CAB/ LEG/24.9/49 (1990), entered into force 29 November 1999. As at 21 February 2013, 47 of the 54 African states had ratified/acceded to this treaty. Article 16 requires states parties to protect children against abuse, including sexual abuse.

14 SAARC is comprised of seven states: Bangladesh, Bhutan, India, Maldives, Nepal, Pakistan and Sri Lanka.

15 SAARC Convention on Preventing and Combating Trafficking in Women and Children for Prostitution, Kathmandu, Nepal (5 January 2002). See http://www.saarc-sec.org/userfiles/ conv-traffiking.pdf (accessed 15 November 2013).

Perhaps the most active geopolitical region in seeking to combat child sexual exploitation is Europe. As is well known, there are two principal groupings within Europe; the Council of Europe (which consists of 47 member states) and the European Union (EU) (which has 27 Member States). There are other groupings (eg the 'Council of Baltic Sea States'[16]), but these tend to work in conjunction with both of the other bodies.

The Council of Europe is best known for its work in human rights, particularly the European Convention on Human Rights[17] (ECHR), but it has, in recent years, been active in seeking to combat exploitative actions against individuals, including the sexual exploitation of children. Most of its work has been on a legislative basis, although it does fund projects that seek to tackle these areas. Some of its legislation relates specifically to the exploitation of vulnerable persons (most notably the Convention on Action against Trafficking in Human Beings[18] and the Convention on the Protection of Children against Sexual Exploitation and Sexual Abuse),[19] but at other times the legislative action is found within more general provisions. Perhaps the most notable example of this is the Convention on Cybercrime,[20] which includes a provision that defines and mandates action against child pornography.[21]

The European Union has become involved in this area only comparatively recently, although this is perhaps unsurprising since prior to the Treaty of Maastricht[22] of 1992 the European Community (as it was then known) was simply an economics vehicle. However, by the mid 1990s there was increased interest in child sexual exploitation (Gillespie 2011: 299), eventually culminating in a number of legislative instruments including a Council Decision on combating child pornography,[23] a Council Framework Decision[24] on combating the sexual exploitation of children and child pornography and ultimately a (legally binding)

---

16 The Council of the Baltic Sea States (http://www.cbss.org) is a political forum for regional intergovernmental cooperation. The Members of the Council are the 11 states of the Baltic Sea Region and the European Commission, namely Denmark, Estonia, Finland, Germany, Iceland, Latvia, Lithuania, Norway, Poland, Russia and Sweden.

17 European Convention for the Protection of Human Rights and Fundamental Freedoms, opened for signature 4 November 1950, ETS No 5, 213 UNTS 221 (entered into force 3 September 1953).

18 Opened for signature 16 May 2005, CETS No 197 (entered into force 1 February 2008).

19 Opened for signature 25 October 2007, CETS No 201 (entered into force 1 July 2010).

20 Opened for signature 23 November 2001, CETS No 185 (entered into force 1 July 2004).

21 Council of Europe, Convention on Cybercrime, CETS No 185 art 9.

22 European Union, Treaty on European Union (Consolidated Version), Treaty of Maastricht (7 February 1992) Official Journal of the European Communities C 325/5 (24 December 2002).

23 Council Decision 2000/375/JHA of 29 May 2000 to Combat Child Pornography on the Internet [2000] Official Journal of the European Communities L138/1.

24 Council Framework Decision 2004/68/JHA of 22 December 2003 on Combating the Sexual Exploitation of Children and Child Pornography [2004] Official Journal of the European Communities L13/44.

Directive.[25] The main purpose of the Directive is to ensure that the laws on child sexual exploitation are harmonised across the Union and it includes minimum levels of punishment. The Directive requires states to act in an extraterritorial manner (explained in the following discussion) and provide programmes of assistance to victims of sexual exploitation.

The European Union's greatest impact, however, has probably been in its non-legislative action. The Treaty of Maastricht of 1992 established a European Law Enforcement Agency, 'Europol',[26] which is designed, inter alia, to facilitate cooperation between the law enforcement agencies of each Member State.

Europol came into existence in 1998 and as early as 2000 it had participated in international operations against child sexual exploitation (Europol 2009: 21), something it continues to do to this day. Its 'Internet Safety Programme and Internet Safety Plus' programme – Akdeniz (2008) provides a useful summary of these initiatives – has led to significant funding becoming available to ensure the safety of children from, for example, child pornography and grooming. Funding has also been used to establish Inhope[27] and Insafe,[28] both of which have been successful in safeguarding children from abuse.

7.2.3   Industry

Whilst we would tend to think of governments as being the key actors of international action, it is not limited to this. In the context of child sexual exploitation it is clear that other actors can become involved and this includes industry. For example, individual companies have sometimes spent considerable resources to combat child pornography. For example, both Google and Microsoft have developed software that provides assistance to law enforcement in the identification and detection of child pornography images (Westlake and others 2012). Microsoft, for example, has created 'PhotoDNA', which allows images to be tracked around the internet and identifies whether they are new but also, perhaps importantly, whether the child is already known or other images exist (Ricanek and Boehnen 2012: 97). The latter is important because it could tell investigators that images they are looking at of a child aged five depict a child in other known images where the child is depicted at the age of 12. This would save the police wasting time searching for a five-year-old when the child is, in fact, much older.

---

25 Directive 2011/92/EU of the European Parliament and of the Council of 13 December 2011 on Combating the sexual abuse and sexual exploitation of children and child pornography, and replacing Council Framework Decision 2004/68/JHA [2011] Official Journal of the European Communities L335/1.

26 See http://www.europol.europa.eu/ (accessed 14 October 2013).

27 See www.inhope.org. This is an international network of hotlines that allows members of the public to report websites they suspect of hosting child pornography or other exploitative material.

28 See www.saferinternet.org. This is a network of contact centres that provide assistance and educational initiatives to the public and educators to safeguard children and young persons online.

Whilst individual companies may contribute, it is perhaps more interesting when industry as a whole cooperates because they then truly become a form of international action. Perhaps one of the best examples of this is in relation to child sex tourism (something discussed in the case study below). Child sex tourism can be best summarised as where an adult travels abroad and engages in sexually inappropriate behaviour with children. In many instances the purpose of the travel will be to abuse a child but in other instances it may be that an opportunity arises whilst the traveller is in a particular country (the hotel, for example, arranges for a child prostitute or a person attends a sexual massage parlour).

Child sexual tourism is a largely hidden form of abuse (Svensson 2006:643), partly because there are concerns that in some instances the families of the children are complicit within it, partly for financial reasons (Montgomery 2008: 909). However, the travel industry is perhaps one of the biggest and most lucrative forms of international commerce. There is a realisation that the industry itself could assist in the combating of child sexual exploitation. The industry created the Task Force to Protect Children from Sexual Exploitation in Tourism, which was highlighted by the Special Rapporteur.[29] The Task Force is a mixture of government agencies, NGOs and industry representatives that seek to gather information on the main trends of child sex tourism.

Perhaps the more notable action by industry was the development of two codes by the industry. The first is the Global Code of Ethics for Tourism,[30] which was developed by the World Tourism Organisation. This is a global umbrella group for tourist providers and the global code of ethics sets out a series of principles for corporate social responsibility, including making reference to child sex tourism (Tepelus 2008: 107). The difficulty with it, as the Special Rapporteur has noted, is that it is not binding and there are no sanctions if organisations simply turn a blind eye to it (Maalla, 2012: 17). Child sex tourism is also included within a long list of other factors, rather than it being the target of specific action.

The more pertinent code is that created by the Sexual Exploitation in Travel and Tourism initiative which is specifically created by the industry to combat sexually exploitative behaviour. Its Code of Conduct for the Protection of Children in Travel and Tourism[31] addresses these issues in more detail and commits the industry to ensuring that it takes positive action to combat child sexual exploitation. It contains very practical initiatives, including the provision of training to hotel employees and the distribution of literature by air carriers. Of course, the difficulty with it is that it relies on cooperation as there are few sanctions but it is a major step forward from what existed before and it has led to the situation

---

29 Human Rights Council, *Report submitted by the Special Rapporteur on the sale of children, child prostitution and child pornography*, Juan Miguel Petit, 7th session, UN Doc A/HRC/7/8 (9 January 2008) para 14.

30 See http://www.unwto.org/ethics/full_text/en/full_text.php?subop=2 (accessed 15 November 2013).

31 See http://www.osce.org/eea/41835 (accessed 15 November 2013).

where, for example, major hotel companies are no longer considered 'safe' places to conduct child sex tourism from (Maalla, 2012: 8).

More can be done, however. There is a strong link between poverty and child sex tourism (Maalla, 2012:10) and it is incumbent on large players, eg tour operators, to use their financial muscle to implement the Code. For example, an independent hotelier in a tourist resort may be heavily reliant on the business from a tour operator (who will block-book the hotel). The Code could, and should, be incorporated into the contract between them. However, the tourism industry also has to look at paying a living wage to employees of hotels etc. It is perhaps unsurprising that an employee who is paid a poverty-level wage will find it an attractive proposition to procure a child for a Western tourist, when the rewards for doing so could be many months' wages as a bribe.

It is not only the tourist industry that is seeking to tackle child sexual exploitation. Another good example is the finance industry. There is still a considerable amount of commercially-available child pornography; in other words, material that is purchased. In 2006 the Special Rapporteur was concerned about the fact that some financial bodies had created anonymous payment systems, which could cause problems in tracing those who purchase exploitative images of children.[32] Whilst some anonymous forms do still exist – and are indeed marketed as being a source of evading law enforcement – the financial industry has taken steps to try to tackle child pornography.

In North America the Financial Coalition against Child Pornography[33] involves many of the major banks, credit card companies and ecommerce bodies (eg PayPal). An equivalent exists in Europe, the European Financial Coalition against Commercial Sexual Exploitation of Children Online.[34] Both coalitions work closely with law enforcement to identify individuals who use their services, inter alia, to purchase child pornography but they also use intelligence to deny banking services to those who market child pornography, in essence making it difficult to trade such material.

These examples show that industry can have an important part to play in combating child sexual exploitation and it is for this reason that governments and governmental bodies are increasingly trying to work with industry. This, as will be seen, is reflected in some international instruments that widen the meaning of cooperation to include all forms of agencies.

---

32 Commission on Human Rights, *Report of the Special Rapporteur on the sale of children, child prostitution and child pornography*, Economic and Social Council, 62nd session, UN Doc E/CN.4/2006/67 (12 January 2006) para 5.

33 See http://www.missingkids.com/FCACP (accessed 15 November 2013).

34 See http://www.europeanfinancialcoalition.eu/ (accessed 15 November 2013).

7.3   International instruments

Having outlined the international action that is being undertaken to combat the sexual exploitation of children, it is now necessary to consider the international legal instruments that exist to tackle this phenomenon.

7.3.1   UN Convention on the Rights of the Child

As has been noted already in other parts of this book (sections 1.2.1 and 3.1), the Convention on the Rights of the Child[35] is perhaps the most important international instrument relating to children's rights. It is a wide-ranging treaty that governs the social, civil and political rights of the child. Many of the provisions within the Convention are not directly relevant to the issue of sexual exploitation, but two Articles are specifically relevant to this issue. The first, and perhaps most significant, is Article 34, although Article 35 is also of relevance in this context. The Special Rapporteur has said of this that: 'the [Convention] promotes a comprehensive system for protecting children from violence and from sexual and other forms of exploitation' (Maalla 2011:9).

Article 34 is the wider provision of the two: see section 3.7.6.3 for the text of this Article. At first sight this appears useful: it provides a clear statement that countries shall protect a child from both sexual abuse and sexual exploitation. Whilst this is a worthy statement, there is, however, difficulty in terms of how it is expressed. Article 34 does not make clear how a state should protect a child from sexual exploitation. Does it mean to take civil steps? Criminal steps? Presumably both, but the Article does not set this out clearly.

Article 34 seeks to define sexual exploitation in paragraphs (a)–(c), but again the specific terms used are not defined and this can lead to questions being raised as to what precisely Article 34 seeks to protect. Some have argued that Article 34 was a fudge and a compromise between the desire to protect children from exploitative practices and, at the same time to ensure that adolescent experimentation was not the subject of mandatory intervention (Alexander and others 2000: 482). The difficulty with compromised wording is that it allows debates to occur as to what its objectives are. For example, paragraph (a) refers to coercion or inducement but these can be said to be opposite ends of the same scale.

What of situations where sexual activity takes place without coercion (which suggests pressure or force) or inducement (which suggests grooming or reward)? In paragraph (b) there is reference to 'child prostitution' but it is not clear what this covers. The term 'prostitute' covers a wide range of behaviour and indeed many argue the term is inappropriate (Pearce 2006).

Without a clear understanding of what the term means, is Article 34 seeking to protect only against, for example, the payment of money to a child for sex or

---

35 Opened for signature 20 November 1989, 1577 UNTS 3 (entered into force 2 September 1990).

does it cover other parts of the sex industry (eg online chatrooms, telephone sex lines etc)? Does it cover situations where an adolescent has sex with someone in return for being given food or shelter?[36] Is this prostitution for the purposes of Article 34?

It may seem pedantic to concentrate on the wording of the Article when it could be argued that, like many of the other Articles within the Convention, it was drafted deliberately widely to allow flexibility.[37] However, the first Special Rapporteur noted that vague terminology can cause difficulties in assessing legal frameworks.[38] This in turn makes the task of protecting children more difficult.

If Article 34 suffers from a lack of precision, Article 35 is perhaps even more problematic: see section 3.7.9.3 for the text of Article 35. This Article does not even expressly mention the sexual exploitation of children. Sexual exploitation is undoubtedly covered since the provision refers to 'for any purpose or in any form', but it is not set out explicitly. Is this problematic? Arguably, it is, because the abduction of a child by a parent is considerably different to the trafficking of children for sex, and yet Article 35 appears to cover both situations. A provision as wide as this raises the same issues as before. How can states be held to account for their legal systems if the benchmark they are being measured against – in this case, Article 35 – is not sufficiently defined itself?

7.3.2   Convention on the Worst Forms of Child Labour (1999)

In 1999 the International Labour Organisation (ILO) (section 2.4.1.4), a specialist agency of the United Nations charged with developing and enforcing labour standards, passed the Convention on the Worst Forms of Child Labour[39] (see generally, section 4.2.3). At the time this Convention appeared, the ILO estimated that 250 million children were at work, with some 80 million involved in what it refers to as 'the worst forms of labour' (NGO Group 2001: 5). The Convention on the Worst Forms of Child Labour defines a child as a person under the age of 18.[40]

This can be contrasted immediately with the Convention on the Rights of the Child which, whilst suggesting that the age of majority should be 18, allows that it can be lowered by domestic legislation.[41] Article 3 defines the 'worst forms of

---

36 Research suggests that this is not uncommon: see for example Chase and Statham (2005) and Pearce and others (2002).

37 See section 3.2 for an account of the Convention on the Rights of the Child's provenance.

38 Commission on Human Rights, *Report of the Special Rapporteur on the sale of children, child prostitution and child pornography*, Economic and Social Council, 63rd meeting, UN Doc E/CN.4/1991/51 (6 March 1991).

39 International Labour Organization, Prohibition and Immediate Action for the Elimination of the Worst Forms of Child Labour Convention, ILO Convention No 182 (17 June 1999). This Convention had 178 parties as at 22 February 2014.

40 Convention on the Worst Forms of Child Labour art 2.

41 *Convention on the Rights of the Child* art 1.

child labour' and paragraph (b) includes 'the use of children for prostitution and pornography'. Paragraph (d) may also be of relevance as it refers to work that 'is likely to endanger the health, safety or morals of children'. The use of the term 'morals' may be of assistance in terms of dealing with some forms of commercial sexual exploitation that do not come within either prostitution or pornography.

Article 7 of the Convention on the Worst Forms of Child Labour commits states parties, inter alia, to take measures to prevent a child's involvement in the worst forms of child labour and to provide assistance to those children who are working. Accompanying the Convention is a recommendation[42] that provides guidance to contracting states on how to implement the Convention. The Recommendation includes, for example, the suggestion that criminal offences should be invoked to tackle those who employ children in the worst forms of labour,[43] and also protocols on how information should be fed back to the ILO.

The ILO Convention does, at least, recognise that the commercial sexual exploitation of children is inappropriate and should be tackled. An advantage of the Convention on the Worst Forms of Child Labour is that it brings together not just governments but also employers, NGOs and trade unions. Their diverse membership means that the issue of commercial sexual exploitation is raised at different levels: see further section 4.3. That said, however, it is focused on very narrow areas, is restricted to commercial forms of child sexual exploitation (since otherwise they would not be 'labour') and does not provide appropriate definitions of the various terms. To an extent, therefore, it can be said to be an additional recognition of the issue but it does not, by itself, take matters much further than the standards as formulated in the Convention on the Rights of the Child.

7.3.3 Optional Protocol to the Convention on the Rights of the Child on the sale of children, child prostitution and child pornography of 2000 (OPSC)[44]

As noted already, shortly after the drafting of the Convention on the Rights of the Child the issue of child sexual exploitation, particularly sex tourism, became of great concern and the United Nations appointed its first Special Rapporteur on the sale of children, child prostitution and child pornography. The Special Rapporteur was concerned about whether the Convention on the Rights of the Child was sufficient to tackle child sexual exploitation, and by 1994 the UN Commission on Human Rights[45] had created a working group to examine the possibility of an Optional Protocol to the Convention on the Rights of the Child,

---

42 See ch 4 (n 11) for the legal status of ILO Recommendations.

43 R190 Worst Forms of Child Labour Recommendation 1999 (No 190), Recommendation concerning the prohibition and immediate action for the elimination of the worst forms of child labour. Adoption: Geneva, 87th ILC session (17 June 1999) para 12.

44 25 May 2000, 2171 UNTS 227 (entered into force 18 January 2002).

45 The UN Commission on Human Rights (UNCHR) was replaced by the UN Human Rights Council (UNHRC) in 2006: see section 2.5.1.1.

specifically related to the issue of (commercial) sexual exploitation.[46] Pressure to change increased with the holding of the first World Congress against the Commercial Sexual Exploitation of Children ('the Stockholm Conference').[47]

An important outcome of this Congress was support for strengthening the international rules relating to commercial sexual exploitation, including the possibility of drafting a new legal instrument. Part of this pressure arose from the unsatisfactory wording of Article 34, and it has been suggested that this was a major reason for the development of the Optional Protocol so soon after the Convention on the Rights of the Child had come into force (Alexander and others 2000: 482).

Ultimately, the demand for change led to the drafting of the OPSC. The Optional Protocol[48] differs from the Convention on the Rights of the Child in that it is more specific in terms of its definitions and its obligations on contracting states. The current Special Rapporteur has noted that the wording of the OPSC is sufficient to allow her to 'implement her mandate within a clear legal framework and yet take into consideration endemic situations and emerging problems' (Maalla 2008: 6). That is not to say, however, that the OPSC is perfect as, like any international instrument, it contains the negotiated wording resulting from the discussions and diplomatic compromises made by various states parties.

Perhaps the most significant issue is that, unlike Article 34 of the Convention on the Rights of the Child, the Optional Protocol is arguably too narrow. The OPSC does not refer to the sexual abuse or sexual exploitation of children (unlike, eg, the Council of Europe's Convention on the Protection of Children against Sexual Exploitation and Sexual Abuse,[49] which does seek to cover most forms), but rather it is focused specifically on commercial sexual exploitation. Indeed, it is clear from Article 1 that it is restricted to three forms:

- child trafficking (the sale of children)
- child prostitution and
- child pornography.

If the sexual behaviour is not within these three heads then it is outside the scope of the OPSC. It is notable that the OPSC is clearer than the Convention on the Rights of the Child in terms of how it defines child prostitution. The wording of Article 2 makes clear that it applies to sexual activity 'for remuneration or any other form of consideration' and, accordingly, the comments made earlier about

---

46 UN Commission for Human Rights, *Need to adopt effective international measures for the prevention and eradication of the sale of children, child prostitution and child pornography*, resolution 1994/90, 66th meeting (9 March 1994).

47 See First World Congress Against Commercial Sexual Exploitation of Children, Stockholm (1996). There have subsequently been two more world congresses: in 2001, held in Yokohama, Japan; and in 2008, held in Rio de Janeiro. See http://www.ecpat.net/world-congress-against-commercial-sexual-exploitation-children for summaries.

48 The OPSC had 166 states parties on 22 February 2014.

49 Opened for signature 25 October 2007, CETS No 201 (entered into force 1 July 2010).

youths providing sex in return for gifts or a place to stay overnight, would come within this definition.

The technological revolution has, in recent years, arguably placed great strain on the OPSC as there is evidence of exploitation which is not within these headings, most notably the issue of sexual solicitation or grooming.[50] This will be discussed further later in respect of the criminalisation of the commercial sexual exploitation of the child.

7.4 States' responsibilities

The international instruments discussed earlier place a number of responsibilities onto state parties. For ease of analysis, these responsibilities will be considered in key themes. The themes are:

- criminalisation of child sexual exploitation
- establishing jurisdiction over child sexual exploitation
- international cooperation and support in tackling child sexual exploitation
- measures to assist victims of child sexual exploitation.

7.4.1 Criminalisation

Perhaps the most significant part of the OPSC is the requirement in Article 3 to ensure that 'as a minimum' a series of acts and actions are subject to the criminal law. The acts and actions are, inter alia:

(a) offering, delivering or accepting, by whatever means, a child for the purposes of its sexual exploitation,
(b) offering, obtaining, procuring or providing a child for child prostitution,
(c) producing, distributing, disseminating, importing, exporting, offering, selling or possessing for those purposes child pornography.

(OPSC art 3(1))

Article 3(2) requires states to ensure that an attempt to commit an offence in Article 3(1) is also an offence. The Optional Protocol does not define what an attempt is but rather leaves this to each domestic legal system to identify.

Article 3(3) requires states to 'make these offences punishable by appropriate penalties that take into account their grave nature'. This is somewhat vague but could, in a positive sense, be read as meaning that there must be recognition that the crimes set out in Article 3(1) are serious and should be reflected in

---

50 See: UN Commission on Human Rights, *Rights of the Child: report submitted by the Special Rapporteur on the sale of children, child prostitution and child pornography*, Economic and Social Council, 61st session, UN Doc E/CN.4/2005/78 (23 December 2004) 7. For a discussion on the meaning of such terms see Gillespie (2002); Craven and others (2006).

strong punishments. However, in the more negative sense it is notable that the Convention has not, for example, suggested that they should ordinarily be punishable by imprisonment, or set minimum punishments. The reasoning behind this approach is that it is most unusual for treaties to set out minimum punishments,[51] in part because each jurisdiction will have its own system of punishments and agreeing a coherent approach could be difficult to negotiate.

It was noted earlier that the Convention on the Rights of the Child has been almost universally ratified and 166 countries have ratified the OPSC to date. The drafters of the OPSC were no doubt careful to ensure that there was nothing in this instrument that would restrict the likelihood of ratification.

7.4.1.1   Sale of children

Article 3(1) tackles the sale of children. The demarcation between this and child prostitution is open to debate but it is likely that this heading is designed to tackle those who treat children as a commodity, to be bought and sold. Whilst the term 'trafficking' is not used expressly, the language of OPSC which refers to 'offering, delivering or accepting, by whatever means, a child' means it is likely that this is what was meant (UNICEF 2009: 9). That said, however, it has been noted that trafficking does not need to involve a child being physically sold (UNICEF 2009: 10), and this demonstrates a potential lacuna in the Optional Protocol in that in the absence of a sale, or if it does not come within the definition of child prostitution, the trafficking of a child may not be included.

It is notable that the wording of Article 3(1) includes 'offering', 'delivering' and 'accepting' and thus it tackles not only the person who sells the child but also an intermediary who 'receives' the child for another. 'Delivering' would seem to include those who are responsible for the actual movement of the child, irrespective of whether they are necessarily involved in the sale itself. So, for example, X asks Y to smuggle V into country A. X is to be paid US$5000 for V. X is the one who has 'sold' V but Y is undoubtedly delivering her and accordingly would be covered under this Protocol. 'Offering' would seem to imply that the actual transaction need not take place, and advertising the sale of the child may be covered also. As will be seen, it is somewhat regrettable that the same is not true for either child prostitution or child pornography.

7.4.1.2   Child prostitution

It was noted in the first section of this chapter that 'child prostitution' is a controversial label and doubt exists over what precisely is covered. Article 3(1)(b)

---

51 Council Framework Decision 2004/68/JHA of 22 December 2003 on Combating the Sexual Exploitation of Children and Child Pornography [2004] Official Journal of the European Communities L13/44, does provide minimum standards but this is not a treaty per se but rather a legal instrument of the European Union.

criminalises the 'offering, obtaining, procuring or providing' of a child for the purposes of child prostitution. The emphasis of the Article would appear to be on those who control the child ('offering', 'procuring' and 'providing' must relate to the person who 'supplies' the child).

What of the person who actually pays to have sexual contact with a child? It could be argued that the term 'obtains' covers this behaviour, although in the context of Article 3(1)(b) the term 'obtains' may be more apposite to describe a person who receives the child in order to control him or her. That said, the Special Rapporteur indicated his belief that the OPSC did mandate the criminalisation of the clients of child prostitutes[52] and, whilst it may have been preferable for the language of the OPSC to be clearer, it is to be hoped that states adopt that reasoning.

UNICEF (2009: 12) has noted that the issue of sex tourism is only mentioned in passing by the OPSC but argues that sex tourism could be considered child prostitution. Presumably UNICEF means by this the fact that many sex tourists will seek to pay either a child or an agency for sexual activity with a child. Where this is the case, it should be possible to read Article 3 in such a way that covers this activity. Certainly this argument is supported by the Special Rapporteur who, in her latest report (which specifically examined the issue of child sex tourism), considered that it fell within the OPSC through child prostitution and possibly child pornography (Maalla, 2012:10). Whilst this is true it is perhaps a matter of regret that it is not expressly mentioned as a form of abuse and exploitation in its own right.

The implicit inclusion of child sex tourism in child prostitution does raise an issue in terms of how child prostitution is defined and criminalised. The definition in Article 2 appears to be focused quite specifically on the individual who supplies the child, but what of the person who controls the activities, or some of the activities, of a child prostitute? In the context of sex tourism this could involve the travel agent who knowingly sends a person to a particular country and, indeed, a particular villa or hotel. Can it really be said that this person has offered, procured or provided a child? The only possibility would be to suggest that he has procured child prostitution, but realistically it may still be one step away. Had the OPSC referred to 'facilitates', then the issue would have been put beyond doubt.

7.4.1.3 Child pornography

Child pornography is something that continues to defy a precise definition (Gillespie 2010), but the OPSC does, at least, define what it considers the term to mean. In Article 2(c) it states that child pornography is 'any representation, of whatever means, of a child engaged in real or simulated explicit sexual activities or

---

52 Commission on Human Rights, *Report of the Special Rapporteur on the sale of children, child prostitution and child pornography*, Economic and Social Council, 62nd session, UN Doc E/CN.4/2006/67 (12 January 2006) 13.

any representation of the sexual parts of a child for primarily sexual purposes'. It is not the place of this chapter to critique this definition,[53] but it should be noted that the OPSC definition is arguably one of the widest and would include all forms of representation, including text, drawings and photographs.

Article 3(1)(c) requires a number of actions relating to child pornography to be criminalised. The first set of offences is concerned with the creation and dissemination of child pornography. The language of Article 3 is deliberate and ensures that for example, there is no doubt that the creation (production) of child pornography should be criminalised as should any form of the dissemination of child pornography. So, for example, the Article is careful to ensure that dissemination includes not only distribution, but also the importing and exporting of material.

The advent of communication technologies has meant that the clear majority of child pornography is hosted online (Taylor and Quayle 2003), which does raise issues about whether information is 'imported' or 'exported' when it is merely accessed on the internet as those terms are traditionally understood to mean the physical moving of an item into or out of the country.

An interesting issue in the wording of Article 3(1) is whether the simple possession of child pornography is criminalised. The wording of Article 3(1) suggests it is not, but that possession with the intention of disseminating the images is criminalised. This can be contrasted with, for example, Article 9 of the Convention on Cybercrime,[54] which states that simple possession of child pornography may[55] be a criminal activity, or Article 20 of the Convention on the Protection of Children against Sexual Exploitation and Sexual Abuse.[56]

UNICEF has noted the potential lacuna in the wording of the OPSC, although it suggests that the Committee on the Rights of the Child has attempted to fill this lacuna by making comments in national reports (Cedrangolo 2009: 9–10). In his first thematic report on child pornography, the then Special Rapporteur also noted this omission and recommended that simple possession be criminalised so as to tackle the 'participant chain' in the production and dissemination of child pornography.[57] This has recently been reinforced by the current Special Rapporteur who, along with calling for simple possession to be criminalised, has argued that liability should additionally be extended to those who knowingly access or watch material online (Maalla 2009: 23).

---

53 See Gillespie (2010) for further discussion.
54 Council of Europe, Convention on Cybercrime, CETS No 185.
55 Although art 9(1)(e) is not equivocal, art 9(4) provides that states may reserve, in whole or in part, the right not to apply that provision.
56 Opened for signature 25 October 2007, CETS No 201 (entered into force 1 July 2010).
57 UN Commission on Human Rights, *Rights of the Child: report submitted by the Special Rapporteur on the sale of children, child prostitution and child pornography*, Economic and Social Council, 61st session, UN Doc E/CN.4/2005/78 (23 December 2004) 23.

7.4.1.4 Missing activities

It was noted previously that the OPSC does not seek to criminalise all forms of child sexual abuse but is restricted to commercial forms of sexual abuse, as is the Convention on the Worst Forms of Child Labour. It will be remembered that the Convention on the Rights of the Child itself does not provide expressly for the criminalisation of any specific forms of behaviour, although Article 34 does, at least, suggest that, inter alia, all forms of sexual abuse should be criminalised.

In response to technological advancements and the ways in which offenders have used information and communication technologies to seek children for abuse, the then Special Rapporteur recommended that states '... introduce legislation creating the offence of "internet grooming or luring" '.[58] This was an interesting call since it would seem to fall outside the definitions put forward in the OPSC (as grooming rarely involves any commercial aspect). The call could be taken as evidence of a desire to move the OPSC beyond commercial sexual exploitation into a wider instrument to address the sexual abuse and exploitation of children.

In the absence of a change to the text of the instrument, however, the Special Rapporteur can only make recommendations rather than ensuring that they form part of the obligations of a state. The effect of this is perhaps evident from the fact that a report of the current Special Rapporteur made the same point about grooming (Maalla 2009: 23). Despite this, few countries appear to have introduced legislation to tackle grooming (Maalla 2009: 12) and there is no indication that the position has changed in recent years.

7.4.1.5 Victims as criminals

It was noted in the preceding discussion that Article 34 of the Convention on the Rights of the Child was considered to be a compromise because of concerns that alternative wording may have led to adolescent sexual experimentation being criminalised.

A more difficult problem is that in some countries it would appear that the victim of child sexual exploitation could be criminalised. It may be thought that this was only so in less developed countries, but it should be noted that, theoretically at least, under English law a child involved in prostitution continues to be subject to the criminal law through, for example, soliciting (Gillespie 2007; Phoenix 2003). The Special Rapporteur has previously denounced the criminalisation of victims of sexual exploitation[59] and the current Special Rapporteur has

---

58 ibid.
59 Commission on Human Rights, *Report of the Special Rapporteur on the sale of children, child prostitution and child pornography*, Economic and Social Council, 62nd session, UN Doc E/CN.4/2006/67 (12 January 2006) 21.

announced an advocacy programme with the intention of urging countries to decriminalise victims (Maalla 2008: 11).

A difficulty, however, is that international instruments are somewhat vague on this issue. The Convention on the Rights of the Child merely states in general that non-judicial alternatives should be adopted where possible,[60] and the OPSC requires only that 'the best interests of the child shall be a primary consideration'.[61] It is notable that the OPSC says it should be *a* primary consideration and not *the* primary consideration. The absence of a definitive statement[62] is undoubtedly causing difficulties for some children – who may not report the fact that they are being exploited for fear of prosecution – and it is to be hoped that the Special Rapporteur is able to develop a presumption against the criminalisation of victims.

7.4.2   Establishing jurisdiction

Article 4 of the OPSC highlights the issue of jurisdiction. Article 4(1) requires states to ensure that their domestic laws establish jurisdiction of the criminal offences discussed earlier when committed in its territory, on board a ship or on an aircraft registered in that state. This can be said to be the traditional approach to jurisdiction (Hirst 2003) and it is relatively uncontroversial. However, the OPSC goes further and suggests that jurisdiction should be extended in certain circumstances.

Article 4(2) requires states parties to ensure that jurisdiction over the offences referred to in Article 3(1) (those discussed in section 7.4.1) should also be secured where the alleged perpetrator is a national or habitual resident of that state or where the victim is a national of that state.[63] Many countries have now adopted so-called 'sex tourism' legislation that seeks to tackle those who commit sexual offences abroad,[64] but few countries secure jurisdiction by reference to victims.

Despite this provision in the OPSC, it would seem that some countries continue to refuse to adopt the principle of extraterritoriality and many apply the principle of double jeopardy (Maalla 2009: 13). In this context, the rule of double jeopardy prevents somebody from being tried twice for the same offence. Accordingly, if D is prosecuted for crime X and is acquitted, then he cannot be prosecuted again.

In the context of extraterritorial jurisdiction this would mean that if D is prosecuted in country X, where the crime took place, he could not then be prosecuted in country Y (the country of his residence). Some are concerned that the principle of double jeopardy can be misused in countries where sexual exploitation of a child will attract a very low penalty (Beaulieu 2008: 12). The Special Rapporteur has urged that double jeopardy should not apply to cases involving the sexual

---

60 Convention on the Rights of the Child art 40(3)(b).

61 OPSC art 8(3).

62 It was originally intended that a definitive clause would be present, but several states objected to this (Cedrangolo 2009: 13).

63 See OPSC art 4(2)(a) and (b) respectively.

64 A useful history of this can be found in Hirst (2003: 268–9).

exploitation of children (Maalla 2009: 23) but, whilst some countries may agree to try individuals who have been prosecuted but not convicted, many countries would baulk at the notion that someone will be punished twice for the same conduct.

Even where countries adopt extraterritorial jurisdiction, some challenges remain. For example, in some jurisdictions there is the requirement of 'dual criminality'. Put at its most basic, this means that the crime must be illegal in both the country that is to try the offence (that is, the state exercising extraterritorial jurisdiction) and the country where the act took place. In many instances this may well be appropriate, but in the context of commercial sexual exploitation, particularly in respect of sex tourism, this can be problematic. In some countries the age of consent remains extremely low and the principle of dual criminality would therefore permit a sex tourist the right to go to this country for the sole purpose of sexually exploiting a child.

Abolishing the principle of dual criminality would mean that the same standard is expected of a country's citizens wherever they may go, but it does mean that a citizen of country X but resident in country Y may be prevented from doing something that is perfectly lawful in country Y. This can be particularly problematic where, for example, a person is a citizen of more than one country. Where dual criminality is no longer recognised, then it is presumably reliant on prosecutors to use their extraterritorial powers only where there is clear evidence of abuse or exploitation.

The far greater challenge for extraterritorial jurisdiction is evidence. Whilst legislating for extraterritorial jurisdiction is relatively easy to do, securing its practical use is more challenging. In many countries the standard of evidence-gathering may be poorer than that which is expected by the courts of the country exercising jurisdiction. There is also the difficulty of securing witness testimony. That said, it can sometimes be a useful provision; an example could be:

> D is a citizen of country X. He went on holiday to country Y where he recorded himself having sexual activity with a child. Upon his return to country X he is arrested for an unconnected matter and his camera is analysed. The images show him sexually abusing the child in country Y. Applying extraterritorial jurisdiction, D could be tried in country X for the crimes committed in country Y, the photographs serving as the principal evidence.

Also, in the context of sex tourism, many would argue that it serves as a deterrent in that offenders know that they are not necessarily safe from prosecution when they return to their country of residence.

7.4.2.1   Refusal to extradite

Article 5 of the OPSC, discussed in the following section, provides for rules relating to extradition. However, some countries adopt an approach of not extraditing their citizens. Article 4(3) states that where an alleged offender is within state borders and the state refuses to extradite him, then domestic legislation should allow that person to be prosecuted in that state. It has been noted that, although Article 4(3) is silent as to nationality, it is likely that it means a citizen of that state (UNICEF 2009: 13). That said, there is no reason why it should be restricted to this and where, for example, domestic or international rules on extradition would prevent the extradition of non-citizens,[65] Article 3(4) could ensure that they do not escape justice.

7.4.2.2   Extradition

Article 5 raises the issue of extradition. It is recognised that international travel makes it relatively easy for an offender to leave the state where a crime was committed or a state that seeks to prosecute him for the offence. The rules of extradition have existed for some time and allow for a country to remove a person from its state borders and deliver him to the requesting country. Extradition operates on a bilateral basis, with countries agreeing treaties amongst themselves as to how the extradition process operates (section 2.2.1). Article 5(1) requires the extradition treaties to be amended (and new treaties to be drafted) so as to include the offences contained within Article 3.

Where an extradition treaty does not exist between parties, then Article 5(2) requires the state to treat the OPSC as a treaty authorising extradition between signatory parties. Obviously this is limited to the offences contained within Article 3(1) but, if state courts take this into account, it will allow for the extradition of an offender. Article 5(3) is related to this issue as it states that where a country is prepared to extradite in the absence of a treaty, it should recognise the offences within Article 3(1) as extraditable offences. This is required because in the absence of such provision it is quite possible that only certain offences would be subject to extradition without a treaty.

Article 5(4) is an important provision in that it requires states to recognise the extension of jurisdiction in Article 4. Extradition ordinarily applies in respect of offences that are deemed to have been committed in the requesting country's territory. As noted in the previous discussion, Article 4(2) asks countries to extend jurisdiction to include situations where a citizen of their country is alleged to have committed, or been the victim of, an offence. Article 5(4) requires countries to recognise this extended jurisdiction, meaning that country X could request country Y to extradite a citizen of country X where it is alleged that he committed an offence within Article 3(1) in country Z.

---

65 For example some instruments prevent extradition to countries where the perpetrator could be tortured or subject to capital punishment (see most notably the European Convention on Human Rights as set out in *Soering v United Kingdom* (1989) 11 EHRR 439 and *Ahmed v Turkey* (1997) 24 EHRR 278.

7.4.3 International cooperation and support

Article 6 of the OPSC requires states to 'afford one another the greatest measure of assistance in connection with investigations or criminal or extradition proceedings ... including assistance in obtaining evidence at their disposal necessary for the proceedings'. It was noted earlier that a difficulty with extending jurisdiction is that the evidence may not be immediately available, and Article 6 seeks to address this in part.

Article 6 is reinforced by Article 7 which, inter alia, requires states to take prompt measures to seize and confiscate goods, materials and proceeds of sexual exploitation,[66] including requests from other states.[67] The mischief of Article 7 is obviously to ensure that those who are involved in commercial sexual exploitation do not profit from their activities. The OPSC does not, however, say what should happen to the monies realised. It would have been useful if, at the very least, the Optional Protocol had recommended that the monies were placed in a fund to assist victims.

International cooperation and support is not restricted to government agencies. Considerable cooperation exists at other levels, something hinted at by Article 10(1) which, along with obliging states to cooperate internationally, requires states to work with international organisations and NGOs. It was noted earlier (section 7.2.3) that this can include cooperation with industry and this has become increasingly important in recent years.

A good example of cooperation can be found from the 2009 annual report of the current Special Rapporteur, which highlights the work of the 'Virtual Global Taskforce' (VGT) (Maalla 2009: 21). The VGT was established in 2003 and is a group encompassing Interpol and agencies from Australia, Canada, Italy, the United Kingdom and the United States. The operation of the VGT allows for quick and efficient cooperation across national borders and its existence led, for example, to the arrest of Christopher Neil who had recorded himself sexually abusing children and placing these images on the internet in such a way as to obscure his identity.[68]

7.4.4 Assisting victims

A difficulty with the global nature of child sexual exploitation is that it makes the identification of victims somewhat difficult. A (local) police unit may receive, for example, a pornographic picture of a child or an advertisement for sex with a child but they may not know who that child is. If they recover children from

---

66 OPSC art 7(1).

67 ibid art 7(2).

68 '"Swirly faced" paedophile sentenced for abusing Thai child', *The Times* (15 August 2008) http://www.timesonline.co.uk/tol/news/world/asia/article4537360.ece (accessed 14 October 2013).

trafficking or prostitution it may not necessarily be easy to identify where they came from. One commentator has noted that cooperation at the international level is necessary to safeguard children (Palmer 2005: 66), and this is reflected within the text of OPSC.

Article 10(2) requires states parties to cooperate 'to assist child victims in their physical and psychological recovery, social reintegration and repatriation'. The OPSC goes further and notes that social and economic deprivation could be a causal link to sexual exploitation and that these matters must be addressed too (Article 10(3)), including by the provision of 'financial, technical or other assistance' at a multilateral, regional or bilateral level (Article 10(4)).

The principal provision that deals with assistance to victims is contained within Article 8 of the OPSC. Article 8(1) requires a series of measures to be adopted 'at all levels of the criminal justice system'. The measures are:

(a)   adapting the court proceedings to recognise the vulnerability of victims as witnesses
(b)   informing the child of their rights, their role and the timing and progress of the proceedings
(c)   allowing the views, needs and concerns of the child victim to be raised
(d)   providing appropriate support services to child victims throughout the process
(e)   protecting the privacy and identity of the child victim
(f)   providing, in appropriate cases, for the safety of the child victim and their family
(g)   avoiding unnecessary delay in the disposition of the case.

These are challenging measures for most judicial systems, including developed countries. It is an area that both the Special Rapporteur and the Committee on the Rights of the Child pay particular attention to, although an annual report of the Special Rapporteur suggests that the broad picture is that there is still inadequate provision of assistance to victims (Maalla 2009: 16).

Article 8(2) of the OPSC states that where there is doubt as to the age of the child this should not prevent the initiation of criminal investigation. It should be noted that this provision does not state that criminal proceedings cannot be initiated – since in many jurisdictions identifying the age of the child would be critical to a prosecution – but it does require an investigation to occur as this may allow the age of the child to be ascertained.

Article 8(6) makes clear that the provisions of the Article are not designed to prevent the accused from receiving a fair trial. This is an important point as other international instruments will uphold the right of a suspect to be treated fairly. The essence of Article 8(6) is to ensure that the various states consider how best to balance the needs of the victim and the rights of the defendant.

7.5   Reporting mechanisms

The reporting mechanism of the Convention on the Rights of the Child is discussed elsewhere (section 3.5) and, obviously, state parties are obliged to follow this in respect of Article 34 (sections 3.7.6.3 and 3.7.9.3). However, in the wider field of commercial sexual exploitation there are additional reporting mechanisms. There are two of primary relevance here: the Special Rapporteur and the mechanism provided in the OPSC.

The office of the Special Rapporteur was outlined earlier (section 7.2.1.2), but part of her work is to visit countries to assess their approach to tackling the behaviour under her remit: see Maalla (2008: 9), who discusses the role of visits in the context of her mandate. These visits are summarised in each annual report and cross-references are also made to the reports submitted by countries under either the Convention on the Rights of the Child or the OPSC. The ability to visit and comment on countries should allow for an additional check to be made on the monitoring process, although it was noted earlier (section 7.2.1.2) that there are concerns about whether the office of the Special Rapporteur is adequately funded.

Article 13(1) of the OPSC requires a state that has ratified the Optional Protocol to provide a report to the Committee on the Rights of the Child giving comprehensive information about the measures taken to implement the Optional Protocol in domestic law. After this initial report, states are required to report every five years.[69] Where a states party has also ratified the Convention on the Rights of the Child, its report on the OPSC should form a discrete part of its wider five-yearly report on the Convention on the Rights of the Child. Where a state has not ratified the Convention on the Rights of the Child but has ratified the OPSC (eg the United States), then its report will focus solely on the Optional Protocol.

It has already been observed that the reporting process of the Convention on the Rights of the Child has suffered from delays, both in terms of the delay of the Committee on the Rights of the Child in processing reports and in the willingness of states to submit their country reports on time (see section 3.5, Table 3.2). This has been a pervasive problem both in the Convention on the Rights of the Child mechanisms and for other human rights treaty bodies, but there appears to be some evidence to suggest that this has improved in respect of the reports relating to the Optional Protocol. It is obviously crucial to the integrity of the process that the reports are considered promptly but also carefully. A 'rubber stamp' is of no assistance, but neither are delays of several years.

---

69 OPSC art 12(2).

Case study 7.1

Child Sex Tourism

The issue of child sex tourism has been discussed briefly already in this chapter but it is also an example of a particular type of child sexual exploitation that requires international cooperation to solve.

Child sex tourism is sometimes presented as a simple form of child sexual exploitation but it is now recognised that it covers a broad range of behaviour. The 'typical' view of child sex tourism is that which was first discovered. This involves an offender (usually male) who travels from a developed (usually Western) country to a poorer country where he engages in sexually inappropriate behaviour with a child. Asian countries, particularly Thailand and Sri Lanka, were some of the earliest countries where child sex tourism developed.

The difference in economic wealth means that access to children can be relatively simple. Early research noted, for example, that many communities 'survived through the prostitution of children' (Montgomery, 2008: 908) and that families would not consider their children to be abused but rather considered the offender as a 'friend' or 'sponsor' to the family (Montgomery 2008: 909). This reflected a particular type of child sex tourism where the abuse and exploitation was not an isolated incident but rather the offender would return to the family on a number of occasions, befriending them.

As we began to understand the behaviour it was discovered that the issue of child sex tourism was more complicated than previously thought. It is now thought that there are two types of child sex tourism; 'core sex tourists' and 'opportunistic sex tourists'. Core sex tourists are sometimes also called 'preferential offenders' and are those that travel to a specific country with the intention of abusing or exploiting a child. An opportunistic sex tourist is someone that goes to a country for a legitimate reason (eg a business trip) but who will take the opportunity to abuse a child if it arises (for example, in a massage parlour or if approached in a hotel bar) (O'Connell Davidson 2000). Of course the reality is that an offender could be both: they will travel to specific countries with the intention of abusing a child but will take opportunities that arise whilst travelling legitimately. However, even if they are both, they constitute one form of this offending on each trip. The fact that there are different types of child sex tourism is important in considering how to tackle it. For example, focusing attention on preferential abusers by, for example, tracking those sex offenders who travel or even preventing travel will not stop those who have travelled for legitimate reasons. Neither would, for example, warning people when booking travel to a certain country that child sex tourism is illegal.

When considering the states involved, it is common to also divide countries into two; those that are 'sending' states (that is, those countries from whom the perpetrator originates) or 'receiving' states (that is, those countries to whom the offender visited and where the victim is based). Whilst this is largely true it can be criticised as being simplistic in that some countries may be both, a good example of this being South Africa (Vrancken and Chetly 2009).

Responding to child sex tourism

The response to child sex tourism is perhaps a good example of how international law and policy can target a particular area. ECPAT, probably one of the most famous international NGOs working in the area of child sexual exploitation, was created specifically to tackle child sex tourism, particularly in Asia (whilst it is still based in Asia its sphere of influence is now global). The charity sought to raise awareness of the issue both nationally, in both sending and receiving countries, and at a global level. Its campaign led to the First World Congress against Commercial Sexual Exploitation, which was one of the first attempts to bring together a global coalition of public and private agencies committed to identifying how to tackle child sexual exploitation.

One of the key components of the drive against child sexual tourism was recognition that there needed to be legislation at both the domestic and international level. Many destination countries were targeted because child protection was largely ignored by these countries (Fredette 2009: 13). In many instances there was no domestic legislation that specifically tackled child sexual abuse, or if it did exist it was widely ignored.

A difficulty in concentrating on destination countries, however, is that even if legislation is introduced it may be ineffective. Legislation is only of use if there are appropriate strategies to detect, investigate and prosecute offenders. Most destination countries did not have the expertise to do this or were populated by police officers and prosecutors who were corrupt and would avoid taking action in return for bribes (Fredette 2009: 15). Even if the police were able to detect the crime, it was not unusual in many instances for the victims of the offence to deny that there had been any crime, partly because the offender was seen as being the benefactor of the family (Montgomery 2008: 909). Once again, this militated against prosecutions occurring.

Extraterritorial legislation

Sending states began to realise that they had a responsibility to protect children from the actions of their own citizens (Montgomery, 2010). Sending states began to consider the use of extraterritorial jurisdiction, that is, the right to prosecute their own citizens for actions they took outside their territorial borders. The advantage of extraterritorial jurisdiction was that it could bypass many of the difficulties that existed in destination countries. However, extraterritorial legislation is far from being a perfect solution as in many crimes there will still be a need for local law enforcement to become involved. For example, the victim and witnesses are likely to be in the destination countries and so either local police forces would need to gather the evidence or, in many countries, facilitate the gathering of evidence by foreign police forces. Of course not every crime would require local evidence. Where, for example, a person filmed himself abusing a child and that footage was found when he returned to his country of origin then extraterritorial jurisdiction would allow an offender to be prosecuted for the sexual acts on the strength of that footage.

Whilst some countries did exercise extraterritorial jurisdiction many did not. Indeed in the latest report from the UN Special Rapporteur it has been noted that only 44 countries have done so (Maalla 2012: 11) although this does cover many sending states. A major barrier in some countries however is the requirement for 'dual criminality'. This is the principle that requires an action to be criminalised in both the prosecuting state and the state in which the crime took place. So, for example, if D (a citizen of England) went to Thailand where he sexually exploited four children, it would be necessary that child sexual exploitation was a crime in *both* England and Thailand. As it has been noted that many destination countries do not have effective child protection laws this was problematic and the Special Rapporteur has called for its abolition (Maalla 2012: 11) although many countries had already independently done so because of the difficulty that this caused to prosecutions (Svensson 2006: 655).

International instruments

The fact that extraterritorial jurisdiction could be an effective method of tackling child sex tourism has been recognised in international instruments. The OPSC expressly includes a call for states to consider using extraterritorial jurisdiction (Article 4) and similar provisions can be found in, for example, the Lanzarote Convention (Article 25). However, the fact that only 44 states have implemented extraterritorial jurisdiction does demonstrate a lack of willingness on the part of some countries since 166 countries have ratified the OPSC. Clearly therefore not all countries are adhering to the provisions they committed themselves to.

Police cooperation

The adoption of extraterritorial legislation is only one part of the solution that can be offered by sending states. Ideally extraterritorial legislation need not be used but instead the local police in destination countries would identify and prosecute abuse. A considerable amount of effort is therefore placed on cooperation between police. This is sometimes in respect of evidence-gathering or part of the extradition process (and the OPSC specifically mentions this in Articles 6 and 10) but it is also frequently beyond this and involves, for example, the sharing of best practice, training events etc. A good example of this is the work undertaken by INTERPOL which has a specific training and capacity building programme. Much of this work is showing destination countries how to detect child sexual exploitation, how to interview children etc. This is vitally important as it means that destination countries begin to take responsibility for tackling child sexual exploitation and send out a signal that such activities will not be tolerated within its borders.

Industry
In section 7.2.3 above it was noted that the tourism industry has become involved in the fight against child sex tourism. This has been welcomed by the Special Rapporteur (Maalla 2012: 17) and it should be welcomed. The tourism industry has a particular responsibility in this regard since it, in essence, facilitates the child sexual exploitation of children. Whilst in many instances this is without their knowledge, this is not always true and there are examples of certain bodies actively marketing child sex tourism (Fredette 2009: 6). Laws should prohibit knowingly facilitating the sexual abuse of children but the industry could (and has) acted by, for example, denying flights or accommodation to those that use these agencies. Together with the training that they offer in detecting child sex tourism and, in many instances, the sponsorship of training for local police forces, demonstrates the advantages of gaining industry cooperation.

A shifting problem
The Special Rapporteur has noted that it is important that countries harmonise their laws to the basic international instruments (Maalla 2012: 12) because the spread of law will mean there are fewer places to hide. One issue of concern is that child sex tourism is a *reactive* phenomenon. As countries begin to develop a strategy against it there is concern that it simply displaces the activity to other countries (Maalla 2012: 7). So, for example, when Thailand began to actively prosecute child sex tourists and created specialist police units to disrupt the behaviour there was a subsequent increase in neighbouring countries such as Cambodia and Vietnam.

It is incumbent on the international community therefore to act proactively. Whilst encouragement should be given to those who are destination countries to introduce new laws, considerable effort needs to be placed in predicting where the next generation of tourists will visit. Early intervention in those countries could help ensure that there is an appropriate framework in place (including international agreements) to combat this.

Whilst enacting laws sends a signal it must be remembered that they are only of use when implemented effectively. Even then however there must be recognition of the root causes of child sex tourism. Almost one-third of child sex tourists convicted in the USA committed their offences in Mexico (Maalla 2012: 6). Mexico is a country that is generally thought to have a well-established system of governance and laws. However, it is also a country that has considerable poverty in areas. Laws to combat child sex tourism will only be effective where the conduct is detected, including by the victim reporting the sexual assault. Where a family is paid the equivalent of a year's salary to gain access to the child it is unlikely that the activities of the offer will be reported and indeed the family may put pressure on the victim not to do so (Montgomery 2008). It is for this reason that work must be done to support victims (something that is expressly found in the OPSC: see Article 8) but the root causes, including poverty, have to be tackled too. This may be in very localised pockets, for example Fredette (2009:11) notes that where local economies collapse as a result of internationalisation (rural areas) or outsourcing then there is a rise in commercial child sexual exploitation. That being the case it is likely that laws will only be of limited use since communities are effectively given little option but to condone the exploitation of children.

Chapter 8

Children and armed conflict

8.1 Children and armed conflict: the international law framework

This chapter discusses the international framework relating to children's involvement and association with armed conflict. This takes a number of forms: the treatment of child civilians in armed conflicts; the damaging impact of armed conflicts on children; the recruitment and use of children by state and non-state armed forces; the reintegration of child soldiers into society; and the international criminal justice available for those (including child soldiers themselves) who may have committed 'crimes against humanity' and 'war crimes'. This involves a consideration of both 'international humanitarian law' and 'international human rights law'.

There are some important contextual points to note before we examine the relevant international law. First, the international legal framework has had to respond to the changing patterns of armed conflicts over the past 60 years; *inter*-state wars are now significantly eclipsed by the proliferation of *intra*-state conflicts. There has also been in recent years an increase in the number of intra-state conflicts that are internationalized, that is where another state supports one side or another and this 'often has the effect of increasing casualty rates and prolonging conflicts' (SIPRI 2013: 2).

Secondly, the proportion of civilian casualties has greatly increased over the same period and the largest proportion of these has been women and children. Thirdly, the ground-breaking 'Machel Report'[1] in 1996 on the impact of armed conflict on children galvanised a unique confluence of humanitarian concern with the growing presence of the children's rights agenda on the international stage (section 8.2.3). Finally, the United Nations has, following a series of Security Council

---

1 General Assembly, *Impact of Armed Conflict on Children: report of the expert of the Secretary-General, Ms Graça Machel*, submitted pursuant to General Assembly resolution 48/157 (Machel Report), UN Doc A/51/306 (26 August 1996). See http://www.un.org/documents/ga/docs/51/plenary/a51-306. htm (accessed 15 November 2013).

resolutions (section 8.2.1), attempted to mainstream issues around children and armed conflict within its primary mission to maintain global peace and security.

This section examines the influences of international humanitarian law, principally the Geneva Conventions of 1949[2] along with the Additional Protocols of 1977,[3] followed by consideration of the main international human rights instruments relevant to this area, that is, the UN Convention on the Rights of the Child[4] along with the Optional Protocol to the Convention on the Rights of the Child on the involvement of children in Armed Conflict (OPAC),[5] the African Charter on the Rights and Welfare of the Child[6] and the Worst Forms of Child Labour Convention.[7]

8.1.1   International humanitarian law

This is the body of law that comprises 'all those rules of international law which are designed to regulate the treatment of the individual – civilian or military, wounded or active – in international armed conflicts' (Fleck 2013: 11). It famously includes the Geneva Conventions of 1949 and two Additional Protocols to these Conventions in 1977, although the term 'international humanitarian law' does not appear in any of these instruments.

---

2 International Committee of the Red Cross (ICRC), Geneva Convention for the Amelioration of the Condition of the Wounded and Sick in Armed Forces in the Field (First Geneva Convention), adopted 12 August 1949, 75 UNTS 31 (entered into force 21 October 1950). ICRC, *Geneva* Convention for the Amelioration of the Condition of Wounded, Sick and Shipwrecked Members of Armed Forces at Sea (Second Geneva Convention), adopted 12 August 1949, 75 UNTS 85 (entered into force 21 October 1950). ICRC, Geneva Convention Relative to the Treatment of Prisoners of War (Third Geneva Convention), 12 August 1949, 75 UNTS 135 (entered into force 21 October1950). ICRC, Geneva Convention Relative to the Protection of Civilian Persons in Time of War (4th Geneva Convention) (12 August 1949) 75 UNTS 287 (entered into force 21 October 1950). At the time of writing, 195 states parties had ratified/acceded to each of the four Geneva Conventions of 1949.

3 ICRC, Protocol Additional to the Geneva Conventions of 12 August 1949, and relating to the Protection of Victims of International Armed Conflicts (Protocol I) (8 June 1977) 1125 UNTS 3 (entered into force 7 December 1979). ICRC, Protocol Additional to the Geneva Conventions of 12 August 1949, and relating to the Protection of Victims of Non-International Armed Conflicts (Protocol II) (8 June 1977) 1125 UNTS 609 (entered into force 7 December 1978).

4 Opened for signature 20 November 1989, 1577 UNTS 3 (entered into force 2 September 1990).

5 Opened for signature 25 May 2000, 2173 UNTS 222 (entered into force 12 February 2002). The OPAC had 129 signatories and 154 ratifications as at 22 February 2014.

6 OAU, African Charter on the Rights and Welfare of the Child, (11 July 1990) CAB/LEG/24.9/4 (entered into force 29 November 1999). As at 21 February 2014, 47 of the 54 African States had ratified/acceded to this treaty. Article 16 requires states parties to protect children against abuse, including sexual abuse.

7 International Labour Organization, Prohibition and Immediate Action for the Elimination of the Worst Forms of Child Labour Convention, ILO Convention No 182 (17 June 1999). This Convention had 178 parties as at 18 November 2013.

8.1.1.1   The Geneva Conventions of 1949[8]

Most of the content of the Geneva Conventions is now considered to be declaratory of customary international law (Fleck 2013: 28). The various Conventions adopted prior to 1949 focused on combatants, not civilians. There was some protection for civilians in regulations annexed to the Hague Conventions of 1899 and 1907.[9] However, the Geneva Convention IV: Relative to the Protection of Civilian Persons in Time of War of 1949 (Geneva Convention IV)[10] was the first treaty to focus on the protection of *civilians* during armed conflict, although it is principally concerned with their treatment while 'in the hands of an opposing party or who are the victims of war, rather than with regulating the conduct of parties to a conflict in order to protect civilians' (Harvey 2003: 7). The Geneva Conventions of 1949 reflected people's experiences of the Second World War:

> Recent wars have emphasized in tragic fashion how necessary it is to have treaty rules for the protection of children. During the last World War, in particular, the mass migrations, bombing raids and deportations separated thousands of children from their parents. The absence of any means of identifying these children, some of whom were even too young to vouch for their own identity, had disastrous consequences. Thousands of them are irretrievably lost to their own families and thousands of fathers and mothers will always suffer the grief of their loss. It is therefore to be hoped that effective measures can be taken to avoid such harrowing experiences in the future.[11]

Geneva Convention IV contains a brief section[12] concerning the general protection of the civilian population against certain consequences of war. Most of Geneva Convention IV[13] addresses the status and treatment of protected persons, of which children form one category. One provision of Geneva Convention IV allows that the parties to a conflict may establish 'hospital and safety zones' in

8 See n 2 above. The full text of the Geneva Conventions of 1949 and the Additional Protocols of 1977, along with commentaries, can be found on the International Committee of the Red Cross (ICRC) website. See http://www.icrc.org/ihl (accessed 16 November 2013).

9 International Conferences (The Hague), Convention (II) with Respect to the Laws and Customs of War on Land and its annex: Regulations concerning the Laws and Customs of War on Land (29 July 1899) (entered into force 4 September 1900). International Conferences (The Hague), Hague Convention (IV) Respecting the Laws and Customs of War on Land and Its Annex: Regulations Concerning the Laws and Customs of War on Land (18 October 1907) (entered into force 26 January 1910).

10 ICRC, Geneva Convention Relative to the Protection of Civilian Persons in Time of War (4th Geneva Convention) (12 August 1949) 75 UNTS 287 (entered into force 21 October 1950).

11 ICRC, *Commentaries on the Geneva Conventions of 1949*, Conv IV art 24, 185. See http://www.icrc.org/ihl.

12 Geneva Convention IV Part II arts 13–26.

13 ibid Part III arts 27–141.

order to protect from the effects of war, the 'wounded, sick and aged persons, children under fifteen, expectant mothers and mothers of children under seven'.[14] Another provision mandates parties to the conflict to 'endeavour to conclude local agreements for the removal from besieged or encircled areas' of a number of vulnerable groups including children.[15]

Subject to certain conditions, there is also a provision that prescribes that states parties to the Convention must allow 'the free passage of all consignments of medical and hospital stores and objects necessary for religious worship', and this requires the free passage of 'essential foodstuffs, clothing and tonics intended for children under fifteen, expectant mothers and maternity cases'.[16]

Geneva Convention IV also contains a *general* child welfare protective clause:

> The Parties to the conflict shall take the necessary measures to ensure that children under fifteen, who are orphaned or are separated from their families as a result of the war, are not left to their own resources, and that their maintenance, the exercise of their religion and their education are facilitated in all circumstances. Their education shall, as far as possible, be entrusted to persons of a similar cultural tradition.
>
> The Parties to the conflict shall facilitate the reception of such children in a neutral country for the duration of the conflict with the consent of the Protecting Power, if any, and under due safeguards for the observance of the principles stated in the first paragraph.
>
> They shall, furthermore, endeavour to arrange for all children under twelve to be identified by the wearing of identity discs, or by some other means.[17]

The International Committee of the Red Cross (ICRC) comments that the principles set out in this Article 'apply to all the children in question who are living in the territory of a Party to the conflict, whether they are nationals of that country or aliens'.[18] The provision regarding accommodating children in a neutral country is based on the belief that '[h]owever well organised child welfare measures may be, they will never be able to protect the children completely from all the various privations suffered by the population of a belligerent country'.[19]

---

14 'Certain definite categories – children under fifteen and mothers of children under seven – were nevertheless chosen because the Conference considered that they were appropriate, reasonable and generally in accord with the requirements of the physical and mental development of children'. *ICRC Commentaries*, Conv IV art 14 at 126.

15 'Unlike Article 14 (Hospital and Safety Zones), the present Article does not fix an age limit up to which children are to be evacuated. The belligerents concerned are free to come to an agreement on the ... subject; the upper limit of 15 years of age, which applies to admission to a safety zone, seems reasonable and would appear to merit adoption in the present instance'. *ICRC Commentaries*, Conv IV art 17 at 138–9.

16 Geneva Convention IV art 23.

17 ibid art 24.

18 ICRC Commentaries, Conv IV art 24 at 187.

19 ibid at 188.

Given the consistent use of the age of 15 years elsewhere in Geneva Convention IV, it is perhaps surprising to see the reference to an age limit of 12 years in relation to the third paragraph of Article 24. This was chosen at an earlier international conference of the ICRC on the basis that 'it was considered that children over twelve were generally capable of stating their own identity'.[20] It would seem that there was some contention over this provision at the Diplomatic Conference in 1949.[21]

There are also provisions that mandate the 'occupying power', with the cooperation of the national or local authorities, to 'facilitate the proper working of all institutions devoted to the care and education of children'. The occupying power is also obliged to 'take all necessary steps to facilitate the identification of children and the registration of their parentage' and cannot change their personal status 'nor enlist them in formations or organizations subordinate to it'.

For children whose identity is in doubt, there is provision for a special section of the 'official information Bureau'[22] to take responsibility for them. The occupying power is also obliged not to hinder any preferential measures regarding food, medical care and protection against the effects of war that were in place before an occupation 'in favour of children under 15 years, expectant mothers, and mothers of children under 7 years'.[23]

With regard to detainment, it is provided that members of the same family 'and in particular parents and children' must be accommodated in the same place of internment, subject to certain exceptions, and internees 'may request that their children who are left at liberty without parental care shall be interned with them'.[24] Furthermore, internees who are expectant and nursing mothers and children under 15 years 'shall be given additional food, in proportion to their physiological needs'.[25]

There is also an obligation on the 'detaining power' to 'encourage intellectual, educational and recreational pursuits, sports and games amongst internees', and specifically the education of children and young people is protected; 'they shall

---

20 ibid at 189.

21 'The idea of identity discs was treated with scepticism by many delegates, who pointed out for instance how mistakes could arise from children losing or exchanging their identity discs. That danger certainly exists and although experience of this method of identification in the armed forces has been generally satisfactory, that does not necessarily prove anything in regard to children'. *ICRC Commentaries*, Conv IV art 24 at 189.

22 This must be set up under the terms of Article 136 on the outbreak of hostilities or in case of occupation. 'The primary function of these Bureaux is ... to transmit to the State of origin all available information concerning measures taken in regard to its subjects by the Power in whose hands they are. The official Bureau which the Occupying Power is thus bound to open in occupied territory is a valuable source of information of all kinds. It is in a position to render useful service, particularly in the case of children whose identity has not been established by the local services concerned'. *ICRC Commentaries*, Conv IV art 50 at 289.

23 Geneva Convention IV art 50.

24 ibid art 82.

25 ibid art 89.

be allowed to attend schools either within the place of internment or outside' and 'special playgrounds shall be reserved for children and young people'.[26] Finally, the rules regarding the release of interned persons by the detaining power privilege 'in particular children, pregnant women and mothers with infants and young children, wounded and sick, and internees who have been detained for a long time'.[27]

However, a significant weakness of the Geneva Conventions is that they apply only to international conflicts and not to the non-international/internal conflicts which, as already noted, have become the predominant mode of armed conflict in recent decades. The exception to this is found in an Article which appears in all four Geneva Conventions and is known as 'common Article 3':

Article 3

In the case of armed conflict not of an international character occurring in the territory of one of the High Contracting Parties, each Party to the conflict shall be bound to apply, as a minimum, the following provisions:

(1) Persons taking no active part in the hostilities, including members of armed forces who have laid down their arms and those placed '*hors de combat*' by sickness, wounds, detention, or any other cause, shall in all circumstances be treated humanely, without any adverse distinction founded on race, colour, religion or faith, sex, birth or wealth, or any other similar criteria. To this end, the following acts are and shall remain prohibited at any time and in any place whatsoever with respect to the above-mentioned persons:

(a) violence to life and person, in particular murder of all kinds, mutilation, cruel treatment and torture;

(b) taking of hostages;

(c) outrages upon personal dignity, in particular humiliating and degrading treatment;

(d) the passing of sentences and the carrying out of executions without previous judgment pronounced by a regularly constituted court, affording all the judicial guarantees which are recognized as indispensable by civilized peoples.

(2) The wounded and sick shall be collected and cared for. An impartial humanitarian body, such as the International Committee of the Red Cross, may offer its services to the Parties to the conflict.

---

26 ibid art 94. 'This provision is one more proof of the interest shown by the Geneva Conventions in child welfare. It represents a most useful addition to the provisions contained in Article 50, which is one of the Articles (14, 17, 24, 26 etc.) laying down exceptions to the ordinary regulations in favour of children and contains special provisions dealing with their care and education'. *ICRC Commentaries*, Conv IV art 94 at 412.

27 Geneva Convention IV art 132.

The Parties to the conflict should further endeavour to bring into force, by means of special agreements, all or part of the other provisions of the present Convention.

The application of the preceding provisions shall not affect the legal status of the Parties to the conflict.[28]

Article 3 'applies to non-international conflicts only, and will be the only Article applicable to them until such time as a special agreement between the Parties has brought into force between them all or part of the other provisions of the Convention'.[29] This Article ensures that a set of minimum standards is recognised and 'provides a legal basis for charitable interventions by the International Committee of the Red Cross or any other impartial humanitarian organization – interventions which in the past were all too often refused on the ground that they represented unfriendly interference in the internal affairs of a State'.[30]

8.1.1.2 UN Declaration on the Protection of Women and Children in Emergency and Armed Conflict of 1974

This (non-binding) Declaration was adopted by the General Assembly in 1974.[31] It condemns and prohibits attacks and bombings on the civilian population, recognising that these inflict incalculable suffering, 'especially on women and children, who are the most vulnerable members of the population'.[32] It severely condemns the use of chemical and bacteriological weapons, recognising that this will inflict heavy civilian losses 'including defenceless women and children'.[33]

States must make 'all efforts' in armed conflicts and military operations 'to spare women and children from the ravages of war' and '[a]ll necessary steps shall be taken to ensure the prohibition of measures such as persecution, torture, punitive measures, degrading treatment and violence, particularly against that part of the civilian population that consists of women and children'.[34] The Declaration of 1974 also indicates the criminal nature of violations of humanitarian law:

All forms of repression and cruel and inhuman treatment of women and children, including imprisonment, torture, shooting, mass arrests, collective punishment, destruction of dwellings and forcible eviction, committed by

---

28 Geneva Convention I art 3; Geneva Convention II art 3; Geneva Convention III art 3; and Geneva Convention IV art 3.
29 ICRC Commentaries, Conv IV art 3 at 34.
30 ibid
31 General Assembly, Declaration on the Protection of Women and Children in Emergency and Armed Conflict, 29th session, UN Doc A/RES/29/3318 (14 December 1974).
32 ibid art 1.
33 ibid art 2.
34 ibid art 4.

belligerents in the course of military operations or in occupied territories shall be considered criminal.[35]

Finally, the Declaration asserts that (civilian) women and children 'shall not be deprived of shelter, food, medical aid or other inalienable rights'.[36]

8.1.1.3   The Additional Protocols of 1977 to the Geneva Conventions of 1949

Protocol I[37] extended the protection of persons affected by international conflicts by, amongst other things, upgrading the standards relating to the conduct of hostilities. It also offered further protection for children in international conflicts, and contains a general child protection clause as follows:

Article 77
1. Children shall be the object of special respect and shall be protected against any form of indecent assault. The Parties to the conflict shall provide them with the care and aid they require, whether because of their age or for any other reason.
2. The Parties to the conflict shall take all feasible measures in order that children who have not attained the age of fifteen years do not take a direct part in hostilities and, in particular, they shall refrain from recruiting them into their armed forces. In recruiting among those persons who have attained the age of fifteen years but who have not attained the age of eighteen years the Parties to the conflict shall endeavour to give priority to those who are oldest.
… [paras 3, 4 and 5 omitted][38]

The remaining paragraphs of Article 77 above: continue the protection offered by this Article for children under 15 years who have taken a direct part in hostilities and have fallen into the hands of an adverse party[39]; prescribe that children who are arrested, detained or interned have separate quarters from adults[40]; and prohibit the death penalty for a child less than 18 years for offences related to the armed conflict.[41]

A further provision of Protocol I[42] provides some ground rules regulating the parties to a conflict in arranging the evacuation of children other than their own

---

35 ibid art 5.
36 ibid art 6.
37 ICRC, Protocol Additional to the Geneva Conventions of 12 August 1949, and relating to the Protection of Victims of International Armed Conflicts (Protocol I) (8 June 1977) 1125 UNTS 3 (entered into force 7 December 1979).
38 Protocol I art 77(1) and (2).
39 ibid art 77(3).
40 ibid art 77(4).
41 ibid art 77(5). Protocol I art 68 also prohibits pronouncing the death penalty on persons under 18 years of age, a provision also adopted in the ICCPR art 6(5).
42 Protocol I art 78.

nationals to a foreign country.[43] This is only permitted for a temporary period 'where compelling reasons of the health or medical treatment of the children or, except in occupied territory, their safety, so require' and parental consent must be obtained.

Article 78 of Protocol I attempts to ensure that 'each child's education, including his religious and moral education as his parents desire, shall be provided while he is away with the greatest possible continuity'. Finally, with a view to returning the children, the party arranging the evacuation and the authorities of the receiving country must establish a prescribed list of identity details for each child, which they shall send to the Central Tracing Agency of the ICRC.

Protocol II[44] was, significantly, the first binding international instrument to deal with the parties' conduct in *non-international* armed conflicts. It develops the basic guarantees of 'common Article 3' of the Geneva Conventions of 1949 (see text in section 8.1.1.1) and contains an abbreviated version of the child protection provisions contained in Protocol I:

Article 4(3)

Children shall be provided with the care and aid they require, and in particular:

(a) they shall receive an education, including religious and moral education, in keeping with the wishes of their parents, or in the absence of parents, of those responsible for their care;

(b) all appropriate steps shall be taken to facilitate the reunion of families temporarily separated;

(c) children who have not attained the age of 15 years shall neither be recruited in the armed forces or groups nor allowed to take part in hostilities;

(d) the special protection provided by this Article to children who have not attained the age of 15 years shall remain applicable to them if they take a direct part in hostilities despite the provisions of subparagraph (c) and are captured;

(e) measures shall be taken, if necessary, and whenever possible with the consent of their parents or persons who by law or custom are primarily responsible for their care, to remove children temporarily from the area in which hostilities are taking place to a safer area within the country and ensure that they are accompanied by persons responsible for their safety and well-being.[45]

---

43 'This is to avoid the risk of removal for the purposes of ethnic cleansing and unnecessary removal of children, representing a major change in practice from World War II when mass evacuation of children took place' (Harvey 2003: 10).

44 ICRC, Protocol Additional to the Geneva Conventions of 12 August 1949, and relating to the Protection of Victims of Non-International Armed Conflicts (Protocol II) (8 June 1977) 1125 UNTS 609 (entered into force 7 December 1978).

45 ibid art 4(3).

Unfortunately, Protocol II is expressly not applicable to 'situations of internal disturbances and tensions, such as riots, isolated and sporadic acts of violence and other acts of a similar nature, as not being armed conflict'.[46] Consequently, it is applicable to a smaller range of internal conflicts than that covered by common Article 3 of the Geneva Conventions of 1949.

8.1.2   International human rights law

In addition to the body of international humanitarian law outlined above, this section considers the principal international human rights instruments impacting on children and armed conflict. It deals, in particular, with the Convention on the Rights of the Child (1989) and the Optional Protocol to the Convention on the Rights of the Child on the Involvement of Children in Armed Conflict (OPAC). It should be remembered that international concern for the plight of children in armed conflicts is not new. Indeed, it is clear that one of the main motivating factors underlying the adoption of the Declaration of the Rights of the Child in 1924 by the League of Nations (Jebb Declaration) (section 3.2) had been the disastrous impact that the war in the Balkans had had on children (Marshall 1999: 106).

8.1.2.1   UN Convention on the Rights of the Child of 1989[47]

From the outset, the issue of children and armed conflict was of particular concern to the drafters of the Convention on the Rights of the Child and to the Committee on the Rights of the Child:

> During the drafting of Article 38, there was a strong move not only to ensure that its provisions did not in any way undermine existing standards in international humanitarian law but also to go beyond existing international standards so that children were protected up to the age of 18, in order to secure consistency with the rest of the Convention. The final version of Article 38 was a compromise.
>
> (Hodgkin and Newell 2007: 574)

Indeed, this topic formed the subject of the Committee's first 'Day of General Discussion' in 1992.[48] The Convention on the Rights of the Child contains two significant Articles relating to children and armed conflict. The first – Article 38 – proved to be one of the most controversial issues dealt with by the drafters of the Convention: see the text of Article 38 in section 3.7.9.5.

46 ibid art 1(2).
47 Opened for signature 20 November 1989, 1577 UNTS 3 (entered into force 2 September 1990).
48 Committee on the Rights of the Child, 'Day of General Discussion' on *Children in armed conflicts*, Report on the 2nd session, CRC/C/10, (19 October 1992) [75(e)].

The first paragraph of this Article ties in states parties' obligations to respect (and *ensure* respect for) the rules of international humanitarian law (section 8.1.1), although it does not appear to raise in any way these (minimum) standards of humanitarian law. The second paragraph obliges states parties to take 'all feasible measures', a formulation allowing states a certain amount of discretion, 'to ensure that persons who have not attained the age of fifteen years do not take a direct part in hostilities'.

As we have seen in the discussion above, the age of 15 years is frequently adverted to in the Geneva Conventions of 1949 and the Additional Protocols of 1977, and was therefore a natural age limit for the drafters of the Convention on the Rights of the Child to alight upon and to do so consistently with the exist-ing body of international humanitarian law and customary international law. However, there was substantial discomfort about the 15-year age limit. These are the only provisions of the Convention on the Rights of the Child that do not apply to all children under 18 years. The third paragraph mandates states parties to refrain from recruiting under-15-year-old persons into the armed forces, and, in recruiting 15 to 17-year-olds, states parties should endeavour to prioritise the recruitment of the oldest.

By contrast, the comparable Article appearing in the African Charter on the Rights and Welfare of the Child[49] does not carry the 15-year limit and is more explicit in its application to internal armed conflicts.[50]

The fourth paragraph of Article 38, for the avoidance of any doubt, makes it expressly clear that states parties must observe their obligations in international humanitarian law to protect children from the impact of armed conflict. There was some general dissatisfaction by human rights groups and states parties about the 15-year threshold.

Several states parties registered declarations or reservations in respect of Article 38, disagreeing with the provisions in paragraphs 2 and 3 of this Article con-cerning the participation and recruitment of children from the age of 15 years.[51] Others likewise rejected the 15-year threshold on the basis that this was, in any event, inconsistent with Article 3(1) of the Convention on the Rights of the Child, which determines that the best interests of the child is a primary consideration.[52] Others expressly declared that 'it would have been preferable to fix that age at 18

---

49 OAU, African Charter on the Rights and Welfare of the Child (11 July 1990) CAB/LEG/24.9/49 (entered into force 29 November 1999).

50 ibid art 22: '1. States Parties to this Charter shall undertake to respect and ensure respect for rules of international humanitarian law applicable in armed conflicts which affect the child. 2. States Parties to the present Charter shall take all necessary measures to ensure that no child shall take a direct part in hostilities and refrain in particular, from recruiting any child. 3. States Parties to the present Charter shall, in accordance with their obligations under international humanitarian law, protect the civilian population in armed conflicts and shall take all feasible measures to ensure the protection and care of children who are affected by armed conflicts. Such rules shall also apply to children in situations of internal armed conflicts, tension and strife'.

51 For example, the declarations of Andorra, Argentina, the Netherlands and Spain.

52 See the declarations of Austria and Germany.

years in accordance with the principles and norms prevailing in various regions and countries'.[53]

The second key provision of the Convention on the Rights of the Child is Article 39, which deals with the recovery and reintegration of the child following armed conflict: see the text of Article 39 in section 3.7.9.5.

This provision recognises, inter alia, the serious and potentially long-lasting effects of armed conflict on children and reflects some aspects of international humanitarian standards. The Committee commented in its 'Day of General Discussion':

> Consideration was particularly given to Article 39 of the Convention: different experiences and programmes were brought to the attention of the Committee, underlying the need for resources and goods (namely, food and medicine). Moreover, emphasis was put on the need to consider a coherent plan for recovery and reintegration, to be planned and implemented in a combined effort by United Nations bodies and non-governmental organizations. Attention should be paid to (a) the implementation and monitoring of adequate strategies and (b) the need to reinforce the involvement of the family and the local community in this process.[54]

The Committee further highlighted the need to provide rehabilitative care in relation to children who were unaccompanied and separated from their parents outside their country of origin in a General Comment in 2005:

> 48. The obligation under Article 39 of the Convention sets out the duty of States to provide rehabilitation services to children who have been victims of any form of abuse, neglect, exploitation, torture, cruel, inhuman and degrading treatment or armed conflicts. In order to facilitate such recovery and reintegration, culturally appropriate and gender-sensitive mental health care should be developed and qualified psychosocial counselling provided.
>
> 49. States shall, in particular where government capacity is limited, accept and facilitate assistance offered by UNICEF, the World Health Organization (WHO), United Nations Joint Programme on HIV/AIDS (UNAIDS), UNHCR and other agencies (art 22 (2)) within their respective mandates, as well as, where appropriate, other competent intergovernmental organizations or non-governmental organizations in order to meet the health and health-care needs of unaccompanied and separated children.[55]

---

53 See the reservations of Colombia and Uruguay.

54 Committee on the Rights of the Child, 'Day of General Discussion' on *Children in armed conflicts*, Report on the 2nd session, CRC/C/10 (19 October 1992) [74].

55 Committee on the Rights of the Child, General Comment No 6: *Treatment of Unaccompanied and Separated Children Outside their Country of Origin*, 39th session, CRC/GC/2005/6 (1 September 2005) [48–9].

The General Comment focuses on states parties' obligations towards former child soldiers in the following extract:

> *Former child soldiers*
> 56. Child soldiers should be considered primarily as victims of armed conflict. Former child soldiers, who often find themselves unaccompanied or separated at the cessation of the conflict or following defection, shall be given all the necessary support services to enable reintegration into normal life, including necessary psychosocial counselling. Such children shall be identified and demobilized on a priority basis during any identification and separation operation. Child soldiers, in particular, those who are unaccompanied or separated, should not normally be interned, but rather, benefit from special protection and assistance measures, in particular as regards their demobilization and rehabilitation. Particular efforts must be made to provide support and facilitate the reintegration of girls who have been associated with the military, either as combatants or in any other capacity.
> 57. If, under certain circumstances, exceptional internment of a child soldier over the age of 15 years is unavoidable and in compliance with international human rights and humanitarian law, for example, where she or he poses a serious security threat, the conditions of such internment should be in conformity with international standards, including Article 37 of the Convention and those pertaining to juvenile justice, and should not preclude any tracing efforts and priority participation in rehabilitation programmes.[56]

The identification of the importance of achieving the recovery and reintegration into society of child soldiers and child victims of armed conflicts increasingly resonated with the more sophisticated analyses given to the impact of armed conflict on children in the debates appearing in the UN institutions, as reflected in the ground-breaking Machel Report: see section 8.2.3 below.

8.1.2.2 The Worst Forms of Child Labour Convention of 1999[57]

As we have seen (section 4.2.3), the definition of the *worst forms* of child labour includes, inter alia, the 'forced or compulsory recruitment of children for use in armed conflict',[58] a definition that controversially fell short of a much broader prohibition on the use of children as soldiers in armed conflicts by some of the delegates to that negotiation (Davidson 2001: 217). The associated Recommendation to the Worst Forms of Child Labour Convention also notes that states parties

---

56 ibid [56–57].
57 International Labour Organization, ILO Convention concerning the Prohibition and Immediate Action for the Elimination of the Worst Forms of Child Labour, ILO Convention No 182 (17 June 1999).
58 The Worst Forms of Child Labour Convention of 1999 art 3(a).

should provide that forced or compulsory recruitment of children for use in armed conflict is made a criminal offence.[59]

8.1.2.3   Optional Protocol to the Convention on the Rights of the Child on the involvement of children in armed conflict of 2000 (OPAC)[60]

In part, precisely because of the unsatisfactory compromises reached in relation to the drafting of Article 38 of the Convention on the Rights of the Child, there was sufficient support to establish OPAC in 2000. The appearance of a landmark report[61] by the expert, Mme Graça Machel, appointed by the Secretary-General, which had followed two years of consultation, extensive research and field visits, was also a key influence in the production of OPAC. The UN Commission on Human Rights (UNCHR)[62] established a working group to draft OPAC in 1994. In 1996 the General Assembly recommended, in response to the Machel Report, that the Secretary-General appoint for a period of three years a Special Representative on the impact of armed conflict on children: see section 8.2.3.

There were delays in the drafting process, not least because of the need to deal with a number of difficult issues: the minimum age of persons participating in hostilities; the issue of direct or indirect involvement in hostilities; the age of recruitment (voluntary or compulsory) into the armed forces; and whether or not a clause should be included to prevent child recruitment by non-governmental armed groups.

The Committee issued Recommendation No 1[63] in 1998 on the subject of children and armed conflict, following its 'Day of General Discussion' on the topic. The Recommendation expressed concerns about the delays in drafting the OPAC. It also reaffirmed the belief that 'this new legal instrument is urgently needed in order to strengthen the levels of protection ensured by the Convention' and referred to its previous suggestion 'on the fundamental importance of raising the age of all forms of recruitment of children into the armed forces to 18 years and the prohibition of their involvement in hostilities'.[64]

In the meantime, another landmark international instrument was gaining attention, the Rome Statute of the International Criminal Court of 1998 (section

59 R190 Worst Forms of Child Labour Recommendation, 1999 (No.190), Recommendation concerning the prohibition and immediate action for the elimination of the worst forms of child labour. Adoption: Geneva, 87th ILC session (17 June 1999) [12(a)].

60 Opened for signature 25 May 2000, 2173 UNTS 222 (entered into force 12 February 2002). OPAC had 129 signatories and 154 ratifications as at 22 February 2014.

61 General Assembly, *Impact of Armed Conflict on Children: report of the expert of the Secretary-General, Ms. Graça Machel*, submitted pursuant to General Assembly resolution 48/157 (Machel Report), UN Doc A/51/306 (26 August 1996).

62 The UNCHR was reconstituted as the UN Human Rights Council (UNHRC) in 2006: see section 2.5.1.1.

63 Committee on the Rights of the Child, Recommendation No 1: *Children in Armed Conflict*, Report on the Nineteenth Session, CRC/C/80 (September 1998).

64 ibid [1, 3 and 5].

8.3.4) which provided a mechanism of accountability for war crimes, crimes against humanity and other serious violations of humanitarian law.

The OPAC entered into force on 12 February 2002. It attempts to lay down a higher standard than the Convention on the Rights of the Child to prevent the direct participation of under-18-year-olds in armed combat or their compulsory recruitment:

Article 1
States Parties shall take all feasible measures to ensure that members of their armed forces who have not attained the age of 18 years do not take a direct part in hostilities.[65]

Article 2
States Parties shall ensure that persons who have not attained the age of 18 years are not compulsorily recruited into their armed forces.[66]

However, the OPAC falls short of achieving an absolute threshold of 18 years for participation and recruitment in armed conflict '... due to the reluctance of certain States, most notably the USA' (Harvey 2003: 13). Article 3 of OPAC provides a mechanism whereby each state party must raise in years the minimum age for voluntary recruitment from that set out in Article 38(3) of the Convention on the Rights of the Child.[67]

Furthermore, states parties must deposit a binding declaration upon ratification of, or accession to, OPAC that sets out the minimum age at which it will permit voluntary recruitment into its national armed forces and a description of safeguards it has adopted to ensure that such recruitment is not forced or coerced.[68] OPAC provides that states that do permit voluntary recruitment under the age of 18 years must maintain certain safeguards:

Article 3(3)
3. States Parties that permit voluntary recruitment into their national armed forces under the age of 18 years shall maintain safeguards to ensure, as a minimum, that:

    (a) Such recruitment is genuinely voluntary;
    (b) Such recruitment is carried out with the informed consent of the person's parents or legal guardians;
    (c) Such persons are fully informed of the duties involved in such military service;

---

65 OPAC art 1.
66 ibid art 2.
67 The requirement to raise the minimum age for voluntary recruitment does not apply, however, 'to schools operated by or under the control of the armed forces' that are in keeping with the education standards set out in the Convention on the Rights of the Child: see OPAC art 3(5).
68 OPAC art 3(2).

(d) Such persons provide reliable proof of age prior to acceptance into national military service.

A significant advance achieved in the OPAC is the explicit recognition that 'armed groups', as distinct from the 'armed forces' of a state, have comparable impacts on children. The preamble of the OPAC states:

> Condemning with the gravest concern the recruitment, training and use within and across national borders of children in hostilities by armed groups distinct from the armed forces of a State, and recognizing the responsibility of those who recruit, train and use children in this regard.[69]

Under Article 4(1) of the OPAC, such (non-state) armed militias or groups are absolutely prohibited from recruiting, or using in hostilities, under-18-year-olds.

One commentator has observed that: '[p]redictably, states have bound potential opponents with stronger obligations than they are prepared to accept for themselves, agreeing to stricter recruitment and deployment standards for rebel groups' (Harvey 2003: 28). States parties are encouraged to prevent any recruitment and use of children in hostilities, including the adoption of 'legal measures necessary to prohibit and criminalise such practices'.[70] This Article also carefully notes that its application 'shall not affect the legal status of any party to an armed conflict'.[71] Nothing in the OPAC shall be construed as 'precluding provisions in the law of a State Party or in international instruments and international humanitarian law that are more conducive to the realization of the rights of the child'.[72]

States parties are under a duty, comparable to that contained in Article 4 of the Convention on the Rights of the Child (section 3.7.1) to take all necessary measures to ensure the OPAC's effective implementation and enforcement within their own jurisdictions and to disseminate its principles and provisions widely.[73] States parties are also under a duty to take 'all feasible measures' to ensure the demobilisation of children who are recruited or used in hostilities in contravention of the OPAC, and must 'when necessary' offer such persons appropriate assistance for their 'physical and psychological recovery and their social reintegration'.[74]

Article 7 of the OPAC mandates states parties to cooperate in the implementation of the Optional Protocol, including the prevention of activity violating the Optional Protocol, and in the rehabilitation and social reintegration of victims. Technical cooperation and financial assistance is undertaken by the states parties and relevant international organisations.[75] States parties that are, 'in a position

---

69 OPAC preamble §11.
70 ibid art 4(2).
71 ibid art 4(3).
72 ibid art 5.
73 ibid art 6(1) and (2).
74 ibid art 6(3).
75 ibid art 7(1).

to do so', must provide assistance through existing multilateral, bilateral or other programmes, 'or, inter alia, through a voluntary fund established in accordance with the rules of the General Assembly'.[76]

The OPAC also contains its own reporting procedure: see section 3.5 for further details of the reporting procedures under the two substantive Optional Protocols. By way of illustrating how the OPAC may be applied in practice, Case study 8.1 below contains some extracts from the Committee's Concluding Observations on China's initial report submitted under the OPAC.

Case study 8.1

[Extract from:]
Concluding observations on the initial report of China submitted under Article 8 of the Optional Protocol to the Convention on the Rights of the Child on the involvement of children in armed conflict, adopted by the Committee at its 64th session (16 September–4 October 2013), CRC/C/OPAC/CHN/CO/1 (29 October 2013).

…[paras 1 – 3 omitted]

II.   General observations
Positive aspects
4. The Committee welcomes the revision of the Law of the People's Republic of China on the Protection of Minors in December 2006 and in October 2012.
5. The Committee further welcomes the progress achieved in the adoption of national plans and programmes to facilitate the implementation of the Optional Protocol, including the adoption in July 2011 of the National Programme for Child Development (2011–2020) for mainland China.

III.   General measures of implementation
Legislation
6. The Committee regrets that the Law of the People's Republic of China on National Defence does not explicitly criminalize recruitment of children up to 18 years.
7. The Committee recommends that the State party consider amending the Law on National Defence to criminalize recruitment and involvement of children under the age of 18 years in the Armed Forces.

76 ibid art 7(2).

Independent monitoring

8. The Committee is concerned about the absence of an independent national human rights institution in line with the principles relating to the status of national institutions (the Paris Principles) to regularly monitor progress in the fulfilment of child rights under the Optional Protocol and to receive and address complaints from children.

9. In the light of its general comment No. 2 (2002) on the role of independent national human rights institutions in the promotion and protection of the rights of the child and of the recommendations made by several United Nations human rights bodies on the necessary establishment of an independent national human rights institution in line with the Paris Principles, the Committee urges the State party to establish an independent mechanism to monitor the fulfilment of rights under the Optional Protocol and to deal with children's complaints in a child-friendly and expeditious manner.

Dissemination and awareness-raising

10. The Committee recommends that the State party ensure that the principles and provisions of the Optional Protocol are widely disseminated among the general public, children and their families.

Training

11. The Committee regrets that the training programmes for members of the Armed Forces and relevant professional groups dealing with children do not fully cover the provisions of the Optional Protocol.

12. The Committee encourages the State party to provide training on the Optional Protocol to all members of its Armed Forces, in particular personnel dealing with children, authorities working for and with asylum-seeking and refugee children, the police, lawyers, judges, military judges, medical professionals, social workers and journalists.

Data

13. The Committee regrets the absence of information on the measures taken to establish a central data collection system in the State party — mainland China, Hong Kong, China, and Macao, China — to register all children within its jurisdiction who may have been recruited or used in hostilities.

14. The Committee recommends that the State party establish central data collection systems in mainland China, Hong Kong, China, and Macao, China, to identify and register all children within its jurisdiction who may have been recruited or used in hostilities abroad, or detained or maimed. The Committee also recommends that the State party ensure that data on refugee and asylum-seeking children who have been victims of such practices are properly collected. All data should be disaggregated by, inter alia, sex, age, nationality, ethnic origin and socioeconomic background.

IV.   Prevention
Voluntary recruitment

15. The Committee expresses concern that the Military Service Law of the People's Republic of China allows voluntary recruitment of children below the age of 18 years into the active military service. It regrets that the State party does not intend to raise the age of voluntary recruitment to 18 years. In addition, while the minimum voluntary enlistment age in the State Party is reported to be 17 years, its binding declaration in respect of the Optional Protocol, made at the time of accession, appears to contain a contradictory statement that citizens who have not yet reached 17 years by 31 December of a given year may be recruited for active service.

16. The Committee is also concerned about:

(a) The high number of total recruits under 18 years enrolled in the Armed Forces; and

(b) The absence of policy and practice to ensure that children under 18 years are not involved in participation in hostilities.

17. The Committee recommends that the State party review and raise the age for voluntary recruitment into the Armed Forces to 18 years in order to promote and strengthen the protection of children through an overall higher legal standard. It further recommends that the State party:

(a) Provide in its next periodic report information on the number and per-centage of recruits under 18 years of age, if any, to the Armed Forces, as well as on the reported cases of recruitment irregularities, the nature of the complaints received and sanctions undertaken; and

(b) Explicitly prohibit the deployment of children under 18 years to areas where they may be at risk of indirect or direct participation in hostilities. The Committee further recommends that until such policy reform is under-taken, the State party put in place effective safeguards, including policies to ensure that children under 18 years are effectively screened before deploy-ment to situations of armed conflict.

Age verification procedures

18. While noting that the State party has established procedures to verify the ages of incoming recruits, the Committee remains concerned at the low level of birth registration, especially among migrant children, in the State party, which may impact on the effectiveness of these procedures.

19. The Committee underlines the importance of birth registration as a measure to prevent recruitment of underage children, and recommends that the State party continue and strengthen its efforts to establish a free national birth registration system for all children, including migrant children.

Military training

20. The Committee is concerned that military training is included in the mainstream education curriculum and schools provide compulsory military education and training activities, including various levels of exposure to the handling of firearms, for all children under 18 years.

21. The Committee recommends that the State party exclude military training from the general education curriculum and take measures to ban military training with the use of firearms for children under the age of 18 in the mainstream education curriculum and schools.

Military schools

22. The Committee notes that the State Council and the Central Military Commission are allowed to recruit 17 year-old students graduating from ordinary high schools on a voluntary basis. The Committee is, however, concerned that:

(a) Although the enrolment plans, specifically aimed at enrolling young students in military colleges and schools, are approved by the Ministry of Education and the General Political Department of the People's Liberation Army, each military college or school sets up its own educational curriculum and military training programmes;

(b) No concrete information on the curriculum and military training activities — in particular regarding the handling of firearms — in military schools is provided;

(c) Children in military colleges and schools lack access to an independent complaints mechanism.

23. The Committee recommends that the State party:

(a) Ban military-type training — including on the use of firearms — for children and ensure that any military training for children takes into account human rights principles, and that the educational content is approved and periodically monitored by the Ministry of Education;

(b) Provide in its next periodic report data, disaggregated by sex, age, nationality, ethnicity and socioeconomic background, on children enrolled in military colleges, vocational colleges and schools, as well as on the types of activities they carry out; and

(c) Set up independent and gender-sensitive mechanisms for complaints and investigation that are accessible to children in military colleges and schools, in order to monitor the welfare of and investigate complaints by children in such programmes.

Human rights and peace education

24. The Committee regrets that human rights and peace education, as well as knowledge on the Optional Protocol, is not specifically incorporated as

a mandatory part of the primary and secondary school curricula and in teacher training programmes.

25. With reference to its general comment No. 1 (2001) on the aims of education, the Committee recommends that the State party, in the context of its education reform, consider including peace education in school curricula at all levels, with special reference to the crimes covered by the Optional Protocol.

... [paras 26–38 omitted]

8.2   The United Nations and children associated with armed forces or armed groups

8.2.1   Security Council resolutions

In the late 1990s the UN Security Council (section 2.4.1) started to express its commitment to address the widespread impact of armed conflict on children in the context of its primary responsibility for the maintenance of international peace and security. On an unprecedented occasion during the Security Council's new annual debate on children and armed conflict, a 14-year-old former child soldier from Sierra Leone addressed the Council.[77]

A Security Council resolution in 1999,[78] reflecting the first Security Council debate on this issue, expressed 'grave concern at the harmful and widespread impact of armed conflict on children and the long-term consequences this has for durable peace, security and development' and strongly condemned the targeting of children in situations of armed conflict, 'including killing and maiming, sexual violence, abduction and forced displacement, recruitment and use of children in armed conflict in violation of international law', and called upon parties to comply strictly with their obligations under international law.

A further resolution in 2000[79] welcomed the appearance of the OPAC and reaffirmed its strong condemnation of the deliberate targeting of children in armed conflicts and the damaging impact such conflicts had on children and the long-term consequences for durable peace, security and development. It extended its list of concerns by, for example, also emphasizing 'the responsibility of all States to put an end to impunity and to prosecute those responsible for genocide, crimes against humanity and war crimes, and, in this regard, stresses the need to exclude these, where feasible, from amnesty provisions and relevant legislation'.[80]

77 'Child soldier asks United Nations for help', *BBC News* (21 November 2001). See http://news.bbc.co.uk/1/hi/world/africa/1667683.stm (accessed 17 November 2013).
78 UNSC Res 1261 (25 August 1999) UN Doc S/RES/1261.
79 UNSC Res 1314 (11 August 2000) UN Doc S/RES/1314.
80 UNSC Res 1314 (11 August 2000) UN Doc S/RES/1314 para 2.

Another resolution in 2001[81] expressed readiness to include provisions for the protection of children when considering the mandates of peacekeeping operations and reaffirmed its readiness to include, where appropriate, child protection advisers in peacekeeping operations. It also committed itself to intensifying, monitoring and reporting activities on the situation of children in armed conflicts. This resolution built on previous ones with a list of concerns, for example; the need to pay attention to the rehabilitation of children affected by armed conflict in order to reintegrate them into society, and to develop and expand regional initiatives.

Furthermore, the resolution requested the Special Representative of the Secretary-General for children and armed conflict (section 8.2.3) to annex to her annual report a list of parties that recruit and use children. There are in fact two lists: one lists the parties that recruit or use children in situations of armed conflict which are on the Security Council's agenda;[82] and the second list includes parties that recruit or use children in situations of armed conflict which are not on the Security Council's agenda.[83]

A subsequent Security Council resolution in 2004[84] expressed deep concern 'over the lack of overall progress on the ground, where parties to conflict continue to violate with impunity the relevant provisions of applicable international law'. Significantly, it also requested the Secretary-General to devise urgently 'an action plan for a systematic and comprehensive monitoring and reporting mechanism', including time-bound measures, that would utilise United Nations, national, regional and NGO expertise to provide reliable information on 'the recruitment and use of child soldiers in violation of applicable international law and on other violations and abuses committed against children affected by armed conflict'.

The resolution also expressed the Security Council's intention to consider sanctions on parties failing to develop such action plans, for example, a ban on the export or supply of small arms and of other military equipment. In a further resolution in 2005,[85] the plans to devise monitoring and reporting mechanisms were strengthened. A working group of the Security Council[86] was established to review reports from the monitoring mechanisms and to review progress in the development of action plans.

---

81 UNSC Res 1379 (20 November 2001) UN Doc S/RES/1379.

82 As at May 2013, there were various parties in this category in the following states: Afghanistan, Central African Republic, Chad, Democratic Republic of Congo, Iraq, Mali, Myanmar, Somalia, South Sudan, Sudan, Syrian Arab Republic, Uganda and Yemen. General Assembly, *Children and armed conflict: Report of the Secretary-General*, 67th session, UN Doc A/67/845–S/2013/245 (15 May 2013) Annex I.

83 As at May 2013, there were various parties in this category in the following states: Colombia, Philippines. General Assembly, *Children and armed conflict: Report of the Secretary-General*, 67th session, UN Doc A/67/845–S/2013/245 (15 May 2013) Annex II.

84 UNSC Res 1539 (22 April 2004) UN Doc S/RES/1539.

85 UNSC Res 1612 (26 July 2005) UN Doc S/RES/1612.

86 The Security Council's Working Group's documents are available at http://www.un.org/children/conflict/english/securitycouncilwgroupdoc.html (accessed 7 February 2010). See the group's latest annual report: SCWG (2009).

The Security Council also expressed grave concern about 'the documented links between the use of child soldiers in violation of applicable international law and the illicit trafficking of small arms and light weapons and stressing the need for all States to take measures to prevent and to put an end to such trafficking'. In a later Security Council resolution on children and armed conflict,[87] the success in bringing to justice some persons alleged to have committed crimes against children in situations of armed conflict was welcomed.

The resolution also expressed a conviction that 'the protection of children in armed conflict should be an important aspect of any comprehensive strategy to resolve conflict'. It reaffirmed the intention to take action against persistent perpetrators of crimes against children in armed conflict, and expressed deep concern that children continue to account for a considerable number of casualties resulting from killing and maiming in armed conflicts 'including as a result of deliberate targeting, indiscriminate and excessive use of force, indiscriminate use of landmines, cluster munitions and other weapons and use of children as human shields'.[88]

In the Security Council's resolution in 2011 on children and armed conflict, it stated, inter alia:

> *Noting* that Article 28 of the Convention on the Rights of the Child recognizes the right of the child to education and sets forth obligations for State parties to the Convention, with a view to progressively achieving this right on the basis of equal opportunity;
>
> 1. Strongly *condemns* all violations of applicable international law involving the recruitment and use of children by parties to armed conflict, as well as their re-recruitment, killing and maiming, rape and other sexual violence, abductions, attacks against schools or hospitals and denial of humanitarian access by parties to armed conflict and all other violations of international law committed against children in situations of armed conflict;
>
> 2. *Reaffirms* that the monitoring and reporting mechanism will continue to be implemented in situations listed in annex I and annex II ("the annexes") to the reports of the Secretary-General on children and armed conflict, in line with the principles set out in paragraph 2 of its resolution 1612 (2005), and that its establishment and implementation shall not prejudge or imply a decision by the Security Council as to whether or not to include a situation on its agenda;
>
> 3. *Recalls* paragraph 16 of its resolution 1379 (2001) and requests the Secretary-General to also include in the annexes to his reports on children and armed conflict those parties to armed conflict that engage, in contravention of applicable international law;
>
>   (a) in recurrent attacks on schools and/or hospitals

87 UNSC Res 1882 (4 August 2009) UN Doc S/RES/1882.
88 UNSC Res 1882 (4 August 2009) UN Doc S/RES/1882.

(b) in recurrent attacks or threats of attacks against protected persons in relation to schools and/or hospitals in situations of armed conflict, bearing in mind all other violations and abuses committed against children, and notes that the present paragraph will apply to situations in accordance with the conditions set out in paragraph 16 of its resolution 1379 (2001); ...[89]

A further resolution in 2012[90] indicates the Security Council's increasing resolve to impose increasing pressures on persistent perpetrators of violations and abuses committed against children in situations of armed conflict. Indeed, some commentators argue that the Security Council should further develop sanctions against governments and other groups who breach their international obligations by using children in armed conflict, rather than focusing on enforcement through the prosecution in international courts and tribunals (section 8.3) of those who recruit and enlist child soldiers (Happold 2005).

The Secretary-General's now annual report on armed conflict[91] includes information on compliance with the relevant international law relating to the recruitment and use of children in armed conflict and other grave violations committed against children affected by armed conflict. It also reports progress on the implementation of the monitoring and reporting mechanism and action plans mandated in the resolutions discussed above, and provides summaries of the situations on the two lists referred to above.

8.2.2 The Paris Principles

At a Conference held in Paris, 'Free Children from War', organised jointly by the French Ministry of Foreign Affairs and UNICEF on 5–6 February 2007, 59 states supported the adoption of the Paris Commitments to Protect Children Unlawfully Recruited or Used by Armed Forces or Armed Groups[92] and the Paris Principles and Guidelines on Children associated with Armed Forces or Armed Groups'[93] (Paris Commitments and Paris Principles respectively).[94] Such international documents are a good example of 'soft law' (section 2.2.6).

---

89 UNSC Res 1998 (12 July 2011) UN Doc S/RES/1998.

90 UNSC Res 2068 (19 September 2012) S/RES/2068.

91 For example General Assembly, *Children and armed conflict: Report of the Secretary-General*, 67th session, UN Doc A/67/845–S/2013/245 (15 May 2013).

92 See http://www.icrc.org/eng/assets/files/other/pariscommitments_en.pdf (accessed 18 November 2013).

93 UNICEF, *Paris Principles. Principles and Guidelines on Children Associated With Armed Forces or Armed Groups* (February 2007). See http://www.refworld.org/docid/465198442.html (accessed 18 November 2013).

94 The last ministerial follow-up forum on the Paris Commitments and the Paris Principles and Guidelines was held at UNHQ in New York on 29 September 2009. Further countries endorsed

The Paris Commitments are intended to strengthen political action to prevent association of children with armed conflict and to ensure their reintegration with society. States commit themselves to uphold and apply the Paris Principles, a set of operational guidelines. The language used in these documents had broadened out from referring to 'child soldiers' to a definition of 'a child associated with an armed force or armed group'.[95] The extract below, concerting the specific situation of girls, provides an illustration of the detail that has been provided in the Paris Principles:

> 4.0 There are almost always a significant number of girls amongst children associated with armed forces or armed groups. For a range of reasons, however, these girls are rarely provided with assistance. While there are commonalities between the circumstances and experiences of girls and boys, the situation for girls can be very different in relation to the reasons and manner in which they join the armed forces or armed groups; the potential for their release; the effects that the experience of being in the armed force or armed group has on their physical, social and emotional well being; and the consequences this may have for their ability to successfully adapt to civilian life or reintegrate into family and community life after their release.
>
> 4.1 From the planning stage onwards, through the design of eligibility criteria and screening procedures for inclusion in release and reintegration programmes and informal release processes through to programming for reintegration, monitoring and follow-up, actors should recognise that girls are at risk of being 'invisible' and take measures to ensure that girls are included and relevant issues addressed at all stages. It is important that the differences between girls' and boys' experiences are understood and taken into account by all actors and that programming for children who are or have been associated with armed forces or armed groups explicitly reflects the particular situation of both girls and boys.
>
> 4.2 Actors should establish the means to share and learn from one another's experience and expertise including findings on research and outcomes of pilot programmes for girls associated with armed forces or armed groups.
>
> 4.3 Issues relating particularly or specifically to girls are considered throughout the Principles.[96]

---

the Paris Commitments, bringing the total number of country endorsements to 84: see http://childrenandarmedconflict.un.org/our-work/paris-principles/ (accessed 18 November 2013).

95 '... any person below 18 years of age who is or who has been recruited or used by an armed force or armed group in any capacity, including but not limited to children, boys, and girls used as fighters, cooks, porters, messengers, spies or for sexual purposes. It does not only refer to a child who is taking or has taken a direct part in hostilities' (Paris Principles, para 2.1).

96 UNICEF, *Paris Principles. Principles and Guidelines on Children Associated With Armed Forces or Armed Groups* (February 2007) [4.0–4.3].

8.2.3   The Special Representative of the Secretary-General for children and armed conflict

A significant landmark in the international attention paid to children and armed conflict was the appearance of the UN commissioned report 'Impact of armed conflict on children' in 1996. The report was authored by Graça Machel, an expert designated by the Secretary-General to undertake the study, and has become known as the Machel Report.[97] It set out a comprehensive and detailed analysis of the problem:

> In 1995, 30 major armed conflicts raged in different locations around the world. All of them took place within States, between factions split along ethnic, religious or cultural lines. The conflicts destroyed crops, places of worship and schools. Nothing was spared, held sacred or protected – not children, families or communities. In the past decade, an estimated two million children have been killed in armed conflict. Three times as many have been seriously injured or permanently disabled, many of them maimed by landmines. Countless others have been forced to witness or even to take part in horrifying acts of violence.[98]

The report observed, for example, that 'the proportion of war victims who are civilians has leaped dramatically from 5 per cent to over 90 per cent'.[99] Furthermore, it noted that children were rarely mentioned in reconstruction plans and advised that 'the seeds of reconstruction should be sown even during conflict'.[100] The report was a powerful call to action and the General Assembly unanimously welcomed the report in a resolution in which it also established the mandate of the Special Representative of the Secretary-General for Children and Armed Conflict.[101] The General Assembly has since extended the mandate several times and there have to date been four successive holders of the mandate.[102] The website of the Special Representative announces its mission thus:

> To promote and protect the rights of all children affected by armed conflict.

---

97 General Assembly, *Impact of Armed Conflict on Children: report of the expert of the Secretary-General, Ms. Graça Machel*, submitted pursuant to General Assembly resolution 48/157, (Machel Report), UN Doc A/51/306 (26 August 1996). See http://www.un.org/documents/ga/docs/51/plenary/a51-306.htm (accessed 15 November 2013).

98 ibid [2].

99 ibid [24].

100 ibid 243.

101 Office of the General Assembly, *The rights of the child*, UN Doc A/RES/51/77 (20 February 1997) [35–7].

102 Mr Olara A. Otunnu (1998 to 2005); Ms Karin Sham Poo, Interim Special Representative in the Fall of 2005; Ms Radhika Coomaraswamy (April 2006–August 2012); Ms Leila Zerrougui (September 2012 to present).

- The Special Representative serves as a moral voice and independent advocate for the protection and well-being of boys and girls affected by armed conflict.
- The Special Representative works with partners to propose ideas and approaches to enhance the protection of children and armed conflict and to promote a more concerted protection response.
- The Special Representative and her Office advocate, build awareness and give prominence to the rights and protection of children and armed conflict.
- The Special Representative is a facilitator, undertaking humanitarian and diplomatic initiatives to facilitate the work of operational actors on the ground with regard to children and armed conflict.

The Office of the Special Representative does not have a field presence but promotes and supports the efforts of operational partners.[103]

The Special Representative makes annual reports to the UN Human Rights Council (UNHRC).[104] In September 2000, at the World Summit for Children, Canada hosted the International Conference on War-affected Children in Winnipeg. In preparation for the conference, Canada commissioned the 'Machel Review 1996–2000', to review progress in protecting war-affected children and to serve as principal background document for the Conference.

This review[105] concluded that there had been some progress; for example, children were now more central to the UN's peace and security agenda and that war crimes against children had started to be prosecuted and violations against children were being documented more systematically, and that more is now known about how small arms and light weapons are damaging children's lives. However, the damaging impact on children by armed conflicts continues:

> In spite of this progress the assaults against children continue. An estimated 300,000 children are still participating in armed combat. Children in 87 countries live amid the contamination of more than 60 million landmines. At least 20 million children have been uprooted from their homes. Girls and women continue to be marginalised from mainstream humanitarian assistance and protection. Humanitarian personnel continue to be targeted and killed. Millions of children are abandoned to cope with the multiple and compounded effects of armed conflict and HIV/AIDS. Hundreds of thousands of children continue to die from disease and malnutrition in flight from

---

103 See http://childrenandarmedconflict.un.org/about-us (accessed 18 November 2013).

104 For example Human Rights Council, *Annual report of the Special Representative of the Secretary-General for Children and Armed Conflict, Radhika Coomaraswamy*, 21st session, UN Doc A/HRC/21/38 (28 June 2012).

105 General Assembly, *The Machel Review 1996–2000: A Critical Analysis of Progress Made and Obstacles Encountered in Increasing Protection for War-affected Children*, 55th session, UN Doc A/55/749 (26 January 2001).

conflict or in camps for displaced persons. Small arms and light weapons continue to proliferate excessively. Millions of children are scarred physically and psychologically.[106]

To mark the 10th anniversary of the landmark Graça Machel study of 1996, UNICEF and the Special Representative of the Secretary-General (SRSG) reviewed the current situation faced by children in armed conflict. The 'Machel Strategic Review'[107] identifies emerging challenges and priorities and the responses required for the next decade. It concludes with 15 recommendations: for example, urging the end of impunity for violations against children; strengthening the monitoring and reporting mechanisms; supporting inclusive reintegration strategies; operationalising the engagement of regional bodies; and integrating children's rights in peacemaking, peacebuilding and preventive actions.[108] The main objectives of the current Special Representative's strategic plan are:

> (1) to support global initiatives to end grave violations; (2) to promote rights-based protection for children affected by armed conflict; (3) to make children and armed conflict concerns an integral aspect of peacekeeping and peace-building; (4) to identify new trends and strategies for the protection of children through research; (5) to secure political and diplomatic engagement on CAAC [Children And Armed Conflict] initiatives and (6) to raise global awareness with regard to all issues relating to children and armed conflict.[109]

The Office of the Special Representative has also instituted a series of working papers 'to assist the community of practice working on the protection of children affected by armed conflict'. The first of these working papers (Kolieb 2009) identifies the legal foundations of 'six grave violations' against children during armed conflict. The normative standards which are examined and clarified in the paper and which address these six grave violations are headlined as follows:

- Parties to a conflict must protect children from being killed or seriously injured
- Parties to a conflict must not recruit or deploy children as soldiers, and must prevent children from participating in hostilities
- Parties to a conflict must not rape or otherwise abuse children
- Parties to a conflict must not abduct children
- Parties to a conflict must not attack schools or hospitals, other education or medical facilities ordinarily used by children and

---

106 ibid 61.
107 General Assembly, *Report of the Special Representative of the Secretary-General for Children and Armed Conflict*, 62nd session, UN Doc A/62/228 (13 August 2007).
108 ibid [103–117].
109 See http://childrenandarmedconflict.un.org/our-work/strategic-plan/ (accessed 20 November 2013).

- Parties to a conflict must not deny humanitarian access for children even in a conflict zone.

Subsequent Working Papers explored the rights and guarantees of internally displaced children in armed conflict (Mooney and Paul 2010) and the ways in which children who have suffered grave violations during armed conflicts can access justice (Hamilton and Dutordoir 2011).

8.3   International courts and tribunals

Over the past two decades there have been important developments in international efforts to prosecute crimes against humanity, war crimes and other serious violations against international humanitarian law, including ending impunity for crimes against children. The arrest and trial of individuals in leadership positions alleged to have committed such crimes sends a powerful message that such behaviour may not be tolerated in the future. Combined with the various initiatives of the United Nations discussed earlier, these international justice mechanisms hold out some hope that relevant parties will be brought into compliance with international law standards in this field.

The sections below focus on the International Criminal Tribunal for the former Yugoslavia (ICTY), the International Criminal Tribunal for Rwanda (ICTR), the Special Court for Sierra Leone (SCSL) and the International Criminal Court (ICC). The international justice system, such as it is, remains challenged by the difficulties of dealing with child soldiers who have themselves been accused of war crimes, a problem that 'illustrates the complexity of balancing culpability, a community's sense of justice and the "best interests of the child"'.[109a]

It would appear, however, that a consensus is emerging from the practice of the ICC and other international tribunals that children below the age of 18 years should not be prosecuted for such crimes by international courts and tribunals. There is also the political difficulty of whether the particular international court or tribunal is dispensing, or is seen as dispensing, 'victors' justice', a problem that undoubtedly impacts on the long-term legitimacy of such bodies. The various international courts/tribunals are discussed below in the chronological order of their establishment.

8.3.1   The International Criminal Tribunal for the former Yugoslavia (ICTY)

In May 1993, the International Criminal Tribunal for the former Yugoslavia (ICTY) was established by the United Nations in response to mass atrocities taking place in Croatia and Bosnia and Herzegovina. The ICTY is situated in The Hague, the Netherlands. The ICTY was the first war crimes court created by the United

---

109a   Machel Report, n97, para 250.

Nations and the first international war crimes tribunal since the Nuremberg and Tokyo tribunals. It was established as an ad hoc court by the Security Council in accordance with Chapter VII of the UN Charter. The Tribunal laid the foundations for what is now the accepted norm for conflict resolution and post-conflict development globally, namely, that leaders suspected of crimes against humanity, war crimes and other serious violations of international humanitarian law will be exposed to face justice.

The ICTY was empowered to prosecute persons responsible for serious violations of international humanitarian law committed in the territory of the former Yugoslavia since 1991, genocide and crimes against humanity.[110] Several leaders, including Momcilo Krajišnik, president of the Bosnian Serb Assembly during the 1992–1995 war, Slobodan Miloševic, former president of the Federal Republic of Yugoslavia and Karadzic were charged with these crimes. The work of the Tribunal showed that the mass murder at Srebrenica, where it is estimated that around 8,000 Bosnian Muslims were murdered, was indeed 'genocide'.

Most of the key cases heard at the Tribunal have dealt with alleged crimes committed by Serbs and Bosnian Serbs, but the Tribunal has also investigated and brought charges against persons from every ethnic background. Its indictments address crimes committed from 1991 to 2001 against members of various ethnic groups in Croatia, Bosnia and Herzegovina, Serbia, Kosovo and the Former Yugoslav Republic of Macedonia. As of May 2013, 69 individuals have been convicted and currently 25 people are in different stages of proceedings before the Tribunal.[111]

Under the Statute of the International Criminal Tribunal for the former Yugoslavia,[112] there is no mention of the crime of child soldiery, although children were used in the conflict. The number of children involved in the 1991–1995 Balkan wars is difficult to identify accurately, but is variously estimated as between around 3,000[113] to 20,000.[114]

8.3.2   International Criminal Tribunal for Rwanda (ICTR)

On 6 April 1994, a plane carrying the Rwandan President Habyarimana, a Hutu, was shot down. Violence began almost immediately after that. Hutu extremists launched their plans to destroy the entire Tutsi civilian population. In the weeks after 6 April 1994, 800,000 men, women and children perished in the Rwandan

---

110 UN Security Council, Statute of the International Criminal Tribunal for the Former Yugoslavia (as amended on 17 May 2002), adopted by UN Doc S/RES/827/93 (25 May 1993) arts 1–5.

111 See ICTY website http://www.icty.org/sections/AbouttheICTY (accessed 18 November 2013).

112 UN Security Council, Statute of the International Criminal Tribunal for the Former Yugoslavia (as amended on 17 May 2002), adopted by UN Doc S/RES/827/93 (25 May 1993) art 3.

113 'Child Soldiers of the Balkans', Radio Free Europe. See http://www.rferl.org/content/Child_Soldiers_Of_The_Balkans/1349516.html (accessed 18 November 2013).

114 See Child Soldiers International, *Child Soldiers Global Report 2001 – Bosnia-Herzegovina, 2001* (n 263). See http://www.refworld.org/docid/4988060e28.html (accessed 18 November 2013).

genocide. Acting again under Chapter VII of the United Nations Charter, the Security Council resolved in 1994 to create the International Criminal Tribunal for Rwanda (ICTR)[115] in response to the recognition of the serious violations of humanitarian law committed in Rwanda between 1 January and 31 December 1994. The Tribunal is located in Arusha, United Republic of Tanzania. The purpose was to contribute to the process of national reconciliation in Rwanda and to the maintenance of peace in the region.

The ICTR was established for the prosecution of persons responsible for genocide and other serious violations of international humanitarian law, including violations of 'common Article 3' of the Geneva Conventions of 1949 (section 8.1.1.1), committed in the territory of Rwanda. It also has jurisdiction to deal with the prosecution of Rwandan citizens responsible for genocide and other such violations of international law committed in the territory of neighbouring states during the same period. However, the ICTR Statute is silent on the conscription or enlistment of child soldiers.

The ICTR is governed by its Statute, which is annexed to Security Council Resolution 955 of 1994. The Tribunal consists of three organs: the Chambers and the Appeals Chamber; the Office of the Prosecutor, in charge of investigations and prosecutions; and the Registry, responsible for providing overall judicial and administrative support to the Chambers and the Prosecutor.

On 2 September 1998, the ICTR issued the first conviction for the crime of genocide in *Prosecutor v Akayesu*.[116] The decision in *Prosecutor v Kambanda* denoted genocide as the 'crime of crimes'.[117] Child combatants were involved in the conflict. In 1994, the Rwandan Ministry of Defence agreed to demobilise all child soldiers – commonly referred to as *kadogo* or 'little ones' in Kiswahili. Estimations of children's involvement is again difficult to state with precision but it would appear both government forces and the guerilla forces used child soldiers and possibly around 15,000 to 20,000 individuals were involved.[118]

It would appear, however, that the genocide in Rwanda, branded the 'crime of crimes', eclipsed any other crimes such as the recruitment and enlistment of child soldiers that occurred during the conflict. The ICTR has convicted 63 persons, 16 of whom are pending further appeal. A further 12 have been acquitted.[119]

---

115 UNSC Res 955 (8 November 1994) UN Doc S/RES/955.

116 *Prosecutor v Akayesu (Judgment)*, International Criminal Tribunal for Rwanda, Trial Chamber I, Case No ICTR-96-4-T (2 September 1998).

117 *Prosecutor v Kambanda (Judgment and Sentence)*, International Criminal Tribunal for Rwanda, Trial Chamber I, Case No ICTR-97-23-S (2 September 1998) [16].

118 See Child Soldiers International, *Child Soldiers Global Report 2001 – Rwanda, 2001* (n 1618). See http://www.refworld.org/docid/498805d326.html (accessed 18 November 2013).

119 See ICTR website http://www.unictr.org/Cases/tabid/204/Default.aspx (accessed 18 November 2013).

8.3.3 Special Court for Sierra Leone (SCSL)

In response to some of the perceived disadvantages of the ICTY and ICTR the international community developed a further model of international justice with the appearance of 'hybrid' or 'experimental' courts/tribunals, involving a blend of international and domestic law (Dickinson 2003). The SCSL was established jointly by the Government of Sierra Leone and the United Nations. It is now located at The Hague, in the Netherlands. It is mandated to try those who bear the greatest responsibility for serious violations of international humanitarian law and Sierra Leonean law committed in the territory of Sierra Leone since 30 November 1996.[120]

Thirteen indictments were issued by the prosecutor in 2003. Two of those indictments were subsequently withdrawn in December 2003, owing to the deaths of the accused. A breakthrough in the legal development of the crime of child recruitment arrived in 2004 with the case of *Hinga Norman*.[120a] The Appeals Chamber decided by a three-to-one majority that the recruitment and use of child soldiers was a crime recognised by customary international law, and had attracted individual criminal responsibility since at least November 1996, the date when the Court's temporal jurisdiction started (Smith 2004, Novogrodsky 2006). The trials of three former leaders of the Armed Forces Revolutionary Council (AFRC) in *Prosecutor v Brima, Kamara and Kanu*[121] (*AFRC* case) have resulted in convictions and sentences. There have also been completed trials of two members of the Civil Defence Forces (CDF)[122] and of three former leaders of the Revolutionary United Front (RUF),[123] including appeals. The *AFRC* case was something of a breakthrough when in 2007 the SCSL convicted three rebel leaders for the crime of using child soldiers. The Appeals Chamber, on 22 February 2008,[124] upheld sentences in the *AFRC* case of 50 years for Brima, 45 years for Kamara and 50 years for Kanu. For the first time, international law proscribed child soldiering as a crime under customary international law in definitive terms. In *Prosecutor v Brima, Kamara, Kanu (Appeal Judgment)*, the Court stated the following:

---

120 UN Security Council, Statute of the Special Court for Sierra Leone (16 January 2002) as established pursuant to UNSC Res 1315 (14 August 2000) UN Doc S/RES/1315 art 1(1).

120a *Prosecutor v Sam Hinga Norman (Moinina Fofana intervening)*. Decision on Preliminary Motion Based on Lack of Jurisdiction (Child Recruitment), Special Court for Sierra Leone, Appeals Chamber, Case No SCSL-2004-14-AR72(E) (31 May 2004).

121 *Prosecutor v Brima, Kamara and Kanu (AFRC case) (Sentencing Judgment)*, Special Court for Sierra Leone, Trial Chamber II, Case No SCSL-04-16-T (19 July 2007).

122 *Prosecutor v Fofana and Kondewa (CDF case) (Sentencing Judgment)*, Special Court for Sierra Leone, Trial Chamber I, Case No SCSL-04-14-T (9 October 2007).

123 *Prosecutor v Sesay, Kallon and Gbao (RUF case) (Judgment)*, Special Court for Sierra Leone, Trial Chamber I, Case No SCSL-04-15-T (2 March 2009).

124 *Prosecutor v Brima, Kamara and Kanu (AFRC case) (Appeal Judgment)*, Special Court for Sierra Leone, Trial Chamber II, Case No SCSL-2004-16-A (22 February 2008).

The Prosecution observes that the Appeals Chamber has already ruled that conscripting or enlisting children under the age of 15 years into armed forces or groups or using them to participate actively in hostilities was a crime entailing individual criminal responsibility at the time of the acts alleged in the Indictment. The Appeals Chamber refers to its dictum that:

> The rejection of the use of child soldiers by the international community was widespread by 1994 … Citizens of Sierra Leone, and even less, persons in leadership roles, cannot possibly argue that they did not know that recruiting children was a criminal act in violation of international humanitarian law. Child recruitment was criminalized before it was explicitly set out as a criminal prohibition in treaty law and certainly by November 1996, the starting point of the time frame relevant to the indictments. As set out above, the principle of legality and the principle of specificity are both upheld.[125]

In the *CDF* case (Appeals Chamber) the Court similarly held that the crime of recruitment by way of conscripting or enlisting children under the age of 15 years into an armed force or group and/or using them participate actively in hostilities constituted a crime under customary international law.[126]

The SCSL is also in the process of processing another high-profile case; that of the former Liberian President, Charles Taylor. He was indicted on 7 March 2003 for his role in the Sierra Leone conflict. He was convicted of, among other charges, using children in armed conflict, and sentenced in 2012 to 50 years in prison, a sentence that was confirmed on appeal on 26 September 2013.[127]

8.3.4   *International Criminal Court (ICC)*

An outline of the origins, establishment and jurisdiction of the International Criminal Court (ICC) has been given in section 2.4.3. The Rome Statute of the International Criminal Court[128] (1998) provides a definition of 'war crimes' that includes, inter alia, '[c]onscripting or enlisting children under the age of 15 years into the national armed forces or using them to participate actively in

---

125 ibid [para 295].
126 *Prosecutor v Fofana and Kondewa (CDF case) (Appeal Judgment)*, Special Court for Sierra Leone, Appeals Chamber, Case No SCSL-04-14-A (28 May 2008) [139].
127 *Prosecutor v Charles Ghankay Taylor (Trial Judgment)*, Special Court for Sierra Leone, Case No SCSL-03-01-T-1283 (18 May 2012); *Prosecutor v Charles Ghankay Taylor (Sentencing Judgment)*, Special Court for Sierra Leone, Case No SCSL-03-01-T-1285 (30 May 2012); *Prosecutor v Charles Ghankay Taylor (Appeal Judgment)*, Special Court for Sierra Leone, Appeals Chamber, Case No SCSL-03-01-A (26 September 2013).
128 Rome Statute of the International Criminal Court, opened for signature 17 July 1998, 2187 UNTS 90 (entered into force 1 July 2002).

hostilities'.[129] It also defines as a 'war crime' other serious violations of the laws and customs applicable in 'armed conflicts not of an international character', within the established framework of international law, including the conscription or enlisting of children under 15 years into 'armed forces or groups or using them to participate actively in hostilities'.[130] The death penalty is prohibited under ICC rules.

The ICC's first trial of Congolese rebel militia leader Thomas Lubanga Dyilo began on 26 January 2009, following an application for arrest made on 12 January 2006.[131] Lubanga was indicted for war crimes consisting of both of the offences referred to above. The number of children involved in fighting forces in the Democratic Republic of the Congo (DRC) conflict was estimated by the United Nations to be around 30,000. Lubanga was the President of the 'Union of Congolese Patriots' and is alleged to have served as commander-in-chief of the former military wing of the Union, namely the 'Patriotic Forces for the Liberation of Congo'. The Union of Congolese Patriots aimed to establish dominance of the Hema ethnic group through violence against mainly Lendu militias and civilians.

Lubanga was originally arrested in 2005 and transferred from the DRC to the ICC a year later, in March 2006. After long delays, his trial started at the ICC on 26 January 2009. Lubanga was charged with responsibility for these crimes because of his alleged political and military leadership roles. The ICC gave its verdict in his case on 14 March 2012 and its sentencing judgment on 10 July 2012: see Case study 8.2 below. There was some disappointment that Lubanga was charged only with child conscription/enlistment offences and not with additional offences of murder and sexual violence.

As this was the first trial in the ICC brought to completion it has naturally attracted much academic and other commentary assessing its significance and contribution to the development of the law in this field (eg Catani (2012); Graf (2012); Lieflander (2012); Roberts (2012) and Steffen (2012)). One point of interest in the Lubanga judgment is the endorsement of the persuasive value of the judgments of the SCSL within the ICC's development of jurisprudence:

> 603. The jurisprudence of the SCSL has been considered by the Trial Chamber. Although the decisions of other international courts and tribunals are not part of the directly applicable law under Article 21 of the Statute, the wording of the provision criminalising the conscription, enlistment and use of children under the age of 15 within the Statute of the SCSL is identical to Article 8(e)(vii) of the Rome Statute, and they were self-evidently directed at

---

129   ibid art 8(2)(b)(xxvi).

130   ibid art 8(2)(e)(vii).

131   *Prosecutor v Thomas Lubanga Dyilo (Warrant of Arrest)*, International Criminal Court, Pre-Trial Chamber I, Case No ICC-01/04-01/06 (10 February 2006).

the same objective. The SCSL's case law therefore potentially assists in the interpretation of the relevant provisions of the Rome Statute.[132]

The person accused of committing crimes as Lubanga's deputy, Bosco Ntaganda, has also been charged with enlisting, conscripting and using child soldiers in armed conflict in the first warrant of arrest issued in January 2006, and following a second warrant of arrest for additional charges in July 2012,[133] voluntarily surrendered to ICC custody on 22 March 2013 and is currently awaiting trial. Of course, the strategy of the ICC and other international courts and tribunals to prosecute what must inevitably be a very small number of commanders remains contentious. As Drumbl (2012: 207) comments: '[t]he current preference to criminally prosecute a handful of adult commanders for unlawful recruitment of children yields only a faint print of justice'.

At the time of writing, 21 *cases* in eight *situations* had been brought before the ICC. Four states parties to the Rome Statute – Uganda, the Democratic Republic of the Congo, the Central African Republic and Mali – had referred situations occurring on their territories to the Court. In addition, the Security Council has referred the situation in Darfur, Sudan, and the situation in Libya – both non-states parties. The prosecutor has opened and is conducting investigations in all of the above-mentioned situations.

Pre-Trial Chamber II, on 31 March 2010, granted the prosecution authorisation to open an investigation *proprio motu* in the situation of Kenya. In addition, on 3 October 2011, Pre-Trial Chamber III granted the prosecutor's request for authorisation to open investigations *proprio motu* into the situation in Côte d'Ivoire.[134]

Case study 8.2

The *Lubanga* Case

The ICC's verdict was given on 14 March 2012 by Trial Chamber I, composed of Judge Adrian Fulford (United Kingdom) as Presiding Judge, Judge Elizabeth Odio Benito (Costa Rica) and Judge René Blattmann (Bolivia). Although the first two judges have written separate and dissenting opinions on some issues, the verdict was unanimous.

Prosecutor v Thomas Lubanga Dyilo (Judgment), International Criminal Court, Trial Chamber I, Case No ICC-01/04-01/06 (14 March 2012) [1351–63]

---

132 *Prosecutor v Thomas Lubanga Dyilo (Judgment)*, International Criminal Court, Trial Chamber I, Case No ICC-01/04-01/06 (14 March 2012) [603].

133 *Prosecutor v Bosco Ntaganda, (Decision on the Prosecutor's Application under Article 58)*, International Criminal Court, Pre-Trial Chamber II, Case No ICC-01/04-02/06 (13 July 2012).

134 ICC website http://www.icc-cpi.int/en_menus/icc/situations%20and%20cases/Pages/situations%20and%20cases.aspx (accessed 20 November 2013).

4. OVERALL CONCLUSIONS

1351. The accused and his co-perpetrators agreed to, and participated in, a common plan to build an army for the purpose of establishing and maintaining political and military control over Ituri. This resulted, in the ordinary course of events, in the conscription and enlistment of boys and girls under the age of 15, and their use to participate actively in hostilities.

1352. As indicated in an earlier section of this Judgment, the Chamber has concluded that from late 2000 onwards, Thomas Lubanga acted with his co-perpetrators, who included Floribert Kisembo, Bosco Ntaganda, Chief Kahwa, and commanders Tchaligonza, Bagonza and Kasangaki. Mr Lubanga's involvement with the soldiers (including young children) who were sent to Uganda for training is of significance. Although these events fall outside the period covered by the charges and are outwith the temporal jurisdiction of the Court, they provide critical background evidence on the activities of this group, and they help establish the existence of the common plan before and throughout the period of the charges.

1353. As further background, the accused was in conflict with the RCD-ML from at least April 2002, and he led a group that sought to bring about political change in Ituri, including the removal of Mr Mbusa Nyamwisi and Governor Molondo Lompondo, if necessary by force. The accused remained in control by delegating his authority, whilst he was detained in the summer of 2002 and he sent Chief Kahwa and Mr Beiza to Rwanda to obtain arms. During that period, Floribert Kisembo, Bosco Ntaganda and Chief Kahwa, three of the accused's principal alleged co-perpetrators, were generally responsible for recruitment and training, which included girls and boys under the age of 15.

1354. The accused and at least some of his co-perpetrators were involved in the takeover of Bunia in August 2002. Thomas Lubanga, as the highest authority within the UPC, appointed Chief Kahwa, Floribert Kisembo and Bosco Ntaganda to senior positions within the UPC/FPLC. The evidence has established that during this period, the leaders of the UPC/FPLC, including Chief Kahwa, and Bosco Ntaganda, and Hema elders such as Eloy Mafuta, were active in mobilisation and recruitment campaigns aimed at persuading Hema families to send their children to join the UPC/FPLC. Those children recruited before the formal creation of the FPLC were incorporated into that group, and a number of training camps were added to the original facility at Mandro. The Chamber has concluded that between 1 September 2002 and 13 August 2003, a significant number of high-ranking members of the UPC/FPLC and other personnel conducted a large-scale recruitment exercise directed at young people, including children under the age of 15, whether voluntarily or by coercion.

1355. The Chamber is satisfied beyond reasonable doubt that as a result of the implementation of the common plan to build an army for the purpose of establishing and maintaining political and military control over Ituri, boys and girls under the age of 15 were conscripted and enlisted into the UPC/FPLC between 1 September 2002 and 13 August 2003. Similarly, the Chamber is satisfied beyond reasonable doubt that the UPC/FPLC used children under the age of 15 to participate actively in hostilities, including during battles. They were also used, during the relevant period, as soldiers and as bodyguards for senior officials, including the accused.

1356. Thomas Lubanga was the President of the UPC/FPLC, and the evidence demonstrates that he was simultaneously the Commander-in-Chief of the army and its political leader. He exercised an overall coordinating role over the activities of the UPC/FPLC. He was informed, on a substantive and continuous basis, of the operations of the FPLC. He was involved in planning military operations, and he played a critical role in providing logistical support, including as regards weapons, ammunition, food, uniforms, military rations and other general supplies for the FPLC troops. He was closely involved in making decisions on recruitment policy and he actively supported recruitment initiatives, for instance by giving speeches to the local population and the recruits. In his speech at the Rwampara camp, he encouraged children, including those under the age of 15 years, to join the army and to provide security for the populace once deployed in the field following their military training. Furthermore, he personally used children below the age of 15 amongst his bodyguards and he regularly saw guards of other UPC/FPLC members of staff who were below the age of 15. The Chamber has concluded that these contributions by Thomas Lubanga, taken together, were essential to a common plan that resulted in the conscription and enlistment of girls and boys below the age of 15 into the UPC/FPLC and their use to actively participate in hostilities.

1357. The Chamber is satisfied beyond reasonable doubt, as set out above, that Thomas Lubanga acted with the intent and knowledge necessary to establish the charges (the mental element required by Article 30). He was aware of the factual circumstances that established the existence of the armed conflict. Furthermore, he was aware of the nexus between those circumstances and his own conduct, which resulted in the enlistment, conscription and use of children below the age of 15 to participate actively in hostilities.

DISPOSITION

1358. For the foregoing reasons and on the basis of the evidence submitted and discussed before the Chamber at trial, and the entire proceedings, pursuant to Article 74(2) of the Statute, the Chamber finds Mr Thomas Lubanga Dyilo:

GUILTY of the crimes of conscripting and enlisting children under the age of 15 years into the FPLC and using them to participate actively in hostilities within the meaning of Articles 8(2)(e)(vii) and 25(3)(a) of the Statute from early September 2002 to 13 August 2003.

1359. Pursuant to Regulation 55 of the Regulations of the Court, the Chamber modifies the legal characterisation of the facts to the extent that the armed conflict relevant to the charges was non-international in character from early September 2002 to 13 August 2003.

1360. At the request of the defence and in accordance with Article 76(2) of the Statute and Rule 143 of the Rules, the Chamber will hold a separate hearing on matters related to sentencing and reparations.

1361. The Chamber communicates to the Prosecutor, pursuant to Article 70 of the Statute and Rule 165 of the Rules, its findings that P- 0143, P-0316 and P-0321 may have persuaded, encouraged, or assisted witnesses to give false evidence.

1362. The Majority of the Chamber withdraws the right of dual status witnesses P-0007, P-0008, P-0010, P-0011, P-0298 and P-0299 to participate in the proceedings as victims.

1363. The Chamber withdraws the right of victims a/0229/06, a/0225/06, and a/0270/07 to participate in the proceedings.

1364. Judges Fulford and Odio Benito append separate and dissenting opinions to this judgment on particular discrete issues.

††††

On 10 July 2012, Trial Chamber I sentenced Thomas Lubanga Dyilo to a total period of 14 years of imprisonment. The time he spent in the ICC's custody will be deducted from this total sentence. He is detained, for the time being, at the Detention Centre in The Hague.

Prosecutor v Thomas Lubanga Dyilo (Decision on Sentence), International Criminal Court, Trial Chamber I, Case No ICC-01/04-01/06 (10 July 2012) [92–110].

IV. Determination of the sentence

92. The prosecution argues that in order "to avoid inexplicable sentencing discrepancies", the sentencing policy of the Court should presume a "consistent baseline" for sentences, which should not be adjusted on the basis that some crimes are less serious than others. It is submitted that the appropriate "baseline" or starting point for all sentences should be set at approximately 80% of the statutory maximum, and this should then be

adjusted in accordance with Rule 145 to take into account any aggravating and mitigating circumstances and other factors relevant to the convicted person and the circumstances of the crimes.

93. No established principle of law or relevant jurisprudence under Article 21 of the Statute has been relied on in support of this suggested approach, which would bind the judges to a minimum starting point of 24 years in all cases. In the judgment of the Chamber, the sentence passed by a Trial Chamber should always be proportionate to the crime (see Article 81(2)(a)), and an automatic starting point – as proposed by the prosecution – that is the same for all offences would tend to undermine that fundamental principle.

94. As set out above, pursuant to Article 77(1) of the Statute, the prison sentence for each crime falling within the jurisdiction of the Court must not exceed 30 years, unless the extreme gravity of the crime and the individual circumstances of the convicted person justify life imprisonment.

95. The prosecution has requested that the Chamber impose a 30-year sentence on Mr Lubanga.

96. A life sentence would be inappropriate in the instant case, given the requirement in Rule 145(3) that imposing this sentence is "justified by the extreme gravity of the crime and the individual circumstances of the convicted person, as evidenced by the existence of one or more aggravating circumstances". Given the Chamber has not found any aggravating factors in this case, a whole life term would be inappropriate.

97. Mr Lubanga has been convicted of having committed, jointly with others, the crimes of conscripting and enlisting children under the age of 15 and using them to participate actively in hostilities in the context of an internal armed conflict. The Chamber has borne in mind the widespread recruitment and the significant use of child soldiers during the timeframe of the charges; the position of authority held by Mr Lubanga within the UPC/FPLC and his essential contribution to the common plan that resulted, in the ordinary course of events, in these crimes against children; the lack of any aggravating circumstances; and the mitigation provided by his consistent cooperation with the Court during the entirety of these proceedings, in circumstances when he was put under considerable unwarranted pressure by the conduct of the prosecution during the trial, as set out above.

98. Under Article 78(3) of the Statute, when the person has been convicted for more than one crime 'the Court shall pronounce a sentence for each crime and a joint sentence specifying the total period of imprisonment'. Taking into account all the factors discussed above, the Majority sentences Mr Lubanga:

1) for having committed, jointly with other persons, the crime of conscripting children under the age of 15 into the UPC to 13 years' imprisonment; 2) for having committed, jointly with other persons, the crime of enlisting children under the age of 15 into the UPC to 12 years' imprisonment; and 3) for having committed, jointly with other persons, the crime of using children under the age of 15 to participate actively in hostilities to 14 years' imprisonment.

99. Pursuant to Article 78(3) of the Statute, the total period of imprisonment on the basis of the joint sentence is 14 years' imprisonment.

Deduction of time spent in detention
100. Pursuant to Article 78(2) of the Statute, the Court shall deduct the time '[...] spent in detention in accordance with an order of the Court. The Court may deduct any time otherwise spent in detention in connection with conduct underlying the crime'.

101. Under this provision, the defence submits that the Chamber should deduct the period of Mr Lubanga's house arrest and detention by the DRC authorities between 2003 and 2006. The defence argues that the detention of Mr Lubanga in the DRC was imposed as a result of the same conduct underlying the crimes for which he has been convicted at the Court, namely his activities as President of the UPC/FPLC in 2002-2003. On this basis, the defence requests that the Chamber deducts this period of domestic detention from Mr Lubanga's sentence.

102. In the judgment of the Chamber, there is insufficient evidence that Mr Lubanga was detained in the DRC for conduct underlying the crimes for which he was convicted at the Court, namely the conscription and enlistment of children under the age of 15 and using them to participate actively in hostilities. This contention has not been established on the balance of probabilities, and as a result the Chamber declines to deduct this period of time from Mr Lubanga's sentence.

103. On 10 February 2006, Pre-Trial Chamber I issued a warrant of arrest against Mr Lubanga and, on 24 February 2006, a request for his arrest and surrender was transmitted to the DRC.

104. On 16 March 2006, the convicted person was surrendered to the Court and transferred to its detention centre in the Netherlands.

V. Fine
105. The VO1 group of victims submits that a fine should be imposed pursuant to Article 79(2) to benefit the Trust Fund for Victims. It is submitted that Rule 146 enables the Court to take into account the financial circumstances of the convicted person. In addition, the VO1 group of victims seeks an

order from the Chamber that any confiscated assets are paid to the Trust Fund for Victims in accordance with Article 79(2) of the Statute.

106. Pursuant to Article 77(2) of the Statute and Rule 146(1) of the Rules, the Chamber considers it inappropriate to impose a fine in addition to the prison term, given the financial situation of Mr Lubanga. Despite extensive enquiries by the Court, no relevant funds have been identified.

VI. Disposition

107. For the reasons set out above, for the crimes of conscripting and enlisting children under the age of 15 years into the FPLC and using them to participate actively in hostilities within the meaning of Articles 8(2)(e)(vii) and 25(3)(a) of the Statute from early September 2002 to 13 August 2003, the Majority of the Chamber passes, by way of a joint sentence, a total period of 14 years' imprisonment.

108. The Chamber orders pursuant to Article 78(2) that the time from Mr Lubanga's arrest on 16 March 2006 until the date of this Decision shall be deducted from his sentence.

109. In line with the approach taken as regards notification of the Judgment, on the basis of Rule 144(2)(b) the Chamber determines that the accused and the prosecution are notified of the Article 76 Decision (for the purposes of an appeal) when the French translation is effectively notified from the Court by the Registry.

110. Judge Odio Benito appends a dissenting opinion to this Decision.

Chapter 9

Indigenous children

9.1 Indigenous children: introduction

9.1.1 Overview

There has been an emerging interest in indigenous *peoples*' rights over the past 30 years. It is estimated that there are more than 370 million indigenous people in some 90 countries worldwide.[1] The United Nations human rights system has contributed greatly to the heightened focus in international law and policy on the human rights protection of indigenous peoples. However, there does not yet exist a dedicated international instrument that addresses exclusively the rights of indigenous *children*. There are some provisions in the Convention on the Rights of the Child that directly address the rights of indigenous children.[2] In addition, there is an ILO Convention concerning Indigenous and Tribal Peoples in Independent Countries.[3] A landmark achievement has been the General Assembly's adoption of the United Nations Declaration on the Rights of Indigenous Peoples[4] (Declaration of 2007).

9.1.2 Who are indigenous peoples?

The definition of who are *indigenous* peoples remains a contested question. The Declaration of 2007 does not define 'indigenous'.[5] The key criteria would appear to be:

---

1 See United Nations Permanent Forum on Indigenous Issues website http://undesadspd.org/ IndigenousPeoples/AboutUsMembers/History.aspx (accessed 24 November 2013).
2 Convention on the Rights of the Child arts 17(d), 29(1) and 30.
3 International Labour Organization, Indigenous and Tribal Peoples Convention, ILO Convention No 169 (27 June 1989), entered into force 5 September 1991.
4 General Assembly, United Nations Declaration on the Rights of Indigenous Peoples, resolution, adopted by the General Assembly, 61st session, UN Doc A/RES/61/295 (2 October 2007).
5 But see Declaration of 2007 arts 9 and 33.

- self-identification
- historical continuity with pre-invasion and/or pre-colonial societies that developed on their territories
- distinctiveness
- non-dominance
- determination to preserve, develop and transmit to future generations their ancestral territories and identity as peoples in accordance with their own cultural patterns, social institutions and legal system[6]
- a strong link to territories and surrounding natural resources
- distinct social, economic or political systems and
- distinct language, culture and beliefs.[7]

Many indigenous peoples retain some autonomy in relation to their political and legal structures and a strong connection with their lands, territories and resources; some practise nomadic lifestyles. Indigenous peoples' relationships with their land and resources are frequently a defining feature. The Inter-American Court of Human Rights stated:

> The close ties of indigenous people with the land must be recognized and understood as the fundamental basis of their cultures, their spiritual life, their integrity, and their economic survival. For indigenous communities, relations to the land are not merely a matter of possession and production but a material and spiritual element which they must fully enjoy, even to preserve their cultural legacy and transmit it to future generations.[8]

The legal status of indigenous peoples is distinct from that of *minorities*, '[but] they are often, though not always, in the minority in the States in which they reside'.[9] Many of the human rights challenges for indigenous peoples are rooted in pressures on their lands, territories and resources often arising from more dominant non-indigenous groups in their countries. However, the historical background of the relationship between an indigenous people and the modern sovereign state will also often shape and perpetuate discriminatory perceptions and practices. It is

---

6 See Office of the UN High Commissioner for Human Rights, *Fact Sheet No 9/Rev 2*, 'Indigenous Peoples and the United Nations Human Rights System' (August 2013) New York and Geneva: OHCHR. http://www.ohchr.org/Documents/Publications/fs9Rev.2.pdf (accessed 22 November 2013). See also the influential report by José Martínez Cobo, *Study of the problem of discrimination against indigenous populations* http://undesadspd.org/IndigenousPeoples/LibraryDocuments/Mart%C3%ADnezCoboStudy.aspx (accessed 24 November 2013).

7 The United Nations Permanent Forum on Indigenous Peoples has stressed these latter elements.

8 *Case of the Mayagna (Sumo) Awas Tingni Community v Nicaragua*, Judgment of 31 August 2001, Series C, No 79 at para 149.

9 Office of the UN High Commissioner for Human Rights, *Fact Sheet No 9/Rev 2*, 'Indigenous Peoples and the United Nations Human Rights System' (August 2013) New York and Geneva: OHCHR 3.

perhaps, above all, in the area of discrimination that issues relating specifically to indigenous children have arisen.

9.2   Indigenous peoples: international law and policy

Although no one discrete international instrument dedicated to protecting specifically indigenous *children's* rights yet exists, rather than indigenous *peoples'* rights, there has evolved a body of relevant international law relevant to all indigenous people. This is explored in the sections below.

9.2.1   United Nations human rights treaties

In addition to the Convention on the Rights of the Child (section 9.2.2), there are four other UN human rights treaties that address indigeneity issues. Many of the provisions discussed below derive from Article 27(1) of the Universal Declaration of Human Rights,[10] which states that 'everyone has the right freely to participate in the cultural life of the community'.

The International Covenant on Civil and Political Rights (ICCPR) contains a right to self-determination[11] and the rights of persons belonging to minorities to enjoy their own culture, to profess and practise their own religion or to use their own language (Article 27). The Human Rights Committee has elaborated on indigenous peoples' rights during the course of its periodic reporting and individual complaints procedures. For example, Francis Hopu and Tepoaitu Bessert, both ethnic Polynesians and inhabitants of Tahiti, French Polynesia claimed to be victims of violations of various Articles of the ICCPR by France in relation to a land tract in Tahiti which they argued they were dispossessed of in 1961 and on which the landowners wanted to construct a luxury hotel complex on the site in 1990. The applicants ('authors') in an individual communication addressed to the Human Rights Committee asserted that the land encompassed the site of a pre-European ancestral burial ground and that the lagoon remained a traditional fishing ground and provided the means of subsistence for some 30 families living next to it. The Human Rights Committee determined, inter alia, that there had been a violation of the applicants' right to respect for family life by interpreting 'family' to include the relationship between the applicants and their ancestral burial grounds.

> The Committee observes that the objectives of the Covenant require that the term 'family' be given a broad interpretation so as to include all those comprising the family as understood in the society in question. It follows that cultural traditions should be taken into account when defining the term

10 UN General Assembly, Universal Declaration of Human Rights (10 December 1948) 217 A (III).

11 International Covenant on Civil and Political Rights, opened for signature 16 December 1966, 999 UNTS 171 (entered into force 23 March 1976) art 1.

'family' in a specific situation. It transpires from the authors' claims that they consider the relationship to their ancestors to be an essential element of their identity and to play an important role in their family life.[12]

The Human Rights Committee has also indicated, in a concluding observation of a United States periodic report, the need to consider the right to self-determination when interpreting Article 27:

> The State party should review its policy towards indigenous peoples as regards the extinguishment of aboriginal rights on the basis of the plenary power of Congress regarding Indian affairs and grant them the same degree of judicial protection that is available to the non-indigenous population. The State party should take further steps to secure the rights of all indigenous peoples, under Articles 1 and 27 of the Covenant, so as to give them greater influence in decision-making affecting their natural environment and their means of subsistence as well as their own culture.[13]

A right to self-determination is also included in the International Covenant on Economic, Social and Cultural Rights[14] (ICESCR) and has been applied similarly to indigenous peoples. The Committee on Economic, Social and Cultural Rights refers to indigeneity issues in three General Comments. In General Comment No 7, it observed that '[w]omen, children, youth, older persons, indigenous people, ethnic and other minorities, and other vulnerable individuals and groups all suffer disproportionately from the practice of forced evictions'.[15] In General Comment No 17, the Committee asserted that 'States parties should adopt measures to ensure the effective protection of the interests of indigenous peoples relating to their productions, which are often expressions of their cultural heritage and traditional knowledge' and should therefore adopt measures to protect scientific, literary and artistic productions of indigenous peoples.[16] Finally, in General Comment No 21,[17] the Committee observed, inter alia, that:

---

12 Communication No 549/1993, *Hopu and Bessert v France*, views of 29 July 1997 [10.3].

13 CCPR/C/USA/CO/3 (15 September 2006) [37].

14 Opened for signature 16 December 1966, 993 UNTS 3 (entered into force 3 January 1976) art 1.

15 Committee on Economic, Social and Cultural Rights, General Comment No 7: *The right to adequate housing (art 11, para 1 of the Covenant: forced evictions)*, 16th session (14 May 1997) [11].

16 Committee on Economic, Social and Cultural Rights, General Comment No 17: *The right of everyone to benefit from the protection of the moral and material interests resulting from any scientific, literary or artistic production of which he or she is the author (art 15, para 1 (c) of the Covenant)*, 35th session, E/C.12/GC/17 (12 January 2006) [32].

17 Committee on Economic, Social and Cultural Rights, General Comment No 21: *Right of everyone to take part in cultural life (art 15, para 1 (a) of the International Covenant on Economic, Social and Cultural Rights)*, 43rd session, E/C.12/GC/21 (21 December 2009).

The strong communal dimension of indigenous peoples' cultural life is indispensable to their existence, wellbeing and full development, and includes the right to the lands, territories and resources which they have traditionally owned, occupied or otherwise used or acquired. Indigenous peoples' cultural values and rights associated with their ancestral lands and their relationship with nature should be regarded with respect and protected, in order to prevent the degradation of their particular way of life, including their means of subsistence, the loss of their natural resources and, ultimately, their cultural identity.[18]

The Committee on the Elimination of Racial Discrimination (CERD) has also addressed indigeneity issues in its monitoring of the International Convention on the Elimination of All Forms of Racial Discrimination.[19] In its General Recommendation XXIII on indigenous peoples, it affirmed that 'discrimination against indigenous peoples falls under the scope of the Convention' and called in particular on states parties to:

(a) recognize and respect indigenous distinct culture, history, language and way of life as an enrichment of the State's cultural identity and to promote its preservation;
(b) ensure that members of indigenous peoples are free and equal in dignity and rights and free from any discrimination, in particular that based on indigenous origin or identity;
(c) provide indigenous peoples with conditions allowing for a sustainable economic and social development compatible with their cultural characteristics;
(d) ensure that members of indigenous peoples have equal rights in respect of effective participation in public life and that no decisions directly relating to their rights and interests are taken without informed consent;
(e) ensure that indigenous communities can exercise their rights to practice and revitalize their cultural traditions and customs and to preserve and to practice their languages.[20]

The Committee against Torture has also issued a General Comment in its monitoring role of the Convention against Torture,[21] which refers to the need for states

---

18 Committee on Economic, Social and Cultural Rights, General Comment No 21: *Right of everyone to take part in cultural life (art 15, para 1 (a) of the International Covenant on Economic, Social and Cultural Rights)*, 43rd session, E/C.12/GC/21 (21 December 2009) [36–37].
19 Opened for signature 7 March 1966, 660 UNTS 195 (entered into force 4 January 1969).
20 Committee on the Elimination of Racial Discrimination, General Recommendation XXIII: *The rights of indigenous peoples*, 1235th meeting, UN Doc A/52/18 (18 August 1997) [2, 4].
21 Convention against Torture and Other Cruel, Inhuman or Degrading Treatment or Punishment, opened for signature 10 December 1984, 1465 UNTS 85 (entered into force 26 June 1987).

parties to ensure that their laws are in practice applied to all persons, regardless of, inter alia, their 'indigenous status' or any other adverse distinction.[22]

9.2.2   Convention on the Rights of the Child

The Convention on the Rights of the Child is the only global United Nations human rights treaty specifically to mention indigenous children. There are several provisions relating to indigenous children to consider.

9.2.2.1   Article 30

Article 30 is the principal provision in the Convention most directly relating to indigenous children: see the text of Article 30 at section 3.7.9.2. There is a close linkage between Article 30 of the Convention and Article 27 of the ICCPR. Both Articles provide for the individual's right, in community with other members of the group, to enjoy his or her own culture, to profess and practise his or her own religion or to use his or her own language. General Comment No 11 states that:

> The right established is conceived as being both individual and collective and is an important recognition of the collective traditions and values in indigenous cultures. The Committee notes that the right to exercise cultural rights among indigenous peoples may be closely associated with the use of traditional territory and the use of its resources.[23]

Article 30 is derived from a Mexican NGO's proposal (Hodgkin and Newell 2007: 456) to dedicate an Article of the Convention to the rights of indigenous children. It was subsequently agreed that the article should also encompass the rights of all minority children. The upshot was that the precedent of *minority* protection contained in the ICCPR[24] was used as the template for the new provision and was extended with the addition to the stated minorities of 'persons of indigenous origin'. The Committee has read into Article 30 a positive duty on states to take measures of protection.[25] It has emphasised that the cultural practices provided by Article 30 must be exercised in compliance with the Convention as a whole 'and under no circumstances may be justified if deemed prejudicial to the child's dignity, health and development'; for example, if harmful practices such as early marriage or FGM are present, 'the State party should work together

---

22 Committee against Torture, General Comment No 2: *Implementation of Article 2 by States parties*, CAT/C/GC/2 (24 January 2008) [21].
23 Committee on the Rights of the Child, General Comment No 11: *Indigenous children and their rights under the Convention*, 50th session, CRC/C/GC/11 (12 February 2009) [16].
24 ICCPR art 27.
25 General Comment No 11 [17].

with indigenous communities to ensure their eradication'.[26] The Committee also recognises, in relation to the child's right to use his or her own language, that bilingual and inter-cultural curricula are important elements in the education of indigenous children.[27] This also resonates with the provision contained in the ILO Convention (section 9.2.3) prescribing that indigenous children are taught to read and write in their own language as well as the opportunity to engage with the official language of the country.[28]

9.2.2.2   Article 17(d)

States parties are under an obligation contained in Article 17(d) of the Convention to '[e]ncourage the mass media to have particular regard to the linguistic needs of the child who belongs to a minority group or who is indigenous': see text of Article 17(1) at section 3.7.4.3. This provision underlines the important role that the mass media can play, for example by producing material and programmes in minority languages. Furthermore, in commenting on states' duties to disseminate material on the Convention,[29] the Committee has often emphasised the importance of ensuring translation into minority and indigenous languages, and the particular importance of the media's participation in this task (Hodgkin and Newell 2007: 224).

9.2.2.3   Article 29(1)(c) and (d)

Finally, the child's right to education provides further material protecting specifically indigenous children (in Article 29(1)(c) and (d) in particular). See generally section 3.7.8.1 on rights to education:

> *Article 29*
> 1. States Parties agree that the education of the child shall be directed to:
>
>   (a) The development of the child's personality, talents and mental and physical abilities to their fullest potential;
>   (b) The development of respect for human rights and fundamental freedoms, and for the principles enshrined in the Charter of the United Nations;
>   (c) The development of respect for the child's parents, his or her own cultural identity, language and values, for the national values of the country in which the child is living, the country from which he or she may originate, and for civilizations different from his or her own;

---

26 ibid [22].
27 ibid [62].
28 ibid.
29 Convention on the Rights of the Child art 42.

(d) The preparation of the child for responsible life in a free society, in the spirit of understanding, peace, tolerance, equality of sexes, and friendship among all peoples, ethnic, national and religious groups and persons of indigenous origin;

(e) The development of respect for the natural environment.

2. No part of the present Article or Article 28 shall be construed so as to interfere with the liberty of individuals and bodies to establish and direct educational institutions, subject always to the observance of the principle set forth in paragraph 1 of the present Article and to the requirements that the education given in such institutions shall conform to such minimum standards as may be laid down by the State.

The Committee view the education of indigenous children as strengthening their ability to exercise their civil rights and contribute to the policy process for improved protection of human rights; 'the implementation of the right to education of indigenous children is an essential means of achieving individual empowerment and self-determination of indigenous peoples'.[30] It also recognises the importance of urging states parties to ensure that 'the curricula, educational materials and history textbooks provide a fair, accurate and informative portrayal of the societies and cultures of indigenous peoples'.[31]

Nevertheless, the Committee has focused specifically on questions relating to indigenous children in one of their 'Days of General Discussion' in 2003.[32] It has also produced a General Comment[33] on this subject in 2009.

9.2.2.4 'Day of General Discussion' (2003)

In the 'Day of General Discussion' the Committee on the Rights of the Child recognised that:

> ... indigenous children are disproportionately affected by specific challenges such as institutionalization, urbanization, drug and alcohol abuse, trafficking, armed conflict, sexual exploitation and child labour and yet are not sufficiently taken into consideration in the development and implementation of policies and programmes for children ...[34]

---

30 General Comment No 11 [57].

31 ibid [58].

32 Committee on the Rights of the Child, 'Day of General Discussion' on *The rights of indigenous children*, Report on the 34th session, CRC/C/133 (3 October 2003).

33 Committee on the Rights of the Child, General Comment No 11: *Indigenous children and their rights under the Convention*, 50th session, CRC/C/GC/11 (12 February 2009).

34 Committee on the Rights of the Child, 'Day of General Discussion' on *The rights of indigenous children*, Report on the 34th session, CRC/C/133 (3 October 2003) preamble.

It called upon states parties, UN agencies, and others to adopt a broader rights-based approach to indigenous children and encouraged the use of community-based interventions. The Committee recognised that 'the right to enjoy one's culture, may consist of a way of life which is closely associated with territory and use of its resources'.[35] It recommended that states parties strengthen mechanisms for data collection on indigenous children. Furthermore, it recommended that states parties work closely with indigenous peoples and organisations to seek consensus on development strategies, policies and projects aimed at implementing children's rights. The Committee emphasised the importance of applying the principle of non-discrimination to indigenous children in order to enjoy all of their rights equally and including equal access to culturally appropriate services including health, education, social services, housing, potable water and sanitation.[36] Importantly, it recommended that state parties, with the full participation of indigenous communities and children: 'develop public awareness campaigns, including through the mass media, to combat negative attitudes and misperceptions about indigenous peoples'.[37]

The Committee pointed out that states parties should respect the methods customarily practised by indigenous peoples for dealing with criminal offences committed by children , but only 'when it is in the best interests of the child' to do so.[38] Rights of identity by indigenous children were supported by the Committee which called upon states to, inter alia, ensure accessible birth registration.[39] As regards the family environment, the Committee recommended that maintaining the integrity of indigenous families and communities should be a consideration in relevant development programmes, social services, health and education programmes.[40] As regards health, the Committee recommended that states parties take all necessary measures to implement the right to health of indigenous children, in view of 'the comparatively low indicators regarding child mortality, immunization and nutrition that affect this group of children'.[41] Special attention should also be paid to adolescents regarding drug abuse, alcohol consumption, mental health and sex education. As regards education, states parties should 'ensure access for indigenous children to appropriate and high quality education while taking complementary measures to eradicate child labour'.[42]

---

35 'Day of General Discussion' on *The rights of indigenous children* [4].
36 ibid [9].
37 ibid [11].
38 ibid [13].
39 ibid [15].
40 ibid [17].
41 ibid [18].
42 ibid [19].

9.2.2.5   General Comment No 11 *(2009)*[43]

The General Comment consolidates, in a more forensic form, many of the recommendations developed in the 'Day of General Discussion' discussed above. It also provides further analysis in particular of Articles 30, 29 and 17 discussed above and announces that '[t]he specific references to indigenous children in the Convention are indicative of the recognition that they require special measures in order to fully enjoy their rights'. It emphasises that one element that prompted the need for the General Comment was the continued serious discrimination experienced by indigenous children.[44] Based on the recommendations provided in the 'Day of General Discussion' of 2003, the objective of the General Comment is 'to provide States with guidance on how to implement their obligations under the Convention with respect to indigenous children.' Furthermore, it seeks to explore the challenges that impede indigenous children from fully enjoying their rights and highlights measures required by states to guarantee their effective exercise.[45] The General Comment then proceeds to note how the rights of indigenous children are applied within the main 'clusters' of rights used for periodic country reporting under the Convention (section 3.5). For example, under the 'general principles' heading, the General Comment emphasises the importance of the non-discrimination principle (Article 2) in this context, in particular the need for states parties to pursue *positive* measures of implementation, including the need for the collection and collation of data suitably disaggregated to enable discrimination to be identified.[46] As regards the 'best interest principle',[47] also perceived as requiring positive measures to implement, the Committee observes that this principle 'is conceived both as a collective and individual right, and that the application of this right to indigenous children as a group requires consideration of how the right relates to collective cultural rights'. However, when applied to individuals it would seem that the principle 'cannot be neglected or violated in preference for the best interests of the group'.[48] With regard to the right to life, survival and development,[49] the Committee notes with concern the disproportionate high numbers of indigenous children that live in extreme poverty and high infant and child mortality rates and recommends that states take special measures to secure an adequate standard of living for indigenous children. The Committee reiterates its understanding of the 'development' of the child as a holistic concept and in this context the use of traditional lands is seen as relevant to the indigenous child's development. It calls upon states to engage with indigenous

43 Committee on the Rights of the Child, General Comment No 11: *Indigenous children and their rights under the Convention*, 50th session, CRC/C/GC/11 (12 February 2009).
44 ibid [5].
45 ibid [12].
46 ibid [23–29].
47 ibid [30–33].
48 ibid [30].
49 ibid [34–36].

peoples to ensure the realisation of the Millennium Development Goals (section 1.1.4). As regards respect for the views of the child,[50] the Committee separates out an individual child's right to express his or her views and the principle of participation, which allows children as a group to be consulted on matters involving them. It recommends that the latter collective rights are applied in particular in the school environment, alternative care settings and in the community in general. Throughout the General Comment, the Committee urges states parties and others to work collaboratively with indigenous groups. It concludes:

> Empowerment of indigenous children and the effective exercise of their rights to culture, religion and language provide an essential foundation of a culturally diverse State in harmony and compliance with its human rights obligations.[51]

9.2.3   *ILO Indigenous and Tribal Peoples Convention*

The Indigenous and Tribal Peoples Convention[52] (ILO Convention of 1989) revises an earlier version of the ILO Convention of 1957.[53] The general frame of reference of the 1957 Convention is said to have been founded on 'governments taking coordinated and systematic action to protect their indigenous peoples and progressively *integrate* them into the life of their countries' (Yupsanis 2012: 434). By contrast, the appearance of the ILO Convention of 1989 marked a policy shift from assimilation to self-determination, a point supported by the text of the Convention itself.[54] The ILO Convention of 1989 is currently ratified by 22 countries, mainly in Latin America.[55] This is a disappointing number of ratifications, caused perhaps by a general tendency for states to avoid subscribing to international instruments that recognise subgroups within their territories, which may undermine national unity.

The Convention provides a description of tribal and indigenous 'peoples'. The latter are:

> (b) peoples in independent countries who are regarded as indigenous on account of their descent from the populations which inhabited the country, or a geographical region to which the country belongs, at the time of conquest

---

50 ibid [37–9].

51 ibid [82].

52 International Labour Organization, Indigenous and Tribal Peoples Convention, ILO Convention No 169 (27 June 1989) (entered into force 5 September 1991).

53 International Labour Organization, Indigenous and Tribal Populations Convention, ILO Convention No 107 (26 June 1957) (entered into force 2 June 1959).

54 Indigenous and Tribal Peoples Convention of 1989 preamble §4.

55 As at 22 February 2014, the countries were: Argentina, Bolivia, Brazil, Central African Republic, Chile, Colombia, Costa Rica, Denmark, Dominica, Ecuador, Fiji, Guatemala, Honduras, Mexico, Nepal, the Netherlands, Nicaragua, Norway, Paraguay, Peru, Spain and Venezuela.

or colonisation or the establishment of present state boundaries and who, irrespective of their legal status, retain some or all of their own social, economic, cultural and political institutions.[56]

Importantly, the Convention also identifies 'self-determination' as 'a fundamental criterion' for determining whether a group can rank as an indigenous people.[57] One advance achieved following the 1957 Convention was the replacement of the term 'populations' with 'peoples'. However, as the right of *peoples* to self-determination is embedded into the UN system,[58] the Convention neutralises it with the explicit recognition in the text of the Convention that: '[t]he use of the term *peoples* in this Convention shall not be construed as having any implications as regards the rights which may attach to the term under international law'.[59] Even so, Yupsanis (2012: 438) argues that 'this restriction does not totally counteract the value of the designation of indigenous peoples as *sui generis* peoples in the context of an emerging recognition of these peoples as such'.

The Convention lays down a series of provisions establishing obligations on states parties for developing action to protect the rights of indigenous peoples and respect for their integrity.[60] Indigenous and tribal peoples also have the right to non-discrimination and governments are urged to adopt special measures for safeguarding 'the persons, institution, property, labour cultures and environment of the peoples concerned.[61] The 'cornerstone' (Yupsanis 2012: 438) of the Convention is arguably contained in Articles 6 and 7, which focus on the participation of indigenous and tribal peoples at all levels of institutional and administrative decision-making. The Convention also states that 'due regard' shall be had to customs and customary laws in applying national laws to the peoples concerned.[62] The Convention contains detailed provisions protecting land and resource rights, conditions of employment, vocational training, handicrafts and rural industries, social security and health, and education and means of communication.[63] The Convention, despite the advances achieved, is not without its weaknesses. For example, the rights of consultation are arguably insufficient to prevent states from going through a procedural process of consultation without any real intent to garner participation; there was a failure to provide a right of veto by indigenous peoples over the exploration of ancestral lands and resources in Article 15. Further concerns relate to the indeterminate language used in some of the provisions made perhaps more opaque by Article 34, which provides that the nature and scope of the measures to be taken to give effect to the Convention shall

---

56 Indigenous and Tribal Peoples Convention of 1989 art 1(a).
57 ibid art 1(2).
58 See UN Charter art 1(2).
59 Indigenous and Tribal Peoples Convention of 1989 art 1(3) (emphasis added).
60 ibid art 2.
61 ibid arts 3 and 4 respectively.
62 ibid art 8(1).
63 ibid Pts II–VI respectively.

be determined in 'a flexible manner, having regard to the conditions character-istic of each country'. Nevertheless, the abandonment of the former *individualistic* approach and the focus on recognising *collective* rights, for example to lands and resources, coupled with an emphasis on self-determination has provided, in the view of one commentator:

> ... a valuable instrument for promoting the case of indigenous peoples by establishing fundamental (and legally binding) *minimum standards* of protec-tion, the further entrenchment of which, in scope and content, must now rely on the willingness of the countries forming the international community to recognise, respect and promote the rights of these long-suffering and most disadvantaged peoples.
>
> (Yupsanis 2012: 455–6)

Another commentator states that, although the Convention falls short of provid-ing a concrete right to self-determination, it 'can be considered as a small step for indigenous persons but a giant leap for indigenous peoples' (Joonal 2010: 260).

9.2.4   United Nations Declaration on the Rights of Indigenous Peoples

The United Nations Declaration on the Rights of Indigenous Peoples (Declaration of 2007)[64] was adopted by the General Assembly on 13 September 2007 with 144 votes in favour, 11 abstentions and four states against (Australia, Canada, New Zealand[65] and the United States of America), although the latter countries have subsequently endorsed it.[66] The Declaration of 2007 is a species of 'soft law' (section 2.2.6) but its formal, non-binding status should not be overplayed. As one commentator states: '[u]nder the complexity and dynamism of contempo-rary international law-making, the relevance of a soft law instrument cannot be aprioristically dismissed' (Barelli 2010: 983):

> *The status of the Declaration under international law*
> While the United Nations Declaration on the Rights of Indigenous Peoples, as a declaration, is not a formally binding treaty, it contains rights and free-doms, such as self-determination and non-discrimination, set out in binding international human rights treaty law, of which some may be considered

---

64 General Assembly, United Nations Declaration on the Rights of Indigenous Peoples, resolution Adopted by the General Assembly, 61st session, UN Doc A/RES/61/295 (2 October 2007).

65 For the impact of the Declaration of 2007 on New Zealand see generally Toki (2010).

66 Office of the UN High Commissioner for Human Rights, *Fact Sheet No 9/Rev.2*, 'Indigenous Peoples and the United Nations Human Rights System' (August 2013) New York and Geneva: OHCHR http://www.ohchr.org/Documents/Publications/fs9Rev.2.pdf (accessed 22 November 2013).

customary international law. It reflects a global consensus on indigenous peoples' rights. Moreover, according to the Office of Legal Affairs of the United Nations Secretariat, 'a "declaration" is a solemn instrument resorted to only in very rare cases relating to matters of major and lasting importance where maximum compliance is expected'. The United Nations Declaration on the Rights of Indigenous Peoples is such a declaration deserving of the utmost respect.[67]

The question of whether the Declaration of 2007, or at least parts of it, may be considered as (binding) customary law remains contentious. Davis (2012: 19) asserts:

> [T]he Declaration exists in an amorphous in-between state of constituting both a 'nonbinding', influential and aspirational statement of soft law but equally an instrument that reflects already binding rules of customary international law.

The Declaration of 2007 provides a more comprehensive instrument than the ILO Convention discussed above. In particular, it contains a concrete right to self-determination (Coulter 2010):

> *Article 3*
> Indigenous peoples have the right to self-determination. By virtue of that right they freely determine their political status and freely pursue their economic, social and cultural development.[68]

This was quite a landmark in international law; one commentator hails the recognition of self-determination in the Declaration of 2007 as a 'breakthrough of great importance in the law of self-determination, probably the most important development of the right since the era of decolonization' (Barelli 2010: 2).

The right to self-determination is viewed as one which informs all the other rights in the Declaration of 2007. However, although self-determination by *sovereign states* is embedded in the UN system, the appearance of self-determination by an *indigenous people* within the borders of a state may pose a threat, or the perception of one, to that state. The solution to this conundrum has been the adoption of a provision in the Declaration of 2007 that provides a right, in effect, to internal self-governance, rather than outright secession:

---

67 Office of the UN High Commissioner for Human Rights, *Fact Sheet No 9/Rev.2*, 'Indigenous Peoples and the United Nations Human Rights System' (August 2013) New York and Geneva: OHCHR 8–9.
68 Declaration of 2007 art 3.

Article 4

Indigenous peoples, in exercising their right to self-determination, have the right to autonomy or self-government in matters relating to their internal and local affairs, as well as ways and means for financing their autonomous functions.[69]

Autonomous self-determination if given further elaboration in a provision which provides a right of indigenous peoples to promote, develop and maintain 'institutional structures and their distinctive customs, spirituality, traditions, procedures, practices and, in the cases where they exist, juridical systems or customs ...'.[70] A dominant theme of the Declaration of 2007 is the provision of equality and non-discrimination in relation to indigenous individuals and peoples.[71]

There are distinct political rights of participation in decision-making on matters that would affect their rights, and duties on states to consult in order to obtain their 'free, prior and informed consent' before adopting legislative or administrative measures.[72] Indigenous peoples' rights to lands, territories and resources are recognised.[73]

A further provision obliges states, subject to the participation of indigenous groups, to establish and implement a fair and independent process 'to recognize and adjudicate the rights of indigenous people's laws, traditions, customs and land tenure systems'.[74] The Declaration of 2007, consistently with the ICESCR, affirms indigenous peoples' economic, social and cultural rights: for example, rights to health, education, employment, housing, sanitation, social security and an adequate standard of living.[75] The Declaration of 2007 contains several provisions to protect against discriminatory and adverse treatment on cultural grounds and positive measures to support indigenous peoples' cultures. In particular, the integrationist policy of the past is put to rest by a provision that provides indigenous peoples and individuals with 'the right not to be subjected to forced assimilation or destruction of their culture'.[76] The Declaration of 2007 is also distinctive as an international instrument in so far as it recognises indigenous peoples' *collective* rights.[77]

Finally, there is some referencing of specifically indigenous *children* in the Declaration of 2007. In particular, the preamble recognises: 'the right of indigenous families and communities to retain shared responsibility for the upbringing, training, education and well-being of their children, consistent with the rights

---

69 ibid art 4.
70 ibid art 34.
71 ibid arts 1 and 2.
72 ibid arts 18 and 19.
73 ibid art 26.
74 ibid art 27.
75 ibid arts 3, 21 and 24.
76 ibid art 8.
77 ibid preamble §22, arts 1, 7(2) and 40.

of the child'.[78] Within the framework of the 'collective right to live in freedom, peace and security as distinct peoples' there is a prohibition on 'forcibly removing children' from one group to another.[79] Further provisions spell out indigenous children's rights to education, and states' obligations to take specific measures to protect indigenous children to have access to 'an education in their own culture and provided in their own language'.[80] States are also obliged to 'take specific measures to protect indigenous children from economic exploitation and from performing any work that is likely to be hazardous or to interfere with the child's education'.[81]

Whatever the precise legal status of the Declaration of 2007 may be, there is no doubt that it has been regarded increasingly as the 'principal benchmark' in international law for the rights of indigenous peoples. That is certainly the view[82] of the Special Rapporteur on the situation of human rights and fundamental freedoms of indigenous people (section 9.3.2). A comprehensive manual for national human rights institutions on the Declaration of 2007 was produced in 2013.[83]

9.3   Indigenous peoples and United Nations mechanisms

Three principal UN mechanisms relating directly to indigenous peoples' issues are discussed in the following sections. They are:

- the United Nations Permanent Forum on Indigenous Peoples
- the Special Rapporteur on the situation of human rights and fundamental freedoms of Indigenous people and
- the Expert Mechanism on the Rights of Indigenous Peoples.

All three (complementary) mandates meet annually to coordinate their activities and share information. Representatives of the Permanent Forum usually attend the annual session of the Expert Mechanism and vice versa. The Special Rapporteur attends the annual sessions of both the Permanent Forum and the Expert Mechanism. In essence, the Expert Mechanism undertakes thematic studies; the Special Rapporteur undertakes country visits, addresses specific cases of alleged human rights violations through communications with governments or others and, in addition, undertakes or contributes to thematic studies; and the Permanent Forum focuses on advice and coordination on indigenous issues within

---

78 ibid preamble §13.
79 ibid art 7(2).
80 ibid art 14(2) and (3).
81 ibid art 17(2).
82 See General Assembly, *Rights of indigenous people: note by the Secretary-General*, 67th session, UN Doc A/67/301 (13 August 2012) [26–32].
83 Office of the High Commissioner for Human Rights, The United Nations Declaration on the Rights of Indigenous Peoples (August 2013) UN Doc HR/PUB/13/2 http://www.refworld. org/docid/5289e4fc4.html (accessed 23 November 2013).

the United Nations and raises awareness about such issues. The Human Rights Council requests all three mandates to carry out their tasks in a coordinated manner. For example, all three bodies have recently participated in organising and preparing for a major World Conference on Indigenous Peoples authorised by the General Assembly,[84] to be held on 22–23 September 2014 at the UN Headquarters in New York.

9.3.1   United Nations Permanent Forum on Indigenous Peoples

The Economic and Social Council (ECOSOC), one of the six principal bodies of the United Nations (section 2.4.1), although losing its direct authority over the former UN Commission on Human Rights,[85] has remained the parent body of, and is advised by, the United Nations Permanent Forum on Indigenous Issues (Permanent Forum). This body was established by an ECOSOC resolution in 2000,[86] which noted in particular 'the striking absence of a mechanism to ensure coordination and regular exchange of information'.[87] The Permanent Forum is mandated:

- to provide expert advice on indigenous issues to ECOSOC
- to raise awareness of indigenous issues with the UN system and
- to prepare and disseminate information on indigenous issues.

The Permanent Forum has 16 members, who serve in their personal capacity for a three-year term. Eight members are nominated by states and elected by ECOSOC, based on the five regional groupings normally used at the United Nations. A further eight are nominated directly by indigenous organisations and appointed by the President of the Economic and Social Council. They represent seven sociocultural regions to give broad representation to the world's indigenous peoples: Africa; Asia; Central and South America and the Caribbean; the Arctic; Central and Eastern Europe, the Russian Federation, Central Asia and Transcaucasia; North America; and the Pacific, with one additional rotating seat among the first three.[88]

---

84 General Assembly, *Indigenous issues*, 65th session, UN Doc A/RES/65/198 (21 December 2010); General Assembly, *Organization of the high-level plenary meeting of the 69th session of the General Assembly, to be known as the World Conference on Indigenous Peoples*, sixty-sixth session, UN Doc A/RES/66/296 (17 September 2012).

85 The UNCHR was replaced by the UN Human Rights Council (UNHRC) in 2006, but the latter body was placed under the authority of the General Assembly.

86 Economic and Social Council, *Establishment of a Permanent Forum on Indigenous Issues*, Res 2000/22 (28 July 2000).

87 ibid.

88 Office of the UN High Commissioner for Human Rights, *Fact Sheet No 9/Rev.2*, 'Indigenous Peoples and the United Nations Human Rights System' (August 2013) New York and Geneva: OHCHR 12.

The Permanent Forum operates annual two-week sessions. It identifies a specific theme[89] as the overall framework for its sessions, alternating with a review every other year. In recent years, the Permanent Forum has focused on the implementation of the Declaration of 2007. The Forum also focuses attention on a specific region each year, as a means of highlighting the situation of the indigenous peoples in that region and the challenges they face. The Permanent Forum additionally undertakes studies on specific matters of concern, expert seminars and, on occasion, country visits. Its annual sessions in New York are widely attended by member states, indigenous peoples' representatives and organisations/institutions, United Nations agencies, non-state actors and others.

9.3.2   The Special Rapporteur on the situation of human rights and fundamental freedoms of indigenous people

While ECOSOC remains the body to which the Permanent Forum (section 9.3.1) reports, the Special Rapporteur on the situation of human rights and fundamental freedoms of Indigenous people (Special Rapporteur) and the Expert Mechanism on the Rights of Indigenous Peoples (section 9.3.3) both report back to and enter into interactive dialogue with the Human Rights Council. The Special Rapporteur[90] is a 'special procedure' of the Human Rights Council. The mandate was established in 2001 by the UNCHR and continued by the Human Rights Council. The mandate involves the Special Rapporteur in:

- examining ways to overcome existing obstacles to indigenous peoples' enjoyment of their rights
- exchanging information about alleged violations of the rights of indigenous peoples
- formulating proposals to prevent and remedy violations
- liaising with other special procedures, treaty bodies and regional human rights organisations.

The Special Rapporteur assesses the situation of indigenous peoples in specific countries (see Case study 9.1 below); carries out thematic studies; communicates with governments, indigenous peoples and others concerning allegations of violations of indigenous peoples' rights; and promotes good practices for the protection

---

89 For example, the theme of the Permanent Forum's 11th session was 'The Doctrine of Discovery: its enduring impact on indigenous peoples and the right to redress for past conquests (arts 28 and 37 of the United Nations Declaration on the Rights of Indigenous Peoples)'. Permanent Forum, *Report on the 11th session: 7–18 May 2012*, UN Doc E/2012/43 E/C.19/2012/13. The upcoming special theme for the 13th session (12–23 May 2014) was 'Principles of good governance consistent with the United Nations Declaration on the Rights of Indigenous Peoples: arts 3 to 6 and 46'.

90 See http://www.ohchr.org/en/issues/ipeoples/srindigenouspeoples/pages/sripeoplesindex.aspx (accessed 23 November 2013).

of these rights. The Special Rapporteur reports annually to the Human Rights Council on particular human rights issues involving indigenous peoples and coordinates work with the Permanent Forum on Indigenous Issues and the Expert Mechanism on the Rights of Indigenous Peoples. Extracts from a recent country report on Canada are shown in the case study below.

Case study 9.1

Statement upon conclusion of the visit to Canada by the United Nations Special Rapporteur on the rights of indigenous peoples, James Anaya

Extracted from:
http://www.ohchr.org/en/NewsEvents/Pages/DisplayNews.aspx?News ID=13868&LangID=E (accessed 20 November 2013).

15 October 2013
I am now concluding my visit to Canada in my capacity as United Nations Special Rapporteur on the rights of indigenous peoples. Over the last nine days I have met with federal and provincial government authorities, and with First Nations, Inuit, and Métis leaders, organisations and individuals in several parts of the country. In addition to being in Ottawa, my meetings have taken me to various places, including indigenous territories, in British Columbia, Alberta, Saskatchewan, Manitoba, Ontario, and Québec.
...
Canada, with its diverse and multicultural society, has been a leader on the world stage in the promotion of human rights since the creation of the United Nations in 1945. And it was one of the first countries in the modern era to extend constitutional protection to indigenous peoples' rights. This constitutional protection has provided a strong foundation for advancing indigenous peoples' rights over the last 30 years, especially through the courts. Federal and provincial governments have made notable efforts to address treaty and aboriginal claims, and to improve the social and economic well-being of indigenous peoples. Canada has also addressed some of the concerns that were raised by my predecessor following his visit in 2003. ...

But despite positive steps, daunting challenges remain. From all I have learned, I can only conclude that Canada faces a crisis when it comes to the situation of indigenous peoples of the country. The well-being gap between aboriginal and non-aboriginal people in Canada has not narrowed over the last several years, treaty and aboriginals claims remain persistently unresolved, and overall there appear to be high levels of distrust among aboriginal peoples toward government at both the federal and provincial levels.

Canada consistently ranks near the top among countries with respect to human development standards, and yet amidst this wealth and prosperity, aboriginal people live in conditions akin to those in countries that rank much lower and in which poverty abounds. At least one-in-five aboriginal Canadians live in homes in need of serious repair, which are often also overcrowded and contaminated with mould. The suicide rate among Inuit and First Nations youth on reserve, at more than five times greater than other Canadians, is alarming. One community I visited has suffered a suicide every six weeks since the start of this year. Aboriginal women are eight times more likely to be murdered than non-indigenous women and indigenous peoples face disproportionately high incarceration rates. For over a decade, the Auditor General has repeatedly highlighted significant funding disparities between on-reserve services and those available to other Canadians. The Canadian Human Rights Commission has consistently said that the conditions of aboriginal peoples make for the most serious human rights problem in Canada.

It is clear to me that Canada is aware of and concerned about these issues, and that it is taking steps to address them. I have learned about numerous programs, policies and efforts that have been rolled out at the federal and provincial levels, and many of these have achieved notable successes. However, it is equally clear that these steps are insufficient, and have yet to fully respond to aboriginal peoples' urgent needs, fully protect their aboriginal and treaty rights, or to secure relationships based on mutual trust and common purpose. Aboriginal peoples' concerns and well-being merit higher priority at all levels and within all branches of Government, and across all departments. Concerted measures, based on mutual understanding and real partnership with aboriginal peoples, through their own representative institutions, are vital to the long-term resolution of these issues.

Importantly, Canada has taken action toward the goal of reconciliation between aboriginal and non-aboriginal Canadians with the 2008 government apology for the residential schools and the creation of the Truth and Reconciliation Commission. The Truth and Reconciliation Commission has been documenting the horrifying stories of abuse and cultural dislocation of indigenous students who were forced from their homes into schools whose explicit purpose was to destroy their family and community bonds, their language, their culture, and their dignity, and from which thousands never returned. Generations of aboriginal children grew up in residential schools estranged from their cultures and languages, with devastating effects on maintaining indigenous identity. It is clear that the residential school period continues to cast a long shadow of despair on indigenous communities, and that many of the dire social and economic problems faced by aboriginal peoples are directly linked to that experience. I urge the Government to ensure that the mandate of the Truth and Reconciliation Commission be extended for as long as may be necessary for it to complete its work, and to consider establishing means of reconciliation and redress for survivors of all types of residential schools. In addition, I would like to emphasise that the mark on Canada's history left by the residential schools is a matter of concern to all of Canada, not just aboriginal peoples, and that lasting healing can only truly occur through building better relationships and understanding between aboriginal peoples and the broader society.

Another aspect of the long shadow of residential schools, combined with other historical acts of oppression, is the disturbing phenomenon of aboriginal women missing and murdered at the hands of both aboriginal and non-aboriginal assailants, whose cases have a much higher tendency to remain unresolved than those involving non-aboriginal victims. Certainly, both federal and provincial governments have taken steps targeted at addressing various aspects of this issue. Yet over the past several days, in all of the places I have visited, I have heard from aboriginal peoples a widespread lack of confidence in the effectiveness of those measures. I have heard a consistent call for a national level inquiry into the extent of the problem and appropriate solutions moving forward with the participation of victims' families and others deeply affected. I concur that a comprehensive and nation-wide inquiry into the issue could help ensure a coordinated response and the opportunity for the loved ones of victims to be heard, and would demonstrate a responsiveness to the concerns raised by the families and communities affected by this epidemic.

These and further steps are required to realise the promise of healing and a new relationship that was made in the 2008 apology. Among all the government and aboriginal people with whom I have met, there is agreement that improving educational outcomes for aboriginal people is a key to addressing many of the other problems facing them. ...

...

By all accounts, increased investment in building self-governing capacity is essential to creating socially and economically healthy and self-sufficient aboriginal communities. One hundred and thirty years of Indian Act policies persistently undermined—and in some cases continue to undermine—many First Nations' and Inuit peoples' historic self-governance capacity. Enhancing economic development opportunities is also crucial to restoring and building healthy and vibrant aboriginal nations and communities. I acknowledge the many initiatives by Canada to strengthen aboriginal governance and catalyse economic development. And I applaud the many successes a number of aboriginal communities have had in building governance capacity and pursuing economic development opportunities.

But at the same time I note the frustration expressed to me uniformly by aboriginal leaders that their self-governance capacity and economic development, and improved conditions more generally, remain impeded by the multiple legacies of the history of colonisation, treaty infringements, assault on their cultures, and land dispossession suffered by their peoples. To address these legacies Canada has developed specific and comprehensive claims processes that in many respects are models for the world to emulate.

There are noteworthy success stories arising out of these procedures. But in their implementation overall, the claims processes have been extremely slow and mired in challenges—challenges that appear in most cases to stem from the adversarial structure of negotiations, in which entrenched opposing positions often develop on key issues and agreement simply cannot be reached. To make this worse, resource development often proceeds at a rapid pace within lands that are the subject of protracted negotiations between aboriginal peoples and the Government, undermining the very purpose of the negotiations.

...

More generally, greater efforts are needed to improve avenues of communication between Canada and aboriginal peoples to build consensus on the path forward. In all my meetings with aboriginal leaders and community members it was evident that there is a significant level of discontent with the state of relations with federal and provincial authorities, as well as a widely held perception that legislative and other decisions over multiple matters of concern to them are being taken without adequate consultation or consideration of their inherent and treaty rights. I urge the federal Government especially to work with aboriginal peoples, through their representative institutions and authorities, to overcome this condition of mistrust. As with the Education Act initiative mentioned earlier, unless legislative and other government actions that directly affect indigenous peoples' rights and interests are made with their meaningful participation, those actions will lack legitimacy and are likely to be ineffective.

...

In addition to historical treaties and constitutional principles, the international standards endorsed by Canada and aboriginal peoples, in particular the United Nations Declaration on the Rights of Indigenous Peoples, should inform the definition of common objectives and goals. Canada's 2010 endorsement of the Declaration marked an important step on the path towards reconciliation with indigenous peoples, and Canada should be commended for joining most all of the rest of the countries of the world in support of this instrument. I was pleased to hear, throughout my visit, references by First Nations, Inuit and Métis people to the Declaration, and about the incorporation of its standards into their work. It is my hope that the provincial and federal governments in Canada, as well as the country's courts, will aspire to implement the standards articulated by the Declaration. The Declaration can help to provide a common framework within which the problems that I have outlined here in a preliminary fashion can be addressed.

I look forward to developing more detailed observations and recommendations beyond these initial comments in my report to the Human Rights Council. My observations and recommendations will be aimed at identifying good practices and needed reforms in line with the Declaration on the Rights of Indigenous Peoples and other international instruments that mark Canada's international human rights obligations. I hope that this process will contribute to ensuring that the indigenous peoples of Canada can continue to thrive and maintain their distinct ways of life as they have done for generations despite the long shadow of a history of misdealing, enriching Canadian society for the benefit of all.

9.3.3   Expert Mechanism on the Rights of Indigenous Peoples

The United Nations Expert Mechanism on the Rights of Indigenous Peoples (the 'Expert Mechanism') was established in 2007 by the Human Rights Council,[91] of which it is a subsidiary body. It comprises five experts on the rights of indigenous peoples, usually one from each of the world's five geopolitical regions, with indigenous origin a relevant factor in their appointment. Its mandate is to provide the Human Rights Council with thematic expertise, mainly in the form of studies and research, on the rights of indigenous peoples as directed by the Council. The Expert Mechanism may also make proposals to the Council for its consideration and approval. The Expert Mechanism has produced a number of major studies to date: one on the implementation of the right of indigenous peoples to education finalised in 2009;[92] another appeared in 2011, which examined indigenous peoples and the right to participation in decision-making.[93] Further studies have been initiated on the role of languages and culture in the promotion and protection of the rights and identity of indigenous peoples in 2011–2012[94] and on indigenous peoples' access to justice in 2012–2013.[95]

The rules governing participation in its annual sessions are relatively open. Hundreds of representatives of indigenous peoples' organisations, indigenous individuals and non-governmental organisations attend the annual sessions.

---

91 Human Rights Council, *Expert mechanism on the rights of indigenous Peoples*, Resolution 6/36 (14 December 2007).

92 Human Rights Council, *Study on lessons learned and challenges to achieve the implementation of the right of indigenous peoples to education*, Report of the Expert Mechanism on the Rights of Indigenous Peoples, UN Doc A/HRC/12/33 (31 August 2009).

93 Human Rights Council, *Final report of the study on indigenous peoples and the right to participate in decision-making*, Report of the Expert Mechanism on the Rights of Indigenous Peoples, UN Doc A/HRC/18/42 (17 August 2011).

94 Human Rights Council, *Role of languages and culture in the promotion and protection of the rights and identity of indigenous peoples*, study of the Expert Mechanism on the Rights of Indigenous Peoples, UN Doc A/HRC/21/53 (16 August 2012).

95 Human Rights Council, *Access to justice in the promotion and protection of the rights of indigenous peoples*, study by the Expert Mechanism on the Rights of Indigenous Peoples, UN Doc A/HRC/24/50 (30 July 2013).

9.4   Concluding remarks

The Convention on the Rights of the Child makes a significant contribution to the corpus of international law relating to indigenous people by establishing the right of the indigenous child to enjoy his or her own culture, to profess and practise his or her own religion, or to use her own language, and by other provisions relating to cultural identity and linguistic needs. The Committee on the Rights of the Child recommendations contained the 'Day of General Discussion', taken further forward by General Comment No 11, also provide a further depth to the emerging jurisprudence in this field.

The ILO Indigenous and Tribal Peoples Convention of 1989 has been helpful in establishing rights of non-discrimination and rights of participation by indigenous people. In addition, it has broadened a development of the concept and importance of *collective rights* applied to indigenous peoples. It also identified importantly *self-determination* as a fundamental criterion to assess indigeneity.

The international law relating to indigenous peoples has undoubtedly received a sharper focus with the arrival of the Declaration of 2007. This instrument carries forward a human rights approach tailored to the particular needs and historical legacies of indigenous peoples. Like most international instruments, it is not perfect and will no doubt require further elaboration and development in the future. It would seem that the gathering moral authority and evidence of impact of the Declaration of 2007 may well eclipse arcane debates about its precise international legal status. For the time being at least, it would appear that the limited notion of self-determination is sufficient to neutralise concerns about secession that might otherwise arise from further recognition of the autonomy of indigenous peoples. The tension between collective and individual rights also poses a significant challenge for the future.

The relevant UN infrastructure relating to indigenous peoples, the Permanent Forum, Special Rapporteur and Expert Mechanism, have all made significant contributions to the development of international law and policy, but there is a growing sense of the need to rationalise their respective mandates to provide a more efficient and focused institutional architecture ready to address the challenges on the horizon relating to, for example, developments in technology and climate change.

Bibliography

Abernethie, L. (1998) 'Child labour in contemporary society: Why do we care?', 6(1) *International Journal of Children's Rights* 81–114.

Agarwal, R.K. (2004) 'The Barefoot Lawyers: Prosecuting Child Labour in the Supreme Court of India', 21(2) *Arizona Journal of International & Comparative Law* 663–713.

Akande, D. (2003) 'The Jurisdiction of the International Criminal Court over Nationals of Non-Parties: Legal Basis and Limits', 1(3) *Journal of International Criminal Justice* 618–50.

Akdeniz, Y. (2008) *Internet Child Pornography and the Law: National and International Responses*, Aldershot: Ashgate Publishing.

Alexander, S., Meuwese, S. and Wolthuis, A. (2000) 'Policies and Developments relating to the Sexual Exploitation of Children: The Legacy of the Stockholm Conference', 8(4) *European Journal on Criminal Policy and Research* 479–501.

Allain, J. (2008) *The Slavery Conventions: The Travaux Préparatoires of the 1926 League of Nations Convention and the 1956 United Nations Convention*, Leiden/Boston: Martinus Nijhoff.

Alston, P. (1989) 'Implementing Children's Rights: The Case of Child Labour', 58(1) *Nordic Journal of International Law* 35–53.

Alston, P. (1992) 'The Legal Framework of the Convention on the Rights of the Child', 91(2) *Bulletin of Human Rights* 1–15.

Alston, P. (2004) ' "Core Labour Standards" and the Transformation of the International Labour Rights Regime', 15(3) *European Journal of International Law* 457–521.

Alston, P., Parker, S. and Seymour, J. (eds) (1992) *Children, Rights and the Law*, Oxford: Clarendon Press.

American Anthropological Association (1947) 'Statement on Human Rights', Executive Board, American Anthropological Association, 49(4) *American Anthropologist* 539–43.

Anker, R. (2000) 'The economics of child labour: a framework for measurement', 139(3) *International Labour Review* 257–80.

Archard, D. (1993) *Children: Rights and Childhood*, London: Routledge.

Archard, D. (2010) 'Children's Rights', *The Stanford Encyclopedia of Philosophy* (Summer 2011 Edition), Edward N. Zalta (ed) http://plato.stanford.edu/archives/sum2011/entries/rights-children/ (accessed 16 January 2013).

Archard, D. (2012) 'Children's rights' in Cushman, R. (ed) (2012) *Handbook of Human Rights*, Abingdon: Routledge, 324–32.

Ariès, P. (1962) *Centuries of Childhood*, London: Cape.

Arnstein, S.R. (1969) 'Eight rungs on the ladder of citizen participation', 35(4) *Journal of the American Institute of Planners* 216–24.

Aust, A. (2010) *Handbook of International Law*, Second Edition, Cambridge: Cambridge University Press.

Bakirci, K. (2002) 'Child labour and legislation in Turkey', 10(1) *International Journal of Children's Rights* 55–72.

Barelli, M. (2009) 'The Role of Soft Law in the International Legal System: the case of the United Nations Declaration on the Rights of Indigenous Peoples', 58 *International and Comparative Law Quarterly* 957–83.

Bean, P. and Melville, J. (1989) *Lost Children of the Empire*, London: Unwin Hyman.

Beaulieu, C. (2008) *Extraterritorial Laws: Why they are not working and how they can be strengthened*, Bangkok: ECPAT International congress III/PDF/Journals/EXTRATERRITORIAL_ LAWS.pdf (accessed 27 January 2010).

Beaumont, P. and McEleavy, P. (1999) *The Hague Convention on International Child Abduction*, Oxford: Oxford University Press.

Betcherman, G., Fares, J., Luinstra, A. and Prouty, R. (2004) 'Child labor, Education, and Children's Rights', Social Protection Discussion Paper Series, No 0412, Washington, DC: The World Bank.

Black, M. (1986) *The Children and the Nations: the story of Unicef*, Sydney: UNICEF.

Black, M. (1996) *Children First: The Story of Unicef, Past and Present*, Oxford: Oxford University Press.

Blagbrough, J. (1997) 'Eliminating the worst forms of child labour – a new international standard', 5(1) *International Journal of Children's Rights* 123–27.

Boéchat, H. and Cantwell, N. (2007) *Assessment of the adoption system in Kazakhstan*, Geneva: International Social Service, December 2007.

Boezaart, T. (2013) 'Listening to the Child's Objection', 2013(3) *New Zealand Law Review*, 357–72.

Bonnet, M. (1993) 'Child labour in Africa', 132(3) *International Labour Review* 371–89.

Bouhdiba, A. (1982) *Exploitation of Child Labour*, E/CN.4/Sub.2/479/Rev.l, U.N., Sales No E.82.XIV.2, United Nations, New York: United Nations.

Boyden, J. (1997) 'Childhood and the Policy Makers: A Comparative Perspective on the Globalization of Childhood', in James, A. and Prout, A. (eds) (1997) *Constructing and Reconstructing Childhood: Contemporary Issues in the Sociological Study of Childhood*, Second Edition, London: Routledge/Falmer 187–226.

Brighouse, H. (2002) 'What Rights (if any) do Children Have?' in D. Archard and C. Macleod (eds) (2002) *The Moral and Political Status of Children: New Essays*, Oxford: Oxford University Press 31–52.

Browne, K. and Chou, S. (2008) 'Child Rights and International Adoption: A Response to Critics', 32(2) *Adoption and Fostering* 69–74.

Buck, T. (2008) 'International Criminalisation and Child Welfare Protection: the Optional Protocol to the Convention on the Rights of the Child', 22(3) *Children & Society* 167–78.

Buck, T. (2011) *International Child Law*, Second Edition, London: Routledge.

Buck, T. (2012) *An Evaluation of the Long-term Effectiveness of Mediation in Cases of International Parental Child Abduction* (104 pp), Leicester: Reunite http://hdl.handle.net/2086/6329

Buck, T. and Wabwile, M. (2013) 'The Potential and Promise of Communications Procedures under the Third Protocol to the Convention on the Rights of the Child', 2 *International Human Rights Law Review* 205–39.

Burnett, J. (1983) 'The History of Childhood', 33(12) *History Today* 1–6.

Burra, N. (1995) *Born to Work: Child Labour in India*, India: OUP.

Calitz, K. (2013) 'The Failure of the Minimum Age Convention to Eradicate Child Labour in Developing Countries, with Particular Reference to the Southern African Development Community', 29(1) *International Journal of Comparative Labour Law and Industrial Relations* 83–103.

Campbell, T. (1992) 'The Rights of the Minor' in Alston, P., Parker, S. and Seymour, J. (eds) (1992) *Children, Rights and the Law*, Oxford: Clarendon Press.

Cantwell, N. (1992) 'The origins, development and significance of the United Nations Convention on the Rights of the Child' in Detrick, S. (ed) (1992) *The United Nations Convention on the Rights of the Child: A Guide to the 'travaux préparatoires'*, Dordrecht/Boston/Norwell: Martinus Nijhoff Publishers 19–30.

Catani, L. (2012) 'Victims at the International Criminal Court: Some Lessons Learned from the Lubanga Case', 10(4) *Journal of International Criminal Justice* 905–922.

Cedrangolo, U. (2009) 'The Optional Protocol to the Convention on the Rights of the Child on the sale of children, child prostitution and child pornography and the jurisprudence of the Committee on the Rights of the Child', Innocenti Working Paper No. 2009-03, Florence: UNICEF Innocenti Research Centre http://www.unicef-irc.org/publications/pdf/iwp_2009_03.pdf (accessed 27 January 2010).

Chamberland, J. (2012) 'Whither the "best interests of the child" in the 1980 Child Abduction Convention?', March *International Family Law* 27–30.

Chase, E. and Statham, J. (2005) 'Commercial and Sexual Exploitation of Children and Young People in the UK – A Review', 14(1) *Child Abuse Review* 4–25.

Chen, X. (2003) '"Parents Go Global": report on an intercountry adoption research project', 2003(1) *Variegations: New Research Directions in Human and Social Development 10–14*, Canada: University of Victoria.

Chiancone, J. (2001) Parental Abduction: A Review of the Literature, US Department of Justice, Office of Justice Programs/Office of Juvenile Justice and Delinquency Prevention http://www.ncjrs.gov/html/ojjdp/190074/index.html (accessed 20 January 2010).

Chou, S. and Browne, K. (2008) 'The Relationship between Institutional Care and the International Adoption of Children in Europe', 32(1) *Adoption and Fostering* 40–48.

Choy, C.C. (2007) 'Institutionalizing International Adoption: The Historical Origins of Korean Adoption in the United States', in Bergquist, K.J.S., Vonk, M.E., Kim, D.S. and Feit, M.D. (eds) *International Korean Adoption: A Fifty-Year History of Policy and Practice*, Binghamton, NY: Haworth Press 25–42.

Cooper, J. (1997) 'Child Labour: legal regimes, market pressures, and the search for meaningful solutions', 52(3) *International Journal* 411–30.

Cordova, E. (1993) 'Some Reflections on the Overproduction of International Labour Standards', 14(2) *Comparative Labor Law Journal* 138–62.

Corsaro, W. (2011) *The Sociology of Childhood*, Third Edition, Los Angeles: Sage/Pine Forge Press.

Coulter, R.T. (2010) 'The Law of Self-determination and the United Nations Declaration on the Rights of Indigenous Peoples', 15 *UCLA Journal of International Law & Foreign Affairs* 1–27.

Craven, S., Brown, S. and Gilchrist, E. (2006) 'Sexual Grooming of Children: Review of the Literature and Theoretical Considerations', 12(3) *Journal of Sexual Aggression* 287–99.

Crawford, J. (2012) *Brownlie's Principles of Public International Law*, Eighth Edition, Oxford: Oxford University Press.

Crawford, J. and Grant, T. (2007) 'International Court of Justice', Chapter 11 in Weiss, T. G. and Daws, S. (eds) (2007) *The Oxford Handbook on the United Nations*, Oxford: Oxford University Press, 193–216.

Crawford, S. (2000) *The Worst Forms of Child Labour: A Guide to Understanding and Using the New Convention*, London: Department for International Development.

Creighton, B. (1997) 'Combating Child Labour: The Role of International Labour Standards', 18(3) *Comparative Labor Law Journal* 362–96.

Cullen, H. (1999) 'The limits of international trade mechanisms in enforcing human rights: the case of child labour', 7(1) *International Journal of Children's Rights* 1–29.

Cunningham, H. (2005) *Children and Childhood in Western Society since 1500*, Second Edition, Harlow: Pearson Education Ltd.

Cunningham, H. (2006) *The Invention of Childhood*, London: BBC Books.

Cushman, R. (ed) (2012) *Handbook of Human Rights*, Abingdon: Routledge.

Dachi, H. and Garrett, R. (2003) *Child Labour and its Impact on Children's Access to and Participation in Primary Education: A Case Study from Tanzania*, No 48, Education Papers, London: Department for International Development.

Davidson, M.G. (2001) 'The International Labour Organization's Latest Campaign to End Child Labour: Will it Succeed Where Others Have Failed?', 11(1) *Transnational Law & Contemporary Problems* 203–24.

Davies, M. (2011) 'Intercountry Adoption, Children's Rights and the Politics of Rescue', 35(4) *Adoption and Fostering* 50–62.

Davis, M. (2012) 'To Bind or Not to Bind: The United Nations Declaration on the Rights of Indigenous Peoples Five Years On', 19 *Australian International Law Journal* 17–48.

DeMause, L. (ed.) (1976) *The History of Childhood*, London: Souvenir Press.

Demetriou, A., Efklides, A. and Platsidou, M. (2000) *The Architecture and Dynamics of Developing Mind: Experiential Structuralism as a Frame for Unifying Cognitive Developmental Theories*, Monographs for the Society of Research in Child Development, Serial No 234, Vol 58, Nos 5–6 (1993, London: Wiley Blackwell.

Dennis, M.J. (1999) 'The ILO Convention on the Worst Forms of Child Labour', 93(4) *American Journal of International Law* 943–48.

Detrick, S. (ed.) (1992) *The United Nations Convention on the Rights of the Child: A Guide to the 'travaux préparatoires'*, Dordrecht/Boston/Norwell: Martinus Nijhoff Publishers.

Detrick, S. (1999) *A Commentary on the United Nations Convention on the Rights of the Child*, The Hague/Boston/London: Martinus Nijhoff Publishers.

Dickinson, L. (2003) 'The Promise of Hybrid Courts', 97(2) *The American Journal of International Law* 295–310.

Dixon, M. (2013) *International Law*, Seventh Edition, Oxford: Oxford University Press.

Doek, J.E. (2003) 'The Protection of Children's Rights and the United Nations Convention on the Rights of the Child: Achievements and Challenges', 22(2) *Saint Louis University Public Law Review* 235–52.

Dorman, P. (2001) *Child labour in the developed economies*, ILO/IPEC working paper, Geneva: ILO/IPEC.

Dorman, P. (2008) *Child labour, education and health: A review of the literature*, International Programme on the Elimination of Child Labour (IPEC), Geneva: International Labour Office.

Douglas, G. (1992) 'The Retreat from Gillick', 55(4) *Modern Law Review* 569.

Drumbl, M.A. (2012) *Reimagining Child Soldiers in International Law and Policy*, Oxford: Oxford University Press.

Dyer, A. (1997) 'The Internationalization of Family Law', 30 *U.C. Davis Law Review* 625–45.

Edmonds, E. (2008) *Defining child labour: A review of the definitions of child labour in policy research*, Working paper, International Programme on the Elimination of Child Labour (IPEC), Geneva: International Labour Office.

Eekelaar, J. (1986) 'The emergence of children's rights', 6(2) *Oxford Journal of Legal Studies* 161–82.

Engle, E. (2011) 'The Convention on the Rights of the Child', 29 *Quinnipiac Law Review* 793–819.

English, J. (1997) ' "Imitating the cries of little children": exploitative child labour and the growth of children's rights', 52(3) *International Journal* 431–44.

Ennew, J. (2008) Conference on Children's Rights, Presentation, Swansea University (19 September 2008).

Erikson, E.H. (1995) *Childhood and Society*, first published in Great Britain 1951, London: Vintage Books.

Europol (2009) *Ten Years of Europol: 1999–2009*, The Hague, Netherlands: Europol http://www.europol.europa.eu/ (accessed 14 October 2013).

Eva, B. (2006) 'Above Children's Heads: The Headscarf Controversy in European Schools from the Perspective of Children's Rights', 14(2) *International Journal of Children's Rights* 119–36.

Evans, M. (ed) (2010) *International Law*, Third Edition, Oxford: Oxford University Press.

Feinberg, J. (1980) *Rights, Justice and the Bounds of Liberty: Essays in Social Philosophy*, Princeton, New Jersey: Princeton University Press.

First World Congress (1996) *Declaration and Agenda for Action, 1st World Congress against Commercial Sexual Exploitation of Children*, Stockholm, Sweden (27–31 August 1996) http://www.ecpat.net/world-congress-against-commercial-sexual-exploitation-chil dren (accessed 24 November 2013).

Fleck, D. (2013) *The Handbook of International Humanitarian Law*, Third Edition, Oxford: Oxford University Press.

Fortin, J. (2006) 'Accommodating Children's Rights in a Post Human Rights Act Era' 69(3) *Modern Law Review* 299–326.

Fortin, J. (2009) *Children's Rights and the Developing Law*, Third Edition, Cambridge: Cambridge University Press.

Fox Harding, L. (1996) *Family, State and Social Policy*, Basingstoke: Macmillan.

Fredette, K. (2009) 'International legislative efforts to combat child sex tourism', 32 *Boston College International and Comparative Law Review* 1–43.

Freeman, M. (2003) *The Outcomes for Children Returned Following an Abduction*, Reunite research unit, Leicester: International Child Abduction Centre.

Freeman, M. (2006) *International Child Abduction: The Effects*, Reunite research unit, Leicester: International Child Abduction Centre.

Freeman, M. (2009) 'When the 1980 Hague Child Abduction Convention does not Apply: The UK–Pakistan Protocol, *International Family Law* 181–85.

Freeman, M.D.A. (1983) *The Rights and Wrongs of Children*, London: Continuum International Publishing.

Freeman, M.D.A. (2007) 'Why it Remains Important to Take Children's Rights Seriously', 15(1) *International Journal of Children's Rights* 5–23.

Freeman, M.D.A. (2011) 'Children's Rights as Human Rights' in Qvortrup, J., Corsaro, W.A. and Honig, M. (eds) *The Palgrave Handbook of Childhood Studies*, Basingstoke: Palgrave Macmillan.

Freud, S. (1920) *Three Contributions to the Theory of Sex* (Nervous and mental disease monograph series), Brill, A.A. tr, Second Edition, New York/Washington: Nervous and Mental Disease Publishing Company.

G8 (2003) Justice and Home Affairs ministerial meeting—Paris (5 May) President's Summary http://www.justice.gov/criminal/ceos/downloads/G8MinistersDeclaration 20090530.pdf (accessed 19 November 2013).

G8 (2009) 'The Risk to Children Posed by Child Pornography Offenders', Ministers' Declaration, G8 Justice and Home Affairs Ministers', Rome (30 May 2009) http://www.justice.gov/criminal/ceos/downloads/G8MinistersDeclaration20090530. pdf (accessed 14 October 2013).

G8 (2013) Foreign Ministers' Meeting Statement (11 April 2013 https://www.gov.uk/ government/uploads/system/uploads/attachment_data/file/185944/G8_Statement_ Document.pdf (accessed 15 November 2013).

Gaer, F.D. (2007) 'A Voice Not an Echo: Universal Periodic Review and the UN Treaty Body System', 7 *Human Rights Law Review* 109–139.

Gay y Blasco, P., Macrae, S., Selman, P. and Wardle, H. (2008) 'The Relationship between Institutional Care and the International Adoption of Children in Europe: A Rejoinder to Chou and Browne', 32(2) *Adoption and Fostering* 63–67.

Gill, T. (2007) *No Fear: Growing up in a risk averse society*, London: Calouste Gulbenkian Foundation.

Gillespie, A.A. (2002) 'Child Protection on the Internet: Challenges for Criminal Law', 14(4) *Child and Family Law Quarterly* 411–26.

Gillespie, A.A. (2007) 'Diverting Children Involved in Prostitution', 2 *Web Journal of Current Legal Issues*, published 27 April 2007 http://webjcli. ncl.ac.uk/2007/issue2/gillespie2. html (accessed 27 January 2010).

Gillespie, A.A. (2010) 'Legal Definitions of Child Pornography', 16(1) *Journal of Sexual Aggression* 19–31.

Gillespie, A.A. (2011) *Child Pornography: Law and Policy*, Abingdon: Routledge.

Goldstein, J., Freud, A. and Solnit, A. (1973) *Beyond the Best Interests of the Child*, London: Collier-Macmillan.

Goldstein, J., Freud, A. and Solnit, A. (1980) *Before the Best Interests of the Child*, London: Burnett Books Ltd.

Graf, R. (2012) 'The International Criminal Court and Child Soldiers: An Appraisal of the Lubanga Judgment', 10(4) *Journal of International Criminal Justice* 945–70.

Guymon C.D. (ed) (2012) *Digest of United States Practice in International Law* 2012, USA: Office of the Legal Adviser, US State Department http://www.state.gov/s/l/2012/index.htm (accessed 11 February 2013).

Guzman, A.T. and Meyer, T.L. (2010) 'International Soft Law', 2 (1) *Journal of Legal Analysis* 171–225.

Haanappel, P.P.C. (2003) *The Law and Policy of Air Space and Outer Space: a Comparative Approach*, The Hague: Kluwer Law International.

Hamilton, C. and Dutordoir, L. (2011) 'Children and Justice During and in the Aftermath of Armed Conflict', *Working Paper No 3*, New York: Office of the Special Representative of the Secretary-General for Children and Armed Conflict http://childrenandarmed conflict.un.org/publications/WorkingPaper-3_Children-and-Justice.pdf (accessed 18 November 2013).

Happold, M. (2005) *Child Soldiers in International Law*, Manchester: Manchester University Press.

Harris-Short, S. (2001) 'Listening to "The Other"? The Convention on the Rights of the Child', 2(2*) Melbourne Journal of International Law* 304–50.

Hart, H.L.A. (1984) 'Are There Any Natural Rights?', in Waldron, J. (ed) *Theories of Rights*, Oxford: Oxford University Press.

Hart, R.A. (1992) *Children's Participation: From Tokenism to Citizenship*, Innocenti Essays No. 4, Florence: UNICEF.

Harvey, R. (2003) *Children and Armed Conflict—A guide to international humanitarian and human rights law*, University of Essex: Children and Armed Conflict Unit/ International Bureau for Children's Rights http://www.essex.ac.uk/armedcon/story_id/000044.pdf (accessed 15 November 2013).

Hassel, A. (2008) 'The Evolution of a Global Labor Governance Regime', 21(2) *Governance: An International Journal of Policy, Administration and Institutions* 231–51.

Hayes, P. (2011) 'The Legality and Ethics of Independent Intercountry Adoption under the Hague Convention', 25(3) *International Journal of Law, Policy and the Family* 288–317.

Hendrick, H. (1997) *Children, Childhood and English Society 1880–1990*, Cambridge: Cambridge University Press.

Heywood, C. (2001) *A History of Childhood: Children and Childhood in the West from Medieval to Modern Times*, Cambridge: Polity Press.

Hirst, M. (2003) *Jurisdiction and the Ambit of the Criminal Law*, Oxford: Oxford University Press.

Ho, J. (2006) 'The International Labour Organization's Role in Nationalizing the International Movement to Abolish Child Labor', 7(1) *Chicago Journal of International Law* 337–49.

Hobbins, A.J. (2001) 'Humphrey and the High Commissioner: the Genesis of the Office of the UN High Commissioner for Human Rights', 3 *Journal of the History of International Law* 38–74.

Hodgkin, R. and Newell, P. (2007) *Implementation Handbook for the Convention on the Rights of the Child*, Third edition, Geneva: UNICEF http://www.unicef.org/publications/index_43110.html (accessed 11 June 2013).

Holt, J. (1974) *Escape from Childhood: The Needs and Rights of Childhood*, New York: EP Dutton and Co. Inc.

Horton, R. (2004) 'UNICEF leadership 2005–2015: a call for strategic change' (editorial) vol 364, issue 9451 *The Lancet* 2071–74.

Hubinette, T. (2006) 'From Orphan Trains to Baby Lifts: Colonial Trafficking, Empire Building, and Social Engineering', in Trenka, J.J, Oparah, J.C. and Shin, S.Y. (eds) *Outsiders Within: Writing on Transracial Adoption*, New York: Southend Press 139–50.

Humbert, F. (2009) *The Challenge of Child Labour in International Law*, Cambridge Studies in International and Comparative Law, Cambridge: Cambridge University Press.

ILO (1996) *Child Labour: What is to be done?* Geneva: International Labour Office.

ILO (2002) *A Future Without Child Labour*, Global report under the Follow-up to the ILO Declaration on Fundamental Principles and Rights at Work, Report of the

Director- General, International Labour Conference 90th Session, Geneva: International Labour Office.

ILO (2002a) *Eliminating the Worst Forms of Child Labour: A Practical Guide to ILO Convention No 182*, Geneva: ILO and Inter-Parliamentary Union.

ILO (2004) *Investing in Every Child: An Economic Study of the Costs and Benefits of Eliminating Child Labour*, International Programme on the Elimination of Child Labour, Geneva: ILO.

ILO (2006) *The End of Child Labour: Within Reach*, Global report under the Follow-up to the ILO Declaration on Fundamental Principles and Rights at Work. Report of the Director-General, International Labour Conference 95th Session, Geneva: International Labour Office.

ILO (2010) *Accelerating Action against Child Labour*, Global report under the follow-up to the ILO Declaration on Fundamental Principles and Rights at Work, Report of the Director-General, International Labour Conference 99th Session, Geneva: International Labour Office.

ILO (2010a) *Towards a World without Child Labour: Mapping the Road to 2016*, The Hague Global Child Labour Conference Report, Geneva, ILO and the Ministry of Social Affairs and Employment of the Netherlands.

ILO (2013) *Marking progress against child labour: Global estimates and trends 2000–2012*, Geneva: International Labour Office.

Invernizzi, A. and Milne, B. (2002) 'Are children entitled to contribute to international policy making? A critical view of children's participation in the international campaign for the elimination of child labour', 10(4) *International Journal of Children's Rights* 403–31.

IPEC (2004) *Helping Hands or Shackled Lives? Understanding Child Domestic Labour and Responses to it*, International Programme on the Elimination of Child Labour, Geneva: ILO.

IPEC (2013) *Global child labour trends: 2008 to 2012*, International Labour Office, International Programme on the Elimination of Child Labour (IPEC), Geneva: ILO.

James, A. and Prout, A. (eds) (1997) *Constructing and Reconstructing Childhood: contemporary issues in the sociological study of childhood*, Second Edition, London: Routledge/Falmer.

James, A., Jenks, C. and Prout, A. (1998) *Theorizing Childhood*, Oxford: Polity Press.

Jenks, C. (1996) *Childhood*, London: Routledge.

Johnson, C.F. (2004) 'Child Sexual Abuse', 364(9432) *The Lancet* 462–70.

Johnson, S.M. (1999) 'Excuse me, but is that football "child-free"? Pakistan and Child Labour', 7(1) *Tulsa Journal of Comparative and International Law* 163–76.

Jonah, J.O.C. (2007) 'Secretariat: independence and reform', Chapter 9 in Weiss, T.G. and Daws, S. (eds) (2007) *The Oxford Handbook on the United Nations*, Oxford: Oxford University Press 160–74.

Joonal, T. (2010) 'International Norms and Domestic Practices in Regard to ILO Convention No 169 – with Special Reference to Articles 1 and 13–19', 12 *International Community Law Review* 213–60.

Joseph, S. and McBeth, A. (eds) (2010) *Research Handbook on International Human Rights Law*, Cheltenham UK: Edward Elgar.

Joseph, S. and Kyriakakis, J. (2010) 'The United Nations and Human Rights' in Joseph, S. and McBeth, A. (eds) (2010) *Research Handbook on International Human Rights Law*, Cheltenham UK: Edward Elgar 1–35.

Kaczorowska, A. (2010) *Public International Law*, Fourth Edition, Abingdon: Routledge.

Kelly, F. (2005) 'Conceptualising the child through an "ethic of care": lessons for family law' 1(4) *International Journal of Law in Context* 375–96.

Kelly, L. (2002) *Journeys of Jeopardy: A Commentary on Current Research on Trafficking of Women and Children for Sexual Exploitation within Europe*, IOM Migration Research Series, MRS No 11, International Organization for Migration, London: Stationery Office Books.

Kempe, C.H. (1978) 'Sexual abuse, another hidden pediatric problem: The 1977 C. Anderson Aldrich Lecture', 62(3) *Pediatrics* 382–89.

Kilbourne, S. (1998) 'The wayward Americans – why the USA has not ratified the UN Convention on the Rights of the Child' [1998] *International Family Law* 104–12.

Kilkelly, U. (2003) 'Economic Exploitation of Children: A European Perspective', 22(2) *Saint Louis University Public Law Review* 321–58.

Kim, H. (2007) 'Mothers without mothering: birth mothers from South Korea since the Korean War', in Bergquist, K.J.S., Vonk, M.E., Kim, D.S. and Feit, M.D. (eds) *International Korean Adoption: A Fifty-Year History of Policy and Practice*, Binghamton, NY: Haworth Press 131–54.

King, M. (2007) 'The Sociology of Childhood as Scientific Communication: Observations from a social systems perspective', 14(2) *Childhood* 193–213.

Kirby, M. (2010) 'Children Caught in Conflict — the Child Abduction Convention and Australia', 24(1) *International Journal of Law, Policy and the Family* 95–114.

Klabbers, J. (2013) *International Law*, Cambridge: Cambridge University Press.

Kolieb, J. (2009) 'The Six Grave Violations Against Children During Armed Conflict: The Legal Foundation', *Working Paper No 1*, New York: Office of the Special Representative of the Secretary-General for Children and Armed Conflict http://childrenandarmedconflict.un.org/publications/WorkingPaper-1_SixGraveViolationsLegalFoundation.pdf (accessed 18 November 2013).

Komanovics, A. (2012) 'The Human Rights Council and the Universal Periodic Review: Is it more than a public relations exercise?' 150 *Studia Iuridica Auctoritate Universitatis Pecs* 119–46.

Kott, E. and Droux, J. (eds) (2013) *Globalizing Social Rights: The International Labour Organization and Beyond*, ILO Century Series), Geneva: International Labour Organization.

Kramer, M.H. (1998) 'Rights Without Trimmings', in M.H. Kramer, N. Simmonds and H. Steiner (eds) *A Debate Over Rights, Philosophical Enquiries*, Oxford: Clarendon Press 7–111.

Lamont, R. (2008) 'The EU: Protecting Children's Rights in Child Abduction', *International Family Law* 110–12.

Lamont, R. (2011) 'Mainstreaming Gender into European Family Law? The Case of International Child Abduction and Brussels II Revised', 17(3) *European Law Journal* 366–84.

Lamont, R. (2012) 'Free movement of persons, child abduction and relocation within the European Union', 34(2) *Journal of Social Welfare and Family Law* 231–44.

Langille, B.A. (2005) 'Core Labour Rights—The True Study (Reply to Alston), 16(3) *European Journal of International Law* 409–37.

Levison, D., Hoek, J., Lam, D. and Duryea, S. (2007) 'Intermittent child employment and its implications for estimates of child labour', 146(3/4) *International Labour Review* 217–51.

Liefländer, T. (2012) 'The *Lubanga* Judgment of the ICC – More than just the First Step?' 1(1) *Cambridge Journal of International and Comparative Law*, 191–212.

Lind, J. and Johansson, S. (2009) 'Preservation of the Child's Background in In- and Intercountry Adoption', 17 *International Journal of Children's Rights* 235–60.

Lowe, N. (2007) 'The Current Experiences and Difficulties of Applying Brussels II Revised', 7(4) *International Family Law* 182–95.

Lowe, N., Armstrong, S. and Mathias, A. (1999) A Statistical Analysis of Applications Made in 1999 under the Hague Convention of 25 October 1980 on the Civil Aspects of International Child Abduction, The Hague: HCCH Publications.

Lowe, N., Atkinson, E. and Horosova, K. (2006) A Statistical Analysis of Applications Made in 2003 under the 1980 Hague Convention on the Civil Aspects of International Child Abduction, Vol 1, Global Report (pp 80); Vol 2, National Reports (pp 492); published as Preliminary Document No 3 for the 5th Meeting of the Special Commission to Review the Operation of the Hague Convention of 25 October 1980 on the Civil Aspects of International Child Abduction http://www.hcch.net/ index_en.php?act=conventions.publications&dtid=2&cid=24 (accessed 25 January 2010).

Lowe N. (2011a) 'A statistical analysis of applications made in 2008 under the Hague Convention of 25 October 1980 on the Civil Aspects of International Child Abduction. Part I – Global Report', Prel Doc No 8 A of May 2011, The Hague: HccH http://www.hcch.net/upload/wop/abduct2011pd08ae.pdf (accessed 7 January 2013).

Lowe N. (2011b) 'A statistical analysis of applications made in 2008 under the Hague Convention of 25 October 1980 on the Civil Aspects of International Child Abduction. Part II – Regional Reports', Prel Doc No 8 B of May 2011 – A statistical analysis of applications made in 2008 under the Hague Convention of 25 October 1980 on the Civil Aspects of International Child Abduction http://www.hcch.net/upload/wop/abduct2011pd08be.pdf (accessed 7 January 2013).

Lowe N. (2011c) 'A statistical analysis of applications made in 2008 under the Hague Convention of 25 October 1980 on the Civil Aspects of International Child Abduction. Part III – National Reports', Prel Doc No 8 C of May 2011, The Hague: HccH http://www.hcch.net/upload/wop/abduct2011pd08c.pdf   (accessed   1   October 2011).

Lowe, N., Everall, M. and Nichols, M. (2014) *International Movement of Children: Law, Practice and Procedure*, Second edition, London: Family Law/Jordan Publishing Ltd.

Lowe, V. and Crawford, J. (eds) (2012) *British Year Book of International Law 2011: Volume 81*, Oxford: Oxford University Press.

Maalla, N.M. (2008) *Report submitted by the Special Rapporteur on the sale of children, child prostitution and child pornography*. UN Human Rights Council, 9th session, A/HRC/9/21 (31 July 2008) http://daccess-dds-ny.un.org/doc/UNDOC/GEN/G08/148/41/PDF/G0814841.pdf?OpenElement (accessed 27 January 2010).

Maalla, N.M. (2009) *Report submitted by the Special Rapporteur on the sale of children, child prostitution and child pornography*. UN Human Rights Council, 12th session, A/HRC/12/23 (13 July 2009) http://www2.ohchr.org/english/bodies/hrcouncil/docs/12session/A.HRC.12.23.pdf (accessed 27 January 2010).

Maalla, N.M. (2011) *Report of the Special Rapporteur on the sale of children, child prostitution and child pornography*. UN Human Rights Council, 19th session, A/HRC/19/63 http://daccess-dds-ny.un.org/doc/UNDOC/GEN/G11/175/13/PDF/G1117513.pdf (accessed 14 October 2013).

Maalla, N.M. (2012) *Report of the Special Rapporteur on the sale of children, child prostitution and child pornography*. UN Human Rights Council, 22nd session, A/HRC/22/54 http://

daccess-dds-ny.un.org/doc/UNDOC/GEN/G13/102/63/PDF/G1310263.pdf (accessed 14 October 2013).

MacCormick, N. (1982) *Legal Right and Social Democracy: Essays in Legal and Political Philosophy*, Oxford: Clarendon Press.

McCrae, D. (2012) 'The Work of the International Law Commission, 2007–2011: progress and prospects', 106 *American Journal of International Law* 322–40.

McEleavy, P. (2005) 'The New Child Abduction Regime in the European Community: Symbiotic Relationship or Forced Partnership?' [2005] *Journal of Private International Law* 5–34.

McEleavy, P. (2008) 'Evaluating the Views of Abducted Children: Trends in Appellate Case Law' [2008] *Child and Family Law Quarterly* 230–54.

Malone, D.M. (2007) 'Security Council', Chapter 6 in Weiss, T.G. and Daws, S. (eds) (2007) *The Oxford Handbook on the United Nations*, Oxford: Oxford University Press 117–35.

Marshall, D. (1999) 'The construction of children as an object of international relations: The Declaration of Children's Rights and the Child Welfare Committee of League of Nations, 1900–1924', 7(2) *International Journal of Children's Rights* 103–47.

Masum, M. (2002) 'Eradication of hazardous child labour in Bangladesh: The need for an integrated strategy', 10(3) *International Journal of Children's Rights* 233–68.

Mayall, B. (2000) 'The sociology of childhood in relation to chidren's rights', 8(3) *International Journal of Children's Rights* 243–59.

Mayall, B. (2003) *Childhood in Generational Perspective*, Bedford Way Papers, London: Institute of Education.

Melrose, M. and Barrett, D. (2006) 'The Flesh Trade in Europe: Trafficking in Women and Children for the Purpose of Commercial Sexual Exploitation', 7(2) *Police Practice and Research* 111–23.

Mezmur, B.D. (2008) ' "As painful as giving birth": A reflection on the Madonna adoption saga', 41 *Comparative and International Law of Southern Africa* 383–403.

Mezmur, B.D. (2009) 'From Angelina (to Madonna) to Zoe's Ark: What are the 'A–Z' lessons for intercountry adoptions in Africa', 23 *International Journal of Law, Policy and the Family* 145.

Mezmur, B.D. (2012) ' "Acting Like a Rich Bully"?: Madonna, Mercy, Malawi, and international children's rights law in adoption', 20(1) *International Journal of Children's Rights* 24–56.

Molfenter, C. (2011) 'Bonded Child Labour in Pakistan – The State's Responsibility to Protect from an Institutional Perspective', 5 *Vienna J. on Int'l Const. L.* 260–320.

Montgomery, H. (2008) 'Buying innocence: child-sex tourists in Thailand', 29(5) *Third World Quarterly* 903–917.

Montgomery, H. (2010) Is extra-territorial legislation the answer? in Botterill, D. and Jones, T. (eds) *Tourism and Crime: Key Themes*, Oxford: Goodfellow Publishing 69–85.

Mooney, E. and Paul, D. (2010) 'The Rights and Guarantees of Internally Displaced Children in Armed Conflict', *Working Paper No 2*, New York: Office of the Special Representative of the Secretary-General for Children and Armed Conflict http://childrenandarmedconflict.un.org/publications/WorkingPaper-2-Rights-GuaranteesIDP-Children.pdf (accessed 18 November 2013).

Moravcsik, A. (2000) 'The Origins of Human Rights Regimes: Democratic Delegation in Postwar Europe', 54(2) *International Organization* 217–52.

Mullerbeck, E. and Anthony, D. (2011) 'UNICEF at 65: Looking back, thinking ahead', Unicef website http://www.unicef.org/about/who/index_60926.html (accessed 25 February 2013).

Muntarbhorn, V. (1998) 'Child rights and social clauses: Child labour elimination as a social cause?' 6(3) *International Journal of Children's Rights* 255–311.

Myers, W.E. (2001) 'The Right Rights? Child Labour in a Globalizing World', 575(1) *Annals of the American Academy of Political and Social Science* 38–54.

Newiss, G. and Fairbrother, L. (2004) 'Child abduction: understanding police recorded crime statistics', *Findings 225*, London: Home Office Research, Development and Statistics Directorate.

Newman, E. (2007) 'Secretary-General', Chapter 10 in Weiss, T.G. and Daws, S. (eds) (2007) *The Oxford Handbook on the United Nations*, Oxford: Oxford University Press 175–92.

NGO Group (2001) *Do You Know About the ILO Worst Forms of Child Labour Convention?* Geneva: NGO Group for the Convention on the Rights of the Child.

NGO Group (2005) *Semantics or Substance? Towards a shared understanding of terminology referring to the sexual abuse and exploitation of children*, Subgroup against the Sexual Exploitation of Children, NGO Group for the Convention on the Rights of the Child, Bangkok: ECPAT International http://www.crin.org/docs/resources/publications/Subgroup_Sexual_Exploitation_Semantics.pdf (accessed 30 January 2010).

NGO Group for the Convention on the Rights of the Child (2006) *A Guide for non-governmental organizations reporting to the Committee on the Rights of the Child*, Third edition, Geneva: NGO Group for the Convention on the Rights of the Child http://www.childrightsnet.org/docs/Reporting%20Guide%202006%20English.pdf (accessed 6 June 2013).

Noguchi, Y. (2002) 'ILO Convention No 182 on the worst forms of child labour and the Convention on the Rights of the Child', 10(4) *International Journal of Children's Rights* 355–69.

Noguchi, Y. (2010) '20 years of the Convention on the Rights of the Child and International Action against Child Labour', 18(4) *International Journal of Children's Rights*, 515–34.

Novogrodsky, N.B. (2006) 'Litigating Child Recruitment Before the Special Court for Sierra Leone', 7 *San Diego International Law Journal* 421–26.

Ochaíta, E., Espinosa, A. and Calvo, E. (2000) 'Child Work and Labour in Spain: a First Approach', 8(1) *International Journal of Children's Rights* 15–35.

O'Connell Davidson, J. (2000) Sex Tourism and Child Prostitution in Clift, S. and Carter, S. (eds) *Tourism and Sex Culture, Commerce and Coercion*, London: Continuum Publishing 54–73.

O'Donnell, C. and White, L. (1999) *Hidden Danger: injuries to children at work in Britain*, London: Low Pay Unit.

Oestreich, J.E. (1998) 'UNICEF and the Implementation of the Convention on the Rights of the Child', 4(2) *Global Governance* 183–98.

Office of the High Commissioner for Human Rights (2012) The United Nations Human Rights Treaty System, Fact Sheet No 30/rev1, Office of the High Commissioner for Human Rights, New York/Geneva: OHCHR http://www.ohchr.org/Documents/Publications/FactSheet30Rev1.pdf (accessed 1 March 2013).

Official Solicitor (1997) *The Hague and European Conventions Child Abduction Unit – Operation of Conventions*, Official Solicitor and Public Trustee website www.offsol.demon.co.uk.

OHCHR (1997) *Manual on Human Rights Reporting: under six major international human rights instruments*, Office of the High Commissioner for Human Rights, HR/PUB/91/1

(Rev.1), 1997, Geneva: OHCHR http://www.ohchr.org/Documents/Publications/manualhrren.pdf (accessed 2 August 2013).

Ost, S. (2009) *Child Pornography and Sexual Grooming: Legal and Societal Responses*, Cambridge: Cambridge University Press.

Palmer, T. (2005) 'Behind the Screen: Children who are the Subjects of Abusive Images', in Quayle, E. and Taylor, M. (eds) *Viewing Child Pornography on the Internet*, Lyme Regis: Russell House Publishing 61–74.

Parra-Aranguren, G. (1994) *Explanatory Report on the Convention on Protection of Children and Co-operation in Respect of Intercountry Adoption*, The Hague: HCCH Publications.

Parsons, T. and Bales, R. (1956) *Family: Socialisation and Interaction Processes*, London: Routledge and Kegan Paul.

Paton, J. (2012) 'The Correct Approach to the Examination of the Best Interests of the Child in Abduction Convention Proceedings Following the Decision of the Supreme Court in Re E (Children) (Abduction: Custody Appeal)', 8(3) *Journal of Private International Law* 545–74.

Pearce, J. (2006) 'Finding the "I" in sexual exploitation: hearing the voices of sexually exploited young people in policy and practice', in Campbell, R. and O'Neill, M. (eds) *Sex Work Now*, Cullompton: Willan Publishing 190–211.

Pearce, J., Williams, M. and Galvin, C. (2002) *It's someone taking a part of you: a study of young women and sexual exploitation*, London: National Children's Bureau.

Pearl, D. and Menski, W. (1998) *Muslim Family Law*, Third Edition, London: Sweet & Maxwell.

Pérez-Vera, E. (1980) *Explanatory Report: Hague Convention on International Child Abduction*, The Hague: HCCH Publications.

Peterson, M.J. (2007) 'General Assembly', Chapter 5 in Weiss, T.G. and Daws, S. (eds) (2007) *The Oxford Handbook on the United Nations*, Oxford: Oxford University Press 97–116.

Phoenix, J. (2003) 'Rethinking Youth Prostitution: National Provision at the Margins of Child Protection and Youth Justice', 3(3) *Youth Justice* 152–68.

Phoenix, J. and Oerton, S. (2005) *Illicit and Illegal: sex, regulation, and social control*, Cullompton: Willan Publishing.

Piaget, J. (1952) *The Origins of Intelligence in Children*, New York: The Norton Library, W.W. Norton and Co. Inc.

Piaget, J. (1960) *The Child's Conception of the World*, New Jersey: Littlefield, Adams and Co.

Pollock, L. (1983) *Forgotten Children: Parent – Child Relations from 1500–1900*, Cambridge: Cambridge University Press.

Quigley, J.B. (2002) 'US ratification of the Convention on the Rights of the Child', Justice for Children Project, Moritz College of Law: moritzlaw.osu.edu/jfc/staff/quigleyratification.pdf.

Qvortrup, J., Bardy, M., Sgritta, G. and Wintersberger, H. (1994) *Childhood Matters: Social Theory, Practice and Politics*, Aldershot: Avebury.

Qvortrup, J., Corsaro, W.A. and Honig, M. (eds) (2011) *The Palgrave Handbook of Childhood Studies*, Basingstoke: Palgrave Macmillan.

Ramcharan, B.G. (2007) 'Norms and Machinery', Chapter 25 in Weiss, T.G. and Daws, S. (eds) (2007) *The Oxford Handbook on the United Nations*, Oxford: Oxford University Press 439–62.

Ranton, D. (2009) 'Hague and Non-Hague Convention Abductions: notes for Reunite Website on Hague Convention Law as at 20th October 2009', Reunite website http://www.reunite.org/edit/files/articles/Notes%20on%20Hague%20Convention %20Law.pdf (accessed 25 October 2013).

Raz, J. (1996) 'Liberty and trust', in George, R. (ed) *Natural Law, Liberalism and Morality*, Oxford: Oxford University Press.

Ricanek, K. and Boehnen, C. (2012) 'Facial Analytics: From Big Data to Law Enforcement', 45(9) *Computer* 95–97.

Richards, A. (2013) 'Bombs and Babies: The Intercountry Adoption of Afghanistan's and Iraq's War Orphans', 25(2) *Journal of the American Academy of Matrimonial Lawyers* 399–424.

Riiskjær, M. and Gallagher, A.M. (2008) *Review of the UNHCR's efforts to prevent and respond to human trafficking*, United Nations High Commissioner for Refugees, Policy Development and Evaluation Service, PDES/2008/07, Geneva: UNHCR http://www.unhcr. org/48eb2ff82.html (accessed 15 November 2013).

Rios-Kohn, R. (1998) 'UNICEF's Mission to Protect the Rights of the Child', 4 *Loyola Poverty Law Journal* 185–94.

Roberts, R.C.E. (2012) 'The Lubanga Trial Chamber's Assessment of Evidence in Light of the Accused's Right to the Presumption of Innocence', 10(4) *Journal of International Criminal Justice* 923–44.

Rosenthal, G. (2007) 'Security Council', Chapter 7 in Weiss, T.G. and Daws, S. (eds) (2007) *The Oxford Handbook on the United Nations*, Oxford: Oxford University Press 136–48.

Roth, P. (2010) 'Child Labour in New Zealand: a job for the nanny state?', 12(2) *Otago Law Review* 245–63.

Rutkow, L. and Lozman, J.T. (2006) 'Suffer the Children? A Call for United States Ratification of the United Nations Convention on the Rights of the Child', 19 *Harvard Human Rights Journal* 161–90.

Sachlier C. (1993) 'The Hague Convention on Protection of Children and Co-operation in respect of Intercountry Adoption: a convention in the best interests of the child', Geneva: International Social Service www.iss-ssi.org.

Sargent, S. (2009) 'The Best Interests of the Child in Intercountry Adoption: A Constructivist and Comparative Account', PhD thesis, Leicester De Montfort Law School, De Montfort University, Leicester, United Kingdom https://www.dora.dmu. ac.uk/handle/2086/3535 (accessed 13 November 2013).

Sarkin, J. and Pietschmann, M. (2003) 'Legitimate Humanitarian Intervention under International Law in the Context of the Current Human Rights and Humanitarian Crisis in Burma (Myanmar)', 33(2) *Hong Kong Law Journal* 371–416.

Sarri R, Baik Y. and Bombyk M. (1998) 'Goal displacement and dependency in South Korean – United States intercountry adoption', 20(1) *Children and Youth Services Review* 87–114.

Sawyer, C. (2006) 'The Child is Not a Person: Family Law and Other Legal Cultures', 28(1) *Journal of Social Welfare and Family Law* 1–14.

Schabas, W. (1996) 'Reservations to the Convention on the Rights of the Child', 18(2) *Human Rights Quarterly* 472–91.

Schuz, R. (2001) 'Habitual Residence of Children under the Hague Child Abduction Convention: Theory and Practice', 13(1) *Child and Family Law Quarterly* 1.

Schuz, R. (2001a) "Policy Considerations in Determining the Habitual Residence of a Child and the Relevance of Context" (2001) 11 *Journal of Transnational Law and Policy* 101.

Schuz, R. (2003) 'Returning Abducted Children to Israel and the Intifada' (2003) *Australian Journal of Family Law* 297.

Schuz, R. (2008) 'In Search of a Settled Interpretation of Article 12(2) of the Hague Child Abduction Convention' *Child and Family Law Quarterly* 64–80.

Schuz, R. (2013) *The Hague Child Abduction Convention: A Critical Analysis*, Oxford and Portland, Oregon: Hart Publishing.

Schwebel, S. (1984) 'Authorising the Secretary-General of the United Nations to Request Advisory Opinions', 78(4) *American Journal of International Law* 869–78.

Schwebel, S. (1988) 'Preliminary Rulings by the International Court of Justice at the Instance of National Courts', 28(2) *Virginia Journal of International Law* 495–508.

Scullion, D. (2013) 'Passive victims or empowered actors: Accommodating the needs of child domestic workers' 21(1) *International Journal of Children's Rights* 97–126.

SCWG (2009) *Annual report on the activities of the Security Council Working Group on Children and Armed Conflict* (1 July 2008–30 June 2009), Security Council, S/2009/378 (22 July 2009) http://www.un.org/children/conflict/english/securitycouncilwgroupdoc.html (accessed 7 February 2010).

Selby, J. (2008) 'Ending Abusive and Exploitative Child Labour through International Law and Practical Action', 15 *Australian International Law Journal* 165–80.

Selman, P. (2002) 'Intercountry adoption in the new millennium: the "quiet migration" revisited', 21 *Population Research and Policy Review* 205–25.

Selman, P. (2006) 'Trends in intercountry adoption: analysis of data from 20 receiving countries, 1998–2004', 23(2) *Journal of Population Research* 183–204.

Selman, P. (2011) 'Intercountry Adoption after the Haiti Earthquake: Rescue or Robbery?', 25(4) *Adoption and Fostering* 41–49.

Selman, P. (2012) 'Global Trends in Intercountry Adoption: 2001–2010', 44 *Adoption Advocate* 1–17 https://www.adoptioncouncil.org/images/stories/documents/NCFA_ADOPTION_ADVOCATE_NO44.pdf (accessed 10 November 2013).

Selman, P. (2013) *Key Tables for Intercountry Adoption: Receiving States 2003–2012; States of Origin 2003–2011*, available on request from the author at pfselman@yahoo.co.uk, or on the Hague website at http://www.hcch.net/upload/2013selmanstats33.pdf (accessed 8 November 2013).

Sharma, A. and Viswanathan, H. (2011) 'Extension of the Hague Convention to non-signatory nations: a possible solution to parental child abduction', 4(4) *International Journal of Private Law* 546–59.

Shaw, M. (2008) *International Law*, Sixth Edition, Cambridge: Cambridge University Press.

Silk, J.J. and Makonnen, M. (2003) 'Ending Child Labor: A Role for International Human Rights Law?', 22(2) *Saint Louis University Public Law Review* 359–70.

SIPRI (2013) *SIPRI Yearbook 2013: Armaments, Disarmament and International Security*, Solna, Sweden: Stockholm International Peace Research Institute (SIPRI). Summary of Yearbook http://www.sipri.org/yearbook/2013/files/SIPRIYB13Summary.pdf (accessed 16 November 2013).

Smith, A. (2004) 'Child Recruitment and the Special Court for Sierra Leone', 2 *Journal of International Criminal Justice* 1141–1153.

Smolin, D.M. (2000) 'Strategic choices in the international campaign against child labour', 22(4) *Human Rights Quarterly* 942–87.

Smolin, D.M. (2006) 'Overcoming Religious Objections to the Convention on the Rights of the Child', 20(1) *Emory International Law Review* 81–110.

Smolin, D.M. (2007) 'Child Laundering as Exploitation: Applying Anti-Trafficking Norms to Intercountry Adoption under the Coming Hague Regime', 32(1) *Vermont Law Review* 1–55.

Smolin, D.M. (2010) 'Child Laundering and The Hague Convention on Intercountry Adoption: The Future and Past of Intercountry Adoption', 48 *University of Louisville Law Review* 441–98.

Stalford, H. and Drywood, E. (2009) 'Coming of Age? Children's Rights in the European Union', 46(1) *Common Market Law Review* 143–72.

Steffen, W. (2012) 'Co-perpetration in the Lubanga Trial Judgment', 10(4) *Journal of International Criminal Justice* 971–96.

Steiner, H. (1994) *An Essay on Rights*, Oxford: Blackwell.

Stone, L. (1990) *The Family, Sex and Marriage in England 1500–1800* (abridged edition) London: Penguin.

Sumner, L.W. (1987) *The Moral Foundation of Rights*, Oxford: Clarendon Press.

Sutherland, P. (1992) *Cognitive Development Today: Piaget and his critics*, London: Paul Chapman Publishing.

Svensson, N.L. (2006) 'Extraterritorial Accountability: An Assessment of the Effectiveness of Child Sex Tourism Laws', 28(3) *Loyola of Los Angeles International and Comparative Law Review* 641–64.

Taylor, M. and Quayle, E. (2003) *Child Pornography: An Internet Crime*, London: Routledge.

Tepelus, C.M. (2008) 'Social Responsibility and Innovation on Trafficking and Child Sex Tourism: morphing of practice into sustainable tourism policies?', 8(2) *Tourism and Hospitality Research* 98–115.

Tetteh, P. (2011) 'Child Domestic Labour in (Accra) Ghana: A Child and Gender Rights Issue?', 19(2) *International Journal of Children's Rights* 217–232.

Thomas, N. (2007) 'Towards a Theory of Children's Participation', 15(2) *International Journal of Children's Rights* 199–218.

Thorp, A. (2011) *Parliament's new statutory role in ratifying treaties*, Library Standard Note SN/1A/5855 (8 February 2011) London: House of Commons Library.

Toki, K.R. (2010) 'What a Difference a "Drip" Makes: The Implications of Officially Endorsing the United Nations Declaration on the Rights of Indigenous Peoples', 16 *Auckland University Law Review* 243–71.

Trimmings, K. (2013) *Child Abduction within the European Union*, Oxford and Portland, Oregon: Hart Publishing.

Türkelli G. and Vandenhole, W. (2012) 'The Convention on the Rights of the Child: Repetoires of NGO Participation', 12(1) *Human Rights Law Review* 33–64.

Türkelli, G., Vandenhole, W. and Vandenbogaerde, A. (2013) 'The NGO Impact on Law-Making: the Case of a Complaints Procedure under the ICESCR and the CRC', 5(1) *Journal of Human Rights Practice* 1–45;

UNAIDS (2006) *International Guidelines on HIV/AIDS and Human Rights, Consolidated version 2006*. Geneva: Office of the High Commissioner for Human Rights / Joint United Nations Programme on HIV/AIDS (UNAIDS) org/Publications/IRC-pub07/jc1252-internguidelines_en.pdf (accessed 1 December 2009).

UNCHR (1993) Programme of Action for the Elimination of the Exploitation of Child Labour, E/CN.4/RES/1993/79, Geneva: Office of the United Nationas High Commissioner for Human Rights.

Unger, J. (1965) 'Hague Conference on Private International Law: Draft Convention on Adoptions', 28(4) *Modern Law Review* 463–65.

UNICEF (1997) *State of the World's Children 1997*, New York/Oxford: OUP/United Nations Children's Fund.

UNICEF (2009) *Handbook on the Optional Protocol on the Sale of Children, Child Prostitution and Child Pornography*, Innocenti Research Centre, Florence: UNICEF http://www.unicef-irc.org/publications/pdf/optional_protocol_eng.pdf (accessed 27 January 2010).

UNICEF (2010) *Core Commitments for Children in Humanitarian Action*, New York: United Nations Children's Fund http://www.unicef.org/publications/files/CCC_042010.pdf (accessed 25 February 2013).

UNICEF (2012) *State of the World's Children 2012: children in an urban world*, New York: United Nations Children's Fund.

UNICEF (2013) *State of the World's Children 2013: children with disabilities*, New York: United Nations Children's Fund.

Van Bueren, G. (1994) *The International Law on the Rights of the Child*, Dordrecht/ Boston/ London: Martinus Nijhoff Publishers.

Van Bueren, G. (1994a) 'Child sexual abuse and exploitation: A suggested human rights approach', 2(1) *International Journal of Children's Rights* 45–59.

Van Bueren, G. (1998) *The International Law on the Rights of the Child*, The Hague: Martinus Njjhoff / Kluwer Law International.

Van Loon, H. (1995) 'Hague Convention of 29 May 1993 on Protection of Children and Co-operation in Respect of Intercountry Adoption', 3 *International Journal of Children's Rights* 463–68.

Van Loon, H. (2000) 'Globalisation and The Hague Conference on Private International Law', 2(4) *International Law FORUM Du Droit International* 230–34.

Van Loon, H. (2011) 'Legal Diversity in a Flat, Crowded World: The Role of the Hague Conference', 39(2) *International Journal of Legal Information* 172–85.

Vesneski, W., Lindhorst, T. and Edleson, J. (2011) 'Judicial Implementation of the Hague Convention in Cases Alleging Domestic Violence' 62(2) *Juvenile and Family Court Journal* 1–21.

Vigers, S. (2011) *Mediating International Child Abduction Cases: The Hague Convention*, Oxford and Portland, Oregon: Hart Publishing.

Vrancken, P. and Chetly, K. (2009) 'International Child Sex Tourism: A South African Perspective', 53 *Journal of African Law* 111–41.

Vygotsky, L. (1962) *Thought and Language*, edited and translated by Eugenia Hanfmann and Gertrude Vakar, Cambridge, MA: MIT Press; 1975 reprint (original Russian edition, 1934).

Walker, L. (2010) 'The Impact of the Hague Abduction Convention on the Rights of the Family in the Case-law of the European Court of Human Rights and the UN Human Rights Committee: The Danger of Neulinger', 6(3) *Journal of Private International Law* 649–82.

Walker, L. and Beaumont, P. (2011) 'Shifting the Balance Achieved by the Abduction Convention: The Contrasting Approaches of the European Court of Human Rights and the European Court of Justice', 7(2) *Journal of Private International Law* 231–49.

Ward, R. and Akhtar, A. (2011) *Walker and Walker's English Legal System*, Eleventh Edition, Oxford: Oxford University Press.

Watkins, D. (2012) 'Intercountry Adoption and the Hague Convention: Article 22 and Limitations upon Safeguarding', 24(4) *Child and Family Law Quarterly* 389–409.

Weiner, M. (1994) 'Child labour in developing countries: The Indian case. Articles 18a, 32 and 36 of the UN Convention on the Rights of the Child', 2(2) *International Journal of Child Rights* 121–28.

Weiss, T.G. and Daws, S. (eds) (2007) *The Oxford Handbook on the United Nations*, Oxford: Oxford University Press.

Wellman, C. (1999) *The Proliferation of Rights: Moral Progress or Empty Rhetoric?* USA: Westview Press.

Westlake, B., Bouchard, M. and Frank, R. (2012) 'Comparing methods for detecting child exploitation content online', European Intelligence and Security Informatics Conference 156–63.

Wilde, R. (2007) 'Trusteeship Council', Chapter 8 in Weiss, T.G. and Daws, S. (eds) (2007) *The Oxford Handbook on the United Nations*, Oxford: Oxford University Press, 149–59.

Wyness, M.G. (2012) *Childhood and Society*, Second Edition, Basingstoke: Palgrave Macmillan.

Yupsanis, A. (2012) 'ILO Convention No 169 Concerning Indigenous and Tribal Peoples in Independent Countries 1989–2009: An Overview', 79 *Nordic Journal of International Law* 433–56.

Index

Note: Page numbers followed by n denote footnotes.

abduction: by parents *see* abduction,
     international parental child; exploitation
     of children 216–17, 278, 365; inter-
     country adoption: safeguards to protect
     children from abduction, sale and
     trafficking 339–42
abduction, international parental child
     40, 274–6, 320; best interests of child
     280, 284, 304, 305, 316–17, 320;
     Convention on the Rights of the
     Child 275, 277, 278–9, 315, 320, 365;
     European Convention 1980 279–80;
     Hague Convention on the Civil Aspects
     of International Child Abduction 1980
     see separate entry; mediation 318–20;
     motivation 277; non-Convention
     countries 314–17, 320; Revised Brussels
     II Regulation 2003 280–3, 307–8, 309,
     318; soft law 317, 320; statistics on
     276–7, 297–8, 303
abortion 133, 143, 195
abuse and exploitation 353–4; *see also*
     exploitation
adolescent health 194–6, 433
adoption: best interests of child 137,
     166, 172–3, 321–2, 326, 328, 331,
     332, 335–9, 343, 346; customary
     174; inter-country *see separate entry*;
     right to know biological parents 154,
     156
Afghanistan 74, 323
Africa 234, 238, 258, 352; African Charter
     on the Rights of the Child 38, 359, 385,
     394; Sub-Saharan 190, 234, 235; *see also*
     individual countries
AIDS *see* HIV/AIDS

Albania 121, 122, 125, 164, 169;
     adoption 174; birth registration 153;
     disability 169, 187, 189, 198; economic
     exploitation 213; education 201;
     health 192, 197; institutional care 172;
     juvenile justice 223; minority groups
     211; poverty 198; refugees 207; sexual
     exploitation 181, 218; street children
     218; views of child 148, 149; violence
     against children 145, 177, 180
Algeria 90, 160
Andorra 119, 121, 122, 128, 134; adoption
     175; age of criminal responsibility 225;
     economic exploitation 213–14; inter-
     country adoption 325; privacy 162;
     refugees 208
apprenticeships 244
arbitration 51
Archard, D. 3–5, 23, 25, 30
Argentina 90, 130, 155
Ariès, P. 2, 3, 5
armed conflict and children 384–5;
     CRC: article 38 90, 110, 219–21, 253,
     393–5; CRC: article 39 183–4, 219,
     221, 395–6; CRC: OPAC 107, 110–12,
     385, 397–404; customary international
     law 415–16; ILO Worst Forms of
     Child Labour Convention 1999
     252–3, 396–7; International Criminal
     Court (ICC) 74, 397–8, 412, 416–24;
     International Criminal Tribunal for
     the former Yugoslavia (ICTY) 412–13;
     International Criminal Tribunal for
     Rwanda (ICTR) 413–14; international
     humanitarian law 385–93, 394; (non-
     state) armed militias: age threshold 399;

armed conflict and children (*cont.*)
Paris Principles 407–8; Security Council resolutions 404–7; sexual exploitation 357; Special Court for Sierra Leone (SCSL) 415–16, 417–18; Special Representative of Secretary-General 405, 409–12; UNICEF 67, 395, 411; war crimes 110, 220–1, 357, 410, 416–24
Armenia 133, 169, 171, 175, 180, 183; disability 190; economic exploitation 214; health 193, 194; juvenile justice 225; social security 199
Asia 340; South Asia 190, 263, 359; *see also individual countries*
association, freedom of 156–7, 158, 159, 160–1, 261, 262
asylum-seeking and refugee children 134, 205, 206–9
Australia 111, 161, 164–5, 376, 437; inter-country adoption 321–2; international parental child abduction 310, 311
Austria 118, 119, 121, 124, 134, 148–9; abandonment 156; abduction, international parental child 302; adoption 174; armed conflict and children 220; disability 187, 189, 190; economic exploitation 214; education 201; health 192, 195; inter-country adoption 327; juvenile justice 223; privacy 162; prostitution 217; refugees 209; sexual exploitation 182, 183; statistical data 123, 171
Azerbaijan 164

Bangladesh 232, 237, 238, 271
Beijing Rules 129, 222
Belgium 159
best interests of child 29–30, 31, 137–42, 165, 373, 394; abduction, international parental child 280, 284, 304, 305, 316–17, 320; adoption 137, 166, 172–3, 321–2, 326, 328, 331, 332, 335–9, 343, 346; child soldiers 412; children with disabilities 189, 190; communications procedure (CRC) 113; criminal justice system 109, 373, 433; indigenous children 433, 434
bilateral trade agreements 272
biological parents, child's right to know 154, 156

birth registration: armed forces 402; child labour 247, 252; CRC : identity rights and 150–6, 159; indigenous children 153, 433
Bosnia and Herzegovina 126, 141, 149, 169, 170; adoption 173, 174; birth registration 152, 153; disability 187, 188, 189–90; discrimination 134, 137; economic exploitation 213; education 201, 202, 203; health 192, 193, 195; juvenile justice 224; privacy 162; refugees 208; social security 199; trafficking of children 217
Bouhdiba, Abdelwahab 240
Brazil 231
breastfeeding 193–4
business sector 125–6, 194, 270, 271–2; action to combat sexual exploitation 361–3, 366, 382; corporate codes 269, 270; corporate responsibility 126, 362–3; industry codes 362–3

Cambodia 352, 382
Canada 120, 123, 135, 169, 171, 437; abduction, international parental child 283–4, 308–9; aboriginal children 135, 177, 182, 192, 211, 220, 443–6, 443–7; adoption 175; armed conflict and children 111, 220; armed forces: minimum age 111; best interests principle 141; birth registration 152; child labour 214–15; citizenship 156; disability 189; education 201; federal systems 119; health 192, 194; inter-country adoption 325; juvenile justice 223, 224–5; mature minor doctrine 28; medical treatment and child's best interests 28–30; refugees 207; sexual exploitation 182, 183, 225, 376; trafficking of children 217; views of child 149; violence against children 177, 182, 183
Cantwell, N. 37, 90, 126, 158, 159, 173, 219, 347–8
Caribbean 234
Chad 132, 352
child labour 18, 227, 240–2; agriculture 213, 214, 217, 228, 233, 236, 237, 245, 253, 266, 272–3; apprenticeships 244; case study 272–3; causes of 231–4, 251; consumer boycotts 271; Convention on the Rights of the Child 212–15, 229,

241, 249; covert nature of 238; cultural relativism and 237–8, 268–9; definition difficulties 227–31; developed countries 236–8, 239, 248, 268, 270–1; education and 231, 232–3, 234, 237, 240, 243, 244, 255–6, 271; 'employment' and 'work' 229, 242–3, 253; enforceability problem 268–9; extent and location of exploitative 234–7; hazardous work 213, 230, 232, 235–6, 242, 246–7, 252, 253, 254, 255; ILO Domestic Workers Convention 2011 257–8; ILO Minimum Age Convention 1973 241, 242–8, 250, 253, 258; ILO reporting, representation and complaints procedures 263–7; ILO Worst Forms of Child Labour Convention 1999 230, 241, 248, 250–7, 258, 365–6, 396–7; ILO's wider role 260–3; informal economy 227, 228, 236, 238, 253; intermittent 231; labelling 271; light work 244–6; measuring extent of 238–40; other international instruments 22–3, 258–60; partnership and coordination 269–70; poverty and 231–2, 233–4, 251; progressing elimination of exploitative 267–72; refugee children 207; rehabilitation and reintegration 251, 256, 271; role of law 268; trade–labour linkage 249, 270–2; 'work' and 'employment' 229, 242–3, 253
child liberationists 33–4
Child Rights Connect 100
child-rearing practices 2–3, 5
child-rights impact assessment (CRIA) 140, 142
childhood 1; active social agent 13, 14, 16; armed conflict and children 220; behaviourist understanding of 10; boundaries, dimensions and divisions 3–4, 6; constructivist model 9, 10–12; cultural relativism 6, 37–9, 237–8, 268–9; deterministic model 9–10; historical perspective 2–6; inequality 10, 13, 17, 231; peer cultures 13; Piaget's stages 7–9, 10–11; psychological perspective 4, 6–9, 10; social policy perspectives 14–18; sociological perspective 9–14; state–family relationship 15–17, 34–5, 38; welfare approach 16

children's rights 21–3; autonomy 9, 13, 14, 16, 25–6, 27–33, 34, 308; basic interests 25, 26; best interests standard 29–30, 31; cultural relativism 6, 37–9, 237–8, 268–9; developmental interests 25, 26; international 35–6; ladder of participation 32–3; movement for 33–5, 91; participation rights 30–1, 32–3; paternalism 22, 31; theories of 23–6
China 73, 127, 143, 233, 400–4; inter-country adoption 323, 325, 326, 352
choice/will theory of rights 24, 25, 26
Clinton, Bill 92
Committee on the Rights of the Child 17–18, 32, 36, 95–7, 377; child labour 249, 250, 260; cultural sensitivity 38–9; delays 104–6, 378; reporting process 98–106, 378; reservations to treaty 46
companies see business sector
complaints procedures (ILO) 265–7
complaints/communication procedure (CRC) 36, 104, 106, 112–14; individual communications 114–15, 184; inquiry procedure 115–16; inter-state communications 116–17
Congo, Democratic Republic of 74, 197, 417–24
Congo, Republic of 145
conscience, religion and thought, freedom of 90, 156–7, 158–60
constructivist model 9, 10–12
Convention on the Rights of the Child 20, 21, 22, 23, 35–6, 42, 49, 87–9, 241, 248; abduction (article 35) 216–17, 278, 365; abduction by parent (articles 9–11) 275, 277, 278–9, 315; adoption (article 21) 90, 166, 172–5, 328, 335; armed conflict, participation in (article 38) 90, 110, 219–21, 253, 393–5; association, freedom of (article 15) 156–7, 158, 159, 160–1; background 89–91; best interests principle (article 3) 30, 137–42, 166, 394, 434; birth registration and identity rights (articles 7 and 8) 150–6, 159; civil rights and freedoms (articles 7, 8, 13–17, 28(2) and 37(a)) 150–65; cultural differences 6, 37–9; declarations 46, 143, 159, 211, 394; definition of child (article 1) 6, 90, 94, 126–30; disability (article 23) 184, 186–90; drafting controversies 90, 158, 173, 219; drugs (article 33) 185, 195,

Convention on the Rights of the Child
  (*cont.*)
  215; economic exploitation (article 32)
  212–15, 229, 249; education, right to
  (articles 28 and 29) 159, 199–203,
  232–3, 431–2; exploitation situations
  (articles 32–36) 181–3, 205, 212–18,
  229, 249, 353, 364–5, 372; express
  views and participate in decisions
  (article 12) 146–50, 282; expression,
  freedom of (article 13) 156–8, 159;
  family environment and alternative
  care 159, 165–75; general measures
  of implementation 118–26; general
  principles (articles 2, 3, 6 and 12)
  131–50; Hague Conventions and 72,
  327–8; health and access to health
  services (article 24) 36, 185, 190–7;
  heard, child's right to be (article 12)
  30, 32; history 89–91; implementation
  117–226; information, access to
  (article 17) 156–7, 158, 163–4, 431;
  international customary law and 49;
  jus cogens 35, 52; juvenile justice 93,
  163, 164–5, 180, 205, 221–6; leisure
  and cultural activities (article 31) 199,
  203–5; life, survival and development
  (article 6) 36, 93, 142–6, 434; minority
  or indigenous group (article 30) 159,
  210–12, 430–1; non-discrimination
  principle (article 2) 131–7, 188, 211,
  434; parental responsibilities, rights and
  duties (articles 5 and 14) 30, 157, 159,
  169; parents, common responsibilities of
  both (article 18(1)) 169; parents, contact
  with both (article 9) 277, 278, 279;
  parents and living conditions (article
  27(2)) 197; participation rights (article
  12) 146–50, 282; privacy (article 16)
  156–7, 159, 161–3, 164–5; ratification
  43, 87; recovery and reintegration of
  child victims (article 39) 183–4, 219,
  221, 251, 256, 395–6; refugee children
  (article 22) 205, 206–9; reporting
  process 98–106, 378; reservations 46,
  120, 143, 154, 156, 159, 164, 211,
  328, 394; sale or trafficking of children
  (article 35) 216–17, 218, 364, 365;
  sexual exploitation and abuse (article
  34) 181–3, 353, 364–5, 372; social
  exploitation (article 36) 218; social
  security (article 26) 185, 199; Somalia
  not ratifying 91–2; South Sudan,
  Republic of 91, 92; special protection
  measures 205–26; standard of living
  (article 27) 35–6, 185, 197–8; street
  children 218–19; thought, conscience
  and religion, freedom of (article 14)
  90, 156–7, 158–60; torture or other
  punishment (article 37(a)) 177–81, 223;
  understandings 211; United Kingdom
  54–5, 120, 125, 129–30; United States
  not ratifying 91, 92–5; victims as
  criminals 373; violence against children
  (articles 19, 37(a), 34 and 39) 175–84;
  violence, freedom from all forms of
  (article 19) 166, 175–7, 179
Convention on the Rights of the
  Child: Optional Protocols 94, 107,
  137; children and armed conflict
  (OPAC) 107, 110–12, 385, 397–404;
  communication procedure (OPIC) 36,
  104, 106, 112–17, 184; reporting regime
  37, 102–4, 105, 107, 109, 112, 378; sale
  of children, child prostitution and child
  pornography (OPSC) 107, 108–9, 184,
  216, 275, 366–77, 378
Cook Islands 164
Cooper, J. 232, 270, 271
corporal punishment 178–80, 181
corporate: codes 269, 270; responsibility
  126, 362–3; *see also* business sector
Corsaro, W. 9, 11, 12, 13
Council of Europe 14, 360, 367
Creighton, B. 243, 247–8, 249, 260
criminal law/justice system 93, 108,
  109, 135, 205, 221–6; abduction 274,
  275; abortion 195; age of criminal
  responsibility 128–30, 225; armed
  conflict and children 399; assembly,
  freedom of 161; child labour 242, 251,
  255, 366, 397; demonstrations 161;
  double jeopardy 373–4; extradition 42,
  108, 374–5; grooming 372; ill treatment
  or torture 180–1; indigenous peoples
  135, 433, 445; international cooperation
  and support 376–7, 381–2; irregular
  migration situations 207–8; jurisdiction,
  establishing 373–5; pornography, child
  368, 370–1; privacy 162–3, 164–5, 377;
  prostitution 217, 364, 369–70; sexual
  exploitation 181–2, 183, 361, 364,
  368–73, 380–3; street children 218;
  trafficking of children 217, 369; victims,

assisting 376–7; victims as criminals 372–3; victims and witnesses, protection of 225–6
cultural activities and leisure 199, 203–5
cultural relativism 6, 37–9; child labour and 237–8, 268–9
Cunningham, H. 5, 34
customary international law 20, 42, 43, 46–9, 51–2, 54, 75, 94; armed conflict and children 386, 394, 415–16; beginning of childhood 130; indigenous peoples 438
customary law: domestic 119, 145, 169; indigenous peoples 436; international *see* customary international law

databases 163, 217; International Child Abduction (INCADAT) 286, 292
debt bondage 252, 253, 258
Declaration of the Rights of the Child 1959 22, 89, 137, 259
Declaration on the Rights of Indigenous Peoples 2007 437–40, 448
DeMause, L. 3, 5
Denmark 280, 307
Dennis, M.J. 253, 256, 257
deterministic model 9–10
Detrick, S. 87, 89, 117, 132, 138, 150, 155, 157, 164, 203, 210, 216, 249, 278, 328, 329
disability 146, 169, 171, 177, 184, 186–90; discrimination 135–6; poverty 198
disappearance, enforced 155
domestic courts 51, 53, 54, 55; United States 93, 94
domestic violence 307
double jeopardy 373–4
drugs 185, 195, 215
dual criminality 374, 381
dualist doctrine 53, 54

economic exploitation 212–15, 229, 249, 440; child labour *see separate entry*
ECPAT (Ending Child Prostitution and Trafficking) 356, 380
education 392, 403–4; child labour and 231, 232–3, 234, 237, 240, 243, 244, 255–6, 271; children with disabilities 189; indigenous children 431–2, 433, 436, 439–40, 444–5; right to 23, 140, 159, 199–203, 232–3, 431–2
Eekelaar, J. 25–6

Egypt 317
El Salvador 155
Erikson, E.H. 6, 8
Ethiopia 321, 325
Europe 322, 325, 360, 363; child labour 237, 239, 240; *see also individual countries*
European Convention on Recognition and Enforcement of Decisions Concerning Custody of Children and on Restoration of Custody of Children 1980 279–80
European Court of Human Rights (ECtHR) 279, 289, 303–5
European Union (EU) 14–15; abduction, international parental child 280–3, 288, 289, 305, 307–8, 309, 318; Charter of Fundamental Rights 282; Revised Brussels II Regulation 2003 280–3, 307–8, 309, 318; sexual exploitation 360–1
Europol 361
exploitation: abuse and 353–4; economic *see separate entry*; sale and trafficking *see separate entry*; sexual *see separate entry*; social 218
expression, freedom of 36, 156–8, 159, 261
extradition 108, 374–5; treaty-contract 42
extraterritoriality 373–4, 380–2

family environment and alternative care (CRC) 159, 165–75
federal systems 93, 119, 121, 127
female genital mutilation (FGM) 134, 183, 430–1
finance industry 363
foetus 94, 130
Food and Agriculture Organization (FAO) 270
forced labour 69, 180, 213, 217, 255, 258, 262, 266, 273
Fortin, J. 23, 24, 26, 31, 34, 35
France 18, 111, 120, 137, 141, 143; corporal punishment 179; inter-country adoption 323, 326; minority or indigenous groups 211; secular public education 159–60
Freud, S. 6, 8

G8 356–7, 359
gender 108, 408; abduction, international parental child 283; child labour 229, 232, 238, 258; discrimination 133–4

genocide 413–14
Germany 111, 127, 359
Ghana 232
good faith 43, 50, 91
Google 361
grooming 372
guardianship 51, 63–5; unaccompanied
  refugees 209
Guatemala 325, 347, 352
Guinea 74, 119, 145, 148, 153, 169; armed
  conflict and children 220; disability
  189; discrimination 134; economic
  exploitation 214; education 201; health
  191, 195; juvenile justice 224; marriage,
  age of 128; poverty 198; refugees 203;
  sexual exploitation 182, 183; violence
  against children 177, 182, 183
Guinea-Bissau 134, 145–6, 148, 152, 156;
  disability 188; economic exploitation
  215; health 191, 197, 198; juvenile
  justice 223; *meninos de criação* 215; sexual
  exploitation 183, 217; standard of living
  198; trafficking of children 217
Guyana 134, 148, 151–2, 170, 171;
  adoption 173; child labour 213;
  disability 189; education 201; health
  195, 196; juvenile justice 226; poverty
  198; sexual exploitation 182

Haanappel, P.P.C. 47
Hague Conference on Private
  International Law 40, 70–2, 284, 320,
  332; International Centre for Judicial
  Studies and Technical Assistance
  346–52; Special Commissions 71–2,
  320, 327, 328–9, 330–1, 333–5, 341
Hague Convention on the Civil Aspects
  of International Child Abduction 1980
  44, 46, 72, 275, 278, 279, 320, 327;
  acquiescence 302–3; age limit 284;
  agreement/amicable resolution 318;
  approach to Article 13 exceptions/
  defences 299–301; Article 15
  declaration 290–1; Article 20 discretion
  to refuse return 309–11, 320; breach of
  custody rights 280; case studies 292–5,
  305–7, 312–14; child's objections
  308–9, 312–14; consent exception 302;
  custody rights 287–8, 301–2; domestic
  violence 307; duty to make return order
  296–8; European Convention 1980
  and 280; exceptions from duty to make

return order 298–311, 320; exercising
  discretion 311–14; explanatory report
  284–5; failure to exercise custody rights
  301–2; grave risk of harm/intolerable
  situation 303–8, 314; habitual residence
  291–6; non-Convention countries
  314–17, 320; *patria potestas* doctrine
  288; Revised Brussels II Regulation and
  280–3, 307–8, 309; settlement exception
  298–9, 309, 320; structure of 285–6;
  time limits 284, 285, 297; wrongful
  removal or retention 286–96
Haiti 323, 352
Harding, Fox 15
Harris-Short, S. 6, 37
Hart, R.A. 32–3
Havana Rules 222
health and access to health services 23, 36,
  140, 185, 190–7, 231, 433; indigenous
  peoples 433, 436, 439
historical perspective on childhood 2–6
HIV/AIDS 127, 128, 136, 144, 167, 169,
  195, 395, 410; prevalence of 196–7;
  trafficking and prostitution 355
Holy See 159
honour killings 145
human rights and children's rights 18–21
human rights education 203
human rights global protection: UN
  machinery 74–86

identity rights and birth registration 150–6,
  159
India 73, 127, 352; abduction,
  international parental child 314; armed
  forces: minimum age 111; child labour
  233, 234, 241, 271
indigenous children 135, 425–7, 448; birth
  registration 153, 433; Canada 135,
  177, 182, 192, 211, 220, 443–6, 443–7;
  Committee against Torture 429–30;
  Convention on the Rights of the Child
  210–12, 430–5, 448; education 431–2,
  433, 436, 439–40, 444–5; ICCPR
  427–8, 430; ICESCR 428–9, 439;
  ILO Indigenous and Tribal Peoples
  Convention 1989 431, 435–7, 448; non-
  discrimination 429, 433, 434, 436, 437,
  439; self-determination and indigenous
  peoples 427, 428, 436, 437, 438–9, 448;
  UN Declaration 2007 437–40, 448; UN
  mechanisms 440–7, 448

industry *see* business sector
inequality 10, 13, 17, 231
information, access to 156–7, 158, 163–4, 431
inter-country adoption 40, 175, 321–3, 352; accreditation 341–2, 344, 345, 346; automatic recognition of adoption decisions 343–4; best interests of child 137, 166, 172–3, 321–2, 326, 328, 331, 332, 335–9, 343, 346; case study 347–52; competent authorities, central authorities and accredited bodies 344–6; cooperation between and within states 342–3; costs and expenses only 328, 340–1; disaster situations 323, 330–1, 332; Hague Convention 1965 326–7; Hague Convention 1993 42–3, 44–6, 72, 137, 173–4, 322, 328–31, 333–46; safeguards to prevent abduction, sale and trafficking 339–42; sending and receiving countries 326; statistics 323–5; subsidiarity principle 172, 328, 339; UNICEF's position 331–2
interest theory of rights 24–6
International Bureau of Children's Rights 109
International Committee of the Red Cross (ICRC) 332, 387, 389, 390
International Confederation of Free Trade Unions 260, 271
International Court of Justice (ICJ) 60, 62–6, 266
International Criminal Court (ICC) 72–4, 110, 219, 397–8; *Lubanga* case 74, 417–24
International Criminal Tribunal for the former Yugoslavia (ICTY) 412–13
International Criminal Tribunal for Rwanda (ICTR) 413–14
International Labour Organization (ILO) 44, 61, 69–70, 212, 228, 232, 241–2; constitution 237, 263; Declaration concerning aims and purposes 1944 261; Declaration on Fundamental Principles and Rights at Work 1998 250, 251, 262, 264; definitions 229–30; Domestic Workers Convention 2011 257–8; Indigenous and Tribal Peoples Convention 1989 431, 435–7, 448; measuring extent of child labour 239–40; Minimum Age Convention 1973 241, 242–8, 250, 253, 258;

reporting, representation and complaints procedures 263–7; soft law 250, 261, 262, 270; statistical data requirement 239; trade–labour linkage 271–2; tripartism 69, 260, 264, 272; wider role of 260–3; Worst Forms of Child Labour Convention 1999 230, 241, 248, 250–7, 258, 365–6, 396–7
international law 40, 268, 279; commencement dates of treaties 42–3; customary *see separate entry*; declarations 38, 45, 46; domestic law and 48, 53–5, 120, 156; dualist doctrine 53, 54; general principles 49–50, 51; good faith 43, 50, 91; hierarchy of sources 51–2; humanitarian law 385–93, 394; incorporation doctrine 48, 53–4; judicial decisions 50–1; *jus cogens* 35, 51–2, 142; labour law 270; monist doctrine 53–4; preparatory works (*travaux préparatoires*) 44–5; publicists' writings 50, 51; reservations 38, 45–6; signature to a treaty 43; soft law 52–3, 68; sources of 41–53, 95; transformation doctrine 53; treaties and conventions 41–6, 49, 51–2; treaty interpretation 43–5
International Law Commission (ILC) 48, 67–8
international parental child abduction *see* abduction
international relations 45, 48
international trade and labour standards 249, 270–2
Interpol 376, 382
Iraq 323
Ireland 288, 302, 310–11
Islamic countries: adoption 328; international parental child abduction 314, 315–17
Islamic law 158, 166, 173
Israel 111, 122, 127, 133, 141, 142, 144–5; adoption 156; armed conflict and children 220; arrest and detention 223–4; disability 189; education 202; family reunification 170; foster care 171; health 193, 196; poverty 198; refugees 208; torture and ill treatment 180–1; unregistered Palestinian children 153–4; water 198
Italy 127, 323, 376

James, A. 13
Japan 233, 241, 322
jurisdiction 373–5, 380–1
jus cogens 35, 51–2, 142

kafalah 166
Kazakhstan 347–52
Khadr, Omar 220–1
King, M. 14
Korea, Republic of 157, 160, 233, 322–3, 326
Kyrgyzstan 128

Latin America 234, 340, 352, 435
League of Nations 21–2, 60, 69, 89
leisure and cultural activities 199, 203–5
Lesotho 238
liberationists, child 33–4
Liberia 119, 122, 128, 132, 136, 145, 148; adoption 175, 352; armed conflict and children 220; best interests principle 141–2; birth registration 152; child labour 214; disability 187, 189; education 201, 202; health 191, 197; juvenile justice 223, 225; poverty 198; refugees 208; sexual exploitation 182, 183; street children 218; trafficking of children 217; violence against children 177, 181, 182, 183
liberty rights 25
life, survival and development 36, 93, 142–6, 434
Locke, John 18
Lubanga Dyilo, Thomas 74, 417–24
Luxembourg 143, 154

Machel Report (1996) 397, 409
Madagascar 158
mainstreaming 76, 120, 242, 251, 262, 385; gender 283
maintenance, recovery of 170
Malawi 155, 321
Malta 126, 127, 128, 133; economic exploitation 214; health 192–3, 195; juvenile justice 224, 225; refugees 207–8; sexual exploitation 182
manifesto rights 35
maternity leave 194
Mauritania 132
maximum extent of available resources 118, 121–2
Mayall, B. 13

mediation 318–20
meninos de criação 215
Mexico 382–3
Microsoft 361
Middle East and North African region (MENA) 234; *see also individual countries*
Millennium Development Goals (MDGs) 17, 57, 91, 190–1, 198, 199; education 232–3; indigenous children 435
minimalist state intervention 34–5
minority groups 159, 210–12; birth registration 153; *see also* indigenous children
monist doctrine 53–4
Moravcsik, A. 47
mortality, child 145, 190–1, 434
mui tsai 258–9
Myanmar 158, 160, 161, 164, 266

name, right to a 22, 154, 155–6
Namibia 124, 145, 168; adoption 173–4, 175; birth registration 153; child labour 214; definition of child 126–7; disability 188; education 202; health 193, 194, 197; indigenous children 135; juvenile justice 224, 225–6; mining and uranium-production 125–6; sexual exploitation 182, 183; street children 219; trafficking of children 217
national courts 51, 53, 54, 55; United States 93, 94
national human rights institutions (NHRIs) 76, 84, 97, 101, 124, 401, 440
national systems of labour inspection 268
nationality 22, 151, 154, 155–6
natural law 18
Nepal 347, 352
Netherlands 159
New Zealand 111, 248, 437; inter-country adoption 321–2; international parental child abduction 288, 292–5
Niger 220
Niue 125, 128, 132, 154, 169; adoption 174; best interests principle 142; corporal punishment 180; disability 187; education 202; health 191, 194; juvenile justice 225; sexual exploitation 181–2
Noguchi, Y. 231, 233, 249, 250, 251, 253, 257, 263, 266–7
non-discrimination 22, 131–7, 169, 188, 211, 262; health status 196–7;

indigenous peoples 429, 433, 434, 436, 437, 439
non-governmental organisations (NGOs) 18, 23, 76, 87, 101; advocacy campaigns 124–5; armed conflict and children 405; care institutions 171; child labour 239, 257, 260–1, 269, 272, 366; communications procedure 112–13; CRC: OPSC 109; CRC, drafting of 90; 'Day of General Discussion' 97; disappearance of children 155; education 203; inter-country adoption 332; juvenile justice 226; monitoring role 100; non-directive support 123; sexual exploitation 356, 380; Somalia 92
North America: Financial Coalition against Child Pornography 363; see also individual countries
North Korea 74, 233
Norway 127

Obama, Barack 94
obesity 192, 195
Occupied Palestinian Territory (OPT) 127, 144–5, 153–4, 170; arrest and detention 223–4; education 202; health 193; poverty 198; torture and ill-treatment 180–1
Ochaíta, E. 228–9
Ombudsman/person 124, 213

pacta sunt servanda 43, 50
Pakistan 134, 160, 238, 272, 317
parents: abduction, international parental child see separate entry; common responsibilities of both (CRC, article 18(1)) 169; contact with both (CRC, article 9) 277, 278, 279; and living conditions (CRC, article 27(2)) 197; parental responsibilities, rights and duties (CRC, articles 5 and 14) 30, 157, 159, 169
Paris Principles 407–8
Parsons, Talcott 10
participation rights 30–1, 32–3, 94, 146–50, 241, 282, 309, 435
paternalism 22, 31
peremptory norms/jus cogens 35, 51–2, 142
Philippines 238
Piaget, J. 7–9, 10–11
Pinheiro, Paulo Sergio 176

Poland 89, 325
political prisoners 158
Pollock, L. 5
pornography, child 353–4, 355, 356–7, 360, 361, 363, 366, 367, 370–1
Portugal 238
poverty 62, 198, 212, 231–2, 233–4, 251, 261; child sex tourism 363, 383; crisis situations due to 169; indigenous children 434, 444
precedent 50–1, 54
prisoners, political 158
privacy 156–7, 159, 161–3, 164–5, 377; private and family life (ECHR, art 8) 16
private international law 67; Hague Conference on see separate entry
prostitution 217, 354, 355, 359, 364–5, 366, 367–8, 369–70
protectionism 270–1
psychological perspective on childhood 4, 6–9, 10

racial discrimination 134
Raz, J. 31
refugee children 134, 205, 206–9
rehabilitation and reintegration of child victims 183–4, 219, 221, 395–6, 399; child labour 251, 256, 271
religion, thought and conscience, freedom of 90, 156–7, 158–60
reporting process: CRC 98–106, 378; CRC: Optional Protocols 37, 102–4, 105, 107, 109, 112, 378; ILO 263–5
Republika Srpska 174
risk aversion 34
ritual killing 145–6
Riyadh Guidelines 222
Roma children 133, 153, 193, 198, 202, 208, 211–12, 213, 217
Roman law 4
Romania 323, 326, 340
Russia 47, 73, 325, 359; see also Soviet Union, former
Rwanda 123, 133, 149, 167–8, 169, 171; birth registration 152, 153; corporal punishment 180; disability 188, 190; education 202; International Criminal Tribunal for (ICTR) 413–14; juvenile justice 225; minority and indigenous children 212; poverty 198; sexual exploitation 183

sale and trafficking of children 252,
355; CRC 216–17, 218, 364, 365;
CRC: OPSC 367, 369; inter-country
adoption 328, 339–42, 346, 352; power
imbalance 354; regional instruments
359, 360
Samoa 352
Sawyer, C. 26
self-determination and indigenous peoples
427, 428, 436, 437, 438–9, 448
Senegal 90
sexual exploitation 126, 196, 217, 228,
353; abuse and exploitation 353–4;
armed conflict 357; CRC: article 34
181–3, 353, 364–5, 372; CRC: article
35 216–17, 218, 364, 365; CRC:
Optional Protocol 107, 108–9, 184, 216,
275, 366–77, 378; criminalisation
368–73; ECPAT (Ending Child
Prostitution and Trafficking) 356, 380;
G8 356–7, 359; grooming 368, 372;
ILO Worst Forms of Child Labour
Convention 1999 365–6; industry
361–3, 366, 382; international
customary law 49; *jus cogens* 52; juvenile
justice 225–6; pornography, child
353–4, 355, 356–7, 360, 361, 363, 366,
367, 370–1; power imbalance 354, 355;
prostitution 217, 354, 355, 359, 364–5,
366, 367–8, 369–70; refugee children
207; regional bodies 359–61; reporting
mechanisms 378; sale and trafficking
of children *see separate entry*; states'
responsibilities 368–77; street children
218; tourism, child sex 108, 126, 359,
362–3, 366, 370, 373, 374, 379–83;
United Nations 357–9
Shaw, M. 49, 50, 51, 53, 58, 61, 66
Sierra Leone 415–16
Slovenia 122, 124, 141, 170; economic
exploitation 213; education 202, 203;
health 196; refugees 209; Roma children
133, 198, 202, 211–12, 213, 217; sexual
exploitation 182, 183
social media 162, 205
social policy perspectives 14–18
social security 185, 199, 436
sociological perspective on childhood 9–14
soft law 52–3, 68, 185, 222, 317, 320, 407,
437; ILO 250, 261, 262, 270
Somalia 43, 91–2
South Africa 380

South Asia 190, 263, 359; *see also individual
countries*
South Korea 157, 160, 233, 322–3, 326
South Sudan, Republic of 91, 92
Soviet Union, former 323; *see also* Russia
Spain 323
Special Court for Sierra Leone (SCSL)
415–16
Special Rapporteurs 57, 76, 82; child
labour 240; indigenous peoples
440, 442–7; safe drinking water and
sanitation 192; sale of children, child
prostitution and child pornography 216,
358–9, 362, 363, 364, 365, 366, 367,
370, 371, 372–4, 376, 377, 378, 381,
382; trafficking in persons 216
Stalford, H. 15
standard of living 35–6, 185, 197–8
stare decisis/precedent 50–1, 54
state sovereignty 268
statelessness 153, 156
state–family relationship 15–17, 34–5;
Convention on the Rights of the Child
35–6, 38, 165–72; United States 94
statistical data 123, 171, 195, 214–15;
abduction 276–7, 297–8, 303; armed
conflict and children 401, 413, 414,
417; child labour 237, 239, 248, 254;
indigenous children 434; inter-country
adoption 323–5
street children 218–19
suicide 192, 193, 196, 444
Sweden 134, 141
Switzerland 327
Syrian Arab Republic 158

Tahiti 427–8
Taiwan 233
Thailand 164, 382
Thomas, N. 33
thought, conscience and religion, freedom
of 90, 156–7, 158–60
torture or other punishment 177–81, 223
tourism, child sex 108, 126, 359, 362–3,
366, 370, 373, 374, 379–83
trade unions 366; International
Confederation of Free Trade Unions
260, 271
trade–labour linkage 249, 270–2
trafficking: sale and trafficking of children
see separate entry; small arms and light
weapons 406

Tunisia 143
Turkey 161, 164, 238

UNICEF (United Nations Children's
Fund) 23, 57, 66–7, 357; annual reports
17, 66–7; armed conflict and children
67, 395, 411; child labour 260, 269–70,
272; child pornography 371; Committee
on the Rights of the Child 97, 106, 192,
197; inter-country adoption 331–2;
juvenile justice 226; rehabilitation
395; sex tourism 370; social policy
framework 14
United Arab Emirates 156
United Kingdom 18, 47, 48, 127, 376;
abduction *see* United Kingdom and
international parental child abduction;
abduction within own borders 275;
armed forces: minimum age 111;
child labour 233; Convention on the
Rights of the Child 54–5, 120, 125,
129–30; criminal responsibility, age of
129–30; extradition 42; *Gillick*-mature
child 27–8; incorporation doctrine
48; inter-country adoption 321–2,
327; relationship between domestic
and international law 48, 53–5; state–
family relationship 15, 16; statutory
interpretation 55; victims as criminals
372; views of child 30n31; welfare
principle 30n31
United Kingdom and international
parental child abduction:
acquiescence 302–3; approach to
Article 13 exceptions/defences 300;
Article 15 declarations 290; Article
20 discretion to refuse return 309–10;
Cairo Declaration 317; child's
participation rights 281–2, 309;
exceptions from duty to make return
order 299, 300, 301, 302–3, 305–7,
309–10; exercising discretion 312–14;
failure to exercise custody rights
301; grave risk of harm/intolerable
situation 305–7, 314; habitual residence
295–6; 'inchoate' custody rights 288;
International Child Abduction and
Contact Unit (ICACU) 279–80; non-
Convention countries 315–17, 320;
Reunite scheme 319–20; settlement
exception 299, 309; UK–Pakistan
Protocol 317, 320

United Nations 18, 48, 55–63, 240,
267; armed conflict and children
404–12; Charter 19, 49, 50, 56, 62,
268; Children's Fund *see* UNICEF;
Declaration of the Rights of the Child
1959 22, 89, 137, 259; Declaration on
the Rights of Indigenous Peoples 2007
437–40, 448; Development Programme
(UNDP) 269–70; Economic and Social
Council (ECOSOC) 58–60, 61, 66,
67, 80, 106, 109, 357, 441; General
Assembly 56–7, 59–60, 61–2, 65, 67,
80, 89, 106, 425; High Commissioner
for Refugees (UNHCR) 206, 332;
Human Rights Council (UNHRC) 57,
60, 76, 80–3, 112, 357, 358, 442, 447;
indigenous peoples and UN mechanisms
440–7, 448; International Court of
Justice (ICJ) 60, 62–6, 266; Millennium
Development Goals (MDGs) 17, 57, 91,
190–1, 198, 199, 232–3, 435; Office
of High Commissioner for Human
Rights (OHCHR) 57, 61, 75–6, 83, 95,
97, 226; Secretariat 60, 61; Security
Council 57–8, 63, 65, 357, 404–7, 413,
414; sexual exploitation 357–9; Special
Rapporteurs *see separate entry*; specialised
agencies 61, 65; SRSG (children and
armed conflict) 405, 409–12; SRSG
(violence against children) 176, 177;
treaty bodies 75, 83–6, 117; Youth
Assembly on 'Malala Day' (2013)
77–80
United States 18, 33, 47, 48, 73, 150,
437; abduction, international parental
child 274, 284, 288, 289, 303; armed
conflict and children 220–1; armed
forces: minimum age 111, 398; child
labour 237, 248, 253, 256, 271, 272;
ILO membership 260; inter-country
adoption 322–3, 325, 326, 345; not
ratifying CRC 43, 91, 92–5; Optional
Protocols to CRC 94, 103, 107; sexual
exploitation 376, 382
Universal Periodic Review (UPR) 82–3
Uzbekistan 145, 153, 157, 160, 163, 171;
child labour 272–3; disability 187;
economic exploitation 213; education
202; health 193, 197; juvenile justice
223, 225; parents: migrant workers
abroad 209; violence against children
180

Venezuela 90, 211
victims: assisting 376–7; as criminals 372–3; protection of witnesses and 225–6
Vietnam 158, 161, 323, 326, 352, 382
views of child 30–1, 32, 113, 140, 146–50, 377, 435; abduction, international parental child 281–2, 283, 308–9, 312–14; adoption 174; separate representation 309
violence 144–6; against children (CRC, articles 19, 37(a), 34 and 39) 175–84; armed conflict and children *see separate entry*; freedom from all forms of (CRC, article 19) 166, 175–7, 179; sexual exploitation *see separate entry*; torture or other punishment 177–81, 223

Virtual Global Taskforce (VGT) 376
Vygotsky, Lev 11, 12

war crimes 110, 220–1, 357, 398, 404, 410, 412–13, 416–24
welfare rights 25
will/choice theory of rights 24, 25, 26
World Bank 260
World Health Organization (WHO) 65, 145, 192, 193, 395
World Summit for Children (1990) 91
World Trade Organization (WTO) 271, 272

Yousafzai, Malala 77–80
Yugoslavia, former 412–13